Odd Fellows

Rediscovering More Than 200 Years of History,
Traditions and Community Service

LOUIE BLAKE SAILE SARMIENTO, J.D.

Text Copyright © 2019 Louie Blake Saile Sarmiento
(Last Updated on March 18, 2021)

Photo and illustration Copyright © are retained by original photographers, artists and owners except those that has since passed into public domain.

Edited by: Madeline Quiamco, PhD, Terry Barrett,
Harald Thoen, Scott Moye, and Cyril Jaymes Plantilla
Layout and cover design by: Louie Blake Saile Sarmiento

All rights reserved. No part of this book may be reproduced, stored in a retrieval system, or transmitted in any form or by any means, electronic, mechanical, photocopying, recording, or otherwise, without written permission of the author and copyright owners of the photos and illustrations in this book. Illegal copying and selling of publications deprive authors, publishers and booksellers of income, without which there would be no investment in new publications. You can help by reporting copyright infringements and acts of piracy to the author and publisher.

The moral right of the author has been asserted. While every effort has been made to trace the owners of copyright material reproduced herein, the author would like to apologize for any omissions and will be pleased to incorporate missing acknowledgements in any further editions.

Full Color Paperback Version
ISBN: 978-1-7338512-0-6
Full Color Hardback Version
ISBN: 978-1-7338512-1-3
Black and White Paperback Version
ISBN: 978-1-7338512-2-0

Published in the U.S.A.

Contents

Dedication and Acknowledgment i

Foreword iii

Ethics of Odd Fellowship v

Abbreviations and Definitions vi

INTRODUCTION 1

THE NAME 7

LEGENDS AND ORIGINS 11

EARLY ENGLISH CLUBS AND THEIR PRACTICES 17

THE INDUSTRIAL REVOLUTION 23

GOVERNMENT SUPPRESSION 27

REVIVAL 33

RISE OF THE MANCHESTER UNITY ODD FELLOWS 37

ODD FELLOWSHIP IN NORTH AMERICA 43

THE GOLD RUSH 51

AMERICAN CIVIL WAR 55

GOLDEN AGE OF FRATERNALISM 61

WORLD WAR I 71

THE GREAT DEPRESSION 79

WORLD WAR II..85

CIVIL RIGHTS AND RACIAL INTEGRATION...95

DECLINE OF FRATERNALISM..105

SIGNS OF REDISCOVERY..121

INTERNATIONAL EXPANSION..137

PROGRAMS AND PROJECTS...159

ORGANIZATIONAL STRUCTURE..165

INITIATION DEGREES, REGALIA, AND CUSTOMS.............................179

BRANCHES..191

RELIGION, FREEMASONRY, AND WOMEN.......................................209

NOTABLE MEMBERS..219

Past Grand Sires and Past Sovereign Grand Masters.........................271

Sovereign Grand Lodge Sessions..275

Notes..281

Bibliography..317

Index..334

About the Author..338

In Memory of

Niceas Saile, Antonia Saile, Christina Saile, Josefa Saile-Martinez,

Ma. Rosario Zamnor Saile-Korrodi, Donald Smith, Lars Ilstam, Thomas Wiley,

Katie Burns, John Cain and Suzie Robertson.

Nota Bene:

Archive section at the International Headquarters of The Sovereign Grand Lodge of the Independent Order of Odd Fellows in Winston-Salem, North Carolina, U.S.A.

This is an organizational analysis and case study scrutinizing more than 200 years of evolution, successes and struggles of the Independent Order of Odd Fellows. The contents of this book do not necessarily represent the personal opinion of the author or The Sovereign Grand Lodge of the Independent Order of Odd Fellows. The facts, statements and opinions herein are based on six years of research study examining more than 500 private journals, books, manuals, pamphlets, newspaper accounts, artifacts, rituals and secret works connected with Odd Fellowship. Over 100 lodges and about 20 Grand Lodges across the United States and Canada were visited. A number of local, national and international leaders of the organization were interviewed and consulted. An online survey study participated by exactly 2,120 members from all over North America, Latin America, Europe and Southeast Asia was also conducted. Moreover, the most recent dissertations, thesis and expert opinions of historians, sociologists and organizational psychologists were read and reviewed.

Dedication and Acknowledgment

This book is dedicated to all devoted Odd Fellows, Rebekahs, Junior Odd Fellows, Theta Rho Girls, and future members who will continue further to give so much of their time, talents, and resources to preserve and bring this fraternal organization into the future. I would not have accomplished this book without the support of many brothers and sisters from around the world whose names I cannot all enumerate here.

First, I am indebted to The Sovereign Grand Lodge of the Independent Order of Odd Fellows (IOOF) for allowing me to spend about three years researching and reviewing the journals, letters, photographs, and historical artifacts related to Odd Fellowship. To Past Sovereign Grand Masters Delmar Burns, Paul Cuminale, George Glover III, Charles Renninger, Harry Lohman, Donald Smith+ and Sovereign Grand Secretary Terry Barrett. To the Sovereign Grand Lodge staff and friends: Suzie Robertson+, Brenda Nelson, Kelly Westbrook, Stacey Layne, John Cain+, Walker Houchins, Amy-Ruth Hallet and William J Hundley, Jr.

Second, the experiences imparted to me by Odd Fellows and Rebekahs from the United States, Canada, Europe, and Australia helped broaden my knowledge about this worldwide fraternal organization: especially sister Jane Nelson and Peter English of the Manchester Unity Oddfellows, Past Grand Sire Harald Thoen of Norway, Grand Sire Erling Stenholdt Poulsen of Denmark, Grand Sire Gordon Bitter of Australasia, Lars Ilstam of Sweden, Past Grand Master Peter Sellars of California, Past Grand Master Dave Burns and Katie Burns+ of Michigan, Past Grand Master Justin Bailey of Pennsylvania, Past Grand Master Scott Aitchison of British Columbia, Past Grand Master Dave Rosenberg of California, Michael Froimowitz Greenzeiger of Massachusetts, Peter Rehnström of Finland, Jyri Siimes of Finland, David Scheer of Oregon and Barbara Rogers of Tennessee.

Third, those who believed in this project and did not hesitate to help with the expenses for the editing, layout design, International Standard Book Number (ISBN) and printing costs: The Grand Lodge of Pennsylvania of the IOOF, Grand Lodge of Denmark of the IOOF, Grand Lodge of Sweden of the IOOF, Grand Lodge of Texas of the IOOF, Grand Lodge of Maryland of the IOOF, Rockville Centre Lodge No.279 of Rockville Centre, New York, Hopkins Lodge No.87 of Bristol, Pennsylvania, Walker Lodge No.306 of

Philadelphia, Pennsylvania, State College Lodge No.1032 of Bellefonte, Pennsylvania, Upper Falls Lodge No.175 of Upper Falls, Maryland, North Point Lodge No.4 of North Point, Maryland, Towson Lodge No.79 of Towson, Maryland, Baltimore City Lodge No.57 of Granite, Maryland, William F. Packer Encampment No.127 of Johnstown, Pennsylvania, Debra LaVergne, Bob Simoni, Johanna Norton, Michael Zurell, Jan-Hugo Nihlen, Hans Thronström, Eilif Henriksen, Isleifur Gislason, James Harrington, Daniel Weinbren, Loretta Kaskey, Jason Walt, Dan Woolever, Bjørn-Arne Connolly, Eddie LeBoeuf III, Lars Kirkeby, Alice Legg, Roy King, Danilo Lopez, Frances Peterson, Michael Milan, Christopher Milan, Len Taylor, Ronald Aughenbaugh, Benjamin Kadow, Antoinette Vasta, Robert Chaney, Jamie List, Tattie Sarmiento, Bernadette Maradane Sarmiento-Faulkner and Christopher Faulker.

Fourth, the support of all brothers and sisters under the Grand Lodge of the Philippines: especially brothers Rex Boyson Olpoc, Armel Cabale, Anatoly Karpov Buss, Sidrake Arnold Mendez, Cyril Plantilla, Ivan Jason Delos Santos, Kahlil Reyes, Willand Uy, Jeff Nicolo Palad, Kerwin Elman, Alejo Villarmea, Jr., Novee Maestrecampo, Glenn Dimayuga, Jonathan Paulo, Apollo Neil Monroy, Kelvin Acebron, Mcaldous Castañares, Rhudyl Ferniz, and sisters Ivana Mae Canlas, Arlene Dominique Uy, Sheema Bajana, Maria Celeste Guimong, Christyriz Tolosa, Gift Olpoc, Sheila Lyn Francisco, Maelene Bastillada, and Corrine Faye Cornelia.

Fifth, Madeline Quiamco, PhD, Terry Barrett, Harald Thoen, Scott Moye and Cyril Jaymes Plantilla whose suggestions as editors helped improve the whole manuscript for readability and flow, and reworked sentences and paragraphs for clarity.

Sixth, my beloved parents and family who supported me through the years: Marcelino Sun Sarmiento, Jr., Maria Isabelita Da'Nordeza Guinto Saile, Antonia Guinto Saile, Bernadette Maradane Sarmiento-Faulkner and Christopher Faulkner, Grand Terence Sarmiento and Rhyza Ira Aragones-Sarmiento and Michale Vincent Sarmiento. My nephews and niece: Ethanne Dacel Sarmiento, Danor Antoine Faulkner and Mikhyra Lourenne Sarmiento.

Lastly, YOU – because you want to learn more about this worldwide fraternal organization and help preserve its history. A Past Sovereign Grand Master of the Independent Order of Odd Fellows once said: "The true effort to revitalize Odd Fellowship should be to educate and inform its own members. Knowledge leads to confidence, confidence leads to enthusiasm; enthusiasm leads to commitment; commitment leads to pride; and these collectively lead to success." It is important that we put in writing all the history and knowledge about Odd Fellowship so that we can pass on this fraternal organization to younger generations. My advocacy is to see a revival of more lodges in many localities and an international growth of Odd Fellowship – establishing lodges in countries where there is no Odd Fellows or Rebekah Lodge. I can only do so little. This is to make information easily accessible to younger generations in hope that someday they might ask, "How can I be a member?" It is my goal that this book will help encourage more people to further continue *"Improving Character, Making Friends, and Helping People"* through Odd Fellowship!

Always in Friendship, Love and Truth,

Louie Blake Saile Sarmiento

Foreword

Evolving from the English trade guilds and journeymen associations nearly 300 years ago, Odd Fellowship was once the largest fraternal organization in the world. During a time when the world was evolving, as new lands were still being explored and new nations were forming, as pioneers were beginning to conquer new lands, and governmental policies were in the process of being formulated, the Odd Fellows were an important part of that evolution. In fact, Odd Fellowship contributed greatly to the early development of many towns, cities, states, provinces and countries.

As the early American settlers began moving westward on their covered wagons, the Odd Fellows in small towns united with one another and established lodges across the country. These lodges were able to develop a sense of community and provided help to its members during those times when governments provided little social and welfare assistance. Furthermore, lodge rituals taught the important lessons of proper decorum, civic responsibility and equality before laws could be enacted to maintain social order. Many of the early Odd Fellows were the pioneer leaders of several towns, cities, states, provinces, and nations. Eventually, membership included presidents, prime ministers, senators, congressmen, governors, mayors and notable people in their respective fields. They spoke out on issues of international, national, and local interest. As the lodges grew, they built Odd Fellows buildings in new communities and these buildings soon became social centers where people met to relax and to exchange the latest news and ideas. The Odd Fellows were the forerunners of homes for the aged and orphanages. They are also the predecessors of the Social Security System and National Health Insurance. At that time, Odd Fellows literally touched the lives of millions of people, following its tenets to "visit the sick, relieve the distressed, bury the dead, and educate the orphan."

The fraternal organization has survived many wars and major world challenges. It came to America aboard a wooden sailing vessel, in the hands of Thomas Wildey, and the organization had been around to witness the building of the first railroad, the first automobile, the first movie, the first radio and television broadcasts, the first submarine, the first guided missile, the first miracle drug, the first airplane, the first space ship, the first computer, and the introduction of the internet. Odd Fellowship was the social network for many people long before the Internet was born. It served communities long before the birth of other service clubs and modern charitable foundations. It had connected and promoted understanding between people from different nationalities before the United Nations was established, and it even partnered with the United Nations for many years to educate young students in world affairs. Odd Fellowship rose to its most glorious time when members actively participated, and in many occasions led, in the development of communities and nations. People recognized the value of Odd Fellowship, and they reciprocated by becoming members of a Fraternity with the prime objective "To improve and elevate the character of mankind" and to serve those in need.

Surprisingly, people today know very little about the history, purposes, and traditions of Odd Fellowship. Volumes of records and books are stored in museums and libraries but there is not one book that has attempted to compile the highlights of the Odd Fellowship's glorious past and its condition in the present century. Members have been longing for a concise and up-to-date book about the Independent Order of Odd

Fellows and this book will attempt to meet this need. Through this book, Brother Louie hopes to preserve the rich traditions and legacy of this worldwide fraternal organization and share them with its members as well as the general public. His goal is to tell people the story of Odd Fellowship and how they have been "*Improving Character, Making Friends, and Helping People*" for over 200 years!

Douglas E. Pittman, Past Sovereign Grand Master
The Sovereign Grand Lodge
Independent Order of Odd Fellows, 2018-2019

Louie Blake Saile Sarmiento has addressed a long overdue historical review of the Odd Fellows. His book, Odd Fellows: Rediscovering More Than 200 Years of History, Traditions, and Community Service, updates the organization and brings it back into the fold of society. From its past achievements, to its current state, Brother Louie paints a vivid picture of the Odd Fellows. A worldwide fraternity gets noticed through the voice of this remarkable work. From its humble beginnings to its recent growth, in parts of Europe and the Philippines, to the picture the author paints in his work, and leading us right to the contemporary moment, he shows us that Odd Fellowship is alive. Brother Louie takes the Odd Fellows from the all-seeing eye to the public eye. This is a fresh and wonderful book.

Peter V. Sellars, Past Grand Master
Grand Lodge of California
Independent Order of Odd Fellows, 2016-2017

Ethics of Odd Fellowship

Odd Fellows believe in a Supreme Being. They base their thoughts and actions on healthy philosophical principles. They know that life here on earth is temporary. They are aware of the vanity of earthly things, the frailty and inevitable decay of human life, and the fact that wealth has no power to stop the sureness of eventual death. They start by asking the question, "How am I going to live my life?" Then, they work towards the improvement and elevation of their character: to fight against their human weaknesses and to live responsibly.

Odd Fellows are advocates of genuine FRIENDSHIP, the strongest bond of fraternity that teaches goodwill and harmony. They never look at people with prejudiced eyes nor base their judgment on outward appearances. They support the idea that all people regardless of race, gender, nationality, religion, political affiliation, social status, rank, and station in life are brothers and sisters. They do not take undue advantage of their power or the weaknesses of those around them. They are humble in a way that they never boast about their 'self.' They know and accept their individual strengths and weaknesses and keep away from badmouthing people and making unreasonable allegations. In this way, they promise never to slander a brother or sister but will defend his or her well-being, advise him or her for his or her best, and will help his or her family in times of need.

Odd Fellows are enactors of unfettered LOVE, the basis for all life's ambitions, service to others, and family. They work for goodwill between humankind, understanding between classes of the community and peace between nations. They fight against selfishness, the natural human weakness that hampers the will to do what is good. They feel jointly responsible for their fellowmen and are prepared to give attention and help wherever and whenever help is needed. They know the application of sympathy, sincerity, unselfishness, and generosity. They accept the fact that nothing is perfect but believe that they have an obligation to contribute in making the world a better place to live by "visiting the sick, relieving the distressed, educating the orphans, and burying the dead."

Odd Fellows are pursuers of inflexible TRUTH, the standard by which they value people and the foundation of their fraternity. They adhere to equality, justice, and righteousness. They are honest not just in words but also through deeds and actions. They will never defraud their lodge, but will prevent unlawful use of its funds and property, and strive at every occasion to promote its welfare. They see searching for the truth as searching for clarity in the sense of their individual lives. Oftentimes, they think before they speak and act. They know that before they start doing something, they can make the choice what to do, can think it over, and consider whether the choice was the right one. They believe that making good and well-considered choices is called "behaving in a responsible way."

Author

Abbreviations and Definitions

DNA: Data Not Available

FLT: Friendship, Love and Truth

Fraternal organization: an organized society of men and/or women associated together in an environment of brotherhood, sisterhood or camaraderie, and for work toward common goals; also known as fraternal order or fraternity

Friendly society: a mutual association for the purposes of insurance, pensions, savings or cooperative banking; also known as mutual-benefit society

GL: Grand Lodge

GUOOF: Grand United Order of Odd Fellows

IOOF: Independent Order of Odd Fellows

MUIOOF: Manchester Unity Independent Order of Odd Fellows; also known as Oddfellows

Odd: out of the ordinary, extraordinary, exceptional, remarkable, different, or rare

Odd Fellow: a member of an Odd Fellows Lodge

Odd Fellows: generic term for all Affiliated Orders of Odd Fellows

Odd Fellowship: the philosophy or way of life of an Odd Fellow as taught in their degrees of initiation

SGL: Sovereign Grand Lodge

17th Century: 1600s

18th Century: 1700s

19th Century: 1800s

20th Century: 1900s

21st Century: 2000s

Chapter 1

INTRODUCTION

"We command you to visit the sick, relieve the distressed, bury the dead and educate the orphan." The Sovereign Grand Lodge, IOOF (1834)

The passage succinctly sums up the essence of being an Odd Fellow. Odd Fellows are members of one of the oldest ethical and humanitarian fraternal organizations that continue to exist today. The name refers to a number of fraternal orders, friendly societies and service organizations operating in about 30 countries worldwide. The historical roots of these organizations date back approximately 280 years, although some claim these to be older.[1]

Evolving from the traditions of the medieval guilds and journeymen associations in England,[2] the early Odd Fellows Lodges were first set up to protect and care for their members and communities at a time when there were still no social security system, national health insurance, service clubs, or modern-day charitable institutions. The aim was and still is to provide help to their members, their families and their communities when they need it as well as to develop friendships and improve human character through the principles taught in the degrees of

The 100th Anniversary celebration of Caritas Odd Fellows Lodge No.34 held at the Petri Church in the City of Malmö, Sweden. Photo courtesy of Bo Nystrand and Lars Ilstam.

initiation usually conveyed through dramatic plays, lectures, symbols and mystic signs of recognition.[3] The most widespread among these affiliated orders, the Independent Order of Odd Fellows (IOOF), was organized on the North American continent on April 26, 1819.[4]

Definition

There is no precise definition for the Odd Fellows because they continue to evolve today. Traditionally, the Independent Order of Odd Fellows is defined as "a society of people for fraternal purposes; an association of individuals of various creeds and ideals, whose business is not only to alleviate each other's troubles in case of necessity, but to cement themselves in unity based on the motto: Friendship, Love and Truth."[5] In 1907, the *Grand Lodge of Ontario* suggested that Odd Fellowship is:

> "...is an organization having its object the elevation of mankind, morally, intellectually, socially, physically, recognizing mankind's individual helplessness and great need of cooperation in all the affairs of life. It requires all its members to aid, assist, and protect each other, to visit the sick, relieve the distressed, bury the dead, and protect the widow and orphan. It teaches the fatherhood of God and the brotherhood and sisterhood of mankind; it strives to breakdown the artificial barriers that separate mankind from his or her fellowmen, and places upon all an equality, as members of one great family."[6]

Purposes

The activities and projects of the organization has also changed and evolved through the years. And due to schisms in the past, the specific purposes and the activities being emphasized now slightly vary between the three major *Affiliated Orders* in existence today: *the Grand United Order of Odd Fellows, Manchester Unity Independent Order of Odd Fellows* and the *Independent Order of Odd Fellows*. But generally, the goals of Odd Fellowship as a way of life can be summarized into three: *Improving Character (ethical), Making Friends (fraternal), and Helping People (charitable).*[7]

Odd Fellowship aims *to improve and elevate the character of humankind* by encouraging their members to work inwardly with one's "self".[8] For some members, the organization is "an educational institution that teaches the ethics of brotherhood, reciprocity and charity."[9] The *IOOF International Council* suggested that the modern mission is "to elevate the character of mankind by bringing forth the principles of friendship, love and truth among all mankind, guided by a belief in a Supreme Being."[10] This starts with the receiving of the degrees of initiation which teaches a positive way of life based on certain ethical principles. Generally, Odd Fellows are bound by the solemn belief in a Supreme Being, a desire to improve their character, a heart to help each other, their families and their communities and a calling to live and promote the principles of "Friendship, Love and Truth" which transcends labels.[11] Odd Fellows support the principle of universal fraternity and recognizes all human beings as members of one common family regardless of race, nationality, religion, political party and social statues.[12] It promotes the value of tolerance which results in harmony and understanding among people from different walks of life. It endeavors to bridge gaps and serves as an avenue where acquaintances and even enemies can become friends using the purest and practical form of fraternity.[13] It inspires members to be more compassionate toward others,

> In 2012, the Sovereign Grand Lodge adopted the author's summary of the general purposes of the Independent Order of Odd Fellows as follows:[1]
>
> - **Improving Character (Ethical):** To improve and elevate the character of humankind by teaching and promoting the principles of Friendship, Love, and Truth; Faith, Hope, and Charity; and Universal Justice, as exemplified in the degrees of initiation and practiced in real life.
>
> - **Making Friends (Fraternal):** To promote goodwill and understanding among people and nations through the principle of universal fraternity, upholding the belief that all men and women regardless of race, nationality, religion, social status, gender, rank and station are brothers and sisters.
>
> - **Helping People (Humanitarian):** To help make the world a better place to live by aiding each other in times of need and by volunteering in or organizing charitable activities and projects that would benefit the less fortunate, the children, the youth, the elderly, the community and the environment in every way possible, guided by our ancient command: "to visit the sick, relieve the distress, bury the dead and educate the orphan".

be honest in all their dealings in life and tolerant of the beliefs of people across nations.[14] Furthermore, it encourages members to be temperate in their desires, and to avoid vices of any form.[15] This is the *ethical* side of Odd Fellowship.

Odd Fellowship aims *to make friends* because it teaches its members to unite together in the bonds of brotherly and sisterly love.[16] From a definitive standpoint, a fraternal organization is a group of people drawn together by bonds of fraternity, mutual-cooperation and a sincere desire for fellowship on a higher plane of unselfishness than what is usually found in everyday life. Fraternity teaches tolerance of race, creed, and religion. It teaches love and friendship for all mankind. It teaches that we are our neighbor's keepers, and we have a duty to make our neighborhood a much better place to live. Ideally, an Odd Fellows Lodge is an avenue for fellowship in all its forms, from discussion and networking on creative and constructive projects, to hanging out and just enjoying each other's company. It purports to be a vehicle where the young and the old are supposed to learn from each other. Where the rich and the poor assist each other in times of need. Where the educated and uneducated share life's wisdom and experiences. Where people from all walks of life, gender, race, religions, political affiliations and social classes unite in working towards global tolerance and understanding. By meeting at least once or twice a month, the members will eventually develop among themselves *long-lasting friendships*.[17] Further, membership serves as an international social network that extends to about 30 countries. When members visit other cities or countries, they are assured that other members in those areas would welcome them and assist them in their enterprise and their travels whenever possible. This is the *fraternal* side of Odd Fellowship in accord with the overall objective to help its members "define in their own individual way how to live in accordance with the ideals and values taught by the organization."[18] The *three links chain* signals to an onlooker the message:[19]

> You can trust me, I am your brother and friend. If you have problems and worries, I would like to help you. You can discuss with me question of ethical values, as I am also searching for truth in order to give myself a more purposeful life.

Odd Fellowship aims to *help people* because the organization also encourages the members to work outwardly to *help each other and their fellowmen*. This is based on the Golden Rule: "*Do unto others what you want others to do unto you.*" One of its degrees of initiation reminds the members that, "Fraternity, unless linked with acts of humanity, is an empty name".[20] It advises members to translate the lessons in the degrees of initiation into deeds and actions as they are commanded "*to visit the sick, relieve the distressed, bury the dead and educate the orphans.*"[21] While not a charity per se, it is an institution formed for the advancement of the principles of benevolence and charity.[22] It teaches a culture of caring and sharing, of not leaving each other behind, of thinking beyond one's self, and of helping others in need. That the hand of an Odd Fellow must always be open to supply the wants of the needy and distressed.[23] The *IOOF International Council* has advanced that the modern public mandate for members is "to promote health, education, personal development and worldwide fellowship"[24] and that "words alone are not sufficient, but these goals must be translated into actions so that each person, according to his ability, may contribute to the improvement of mankind."[25] If a member asks: Which good works do I have to do? The answer depends on the members and the lodge. One of its degrees tells the member to "make the most of the ups and downs of life as you will meet them,"[26] further noting that, "The vital importance is not the nature or size of the deed, but the right attitude of love."[27]

At a time when social security services and national health insurance were virtually non-existent in almost all countries in the world, the Odd Fellows functioned as a *mutual-benefit corporation* that provided their members and their families emergency relief, job placement assistance, sickness benefits, and death benefits.[28] The outward work of Odd Fellowship was apparent during the 19th and 20th centuries when the IOOF literally built and managed numerous homes for the elderly, orphans and widows, and cemeteries for the deceased. Although many of the social services offered by the Odd Fellows were eventually taken over by the government and commercial insurance companies, its lodges continue to be large contributors and fundraisers of local, national and international charities. Today, the IOOF still raise millions of dollars annually to support its philanthropic programs such as the IOOF Pilgrimage for the Youth, Odd Fellow

An Odd Fellows Lodge is considered a neutral ground where debates about politics and religion are prohibited. This is to develop respect and understanding between people from various political, religious, social, racial and ethnic backgrounds. Within the lodge, there shall only be Friendship, Love, and Truth among members. Photo by the Author, 2019.

and Rebekah Retirement Homes, Odd Fellows and Rebekahs Arthritis Board, IOOF Educational Foundation, Odd Fellows and Rebekahs Visual Eye Research Foundation, IOOF Living Legacy Program and the Odd Fellows and Rebekah World Hunger and Disaster Fund.[29] This is the *humanitarian* side of Odd Fellowship.

What it is Not

Odd Fellowship is non-political. It does not claim any access to political and government power. It is non-sectarian. It is not limited to people belonging to a particular religious sect. It is not a religion. It does not promise spiritual salvation. It is not an esoteric, occult or mystical Order. It does not claim to possess any hidden or secret knowledge or purpose. It is not a financial institution. It does not promise financial wealth to its members. It is non-elitist. It does not rub shoulders with the rich and famous to gain attention. Its history is not tainted with accusations of conspiracy, crimes and abuse of power. As an organization, the aim of Odd Fellowship is only the improvement and upliftment of human character by instilling in each member practical and benevolent values and by encouraging its members to exemplify these principles into actions through: character improvement, tolerance and understanding of people from different racial, political and religious backgrounds, and human compassion through mutual-assistance in times of need and participation in local, national and international charities.

Membership

To be a member, one must believe in a Supreme Being, of good character, and at least sixteen (16) years old. This is regardless of gender, race, creed, religion, political affiliation or social standing.[30] Being a non-political and non-sectarian organization,[31] its membership is open to people of all faiths, and the lodge is always considered a *neutral ground* where debates about religion and politics are highly discouraged.

Internationally, membership today comes from all walks of life including businesspeople, doctors, lawyers, teachers, students, government officials, retirees, blue collar or white collar workers and others. Depending on the country, there are lodges for men only, there are lodges for women only, and there are lodges open for both men and women. Membership is diverse and is represented by the poor, the average and the rich, the educated and the uneducated. There are members who are white, black, Asian, and Hispanic as well as Protestants, Catholics, Muslims, Jewish and others.

Non-Discrimination Policy

The Independent Order of Odd Fellows will not exclude any individual based on disability, age, ethnicity, gender, race, sexual orientation, religion or other social identity from the full and equal enjoyment of its services and facilities, unless the individual poses a direct threat to the health or safety of others, or himself or herself, that cannot be eliminated by a modification of policies, practices, or procedures or by the provision of auxiliary aids or services. The IOOF will not exclude any individual from the full and equal enjoyment of its services and facilities because of the individual's association with a person of disability, age, ethnicity, gender, race, sexual orientation, religion or other social identity.

Chapter 2

THE NAME

A number of theories have attempted to explain the name Odd Fellows through the years. There is no absolute answer but the widely accepted beliefs today, as had been passed from generation to generation, are derived from any or a combination of a number of explanations.[1]

Association for Odd Trades

The origin of the name had been traced from the system of trade guilds in England.[2] Usually, guilds were composed of workers belonging to the same trade or craft such as stonemasons, gardeners, cabinet-makers, and so on. In smaller towns and villages, however, there were too few people practicing the same trade to form a guild of their own. Hence, a group of "fellows" from a mixture of smaller trades such as tailors, smiths, dyers, bakers, merchants and what-not workers joined forces to form an *omnium gatherum* or a brotherhood from an assorted or "odd" collection of workers, hence, the name "Odd Fellows".[3] Indeed, journeymen associations or *compagnons* existed during the 17th

There were other crafts not strong enough to establish a guild of their own so a combination of these "fellows" representing different or "odd" trades, joined forces to form their own trade association and called themselves "Odd Fellows".
Illustration by Asher Alpay as commissioned by the author, 2015.

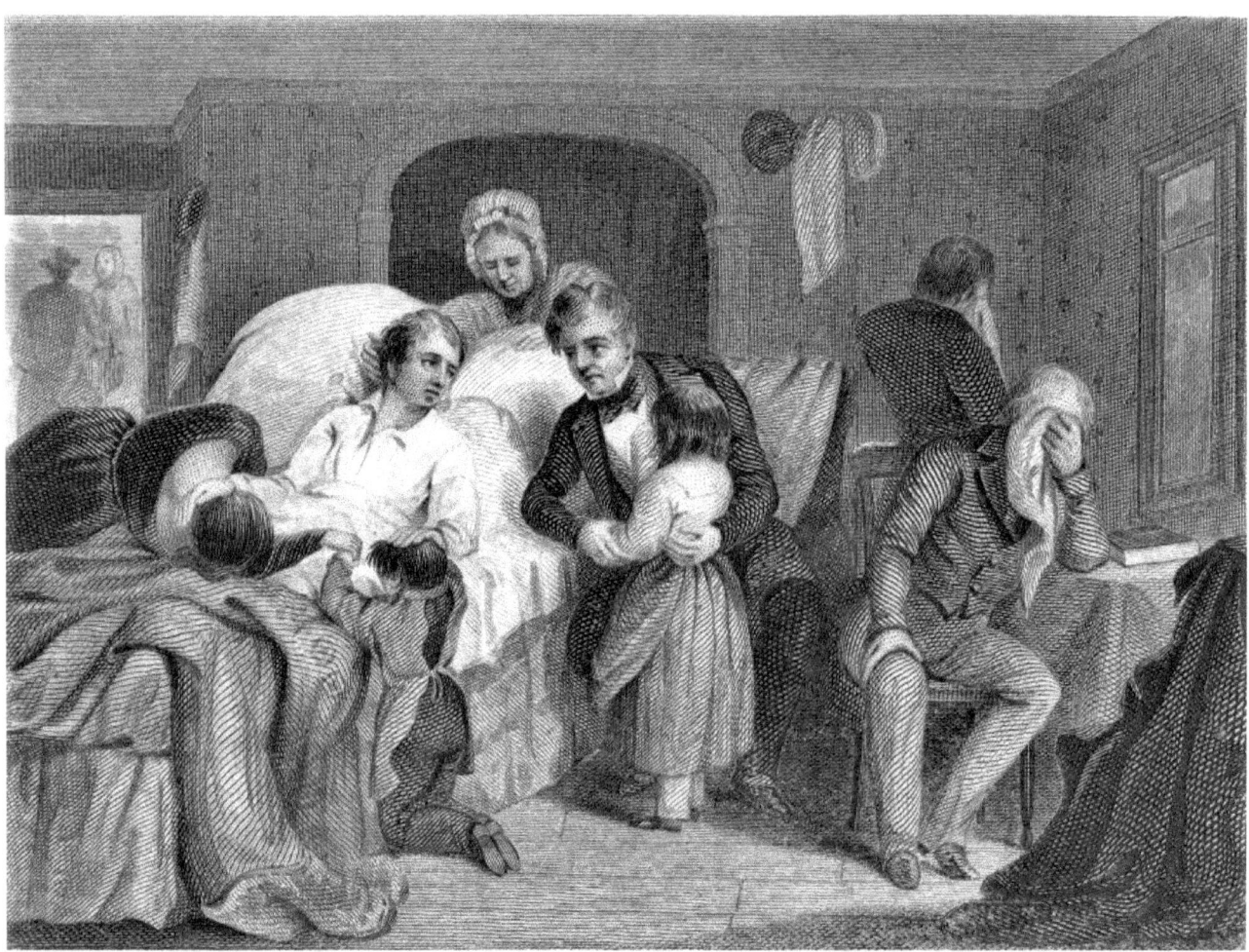

Traditionally, Odd Fellows take an oath promising to visit sick members and help the widows and orphans of their deceased members. From *The Odd Fellows' Offering*, 1847.

century as some kind of deviation from the guild system.[4] In contrast with the trade guilds which accepted only those practicing the same craft, journeyman associations consisted of tradesmen from numerous trades or crafts (See Chapter 3).[5] The *Prologue to The Canterbury Tales*, written by Geoffrey Chaucer (1387 to 1400), mentioned an association of journeymen belonging to different trades at an Inn in Canterbury, Kent, in England:

> It happened that in that season on one day,
> In Southwark at the Tabard Inn as I lay
> Ready to go on my pilgrimage
> To Canterbury with a very devout spirit,
> At night had come into that hostelry
> *Well nine and twenty in a company*
> *Of various sorts of people,* by chance fallen
> In fellowship, and they were all pilgrims,
> Who intended to ride toward Canterbury

Ordinary People Doing Good Deeds

More than 200 years ago, people were facing a lot of challenges. Life was tough, often lawless and desperate. There were still no social security programs or national health insurance, so people who fell upon hard times found very little help or resources available to them. Being out of work even

An Edifying Explanation

The oldest surviving written reference to the meaning of the organization's name can be found in the *Revised Ritual of the Order of Patriotic Odd Fellows* in 1797. In the *White* or *Covenant Degree*, the Vice Grand says:[1]

"…But I tell you, brother, it is this that contracts our sphere of usefulness. It fills the world with sects and parties, who are each one saying, mentally, give place – my opinions are superior to yours; but you, as an Odd Fellow (*which really means that you are singled out from the general mass with a desire for true knowledge*), should look beyond the surface, and view with a friendly eye, all mankind".

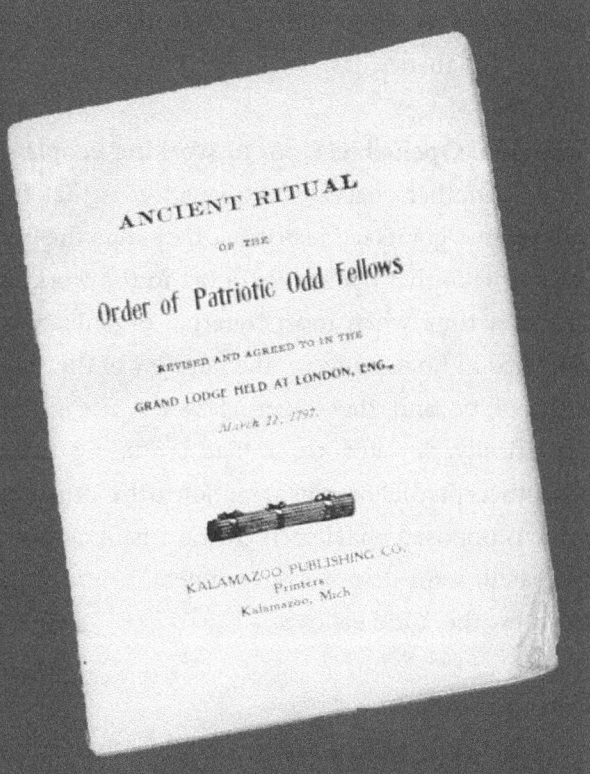

What is certain, therefore, is that the word "Odd" in Odd Fellows was not intended to mean "weird" or "foolish." In fact the passage above points to an edifying origin of the name "Odd Fellows." It strongly suggests that the name was intended to be a title of commendation for people who believed in the ideas of social unity, religious tolerance, benevolence, and charity, which were believed to be "out of the ordinary" or "odd" at that time. Correctly, dictionaries provide that the word "odd" is also synonymous for "remarkable" or "extraordinary." This explanation – documented in writing and attributed to a leader of the organization in its early years – is the most plausible one. It explains to the member the meaning of being "odd," even as it encompasses the essence of the other explanations previously mentioned.

temporarily could mean that one's family was not only going to go hungry but may starve to death. Medicine was still crude. There were many sick people, orphaned children, and widowed mothers, and many could not afford a decent burial for the dead. Morally, people were given over to selfishness and indifference. A chasm existed between the rich and the poor. Most people fended only for themselves, living without much care for others (See Chapter 5).

However, a group of ordinary people from different trades and walks of life deviated from the trend during those times and found it necessary to group together into a fraternity for fellowship and mutual assistance. Because it was rather peculiar or "odd" to see a group of ordinary people helping one another, coming to each other's aid and offering social relief to those in need, they were labeled as "Odd Fellows".[6] Because of the appropriateness of the name, those engaged in forming these associations accepted it. When legally incorporated, the title "Odd Fellows" was purportedly adopted.

The benevolence, charity and fraternalism of the organization continue up to this day and somehow support this theory.[7]

Lodge that Opened its Door to Working People

Another suggested explanation is that the Odd Fellows got its name because they were the first lodge or club that opened its doors to the working class at a time when most fraternal organizations and clubs in England were "the purview of the elite, the nobility, and the upper classes."[8] The group theoretically deviated from that prevailing trend when it accepted laborers as a reaction to the "crushing burdens imposed on laborers by the aristocracy of a dissipated, semi-despotic government,"[9] and thus, they were the "Odd Fellows".

Sworn Brothers

Historical linguistics, on the other hand, suggest the possibility that "odd" is a corruption of the word "ad" or "oath".[10] One of the prominent features of the guilds and early lodges was taking an "ad and wed" – oath and pledge. It is probable that the name Odd Fellows was derived from "ad fellows" or "oath fellows", meaning "sworn brothers".[11] Since its inception members of the Odd Fellows make firm promises or oaths upon joining.

True Reason is a Mystery

Modern references do admit that the exact reason for the choice of name is not categorically known. The origin remains a mystery probably because the explanation may have meant differently in the course of time and has been interpreted differently by various members. Undeniably, the explanations mentioned above were passed on from generation to generation of members by *word-of-mouth*. But whatever the true reason may have been, the unusual name has been the object of public curiosity, criticism, and even ridicule for more than 200 years now.

Chapter 3

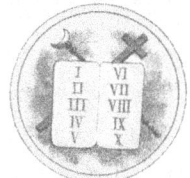

LEGENDS AND ORIGINS

Fraternities and brotherhoods have existed since the beginning of early civilizations - first among sworn kinsmen, monks, knights, Roman *collegia*, craft guilds, burial clubs - and later evolving into fraternal organizations and civic clubs.[1] Owing to their human nature, people desire to associate with each other for social, philosophical, political, religious, charitable, mutual-benefit, or business purposes. During the middle Ages, Orders of Knighthood, revolutionary brotherhoods and craft guilds existed and were part of the social order. During the Industrial Revolution, fraternal organizations became numerous "to meet the social and economic needs of people whose very lives were affected by the shift from agrarianism to industrialism."[2] The Odd Fellows, as well as several other fraternal organizations or friendly societies, appear to have evolved or inherited ideas from these

Mythical history of Odd Fellowship alleged that John De Neuville and five French knights met at Bull and Mouth in Sheffield, London, and established the Grand Lodge of Honour. Illustration by Ric Anton Silot as commissioned by the author, 2017.

numerous early sources.[3]

Sworn Knights

Folk tradition tells the story that the parent organization of Odd Fellowship was founded in 1452 by John De Neuville and five French knights who met at Bull and Mouth in London and established the *Loyal Grand Lodge of Honour*.[4] This society supposedly survived up to the 18th century until they began to form themselves into an *Affiliated Order*, which had been called at different periods by the names *Loyal Ancient Odd Fellows*, the *United Odd Fellows*, and eventually the *Manchester Unity Odd Fellows*.[5] Whether this claim is true or not, nobody can prove. Large meetings were treated with suspicion in those days. Many groups met in secret for fear of prosecution, hence, common sense dictated the wisdom of keeping records only of matters of great importance. But this is most likely just a mythical origin of Odd Fellowship. During the 19th century, members were fond of tracing the lineage of their fraternity to medieval Orders of Knighthood because it can provide their organization with a feeling of longevity, respectability, and mystery.

The Freemasons, for example, claim to have been descended from the Knights Templars but they also do not have any conclusive proof of lineal connection with that ancient order.

Roman Collegia

Another legend suggests that the roots of Odd Fellowship can be traced to a group of exiled Israelites who banded together into a brotherhood for mutual support. After the fall of Jerusalem, the brotherhood is said to have continued among Jewish soldiers in Roman Camps during the reign of Titus Caesar in 79 CE.[6] This, of course, can never be proven and could be just a mythical legend, although similar associations did exist from classical times.

At a time when the Roman Empire dominated, there were, indeed, groups of skilled workers who followed the legions of Rome throughout Europe, building roads, bridges, and military defenses. They included soldiers, artisans, gladiators, weavers, stonemasons, dyers, and other craftspersons.[7] As the Roman Empire spread over the continent, these workers structured their groups into formal organizations called *collegia* that could function as guilds, social clubs, or burial clubs.[8] Members usually met once a month for conviviality, paid entrance fees, and were guaranteed a decent burial for their dead. There were also initiatory societies among Romans with initiation rites and degrees of membership. Such groups, whatever they were named, roamed the European continent for centuries, going wherever their skills and efforts were required. Many of these groups were suppressed following the adoption of Christianity while others adapted and became the basis for corporations,

Circa 1794, a Provincial token bearing the name "Odd Fellows," the "heart and hand" symbol commonly used by the Odd Fellows, and the word "Honour."
From the collection of the author.

Free Gardeners

The Guild of Gardeners can be traced back to the 14th Century England. The earliest surviving record of a Free Gardeners Lodge in Scotland dates back in 1676. Some of these groups had evolved into friendly societies by the 18th Century. Their emblem is a square and compass with a pruning knife in the center as representation of "the simplest tool of gardening." They have three degrees of initiation: *Apprentice, Journeyman* and *Master Gardener*. Like many other 18th and 19th century English or Scottish fraternal organizations, they use collars and aprons as regalia which they adopted from the customs of the craft guilds.

By the 20th century, the Free Gardeners had become almost extinct. Today, there are few surviving and newly established lodges in Australia, Belgium, England, France, Monaco, Philippines, Scotland and South Africa.

confraternities, and guilds.[9]

Craft Guilds

The origin of English fraternal organizations can be more clearly traced from the demise of craft guilds. The historical connections are manifest in the rituals, terminology and functions shared by both the guilds and fraternal orders.[10] In England, organizations and clubs with benefit systems took the form of the guilds and reach back to the Middle Ages. Even as far back as the early 14th century, the early guilds were charitable associations, giving relief in sickness and adversity, and making provision for old age and for burial, and in this can be seen the origin of Odd Fellowship. Great good was done by these old English guilds, and in this respect they are the forerunners of fraternal organizations which, under the government of free and enlightened principles, on English soil, and among English-speaking people, finally culminated into the Odd Fellows.

Contrary to popular misconception, it was not just the operative masons who guarded their trade secrets from others. Other craftsmen also joined forces and formed their own guilds or trade fraternities. In fact, there were more than one hundred early guilds in England during the Middle Ages.[11] The *Fraternity of Butchers*, for example, owned a meeting hall as early as year 975 and had charters dating back to 1605 and 1637.[12] A record dated 1345 shows that the *Fraternity of Gardeners* petitioned the Lord Mayor to sell produce in front of the church of St. Austin.[13] The Gardeners in London had charters dated 1605 and 1659, and a few other surviving documents in Scotland, too.[14] The *Worshipful Company of Carpenters* had charters dating 1477, 1558, 1560, 1607, and 1868, and controlled the craft with religious and charitable aims.[15] There is a reference to the "Masters of the mysteries" of the *Fraternity of Cooks, Pastelers and Piebakers* from 1312 to 1438.[16] These "Mysteries" suggest that they also had degrees of initiation and

Ancient Noble Order of Bucks

A manuscript of the Constitution of the *Most Antient and Honourable Society of Bucks* holds a peculiar interest for Odd Fellows. This society was perhaps formed in a London tavern sometime not later than 1722[1] and flourished between 1770 and 1820.[2] The framework and purposes of the said organization seemed to indicate a link between the ancient guilds and the early lodges of Odd Fellows, or at least, showed that both existed along the same line under a different name.[3]

The presiding officer of the *Most Antient and Honourable Society of Bucks* was called "Most Noble Grand,"[4] the same title used by the Odd Fellows in its installation ceremony up until 1832.[5] The next officers were a Senior and Junior "Vice Grand."[6] The "bundle of sticks" was used as a symbol for teaching unity. Furthermore, one of the principal emblems was three bucks' heads with antlers joined together, as if forming the three links emblem of the Odd Fellows.[7] The activities of this society included innocent mirth and good fellowship,[8] one of the prominent characteristics of the early lodges of Odd Fellows.[9] This "Ancient Order" began to decline after 1780. There is a reference to it in 1802 as the "United Order", the name "Buck" having been disused.[10] Odd Fellows history mentions antecedent organizations called an "Ancient Order", then a "Patriotic Order" and followed by the "United Order", from which the "Independent Order" separated.[11]

trade secrets.

A *guild* was a benevolent association for mutual help that usually consisted of craftsmen belonging to the same trade or living in the same neighborhood.[17] Guilds were sworn brotherhoods that had binding oaths to support one another in times of adversity and back one another in trade ventures alongside their religious and ceremonial roles. Meetings involved proper decorum and wearing of regalia such as chains of office, special robes, and others. Guilds charged entrance fees and indulged in feasting and merry-making. They also had close ties with the church, so that many of the early guilds were often named after patron saints and their ceremonies usually had religious themes. Membership was ordinarily by apprenticeship, which usually lasted up to seven years to learn the "mystery" of the trade. Upon completing *apprenticeship*, one became a *fellowcraft* or *journeyman* of his guild and may serve as *master* of the craft or set up his own guild.[18]

Different types of guilds existed, including religious or social guilds, merchant guilds, and craft guilds.[19] Social guilds were termed simply as "guilds and brotherhoods" while the craft guilds were described as "mysteries and crafts."[20] Within guilds were also offspring fraternities, clubs within clubs, or clubs exclusive for the elite of a particular craft, for instance, only the top men of the trade and other dignitaries.[21] Some guilds eventually admitted other people although they did not practice the same trade. The *Guild of Weavers*, for example, originally consisted of members of the trade when they were founded in 1155, but they later admitted sons of members and noblemen.[22] The *Guild of Merchant Taylors*, on the other hand, admitted King Edward III as a member after they lent him money to pay his wars.[23] The *Company of Masons'* book of accounts mentioned a lodge of "Accepted" masons in 1620 and 1621.[24] This is the earliest reference to the Masons accepting people not practicing their craft. It was advantageous for guilds to admit noblemen because they increased the social prestige of their society.[25]

When King Henry VIII broke away from the Roman Catholic Church, he confiscated the properties of the guilds. Allegedly, he thought that they supported the Pope because of their link with the church. During the reign of Queen Elizabeth I, the *Statute of Apprentices* was passed, which took the responsibility for apprenticeship away from the guilds.[26] The nature and scope of work was also changing, thus, the role of the guilds eventually went into decline. This removed an important form of social and financial support among ordinary workers.[27] Some guilds continued to survive but some adapted to the changing times and evolved into fraternal lodges and social clubs with a combination of social, moral, and charitable or mutual-benefit functions. By the 18th century, there seemed to be a number of such groups that were formed in England. Some lodges of the operative masons allegedly evolved to become the *Free and Accepted Masons*. The Gardeners' guilds eventually formed into the *Ancient Order of Free Gardeners*. Several other fraternal organizations and clubs with a guild-like name, such as the *United Order of Cabinet Makers*, also came into existence during the same period. What happened to the other guilds and trade associations? One historian noted that the Odd Fellows is an "interesting deviation from the London Guild model."[28]

Journeymen Associations

Some groups fell outside the system of craft guilds. During the 17th century, French journeymen formed *compagnons* (companions) or journeymen associations "to defend their collective interests against the guild Masters and to provide food, lodging, and guidance for one another when they travel to search for work."[29] Unlike the other guilds, these associations consisted of *apprentices* and *fellowcrafts* from numerous trades or crafts – stonecutter, roofer, cutter, mechanic, blacksmith, and others.[30] They also had "an elaborate initiation rite in which a young journeyman who joined the association would go through a system of degrees intended to test courage and loyalty and to ascend into hierarchy

An 'ancient Odd Fellow' on a tramp

From Shaffner, *Odd Fellowship Illustrated*, 1875.

within the association."[31] These journeymen traveled throughout France and neighboring countries for three to seven years to gain training and become masters. Some artisans, however, remained as journeymen because of lack of opportunities to achieve the status of a Master of the craft.

The practices of the early Odd Fellows bore much closer resemblance to the traditional journeymen associations than to the craft guilds.[32] In the early times, members were helped by penny subscriptions collected by the Lodge Secretary.[33] Whenever a member was sick or in need of assistance, the lodge by vote appropriated such sum as the exigency of the case demanded.[34] If out of employment, he was furnished with a card, a password, and sufficient funds to reach the nearest lodge. If he was not successful there, then that lodge will provide assistance for his further travels until he found employment.[35] The first Odd Fellows Lodges did not carry any "Old Charges" or charters issued to them as a craft guild. The structure and degrees of initiation also did not follow the craft guild model: *apprentice*, *fellowcraft or journeyman* and then *master*. The oldest degree in the Odd Fellows, called the *Making* or the *Initiatory Degree,* is similar to the early initiations into journeymen associations. Thus, it is more probable that the early Odd Fellows were a derivation or, at least, the English equivalent of the *compagnonnages*.

Chapter 4

EARLY ENGLISH CLUBS AND THEIR PRACTICES

Admittedly, the exact date of the first founding of Odd Fellowship is already lost in the fogs of antiquity. It must be admitted, too, that the first Odd Fellows had "originated in obscurity as it was possibly not popular to claim any public attention of its early operations."[1] This also was because record keeping was not given much importance in the past and because most of the early records were destroyed as a result of government regulations aimed at suppressing fraternal organizations many years ago (See Chapter 6). Nevertheless, fragmentary surviving records, newspaper accounts, and artifacts do prove the existence of the Odd Fellows in the 1700s.

Friendly Societies

The first of these groups emerged in England as "a number of independent lodges or clubs

1789 satirical depiction of a "Meeting Night of a Club of Odd Fellows". Illustration published by Bentley and Co., 1789.

Early English Clubs and Their Practices | 17

Surviving Fragmentary Records and Artifacts

Among the few surviving documentations and relics of early Odd Fellows Lodge activities in the 18th century are the following:

1736 – The *Loyal Rose of Sharon Lodge* was first self-instituted in Hathersage, Derbyshire, on January 29, 1736. This lodge later affiliated with the Manchester Unity Independent Order of Odd Fellows in 1836.

1748 – A minutes of meeting and rules of *Aristarcus Lodge No.9* of the Order of Odd Fellows, which met at Globe Tavern, London on March 13.

1750 – Records possessed by the *Loyal St. Olives Lodge* that proved that the lodge was in existence in London as far back as 1750, discovered when it transferred dispensation under the Manchester Unity Independent Order of Odd Fellows in 1822.

1775 - A lodge of the Union Order of Odd Fellows existed in Derby.

1780 - King George IV, while still Prince of Wales, was initiated into a lodge of Odd Fellows that held its meeting in a private house at Grosvenor Street, in West England.

1789 – Bentley and Co. published a satirical depiction of a meeting night of a *Club of Odd Fellows*, drawn by English artist and caricaturist Samuel Collings.

comprised mostly of working-class people who were not rich, not royalty, and whose very lives depended on each other, each one being vulnerable if ever one of their members got sick, became disabled, lost a job, or died."[2] Like in cooperatives and labor unions today, members would contribute some of their hard-earned wages to a common fund that they could use in unfortunate events such as in times of sickness, job loss, or death of a member.[3] By uniting themselves, workers were able to build up funds to aid each other, their families, and their communities in times of need. Such groups were known as *friendly societies* or *box clubs* and had been in existence at least since the middle of the 17th century.

Daniel Defoe in his book, *Essay on Projects*, wrote about friendly societies in 1697 and defined them as "a number of people entering into a mutual compact to help one another in case any disaster or distress fall upon them, and emphasized the contributory nature of these societies as a way to lower the poor rates and raise the self-respect of working people".[4] He recommended the creation of these societies as "a means to prevent the general misery and poverty of mankind and at once secure the country against beggars, parish poor, almshouses, and hospitals".[5] Other advocates shared the desire to use friendly societies to decrease the cost of poor relief. By the end of 18th century, a number of clubs or lodges developed in virtually every English town and village.[6]

Self-Institution

The early lodges followed the ancient usage of *self-institution*. This meant that any person can gather at least five people to form a lodge without need of approval from any national association or Grand Lodge. Each lodge governed itself according to its own rules, traditions, and practices. Hence, there were actually so many early clubs named "Odd

During the 1700s up to the early 1800s, lodges could not legally own a building so they met inside pubs. Many pubs in the United Kingdom are named "The Oddfellows" or "Oddfellows Arms". Obviously, these were past meeting places of Odd Fellows.

1790 – The *Public Advertiser* issue on July 27 mentioned a "Grand Original Lodge of Odd Fellows."

1792 – A song written by James Montgomery starts with the line, "When Friendship, Love, and Truth abound among a band of brothers."

1793 – The *Morning Chronicle* issue of July 20 mentioned the celebration of the union of the "United Order of Odd Fellows" and the "Imperial Order of Odd Fellows."

1794 - Provincial or Conder tokens bearing the name Odd Fellows dating back to 1794-1795 have survived and are in the hands of several collectors today.

1796 – The *Lloyd's Evening Post* issue of February 17 mentioned "a Society of Odd Fellows with a Vice Grand, a Most Noble Grand and a Secretary."

1797 – The *True Briton* issue on December 4 mentioned a "Society of Odd Fellows" in Gravesend. The *Revised Ritual of the Patriotic Order of Odd Fellows* was adopted on March 12. The *Oddfellows' Magazine of 1838* included a picture of a medal presented to the Secretary of the Grand Independent Order of Odd Fellows, 1796-1797.

1798 – The *Morning Post and Gazetteer* issue of January 16 mentioned "a meeting of the Loyal and Constitutional Third Lodge of Odd Fellows" in Birmingham. The *Whitehall Evening Post* issue of April 7 mentioned the "Town Lodges of the United Order of Odd Fellows."

Fellows" but were not necessarily connected with each other.

The early friendly societies practiced a ritual similar to what lodges still do today. They gave no benefits apart from helping widows and the families of deceased members. They had no Grand Lodge of any kind; they were all independent and unconnected lodges. The only one thing the lodges did together was to implement a system of providing travel assistance to their members who were traveling in search of work. If a member went to another town, he was given a traveling password and certificate to show to the Odd Fellows Lodge in that town, which gave him assistance in terms of food and lodging. His own lodge would then reimburse the lodge that hosted him. Unfortunately, trouble occurred among the lodges in claiming reimbursements, so they decided to form a Grand Lodge for better administration.[7]

The *Gentleman's Magazine of 1798* mentioned that the "Original United Lodge of Odd Fellows consisted of 50 lodges, 39 of them in London and its environs." An *Amicable Bond of Union* of the Grand United Order of Odd Fellows in London was signed on January 6.

1799 – The *General Evening Post* issue of March 7 mentioned "Odd Fellows, Free and Easy and the Jolly Friars," which met at the Goose and Gridiron tavern in London.

1800 – The *Star* issue of May 19, *Lloyd's Evening Post* issue of June 25, and the *Caledonian Mercury* issue of June 30 recorded that Hadfield confessed that he was a member of the Odd Fellows Society.

1806 – T. Tegg Cheapside published a caricature entitled *Making a Sailor an Odd Fellow*, on December 1.

1808 – The journal *Odd Fellows Miscellany* was first published in London.

1811 – The *Dictionary of the Vulgar Tongue* provided a definition of Odd Fellows as "a convivial society: the introduction of the 'Noble Grands' arrayed in royal robes is well worth seeing at the price of becoming a member."

Mergers and Acquisitions

The first *Affiliated Orders* of Odd Fellows appear to be an amalgamation of these numerous independent friendly societies and box clubs that eventually realized the need to federate themselves into a national organization for better coordination. Historical accounts demonstrate individual lodges or clubs that formed themselves into a regional organization or later merged with existing *Affiliated Orders* and adopted the name *Odd Fellows*. The *Naylor's Amalgamated Society*, for example, was a local friendly society founded in Salford in 1808.[8] It merged with *Prince Regent Lodge* to form the *Lord Abercrombie Lodge No.1* of the Manchester Unity Independent Order of Odd Fellows in 1810.[9] The *Loyal Rose of Sharon Lodge* was first established in Hathersage, Derbyshire, on January 29, 1736 as an independent local friendly society. This lodge later affiliated with the Manchester Unity Independent Order of Odd Fellows in 1836. The different Orders of Odd Fellows really was a product of mergers and acquisitions that involved various early English clubs and lodges.

Conviviality

It must be noted that there was still no clear distinction between fraternal organizations and friendly societies before the 19th century. In fact, the early Odd Fellows also functioned as social clubs that held their meetings in *pubs* or *taverns*. Conviviality was a very common habit in those days. Along with the purpose of giving relief to each other in times of need, jolly practices were another objective in almost all associations and gatherings of men everywhere in England. It was commonplace for English social and moral societies, such as the Odd Fellows, Free Gardeners and Free Masons, to hold meetings in pubs. During the meetings, they were provided freely with alcoholic drinks and fumes

During the 18th up to the early-19th centuries, all lodges and clubs in England held their meetings inside pubs where they would drink and socialize. Shown is a satirical illustration of "Making a Sailor an Odd Fellow" in 1806.

Illustration published by T. Tegg Cheapside, 1806.

A Society of Odd Fellows from Downing Street, complaining to John Bull for the loss of their Lodge cash and accounts was depicted in a satirical illustration in 1808.

Illustration published by Thomas Rowlandson, 1808.

Early English Clubs and Their Practices | 21

> ### Odd Fellows Song
>
> British poet, James Montgomery (1771-1854), joined the Odd Fellows after being introduced to Odd Fellowship by his employer Joseph Gales, who was a bookseller, auctioneer, and newspaper owner. Apparently, Montgomery wrote a poem for a Lodge of Odd Fellows sometime between 1788-1792:[1]
>
> When Friendship, Love and Truth abound, among a band of brothers,
> The cup of joy goes gaily round, each shares the bliss of others.
> Sweet roses grace the thorny way along this vale of sorrow;
> The flowers that shed their leaves today shall bloom again tomorrow.
> How grand in age, how fair in youth, are holy Friendship, Love and Truth!
>
> On halcyon wings our moments pass, life's cruel cares beguiling;
> Old Time lays down his scythe and glass, in gay good-humour smiling;
> With ermine beard and forelock grey his reverend front adorning,
> He looks like Winter turned to May, night softened into morning.
> How grand in age, how fair in youth, are holy Friendship, Love and Truth!
>
> From these delightful fountains flow ambrosial rills of pleasure;
> Can man desire, can Heaven bestow, a more resplendent treasure?
> Adorned with gems so richly bright, we'll form a constellation,
> Where every star with modest light shall gild his proper station.
> How grand in age, how fair in youth, are holy Friendship, Love and Truth!

of tobacco, and the proprietor of the tavern was usually the "host."[10] This changed with the advent of the *Temperance Movement* at the beginning of the 19th century. Drinking and smoking were publicly criticized as immoral, so all fraternal organizations began to conform by passing rules that banned convivial practices in the lodge.

Chapter 5

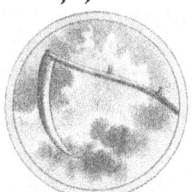

THE INDUSTRIAL REVOLUTION

In 1770, England began shifting from an agricultural to an industrial economy.[1] The rise of the factory system compelled people to move from small towns to bigger cities such as London to work. People left behind their network of families and friends whom they could call upon during hard times.[2] Unemployment and poverty were gaining high profile and becoming a national concern. Many industrializing towns exploited casual, cheap, and part-time labor who worked long hours for low wages in smelly factories and unsafe mines. A number of people died due to typhus, respiratory diseases, small pox, whooping cough and diarrhea. Illiteracy was widespread, many banks failed, and drunkenness was common.[3] This period filled with economic and moral challenges created a need for

In London, many workers lived in an overcrowded, damp, poorly lit, inadequately ventilated and unsanitary environment.
Illustration by Asher Alpay as commissioned by the author, 2015.

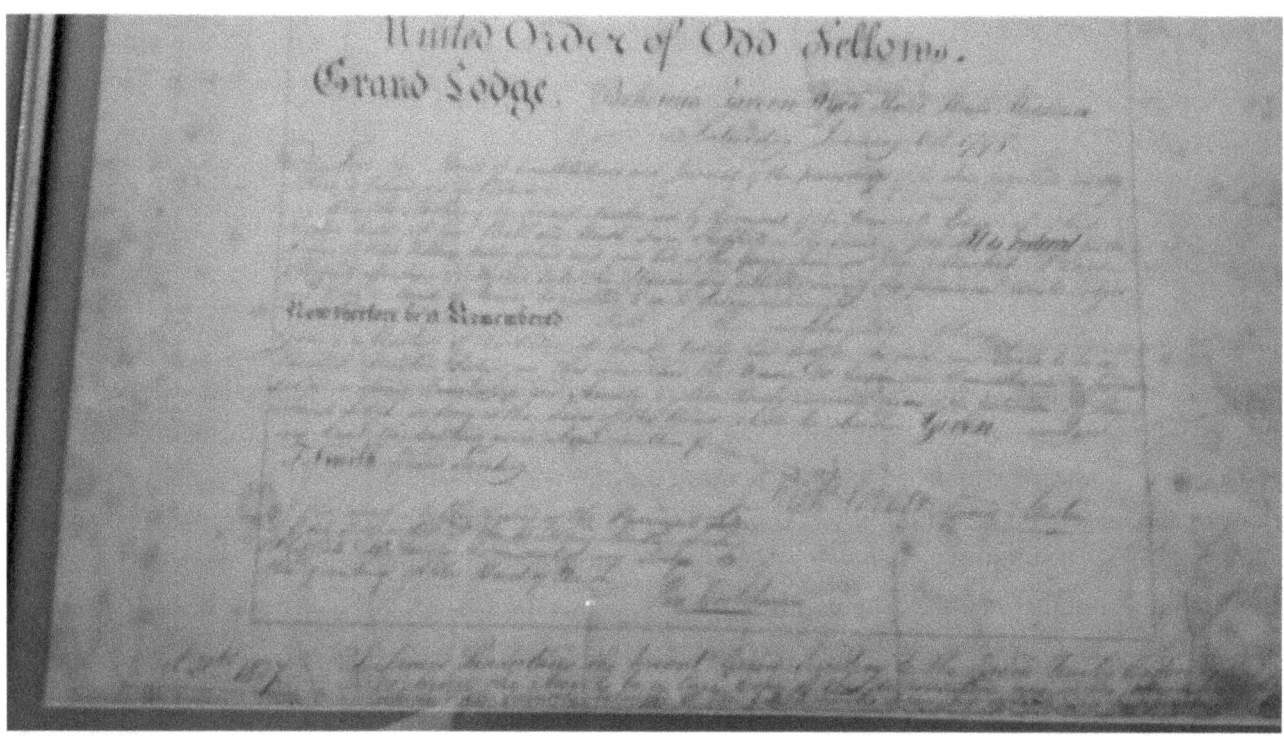

A bond of union to establish Amicable Lodge, in Sheffield, dated January 6, 1798, and signed by the Grand Master and the Grand Secretary on behalf of a meeting of the Grand Lodge of the United Order of Odd Fellows is displayed at the GUOOF headquarters in the United Kingdom today. Photo courtesy of Neil Robinson, 2014.

fraternal organizations especially among working people. Many lodges or clubs were founded because they offered social, moral and financial support at a time when governments barely provided social and welfare services.

Membership allowed people to meet acquaintances and secure real friends and was a means of gaining financial security. By joining, members could be contributors or recipients of charity and could protect themselves and their families against the harsh impact of illness, accident, injury, or death. The network of lodges provided proxy families that could help disabled and distressed members and, at the same time, also served as a social network for traveling members looking for a job in a new town or city.

Lodge rituals taught moral codes that promoted civic virtues, proper decorum and equality before the law. Rules helped maintain social order as lodges fined swearing and drunkenness and forbade debates on religion and politics during meetings. Furthermore, convivial meetings, annual feasts, and public parades fostered togetherness and provided entertainment to members and communities.

Perhaps as a result of growth, some lodges started assuming the role of a "Grand Lodge" and chartered other lodges in their area. The formation of several national federations led to the disintegration of others and prevented the union of some. For example, the Order of Patriotic Odd Fellows thrived until 1798, when it eventually merged with another group to form the United Order of Odd Fellows. Thus, at the close of the 18th century, the following regional Odd Fellows' organizations existed:

- Imperial Order of Odd Fellows in

Merit jewel belonging to the British United Order of Odd Fellows and a 100th anniversary medallion belonging to Sir John Falstaff Lodge of the Loyal Ancient and Independent Order of Odd Fellows founded in 1799. From the collection of the author.

Nottingham
- Ancient Noble Order of Odd Fellows in Bolton
- Grand United Order of Odd Fellows in Sheffield
- Economical Order of Odd Fellows in Leeds
- National Order of Odd Fellows in Salford

This federated system, with its centralized funds and arrangements for the transfer of benefits for migrants' workers, ensured financial and organizational stability for collective self-help during the members' hour of need.

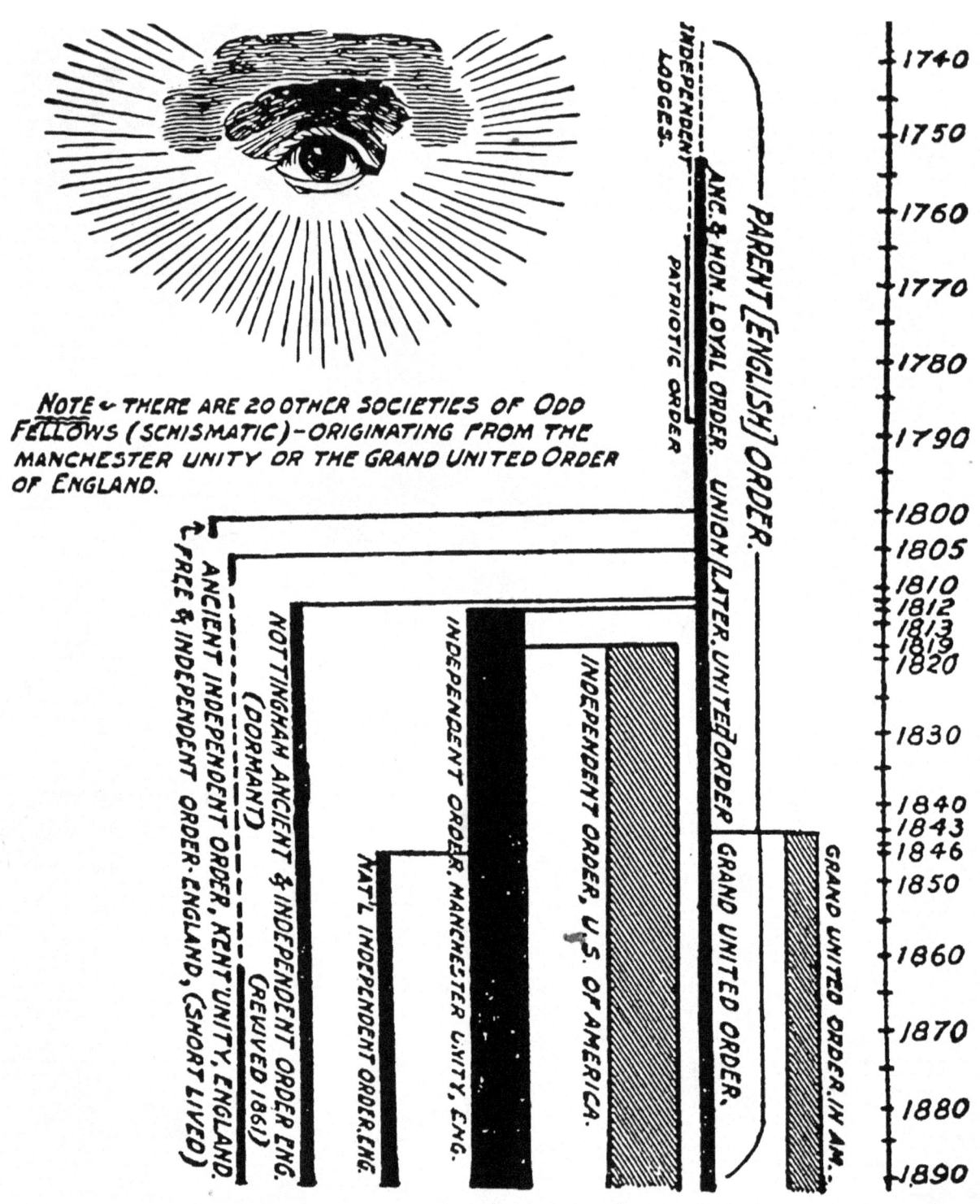

Chart showing the larger and more prominent English and American Orders of Odd Fellows, ancestry of each and dates of origin. From public domain

Chapter 6

GOVERNMENT SUPPRESSION

Religious and political intolerance and bigotry were very common in England until the end of the 18th century. When the monarchy and the churches still held absolute power and influence, any group or person who possessed a new way of thinking was at once branded as blasphemous, heretic, a cult follower, a witch, or even a devil-worshipper. In fact there was a time when churches condemned their followers for intermingling with those professing other religious beliefs.[1] Those who were found guilty of going against their commands were subjected to torture or were persecuted to death and, in many cases, burned at the stake. Thousands of people across Europe, mainly women, were

Believing that the earth rotated around the Sun, Galileo faced Roman Catholic Inquisition. Photo from wiki-commons, painting by Christiano Banti, 1857.

At the time of the Gordon Riots in 1780, John Wilkes and Sir George Savile, both politicians, were said to be members of the Odd Fellows. Photo from wiki-commons, painting by Charles Green, 1840-1898.

charged with witchcraft and were burned for petty reasons. William Tyndale was burned at the stake for his criticisms against the King and for translating the Bible into the English language.

Fraternal organizations and friendly societies faced similar opposition from the monarchy and the church during their formative years. During the 18th century, it was still possible for one to be burned at the stake if one held ideas dissimilar from those of the established religions. In fact, the last person burned at the stake died in 1781 and the *Anti-Witchcraft Law* was only repealed in 1951.[2]

Age of Enlightenment

The Age of Enlightenment was a time when religious fanaticism, violent executions by the church, and power abuse by the ruling class were beginning to be publicly criticized by intellectuals. A new way of thinking based on reason over superstition emerged. New ideas such as democracy, working men's freedom and right to vote, fair wages, access to education, and religious tolerance began to awaken the minds of the common people.[3] It was during this era that the *American Revolution*, the *French Revolution* and subsequent European wars ensued and were greeted with great approval by many Englishmen of radical learning.

Several freethinkers, radicals, and social reformers of that era who opposed the superstition, prejudice, and abuses of State power allegedly established or held membership in so-called *secret societies* or *clubs* that were believed to be revolutionary in nature and were becoming a threat to monarchical governments. In France, for example, left-wing revolutionary political movements called *Jacobin Clubs* spread beginning the year 1789.[4] Adam Weishaupt, a freethinker and promoter of religious equality, founded the *Bavarian Illuminati* in 1776. This society aimed at bringing men of wisdom into politics to create a society based on the teachings of ancient philosophers as well as newer thinkers.

When the authorities learned of their existence, they outlawed them. For instance, the Illuminati and several other similar societies were banned in Bavaria.[5] Comte Cangliostro, whose real name was Joseph Balsamo, played an important role in the political intrigues that resulted in the French Revolution. Balsamo was believed to be the founder of two secret societies, the *Asiatic Brethren* and *Knights of the Light* and was believed to be a member of the Illuminati and Freemasons.[6] Jacobite clubs, the Illuminati, and the French Freemasons were accused of conspiracy resulting in the French Revolution.[7] These incidents in neighboring countries made the English authorities fear that similar societies and clubs were planning a revolutionary plot against the government. Undoubtedly, Odd Fellowship was also a product of the Enlightenment.

Government Suppression

Fraternal organizations and friendly societies caught the attention of the ruling class when they became numerous at the close of the 18th century. When the French Revolution occurred, it became the opinion of the government that large gatherings of ordinary people were plotting against the parliamentary monarchy.

Undeniably, England at that time was rife with radical protests. There was a propaganda war between radical advocates of political and economic reform and the loyalist defenders of the status quo. The government at that time was probably apprehensive about the ideas of democracy reaching to the working classes. Freedom of association and freedom of speech among common people were still not widely acceptable during that period. Using spies and informers, the government tried to infiltrate and investigate any potential threat to parliamentary monarchy. The government eventually passed legislations to manage this growing domestic unease and to make sure that English people will not follow the example of the French who waged a revolution against their monarchy in 1789.

The English government first responded by passing the *Rose Act of 1793*, which required such societies to register, given that they conformed with the government's scrutiny of how they should be organized.[8] This was followed by the *Treasonable and Seditious Practices Act of 1795,* which banned people from speaking or printing grievances or anything against the government while the *Seditious Meetings Act of 1795* banned meetings of more than fifty people. The *Unlawful Oaths Act of 1797* further made illegal oath-taking and various other methods in any society or association. The *Corresponding Societies Act of 1799* made merger and communication between lodges and clubs illegal. Ultimately, the *Unlawful Societies Act of 1799* made membership in almost all fraternal organizations and friendly societies a criminal offence. Through lobbying by aristocrats and Dukes who were members, the Freemasons were exempted from the ban provided they submit a list of its members to the local Magistrates. All other fraternal organizations and friendly societies tried to apply for a similar exemption but to no avail.[9] The exemption is most likely the reason why many of the early records belonging to Freemasonry remained intact. On the other hand, most of the early records belonging to other fraternities were destroyed.

Fear of revolution was not the only reason for the persecution. Fraternal organizations and friendly societies, like the Odd Fellows, were "the predecessors of modern-day trade unions and could facilitate an effective local strike action by collecting additional contributions from their members for their benevolent funds."[10] Out of these funds, payments could be made to the families of members

From the collection of the author.

18th Century Provincial Tokens

There survived several 18th-century *Provincial* or *Conder tokens* that bore the name "Odd Fellows." These were made by Thomas Spence, an English radical who was an advocate of common ownership of land. Several of these tokens have the "heart and hand" symbol on the obverse side - the oldest symbol popularly used by Odd Fellowship until today. Other tokens suggest a connection with government suppression experienced by fraternal organizations during the late 18th century.

The first token shows on obverse two faces of British politicians, William Pitt and Charles Fox, and the text "Quis Rides" which is Latin for "Who is laughing." In reverse is the text, "We were born free and will never die slave." The second token shows on obverse the head of King George III entwined with the head of an ass or donkey. In reverse shows a common man being harassed by an aristocrat and the text, "British Liberty Displayed." On the observe side of other tokens are the following messages: "The Beginning of Oppression," "Noted Advocates for the Rights of Man" and "Let Tyrants Tremble at the Crow of Liberty." Newspaper accounts during this period suggests that the early Odd Fellows' functioned like labor unions, and some lodges actually supported the early labor movement. Presumably, these tokens were a radical protest by some Odd Fellows against government regulations aimed at suppressing fraternal organizations, friendly societies, and trade unions during the late 18th century, which were indeed a violation of people's freedom of association if based on human rights acceptable today.

who were on strike.[11] Moreover, many lodges served as avenue for social mixing – where working class, middle-class and even some aristocrats could fraternize with each other – a practice that was not yet common at that time.[12]

The possibilities of the lodge may have been perceived as a threat to those in authority and power because some aristocrats who were in opposition to the parliament may help finance revolutions. Thus, the ruling class was suspicious of meetings and gatherings of many groups and organizations at that time. Consequently, many of the early Odd Fellows lodges closed down while some went underground and developed secret ciphers and codes for their meetings. This meant that many documents were deliberately destroyed to protect members from identification and arrest. Undoubtedly, this is one reason why very few of the early records and artifacts of the Odd Fellows have survived until today.

Oldest Surviving Record

Allegedly, the oldest surviving record of an Odd Fellows Lodge is the minutes of meeting of the *Aristarcus Lodge, No. 9*, which met at the Globe Tavern on March 12, 1748. The said minutes of the lodge were transcribed in 1867.

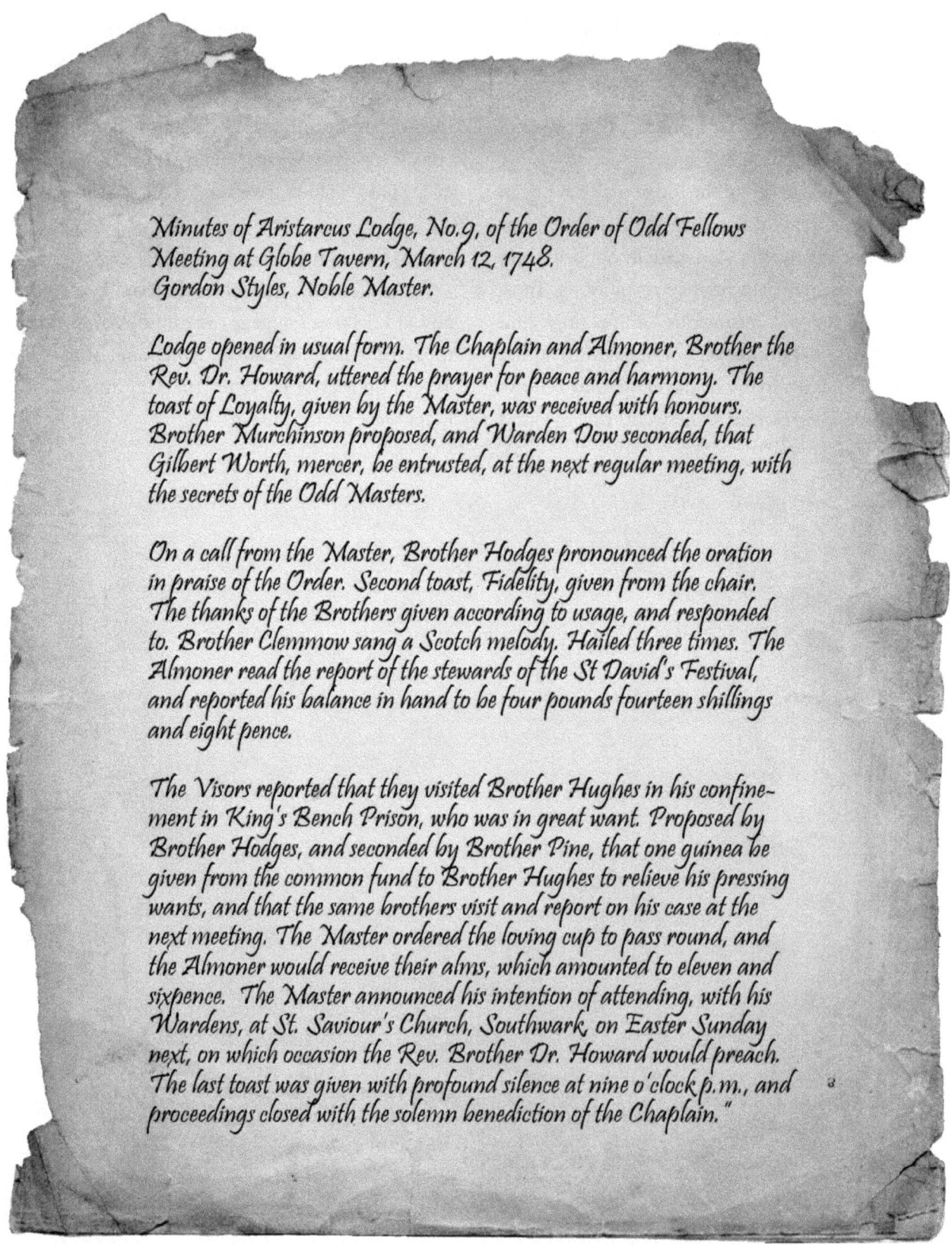

Minutes of Aristarcus Lodge, No.9, of the Order of Odd Fellows Meeting at Globe Tavern, March 12, 1748.
Gordon Styles, Noble Master.

Lodge opened in usual form. The Chaplain and Almoner, Brother the Rev. Dr. Howard, uttered the prayer for peace and harmony. The toast of Loyalty, given by the Master, was received with honours. Brother Murchinson proposed, and Warden Dow seconded, that Gilbert Worth, mercer, be entrusted, at the next regular meeting, with the secrets of the Odd Masters.

On a call from the Master, Brother Hodges pronounced the oration in praise of the Order. Second toast, Fidelity, given from the chair. The thanks of the Brothers given according to usage, and responded to. Brother Clemmow sang a Scotch melody. Hailed three times. The Almoner read the report of the stewards of the St David's Festival, and reported his balance in hand to be four pounds fourteen shillings and eight pence.

The Visors reported that they visited Brother Hughes in his confinement in King's Bench Prison, who was in great want. Proposed by Brother Hodges, and seconded by Brother Pine, that one guinea be given from the common fund to Brother Hughes to relieve his pressing wants, and that the same brothers visit and report on his case at the next meeting. The Master ordered the loving cup to pass round, and the Almoner would receive their alms, which amounted to eleven and sixpence. The Master announced his intention of attending, with his Wardens, at St. Saviour's Church, Southwark, on Easter Sunday next, on which occasion the Rev. Brother Dr. Howard would preach. The last toast was given with profound silence at nine o'clock p.m., and proceedings closed with the solemn benediction of the Chaplain."

Transcribed Minutes of Meeting of the Loyal Aristarcus Lodge No.9 of the Ancient Order of Odd Fellows held on March 12, 1748.

Chapter 7

REVIVAL

Despite government suppression, some clubs and lodges continued to exist although mostly in remote areas. This isolated condition of the Odd Fellows continued until the fear of revolution and sedition began to fade, and surviving lodges started constituting themselves into regional or national organizations, commonly known as a *Unity* or *Grand Lodge*.

United Order of Odd Fellows

In 1803, several lodges in London were apparently revived by the *Union* or *United Order of Odd Fellows*, which later claimed itself as the "Grand Lodge of England" and assumed authority over all lodges in the country.[1] This Grand Lodge was partially successful in placing all lodges under its control until 1813, when lodges that seceded years prior organized themselves into a reformed fraternal organization.[2] For a period, there were disagreements and miscommunications between some lodges in Manchester area and the United Order. When the Manchester lodges finally seceded, they ultimately formed the *Manchester Unity Independent Order of Odd Fellows* (See Chapter 8).[3]

In spite of the secession, the Grand United Order of Odd Fellows (GUOOF) continued to exist

Members of the Rose of Hamilton Lodge of the Grand United Order of Odd Fellows pose for a photo, circa 1930. From the collection of the author.

Early print of a "Toast Song" belonging to the Grand United Order of Odd Fellows. From the collection of the author.

34 | Odd Fellows

and even chartered lodges in the United States in 1843, which were primarily composed of African-American members.[4] The GUOOF still exists today with lodges in Africa, Australia, Canada, Cuba, Dominican Republic, Grand Turks, Netherlands, New Zealand, West Indies, United Kingdom, and the United States of America.[5]

Numerous Affiliated Orders

Surviving Odd Fellows in other regions also organized themselves into a *Regional Unity* or *Affiliated Order,* often without knowledge of the existence of similar associations. In 1805, the *Ancient Independent Order of Odd Fellows Kent Unity* was formed. The *Free and Independent Order of Odd Fellows* was apparently formed in Dover in 1807.[6] Subsequent breakaways from older associations further resulted in the formation of about 34 different Affiliated Orders of Odd Fellows in the United Kingdom by the end of the 19th century.[7]

Among these were the following:
- Grand United Order of Odd Fellows
- Independent Order of Odd Fellows, Manchester Unity
- Nottingham Ancient Imperial Order of Odd Fellows
- Ancient Noble Order of Odd Fellows, Bolton Unity
- British United Order of Odd Fellows
- Improved Independent Order of Odd Fellows, London Unity
- Albion Order of Odd Fellows
- Independent Order of Odd Fellows, Kingston Unity
- National Independent Order of Odd Fellows
- Ancient Independent Order of Odd Fellows, Kent Unity
- Independent Order of Odd Fellows, Wolverhampton Unity

Chapter 8

RISE OF THE MANCHESTER UNITY ODD FELLOWS

By the early 1800s, fraternal organizations and friendly societies had "replaced the craft guilds as working people's most important means to avoid pauperism".[1] Lodges helped eradicate poverty and cultivated the virtue of protecting fellow members, women and children from distress.[2] As government regulations became relaxed, small independent lodges and benevolent clubs eventually joined together to form regional or national Affiliated Orders.

In 1810, *Naylor's Amalgamated Society* and *Prince Regent Lodge* of Odd Fellows in the City of Salford, Manchester, united to form the *Lord Abercrombie Lodge No.1* by self-institution and focused on the purpose of mutual relief for its members.[3] It was argued that they were convivial, political, and charitable in the beginning and, on their merger, the benevolent aspect became the principal aim. This new feature resulted in membership growth and financial strength and other lodges in the area eventually followed their example. *Lord Abercrombie Lodge No.1* and six other lodges declared themselves "independent" from the *Grand United Order of Odd Fellows* and spontaneously formed the *Manchester Unity Independent Order of Odd Fellows* (MUIOOF).[4]

At first, all their lodges were located within or near the Manchester area. But with their improved system, the MUIOOF were able to influence other independent lodges and associations throughout England to join their Unity (including small benefit clubs formerly not named as Odd Fellows). In just a few years, they also chartered lodges in the United States and Canada. By 1845, there were Manchester Unity lodges in every English county. Lodges also were established in Ireland, Scotland, Germany, New

Annual Movable Conference of the Independent Order of Odd Fellows, Manchester Unity, held in Portsmouth, Hampshire, England, in 1929. Photo collection of the author.

The Manchester Unity Odd Fellows has always promoted international brotherhood regardless of race, nationality, and social status. Photo taken during the Annual Movable Conference of the Manchester Unity in 1910. Photo courtesy of Manchester Unity Oddfellows.

Zealand, Australia, and other parts of the kingdom. In 1860, lodges were opened in South Africa, South America, and Istanbul. As membership grew, Manchester Unity Odd Fellows eventually registered with the government and complied with regulations to avoid persecution.[5]

When Manchester Unity IOOF lodges became legal entities, many built or purchased their own meeting halls instead of gathering in taverns and pubs. This helped the organization gain respectability and served as physical manifestations of the stability and permanence of the organization.[6]

By 1850, Manchester Unity Independent Order of Odd Fellows became influential, and attracted

1808
Robert Naylor formed a social and benevolent club known as *Naylor's Amalgamated Society,* which met at the Ropemakers Arms in Salford, Manchester, England.

1809
A member from London named "Bolton" became a resident of Manchester and was able to get a dispensation from London to form *Victory Lodge of Odd Fellows.*

1813
A convention of past and present officers of all lodges of Odd Fellows in and around Manchester was held and the name, *Manchester Unity Independent Order of Odd Fellows,* was officially adopted.

Customs of the Manchester Unity Odd Fellows include ritualistic ceremonies, wearing of regalia, signs, passwords, and symbolism. In the lodge room, Odd Fellows are required to conduct themselves with propriety and decorum. Photo courtesy of Keith Potter

men of education, affluence, and high social and political standing. Many educated citizens became familiar with the Odd Fellows and became devoted enthusiasts. MUIOOF became one of the largest and richest friendly societies in the United Kingdom during the mid-19th and 20th centuries. The peak of membership was sometime in 1922, when MUIOOF had more than 2 million members.[7] The adoption of the welfare state, national health insurance, and other factors resulted in the decline of membership of fraternal and friendly societies in general.

Ceremonial Work

The MUIOOF has various levels of

1814

A *Grand Committee* was formed and a Grand Master was elected.

1817

Facing problems of lack of uniformity and having issues with local travel relief, Manchester Unity IOOF further revised the "old" ritual ceremonies and proceeded to standardize the degree work for their lodges.

1820

The *Duke of York Lodge* of the Manchester Unity IOOF chartered *Washington Lodge No.1* in Baltimore, Maryland, and gave the members there the authority to charter other lodges in North America.

Rise of the Manchester Unity | 39

Visit of the Manchester Unity Odd Fellows to the grounds of Osborne House in 1893. Photo from the collection of the author.

Annual Movable Conference of the Manchester Unity Odd Fellows in Bradford, 1909. Photo from the collection of the author.

initiation. The first is the *Welcoming* or *Initiation Ceremony*.[8] This is followed by Minor Degrees to educate new members of the aims and objectives of the organization, namely: *Gold*, *Scarlet*, *Blue* and *White* degree.[9] Past Officers' Degrees are also conferred such as the *Past Noble Grand's Degree*, *Past Vice Grand's Degree* and *Past Elective Secretary's Degree*.[10] A member who has served the office of Immediate Past Noble Grand of a Lodge, and has taken the four minor degree and the *Degree of Past Noble Grand*, will be qualified to receive the *Purple Degree*.[11]

At the District or Provincial level, the *Past District Deputy Grand Master's Degree* is conferred to a member who has successfully completed his term of office of *District Grand Master*. The highest degree is the *Grand Master's Degree* conferred prior to a member's installation as Grand Master.[12] The final ceremony to pay respect to a deceased member is called the *Lodge of Remembrance*.[13]

Fraternal or Beneficial

At present, the lodges under the MUIOOF are categorized as *Ritual and Social* on one side and *Financial* on the other.[14] Basically, there are two kinds of membership: *fraternal* and/or *beneficial*. Fraternal members still undergo traditional degrees of initiation and hold ritualistic meetings, while the beneficial members join mainly for the insurance and other financial benefits with an option not to undergo ceremonial work. Also, it is now left to the individual lodges to decide whether or not to use ritual ceremony during meetings.[15]

Today, the MUIOOF, also known by their trade name *Oddfellows*, is a worldwide organization with autonomous Grand Lodges in the United Kingdom, Australia, and New Zealand. There are also lodges that are referred to as *Overseas Districts* or *Branches* attached to the mother organization in the United Kingdom and operating in North, Central, and South America and the Mediterranean area.[16] The organization currently has 314,000 members[17] based in the United Kingdom, Australia, Gibraltar, Guyana, Malta, Natal, New Zealand, Otago, Dominican Republic, Transvaal, South Africa and some in the United States and Canada. At least 50,000 are fraternal members while the rest are beneficial members.

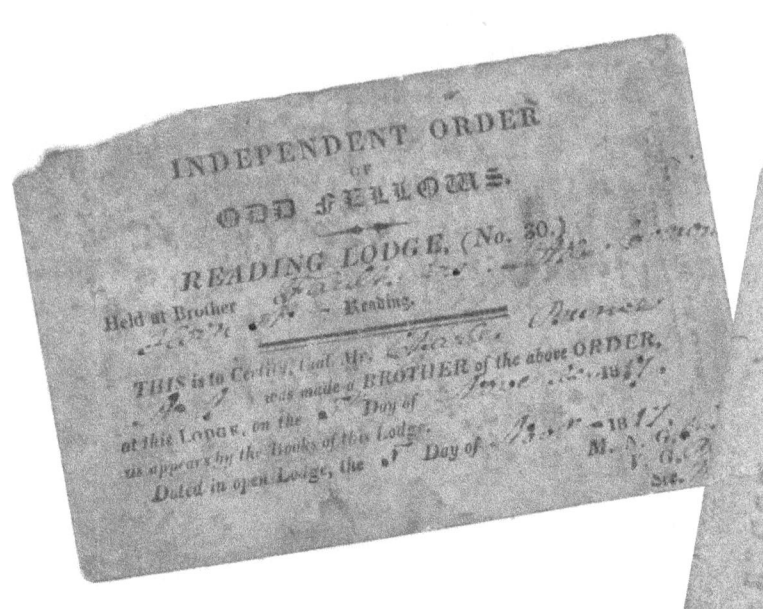
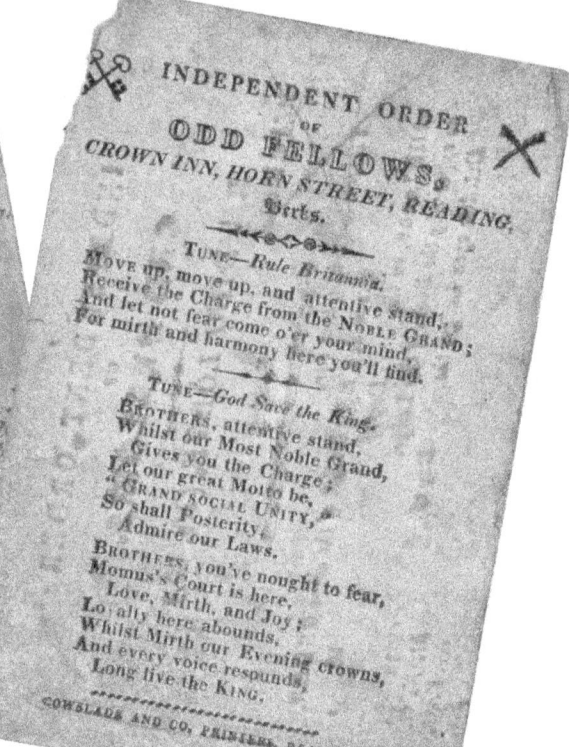

Certificate of Membership belonging to a member of Reading Lodge No.30 of the Independent Order of Odd Fellows, based in Reading, Berkshire, England, dated November 5, 1817. Photo from the collection of the author.

Chapter 9

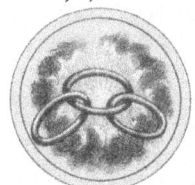

ODD FELLOWSHIP IN NORTH AMERICA

Several attempts were made to establish Odd Fellowship in North America in the 18th century but these early lodges failed to obtain a charter from England.[1] Thus, because of its charter relationship with the Manchester Unity Independent Order of Odd Fellows in the United Kingdom, the official institution of Odd Fellowship in North America is regarded by many as being founded by Thomas

Thomas Wildey and four other members met and instituted Washington Lodge No.1 inside the Seven Stars Tavern in Baltimore, Maryland, on April 26, 1819. *Illustration by Ainslie Heilich as commissioned by the author, 2016.*

Wildey and four other English immigrants namely: John Welch, John Duncan, John Cheatham and Richard Rushworth.[2]

Washington Lodge

In 1817, Thomas Wildey immigrated to the United States from England and found employment in Baltimore. He was a stranger in the land and felt the need for companionship. At that time, the United States was still a young nation recovering from the adverse effects of the War of 1812.[3] The State of Illinois had just been admitted into the Union as the 21st state and Alabama was still seeking for admission.[4] Baltimore was suffering both a yellow fever epidemic and mass unemployment, which underscored the urgent need for a benevolent institution.[5]

The following year, Thomas Wildey met John Welch who was also an Odd Fellow from England. After spending time together they discussed the possibility of establishing a lodge in the City. But the ancient usage established a rule that a minimum of five people are needed to institute a lodge.[6] They needed to find at least three more members, so they advertised their plans of forming a lodge in the *Baltimore American* on February 13, 1819. John Duncan and John Cheatham responded and attended the meeting. The two proved themselves to be worthy members and were duly qualified. They still needed one more member but private search left them unsuccessful. Again, they advertised in the *Baltimore American* on March 27, 1819. Finally, Richard Rushworth responded to the second advertisement and proved himself to be a worthy member. They cross-examined each other and all four were believed to be affiliated with the United Order of Odd Fellows in England. John Duncan, on the other hand, was also able to prove himself as an Odd Fellow through the ancient password, sign, and grip.[7]

They met again on April 26, 1819, this time at the *Seven Stars Tavern* in Baltimore, Maryland, and self-instituted *Washington Lodge No.1*. Within one month, they aligned their work towards the Manchester Unity Independent Order of Odd Fellows and took the initiative to obtain a charter. *Abercrombie Lodge* in Manchester issued them a dispensation but this never reached them. Through John Crowder, who visited Baltimore in 1819, the lodge finally received a charter from the *Duke of York Lodge* in Preston, England, in 1820. This gave them the authority to charter other lodges in the continent.[8]

Early Purposes

The early lodges in the United States were

1799	1802	1806
Masonic historian, Robert Macoy, wrote that Odd Fellowship "was introduced into the United States as early as 1799, at which time a lodge was constituted in Connecticut."	John Duncan, who was a charter member of Washington Lodge No.1 in 1819, was initiated in a Lodge of Odd Fellows in Baltimore in 1802.	*Shakespeare Lodge No.1* was instituted in New York on December 23, 1806. The lodge dissolved in 1812 and was revived in 1818. Other lodges were also instituted in Philadelphia and New York through the efforts of Shakespeare Lodge.

Three Odd Links

Sometime in 1822, a secret fraternity within the IOOF was formed called the "Three Odd Links" with Thomas Wildey, John Boyd, and William Couth as first members.[1] Whatever was the purpose of the trio for the Three Odd Links was not clear. It was suggested by some that it was a "commemoration of the first half decade, others that it was a secret pledge never to abandon the Order, and others to secure a private celebration of the founding date of Washington Lodge and a renewal of the vows of brotherhood of the old members."[2] What is known is that the Links privately met every 26th day of April every year and parted with tokens of friendship.

When William Couth died, Augustus Mathiot was selected as his successor. On Wildey's death, Richard Marley became his replacement. But because of old age, Marley passed away before he had any successor.[3] Mathiot was the last member but the seats were left unfilled until he passed away, hence, he was the last of the "Three Odd Links."

mostly convivial in character with a mixture of moral and charitable purposes. Members met in taverns or saloons to have a good time while taking a solemn obligation of mutual assistance in times of unemployment, sickness, death and distress.[9] Lodges served as a social network and source of aid for traveling members. But when college-educated men became members, the ethical and intellectual purposes became the dominant feature over the social and charitable aspect.[10] Applicants for membership would undergo a series of lectures and ceremonies that taught lessons of mortality, benevolence, brotherly love and charity with emphasis on moderation of personal desires.

Grand Lodge of the United States

For a time, the lodges in Maryland and other states were unaware of each other's existence. There was no state or national governing body in Maryland or in the United States. A *Committee of Past Grands* was formed consisting of past officers of all lodges in Maryland but with advisory powers only.[11] This changed in 1821, when the *Grand Lodge of Maryland and the United States* was formed. Thomas Wildey was elected as the first Grand Master, along with a Deputy Grand Master, Grand Warden, Grand

1815	1816	1817
Two Odd Fellows lodges existed in Halifax, Canada, as early as 1815.	*Prince Regent Lodge* of Odd Fellows was instituted in New York but eventually disbanded or became unheard of.	*Massachusetts Lodge No. 1* was self-instituted in Boston. The lodge later affiliated with the IOOF and received a charter from the Grand Lodge of Maryland and the United States on March 20, 1820.

Thomas Wildey (1782-1861) is revered as founder of the Independent Order of Odd Fellows in North America. He was born in London, England, on January 15, 1782. At age 21, he joined the Odd Fellows Lodge No.17 in London and became a Past Grand at the age 23. Three years after, he was instrumental in organizing Morning Star Lodge No.38 in another city in England where he was also elected as presiding officer and became its Past Grand. In 1819, Wildey was elected as the first Noble Grand of Washington Lodge No.1. He was unanimously elected as the first Grand Master when the Grand Lodge of Maryland and the United States was created in 1821. He then served as the first Grand Sire of the IOOF in 1824 when the Grand Lodge of the United States became a separate organization composed of Grand Lodge representatives from all over North America. Photo courtesy of The Sovereign Grand Lodge, IOOF.

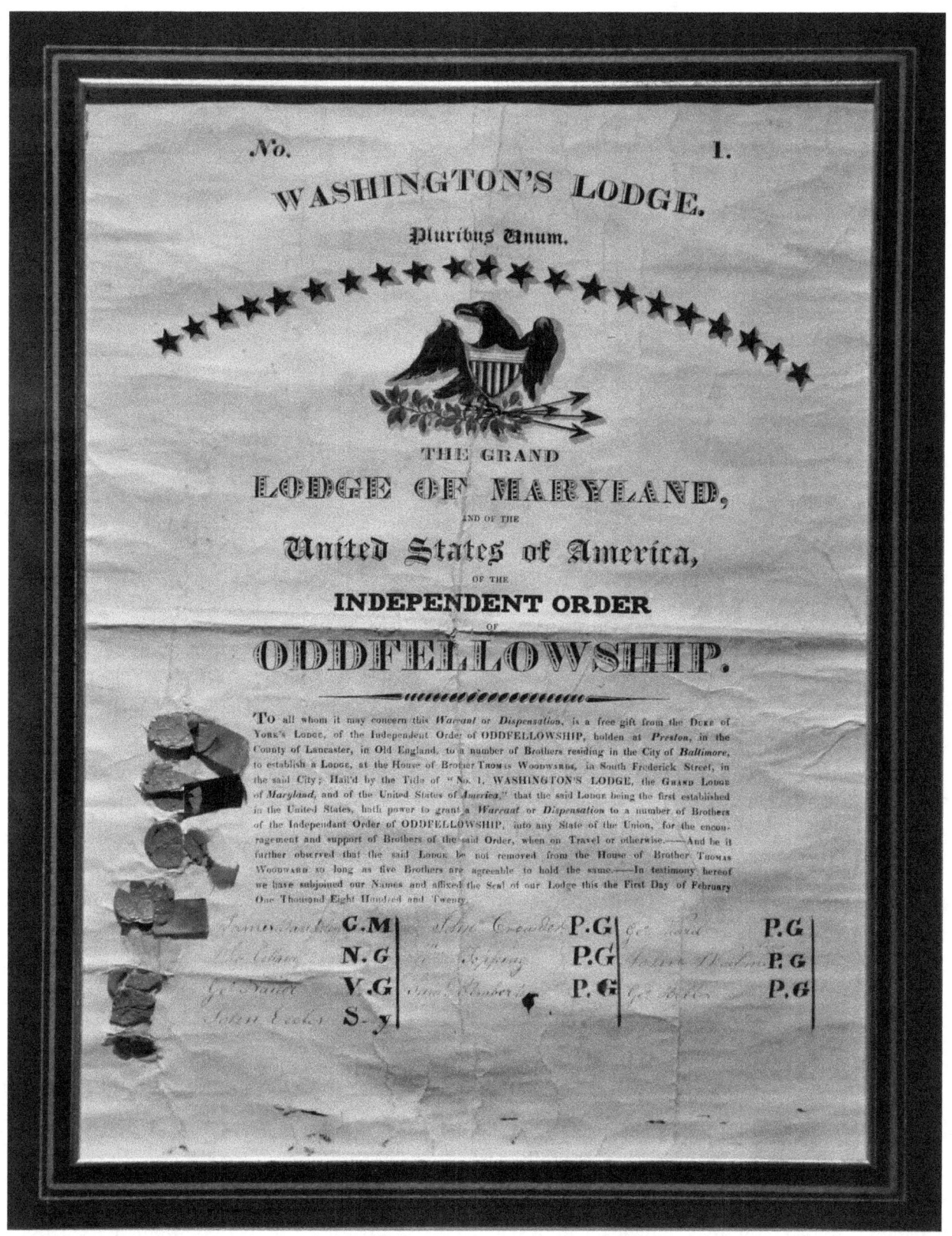

Dispensation of Washington Lodge No.1 under the Grand Lodge of Maryland and of the United States of America granted by the Duke of York Lodge in Preston, United Kingdom, on February 1, 1820. Photo by the author.

Odd Fellowship in North America | 47

Secretary, Grand Treasurer, and Grand Guardian. Soon, existing self-instituted lodges in Philadelphia, New York, and Boston made efforts for a general union and applied for charter from the Grand Lodge. By 1823, the Grand Lodge of Massachusetts, Grand Lodge of New York, and the Grand Lodge of Pennsylvania were instituted.[12]

On January 15, 1825, the *Grand Lodge of the United States*, now known as *The Sovereign Grand Lodge*, became a separate entity from the Grand Lodge of Maryland. This gave the Grand Lodge of Maryland the power to exercise jurisdiction over lodges in Maryland only and allowed the Grand Lodge of the United States to be made up of representatives of several Grand Lodges in North America. This enabled the IOOF in the United States to become a democratic and united system under one acknowledged head. In the same year, the Grand Lodge of the United States outdid other social organizations of that era when it took the initiative to ban drinking and smoking during lodge meetings in conformity with the growing *Temperance Movement* at that time.[13]

By the 1840s, the Grand Lodge of the United States of the IOOF chartered Grand Lodges of Alabama, Arkansas, Canada, Connecticut, Cuba, Delaware, District of Columbia, Georgia, Illinois, Indiana, Iowa, Kentucky, Louisiana, Maine, Mississippi, Missouri, New Hampshire, New Jersey, North Carolina, Ohio, Rhode Island, South Carolina, Tennessee, Texas, Virginia, and Wisconsin.[14] The IOOF began to attract people from every profession and social status.[15]

Separation from Manchester Unity

In 1834, six farm laborers known in history as the *Tolpuddle Martyrs,* were arrested for taking an oath of secrecy and were sentenced to seven years' imprisonment.[16] The verdict shocked many fraternal organizations in England. As a result, Manchester Unity Odd Fellows abolished their oaths and simplified their initiations for fear of a backlash against their organization.[17] In 1839, both the MUIOOF in the United Kingdom and the IOOF in North America revised their ceremonies and initiation rituals with disastrous results.[18]

The changes made were radical in nature, so that Manchester Unity members who visited lodges in North America found it difficult to pass the necessary tests and were denied admission in lodges. This eventually led to the official separation of the two affiliated orders in 1843.[19] What was not clearly understood by the Odd Fellows in North America during this period was the objection by the British government against fraternal organizations and friendly societies.[20] As mentioned earlier, the reason was fear that these groups were plotting against the English King, so any association that wanted to remain in existence was required to register with the government or close down. To register, the MUIOOF had to dispense with certain ways by which they conducted their ceremonies, particularly in giving degrees of initiation and in administering the oath of membership.[21] They had to revise their degrees from dramatic form to purely lectures.[22] It had been often erroneously alleged that the IOOF in the United States absolved their allegiance and affiliation with the Manchester Unity Odd Fellows because the latter granted dispensation to an African-American Lodge in New York City.[23] However, the Manchester Unity IOOF in the United Kingdom never chartered a lodge for black men. It was the Grand United Order of Odd Fellows that did, and the year 1843 was just a mere coincidence.

First to Officially Accept Women

During this period, women were not yet allowed to own property, go to school, practice a

African-American Odd Fellows

During this era, it was publicly unacceptable for white and black Americans to commingle in the same school, church, comfort room, or fraternal lodge (see Chapter 16). Many countries followed racial segregation in their customs and laws. Thus, the IOOF was constrained from accepting blacks as members especially in the United States where racial segregation laws were enforced. Prior to 1843, several groups of white men in Pottsville, Pennsylvania, and the vicinity were operating under the name *Grand United Order of Odd Fellows*. This latter order also was prohibited from accepting black members due to the existing racial prejudice of the times.[1]

Peter Ogden, revered as the founder of the GUOOF in the United States.

So in 1843, African-Americans formed *Philomathean Lodge No. 646* in New York and was granted a dispensation by the *Grand United Order of Odd Fellows* (GUOOF) of England through the effort of Peter Ogden who was a member of *Victoria Lodge No. 448* in Liverpool.[2] The GUOOF of the United States eventually became the Odd Fellows' group for blacks. Many of the founding members of the GUOOF lodges in the United States were known abolitionists and civil rights activists including John C. Bowers, who served as the Grand Master of the GUOOF of Pennsylvania. The early purposes of the GUOOF were the following:[3]

"1st, To unite fraternally all male colored freemen of sound bodily health and good moral character who are socially acceptable and above the ages of twenty one years.
2nd, To give all moral and material aid in its power to its members and those dependent upon them.
3rd, To educate its members socially, morally, and intellectually.
4th, To establish a fund for the relief of sick and distressed members."

Beginning in the late 1800s, nearly every prominent African-American was a member of the GUOOF.[4]

profession, vote, hold public office, or join fraternal organizations. The Independent Order of Odd Fellows started to deviate from this trend when a resolution to extend fraternal care and protection to women was passed by the Grand Lodge of the United States in 1845.

"Resolved: That it is expedient for this Grand Lodge to adopt some measure by which wives of Odd Fellows may be enabled to make themselves known to members of the Order and prove themselves when among strangers."

This further improved when the Independent Order of Odd Fellows became the first international fraternal organization to officially accept women on its adoption of the "Rebekah Degree" on September

The IOOF became a family affair. Sons of members joined an Odd Fellows Lodge while the daughters joined a Rebekah Lodge as early as age eighteen. Photo from the collection of the author.

20, 1851. This degree was written by Schuyler Colfax, who later became the Vice President of the United States from 1869 to 1873. By September 25, 1868, the Rebekah Lodges were given full freedom to elect and vote for their own set of officers, collect fees and dues, and organize their own philanthropic projects. With their example and success, many other fraternal organizations also opened their doors to women by establishing auxiliary groups for women. This was way ahead of the times, noting that the United States of America only recognized women's rights and suffrage in 1920.

Inter-fraternal Recognition with IOOF

In 1876, a movement for the restoration of friendly relations between the IOOF and the MUIOOF began but made little progress.[24] The experiences during World War I and World War II played an important role in making the two organizations realize the importance of a friendly relationship. In 1944, a committee was formed to explore possibilities for more friendly ties between the two Affiliated Orders.[25]

But owing to the big differences in the degrees of initiation, finances, and general method of operations, the possibility of an organic union is remote, if not impossible. Both affiliated orders were able to create a system that would allow inter-visitation without need for departure from any of the well-established operations and organizational structure of either organization. This was done by adopting an *inter-fraternal sign of recognition*.

Chapter 10

THE GOLD RUSH

In the beginning of its colonization, North America was a land of farmers.[1] This was changed when gold was discovered in California in 1848 followed by discoveries of the precious metal in Canada, Australia, and New Zealand in the 1850s. As a result, an immense number of people from all over the world immigrated to these areas in search of gold. Thousands of men and women abandoned their livelihood elsewhere and risked their lives to travel in hopes of making a fortune from gold or from services provided to the miners. Many people voyaged with just enough money to pay their trip and were broke on arrival. The journey was not easy since fever, diarrhea, and scurvy were prevalent.[2] Many people got sick on the way or upon arrival. Some did not even reach their destinations; they died on their way to these presumed gold-rich areas. Some people became rich while many did not. This period in history is known as the *Gold Rush*.

Traveling Odd Fellows

As people traveled, the fraternal and benevolent purposes of Odd Fellowship were put into practical use. In 1849, for example, a group of young men started out on the long journey on their horses but one became ill about half-way.[3] The others believed that there was no use delaying their journey on account of the person who fell ill, and decided to abandon him. In desperation, Thomas K. Hook gave the "Odd Fellows sign of distress,"[4] which was recognized by other Odd Fellows who rescued and nursed him back to health. In later years, he became the county sheriff, president of the Council of Stockton, and mayor of the city.[5] During the same year in Sacramento, Dr. John F. Morse, General A.M. Winn, and over a hundred Odd Fellows organized an *Odd Fellows Relief Association* and elected General Winn as the first president. This association provided aid to those who got sick associated with traveling or working in the gold mines. In the absence of government social

A forty-niner peers into the slit of California's American River in 1850. Many of these miners helped establish early lodges in California. Photo source: wiki-commons, public domain.

The first gold rush in North America was in Tennessee in 1827. But because Cherokee Indians settled in the area, it was only in 1836 that gold mining really started. Shown on photo is the meeting hall of Gap Creek Lodge No.72 of the IOOF located inside a cave in Carter County - one of the gold mining areas in the State. Photo from Henry Stillson, *The Three Link Fraternity*, 1900.

services and charity organizations at that time, the benevolence of the Odd Fellows was not limited to their members. During the Cholera epidemic of 1850, for example, the Odd Fellows spent about $27,000 to set up a temporary hospital for the community and donated coffins for the deceased.[6] In the hospital, members would nurse the sick for free, prepared meals, and buried the dead.[7] During the same year, they established the first hospital in California in partnership with the Freemasons.[8]

Devoted Odd Fellows like Dr. Morse also generously gave free services to the sick who could not afford to pay. And when General Winn became the executive officer of the Sacramento City government in 1849, no man was refused a coffin for burial.[9]

Expansion

Before the start of the gold rush, there were already Odd Fellows in the western part of the United States as well as overseas. Many of them established

Many people took great pride of their membership in the Odd Fellows that they would often hold public parades wearing their fancy regalia and bringing with them their lodge paraphernalia. Photo courtesy of the Grand Lodge of Illinois, IOOF, 1878.

lodges although often without a charter. In 1836, a group of Englishmen formed an Odd Fellows Lodge in Sydney, Australia.[10] In 1840, English Odd Fellows first held their meeting in Melbourne, Australia, and elected Dr. Augustus Greeves as their Noble Grand.[11] In 1847, a meeting of Odd Fellows transpired in San Francisco, California, and a lodge was opened but eventually closed when most of the members left for the gold mines. Several other attempts to officially establish a lodge in San Francisco was tried but unsuccessful because not enough people would stay within the same area.

When members returned to the city, however, they had *California Lodge No.1* officially chartered on September 9, 1849.[12] As more people came to California, more lodges were also established in neighboring towns. The growth was so rapid that the Independent Order of Odd Fellows became incorporated on April 12, 1852 and the *Grand Lodge of California* was formed on May 17, 1853.[13] From thereon, more lodges were established rapidly across the State and in other places where miners would travel in search of gold. On March 10, 1864, Odd Fellows from California instituted *Victoria Lodge No.1* in British Columbia, Canada.[14] In Australia, gold seekers were on the move and also opened lodges in towns where gold reserves were found. In 1867, for example, the strongest lodge was in the gold town of Wahalla. From Australia, miners traveled to New Zealand and also established lodges

The Gold Rush | **53**

The California Seal

California Lodge No.1 of the IOOF was instituted exactly one year before California was admitted as the thirty-first State. Original steps to officially form a lodge were undertaken in 1847 but were put on hold because many members left for the gold mines.[1] Prior to the establishment of the lodge, a seal was designed and adopted.

The California Lodge No.1 seal adopted includes the goddess of wisdom, Minerva, looking to the right, a miner digging near the water's edge, ships at the harbor and mountains in the background. In 1849, a similar seal was adopted by the State of California which also features the goddess Minerva, but looking to the left, a miner digging near the waterfront and ships at the harbor. At the feet of Minerva stands the California grizzly bear.

Credit for designing the State Seal went to Robert S. Garnett, a member of the Independent Order of Odd Fellows.[2] It is believed that he may have designed both the seal of the lodge and that of the state, or at least used the lodge seal as pattern. Unfortunately, written records concerning the seal of California Lodge No.1 and the seal of the State of California were destroyed during the San Francisco earthquake in 1906.[3]

in areas where they settled.[15]

As members voyaged, they brought Odd Fellowship with them. Shortly, it became typical for developing towns during this era to have an Odd Fellows Lodge. Usually, the lodge owned a building right in the center of town. These buildings served not only as a meeting place for members but also as the first school, courtroom, and community center.[16] Many of the early town leaders and pioneers were members of the Odd Fellows.[17] Hence, the organization somehow helped with the establishment of law and order in these developing localities. Soon, the Odd Fellows were also building cemeteries and homes for widows and orphans.

Chapter 11

AMERICAN CIVIL WAR

From the beginning of its colonization, slavery was acceptable across North America. With the growth of the factory system and the increased number of immigrants, however, the need for slaves in Northern states decreased but not in Southern states.[1] The South was much more stationary since there was scarce immigration, there were few cities, and the factory system showed slow progress.[2] The continued growth of the cotton industry in the South made slavery an essential element because cost of production was cheaper with slave labor. In 1860 alone, cotton exports were worth $191 million, which was 57% of the value of all American exports.[3] Nearly 4 million slaves were employed and slave property was worth at least $2 billion. Abolition of slavery meant the collapse of the whole Southern economy and a big financial loss for slave owners in the South.[4]

During the 1860 presidential election, Republicans led by Abraham Lincoln opposed

President Lincoln, writing the proclamation of Freedom. Odd Fellows symbolism can be seen on the background such as three links chain engraved on a book, the globe, and the weighing scale. Illustration by David Gilmour Blythe, 1863.

> ### Andersonville Prison Camp
>
>
>
> Sergeant Leroy L. Key, gained a brief amount of fame as founder of the "Regulators" in Andersonville Prison. He was a member of the Independent Order of Odd Fellows. He died on December 2, 1880 and was buried at an Odd Fellows lot at Oakridge Cemetery in Springfield, Illinois.
>
> Meanwhile at Andersonville Prison Camp, Georgia, the condition of the prisoners was tough. They drank water, washed and bathed from the same creek and their wastes were drained into the same source. Their shelters were only made of tree branches, wood planks, a few tent parts, and shreds of blankets. As a result, the prisoners would suffer from the heat of the summer and the cold of the winter.[1] The members of Odd Fellows were fortunate because they remained true to their pledge of brotherhood and were sympathetic towards each other despite the war. Prisoner Odd Fellows received special aid from their fraternity brothers from inside and outside of prison.[2] When the tents finally arrived, the Confederate prison guards who were Odd Fellows even made sure that prisoners who were Odd Fellows were first served.[3]
>
> But inside the prison there was a gang of about 150 to 500 Union prisoners called the "Raiders" who traded information to the Confederate troops for food and better treatment, and they robbed, beat, killed, and controlled their fellow inmates.[4] In 1864, a group of Union prisoners led by Sergeant Leroy L. Key organized the "Regulators" as an internal force to counter the mischief of the "Raiders." Eventually, the leaders of the "Raiders" faced trial and six of them were hanged inside the prison on July 11, 1864.[5]

the expansion of slavery in the United States. As a result, seven states in the South with cotton-based economies seceded from the United States before the inauguration of Lincoln as president on March 4, 1861, and formed the Confederacy with Jefferson F. Davis as their president. The civil war began and about 2.1 million Northerners and 880,000 Southerners took up arms and fought each other from 1861 to 1865.[5]

During the Civil War

At the start of war, many Odd Fellows' buildings in the South were deserted and all the regalia, books, and records were left behind. Some buildings were forcibly taken by soldiers and used as barracks.[6] Others served as hospitals, canteens, and even makeshift morgues.[7] The books, records, and paraphernalia were exposed to idle and vicious curiosity and destroyed. In some instances, Odd Fellows buildings were wrecked and the treasuries of lodges were robbed. Some soldiers, who were members of Odd Fellows themselves, made efforts to collect these books and surrendered them to the Grand Lodge of the United States for safe-keeping.[8]

When the Grand Lodge of the United States (now called Sovereign Grand Lodge) held their annual meeting in 1861, Grand Sire R.B. Boylston and thirty Grand Representatives of the eleven Grand Lodges located in the South were absent.[9] The officers and Grand Representatives present during their meeting adopted resolutions declaring that Odd Fellowship was "above and beyond divisions and classifications of political party and sect, reaffirming the perpetuity of Odd Fellowship, and urging members everywhere to leave all political differences beyond the portals of the Order."[10] This was passed unanimously and religiously observed. The fraternal ties with the members of Southern states were affirmed by the practice of leaving their chairs vacant until their return.[11] Thomas Wildey attended the sessions of the Grand Lodge of the United States for the last time. One month later, the founder of Odd Fellowship in North America died.[12]

In 1862, Deputy Grand Sire Milton Herndon congratulated the IOOF for the fact that it continued to minister to those in need. Despite the two sides fighting against each other, Odd Fellows were still true to one another and in their solemn pledge to help the widows and orphans of fallen Odd Fellows and in performing funeral rites for deceased members.[13] Efforts to establish lodges in other countries such as Canada and Australia were also ongoing.[14] In 1863, the Grand Representatives re-affirmed their non-partisan feelings towards the Odd Fellows in Southern states and directed the Grand Secretary to send printed copies of the proceedings of the meeting to the representatives of Southern states who were absent.[15] They also adopted a program of benefits that gave its members a fixed and stipulated amount. In 1864, it was reported that the total amount of $462,196 was spent for the relief of distressed members and their families, for the education of orphans, and for burying the dead.[16] Exactly $12,077 was placed in the treasury for the construction of a monument to honor Thomas Wildey.[17]

End of the Civil War

On April 9, 1865, General Robert E. Lee of the Confederacy surrendered to General Ulysses S. Grant of the Union. Five days after, President Lincoln was shot and died early the next morning. On May 10, 1865, Jefferson F. Davis was arrested on the accusation that he was the mastermind of the assassination of President Lincoln. Other Confederate Generals eventually surrendered by that summer and peace began to spread across the United States.

As soon as communication to the Southern states became accessible, letters were sent by the Grand Lodge of the United States to all IOOF Grand Lodges in the Southern states inquiring about their condition and giving advice and encouragement.[18] The Grand Lodge of the United States adopted a proclamation declaring "the unbroken unity of the Order and made known that there exists no hindrance to the re-establishment of the fraternal relations between Grand Lodges in the Northern and Southern states."[19] All Grand Lodges and Grand Encampments in which the Independent Order of Odd Fellows may have been disorganized were encouraged to reassemble and proceed with the work of the organization.[20] The Grand Lodge of the United States further furnished whatever necessary supplies that the lodges in the Southern states needed.[21]

On April 26, 1865, Grand Sire Isaac Veitch, together with members and citizens, met in Baltimore, Maryland and laid the cornerstone for the Wildey Monument.[22] Odd Fellows were dressed in dark clothes while some members wore robes of the High Priests embroidered with crossed shepherds' crook as symbol.[23] This was just before

Jefferson F. Davis, who was the President of the Confederate States of America from 1861-1865, and Ulysses Grant, who served as Commanding General of the United States Army from 1864-1869, were both members of the Independent Order of Odd Fellows.

The Essence of Fraternity

Sometime during the dedication ceremony, a member from the South named William Barnes stood next to a member from California named Dan Norcross who asked him, "Dixie, you have no regalia?" Barnes replied, "No, nor have any money to buy one." Removing his beautiful collar, Norcross said to Barnes, "Take mine." Barnes later became a Past Grand Master of the IOOF Grand Lodge of Georgia and the Grand Scribe of the Grand Encampment of California. He kept the regalia throughout his life, and proudly shared this story about the essence of fraternity in 1915.[1]

the war ended and was believed to be the *"first fraternization between the North and South."*[24] People who were engaged in war and conflict during the civil war marched side by side as brothers, wearing the regalia of the IOOF.[25] On September 18, 1865, all the representatives from the Southern states were represented during the sessions of the Grand Lodge of the United States except for Florida and North Carolina due to the sudden death of their respective Grand Representatives.[26] Handshakes, warm embraces, cordial greetings, voices of emotion, and shouts of joy ensued. Past Grand Sire John Kennedy, with tears on his cheeks, reached out his hand and said, "Georgia, I'm glad to see you."[27] Grand Sire Veitch, on the other hand, stepped on his chair and onto the top of his desk, shouting and dancing.[28] There was one unanimous voice of joy and one prayer, "Thank God the war is over and our Brothers have come back home!"[29] This time, almost all of the seats were filled, unlike in previous meetings when the seats of the IOOF representatives from Southern states were vacant. The Grand Sire welcomed back Odd Fellows from the Southern jurisdictions and spoke about the principle of Fraternity as an essential and fundamental truth that cannot be shaken by wars.[30] The Grand Lodge of the United States reported that a total of $507,957 was spent for the relief for those in need.[31]

Dedication of the Wildey Monument

After the Civil War, Jefferson Davis was in Federal prison waiting for his trial. He was despised by the prison guards assigned to him and was poorly treated.[32] He was allowed no visitors and guards were not permitted to speak to him. At that time, preparations were being made for the dedication of the Thomas Wildey monument.[33] Davis heard about the incoming ceremony and would ask about it from time to time. One day, a new prison guard was assigned to Davis who treated him more kindly.[34] In the course of a conversation, he learned that one of the generals on the post was an Odd Fellow.[35] So Davis persuaded the young guard to take a note to the general.[36] Days passed and he never heard from the general until the day before the dedication ceremony when the general appeared at his cell and commanded the guard to open the door and he and Davis extended the handgrip of the fraternity.[37]

More than 50,000 members and guests from all over the United States attended the dedication ceremony of the Thomas Wildey monument. Illustration from the collection of The Sovereign Grand Lodge, IOOF.

On September 20, 1865, the City of Baltimore declared a holiday. The best carriage on the post arrived at the Federal prison, and Jefferson Davis was escorted to the site of the dedication and sat beside the dignitaries as a special guest to witness the event.[38] All officers and members in attendance were in black suits.[39] The members and officers of the lodges wore white gloves while those representing the Encampments wore black gloves.[40] During the procession, Outside Guardians marched in front with drawn swords and banners followed by officers and members and the last person in line for each lodge was the Inside Guardian with a drawn sword.[41]

A section of the police and military, all members of the Odd Fellows were also in procession wearing their Odd Fellows regalia.[42] Five big cars, each containing about 30 orphaned children in the care of the IOOF in Baltimore, caught great attention.[43] The girls were all dressed in white and carried shields bearing the name of all states and territories where Odd Fellowship is represented.[44] The cars were decorated with colors representing each degree in the Odd Fellows lodge – white, pink, blue, green and scarlet – and each car was escorted by a team of six horsemen attired in white suits.[45] Following the cars, and on foot, were about 350 older orphaned boys also under the guardianship of the IOOF. They were followed by thousands of members representing lodges and encampments from various states. Accompanying the encampments was a tent in wheels made of crimson cloth, surmounted by a golden eagle, and pulled by six horses.[46] Beneath the tent sat the High Priest wearing his robe of purple velvet, and surrounding the tent were the Guardians armed with spears.[47] The last on procession were the dignitaries of the Grand Lodge of the United States. Moreover, there were about fifteen brass bands playing music during the procession.[48]

Chapter 12

GOLDEN AGE OF FRATERNALISM

The American Civil War was an economic and moral disaster. Many lost their families and homes. This resulted in a "heightened sense of nationality which brought people together to join lodges."[1] Using the Odd Fellows and Freemasons as model, many fraternal organizations and social clubs were formed in the United States as "a vehicle by which men, who were engaged in war, became brothers again and recreated the fraternal relationship severed by the war."[2]

Immigration also helped with membership growth because more than 18 million people entered the United States between 1890 and 1920.[3] This encouraged the proliferation of hundreds of different fraternal organizations, benefit societies, college fraternities and sororities, and ethnic associations for almost every person or group. There were separate groups for Englishmen, Scotsmen, Nordics, Irishmen, Protestants, Catholics, Anti-Catholics, pro-temperance, railroad men, mechanics, and

During this period, one Odd Fellows lodge could have more than 100 people in a meeting. There were also individual lodges with more than 500 members. Thus, many lodges constructed huge buildings. From the photo collection of the author.

others.[4] Fraternal organizations had to translate and print their initiation ceremonies in various languages. Noting the racially segregated nature of North American culture at that time, African-Americans also formed their own fraternal groups and benefit societies which grew in numbers. By 1860 to 1870, many other fraternal organizations followed the example of the Independent Order Odd Fellows in forming auxiliary organizations for women when the Rebekah Lodge became a fruitful experiment at a time when American society was still debating whether or not women should be allowed to join fraternal organizations.[5]

In 1896, there were nearly 70,000 lodges belonging to more than 150 organizations. Their memberships included some 810,000 Odd Fellows, 750,000 Freemasons, 475,000 Knights of Pythias, and thousands more belonging to other groups.[6] During the same year, African-American fraternal organizations such as the Prince Hall Freemasons had a membership of 224,000 and the Grand United Order of Odd Fellows had 130,350.[7] Overall, the membership of fraternal organizations in the United States during that year was around 6.4 million of a population of about 19 million.[8] This meant that at least one out of eight men at that time were members of a fraternal organization.[9] Many of these fraternities and benefit societies competed to attract prominent people by revising their rituals, improving their regalia, and employing an attractive benefit system.[10] Soon, nearly every prominent man was an Odd Fellow or a Freemason, or both[11] because it became common for people to hold membership in two or more organizations. Moreover, the fraternal organizations were widely involved in early-day philanthropic works and spent over $649 million in relief assistance in 1897.[12] The three largest fraternal organizations of the era – Odd Fellows, Freemasons, and Knights of Pythias – spent an estimated $176 million per year in aid of members in need, excluding private monetary gifts of the members.[13] This phenomenal period of people rushing to join fraternal organizations between the years 1870 to 1920 is referred to as the "*Golden Age of Fraternalism.*"

Largest Fraternal Organization

As soon as the civil war ended, steps were taken to revive lodges in impoverished and nearly annihilated areas. An important addition was when the *Ancient Independent Order of Odd Fellows* in Australia affiliated with the Grand Lodge of the United States in 1869.[14] During the same year, the IOOF also achieved the distinction of being the first national organization to cross the North American continent by train from one seaboard to another, when it held its annual session in San Francisco, California. Further steps to open lodges in other countries were taken and a lodge under the IOOF was established in Germany in 1870.[15] By the end of the 19th century, the IOOF had spread to most of the rest of the world. Lodges were established in the Americas, Australia, New Zealand, Asia, Africa and most of Europe.

From 1900 to 1910, the IOOF initiated an average number of 124,175 new members annually. At the close of 1910, the IOOF had more than 1.5 million active members and 17,705 lodges in North America.[16] The peak was probably in 1921 when the IOOF had more than 1.9 million active members, 16,986 lodges and a hefty $85 million in invested funds.[17] Combined with the two other major Affiliated Orders of Odd Fellows - the Manchester Unity Independent Order of Odd Fellows and the Grand United Order of Odd Fellows - there were more than 3.5 million Odd Fellows during that year.[18] In addition to those numbers were the Rebekahs under the IOOF numbering more than 1 million

Odd Fellows Parade in Winnipeg, Canada, circa 1912. Photo courtesy of the Sovereign Grand Lodge, IOOF.

women in 9,793 Rebekah Lodges and having more than $1.3 million in invested funds.[19] In 1929, Grand Sire Frank Martin of the Sovereign Grand boasted that "Odd Fellowship have more than two and one-quarter million members in the United States and more than three million members in the world".[20] The Odd Fellows eventually gained international popularity, so that many people were interested in obtaining a charter for an Odd Fellows Lodge in a location as far as Syria.[21]

Elaborate Ceremonies

Fraternal organizations became so numerous in North America. This somehow created a healthy competition among the various groups. Groups such as the Odd Fellows and Freemasons revised their initiation ceremonies to make them more elaborate and longer. Instead of the usual lectures and catechism, many fraternal organizations converted lessons into dramatization and added extravagant costumes, spears, and swords. The dramatic-type of ceremonies was not just a way of teaching the candidates moral principles but it was a form of entertainment and fund-raising. The candidates had to pay a fee for each degree and attending an initiation was similar to attending a dramatic play at the theatre. The fancier the initiation rituals, the more people were interested to join.

Belief in a Supreme Being

Religious Americans were threatened when atheism rose to prominence in the latter half of the 19th century. Thus, the representatives of the IOOF Sovereign Grand Lodge at the time, who were firm believers in the existence of a deity, introduced the "Belief in a Supreme Being" as a qualification

1913 Sessions of the Grand Lodge of Texas of the IOOF held in Houston, Texas.

Photo from collection of the author.

1918 Sessions of the Grand Lodge of Indiana of the IOOF

Photo from collection of the author.

1921 Sessions of the Grand Lodge of Michigan of the IOOF held in Lansing, Michigan.

Photo from collection of the author.

Golden Age of Fraternalism | 65

for membership in 1893.²² "Belief in a Supreme Being" was a common requirement among fraternal organizations of this era.

Largest Provider of Sickness and Death Insurance

Many fraternal organizations started as a way to care for their members at a time when there were no systems in place to insure one's welfare, health or to protect one's job. In those days, insurance companies and government programs that provided sick and death benefits did not exist. Sickness or death of the breadwinner frequently meant poverty and the responsibility of burial depended on the family.

Before the 20th century, life insurance was available only to the wealthy and was beyond the financial ability of the average working class. For these reasons, the Odd Fellows in the United States took on the responsibilities of visiting the sick, burying the dead, educating the orphans and caring for the widows and elderly as a way to support families in need. Aside from the social aspects of being a member, the main draw was the Odd Fellows' dedication to protect and care for their members and families at a time when many charitable and welfare services that people enjoy today were still absent.

Initially, the Odd Fellows provided funds for members as a matter of charity. Several *Odd Fellows' Relief Associations* were founded by members although as a separate entity from the lodge. In 1863, however, the IOOF "became a major trendsetter and was a predecessor of the Social Security System when the organization adopted a clear schedule of guaranteed benefits over the haphazard ways of granting financial assistance previously followed by most fraternal organizations".²³

The Odd Fellows also helped revise the language of fraternalism by using the terms "benefit" and "right" as compared to "charity" and "relief" to describe the aid given to its members.²⁴ Hence, help from an Odd Fellows Lodge was not looked upon as a donation but a member's right, and was paid to every member who was sick, whether he was high or low, rich or poor. Perhaps, these terms were preferred so that members who received financial aid would not feel ashamed or lose his self-esteem for accepting assistance from the lodge during a temporary crisis.²⁵ Mutual-aid triumphed so that a member might be a donor one day and a recipient of help the next.²⁶

From 1863 to 1925, the IOOF was the largest provider of sickness insurance in the United States and Canada. Sick members could claim a regular stipend of around $3.00 to $6.00 per week to compensate for working days lost.²⁷ The lodges' shared resources helped members pay doctor's fees or buy medicine. Other than this, burial for a deceased member was usually covered by the lodge and the widowed families and orphans also received help. This ensured families against the disgrace of alms houses' and the embarrassment of a pauper's grave. From 1900 to 1910, the organization's financial

Many started mutual-benefit corporations within their lodges. As early as the 1870, the Ridgely Protective Association existed. This was named after James L. Ridgely, a prominent Odd Fellow who served as Grand Secretary of the Grand Lodge of the United States from 1840 to 1881. Aside from secret signs and passwords, members wore rings, pins, suspenders and dog tags for identification purposes in times of sickness or accidents.

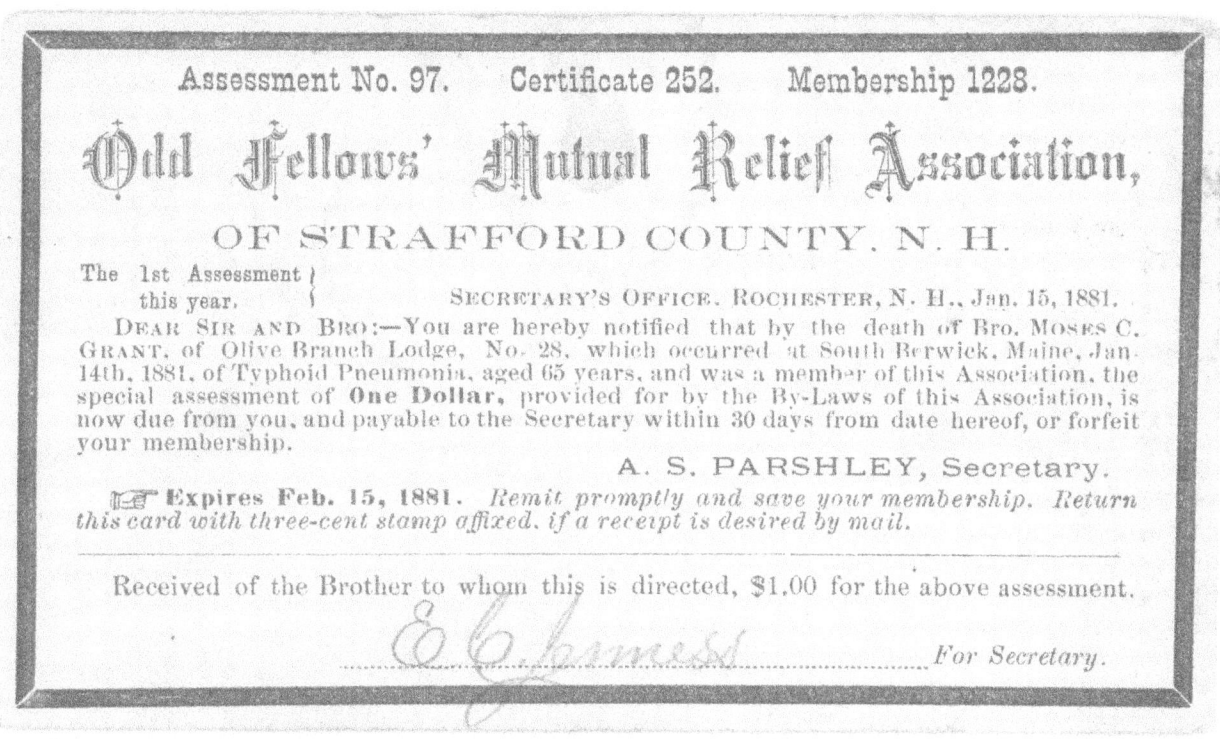

An 1881 Odd Fellows' Mutual Relief Association card used to notify members to contribute $1 special assessment for a member who died due to typhoid. Photo from collection of the author.

strength greatly improved, so that IOOF was able to disburse an average amount of $4.4 million annually for the relief of distressed members, widowed families, orphans, burial for the dead, and other charities.[28]

Other branches such as the Encampments spent an average amount of $300,000 annually. The Rebekah Lodges spent an average of $77,000 a year for relief and charity.[29] At the end of 1910, the IOOF had already expended a grand total of more than $136 million for relief and charity and the organization's overall annual revenue was more than $275 million.[30] These were tremendous amounts during this era if calculated based on today's standards. In the IOOF, the poor were able to help the poor through mutual-aid. This implied a lesson that "the working classes were capable of creating effective, organized self-help efforts on a vast scale and distinguished fraternal organizations from some of the large, bureaucratically organized charities of the day, which practiced hierarchical relief wherein donors often came from a different economic class and social status than the recipients."[31]

Philanthropic Works

The IOOF further proved its administrative abilities by establishing several significant major social welfare institutions such as orphanages, retirement homes, and medical clinics emphasizing preventive care and cemeteries. In 1872, the IOOF became the first fraternal organization to build a home dedicated to the care and education of orphans and the assistance of widows and the elderly when the Grand Lodge of Pennsylvania built the *Odd Fellows Home of Western Pennsylvania* in 1872.[32] Soon, almost every state in the United States, Canada, and

CLINTON LODGE
NO. 98, I. O. O. F.

LOCK HAVEN, PA., MAY 24, 1904.

To the N. G., V. G., Officers and Members of ...Seely Creek......

Lodge, No. ..641.. I. O. O. F.

DEAR SIRS AND BROTHERS:—

It is with deep regret that, for the first time in the history of this Lodge (which was instituted in 1844) we are compelled to appeal to our sister Lodges in this Jurisdiction to solicit aid in behalf of our worthy Brother, P. G. J. D. Miller, who as you can see in this picture, had both legs cut off on a railroad on March 31, 1903, on his way home from his work (he being an axe maker by trade) by avoiding one train of cars he stepped in front of another train and was in this way crippled for life.

Brother Miller is a poor man; he is 41 years of age; he has a wife and two children to support and he has no means of support except what aid he receives from this Lodge and his Brothers in the Fraternity, and this Lodge is not conditioned financially to make further donations.

Now Brothers, this is a very deserving case, and we hope it will receive a generous consideration at the hands of the Fraternity. Our aim is to start the Brother in a small business to make a living for himself. Therefore, Whereas, Clinton Lodge never refuses to assist Brothers in distress by appeal, we feel justified in making this our first appeal to our sister Lodges in time of need.

Send all contributions to GEORGE A. MILLER.
No. 518 E. Main St.,
LOCK HAVEN, PENNA.

We hereby submit the following as a true and correct report of this Lodge:

Number of members in good standing	55
Amount paid by the Lodge or its members to the petitioner	$266.50
The fee for initiation	8.00
Weekly dues	.10
Funeral assessments	member 75 cents; Wife 35 cents
Weekly benefits	$3.50 first 15 weeks; 37 weeks $2.00, after $1.00
Funeral benefits	Member $50.00; Wife $25.00
Invested funds	....
Cash in hands of officers	....

Resolved, That should the prayer of our petition be granted, we do hereby promise and agree to yield a strict compliance with the requirements of Sections 2 and 3 of Article XXXII of the By-Laws of the Grand Lodge.

Fraternally submitted,

S. G. DAVIS, Noble Grand,
GEORGE A. MILLER, Secretary.

I. O. O. F.

Office of the Grand Master of the
Grand Lodge of Pennsylvania.

Approved, Philadelphia, June 24, 1904.
GEORGE HAWKES, Chairman
AMOS H. HALL
CHARLES CHALFANT
JAMES H. AVERY
J. P. HALE JENKINS
Committee on the State of the Order.

Approved, ROBERT GRAHAM,
Grand Master.

SEAL OF GRAND LODGE

ATTEST:
JOSEPH H. MACKEY, Grand Secretary.

It has been a duty and tradition for Odd Fellows to help other members overcome struggles in life. *From the collection of the author.*

Besides building orphanages, homes for the elderly, and cemeteries, the Odd Fellows and Rebekahs also purchased and built several camps and parks in the United States and Canada to provide recreation facilities for families and children.
From the collection of the author.

Australia had an Odd Fellows Home. These facilities were a fully functioning self-sustaining micro-community where widows, orphans and the elderly were cared and provided for. In 1909, the IOOF in Denmark also helped build a hospital for lepers in St. Croix, Virgin Islands.[33]

Yet the benevolent works of the IOOF was not limited to material and financial aid. Ethical or moral aid was often mentioned as the main objective of the fraternal organization. Through the teachings imparted during the ceremonies of initiation, members were taught to be compassionate to their fellowmen, be tolerant to other people's beliefs and to avoid excessive drinking or fight vices of every form.

Odd Fellows visited each other in times of sickness and distress. If a member needed a job, Odd Fellows would also help him find one. If they could not find one locally, they would pay his way to the next lodge and this would continue until he got a job. When a member dies, the officers of the lodge would seek permission from the family to have their own private moment with the deceased as they perform a funeral ceremony to honor their departed brother Odd Fellow or sister Rebekah. Odd Fellowship substantially grew in numbers because its members really propagated a culture of caring and sharing.

Built in 1898, the Odd Fellows' Old Folks Home in Mattoon, Illinois, was a residential community for orphans, widows and retirees. It was equipped with a farm and housing staff.

The Odd Fellows literally "buried the dead" that almost all Odd Fellows' lodges owned cemeteries or burial plots. Photo shows the IOOF Cemetery in Newtonia, Missouri, built in 1894.

Chapter 13

WORLD WAR I

The declaration of World War I came as a shock to the whole civilized world. This had the effect of temporarily paralyzing almost all financial, commercial and industrial enterprises.[1] The changed face of nature, the world unrest and the number of men involved in foreign wars made it hard for many civic and fraternal organizations to continue holding meetings.[2] The Odd Fellows suffered a membership decline largely because a big percentage joined the Armed Forces to fight the war in Europe and Asia.[3]

In 1916, the Grand Secretary of the Independent Order of Odd Fellows in Australia reported that "the war was responsible for a great discontentment".[4] The IOOF in Australia lost members very fast with over 4,000 of their members in training camps or at the warfront.[5] There was also a heavy drain in the lodge funds due to claims for relief by the sick and wounded, and for funeral

World War I Veteran's Degree Team of Manufacturer's Lodge No.15 of the IOOF in Providence, Rhode Island, 1918.
Photo from the collection of the author.

benefits by relatives of those killed in action.[6] In Alberta and Ontario, a large number of members volunteered for active service in the military.[7]

In 1917, the IOOF Grand Lodge of British Columbia estimated that nearly 10,000 of their members volunteered to join the armed forces.[8] Overall, the IOOF Sovereign Grand Lodge reported 67,858 Odd Fellows serving in the military in 1917 alone.[9] The Odd Fellows in Switzerland reported a gain in membership and a good financial condition but shared that the European war affected the prosperity of many lodges.[10] In contrast, the Odd Fellows outside mainland North America and Europe experienced an increase in membership due to immigration. In 1916, for example, the lodge in Japan reported membership growth because of the number of foreigners coming to their country.[11] The same happened to lodges in Alaska, Cuba, Hawaii, Japan, Mexico, Panama, and the Philippines.

Economic Problems

While some states and provinces in the United States and Canada reported an increase in membership, the net increase was really considerably less compared with those of previous years. Many Grand Lodges reported a loss in membership not just because many members were in the Armed Forces but also because of the economic conditions in several states and provinces.

In Colorado, a coal strike affected industries in general such that many lodges had great difficulty in retaining members in good standing.[12] In Kansas, crop failure in rural areas at the end of 1913 resulted in membership loss. In California, hundreds of railroad men and mechanics were laid off for a season and the Odd Fellows felt the adverse effects of the withdrawal by a good number of members in the entire state.[13] Georgia and North Carolina, being agricultural states, were severely affected by the drop in prices of cotton as a result of the war in Europe.[14] In North Carolina, famine overran the fishing sector on the coast for two years as many members lost their entire year's earnings while others became unemployed.[15]

In Washington, lumber and the shipping industry fell, which forced many laborers to seek work in other locations.[16] In Australia, a very serious drought devastated a great part of Australia and brought about bad economic conditions.[17] In 1918, an influenza epidemic hit North America, so that a huge number of lodges in Illinois, Indiana and Iowa, Massachusetts and Minnesota, Nevada, New Hampshire, New York, North Dakota, Ohio, Quebec, Saskatchewan, and Utah were forbidden by the health authorities to hold meetings for several weeks.[18] Iowa reported that they closed for about 2 to 3 months.[19] In Oregon, the influenza epidemic prevented lodges from holding meetings for about 4 months.[20] During the same year, Northern Minnesota was swept by a devastating fire that burned over a tract as large in extent as the states of Massachusetts and Connecticut combined.[21] Many homes and entire villages, and even towns of 10,000 inhabitants were totally destroyed. In response, the Sovereign Grand Lodge and Grand Lodges across North America raised $28,574.41 for the purpose of aiding the victims.[22]

These conditions caused many members to drift away from lodge meetings and become negligent in paying their annual dues. In Tennessee, the Odd Fellows showed a loss of 544 members in 1915.[23] In Puerto Rico, the lodge was unable to hold a quorum for any meeting and ultimately surrendered their charter in 1915.[24]

Brotherhood during the War

The war did not only leave members injured and disabled; it also left many widows and orphans.[25]

Steps were taken to provide assistance and care for members and their families in every manner possible both in North America and in foreign countries.[26] To counter the problem of members unable to pay annual dues because of unemployment or military service, the Grand Lodges and lodges made every effort "to avoid suspending a member for not paying dues"[27] and emphasized that "members who are unemployed or suffering financial problems need help from the entire brotherhood and should receive it."[28]

At the beginning of the war, the Sovereign Grand Lodge made it clear that the Independent Order of Odd Fellows "only supports peace and not war but it has a huge responsibility towards its members' comfort and fair treatment while in war."[29] The organization emphasized that "the IOOF is an international organization so a member who enters military service of a nation other than that of the country to which he belongs, while engaged in military service, gets sick, is entitled to receive help from the organization."[30] The Sovereign Grand Lodge subsequently adopted a bill to provide relief for Odd Fellows in the military and naval forces. This bill declared that "no member shall be suspended for non-payment of dues and shall not lose any right or privilege while serving in the military and naval forces".[31] To attain this, many Grand Lodges and lodges raised funds to cover the dues of these members.[32] In 1917, a *War Relief Commission* was created by the Sovereign Grand Lodge and $75,000 was set aside to assist members or others abroad connected with the war and those who may return needing assistance.[33] During the same year, the *Odd Fellows' Soldiers' and Sailors' Relief Fund* was also adopted and all members were assessed less than $1.00 to assist those in need.[34]

The IOOF also made sure that all lodges kept records of all military members and their dependents.[35] Moreover, many lodges were also involved in providing services and donations to the Red Cross, YMCA and other War Relief Works.[36] Internationally, the IOOF Grand Lodge of New Jersey provided rooms at General Pershing's Headquarters in France for use of members as well as non-members who were doing military service in that country.[37] When a ship carrying explosives accidentally exploded in Halifax, Canada, the Sovereign Grand Lodge started the *IOOF Halifax Relief Fund* with a $38,834.51 donation.[38]

During this period, the IOOF had 55 homes for widows, orphans, elderly and poor members. In 1919, it spent over $7 million for relief and charity, which meant that it distributed $10 every minute, $600 every hour, and $15,000 every day.[39] In 1918, it assisted about 9,000 families, aided 140,000 Odd Fellows, and paid relief for about 70,000 orphans and about $225,000 for their education.[40] More than 125,000 Odd Fellows fought for their country in WWI.[41] From the beginning of WWI in 1914 until it ended in 1919, the IOOF provided sickness and relief assistance to its members, burial expenses, financial assistance to widows, and for education of orphans that amounted to more than $32.1 million. The amount benefited a total of 957,657 members and 58,972 widowed families for a span of five years.[42]

Women at Work

While many men joined the Armed Forces and left their respective countries for the war zones, women members of the Rebekah Lodges took care of many things in their homelands. Because the casualties of war left many widows and orphans, the Rebekahs played a significant role in assisting and taking care of them. In New York, Rebekahs spent most of their time taking care of the residents in four Odd Fellows' Homes for the widows and aged,

Odd Fellowship served as a social network for members of the Armed Forces assigned in Europe and Asia. In 1919, a banquet was organized by the 'Odd Fellows Club' in Germany. Photo from the collection of the author.

two homes for orphans, and several other facilities.[43] In Kansas, a new Odd Fellows Home for elderly members and orphans was built at Eureka Lake, Manhattan.[44]

The Rebekah members throughout the United States and Canada also did considerable volunteer work for the Red Cross and other war relief associations.[45] In Ontario, they volunteered work hours relentlessly on behalf of the Red Cross and other patriotic societies.[46] In Michigan, the Rebekahs also took up volunteer work with the Red Cross and took care of young orphaned boys.[47] In Oklahoma, many of the Rebekah Lodges organized the Red Cross Unity.[48] In Ontario, they sent hundreds of boxes overseas to cheer up Odd Fellows in the war front.[49] In 1917, the Rebekah Assembly of Illinois donated $ 6,000 to the National Headquarters of the Red Cross to purchase two large ambulances for service in France and were involved in food conservation as requested by the United States government.[50]

As a result, the Rebekahs registered

Food Conservation	League to Enforce Peace	Investigation Committee
Beginning in 1918, the IOOF supported the United States Food Administration in conserving food by decreasing food consumption at IOOF events and by sending volunteers to help the local or State Food Administrator.	Former President William Howard Taft invited the IOOF to join the League to Enforce Peace and a committee of four was sent by the Sovereign Grand Lodge to participate in the convention.	In 1918, Rev. Stevenson of the Independent Order of Odd Fellows and Hon. Moore, Inspector General of the Ancient and Accepted Scottish Rite Southern Jurisdiction, formed the *Committee to Investigate the*

membership growth as compared to its male counterpart, the Odd Fellows Lodges. Rebekahs in New York, for example, reported an increase of 2,000 new members and 10 newly instituted Rebekah Lodges in 1917 alone.[51] By 1919, there were 824,901 women belonging to 9,625 Rebekah Lodges.[52] From the onset of the war up to its end, the Rebekahs raised a total of $707,451.73 as relief assistance for the sick and distressed, widowed families, and for education of orphans.[53]

Membership Growth at the End of the War

When World War I ended in 1919, the IOOF experienced the greatest increase in membership since it was established in the United States. The IOOF of California reported a total of 46,292 active members in the entire State.[54] Connecticut initiated 1,080 new members and garnered a total membership of 26,901 Odd Fellows.[55] IOOF in Ohio boasted a total of 94,835 Odd Fellows and 51,439 Rebekahs in the entire state.[56] In Illinois, the IOOF initiated 8,682 new Odd Fellows and 4,500 Rebekahs.[57]

By the end of 1919, the IOOF in four states reported the following total numbers of active members: Illinois - 117,956;[58] New York - 137,245;[59] Pennsylvania - 180,227;[60] Oklahoma, - 40,180 active members in 495 Lodges.[61] Overall, the IOOF boasted more than 2.5 million active members in North America.[62] In the same year, the MUIOOF had 932,063 active members[63] while total active membership of the GUOOF can be rounded off at 300,000.[64] Combining these three major *Affiliated Orders*, there were more or less 4 million Odd Fellows across North America, Europe, Africa, and Asia at that time.

Philanthropic Works

The IOOF organized philanthropic projects to help those suffering from the consequences of the war. When the war ended, the Sovereign Grand Lodge reported that approximately 70,000 Odd Fellows were killed in active service during WWI and 150,000 died because of tuberculosis.[65] In response, the IOOF built additional cemeteries and paid for the burial expenses of their deceased members.[66]

In 1919, Odd Fellows of Sweden raised funds to cover traveling expenses, food, and clothing for impoverished children from Central Europe who were received in Odd Fellows' private homes for six months to recover from the effects of war.[67] The Grand Lodge of Sweden also donated partly in cash and partly in food and clothing to Berlin and Vienna to assist those who were suffering. More than 100,000 Kronen was sent to Odd Fellows in Vienna as fund for a home for suffering babies.[68] The Odd Fellows of Denmark managed two Homes for Orphans in the country. One was a ten-acre property with two buildings serving as home for foundlings.[69] A home also was built in Copenhagen where Odd Fellows living outside the city may, for

---

	Emergency Fund	**Branches for the Youth**
Condition of Fraternal Societies and Members Abroad. They visited Europe to investigate the condition of Odd Fellows and Freemasons in the military service and determine their needs.	In 1919, the Sovereign Grand Lodge created an Emergency Fund in the amount of $100,000 which was used for calamities and relief expenses of affected members.	To help the large number of youths that the war left fatherless, a bill was submitted to the IOOF Sovereign Grand Lodge to form a branch for the youth aged 16 to 21.

The Great Parade

On September 29, 1920, the IOOF in Massachusetts organized one of the biggest parades ever held by the IOOF in history. Thirty-two divisions were lined up and the total number of people who participated in the parade was estimated at 40,000.[1] The parade required hours to pass a given point. The streets along the line of march were thronged with thousands of people, many of them on reviewing stands erected for the purpose.

> **Illinois Degree Day**
>
> An outstanding event occurred on November 19, 1919 when the Third Degree or the Degree of Truth was conferred upon a class of 2,003 candidates in Springfield, Illinois.[1] Among the distinguished candidates for this Degree were Governor of Illinois Frank O. Lowden and Secretary of State Louis L. Emerson.[2] The memorable class received the Third Degree in the presence of 10,000 members.[3]

a nominal fee, have their children stay while they attend school or university.[70] In 1921, the Swedish Odd Fellows took charge of caring for 130 orphaned Austrian children while Danish Odd Fellows took care of 400 orphans.[71] The members welcomed the orphans in their private homes for six months or more, traveling expenses, clothing and everything paid by voluntary contributions of the members. In Queensland, Odd Fellows of Australia established a Home for the elderly and orphans whose sons or fathers were killed during the war.[72]

Beginning 1921, the IOOF started developing Junior Lodges for Boys and Theta Rho Clubs for Girls to offer moral guidance and leadership training among the youth. Many of the first members were children who lost their fathers during the war.[73] In 1927, the IOOF Educational Foundation was also established by the Sovereign Grand Lodge to financially assist the youth in obtaining higher education.[74]

Chapter 14

THE GREAT DEPRESSION

From 1870 to 1920, the Odd Fellows was the largest fraternal organization in the world.[1] The *Research Committee of The Sovereign Grand Lodge* reported that the peak of membership was attained in 1921.[2] However, membership began to decline at the beginning of 1922.[3] The decline became more apparent at the advent of the *Great Depression*, when thousands dropped their membership because they lost their jobs.

Impact of the Great Depression

At the beginning of 1929, Wall Street crashed and a major worldwide economic recession ensued. Many financial, business, and agricultural institutions closed and many people became unemployed.[4] Banks in every section of the United States crashed and, by order of U.S. President Hoover, those banks were able to control the drain of their resources by closing down, thus producing an almost complete collapse of the financial system.[5] Under these circumstances, many members lost their life's savings, and distress and suffering prevailed everywhere.[6]

The stress of the economic condition and the accompanying failure of banks left their impact on many working people whose savings were wiped out overnight.[7] It was almost impossible for many lodges to secure applications for membership or reinstatement because people could not afford membership fees or annual dues.

In 1931, the Sovereign Grand Lodge reported that admission of new members had

Millions of people lost their jobs and livelihood during the Great Depression. Photo source: wiki-commons, public domain.

fallen from more than 100,000 to less than 40,000 new members annually.[8] The Grand Lodge of New York conveyed that approximately 4,000 dropped their membership.[9] In British Columbia, the IOOF had admitted only 24 new members which was the smallest gain in ten years.[10] The Grand Lodge of Georgia became busy reorganizing, consolidating, and closing weak and delinquent lodges.[11] The Grand Lodge of Australia, on the other hand, faced a grave situation with regard to finances, so that they considered postponing their next triennial session.[12] In Europe, the Grand Lodge of Germany reported that due to the economic conditions and the banks crashing, they were finding it impossible to fulfill all obligations.[13] One of their main concerns was their fear of the outcome of the agitation all over Germany at that time.[14] The taxes and the industrial interests imposed were weighing them down and the entire country was in a chaotic situation.[15]

Dr. August Weiss, Grand Sire of the IOOF Grand Lodge of Germany, had to cancel his trip to attend the Sovereign Grand Lodge Sessions in 1931.[16] At the end of December 1931, the condition in Germany reached a magnitude of disaster and it was estimated that at least 20 percent of the German Odd Fellows and their families were in dire need.[17] In response, the *Special Relief Committee of the IOOF* forwarded $5,000 relief for its German members.[18] But due to social instability in the country and the growing mistrust by the German public for fraternal organization, the Grand Lodge of Germany was forced to dissolve its national organization in 1933 although some lodges continued to meet in secret.[19] In Latin America, the three Odd Fellows Lodges in Mexico closed.[20] Outside North America, only the Odd Fellows in Hawaii and the Philippines reported steady or increased membership.[21]

Moreover, many of the lodges that built large buildings and Homes for the Elderly and Orphans felt the growing demand and increased cost of maintenance.[22] Lodges found taxes heavier than they could bear and eventually surrendered their charters. As a result, a number of the properties owned by the Odd Fellows were foreclosed or abandoned.[23] This negative impact was equally experienced by all organizations including the Knights of Pythias and the Freemasons.

Decline of Fraternalism

The continued economic depression had been a large contributing factor in membership decline in all fraternal organizations in North America. Nevertheless, there were other contributing factors that led to the decrease in membership (See Chapter 17). In general, they were the outgrowth of changed conditions in the social and economic life.[24] A different time, a new age, a changed mode of living had the greatest influence on those who have dropped out.[25]

The *Sovereign Grand Lodge Committee on Research* opined that people during this time were generally giving more thought and attention to the setting up of "superfluous standards of living, the accumulation of wealth and acquisition of profits, rather than to participation in civic associations and doing philanthropic works."[26] They found out that the younger generations regarded the objectives of Odd Fellowship as "idealistic rather than practical in a practical age, and its principles have largely developed into ideals which appeal strongly only to the past generation."[27]

Further investigation conducted proved that it was not Odd Fellowship alone that was affected by the prevailing conditions, but all other fraternal organizations and civic associations - including the Freemasons and Knights of Pythias - were similarly affected. Most, if not all, of these organizations "struggled and failed to adapt their methods to the

The economic depression drove many lodges to bankruptcy. Many Odd Fellows' buildings were sold or abandoned.

liberal spirit of the age."[28] The traditional methods failed to grip the imagination and interest of younger men and women to sufficiently persuade them to play an active role in fraternal lodges.[29] Some members believed that "the young men of this era demanded results without unnecessary ceremony"[30] and "questioned whether there exists any valid reason for the continuation of much of its traditional ceremonies, the signs and tests and numerous cards and machinery, or the secrecy which is thrown

The Great Depression | 81

President Roosevelt and the New Deal

Franklin Delano Roosevelt joined Park Lodge No.203 of the IOOF in New York on January 24, 1912. At the beginning of his term as U.S. President, he introduced the *New Deal* to combat mass unemployment. One of these programs, the Social Security System, was apparently modeled after the system of financial benefits previously offered by the Independent Order of Odd Fellows. On July 23, 1940, fifteen members of his lodge assembled at his home and presented to him his 25-year membership jewel. He remained an active member of the IOOF up until his death in 1945. Photo courtesy of The Sovereign Grand Lodge, IOOF.

around in the degree work."[31]

It was observed that members were no longer content to sit upon the benches and listen to ritualistic ceremonies and ordinary lodge routine, but they longed to be entertained.[32] Some members believed that it was time for the Odd Fellows to go back to the basics when lodges focused on the social and charitable aspect. That it would be easier to expand if the Odd Fellows would again allow lodges to hold meetings in pubs and restaurants, with lesser ritualistic activities, more flexible rules and regulations, and control from state and national governing bodies.

This new way of thinking was evident with the formation of so-called *service clubs*, like the Rotary and Kiwanis, which focused on professional networking and community service. These service clubs offered a simpler membership process without degrees of initiation, without the fancy trappings of robes and regalia, and without the need of a lodge room for their meetings. This made the service clubs more conducive for international expansion.[33] True enough, the Sovereign Grand Lodge reported that "membership in fraternal organizations suffered tremendous losses for the past 25 years while service clubs made huge gains in membership and number of new clubs."[34] The Odd Fellows in Switzerland communicated that "Rotary Clubs proved to be quite a competition when it comes to recruitment."[35] Thus, the Sovereign Grand Lodge encouraged its leaders "to give lodges greater liberty in engaging in the necessary activities and in enlarging their activities in community affairs"[36] and also permitted members "to form Odd Fellows' Clubs for purely social and charitable purposes."[37] But many of its lodges still failed to make necessary changes to adapt to the times.

Welfare State and Commercial Insurance

After the Great Depression, commercial life insurance companies began to actively compete with the sick and death benefits offered by fraternal organizations.[38] President Franklin Roosevelt, who was an Odd Fellow member, later introduced the *New Deal* that provided federal programs and public work projects to mitigate the effects of the Great Depression.[39] Beginning 1934, Congress passed government measures that provided unemployment compensation, old-age and disability insurance, and aid to dependent children.[40] Later, the government focused on foster homes, which replaced the importance of the orphanages owned and managed by the Odd Fellows across North America.

In time, the social services offered by the Odd Fellows and other fraternal organizations were taken over by the government with the introduction of the *Social Security System* and *National Health Insurance*. The social safety net offered by these fraternal groups were no longer viewed as necessary to the point that many members ultimately gave up their membership.[41] As a result, nearly all fraternal organizations and friendly societies across the United States, United Kingdom, Australia, and New Zealand substantially lost membership.[42] Owing to their failure to adapt to needed changes promptly, many of these organizations never recovered and eventually went out of existence.

By the end of 1931, the Sovereign Grand Secretary reported considerable loss in membership in North America. An annual statistical records since 1830 up to the close of 1931 showed that the IOOF initiated 5,849,141 men in Odd Fellow Lodges but they lost a total of 3,597,540 members due to death and by suspension of membership due to non-payment of dues.[43] From more than 2 million Odd Fellows affiliated with the IOOF, the number went down to 1,280,121 members. The membership in the Encampments also decreased to 207,496 and the Rebekahs to 830,114.[44]

Only the Independent jurisdictions of the IOOF in Europe made a satisfactory showing of substantial gains in membership.[45] In 1951, Sovereign Grand Master Miles Peck saw "the need to develop fresh national and international projects that can be particularly identified with the Odd Fellows and Rebekahs."[46] He concluded that the necessity and use of past projects - such as sickness and death benefits and homes for widows and orphans - had been eliminated by the changing times.[47] Eventually, the Sovereign Grand Lodge of the IOOF eliminated its compulsory requirement for the payment of stipulated sick and death benefits, and many of its orphanages stopped operations.

Community Involvement

Despite the financial challenges, the Sovereign Grand Lodge still encouraged its lodges to "make special efforts to relieve those suffering of unemployment and make the Odd Fellows a real service organization in the community."[48] That each member "become obsessed with the beauty and glory of the mission of fraternity, fellowship, and brotherly love, so that the influence and usefulness of the Order may be extended."[49] Remaining lodges took active interest in community projects in their jurisdiction. They organized charitable projects and provided individual support for its members.

During this era, the IOOF in the United States alone spent more than $6 million every year for the relief of suffering and distress.[50] This excluded voluntary contributions by its members to help other members and other philanthropic causes at the local or state level.[51]

Chapter 15

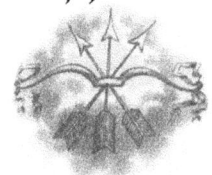

WORLD WAR II

A war between Japan and China in Asia and the Pacific started in 1937. This escalated into WWII in 1939 when Germany invaded Poland, and the United Kingdom and France declared war against Germany.[1] By 1941, Germany controlled most of continental Europe and formed the *Axis Alliance* with Italy and Japan through a series of campaigns and treaties. Within the same year, Japan bombed Pearl Harbor and the American air base in Manila, Philippines.[2]

The Odd Fellows in European countries suffered greatly. Many members served the armed forces or fled to other countries for safety. War and invasion meant that the lives and properties of the lodges and members were destroyed.[3] In countries where war was happening, buildings owned by the Odd Fellows were confiscated or damaged.[4] To those that remained, members were forbidden by the Nazis to hold meetings within their buildings.[5] The Nazis banned people from joining fraternal organizations and humanitarian clubs. A black propaganda against fraternal groups and similar organizations was implemented.[6] As a consequence, many lodges in Europe and Asia suspended public activities and met in secret.

In Norway, the Odd Fellows continued as a countrywide underground movement with contacts in Denmark and Sweden.[7] In China, an *Odd Fellows Society* was formed by German refugees.[8] They petitioned for a charter to officially institute a lodge under the IOOF but the difficult war times made it impossible for the Sovereign Grand Lodge officers to travel and institute lodges in the area.[9] For a time, the Odd Fellows Lodge in Japan continued their operations unobtrusively by mutual understanding among members to meet without publicity to avoid persecution but this arrangement did not take long; eventually they disbanded, in 1943.[10]

Lodges in the Philippines and Panama also suspended their activities because majority of their members served the military and a number became prisoners of war. All four lodges in Austria went out of existence.[11] For a time, gatherings of more than fifty people were also banned by the United States Government. This became a problem for

The IOOF raised large sums of money, which was donated to the U.S. and Canadian governments for the purchase of ambulances and airplanes used in medical missions at the war front. Photo courtesy of Grand Lodge of Texas, IOOF.

many Grand Lodges because they cannot hold their annual sessions and adopt needed legislations.[12] In 1943, IOOF lost 130,359 members due to death and 463,646 became inactive for non-payment of dues.[13]

Benevolence and War for Democracy

When the news about the war reached North America, the Sovereign Grand Lodge expressed the desire "to devise ways and means and to work out plans to carry out the doctrine of Brotherhood of Man, an effort to fraternize the world, and establishment of world peace between the nations of the earth."[14] Because of the oppression involved during wars, the leaders of the IOOF were of the opinion that the global condition then presented an opportunity for universal service.[15] Thus, more than 1 million members of the IOOF acknowledged the importance of the joining of two nations - Canada and United States – across the international boundary in a mutual defense program to defend liberty and freedom.[16]

Many lodges raised funds and provided support for the wartime effort "to preserve democracy and freedom of association."[17] The Sovereign Grand Lodge cancelled its annual meetings in 1942 and 1945 to save resources and instead, supported the war and future rehabilitation efforts. They donated the funds to both the United States and Canadian governments and invested millions in war bonds.[18] All available resources of the IOOF were further conserved to support respective governments in the war and a reserve fund was set aside for continuation of fraternal activities in the postwar reconstruction period.[19]

The Sovereign Grand Lodge further expressed the urgency of community service in every locality. It emphasized that the Odd Fellows Lodges "derived their strength, manpower, and finances from the community in which they were located, and the people of that community have a right to expect some return of that strength in local affairs."[20] In the midst of war, lodges in North America wrote cheerful letters to members in military service so the latter did not feel forgotten. They took care of the families left by members who joined in the war effort. In addition, lodges involved themselves in community service and took active interest in civic affairs in their respective localities, doing active work with the Red Cross, *Unites States Service Organization* and engaged in bond sales, purchase of field kitchens, ambulances, airplanes and other supplies needed at the warfront.[21]

By 1943, the whole IOOF membership became active in the sale and purchase of defense bonds, war savings stamps, volunteer work for the Red Cross, civilian defense, and victory book campaigns.[22] Although complete reports have not been received from all Grand Lodges and Lodges, conclusive evidence showed that the general membership of the IOOF exceeded $100 million in the purchase of war bonds and victory bonds at the close of the year 1943 and helped supply more than 100,000 pints of blood to the Red Cross.[23]

During the same year, sums of money from some Grand Lodges, varying in amounts up to approximately $20,000.00, were used in the purchase of suitable equipment and paraphernalia for the hospitals, and in the rehabilitation work carried out for people who were injured in the service of their country.[24] Several Service Centers were also operated under the auspices of the Odd Fellows and Rebekahs. These provided entertainment and food to the Armed Forces.[25] In Toronto, the Odd Fellows donated one of their buildings to the government and the "refugees from the United Kingdom benefited greatly from it."[26]

The IOOF further mobilized its lodges and members in providing materials to help servicemen

On August 14, 1941, President Franklin Roosevelt and Prime Minister Winston Churchill proclaimed the Atlantic Charter, which outlined eight "common principles" that the U.S. and U.K. would be committed to supporting in the post-war world. President Roosevelt was a long-time member of the Independent Order of Odd Fellows in the U.S., while Prime Minister Churchill was a member of the National Independent Order of Odd Fellows in the U.K. Photo from public domain.

and made sure that the dependents of soldier-members were taken care of.[27] Lodges were given power to enact laws that authorized them to prescribe for the care of their sick and disabled members who needed the assistance of nurses or watchers and the lodges paid for their services.[28] Funeral benefit and expense funds for the purpose of providing for the payment of funeral benefits or expenses of and for deceased members of the lodge were also approved.[29] An emergency fund was also started to assist in the rehabilitation of lodges outside the continental limits of North America, for the relief of distressed members, and for the re-establishment of Odd Fellowship in the several war-torn countries once peace was restored.[30]

In 1946, a sum of $250,000 was set up by the Sovereign Grand Lodge as "Odd Fellows War Relief Fund" to help members in war zones.[31] An *Odd Fellows Care Committee* was formed to help those who suffered under the Nazi regime, were forced to flee their homes as refugees, and traveled long distances by foot leaving behind almost all their possessions.[32] Within twelve months, the Committee sent 689 Care Packages to needy Odd Fellows and their widows in Germany and Austria.[33] This IOOF project of sending 500 to 800 care packages to Europe continued for nearly ten years.

Universal Fraternity

Although the Manchester Unity Independent Order of Odd Fellows and the Independent Order of Odd Fellows became separate organizations in

During World War II, all Grand Lodges and Lodges submitted thousands of records to the Sovereign Grand Lodge of Odd Fellows serving in the Armed Forces and their dependents. The Odd Fellows recognized members who had fallen during the war, paid tribute to those injured, and made sure their dependents were taken care of. From the collection of the Sovereign Grand Lodge, IOOF.

```
Sovereign Grand Lodge Record.

            WORLD-WIDE-WAR RECORD OF I. O. O. F.
            Date of making this Record    8/27/18

Jurisdiction          Illinois
Name of Member        Irving H. Magee
Residence             Palmyra, Illinois
Occupation            Physician
Born at               Barr, Illinois          Date  36 yrs.
Married to            Nona, Arras
Children              2          Age of each
                      Mary Louise             6 yrs.
                      Keith                   1 yr. 2 mos.

                              (Over)

                         LODGE RECORD.
Joined                Palmyra         Lodge No.   348
Location              Palmyra, Ill.   Date  5/8/05
Lodge Rank            3rd.

                        MILITARY RECORD.
Joined                Army     of    U.S.A.
                  (Army or Navy)          (Country)
At                    St. Louis, Mo.   Date  8/21/18
Name of Military Organization in full  In Marine Hospital
                                       St. Louis, Mo.
Rank                                        Lieutenant
            RECORD OF SERVICE. (To be filled in later.)

                              (Over)
```

1843, the members of the MUIOOF extended many courtesies to the members of the IOOF stationed in the United Kingdom during WWII. In some instances, Manchester Unity Lodges conferred honorary membership upon members of the fighting forces who were able to identify themselves as Odd Fellows.[34] Because of this, the Sovereign Grand Lodge adopted a resolution to bring together the two organizations in creating a closer relationship.[35] In return, the members of the MUIOOF who were in military services training in the United States and Canada were welcomed by lodges of the IOOF and were assured of companionship and fellowship.[36]

The international set-up of the Odd Fellows gave members the opportunity to break down and destroy antagonisms and misunderstandings resulting from excessive nationalism. During WWII, Norway was invaded by Germany and there was some enmity between the two nationalities that continued after the war. But in an Odd Fellows meeting in Stockholm, Sovereign Grand Master G.J. Bianchi witnessed representatives of Germany sitting next to those of Norway and mingling with those from invaded countries. Odd Fellowship made it possible to bring about international friendship and understanding.[37]

Post-War Efforts

When the war ended in 1945, Odd Fellows and Rebekah lodges continued to become an active part of their respective communities. In 1948, the Sovereign Grand Lodge reported that many lodges in the United States and Canada collaborated with other organizations in the control of juvenile delinquency, employment of the physically handicapped, polio and cancer drives, Red Cross and Veterans Hospital activities.[38] Odd Fellows and Rebekahs also participated in the National Safety Council, with headquarters in Chicago, in an endeavor to reduce traffic accidents. Moreover, lodges cooperated with school boards and parent-teachers' associations and municipal authorities in clean city campaigns.[39] During the same year, the Sovereign Grand Lodge donated $58,000 to the Grand Lodges in Denmark, Netherlands, Norway, Sweden, and Switzerland as aid and for rehabilitation after the war.[40] The following years, Odd Fellows and Rebekahs in the United States and Canada donated $500,000 for aid to Europe.[41]

In Europe, the Grand Lodge of Switzerland spent 26,000 Francs for relief work in Austria, Czecholovakia, Holland and Germany.[42] Many refugees from these countries who were members of the Odd Fellows received help.[43] In Denmark, the Odd Fellows maintained a nursery that accommodated about 50 abandoned babies.[44] They were cared for in the facility for about two years while efforts were made to locate their parents. If unsuccessful or if the parents did not have the means to support the baby, the Odd Fellows found people who would adopt them.[45] In the United States, the Odd Fellows of California constructed a hospital at the cost of approximately $250,000 and donated the facility to the State of California as a memorial for those who served the war.[46] Odd Fellows and Rebekahs in Ohio and other states also built similar facilities including recreation camps for the youth.[47]

International Goodwill

As head of one of the largest international fraternal organizations of the time, the Sovereign Grand Lodge of the IOOF proclaimed in 1946 that "lodges embrace opportunities as an international force for world peace."[48] Numerous goodwill causes were initiated, study clubs were formed for the education of the membership in international affairs, and a number of lodges sponsored public meetings where the United Nations was discussed by outstanding leaders.[49]

United Nations Pilgrimage for the Youth

The Odd Fellows and Rebekahs United Nations Pilgrimage for Youth Educational Program was established by Sovereign Grand Lodge in 1949 when the United Nations was just four years old.[50] The purpose was to bring together high school students from around the world to study and learn about the United Nations as well as international relations, economics, political sciences while exchanging views on education, politics and religion.

IOOF International Council

During WWII, communication between the Sovereign Grand Lodge and the Grand Lodges

In 1972, members of the IOOF International Council held their triennial meeting in Reyjavik, Iceland, in the capital city's Odd Fellows building at 10 Vonarstraeti. Photo from the collection of the Sovereign Grand Lodge, IOOF.

outside North America was severed. In 1946, the Sovereign Grand Lodge and the Post-War Planning Committee created the *International Council of the Independent Order of Odd Fellows* to cultivate, extend and maintain collective measures of social and fraternal relations among members, as well as advance its principles, and develop friendly and international cooperation between Odd Fellows in several nations.[51] The purpose of the Council, among other things at that time, was to provide a forum by which former combatants could meet in the spirit of Odd Fellowship to resolve conflicting ideologies and to promote the principles of Odd Fellowship worldwide. The preliminary meeting was attended by leaders of the Sovereign Grand Lodge in North America and those of the Grand Lodges of Norway, Sweden, Denmark, and Switzerland.[52] Similar to the United Nations, the IOOF International Council served as avenue for leaders of the Odd Fellows representing various countries to deliberate on matters and work toward closer cooperation among Odd Fellows all over the world.[53]

Moral Education for the Youth

The increasing juvenile delinquency in the United States was brought to attention by the Sovereign Grand Lodge at the start of the year 1939.[54] The organization saw the problems of the youth accentuated by the emotional upset of recent wars and the fear of another world war.[55] With increasing juvenile delinquency and worsening international moral breakdown among the youth who were left without fathers due to the war, the IOOF developed a *Moral Education Program* to emphasize the importance of raising children with an understanding and respect for authority and democracy.[56] This program gained the attention of government leaders who were not members of the fraternity. It had been responsible for many visitors attending the open meetings of the Odd Fellows during this period. The Grand Sire received calls from the U.S. Senate inviting him to attend their sessions to discuss this program. In California, the Grand Sire was able to speak to the State Senate and Legislature; and the *Moral Education Bill* was passed in 1941.

This advocacy for moral education for the youth was also implemented within the organization of the IOOF through the establishment of youth branches: the Junior Odd Fellows Lodges and Theta Rho Girls' Clubs. The goal was to afford the youth an opportunity to be united in friendship and to work together to promote the concepts of service to others, helping one another, and personal growth and development physically, mentally, morally and socially.[57] The Junior Odd Fellows focused on learning the importance of exerting effort to improve and develop character with emphasis on sound citizenship, patriotism, honesty and truthfulness.[58] Theta Rho Girls, on the other hand, were taught to exert all effort to improve oneself physically and mentally, build character that is necessary for happiness in the home, and create an influence toward good in the community.[59] By 1950, there were 9,104 active Junior Odd Fellows and 24,303 active Theta Rho Girls in the United States and Canada.[60]

Membership

Membership increased at the close of the war largely because of veterans seeking camaraderie with others like themselves.[61] The *Odd Fellows Society* in Shanghai, China, eventually formed themselves into the *Franklin D. Roosevelt Lodge No.1* with a membership of approximately 100.[62] A Rebekah Sisters Club for women was also formed in China.[63] Many military lodges or Odd Fellows Clubs, which held regular meetings for fellowship, fraternity, and study of the initiation rituals, were reported to exist in the Southwest Pacific, Aleutian Islands, Asia, and many parts of the globe where the *Allied Armies* advanced.[64] Remaining Odd Fellows in Germany held meetings in the form of clubs without any charter from the Sovereign Grand Lodge until the *Grand Lodge of Berlin* sought recognition from the Sovereign Grand Lodge.[65]

By the end of 1945, the Odd Fellows had initiated 47,071 new members, while the Rebekahs had initiated 47,197.[66] Despite the tremendous philanthropic contributions and volunteer works

Many Odd Fellows' Homes in North America, Europe, and Australia served as safe haven for the widows and orphans of deceased members. Photo from the collection of the author.

rendered by the Odd Fellows and Rebekahs, however, the IOOF in North America never really regained its former statistical strength. The total membership was much less than it was before the war.[67] In 1946, records showed that from a total pre-war membership in the millions, post-war membership was less than a million each for each category: 838,254 active Odd Fellows, 670,642 active Rebekahs, 8,441 active Junior Odd Fellows, and 20,777 active Theta Rho Girls.[68] By 1951, the IOOF in North America began losing more or less 10,000 members annually mostly due to old age.[69]

The Sovereign Grand Lodge also noticed a decrease in the solemnity of the initiation ceremonies by lodges, an unsound financial setup, lack of cleanliness of lodge halls, and a number of lodges suffering because of failure to take in and retain new members.[70] Some members argued that the Odd Fellows failed to cope with its sister organizations such as the Moose, Elks, and Rotary because the IOOF had not taken advantage of publicity.[71] Unlike the service clubs that often publicized their philanthropic works, the good works of the Odd Fellows and Rebekahs were virtually unknown to the general public because of their tradition of discreetness and secrecy. Some of the leaders realized the need to change this mindset. But a study by the *SGL Commission to Study Odd Fellowship* blamed the delay and procrastination of the Sovereign Grand Lodge in financing and implementing public relations for the IOOF.[72] In addition, the organizational structure of having an international governing body made implementation slow in North America because the approval of the majority of the representatives to the Sovereign Grand Lodge was always sought.

The Commission further observed that more and more, the Sovereign Grand Lodge became too much of a legislative body and much of the legislation passed was the "thou shall not" type, or had been drafted to meet the ideas of a particular jurisdiction or of the individual representative.⁷³ One Past Sovereign Grand Master of the Sovereign Grand Lodge observed that discouragement came from so-called "*Code Fellows* - the type of member who devotes so much time and energy in search of an IOOF Code of laws, rules, and regulations in an effort to find some technical reason why any progressive program, which may have otherwise met an enthusiastic response from the members, cannot be put in effect or carried through."⁷⁴ The web of rules stripped the Grand Lodges and Lodges in North America of the needed autonomy and became unnecessary hindrances to progress. At the same time, some Grand Lodges became too dependent on the Sovereign Grand Lodge.

Moreover, the constant amendment of rules and programs by the Sovereign Grand Lodge made implementation at the local level difficult because what was enacted in one year was often changed at the next session the following year.⁷⁵ The continuous revision of the initiation rituals also created unrest and confusion.⁷⁶ Most members felt that "the changes made resulted in no improvement but rather added difficulty in getting members of the Degree Teams to relearn parts that they have been performing for years."⁷⁷

Poor presentation of the initiation rituals resulted in a failure to impress the candidates with the teachings and ceremonies of the fraternity.⁷⁸ Furthermore, the cost of replacement of regalia and paraphernalia increased, so that lodges in many localities were using regalia and robes that were worn and dirty.⁷⁹ The Commission further opined that not sufficient education and information was given to a new member regarding the standing and importance of the organization.⁸⁰ Little, if any, effort was made "to impress the candidate with the worldwide nature of Odd Fellowship and the extent

Prince Bertil, Duke of Halland in Sweden, desired membership in a lodge that bore the name of his friend, Folke Bernadotte, and was initiated as a member of the Independent Order of Odd Fellows in Sweden on May 22, 1950.¹

of the services it renders to humanity." ⁸¹ All this made Odd Fellowship in North America appear to have "lost its prestige over the years and by reason thereof does not attract membership to the same extent as it previously had."⁸²

On the other hand, the Odd Fellows and Rebekahs in Europe and Latin America were steadily growing after the war. The IOOF in Denmark, Iceland, Norway, Sweden, and Switzerland all showed membership growth by 1950.⁸³ Being *quasi-independent* in their internal governance, these jurisdictions enjoyed the needed autonomy to implement the necessary actions unlike the Grand Lodges in North America.

When Sovereign Grand Master Edward Sharpe traveled around Europe, he observed that

From the 1700s to the early 1900s, Odd Fellows proudly wore their regalia during public parades, and would often take group photos outside their buildings. This custom of public parades and public use of lodge regalia changed during World War II, when all fraternal organizations were persecuted by the Nazis. Many lodges became secretive, perhaps because of fear of persecution. Today, almost all of the IOOF lodges in European countries refrain from wearing their lodge regalia in public. Photo from the collection of the author.

the European Independent Order of Odd Fellows differed in that "they select one of the best and outstanding people in their communities for membership."[84] In some occasions, noblemen themselves sought membership in the Odd Fellows.[85] The degrees of initiation were "conducted with profound dignity and solemnity."[86] A lapse of at least one year after admission was required before one can be advanced to a higher degree.[87] It was necessary for a third-degree member to wait three years before he is admitted to the higher branch – Encampment.[88] Grand Master Sharpe further noted that their meetings were conducted with decorum and dispatch. Their buildings were perfect examples of the manner in which they revere the fraternity. Their lodges are an integral part of their communities and their families gathered in their lodge buildings at frequent intervals for a social evening.[89] Moreover, there was a social hour after every lodge meeting where food and beverages were served.[90] What he described used to be the exact condition of the Independent Order of Odd Fellows in North America before the Great Depression and the war.

Chapter 16

CIVIL RIGHTS AND RACIAL INTEGRATION

As an organization, Odd Fellowship teaches universal fraternity among humankind. From its inception, the English Odd Fellows admitted "free men" regardless of race, creed, or economic status. There were no racial restrictions in its By-Laws and rituals when the IOOF was established in 1819. In fact, prior to 1853, several Mongolians and descendants of similar races were admitted as members of the IOOF in the United States on the decision of the Grand Lodge of the United States.[1]

Thereafter, the membership in the Independent Order of Odd Fellows became predominantly white because of the imposition of racial segregation laws by American society. But years prior, black Americans already established the *Grand United Order of Odd Fellows* in America and Jurisdiction as the predominantly African-American branch of Odd Fellowship in North America. It is argued that this culturally imposed racial segregation within fraternal organizations was mainly of North

African-American Odd Fellows Annual Banquet attended by notable African Americans at the time such as Booker T. Washington, Ex-Register J.C. Napier, former Register J.D. Lyons, Ex-Recorder of Deeds Lincoln Johnson, The local Grand Master, and others equally well known. Photo from public domain.

American origin because of the long history of slavery in the continent. The Odd Fellows outside North America, however, were more relaxed in allowing people from different racial and ethnic backgrounds to join their lodges.

African-American Odd Fellows

Fraternal organizations had links to the "freedom struggle."[2] Long before the *African-American Civil Rights* movement in the United States, the black community already created their own parallel fraternal groups that provided sacred spaces of community solidarity and civic courage among former slaves. These groups also provided assistance to African-American families in times of unemployment, illness, death, and other vicissitudes in life.

Undeniably, many of the early African-American leaders who fought against slavery during the American Civil War and for equality during the Civil Rights Movement were affiliated with the Grand United Order of Odd Fellows (GUOOF).[3] A number of the founding members of the first African-American Odd Fellows were notable abolitionists and civil rights activists. For example, John C. Bowers, who played an active role in the anti-slavery movement in Philadelphia, was a founding member of the first African-American Odd Fellows Lodge in the State of Pennsylvania.[4] Abolitionist Patrick Henry Reason was the founder of *Hamilton Odd Fellows Lodge No.710* and founder of the *Household of Ruth* for African-American women.[5] George Morton, Jr. was the Grand Secretary of *District Lodge No.28* of the Grand United Order of Odd Fellows in Canada. He played a part in the civil rights movement, and had been a member of a delegation that met Sir Oliver Mowat, Premier of Ontario, on the issue of segregated schools in the Province of Ontario.[6] Frederick Douglass was also one of the early members of the GUOOF in the United States.[7]

John C. Bowers, a known abolitionist and civil rights activist, served as the Grand Master of the Grand United Order of Odd Fellows of Pennsylvania in 1870.

Through Odd Fellowship, African-American members created a network that was instrumental in the *Underground Railroad* movement - a system of secret trails and safe houses used by African-American slaves to escape into free states with the aid of abolitionists and allies. Several of the houses that served as safe havens for hiding these escaping slaves were homes of Odd Fellows. In fact, some of the marks to identify these houses consisted of symbols of the Odd Fellows placed on the brick chimneys or exterior woodwork. In Guilford College Campus in Greensboro, some trees have the three links emblem carved on their trunks, which pointed the direction to the safe houses. GUOOF buildings also hosted community and social events for African-Americans. These buildings were important during the *Jim Crow* era, when African-Americans were barred from using many public spaces.

The fraternal organization also allowed African-Americans to "develop business contacts and leadership skills, and were involved in a variety of reforms"[8] and meetings generated "a feeling of black pride and comradeship."[9] Annual gatherings of the African-American Odd Fellows in North America were attended by prominent abolitionists and social reformers.

In July 1848, for example, Frederick Douglass delivered a speech in front of five thousand members during the Annual Odd Fellows Conference in New York.[10] In 1854, Douglass again addressed the African-American Odd Fellows in Rochester, New York, where he emphasized that the main pillar in

Arnett and McKinley

Benjamin William Arnett, one of the first African-Americans to serve in the Ohio State Legislature, played an important role in organizing lodges for the Grand United Order of Odd Fellows. He became a close friend of President William McKinley and even provided the Bible upon which he took the oath of Office of the President in 1897. He later became "the President's informal adviser concerning matters of race, and it was widely believed that Arnett exerted more influence on McKinley than any other African-American."[1] Innocently, President McKinley was also an Odd Fellow affiliated with the IOOF.

friendship is trust – "when there is no trust, there is no friendship."[11] True to their pledge, the members of the Grand United Order of Odd Fellows even escorted Douglass, then Federal Marshal of the District of Columbia, from the home of his host to the Salisbury courthouse where he delivered his famous speech "Self-Made Men" in 1880.[12]

Douglass was appointed by President Rutherford Hayes as Federal Marshal of the District of Columbia, the first appointment of an African-American to require United States Senate confirmation. President Hayes "valued and respected Douglass' opinions and consulted him at various times during his administration."[13] Interestingly, President Hayes was an Odd Fellow affiliated with the IOOF and Douglass was affiliated with the GUOOF.

By the time of its 1886 convention in Philadelphia, the GUOOF had grown to be the largest African-American fraternal organization in the United States with lodges in Canada, Central America, Bahamas, Bermuda, and the West Indies and Africa.[14] At the peak of its organizational success, the GUOOF was keeping more than $7.8 million in fraternal insurance,[15] more than 4,000 lodges, and 300,000 members in North America, which was about twice the membership of the Prince Hall Freemasons.[16]

Racial Segregation

After the American Civil War of 1865, slavery was abolished in the United States but a large majority of white Americans were hesitant to comingle on equal terms with the former slaves. In 1870, African-Americans were given the right to vote under the law but many were prevented from registering as voters by means of violence or intimidation. *Jim Crow laws* were passed in the South, which refused blacks from using the same facilities as whites. In 1896, the Supreme Court of the United States even ruled, by a majority of 7 to 1, that segregated washrooms, railroad cars, or lunch counters were constitutional.[17]

Ultimately, "separate but equal" became the norm across the United States.[18] In fact, many states passed *anti-miscegenation laws*, which banned marriages between whites and other races, and prohibited sexual relations between blacks and whites. In some States, there was an unwritten policy called the "sundown rule" where black people were not allowed to go to certain towns or cities after 6:00 o'clock in the evening.[19]

Racial segregation was enforced in schools, churches, military units, restaurants, cemeteries. Various establishments were labeled either as "white only" or "colored only". In the federal work force and the United States Armed Forces, "colored units"

Civil Rights and Racial Integration | 97

2nd row, far right: Mr. Maa Mon Chinn (1846-1923) was a highly respected clan headman, storekeeper, and tin miner who lived in Weldborough, North East Tasmania, for most of his life. He was among the first Chinese to migrate to Tasmania. He joined the Odd Fellows in Weldborough sometime in the 1870s. Photo courtesy of the Museum of Chinese Australian History

were stereotypically separated from "white units". An all-white government in South Africa also passed a similar system of racial segregation called *apartheid*. Because fraternal organizations were influenced by societal norms in general, the "free white male" qualification eventually became a common policy among all organizations and clubs in the United States, Canada and South Africa.

Before the Civil Rights Movement

The IOOF in North America was caught in the middle. It had leaders and members who were for and against racial segregation. As the Speaker of the House of Representatives and an influential member of the IOOF, Schuyler Colfax was an advocate of advanced position for African-Americans such as emancipation, military service, and voting rights.[20] But the IOOF also had members whose beliefs were on the opposite side of the spectrum. If the IOOF in the United States allowed non-whites inside their meeting rooms during this era, the whole organization would face internal factions and many of the lodges in the Southern states would probably disaffiliate. The IOOF would also face public condemnation from a great majority of white Americans at the time, including the government and other establishments, because racial segregation was a national policy that was strictly enforced. In fact, a number of white people were threatened, intimated or murdered by other whites for being

> **Brotherhood beyond Race**
>
> Although GUOOF and IOOF members were separated by the racial divide imposed by American culture, newspaper accounts documented instances when the two groups exchanged correspondences and assisted each other even prior to the African-American civil rights movement. In 1899, for example, it became publicly known that the GUOOF District Grand Lodge in Springfield, Illinois, was struggling to raise funds for the purpose of building a home for widows and orphans. In response to this need, the IOOF Grand Lodge of Illinois donated to the GUOOF $100 to help build the home.[1]
>
> The Deputy Grand Master of the GUOOF, F.W. Rollins, in his thank you letter to IOOF members, addressed them as "brothers."[2] In response, the Grand Secretary of the IOOF of Illinois, J.R. Miller, wrote: "Odd Fellowship found in either one of the branches of our Order, teaches one and the same lesson, and it is not at all surprising or strange, that members of the IOOF should entertain a friendly regard and a Brotherly interest in the good work performed by the Grand United Order of Odd Fellows even though composed of men and women to a different race."[3]
>
> During the Installation of officers of the Key of the West Lodge No.1692 and Memphis Star Lodge No.1501 of the GUOOF in the State of Tennessee in the 1920s, thirteen representatives from five IOOF lodges were present on the stage as guests. Past Grand Master J.D. Danbury of the IOOF was introduced by Senior Past Grand Master D.W. Washington of the GUOOF and he remarked that the IOOF guests were well pleased with the ceremonies of the evening.

identified as "black sympathizers."

Defying societal norms, some IOOF members challenged racial segregation and admitted *colored individuals* into their lodges.[21] In 1873, Ben Christian, a Past Grand Master of the IOOF in Texas, initiated American Indians into the fraternity. This resulted in a complaint filed against him by those who still had animosity toward American Indians, although the charges were eventually dropped. Christian was instrumental in instituting the first Choctaw Nation IOOF Lodge, *Caddo Lodge No.1*, on May 8, 1875.[22] In 1879, efforts were made to remove the qualification of "free white male" so far as native Indians. This had been vehemently raised by members in Hawaii, Australia, and New Zealand.[23] By 1888, American Indian wives of IOOF members were already initiated into the Rebekahs.[24]

Chinese were among the first Asians to be admitted into an Odd Fellows Lodge when a tea merchant and tea shop owner, Quong Tart (Mei Guangda), was admitted as a member in Sydney, Australia, in 1885.[25] In 1902, a Japanese named "Brother Shimidzu" was initiated by Dexter Lodge of the IOOF in New York. In 1911, Past Grand Sire Fulton reported that a colored man had been admitted in an IOOF Lodge in Victoria.[26] The same situation was witnessed in Queensland in 1913. In New Zealand, the IOOF also declared that they had no provision against men of color. In 1920, Grand Sire Henry Borst noticed a "colored man" among those attending a reception for the Grand Sire given by the Odd Fellows in Sydney and his right to admission was not questioned.[27] It was also recorded that a number of *Maoris* have been accepted as members by IOOF Lodges on the North Island of New Zealand.[28] In its communication to the Sovereign Grand Lodge in 1920, the Grand Secretary of the Grand Lodge of Australasia mentioned that, "we draw no color line against a candidate and I have seen brethren dyed black representing their IOOF lodges at various Grand Lodges."[29]

International Pressure

Beginning 1904, various national leaders of the IOOF in Europe, Australia, and Hawaii were vocally opposed against racial segregation in North America.[30] They raised the issue that while previously they understood the great difficulties because of the United States' domestic policy of racial segregation, they nonetheless believed that segregating people based on race, skin color, or religion was contrary to the principles of Odd Fellowship.[31] Many of these leaders considered racial discrimination "incompatible to the principles of the fraternity."[32]

Grand Sire Dahlgren of Sweden spoke that "the world now has new norms and one of the most important is the equality of races."[33] He reported that members in Sweden and Finland were opposed to fact that some lodges were mostly composed of white men. Several Caucasian members have resigned their membership as a result of lodges having "white-only" restriction.[34] The IOOF in Denmark, Germany, Iceland, The Netherlands, Norway, Sweden, Switzerland, Australia, and New Zealand moved to remove the word "white blood" in the old charters issued by the Sovereign Grand Lodge of the IOOF.[35]

Grand Sire Brynjofsson of Germany also passionately opined that racial discrimination contradicts the fundamental and moral substance of the fraternity. He pointed out that "the ethics of Odd Fellowship teaches the message of Fatherhood of the Creator and that all people dwelling on earth are his children."[36] He said that segregating people based on race, skin color, or religion was contrary to the principles of Odd Fellowship. Blum, a representative of the IOOF in Chile, emphasized "the universality of Odd Fellowship, which teaches that the fraternity must favor those who have consistent principles of value and talked about the importance of human rights, assurance of spiritual freedom, and individual freedom."[37] Canadian IOOF leaders also raised the issue of racial segregation and emphasized that, "as a Universal Brotherhood, Odd Fellows profess to be and should be big enough to forget petty prejudices and join those who are trying to make conditions a little better in the troubled world."[38]

Civil Rights Movement

By 1944, many people of *Malayan race* already joined the IOOF in the United States and many became "members of outstanding quality."[39] Several full- and half-blooded American Indians began holding state and national leadership positions in the IOOF. The culture of racial segregation in the United States further weakened when President Harry Truman signed *Executive Order Nos. 9980* and *9981* in 1948, which ordered the desegregation of the federal workforce and the U.S. Armed Forces. During his presidency, he established a *Civil Rights Committee* tasked to examine violence against African Americans in the United States. Rosa Parks' refusal to be moved to the back of a bus for a white passenger in 1955 became an important event in the Civil Rights Movement. Each day eventually brought a story of a strike, a boycott, a peace march, or a sit-in against racism.[40] Racism and racial integration then became a priority discussion in the annual meetings of the Sovereign Grand Lodge of the IOOF.

By 1962, IOOF membership in the United States was opened to "pure Polynesian, Chinese, Japanese, and Korean blood."[41] During the same year, persons of Polynesian and Oriental ancestry were initiated as members in Hawaii. The first Asian-American member in the United States was a woman of Korean ancestry who was initiated into

The Household of Ruth is the female branch in the Grand United Order of Odd Fellows in America and Jurisdiction.
Photo courtesy of David Scheer.

Pacific Rebekah Lodge in Honolulu.[42] In 1964, the Rebekah Assembly president in Switzerland was half-Indonesian.[43] Many of these members became very active; in 1966 it was passionately announced that a woman of Malayan blood became the president of the Rebekah Assembly in the Netherlands.[44]

Racial integration was quickly embraced in many countries outside the North American continent, but implementation in the United States was a challenge because the tension between white and black Americans appeared to be greater. Even when President Johnson already signed the *Civil Rights Act of 1964* and the *Voting Rights Act of 1965*, a number of white Americans were still hesitant to assimilate with black Americans. Yet this was not one-sided because black Americans were also cautious. They refrained from joining organizations and clubs that were predominantly white. This attitude continued until the 1980s.

In 1988, Vietnam veteran Clarence Plant became one of the first African-Americans to join the predominantly-white Independent Order of Odd Fellows in the United States. He ultimately served as the first black Grand Master of the Grand Lodge of Massachusetts. He held various offices in the Sovereign Grand Lodge and serves as the CEO

Despite the imposition of racial segregation, there were Odd Fellows lodges that defied the norm. Photo shows an Odd Fellows lodge in New Bedford, Bristol County, Massachusetts, with a mixed membership of white and black men gathered in the 1920s. Photo courtesy of Leonora Hepsabeth Kydd White.

In 1951, President Truman met with the leaders of the Odd Fellows and Rebekahs in California. It is rumored that he joined the Odd Fellows the following year. His subsequent letters to the Sovereign Grand Lodge addressed the officers of the IOOF as "brothers," which suggests that he was a member. Photo courtesy of Peter Sellars.

of the Odd Fellows Home of Massachusetts until the present. Other African-Americans also joined the IOOF, and several of them now hold important leadership positions in the Grand Lodges and the Sovereign Grand Lodge of the IOOF. In 2007, Richard Kim became the first Polynesian-American to hold the position of Sovereign Grand Master of the IOOF. In 2016, Darlene Parker became the first African-American woman to be the Grand Master of the IOOF in the State of Maryland.[45]

GUOOF-IOOF Relationship

At present, the relationship between members of the GUOOF and IOOF in North America remain unofficial. In 1989, Representative Dag Wallén of Sweden met a Past Grand Master of GUOOF in Ghana, Africa, who showed him their initiation rituals and secret work which was a little similar to the one used by the IOOF.[46] Beginning 1993, leaders of the IOOF from Europe, North America and Australia discussed about building better cooperation with other Odd Fellows organizations such as the Grand United Order of Odd Fellows.[47] Australians were the first to establish an *Odd Fellow Network* for better cooperation between the GUOOF, MUIOOF and GUOOF. In the United States, a number of people began joining both the IOOF and the GUOOF but the progress was slow.

In 2008, representatives of the two organizations in Texas met to see greater cooperation, joint projects, and dual membership. Eventually, many members of the IOOF established informal fraternal relations with members of the GUOOF in the United States, United Kingdom, Africa, Puerto Rico, and Cuba. This resulted in a proposal to establish an official inter-fraternal relationship between the IOOF and the GUOOF similar to the agreement between the Manchester Unity IOOF and the IOOF. This proposal was presented by the author and Past Grand Master Peter Sellars of California through the *Revitalization Committee* of the Sovereign Grand Lodge in 2015 but was set aside by majority of the Sovereign Grand Lodge representatives. In 2017, Past Sovereign Grand Master Jimmy Humphrey of the IOOF joined the GUOOF as a preliminary step towards building a formal relationship between the two Odd Fellows organizations. More recently, Emanuel Page, Sr., Past Noble Father of Wayman Lodge No. 1339 of the GUOOF, spoke in front of the leaders of the IOOF during the 192nd Annual Communication of the Sovereign Grand Lodge held in Baltimore, Maryland, from August 17 to 23, 2018. A bill to recognize the GUOOF was submitted to the IOOF Grand Lodge of Georgia soon after that and is currently awaiting approval.

However, should an official amity between the GUOOF and the IOOF be established soon, this will only be similar to the "inter-fraternal visitation" rights developed between the MUIOOF and the IOOF. After how many decades, these three major Affiliated Orders of Odd Fellows have already developed diverging rituals, customs, practices, and organizational structure that it has become impossible to merge them into one single organization. Thus, a complete unification between the three major Odd Fellows' organizations will not be possible unless these groups will allow major revisions in their ritualistic works, unwritten work, and organizational structure to decrease substantial differences. Interestingly, some dual members of the IOOF and GUOOF have developed what they call the *Unified Initiatory Degree,* which is a combination of the IOOF and GUOOF initiation ceremony.

Racial diversity has played an important role in the growth of some Odd Fellows Lodges across the world. These lodges serve as a bridge for understanding among people from different racial and ethnic backgrounds. Photo by the author, 2012.

Several people hold membership in both the IOOF and GUOOF. In 2017, Past Sovereign Grand Master Jimmy Humphrey of the IOOF joined Florence Lodge No. 2122 of the GUOOF in Columbia, South Carolina. He is currently holding the position of Worthy Chaplain of Wayman Lodge No.1339 of the GUOOF. Photo courtesy of Emmanuel Page, 2017.

Chapter 17

DECLINE OF FRATERNALISM

For over 150 years, the Odd Fellows enjoyed tremendous success. This success stemmed from the fact that the organization, through its highly committed members, pursued a focused purpose while enjoying little competition. Whether the individual joined primarily for the social relationships, the benefits, entertainment, leadership development opportunities, or an inner satisfaction that arose from belonging to a prestigious fraternal organization, responsible members of the community flocked to membership by the hundreds of thousands.[1] Odd Fellows was remarkably successful because lodges "reached out into their communities and were very visible to the public eye."[2] As its success continued and thousands of novitiates crowded its lodge halls, ancillary units

Historic Odd Fellows Hall in Crockett, California currently houses a train museum, an Odd Fellows Lodge and a Masonic Lodge. Photo courtesy of Matthew X. Kiernan / New York Big apple Images, 2018.

were added without any overall goal, strategy, or plan in mind.[3]

By the 20th century, however, membership in all fraternal organizations and service clubs in North America began to decline. In 1969, Past Sovereign Grand Master Donald Smith and Past Sovereign Grand Master Charles Worrell attended a *Brotherhood 2000 Conference* in New York City with many other fraternal organizations represented. Odd Fellowships' sister fraternities such as Freemasonry raised the concern of dropping membership and all other organizations represented shared similar problems.[4] At the beginning of 1922, there were nearly 4 million Odd Fellows who belonged to the IOOF, GUOOF and MUIOOF. Out of that number, almost 2 million were affiliated with the IOOF.[5] But the total membership of all the three major *Affiliated Orders* of Odd Fellows decreased to 1 million members by 1983.[6] Membership in Freemasonry also went down from 4.1 million members in 1959 to 1.3 million in 2012.[7] The documentary film, *Inside the Freemasons (2017)*, mentioned that at least 100 Masonic lodges close every year. Rotary International was not exempted because "it had been losing about 112,000 members each year."[8] There is no single or simple reason for the decline; the causes are complex.

Automobiles

The horse and buggy were completely replaced by cars.[9] The start of the membership decline among fraternal organizations and service clubs is partly attributable to Henry Ford and his Model T. In 1962 alone, the United States produced and sold about 6 million cars at prices mostly over $2000.[10] The universal possession of cars resulted in the elimination of not only the small local lodges but also of other institutions, such as rural schools and churches.[11] International Association of Rebekah Assemblies President Joyce Sommerville reported in 1967 that "the advent of automobiles made small lodges in rural areas unnecessary because of the ease of travel."[12] In addition, the parking problem created by the number of cars also proved detrimental to the lodges in larger cities because many IOOF buildings were structurally designed and built at a time when cars did not exist.[13]

With increased mobility, many people began to move outside the cities and established their homes in newly developed suburban communities, thereby living far away from the lodges in old towns and metropolitan cities. In fact, increased mobility dramatically decreased the population of some towns and generated so-called *ghost towns*.

Old Towns and Buildings

Many lodges constructed their buildings more or less 100 years ago. As their cities grew and aged, many lodge buildings ended up in the old or rough side of the town. Together with the fact that they were two-storeys or more with no elevators made it difficult for senior members to attend meetings.[14] The outmoded architecture and outward appearance of many Odd Fellows buildings, and some Homes, also presented little inducement for young men and women to become members.[15] There was a growing need for "meeting places that are convenient, clean, and inviting, and situated on ground floors, or on upper floors but with modern conveniences such as elevators."[16] In some cases, there was a need to abandon present locations of meeting places to locations where population growth has increased because of housing developments.[17] Thus, the existence of many large tracts of land owned by the IOOF that were sitting idle and buildings that were underutilized and, in many instances, in very poor state of repair.

The cost of holding these lands and buildings

had become expensive. As taxing policies changed in many countries, this problem became acute.[18] The Sovereign Grand Lodge suggested that the affected lodges sell their old properties and buy new ones located in a better part of the community and with parking area available.[19] Many lodges sold their buildings but they did not use the proceeds from the sale to buy a new building that is manageable in size and condition. Instead, they opted to rent a space from other fraternal organizations and clubs. With no own property and not enough income, many of these lodges eventually struggled to pay the rent. The funds from the sale became depleted to the point that they can no longer afford to buy a new building.

In 1964, the Sovereign Grand Lodge shared that the Odd Fellows Home Endowment Funds equaled almost $21 million, and urged the Grand Lodges to invest at least part of the funds for lodge building improvement.[20] But development and implementation were a problem because of the depreciated value of the dollar at the time. The Odd Fellows have done a lot for humanity in time and money, but the low cost of membership fees and annual dues in North America were also becoming unrealistic in terms of meeting the internal needs of the organization. This apparent "lack of putting real values in the fees was somehow responsible in a large measure for the loss of the prestige the Odd Fellows once held."[21] Many lodges just could not afford to remodel their buildings with the low fees and dues they charged.[22] On the other hand, the Sovereign Grand Lodge and Grand Lodges continued to collect a percentage of the annual dues that was higher than the amount that would be left to the local lodges. These funds were mostly spent for the travel and dinner expenses of their officers instead of being used in developing programs focused on opening new lodges, and helping revive many of the struggling lodges and their constituents.

With increased mobility and development of new cities, the town's population declined and this once booming railroad community in Goode, Virginia, turned into a ghost town for many years. Photo courtesy of Eric Lowenbach, 2019.

Television, telephone, computer and other technological advances

The telephone enabled instant communication, while movies, radio, photograph and computers offered instant entertainment.[23] Ultimately, television brought entertainment right into the houses so there was little reason for people to go out. Many lodges, however, failed to provide the organization with the most recent technology and modern tools of communication. It took many years until some lodges incorporated television sets and other technology into their buildings. Still, many Grand Lodges and lodges still do not use e-mail and social networking websites in their communications. This resulted in a drop in attendance at lodges and ultimately loss of membership.[24]

Commercial Insurance, Welfare State and Medical Advances

At the same time, commercial insurance companies became more stable and their products became more attractive to the average person.[25] With the improvement of labor laws, employers began to offer health and pension benefits. Medical advances significantly increased life expectancy and reduced people's worry about mortality.[26] Furthermore, the government created "a massive welfare bureaucracy emulating the charitable and beneficial activities of religious and fraternal organizations in its effort to eliminate pain and suffering among the general population."[27] These welfare state programs essentially replaced the mutual-aid services formerly offered by the Odd Fellows. Many lodges struggled to shift from a fraternal lodge that offered sick and death benefits to an organization that focuses on character improvement and community service.[28]

Individualism

Societal and technological advances have caused the world to change radically in values, ideologies, principles, and goals. With increased incomes and improved standards of living at the beginning of the 1940s, many people were becoming more independent and individualistic. Along with these advances came the disregard for the human element – the "getting away from person to person relationships and decrease of sense of community."[29] During this period, the leaders of the IOOF observed that there was "callous indifference to welfare or safety of others with consequent rejection of any personal responsibility."[30] That there was "general apathy to religion or any organization advocating moral standards, militant opposition in supposedly educated circles, and to restraints of any kind upon individual conduct."[31]

By the 1990s, a great number of people belonging to the younger generations preferred to stay at home after work or during weekends either to watch a movie or play computer games rather than interact with their neighbors or join community organizations.[32] Lodge members also became individualistic in mindset by focusing on their own lodge only and not helping or working together with other lodges which was contrary to the "sense of community" that Odd Fellowship sought to espouse.

Communism and Anti-establishment Views

Furthermore, a worldwide struggle against communism resulted in open warfare in Vietnam from 1963 to 1969.[33] But instead of receiving support from its citizens, the United States faced protests. Young men subject to military draft tore and burned their draft cards in public demonstrations. Opposition to the Vietnam War in the United States bitterly divided Americans. Leaders of the IOOF observed that the anti-establishment views, which developed as a result of the Vietnam War, led many members of the younger generation to cast off membership in organizations where there was any kind of exclusiveness or conditions for membership.[34] The existing order of things was under attack and the youth were involved in anarchic protests against entrenched power. There was "a struggle between established authority and individual conscience."[35]

Vietnam War protesters in Wichita, Kansas, 1967.
Photo source: wiki-commons, public domain.

It was observed that there was "impatience by the younger generations of this era with the process of law and old ideas rooted in tradition."[36] Thus, many lodges experienced difficulty in attracting younger people to join fraternal organizations and civic groups during this period.

Conspiracy Theories

Fraternal organizations had their greatest day when the love for mystery was popular and certainly no welfare state programs to educate the orphan, or care for the widow, or bury the dead.[37] For a time, the method used by fraternal groups to attract people was that "sense of exclusivity", "mysterious awe" and "secrecy" which generated public curiosity. There was little need for recruitment because the people themselves asked to join.

When the government took over most of the social work done by the Odd Fellows, many lodges somewhat "turned inward, became focused more on secret ritual, regalia, grips and passwords and less about community".[38] At the advent of the 20th century, however, the love for "mystery" and the popularity of "secrecy" declined and were replaced by more socially-relaxing and more inclusive service clubs. Scandalous incidents within Freemasonry, such as when an applicant for membership was shot inside a Masonic Lodge in New York,[39] created a "stigma" against so-called "secret societies" and their rituals. Partly, such incidents subjected all fraternities to negative speculations and conjectures by conspiracy theorists. By 1992, the Sovereign Grand Lodge observed that most people, the media and the general public believe that all fraternal organizations are secret societies.[40]

Public Relations

Poor public relations programs by the Odd Fellows also affected the membership. In 1981, the Grand Lodge of Virginia raised the concern of "a decline in public awareness about the Odd Fellows."[41] Studies and surveys conducted for the past 50 years showed that the public is indifferent to the cause of Odd Fellowship primarily because they do not know what it is.[42] It was noticed that the name Odd Fellows was not well-known anymore to those 50 years of age and younger.[43] The Sovereign Grand Lodge noted that the name had a very different meaning to the younger generations. Worse, there were instances where members were ridiculed in public parades and other functions because of the name.[44] This may be because many Odd Fellows and Rebekah lodges have "operated in secret, separate and apart from the community for too long."[45] This is similarly true to the IOOF in the European continent where many people do not even know that an organization like the Odd Fellows actually exists.

In a nationwide survey conducted in the U.S. by the Sovereign Grand Lodge in 1974, it was reported that the general membership wanted the Sovereign Grand Lodge and Grand Lodges to get more publicity, do more advertising, communicate more, and do more promotional work.[46] There was a dire need for a public relations program geared towards promoting and publicizing local efforts and assisting local branches to get better coverage of their activities.[47] It was also suggested that there was a need for more joint social meetings between the Odd Fellows and Rebekahs, family gatherings, social events, and entertainment.[48] But many lodges struggled because there were senior members who actually believed that anything about the Odd Fellows should be private or a secret.

Aging Membership

Because of the organization's failure to implement most of the needed changes and publicity for the past 50 years, recruitment and retention of younger people became scarce especially in North America. As years passed, IOOF membership became older with less or no younger members replacing them.

On the basis of surveys conducted in some jurisdictions in 1994, the average age of the membership in the Odd Fellows was near or over 70 years, and the average age of the Rebekahs was slightly older.[49] Years prior, only one Grand Representative indicated that he was retired. In 1994, over two-thirds indicated that they were retired.[50] Although there were lodges that were taking in a sufficient number of new members to offset the losses due to retirement, membership was still decreasing in number because of age and infirmity.[51] For example, the IOOF initiated 11,807 new members in 1981 but it also lost about 7,427 due to death alone.[52]

Membership age has also been a concern in Australia and several parts of Europe. At the end of 2017, the average age of Odd Fellows in Norway was 65 for men and 68 for women. The Odd Fellows in Finland shared that a weakness of the IOOF in their country "is still aging membership and not being known in the community."[53]

For the past 50 years, the leaders of the IOOF have been stressing the need for members under 40 and the desire that each Odd Fellows and Rebekah lodge be involved in community service in their areas.[54] Statistics in 1999 showed an increase in membership within the group of 55 to 60, even more for group of 60 to 70. On the other hand, it was a struggle to get members below 50 years old.[55] In due course, many lodges closed mainly because there were no younger people who could succeed the older generation of members.

Generation Gap

A significant generation gap eventually developed as a result of Odd Fellows' aging membership. The Sovereign Grand Lodge observed that there were individual lodges who were "out of contact with reality and needed some outside intervention from the Grand Lodge in their area."[56] Lodges that were experiencing low attendance needed to evaluate the cause of the obvious lack of interest and create a more positive and active meeting atmosphere. But progress was a challenge because there were long-time members who were totally resistant to change. In 1986, the Sovereign Grand Lodge reported that there were many situations where the senior members would go up to the younger members and tell them, "That isn't the way we used to do it."[57] This created distrust in some lodges and "killed the younger members' desire and enthusiasm for work in Odd Fellowship."[58]

This clash between senior members resulted in younger members resigning from the organization.[59] It was observed that younger generations did not tolerate antiquated and obsolete ideas. Younger members aged 50 and below did not stay active because they perceived "older members' attitudes of being too comfortable, complacent, and close-minded."[60]

Some of the long-time members became so entrenched in the status quo that they did not want to change the way things were. For the past 20 or more years they have become too comfortable doing things the same way.[61] It appeared that some of them just wanted "to keep their small world to themselves and ignore the next generation and the future existence of their lodge."[62] There was even an occasion when a group of college students and young professionals wanted to join an Odd Fellows Lodge with only eight remaining elderly members but the latter turned them down saying, "We are good. We are not interested." The same people have been holding officer positions for years and the younger ones were often left to sit on the sidelines. As a result, younger people did not stay because "they perceived Odd Fellowship, in its present form, had little to offer."[63]

Younger people were not interested in joining boring and stodgy lodges "where the members don't smile, don't offer a handshake, don't do much more than sit around in meetings, hold a monthly potluck, and write a check or two to a charity."[64] Rather, younger generations were "seeking exciting, rewarding, meaningful, and satisfying use of their time and energies as they grow."[65]

Training and Education

Because they struggled to recruit and retain new members, many lodges in North America made joining quick and easy. Degree rallies became common and this allowed the new candidates to receive all degrees in one day.[66] This resulted in a position where "the deep meaning of the rituals, signs and passwords has not been fully understood."[67] In many cases, when a member received his last degree "he is told nothing much except asked to make a speech about an organization he knows nothing about."[68] The ethical teachings of Odd Fellowship through the rituals was widely ignored.[69] The implementation of this quick-fix solution resulted in "poor selection of candidates, inefficient officers, and failure to properly acquaint new members with the history, aims, objectives and achievements of Odd Fellowship."[70]

In 1982, Past Sovereign Grand Master D.D. Monroe reiterated that one of the weakest links in the various lodges and branches in North America was the lack of information and membership development.[71] As a result, the Odd Fellows "did not spark an interest in the new member"[72] and "that member eventually let his membership lapse."[73] In 1993, Past Sovereign Grand Master Lloyd Shelvey noted that there seemed to be apathy towards the organization. For the most part, this was caused by "a lack of understanding of the organization's very existence and a feeling that the IOOF is out of touch of today's issues."[74] He believed that "this can only be corrected and improved by better education of its members and more information being presented and understood by these members."[75] In a 1994 Sovereign Grand Lodge study, it was found that the biggest shortcoming of the Odd Fellows in North America is the education of its members.[76] A membership survey conducted made it clear that "a significant portion of the membership lacked even the basic knowledge about the organization."[77]

In 1994, Past Sovereign Grand Master J.W. Frederick Laycock emphasized that "the IOOF in North America cannot get the membership to sell Odd Fellowship to a sufficient number of new members to keep pace with the losses until members themselves are schooled in what the Odd Fellows is all about, what its goals and principles are, and have more than a little knowledge about its history."[78] There was a growing need to institute a training program for its members telling them how to conduct meetings, how to participate in community activities, how to obtain publicity, and how and what activities can be promoted.[79] Many leaders urged Grand Lodges and lodges to get quality members, provide them with programs they want, and encourage them to participate actively at all levels.[80] Ian Witton of Australia opined that people will not join lodges unless the Odd Fellows can impress them with a "clearly explainable vision of Odd Fellowship, an attractive building, an impressive dress code, competent ceremonies, and confident officers."[81] He suggested that the "true effort to revitalize the organization should be to educate and inform its own members."[82] He opined that "knowledge leads to confidence; confidence leads to enthusiasm; enthusiasm leads to commitment; commitment leads to pride; and these collectively lead to success."[83] However, many of these recommendations were left unheard. The officers and committees of the Sovereign Grand Lodge and many Grand Lodges took little action so they were unable to deliver the needed results.

Poor Management

Lack of training and education resulted in a failure to effectively inculcate the core values of the IOOF as taught in the degrees of initiation. This resulted in additional problems in some Grand Lodges and lodges. Beginning in 1983, there had been a concern in the United States regarding the utilization of the organization's assets.[84] There were questions regarding the management of many large endowment funds and thousands of small funds which, together, constituted millions of dollars.[85] There were also some instances when "long-time members looked upon lodge funds and properties as their own and not the reversionary property of their Odd Fellows or Rebekah Lodge."[86] There occurred cases of illegal transfer of lodge funds and property to individual members and the outright embezzlement of funds and properties by officers.[87] Professional management had been recommended but not many Grand Lodges were successful at this. Yet some Grand Lodges and lodges still elected officers and hired employees even if they lacked the needed management style and leadership skills. Some members kept people in the same office for too long even though they had done the organization more damage than good. Many lodges were left with no buildings and not enough funds in their treasury. Without endowment funds and the sale of lodge halls, many lodges eventually faced difficulty operating.[88]

Resistance to Change

When the prolonged decline set in, the IOOF failed to seriously re-evaluate its priorities. Instead, it "added numerous programs without any abandonment of older unproductive programs."[89] For many years, members especially in North America have been warned that the Odd Fellows had been drifting. That "the leadership could not continue to hold outmoded ideas and systems of conducting its Sovereign Grand Lodge, Grand Lodges, or Lodges if the IOOF is to catch up with other international organizations."[90]

First, there is a need for change in the organization, which is concurrent to the present society.[91] Second, there is a need to embrace new needs and attitudes of younger generations.[92] However, it has been shown that the complex organizational structure and bureaucracy developed in the 19th century was already ineffective in the present century. The *SGL Ad Hoc Committee* assigned to study the condition of the IOOF in North America in 1968 suggested that there was "a need to simplify procedures and that the organization should spend less time talking about what not to do and more in talking about what they can do and should do."[93]

In 1968, Past Sovereign Grand Master Gene Bianchi wrote a list of things that needed immediate change if the organization was to have a future. This list was "tossed into the waste basket and that no changes that he recommended have been made."[94] European members of the IOOF International Council also noted that there had been many propositions discussed for the past 50 years that were adopted during their meetings but very rarely have actions been taken by Representatives of the Sovereign Grand Lodge consisting of leaders from the United States and Canada.[95] In 1993, Sovereign Grand Master Lloyd Shelvey observed that the IOOF was "taking a year to plan, a year's layover for the funding to be voted upon, and a year to adjust the program for the amount of revenue allowed."[96] He opined that "checks and balances are absolutely necessary but a procedure must be put into place which will allow oversight of the expenditures while permitting orderly and timely decision-making and implementation."[97]

According to a study conducted by the Sovereign Grand Lodge, the greatest challenge that confronted the IOOF during this era was "how to change the thinking of their members".[98] Several leaders urged that it can no longer deny the need for change both structurally and fundamentally.[99] As early as 1968, a national study recommended that the organizational structure of the IOOF needed to be simplified.[100] There was a need to change the routine business meeting into interesting and educational ones by adopting new ideas and new methods.[101] It had become very obvious that to attract new and younger members, the fraternity must "make changes to conform to the thinking of future generations without damaging the high precepts of Odd Fellowship maintained since its inception."[102]

Past Grand Sire Dag Wallen of Sweden in his speech to the Sovereign Grand Lodge in 1993 said that "for fifty years we have heard: Think it over, we have plenty of time, but now, there is not enough time."[103] He challenged the leaders of the Sovereign Grand Lodge to "take action, or admit we have no hope in the future of this Order."[104] That "if the Grand Bodies and Lodges will continue to refuse change, then the eventual and inevitable demise of the IOOF can happen."[105] Inevitably, many lodges that failed to adapt to the times closed; many Grand Lodges that continue with the same management style were left with less than ten lodges in the entire state, and the number of members of the IOOF in general have dwindled.

Organizational Structure

In 1994, a research conducted by a Committee of the Sovereign Grand Lodge observed that the "organizational structure of the IOOF has evolved without any ultimate design or purpose in mind, and has become excessively complex."[106] It reiterated the *1982 Ad Hoc Committee* results that the IOOF is "overloaded and over-organized with its present membership."[107] There was a demand to simplify the organizational structure. Many of its jurisdictions with small memberships were trying to staff a Grand Lodge, a Rebekah Assembly, a Grand Encampment, a Department Council, and Ladies Auxiliary Patriarchs Militant, plus all the lodges necessary to support these grand bodies.[108] The expenditure in time, effort, and money was draining the organization. The Committee felt that jurisdictions would be better served with only one grand body or state organization. This is the case in Europe where all IOOF branches fall directly under their Grand Lodge.

In the same study, the *SGL Ad hoc Committee* also suggested that changes be made to, or within, the structure of the Sovereign Grand Lodge. The structure of the Sovereign Grand Lodge may have been well-suited during the rise of fraternal organizations in the 19th and early 20th centuries. But in the midst of the era of the decline of fraternal groups, the structure of the Sovereign Grand Lodge has become an impediment. It was observed that it was "not getting the job done and does not justify the expense."[109] In fact, the possibility of secession from the Sovereign Grand Lodge had been discussed in some jurisdictions.[110]

Unlike the Masonic lodges, which are governed within each state without a higher authority, the IOOF in North America is governed by a national and an international governing body. It has been observed that the autonomy in the Masonic

Sessions of the IOOF Grand Lodge of Denmark are held once every two years. This minimizes expenses in holding sessions; the saved resources are used for other programs instead. This also gives the officers enough time for planning and implementation. Photo courtesy of the Sovereign Grand Lodge, IOOF.

fraternity provided each jurisdiction more leeway to adopt changes at a faster rate as long as they do not violate the generally accepted landmarks. In the IOOF, however, the organization is slower to react and adapt because the Sovereign Grand Lodge has to take into account all of the jurisdictions it governs. Any change or idea must pass through all levels of bureaucracy from the lodge to the Grand Lodge of each state to the Sovereign Grand Lodge. But before it is voted upon within the Grand Lodge or Sovereign Grand Lodge, proposals will have to undergo review by a certain Committee who makes the recommendation. If the Committee is ineffective or resistant to that change, then the whole process will be delayed. For example, it took the Sovereign Grand Lodge nearly 10 years to update the design of their website because of red tape and inefficiency of the members of the Committee members assigned.

In 1994, the *Ad hoc Committee* recommended that the Sovereign Grand Lodge will better serve its members if it will become "a planning and policy-determining body with minimal legislation."[111] It was also recommended that the Sovereign Grand Lodge should "focus more on becoming a public relations vehicle like the Lions International or Rotary International."[112] Should the Sovereign Grand Lodge continue to exist as an international governing body, it must be quick to react to the needed improvements.

The Committee concluded that major changes in the Sovereign Grand Lodge Sessions must also be made. Beginning 1994, it had been observed that a longer term for the Sovereign Grand Lodge officers was needed. It was recommended that the term of office be changed from one year to two years and the office of the Sovereign Grand Warden be eliminated.[113] The high cost of holding the Annual Communications of the Sovereign Grand Lodge also pointed out the need and advantage of holding sessions on a Biennial basis or once every two years.[114] This had been proven effective by IOOF in Europe where the Grand Lodge meetings vary from once every two years to once every five years while Grand Lodge officers are elected for a term of at least two years. This lessened the expenses of the European organization and allowed the national officers more time for program implementation and expansion projects. *Term limits* for the Representatives of the Grand Lodges and the Sovereign Grand Lodge were also recommended. Studies have found that some officers in the Grand Lodge and Sovereign Grand Lodge have been holding the same office or have been members of the same Committee for the past twenty or more years. Some have become so old that they are so disconnected to the present needs of the organization, while some have become a hindrance to new ideas because they want to continue holding on to their positions even if they were already ineffective.

In addition, the European IOOF Federation proposed to make the Sovereign Grand Lodge a truly international governing body consisting of representatives from all over the world with greater authority for worldwide Odd Fellowship.[115] Past Grand Sire Daniel Corrodi of the Grand Lodge of Switzerland emphasized that "the Odd Fellows as a non-profit organization should follow the example of other successful international associations."[116] For example, the Rotary International was formerly a purely American organization whose international presidents in the past were all Americans. In recent years Rotary has had International Presidents from India, Switzerland, and other countries.[117] But the Sovereign Grand Lodge, consisting of representatives in the United States and Canada, has rejected this idea year after year.[118] At present, there is an IOOF International Advisory Board but the body has no legislative power within the Sovereign Grand Lodge (See Chapter 21).

Closing and Consolidating Lodges

It also was recorded that the traditional management style and poor leadership skills of some of the officers of the Sovereign Grand Lodge and the Grand Lodges in North America has contributed to the demise of a number of lodges. In 1964, Sovereign Grand Master Murphy noted that "what the organization had been doing in the past 20 years was consolidating and taking charters instead of instituting new lodges and finding ways to revitalize dormant lodges."[119] The leadership in some states basically watched lodges go defunct. Leaders expected that "fewer remaining lodges will recruit more members, but failed on membership recruitment directed to hundreds of communities where an Odd Fellows Lodge does not exist."[120] Past Sovereign Grand Master Reynolds suggested that it might be "more beneficial to use some of the money from defunct lodges to start new lodges in other communities."[121] Controversially, he suggested that "if Grand Lodges are strapped for funds they should raise their dues rather than continue trying to live off the bones of lodges they have left to go defunct."[122] In some jurisdictions, only five lodges and less than 100 members remain in the entire state. This is partly the fault of the officers of the Grand Lodges in these areas because they revoked the charters of struggling lodges instead of helping them, and some officers allegedly misspent the funds collected from the lodges they closed instead of using them to open new lodges in other localities.

Growth in Europe and other Countries

While both the Odd Fellows and Rebekahs in North America had been laboring under the problem of decline in membership,[123] foreign countries showed much activity in promoting the organization.[124] Beginning 1969, many lodges were being instituted in the South American continent. Lodges in Chile were growing tremendously in number, as well as lodges in Venezuela, Colombia, and Peru.[125] There was also some membership

In 1970, Sovereign Grand Master Donald R. Smith was the only representative of a fraternal organization to be invited by the Freedoms Foundation to participate in a pilgrimage to Vietnam. He presented a silver Sesquincentennial medallion to President Nguyen Van Thiu of the Republic of Vietnam. Photo courtesy of Peter Sellars

Meeting Presidents

Despite the problem of declining membership, charitable work of the IOOF during this era was tremendous and these contributions have been recognized by several U.S. Presidents.

In 1961, Past Sovereign Grand Master Anglea, as Chairman of the *People-to-People Program*, spent two days in Kansas City, Missouri, to meet with former U.S. Presidents Eisenhower and Truman and Mr. Joyce Hall and the Hallmark Foundation.[1] In 1963, the leaders of the IOOF held a conference with President John. F. Kennedy who recognized the IOOF with a presentation honoring the 15th Odd Fellows and Rebekahs Youth Pilgrimage to the United Nations.[2] In 1970, Sovereign Grand Master Donald Smith participated in a *Pilgrimage to Vietnam* under the sponsorship of Freedoms Foundations.[3] The IOOF was the only fraternal organization represented among more than 20 national and international organizations that participated.[4] Afterwards, the entire group was invited by President Richard Nixon to the White House. In 1982, the IOOF was invited by U.S. President Ronald Reagan to a conference at the White House.[5] The President recognized the IOOF "for the work it had been doing, expressed appreciation, and requested that Odd Fellows, along with similar fraternal bodies, relieve the Government from the great responsibility it has borne in the past in caring for the elderly and indigent."[6]

growth in Montevideo, Uruguay.[126]

Odd Fellowship in Norway was constantly progressing in terms of number of new lodges and total number of members.[127] In Iceland, there had been a steady increase in membership and its philanthropic works were promising.[128] Many lodges were instituted in Finland, and a lodge was re-established in Austria.[129] In 1993, the Grand Lodge of Finland instituted an Odd Fellows Lodge and a Rebekah Lodge in Estonia.[130] Months after, a new lodge in Wroclaw, Poland, was chartered with nearly 60 members.[131] The Encampments were also operating with success in Europe that a study was conducted as to how to adopt their methods in North America.[132]

During his visit, Sovereign Grand Master Verdie Dodds observed that "the dignity and pride exemplified in the decorum of Odd Fellows meetings in Europe is beyond comparison."[133] Every officer and member is dressed in formal attire with the collar regalia and jewels of their respective officers and members resplendent in their appearance. The membership is also at complete attention to the business on hand. There also are realistic approaches to application fees and annual dues.[134] It was observed that lodges in Europe are experiencing growth and interest from younger members by delivering "high quality degree work."[135]

Instead of resorting to one-day degree rallies and functioning more like service clubs, the Odd Fellows in Europe place "first emphasis on the ethical work of Odd Fellowship which was to teach members friendship, love and truth, tolerance, and being charitable through the rituals."[136] Secondly, lodges are involved in humanitarian work for old and sick members as well as for people and institutions who are not part of the organization.[137] The European IOOF were against the suggestion of the Sovereign Grand Lodge to reduce the degree work to only one.

The German IOOF leader opined that "the degree work can still be attractive if it is explained and taught with precision and persuasion, and by choosing the appropriate words to make it more suitable to the current generation."[138]

In Europe, the lodge meetings are still conducted with the traditional ritual ceremonies while social activities are held afterwards.[139] Their strength depends on the education in which a member progresses.[140] Usually, it takes about six months before a candidate can apply for membership. During the period, the officers of the lodge will contact him and his family. His wife has to agree with his admission into the Odd Fellows. A new member must be firmly convinced that it is a special favor to become an Odd Fellow. The lodges make sure that those who wish to join are of good reputation. After receiving the initiatory degree, a new member is required to participate in at least 65% of all meetings and events of the lodge until he can receive the third degree.[141] They must also pledge to visit at least 10 sick and elderly members per year and to visit other lodges in nearby towns at least 3 times a year. New members are also assigned to deliver speeches and accept different duties. Generally, it will take at least one year to receive all degrees of the lodge and the new member may apply for membership in the Encampment after five years.[142] In some European lodges, a new member has to work actively for about three years within the lodge until he is promoted into the third degree.[143]

By 1996, jurisdictions under the Sovereign Grand Lodge in the United States and Canada had lost almost 30% of their membership while the Independent European jurisdictions increased their membership by 11%.[144] By 1999, IOOF membership in Europe had surpassed the membership in North America.

Community Service

The issue of membership decline notwithstanding, the Odd Fellows and Rebekah Lodges continued to provide funds for a variety of public services. In the 20th century, the finances were still in a stable condition – total revenue in 1968 was $1.3 billion.[145] The total invested funds of the IOOF in North America alone was $91.8 million and its Homes for the Aged had $26.6 million in investments.[146] There was a great desire by the general membership to be of service to humanity. While not losing sight of the obligations to members and their families, there was an increasing belief in IOOF that the principles of Odd Fellowship must be applied to all people.[147] The IOOF International Council encouraged the Odd Fellows to participate in helping poor people in underdeveloped countries and the organization did.[148]

In addition to continuing its traditional public services, the organization moved into "the fields of ecology, solutions to drug addiction, and aid to good education."[149] During this period, the Odd Fellows and Rebekahs began sponsoring hundreds of students on an educational trip through the IOOF Educational Pilgrimage for the Youth Program. It had established the IOOF Visual Research Foundation, which raised the initial sum of $1 million for visual research at the John Hopkins University.[150] It provided low-interest student loans to students through its IOOF Educational Foundation. Moreover, the Odd Fellows and Rebekahs constructed the entrance gate of the *Peace Garden* in Manitoba, participated in the *People-to-People* programs and took wide interest in various educational programs.[151] In fact, a Committee was formed in 1962 to investigate the possibility of establishing an Odd Fellows University in the United States.[152] Moreover, it provided relief assistance of over $7.5 million annually to aid victims of natural disasters such as the California and Texas Flood and the Great Alaskan Earthquake.[153]

By 1976, fifty states still continued to provide Homes for orphans, the aged, the infirm, and widows with a valuation of $40 million. Over 58,380 residents of these Homes experienced the caring aspect of Odd Fellowship.[154] Over 2,167 students received loans totaling $1.9 million to continue their education in colleges and universities of their choice.[155] Relief in helping others in times of natural disasters, personal difficulties, and financial problems was at $453,915,159.48 by 1977.[156] Beginning 1982, the Odd Fellows and Rebekahs in North America rapidly acquired a reputation as "a leader in the construction of Retirement Homes for the elderly."[157]

In Europe, the Odd Fellows and Rebekahs also raised millions of dollars for Retirement Homes, Cancer Examination Centers, and other causes. Odd Fellows in Switzerland had the pleasure to grant $90,000 for the construction of a new Home for Children with Special Needs.[158] The Odd Fellows in the Netherlands and Belgium sponsored camps and boat trips for handicapped children.[159] Two lodges in Iceland donated to the local hospital an equipment for blood examination. During the last five years, six lodges in Reykjavik donated about $2 million to the Recreation Home for Retired People.[160]

Odd Fellows and Rebekahs in Norway donated 750,000 Kroner worth of heart diagnostic apparatus to the Oslo Municipal Hospital.[161] They also established a *Grand Lodge Humanitarian Fund* which donates about $100,000 annually to various charitable causes and $120,000 as principal for a foundation for research into Multiple Sclerosis.[162] In 1965, the Grand Lodge of Norway constructed a nursing home for persons with Multiple Sclerosis. In 1973, Odd Fellows of Norway donated a rescue boat to the Norwegian Coast Guard named "Odd Fellow" which cost about 2 million Kroner.[163] In 1979, the

Several Grand Lodges of the Independent Order of Odd Fellows owns Odd Fellows and Rebekahs Youth Camps equipped with cabins, RV site, camp grounds, pavilion and a lake. Photo courtesy of Tall Oaks Odd Fellow and Rebekah Camp, Baldwin, Michigan, 2016.

Odd Fellows Retirement Home in Lockport, New York. Photo from the collection of the author.

Norwegian Rebekahs raised 750,000 Kroner for a special medical echo instrument to be used in the children heart division of the National Hospital in Oslo.[164]

In 1983, Odd Fellows in Sweden established a Grand Lodge Humanitarian Fund with a starting capital of 3.5 million Kroner and an annual donation of about 1 million Kroner.[165] They donated around 430,000 Kroner for the Cancer Examination house and 950,000 Kroner to the national confederation of heart patients.[166] From 1990 to 1995, the Swedish Grand Lodge allotted over 5.8 million Kronor for medical research, rescue boats, overseas aid and others.[167] In Denmark, the Odd Fellows developed substantial charitable activities. Every year, the Grand Lodge of Denmark allocates at least 4 million DKK to humanitarian and cultural activities.[168] In 1993, they also donated more than 1 million DKK to the Red Cross for the restoration of an infant house in Romania where about 100 infants were kept by the communist regime.[169] In Germany, the Odd Fellows and Rebekahs donated several ambulances equipped with radio communication to the Red Cross.[170]

Besides these, individual lodges located around the world spent great amounts for general relief in their home districts. In fact, most of the lodges supported various humanitarian causes regarding the blind, the sick, and the youth.[171] Sponsoring students and their activities seems to be a popular project for many lodges. They sponsored basketball and baseballs teams, purchased team uniforms, and served refreshments. One lodge served dinner annually to 5th grade students going into middle school. Shoes for kids was popular as well as warm coats and mittens in areas where they are needed. There are several lodges that filled backpacks with school supplies for homeless children. Tutoring students and donation of teddy bears to local firemen, police, and hospitals were also a popular volunteer program of several lodges.[172] Some lodges sponsored Easter egg hunts while others sponsored community fireworks displays and the annual Christmas parades. Many lodges donated to shelters for abused women and children.[173] And when a tornado devastated many areas in Texas, the Odd Fellows and Rebekahs collected loads of foods and supplies. Amazingly, an eighteen-wheel tractor trailer was necessary to transport the vast amounts of necessities collected to alleviate the needs of the stricken area.[174]

Chapter 18

SIGNS OF REDISCOVERY

Times have dramatically changed. There are many opportunities and competitions in today's world. Much of the assistance provided by fraternal organizations and service clubs has been absorbed by hospitals, funeral homes and government agencies.[1] Priorities have evolved. Both men and women now work for a living. They have family commitments. They have other leisure activities. For their valuable time, people now "have the option of joining a multitude of other groups, organizations, clubs and lodges."[2] Yet many of these century-old organizations have hardly changed the way they do business and still continue to function virtually in the same way they did over 50 years ago.

Along with other complex factors, the failure of many fraternal organizations, service clubs, and similar organizations to adapt to the needs of the modern times resulted in a failure to attract and retain people belonging to the younger generations. Lodges and clubs that failed to offer something exciting to the younger generations eventually surrendered their charters while some have become stagnant. Membership in some lodges literally skipped two generations and are currently suffering an aging membership.[3]

For many years, the Sovereign Grand Lodge of the IOOF had raised concerns on "increasing the membership, reducing the average age, and educating members as to the meaning of the degrees of initiation."[4] But the leaders found themselves faced with many varied opinions as to the proper steps to take to address membership problems and organizational development concerns.[5] Year after year, the representatives through bills or resolutions and committees have suggested "about the same panacea to put the IOOF on the progress trail but there was nothing new under the sun."[6]

Recently, "the fancy trappings of dwindling fraternal organizations have caught the attention of Hollywood, musicians, artists and historians alike."[7] Fraternal regalia and antiques have been popping up all over the internet, television shows, and art exhibits. Movies and documentary exposés about so called "secret societies" caught the attention of some people, particularly the younger generations. The internet has become one of the best forms of advertising Odd Fellowship and communication for members. The popularity of social networking websites such as *Facebook* and *Instagram* and sharing services such as *Youtube* have made it a lot easier for younger generations to learn about these organizations. Lodges and Grand Lodges that are visible in their communities and combine the use of the most recent technologies are now getting the publicity they need[8] with little or no cost at all.

As a result, there seems to be renewed interest from some men and women to join fraternal organizations like the Odd Fellows and rediscover new forms of community in the lodges. Some people have become interested in returning to basic beliefs of years ago such as "respect for our fellowmen, strong support to our communities, and sharing

The ornate meeting rooms, symbolism, and initiation ceremonies of Odd Fellowship has intrigued people belonging to the younger generations to join. Photo courtesy of Columbia Odd Fellows Lodge No.2, 2017.

with others."[9] Lodges that made extra effort to catch up with the needs of modern times are now coming back to life in a dramatic way. A number of lodges are experiencing a resurgence of membership from different groups of young people - history buffs, tattoo artists, bikers, community activists, musicians, lawyers, businessmen, and the like.

Beginning 2001, a group of motorcycle enthusiasts have revived a handful of Odd Fellows and Rebekah Lodges in Northern Illinois and Wisconsin. In 2005, five new Odd Fellows lodges were instituted in Alberta, California, Georgia, and Arkansas.[10] Between 2007 to 2008, new Odd Fellows lodges were chartered in the Dominican Republic and Nigeria, and United Youth Groups were established in Hawaii, Missouri, and Minnesota.[11] In 2009, Odd Fellowship was revived in the Philippines[12] and fourteen new lodges have been established in the country since then. Recent records show that the number of new members admitted to the IOOF in North America increased from 3,097 in 2012 to 4,578 in 2013.[13] Although a large number of lodges are still struggling with membership at present, there are success stories from different parts of the world about lodges that grew from less than 5 members to more than 100 members. So, what are the secrets of success of these growing lodges?

Rich History, Symbols and Rituals

The long history of fraternal organizations such as the Odd Fellows, their rituals, symbols, regalia, and tradition of camaraderie are a preliminary attractive reason why some people inquire about and consider membership. For the past 50 years, the older members have been debating about how to modernize the organization. Some of the older generations were even ready to abolish the rituals and passwords. Younger members at present, however, see it differently. Many actually joined the Odd Fellows because it is different from service clubs and because of their interest in the traditional ritual ceremonies.[14] They see lodges as an avenue for "preserving long-lost traditions, fellowship, community service, and leadership."[15]

Rick Braggy, one of the youngest members of the recently rejuvenated Sycamore Odd Fellows Lodge No.129 in Hayward, California, opined that "younger people nowadays are looking for a sense of belonging, a sense of history, and of knowing their past."[16] He believes that joining the Odd Fellows is "an opportunity for younger generations to feel a sense of belonging, to feel being a part of something historical, something long-lasting, and something much bigger than one's self."[17] One reason Vic Anton Somoza of Watchdog Odd Fellows Lodge No.1 in Dumaguete, Philippines, joined is because of "the customs and rituals that have been followed through the years."[18] Thomas Roam, a member who recently helped revive an Odd Fellows Lodge in his town, added that "people my age prefer the originality of the rituals and there is something about acting it out that is quite intriguing."[19] He even suggested "memorization" to add drama to the ceremonies. Graham Fullerton, who recently joined at the age of seventeen, shared that he "enjoyed the chance to meet people who share my values, plus the initiation was kind of cool."[20] In fact, many younger members throughout the world are even calling for an improved performance in the exemplification of the degrees of initiation.

Nevertheless, no person is going to stay active as a member just because that lodge has a rich history, ancient rituals, secret grips, passwords, and signs, and because the members wear stylish regalia.[21] There must be more. Successful lodges are those that expanded their lodge activities into hosting social events for the members and their families and doing good works in the community.

Social Events and Activities

Odd Fellowship originated in the pubs and taverns of England where members could experience an enjoyable social life with other members. That "old-fashioned and old-time connection is valuable today in our disconnected society."[22] People still seek a social network where they can have a good time and enjoy activities with others. Nobody wants to continue their membership in a lodge that is always serious and rigid. It had been observed by leaders of successful lodges that "a lodge cannot attract younger members if the only activity it can offer is a 30-minute formal meeting once or twice a month"[23] and "an occasional potluck with little else going on."[24]

The lodges that are growing are those that do not just rely on the formality of opening and closing rituals. There are many instances when a young member "expressed frustration that his lodge seemed to be locked in a time warp."[25] This happens when the members do not do much of anything except go through the ritual book and plan some dinners or potlucks for the lodge. One member said that "he is bored and added that he does not want to bring in potential new members into his lodge because they will just be as bored as I am."[26]

Clearly, monotony and boredom do not attract new members, and certainly do not retain them. Growing Odd Fellows' lodges today are those that allow their members to unwind and socialize at the lodge after a busy day at work. The early Odd Fellows lodges in the 1700s did offer food and liquor after meetings and this practice continued until alcoholic drinks were banned by the IOOF at the beginning of 1825 in compliance with the growing *Temperance Movement* that advocated against consumption of alcoholic beverages. This resulted in the passage of *Prohibition laws* in the United States that made the manufacture, sale or distribution of intoxicating liquors illegal. These laws were eventually repealed in all states from 1933 to 1966, bringing the *Prohibition era* to a close.

But while liquor is already legal in almost all countries today, many lodges failed to update their old prohibition rules and still continue to ban alcoholic beverages within their buildings. More successful and vibrant lodges today are those that have already allowed alcoholic beverages inside their lodge buildings. Some of these growing lodges actually have a bar as additional amenity for their buildings. Obviously, this encourages younger members to regularly attend lodge meetings and essentially stay at the lodge after the meeting to socialize with other members. From a psychological perspective, this also helps develop a stronger bond between members and can boost the morale of the lodge. Studies conducted by the Sovereign Grand Lodge in 1970 revealed that growing lodges are those that do not just hold ritualistic meetings or merely pass through a fixed agenda, but also bring its members together before or after the meetings so that they can "get acquainted and can be united in true friendship, and that they can leave from lodge meeting with a more fortified feeling."[27] Successful lodges are "those that provide an active social life within the lodge, because without a little fun, the lodge loses the friendship that Odd Fellows purports to espouse."[28] This means that there is a need to incorporate activities that would serve the common interests and hobbies of its members.

Scott Shaw, a Past Grand of Columbia Odd Fellows Lodge No.2 in British Columbia, Canada, sees Odd Fellowship as "a group of people coming together, working as a big family, supporting the local community, fund-raising together, and meeting each other's families."[29] Thus, a dinner before or after a formal meeting is just not a selling point. The lodge must organize social events that bring members together to enjoy each other's company and socially interact, whether it be biking, hiking trips, movie nights, game nights, wine tasting, beer brewing, dances, or concerts.

In Europe, younger members envision the Odd Fellows lodge as a place that is different from daily life. They want the lodge to be "a place to rest, to think, to get energy, to obtain ethical education, to learn to get to know fellow citizens and next-door neighbors."[30] In response, most lodges in Switzerland and other parts of Europe hold lectures on ethical topics at least twice a month and this had been met positively.[31] Other lodges whose membership has tremendously increased developed their own "signature events" that their lodge organizes annually for their members and the whole community. Some examples of popular social and community events organized by Odd Fellows today are the "Odd Fest," "Oddtober Fest," "Oddventure," and "Odd Market." These are events that provide volunteer opportunities and showcase the talents of their members by providing music, arts, and other activities for the public to participate in. The funds raised will then be used to support local charities. When lodges have a full slate of such social activities, recruitment of new members is dramatically enhanced.[32]

Community Involvement and Volunteerism

One fraternal lesson from the history of Odd Fellowship is the necessity of community participation and involvement. Odd Fellowship rose to its "most glorious hour when members were active in the growth of communities and nations."[33] Citizens of early days recognized the value of Odd Fellowship, hence, they reciprocated by becoming members of "a Fraternity with the prime objective to serve."[34] Indeed, Odd Fellowship is one of the earliest forms of service organizations that provided its members opportunities to help each other and

The *Temperance Movement* (1784-1933) advocated against the consumption of alcohol and had a big influence on North American society, such that the manufacture, sale, or distribution of alcoholic beverages became illegal not just within the lodges but throughout the country. The prohibition became a nationwide constitutional ban in the United States from 1920 to 1933. After that, the manufacture of beer, wine, and distilled spirits became legal. Growing lodges today have updated their rules regarding consumption of alcoholic beverages and have incorporated in their buildings an industrial kitchen, a bar, and a reception area to allow their members to socialize before and after meetings. Photo courtesy of Scott Aitchison, 2019.

Lodges that are growing are those that organize social events that cater the hobbies and interests of their members whether it be about motorcycles, wine-tasting, and the like. Photo courtesy of Columbia Odd Fellows Lodge No.2, 2017, and Odd Fellows Motorcycle Club, 2016.

The work of Odd Fellowship is not serious all the time. Many lodges are also about having fun by hosting and organizing social and community fund-raising events. The "Odd Fest" or "Oddtober Fest" organized annually by some lodges in the United States and Canada have become one of the "signature events" of the Odd Fellows in specific localities. The event is usually a mix of fellowship through music and arts and a fund-raising event to benefit a particular charity. These events are also a time when the bonds of friendship between members can become stronger.

Photo courtesy of St. Helena Odd Fellows Lodge No.167, 2017.

Signs of Rebirth | 127

Lodges must do more than just handing-out a check to charities. Offering volunteer opportunities for the membership outside the lodge rooms have also been proven effective in increasing membership in countries such as the United States, Canada, and the Philippines. Photo courtesy of Columbia Odd Fellows Lodge No.2, 2017.

their fellowmen.

During the 19th century, the Odd Fellows and Rebekahs were a major presence in every town, providing essential medical aid, sick pay, and generally helping those who fell on hard times. IOOF in every state operated the first cemeteries, retirement homes, and orphanages. When these services were taken over by government programs and other agencies, many lodges eventually became stuck inside their lodge rooms and became virtually invisible in their towns. Today, there are people who are uncomfortable and uneasy over the economy, energy, morality, defense of their countries, the role of government in their lives, and myriad other problems. With several governments increasingly unable to provide adequate funding for health care, education, retirement, and unemployment and with the growing moral breakdown among citizens, the role of fraternal organizations such as the Odd Fellows is finding some relevance once again.

Growing lodges are those that become more involved with problems facing many communities today. *Davis Odd Fellows Lodge No.169* in Davis, California, has grown from less than 20 active members[35] to over 300 members at present. Dave Rosenberg, a Past Grand of the Lodge, shared that their lodge "went in the direction of serving the community, reaching out into the community, being visible and doing good things, and having fun."[36] One of the reasons new members are attracted to join their lodge is because they actively do good works and are highly visible in their community.[37] Graham, the youngest member of Davis Odd Fellows, emphasized that he "joined because of the opportunity to do something good in the community."[38] Oliver Peck, one of the judges of the reality television show, *Ink Master*, is instrumental in rejuvenating the membership of *Waxahachie Odd Fellows Lodge No.80* in Texas. He opined that "most people just go to the bars and hang out or do whatever and nobody really has a sense of community anymore, and I think that's kind of what got me into the Odd Fellows."[39] He thinks of Odd Fellowship as "doing something social that didn't have to do with going to a bar, and doing something community-minded."[40]

However, community involvement must be more than just handing out a check to charities. Lodges of today must provide volunteer opportunities and community events that allow members to work together. For growing lodges, increasing visibility and hosting an annual event open to everyone in the community has been a great way to attract new members.[41] These lodges also made their buildings available for the public for appropriate events.[42] For example, one lodge in North Dakota allowed their building to be a venue for hosting community plays.[43] Several lodges joined other civic organizations in decorating trees for the festival of trees program and participated in walk-a-thons. Some lodges create floats and rode in local parades. Others volunteered to clean streets and highways. Some served coffee and cookies at rest stops to keep drivers more alert.[44] Food drives have also proved very popular and one lodge filled shoe boxes with small gifts, including toys, candy, toiletries, and school supplies for *Operation Christmas Child* for needy children in Central America and South East Asia.[45] Other lodges volunteered in local hospitals, the Red Cross, Salvation Army, schools, and nursing homes.[46] All these have been proven as a great way to expose the Odd Fellows to the community, to build a stronger bond among members, and to generate applications for membership.[47] Convincingly, a lodge grows when it identifies itself in some way with its community.

Active Recruitment and Open Houses

Increase in membership will only happen when everyone involved is giving their all in the recruitment and reinstatement of members. The Sovereign Grand Lodge and the Grand Lodges can only do so much to increase the general membership. Efforts to attract new members must be sustained and has to happen at the "grassroots" level. That is, the individual lodge members must make the effort.[48] Complacency is a big issue. Lodges that became stagnant and still continue losing members are those that do not recruit but simply wait and hope someone will join.

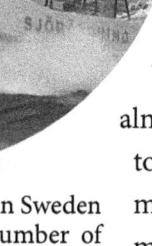

The Odd Fellows and Rebekahs in Sweden and Norway have donated a number of rescue boats to the Swedish and Norwegian Coast Guard.

Photo courtesy of the IOOF Grand Lodge of Sweden.

This is a serious problem in both North America and Europe, where the general public barely know if a lodge exists in their area. It has become obvious that "long-time members' idea of secrecy about the lodge has come at the expense of the membership because many of their lodges almost secreted themselves to death."[49] These long-time members appear to send a message "that they don't wish to bring in younger members and are contented with the status quo of their lodge even when the aging of their membership is already significant."[50] They just want to "keep it going in the same way as they have always known it probably until they pass away."[51]

Lodges that are growing, on the other hand, are those who actively recruit every year. These lodges either send invitation letters to people or advertise in newspapers that they are looking for new members. Some do it by increasing their lodges' visibility and relevance in their community. Others organize "open houses" where prospective members are given tours inside Odd Fellows' buildings. Also, posting photos and videos about Odd Fellowship on social media websites like facebook.com has tremendously helped with recruitment. Still other lodges have grown simply because many of their current members asked their friends, families, and co-workers to join. Bottom line: members must get out of their lodge halls, let the public know about their existence, ask people to join, and create a new approach to meet and attract younger generations to join their lodges.

Mentoring Process

When membership decline set in, many lodges became so desperate for new members that when they got an applicant, they immediately rushed him or her into initiation. Some lodges became so small that "it became difficult to form a team of adequate members to properly present the degrees of initiation."[52] Members and candidates alike did not understand some of the language of the degrees.[53] Once the new member was initiated, the lodge never saw him or her again.[54]

Growing lodges do not make joining too quick and easy for the prospective new members. They make them go through a "mentoring process" that takes about six months before conferring to them all the degrees of initiation. During this period, the candidates are educated about the history, principles, purposes, and organizational structure of Odd Fellowship. In Davis Odd Fellows Lodge No.169, Dave Rosenberg shares that "the candidates are required to meet and interview a minimum of 13 of our members, and to attend a minimum of 8 of their social meetings, join and participate in the committees, plan events for the lodge and the community."[55] This gives them "a chance to meet the members and for the members to meet them and determine if Odd Fellowship is the right organization to join."[56] This process will also help prepare a new member to become a well-informed future leader of the lodge. A similar membership procedure had been proven successful in Europe (See Chapter 17).

Embracing Younger Generations and New Ideas

Getting new members is not enough. If Odd Fellowship is to survive in the coming age, the organization must survive on the feet of the younger generations. Many stagnant and declining lodges frankly need new ideas, new approaches, and new visions. However, a lodge cannot get younger generations to stay active where majority of its members and officers are all in their 60s and 70s and have been the same officers for the past 10 years or so. At some point, long-time members have to allow a younger generation of leaders to develop and to grow. They cannot continue to dominate their Grand Lodge and lodge and impose the ways they are used to doing.

A big problem in several Grand Lodges and lodges is the presence of some long-time members who just cannot let go of the "control" they have exercised for many years. This often results in a situation that is detrimental "to the organization and to the good fellowship among new and long-time members."[57] Situations could occur when a new member suggests a new idea for the lodge, but long-time members would vehemently reject this idea with statements such as "We can't do that," "It won't work," or "It's against the Code."[58] In many instances, this would make the young member feel that he doesn't have a voice in the lodge. So, he or she stops attending meetings because of frustration over being shut out of the decision-making.

Undoubtedly, a change of attitude on the

part of the senior members is important if the organization is to overcome the great "generation gap."[59] There is a need to allow younger generations to offer new ideas, take leadership roles, and make decisions for the organization if the old timers want them to stay active. This approach has been proven effective in lodges that continue to grow despite the challenging times. In one example, one lodge separated their younger group of members aged 18 to 45 and gave them a meeting room in the lodge hall, which they ran as their own lodge in implementing their own local programs. This way, they worked in their own age group and, after one year, they brought in three times the number of members that the older group secured.[60]

Growing lodges are those who have long-time members who train the new members to assume leadership responsibilities. Lodges that are experiencing membership growth today are those who are able to develop new leaders every year. One way of knowing whether the lodge is producing new leaders is by finding out if younger and newer members are taking on leadership roles and positions.

Yet the organization cannot simply ask younger members to join and then turn them loose. The senior members must allow younger members to demonstrate strengths within the harness of what Odd Fellowship is all about for them in this day and age. Younger members, on the other hand, must also be willing to learn from the experience and wisdom of the senior members. Emmett Horace Bratcher, 92 years old and the oldest active member of the Waxahachie Odd Fellows Lodge No.80 in Texas, is a living example of the positive outcome when a long-time member is open to new ideas and willing to work with the younger members.[61] Unless fraternal organizations conduct their affairs in a way that will keep the interest and attention of younger members, they will lose the latter to other activities. Undoubtedly, each Odd Fellows lodge needs to develop an environment that will allow younger and older generations to effectively work together.

Diversity

It has been suggested that "lodges that are diverse - with men and women, coming from different ethnic origins, different ages, religion, and professions - are the lodges that will thrive in the future."[62] Bringing in members who are of the same age as existing members is not sustainable. Lodges that have become viable, vibrant, and active are those that have members who encompass all generations (those who are in their 20s, 30s, 40s, 50s, 60s, 70s, and 80s).

The admission of women in the Odd Fellows Lodges has been proven effective for their growth and sustainability especially in areas where there are no Rebekah or Sister Lodges. *Dallas Odd Fellows Lodge No. 44* in Oak Cliff, Texas, is composed of both men and women, and is currently one of the fastest-growing lodges in the United States.[63] Astonishingly, the lodge members' median age is 40 and there are more women members than men.[64] *Victoria Odd Fellows Lodge No.1* in British Columbia has similarly grown by admitting women, and many of the new members are in their 20s and 30s.[65] Likewise, *Ocean View Odd Fellows Lodge No.143* in Half Moon Bay, California has grown to more than 80 members and women comprise a substantial part of the membership.[66]

One reason for the attraction is that some women want to do something together with their husbands. In other areas, the number of men or women is just not enough to organize two separate lodges for men and women. Single-sex lodges seem to work best only when the number of women and men members have substantially grown to at

In the middle, 92-year-old Emmett Horace Bratcher is revered as the backbone of the lodge and continues to serve as role model and mentor to younger members of Waxahachie Odd Fellows Lodge No.80 in Texas. Photo courtesy of Waxahachie Odd Fellows Lodge No.80, 2016

least 50 because it is only at this point that having separate branches for men and women may become practicable. In a social experiment conducted by the author with lodges in the Philippines, it was observed that mixed or co-ed lodges work effectively when there is a balance between the number of men and of women members. But a lodge that is male-dominated will often attract only male recruits. A lodge that is female-dominated will likewise attract mostly women only. Absent any activity that will serve the needs of both sexes, male members who are in the minority may eventually stop attending meetings and vice-versa.

Another contentious issue with a mixed or co-ed Odd Fellows Lodge is when couples in a romantic relationship break up or get divorced. It is likely that one or both of them will stop attending lodge meetings and activities. Sometimes, the tension between the two parties is brought inside the lodge and this affects the harmony within. In some incidents, men do not join mixed or co-ed lodges because their girlfriends or wives do not allow them to do so. This is because some women do not feel comfortable with allowing their boyfriends or husbands to go to the lodge in the evening, knowing for a fact that there are other women there. So, in areas where there are enough male and female members to form two lodges, adding a Rebekah Lodge or Sister Lodge to serve the specific interests and hobbies of women may still be effective. But having joint meetings and projects from time to time is always needed to develop solidarity between the Odd Fellows and Rebekahs. Otherwise, one lodge open for both men and women will work best for the organization.

Embracing members from various ethnic and racial backgrounds also has helped sustain the charters of several lodges. One of the most diverse lodges in the United States, *Yerba Buena Odd Fellows Lodge No.15* in San Francisco, California, has proven that embracing people from different ethnic and social backgrounds grow the membership of

With men and women members representing different age brackets, Dallas Odd Fellows Lodge has grown from 40 members a few years ago to 120 members in 2017. Photo courtesy of Scott Wayne McDaniel of Dallas Odd Fellows Lodge No.44, 2017.

the lodge. With globalization, those lodges whose members show racial prejudice will diminish and face negative public criticism. Indeed, many IOOF lodges in South Carolina and some parts in Latin America closed because some members simply refused to accept non-whites in their lodges. The problem can occur when the people who control the lodge still hold prejudicial attitudes towards people from other racial backgrounds.

Well-maintained Buildings and Technology

For many lodges, the Odd Fellows building is their most prized possession. Many Odd Fellows buildings are located in the center of town. It is fascinating that memberships have been revitalized in some lodges because of non-members' curiosity about historic Odd Fellows' Halls. In 2009, a group of people in Arbuckle, California, were able to successfully revive the *Spring Valley Odd Fellows Lodge No.316* because of their interest in the abandoned historic IOOF building in their area.[67]

However, many of these buildings are now in bad condition and need renovation. There are many lodges that do not even have a signboard telling the public that an Odd Fellows or Rebekah Lodge meets inside the building. There are lodges whose officers do not use e-mail or facebook and do not have Wi-Fi capability in their lodge halls.[68]

Many buildings owned by the Odd Fellows in the United States and Canada are historic buildings and are attractive to historians and artists. Growing lodges of today are those who take great pride in their building's appearance and amenities. Their members have made sure that these are well-maintained and clean. They placed sign boards outside their buildings. Some made their buildings the hangout for their members by adding up-to-date technology – flat screen televisions, LCD projectors, Wi-Fi, PlayStation, etc. Pairing the rich history and antiquity with new technology undoubtedly aided several lodges to exponentially grow. However, some Odd Fellows buildings are located on the seedy side of town. The best option for some lodges in this situation is to sell their old building and relocate their lodge to a better area for it to attract more members. But they should use the proceeds of the sale of their old building to buy a new one. The mistake of many lodges in the past was selling their building and opting to lease a room from other similar organizations. After a few years, they eventually found themselves struggling to pay the rent and regretting why they did not use their lodge money to purchase a new one that is income-generating.

Solemn Initiation Ceremonies

The IOOF Grand Lodges in the continent of Europe have been worried about all the amendments to the Odd Fellows practices in North America, which have led to "a broader, more popular base, instead of going into the depth of improving the ritualistic work."[69] The leaders of the IOOF in European countries expressed agreement that the rituals need to be revised and the words used need to be changed from time to time in order that the teachings of Odd Fellowship will remain attractive and effective to younger members.[70] During the meetings of the IOOF International Advisory Board, the leaders agreed that they cannot allow Odd Fellowship to become a museum. On the contrary, the European IOOF leaders agreed that the lodge has to be a "constant ethical power station"[71] and "provision should be made for modernizing such ceremonies."[72]

The Sovereign Grand Lodge in North America, however, unsuccessfully revised the degrees of initiation by simplifying the degrees to the point of "dumbing it down" and allowing lodges to sloppily perform the initiations. It also failed to remove some sectarian practices in the rituals, e.g., the exclusive use of the term "Holy Bible" and reciting of the "Lord's Prayer" during meetings. Such prayer was added by the Sovereign Grand Lodge in the early 1900s when majority of the members were Christians. Somehow, this discourages some people outside of the Judeo-Christian religion from joining. The use of the term "Holy Book" or "Book of Sacred Law" may be a more inclusive term to use if the IOOF wants to show that it is really a non-sectarian fraternal organization that is open to all regardless of religion.

On the other hand, the IOOF in European countries have proven that it is possible to update the organization and meet the demands of modern people without totally abandoning some of the customs. Instead of simplifying the rituals, they moved towards further enriching the degrees so that its ethical lessons will be interesting to the younger generations. They removed terms and practices that may be considered as sectarian or politically incorrect in today's era. Many of their lodges also made sure that the degrees of initiation are performed in a dignified manner – their lodge rooms are clean, the members and candidates wear formal attire during ceremonies, and the charges in the rituals are mostly delivered by memory. The Danish version of the degrees of initiation has been positively accepted by members in their 20s, 30s, and 40's in the Philippines and is now used by the lodges

The dramatic ceremonies of the degrees of initiation are attractive to younger generations if performed with dignity and enthusiasm. Photo courtesy of Jim Walterman, 2019.

in the country. A similar version of the Danish IOOF Ritual is being used by the IOOF in Norway, Sweden, Finland, and Iceland.

Strong Risk Management

The biggest problem of most lodges is when internal issues or conflicts occur between members. Lodges that are declining are also those whose membership resort to back-biting and gossiping against each other. Infighting over lodge money or other petty disagreements is one of the major causes why many members quit. This usually happens when the leadership and membership fail to understand and internalize the true meaning of Odd Fellowship. Depending on how effective the risk management is, conflicts and misunderstandings can ruin the relationship between members and could lead to the closure of the lodge.

Successful lodges of today are those that have put a solid risk management plan in place to prevent this from happening. These are lodges that put greater importance on relationships over finances, position, and individual pride. These are the ones whose members do not necessarily agree all the time, but nevertheless have mutual-respect for each other. If effectively conveyed, the Odd Fellows motto - Friendship, Love, and Truth - and the teachings in the degrees of initiation will show the members how to capably deal with their differences.

Relevance of Odd Fellowship Today

The world today is facing many complex, bewildering, and sometimes frustrating problems. Living in concrete and asphalt jungles of metropolitan cities are many lonely people who do not have a feeling of belonging.[73] There are thousands of men and women hungry for sincere friendship.[74] Violence and hate continue to hook their tentacles around people of many lands. Vice, corruption, drugs and narcotics, with their soul-and-character-destroying power have wrought havoc on people's lives in all parts of the globe. They are not new but they have grown strong roots in today's fertile ground of apathy, indifference, and permissiveness. We are living in a time when the global society is saying: "The sky is the limit, nothing is too extravagant, and no sensation is forbidden." Literally by the thousands, younger generations are turning to drugs and narcotics for new kicks, for new sensations, and new ways to escape reality. Some people are struggling because of lack of a sense of direction in life.

A number of people belonging to the younger generation are now reaching out for a better way of life. On the other side of the spectrum, the elderly are looking for a social outlet and some friends to spend time with. Now, more than ever, Odd Fellowship can be of great help. Its ethical teachings as provided in the rituals may still provide the younger generation with a deeper meaning of and direction for their life. People can still do a lot more to help their communities and the world at large if they work together as a group. Organized at the international level, Odd Fellowship not only promotes goodwill but also gives members an opportunity to enjoy better understanding of people from nations other than their own.

However, the fraternal organization must first accept the fact that change is necessary. To be able to compete with other more modern organizations, the leadership in all levels of the IOOF must infuse new and fresh methodologies aside from what they have been accustomed to in the past. Unless the Odd Fellows modernize and make the organization relevant to the men and women of the present century, membership will continue to diminish. Organizational survival depends upon its ability to develop strategies and activities that can be adapted to changing times. Nevertheless, this does not mean the total abandonment of Odd Fellows principles, customs, and traditions that guide its practices. Rather, the task is to find ways on how to apply these principles to modern times.

Odd Fellowship, as an international movement, cannot also continue moving towards different goals. Unless the leadership in all levels of the organization can get their act together, it will be difficult for the organization to expand and grow like it did over a hundred years ago. Ways must be developed to make Odd Fellowship into a cohesive worldwide ethical and humanitarian movement by pursuing one universal goal or purpose. Members everywhere also must know one common set of general objectives, vision, mission, and core values. However, the international and national leadership cannot expect everyone to follow specific rules and regulations. There will always be cultural and regional differences between the jurisdictions, so each lodge will have to apply the general mission and vision in ways that fit their specific environment.

Odd Fellowship is not just facing social and technological changes; it is also competing with many other organizations with similar purposes and services. Planning for expansion locally, nationally, and internationally needs to be accelerated by Grand Lodges and the Sovereign Grand Lodge. An effective program needs to be put in place or Odd Fellowship will be left behind by similar international organizations. The Sovereign Grand Lodge and the Grand Lodges need to stop revoking charters as the first remedy for struggling lodges. Instead, the leadership should use available resources to assist these lodges to get back on their feet and increase membership. Grand Lodges should focus more on recruitment and expansion within their jurisdictions and invest a substantial part of their funds in opening new lodges in localities where the Odd Fellows does not exist. They cannot continue to depend on the remaining lodges. There are many towns and cities today where there is no Odd Fellows or Rebekah Lodge. Lodges must also start helping other lodges because there is little point in assisting and donating to other organizations when the next door lodge is struggling. Odd Fellows can do more if more lodges continue to exist.

But the Sovereign Grand Lodge cannot also continue charging the same rate of SGL annual dues for every country if it wants to expand internationally. Instead, it must consider the purchasing power of the currency per country. Otherwise, it will be hard to spread Odd Fellowship to other countries. The Sovereign Grand Lodge and Grand Lodges should also develop new ways of raising funds for their programs and charities without depending too much on the annual dues and contributions from its lodges. Now more than ever, membership development, training, and public relations should also be given high priority. It has been noted by many researchers that majority of the people do not know who and what the Odd Fellows are, and that the biggest problem within the Odd Fellows is its failure to educate its new members of its history, principles, and customs.

To respond to issues of poor management and lack of leadership and interpersonal skills of some of its officers, the Grand Lodges and Sovereign Grand Lodge must also invest in developing leadership training, interpersonal relationship improvement programs, and effective non-profit management seminars to improve leadership in all levels of the organization. In the end, the IOOF will be better benefited if their officers have the needed attitudes and skills that could lead the IOOF to become a successful and more effective non-profit organization. But more importantly, the members and leaders of each lodge must make the organization relevant and useful within their local communities.

Chapter 19

INTERNATIONAL EXPANSION

At present, the estimated grand total membership of the three major Affiliated Orders - the *Independent Order of Odd Fellows* (IOOF), *Manchester Unity Independent Order of Odd Fellows* (MUIOOF), and the *Grand United Order of Odd Fellows* (GUOOF) - is more or less 600,000 members. Annually, at least 10,000 new members are admitted to more than 10,000 lodges located in about 30 countries. In addition, there are other smaller organizations such as the *Caledonian Lodge of Odd Fellows* in Scotland.

NORTH AMERICA AND TERRITORIES

Barbados

Early in 1879, Grand Sire John Harmon of the IOOF authorized Archibald Bayne to initiate Odd Fellows and establish a lodge in Barbados, West Indies.[1] After admitting several members, the IOOF was officially established with the institution of *Americus Lodge No.1*, at Bridgetown, Barbados, on November 4, 1879.[2] Racial prejudice hindered its progress. The last report in 1882 noted that "notwithstanding earnest efforts to induce the Brethren in Barbados to continue the lodge and outlive the prejudices against color discrimination, the charter of Americus Lodge of the IOOF was surrendered."[3] The lodges affiliated with the Grand United Order of Odd Fellows and the Manchester Unity Independent Order of Odd Fellows were the ones that thrived in this country.

Canada

The precise date of the first introduction of Odd Fellowship in Canada cannot be determined because of the absence of early records. Newspaper accounts, however, show that a *Royal Wellington Lodge* and *Loyal Bon Accorde Lodge* of the Odd Fellows existed in Halifax, Nova Scotia, prior to 1815.[4] It seems that both lodges were working together under either the *United Order* or the *Manchester Unity IOOF* because the meeting place of these two lodges was the same. Apparently, they were already well established because they owned an Odd Fellows Hall as early as 1815. But without a national authority, they soon succumbed.

The first lodge in Canada under the IOOF was chartered on August 10, 1843 as *Prince of Wales Lodge No.1*.[5] In a few months, more lodges were instituted in the country. On April 2, 1844, *Hochelaga Encampment No.1* was instituted in Montreal.[6] The first women's group, *Victoria Rebekah Lodge No.1*, was instituted on December 3, 1869.[7] When members became numerous, the *Grand Lodge of British North America* was established on November 16, 1844 with Montreal as its center.[8] For a time, lodges under this Grand Lodge prospered with many prominent men in its ranks. The early Odd Fellows in Canada included the *very elite* of Canadian society: Sir Dominic Daly, Sir W.B. Robinson, Sir Allan McNab, Sir Hugh Allan, Sir John A. MacDonald, Hon. L.H. Holton, Hon. G. Sherwood, Rev. Doctor Methieson, Rev. Doctor Cordner, Hon. P. McGill, Hon. J. Pangman, Hon. John

Young, Hon. Edmund Murney, R.F. Hamilton, Ogle R. Gowan, J. Moir Ferres, T.D. Harrington, Thomas Keefer, J. Molson, E.L. Montizambert, J. Torrance, William Workman, W.H. Boulton, George B. Hall, Colonel Dyde, J.C. Becket, William Ewan, etc. They were leading statesmen, members of Parliament, prominent merchants, and manufacturers at that time.[9]

However, the charter of the Grand Lodge of British North America was surrendered on October 14, 1853 when many lodges in Montreal area closed.[10] This led to many lodges being disbanded while several others continued and worked directly under the Grand Lodge of the United States. Shortly, the remaining members opened additional lodges so that the *Grand Lodge of Canada West* and the *Grand Lodge of the Lower Provinces* were ultimately instituted in 1855.[11]

When the federal dominion of Canada was formed in 1867, the country was divided into eight provinces. The Grand Lodge of Canada West was renamed as the *Grand Lodge of Ontario* in 1867. Next the *Grand Lodge of British Columbia* was instituted in 1874,[12] the *Grand Lodge of Quebec* in 1878[13] and the *Grand Lodge of Manitoba* in 1883.[14] The Grand Lodge of Lower Provinces was renamed as the *Grand Lodge of Maritime Provinces* in 1892. A large number of lodges and members under the Manchester Unity IOOF ultimately transferred dispensation to the IOOF.[15] At present, the IOOF in Canada has seven Grand Lodges namely, the *Grand Lodge of Alberta*, *Grand Lodge of Atlantic Provinces*, *Grand Lodge of British Columbia*, *Grand Lodge of Manitoba*, *Grand Lodge of Ontario*, *Grand Lodge of Quebec*, and *Grand Lodge of Saskatchewan*. In 2012, they reported about 4,000 members belonging to 178 Odd Fellows Lodges and 2,209 members in 83 Rebekah Lodges. There are also few lodges operating under the GUOOF.

Cuba

The first lodge under the IOOF in Cuba was instituted in Havana on August 26, 1883, known as *Porvenir Lodge No.1*.[16] More lodges were instituted all over Cuba but almost all perished or had to meet secretly during the Cuban Revolution from 1895 to 1896. After the war, the Odd Fellows became prosperous. *Sagua Encampment No.1* and *Sagua Rebekah Lodge No.2* were instituted on March 5, 1924.[17] During the same year, an American member visited Cuba and reported to the Sovereign Grand Lodge that "more than majority of the members of the Cuban House and Senate were either members of the Odd Fellows or Freemasons, or both."[18] Because of the enormous membership growth in the country, the *Grand Lodge of Cuba* was instituted on February 28, 1925.[19]

At present, there are approximately 15,000 members in 130 Odd Fellows Lodges and about 3,000 members in 51 Rebekah Lodges spread all over Cuba,[20] as well as 33 Encampments, 12 Cantons, and 14 Odd Fellow Youth Association Group (GAJO).[21] There are also lodges in Cuba that are operating under the GUOOF, reportedly with a membership of about 8,000.

Dominican Republic

Because of history of racial segregation, lodges under the Grand United Order of Odd Fellows prospered better than those of IOOF in this country. The first lodge under the IOOF was only established when *Joaquin Balaquer Lodge No.1* was instituted on February 24, 2007 in San Cristóbal.[22] Currently, the lodge works directly under the jurisdiction of the Sovereign Grand Lodge.

Mexico

The first lodge under the IOOF was *Ridgely Lodge No.1*, instituted in Mexico City on August 5,

1882.²³ This was followed by *Juarez Lodge No.2* in 1885.²⁴ The number of lodges reached to 10 in 1906 and the *Grand Lodge of Mexico* was chartered as its national governing body. However, the political and economic situation in the country affected the progress. For a time, the remaining lodges worked under the jurisdiction of the *Grand Lodge of Texas* while some worked under the *Grand Lodge of Arizona,* until all these Mexican lodges closed in the mid-20th century.

On February 3, 1996, the IOOF was re-established in the country when *Colotlán Lodge No.1* was instituted in Colotlán, State of Jalisco, Mexico.²⁵ This was followed with the institution of *Casiopea Rebekah Lodge No.1* on December 14, 1996.²⁶ Both lodges currently work under the direct jurisdiction of the Sovereign Grand Lodge.

Puerto Rico

The IOOF established its first lodge in San Juan City on December 12, 1905, known as *San Juan Lodge No. 1.*²⁷ More lodges were opened after that, but all closed during World War II. A second attempt to establish IOOF began when *Puerto Rico Lodge No.1* was chartered in 1972.²⁸ *Jose Marti Lodge No.2* and *Lola Rodriquez de Tio Rebekah Lodge No.1* followed in 1974.²⁹ At least three more lodges prospered until 1986, but all perished in due time.

On November 7, 1999, the IOOF was re-established in the country when *Boriken Lodge No.1* was instituted with the help of members from New Jersey, Florida, and New York.³⁰ On August 23, 2003, *Naborias Rebekah Lodge No.1* was chartered.³¹ Both lodges currently work directly under the jurisdiction of the Sovereign Grand Lodge. Lodges affiliated with the GUOOF have more members and are more

Even though Cuba came under Communist rule, the Odd Fellows continue to have a strong presence in the country.
Photo courtesy of the Grand Lodge of Cuba, IOOF, 2005.

numerous in Puerto Rico.

United States

Presumably, there were several self-instituted lodges in the country as far back as the late 1700s. One historian wrote that "Odd Fellowship was introduced into the United States as early as 1799, at which time a lodge was constituted in Connecticut."[32] There were indeed many other early Odd Fellows groups that existed, but the Independent Order of Odd Fellows dominated because it formed a national organization and issued charters to existing self-instituted lodges across the country. At one time, there were more than 2 million Odd Fellows affiliated with the IOOF belonging in more or less 16,000 lodges on the North American continent alone. When the decline of fraternal organizations began, more than half of all its lodges closed or were left abandoned. Due to many factors, such as complacency of the members and officers, failure in timely adaptation to the needed changes, and an aging membership, the number of lodges and members have dwindled. This is partly due to the fault of the officers of the Grand Lodges and the Sovereign Grand Lodge for leaving so many lodges to close and not investing much of their time and funds in opening new lodges and assisting struggling ones. It was only recently when a number of younger people began to revive the membership of some of IOOF's lodges.

As of this writing, there are 111,167 members in 1,309 Odd Fellows lodges and 71,017 members in 913 Rebekah Lodges located in 49 states including Hawaii and the District of Columbia. There used to be many lodges in Alaska but all had closed by the end of the 20th century. There are also few lodges in some States that work directly under the Manchester Unity IOOF. Furthermore, there are lodges in the United States that are affiliated with the *GUOOF in America and Jurisdiction* with more or less 3,000 members. More recently, the GUOOF is experiencing a revival of its lodges across the United States. The GUOOF also has lodges in Haiti, Bermuda, Bahamas, Jamaica, West Indies, Costa Rica, Nicaragua, Virgin Islands, Honduras, Trinidad, and Barbados.

SOUTH AND CENTRAL AMERICA

Argentina

The IOOF instituted *Buenos Aires Lodge No. 1* in the country on January 25, 1901.[33] But in 1909, the Noble Grand's brother who was in possession of all lodge property mysteriously disappeared.[34] It is believed that he was shot on his way to the station by a stray bullet during the labor riot, and was buried with many others who are known to have shared the same fate. It was reported that a public official took possession of everything they found in his apartment including the properties of the lodge. This unfortunate development was followed by the sudden death of the experienced District Deputy Grand Sire of Argentina, William Henry Raymond, in 1911.[35] Without a competent leadership in the country, the lodge closed a few years thereafter.

Belize

The IOOF was established in the country when *Belize Lodge No.1* was instituted in the town of San Ignacio on January 15, 2004.[36] The lodge currently works directly under the jurisdiction of the Sovereign Grand Lodge.

Bolivia

In 1876, a group of Odd Fellows based in Antofagasta applied for a charter from the Grand Lodge of the United States.[37] This group progressed rapidly and held meetings at the Leavenworth Hall.

Within the same year, a warrant and a blank charter was issued to the Grand Lodge of Chile to institute the lodge.[38] For an unrecorded reason, the lodge never prospered.

Brazil

In 1847, a group of Odd Fellows based in the country petitioned for a charter with the Grand Lodge of the United States to officially institute a Lodge in Brazil but was denied. In 2019, a petition to charter three IOOF lodges in the country was submitted. Brazil Lodge No.1 was instituted in 2020.

Chile

The first lodge under the IOOF was *Valparaiso Lodge No.1* instituted on April 15, 1874.[39] Four additional lodges were instituted the following year. Their success led to the institution of the *Grand Lodge of Chile* and *Southern Watch Encampment No.1* on November 18, 1875.[40] But due to the political situation in the country, the lodges were reduced to 3 Odd Fellows lodges in 1888 which led to the surrender of the charter of the Grand Lodge.

The *Grand Lodge of Chile* was re-instituted on May 29, 1965.[41] The growth went fairly well so that, in 1967, *Juventus Lodge No.10* was formed in a university by a group aged 21 to 26 years.[42] In 1996, however, it was reported that there remained two Odd Fellows lodges under the IOOF namely, *Santiago Lodge No.1* and *Andes Lodge No.2*.[43] There were also three Rebekah Lodges namely, *Copihue Rebekah Lodge No.1, Progresso Rebekah Lodge No.6,* and *Esperanza Rebekah Lodge No. 13*.[44] Thus, the Grand Lodge of Chile again surrendered its charter in 1996 for having fallen below five lodges required to form a grand body.[45] In 1999, new lodges were chartered namely, *Logia Futuro No.25* in Santiago, and *Logia de Rebekah Alegria No.14* in Santiago.[46]

Peru

Lima Lodge No.1 was instituted by the IOOF on January 3, 1872. Next to be instituted was *Atahualpa Encampment No.1* on September 22, 1876. During the same year, *Fortschritt Lodge No.3* in Lima and *Chalaco Lodge No.4* in Callao were chartered.[47] The peculiar political affairs of the Republic of Peru at that time caused extreme business depression and retarded the growth of the IOOF, such that all lodges ultimately surrendered their charters in 1901.[48] A revival was accomplished when *Lima Ner Lodge No.1* was instituted in Lima on November 16, 1966.[49] Nonetheless, the lodge ceased to exist in the 21st century.

Panama

On September 10, 1907, a charter was issued by the Sovereign Grand Lodge to *Isthmian Canal Lodge No.1* at Gorgona, Canal Zone.[50] This was followed by *Cristobal Lodge No.2* in Cristobal on May 16, 1908 and by *Canal Zone Lodge No.3* in Culebra on May 29, 1908.[51] On October 10, 1908, *Isthmian Canal Rebekah Lodge No.1* was instituted.[52] *Isthmian Canal Lodge No.1* and *Canal Zone Lodge No.3* closed during the war years. *Wirz Memorial Lodge No.1* was chartered on August 13, 1952[53] but *Cristobal Lodge No.2* had become inactive by 1955. *Isthmian Canal Rebekah Lodge No.1* existed until 1970.[54] None of the lodges under the IOOF survived today.

Uruguay

The first IOOF lodge in Uruguay, *Artigas Lodge No.1,* was established on February 9, 1966.[55] This was followed by *Amanecer Rebekah Lodge No.1* on November 19, 1966.[56] Additional lodges, *Uruguay Lodge No.2, Horizontes Rebekah Lodge No.2,* and *El Ceibo Rebekah Lodge No.3,* followed. In 1996, the Sovereign Grand Lodge reported two Odd Fellows lodges and three Rebekah lodges operating in the country.⁵⁷

Venezuela

The first lodge under the IOOF was *Venezuela Lodge No.1* instituted on October 1847 in Caracas.⁵⁸ This lodge ceased shortly after due to the revolutionary state of the country.⁵⁹ The IOOF was re-established in Venezuela when *Prakritti Lodge No.1* was instituted on August 1, 1986 by 11 new members and 4 former members from Bolivia, Cuba, and the United States.⁶⁰ *Samaritan Lodge No.2* followed on May 16, 1987.⁶¹ *Ammancer de Oriente Lodge No.3* was added on September 11, 1993.⁶² The first women's group, *Aurora De Oriente Rebekah Lodge No.1,* was instituted on May 11, 1994.⁶³ However, all lodges in Venezuela ceased to exist a few years ago. This is partly because the members there cannot keep up with the rate of annual dues charged by the Sovereign Grand Lodge.

EUROPE

Austria

In February 1898, some residents of Reichenburg, Bohemia, Austria, applied for membership and one of them was initiated into *Berolina Lodge No.15* of Brandenburg, Berlin, under the jurisdiction of the Grand Lodge of Germany.⁶⁴ Special Deputy Grand Sire Block, being advised of the initiation, objected to the Grand Sire of Germany on the ground that it was a violation of the law and was equivalent to the introduction of the IOOF in a foreign country because Odd Fellowship was not yet established in Austria at that time.⁶⁵ The Grand Lodge of Germany respected the objection and directed that no further initiations should be made until questions involved could be properly disposed of.

In 1906, a group of Odd Fellows from Prague and members of the American Embassy founded a humanitarian Odd Fellows Club in Vienna. Because of the political condition at that time, the Odd Fellows group was first called the *Society of Friends for Human Beings* in 1911.⁶⁶

When the situation changed after WWI, the club was instituted as *Friedens Lodge No.1* on June 4, 1922.⁶⁷ A committee consisting of the Grand Sire of Germany, Grand Sire of Holland, Grand Sire of Switzerland, Grand Sire of Denmark met with the President of the Austrian Republic to explain Odd Fellowship to him. After hearing them, the President approved the existence of the IOOF in the country and even offered a room in his palace for the official institution of the lodge.⁶⁸ This was followed by the institution of *Ikarius Lodge No.2*, *Pestalozzi Lodge No.3* and *Fridtjof Nansen Lodge No.4*. The first Encampment named *Mozart Encampment No.1* was founded on June 3, 1932. All lodges were closed during World War II. In 1968, the Odd Fellows was revived in Austria when *Peace Lodge No.1* was instituted,⁶⁹ but this lodge surrendered its charter in 1974 because there was no longer a building for their regular activities.⁷⁰

On October 29, 1999, the IOOF was re-established in the country when the *Paracelsus Lodge No.1* in Salzburg was chartered by the Sovereign Grand Lodge without correspondence with the European IOOF Federation (precursor of the Grand Lodge of Europe).⁷¹ Due to the controversy, the lodge refused to be under the jurisdiction of the Grand Lodge of Europe and ultimately surrendered its charter in 2007.

Belgium

The first lodge under the IOOF in Belgium was *Belgia Lodge No.1*, instituted on June 13, 1911 in Antwerp, Belgium⁷² and a second lodge, *Fiat*

Lodge No.2, in Brussels.[73] April 20, 1929 marked the institution of the third lodge, *Vae Soli Lodge No.3,* in Antwerp.[74] *Aurora Rebekah Lodge No.1* was instituted in the same City on March 15, 1975. Two more Odd Fellows lodges were established and all thrived for several years. Sooner or later, membership declined partly because of the strong Catholic resistance against secular fraternal organizations in the country. At present, two Odd Fellows lodges remain in Belgium, *Belgia Lodge No.1* in Antwerp[75] and a mixed or co-ed lodge named as *Brabo Gemengde Lodge No.3* in Zandhoven.[76]

Czech Republic

When *Friendship Lodge No.1* of the IOOF was founded in 1905, the country was still a part of the former Austrian Empire where all fraternal organizations, except those of the Catholic Church, were prohibited.[77] Therefore, the IOOF lodges existed under fictitious names in order to hide the organization from persecution. Those precautions had been necessary until October 1918 when the war came to an end.[78] Until that time, there were only three lodges, one each in Prague, Teplitz, and Pilsen. These lodges doubled its membership within a span of five years.

When the new country of Czecho-Slovakia was formed, a portion of Germany where several lodges were located was taken from German territory. These lodges eventually formed the *Grand Lodge of Czecho-Slovakia* on January 10, 1924.[79] For a time, the Grand Lodge reported 18 Odd Fellows Lodges, 7 Odd Fellows Clubs, 1 Rebekah Club, and 3 Youth Clubs with a total membership of 1,400. Conversely, the unstable political and social condition of the country during the war years hampered its development. During WWII, the Nazis banned all fraternal organizations so all lodges were closed. There was an effort to re-open these lodges in 1948, but failed because of the Communist dictatorship.

Conditions had changed by March 1994 when a lodge in Copenhagen, Denmark, admitted four new members from Czech Republic for the purpose of establishing a lodge in Prague.[80] This number increased to ten new members in 1995,[81] so that an *Odd Fellow Club* was formed in the town of Zatec on June 15, 1996.[82] This club was eventually instituted as *Bohemia Lodge No.1* on October 12, 1996.[83] At present, there are three Odd Fellows Lodges in the country named *Bohemia Lodge No. 1, Concordia Lodge No. 2,* and *Martel Lodge No.4.* All lodges in Czech Republic currently fall under the jurisdiction of the Grand Lodge of Denmark.

Denmark

The first lodge under the IOOF was instituted in Copenhagen on June 29, 1878, named *Denmark Lodge No.1.*[84] *Valdemar Encampment No.1* and *Caroline Amelia Rebekah Lodge No.1* followed in 1881.[85] In 1883, a uniformed branch, *Excelsior Camp*, was formed in Copenhagen. This group was eventually mustered as *Canton Excelsior No.1* of the Patriarchs Militant in 1889. The lodges in Denmark worked under the jurisdiction of the Grand Lodge of Germany until June 9, 1892, when the *Grand Lodge of Denmark* was instituted. Notably, the Rebekah Lodges in Denmark were renamed as *Sister Lodges* or *Odd Fellow Sisters* in 1996 to promote equality among the branches of the IOOF.[86]

The IOOF in Denmark experienced a decrease in membership for many years, but membership is now increasing.[87] As of this writing, the IOOF in Denmark has over 113 Odd Fellows or Brother Lodges, 94 Rebekah or Sister Lodges, 16 Patriarchs Encampments, and 13 Ladies Encampments, with a total membership of close to 13,000.[88] Denmark and Iceland together also have 4 Cantons of the Patriarchs Militant and 4 Cantons of

Built in 1751, the Odd Fellows Palace in Copenhagen is one of the most magnificent buildings owned by the Odd Fellows in Denmark. The building houses the national headquarters of the Grand Lodge of Denmark and over 30 lodges in the area. Photo courtesy of the Grand Lodge of Denmark, IOOF.

2017 Session of the IOOF Grand Lodge of Denmark. Photo courtesy of Morten Buan, Grand Sire of IOOF Norway, 2017.

the Matriarchs Militant under its own *Department Council of Denmark* established in 1991. All Cantons work under the *General Military Council of Europe*, chartered on November 17, 2012, with the Grand Sire of Denmark as its head.[89]

Estonia

In 1990, several Estonians joined the IOOF in Finland. Their growing number led to the formation of the *Estonian Odd Fellows Society* on April 24, 1992.[90] This society was subsequently chartered as *Maarjamaa Lodge No.1* on November 20, 1993, with 28 charter members.[91] On June 10, 1995, *Linda Rebekah Lodge No.1* was instituted with 12 charter members.[92] The number of members in the country already is more than 100 and are currently working under the jurisdiction of the Grand Lodge of Finland.

Faroe Islands

In 1986, a lodge was instituted in this North Atlantic archipelago with 16 charter members. The lodge operated under the Grand Lodge of Denmark.[93]

Finland

In 1901, a letter of intent to form a lodge in Finland was sent to the Grand Lodge of Sweden. Taking into consideration the political and social situation of Finland as part of the Russian Empire at that time, the Grand Lodge of Sweden advised the applicant to abandon the whole idea. Interest in forming an Odd Fellows Lodge was brought up again after Finland became an independent country in 1917 but progress was slow. In 1924, seven men from Vaasa, Finland, traveled to Haparanda, Sweden, and were finally initiated as Odd Fellows. They were all under a lodge in Sweden until 1925 when the Sovereign Grand Lodge authorized the Grand Lodge of Sweden to officially institute lodges in Finland.[94] The first lodge established was named *Vaasa Lodge No.1* located in the town of Vaasa.[95] Additional lodges were formed in Helsinki in 1927 and in Turku in 1931.

The war years (WWII) hampered further expansion in Finland but the three lodges continued their activities almost without interruption. After the war, a fourth lodge was instituted in 1951. This was followed by the institution of *Finlandia Encampment No.1* on May 9, 1952, in Helsinki. The first women's branch, *Mathilda Wrede Rebekah Lodge No.1*, was instituted in 1967.[96] Further expansion resulted to the opening of more than 35 Odd Fellows lodges and 19 Rebekah lodges by 1980. This success led to the institution of the *Grand Lodge of Finland* on June 1, 1984.[97] Currently, there are more or less 9,000 members belonging to 65 Odd Fellows Lodges and 53 Rebekah Lodges in the country.[98]

France

De La Concorde Lodge No.1 was instituted on March 2, 1887, in Havre, France, by five Charter members of *Concorde Lodge No.43* in New York.[99] This lodge grew to 75 members by the end of December 1887.[100] The second lodge in France was *Fraternité Lodge No.2* on August 3, 1888.[101] In 1893, differences between the members in France and the Sovereign Grand Lodge began when the Representatives in the United States introduced the *"Belief in a Supreme Being"* as a qualification for membership. Members of *Fraternité Lodge No.2* vehemently argued that, "our duty as Odd Fellows does not permit us, in our meetings, to discuss political or sectarian matters which may completely destroy the confidence of future members, who are already frightened by the term 'Lodge', we beg you not to authorize any alterations in the customs, and moreover reject every proposition concerning religion, which is maintained in the manners of the French nation."[102]

Business depression followed, which resulted in several members' failure to pay their annual dues. Thus, both lodges struggled to pay a room for their meetings.[103] The situation worsened when the two lodges in France sought permission from the Sovereign Grand Lodge to solicit funds to construct their own meeting room.[104] The request was left unheeded by the Grand Lodges and lodges in the United States, except for Concorde Lodge No.43 in New York which donated $200.[105] This discouraged the members in France and many ultimately resigned by 1901.[106] The effects were so bad that, in 1905, District Deputy Grand Sire D. Périn of France reported that "the number of members has not increased."[107] An effort to revive the lodge under the leadership of John K. Gowdy, a Past Grand of Franklin Lodge No.35 in Indiana and Consul-General at Paris at that time, was tried but all efforts failed.[108]

On April 20, 1908, *Louis Pasteur Lodge No.1* was instituted under the Grand Lodge of Germany. The lodge was in Strasbourg, which passed into French Possession as a result of WWI. Thus, it was transferred to the jurisdiction of the Grand Lodge of Switzerland.[109] In 1926, an *Odd Fellows Club* was organized in Paris which resulted in the institution of *Lutetia Lodge No.2* on July 7, 1929.[110] A *Rebekah Club* was also organized in Paris during the same year in the hope of instituting it into a Rebekah Lodge within one to two years.[111] However, *Lutetia Lodge No.2* and the Rebekah Club ceased to exist in 1933 and 1938, respectively. The *Louis Pasteur* Lodge No.1 subsequently dissolved due to a crisis. In 1990, a new lodge was established, *Victor Schoelcher Lodge No.3*, composed of French and Swiss members but this lodge failed.[112] A third attempt to re-establish the IOOF in France was made when *French Phocea Lodge No.4* in Marseille was instituted by officers of the Grand Lodge of Switzerland in 1998.[113] The requirement "Belief in a Supreme Being" did not go well among the French people, so this lodge was also short-lived.

Germany

In September 1869, the Sovereign Grand Lodge agreed to introduce the IOOF to the European countries of Germany and Switzerland. As a first step, E.D. Farnsworth sought help from influential IOOF members, U.S. Vice President Schuyler Colfax and U.S. Senator Joseph Fowler, to explain Odd Fellowship to the German Minister.[114] But it took them about a year, waiting until they were sure that there was no objection to the introduction of Odd Fellowship in Germany.[115]

On December 1, 1870, Dr. John F. Morse, a Past Grand Master of California, and B.F. Austin, a member of *California Lodge No.1* in San Francisco, California, finally instituted *Würtemberg Lodge No.1* in Württemberg, Southern Germany.[116] This was followed by the institution of *Germania Lodge No.1* in Berlin on March 30, 1871.[117] During the first decade, many lodges were instituted, numbering more than 56 lodges. *Farnsworth Encampment No.1* was founded on May 23, 1871 in Berlin.[118] And on February 25, 1871, *Würtemberg Lodge No.1* admitted 13 women in what they called a *Sister Circle*, some kind of auxiliary lodge for women. This group culminated into the *Einigkeit Rebekah Lodge No.1* on April 28, 1871.[119] Such tremendous success led to the institution of the *Grand Lodge of Germany* on December 28, 1872.[120]

The number of members went up and down as a result of different wars. In 1925, there were over 12,000 members in 160 lodges. But because of the challenges brought by the economic depression and political hostility in Germany, the membership

Oddur and Odd Fellow Golf Club

The Odd Fellows in Iceland owns a 162-acre golf course in Reyjavik. They founded a private golf club in 1990. Seven years after, the Odd Fellow Golf Club (GOF) built a magnificent 18-hole golf course called the Oddur Golf Club. The golf course is the regular venue for Icelandic championships and is one of the country's most beautiful 18-hole courses.

dropped to 8,000 in 1932. The condition worsened when the Nazis took control of the government. In 1933, the Grand Lodge of Germany decided to dissolve the national governing body due to growing mistrust by the public. It was looked upon as a sort of Freemasonry and misunderstood to be an international secret society opposed to the church.[121] The general opposition to all fraternal organizations on the part of the masses caused a great many of the members to resign, fearing for their life.[122]

After WWII, efforts to revive the IOOF in the country started in Hamburg through the effort of about 1,300 German members who survived the war. These lodges re-instituted the *Grand Lodge of Germany* in 1949, but only received their new charter from the Sovereign Grand Lodge on July 6, 1952.[123] As of this writing, there are nearly 800 members belonging to 40 Odd Fellows Lodges and 12 Rebekah Lodges in the country. There is also one co-ed Odd Fellows Lodge in Germany whose membership is open to both men and women.

Iceland

Odd Fellows was first introduced in the country in 1892 by Danish Odd Fellows who donated to the government of Iceland a hospital for leprosy patients.[124] Inspired by this humanitarian project, five prominent citizens in *Reykjavik* decided to join. This led to the institution of *Ingolfur Lodge No.1* on August 1, 1897.[125] *Bergthora Rebekah Lodge No.1* was instituted.[126] A *District Grand Lodge of Iceland* was founded On August 1, 1933.[127] This grand body ultimately became the *Grand Lodge of Iceland* in 1984.[128]

As of this writing, there are nearly 4,000 members belonging to 28 Odd Fellows Lodges, 18 Rebekah Lodges, 6 Patriarchs Encampments, 5 Ladies Encampments, 1 Patriarchs Militant, and 1 Matriarchs Militant. The Odd Fellows is quite well-known in the country with a membership of about 1% of the whole population. Each new member is given a manual to explain Odd Fellows and what is expected of them. With each advancement in the degrees the member gets additional information.[129]

Italy

In 1893, the Sovereign Grand Lodge received an application from several Italians to establish the

IOOF in Naples.[130] This led to the institution of *Colombo Lodge No.1* on March 12, 1895.[131] This lodge was placed under the *Grand Lodge of Switzerland* but, for one reason or another, it surrendered its charter in 1898.[132] There were several efforts to re-establish the IOOF in the country but each failed after a short period of time.

At present, there are two Odd Fellows Lodges in the country, *San Giorgio Lodge No.1* in Genoa and *Sant'Ambrogio Lodge No.2* in Milano, working under the Grand Lodge of Switzerland. There are also other smaller groups bearing the name Odd Fellows that are not associated with either the IOOF, MUIOOF, or GUOOF.

Netherlands

Interest to form the IOOF in the Netherlands started in 1876 but was delayed due to problems with translation of the initiation rituals. After translations were completed, *Paradise Lodge No. 1* was instituted in Amsterdam, Northern Holland, on March 19, 1877.[133] Many lodges were instituted thereafter until the number was more than enough to form the *Grand Lodge of Netherlands* on May 2, 1900.[134] When *Belgia Lodge No.1* was instituted in Belgium, the Grand Lodge was renamed as the *Grand Lodge of Netherlands and Belgium* to cover both countries. By 1920, there were 30 Odd Fellows Lodges, and *Hollandia Rebekah Lodge No.1* was instituted on January 28 of that year.[135] On September 9, 1922, *Hollandia Encampment No.1* was established, and was followed by four more Encampments on December 10, 1922.

World War II stalled the progress as people in the Netherlands and Belgium faced oppression. This was particularly true with the lodges in Amsterdam that had a large number of Jewish members. After the war, efforts to re-establish several of its lodges were successful. As of this writing, there are about 3,500 members in 60 Odd Fellows Lodges, 35 Rebekah Lodges, 7 Patriarchs Encampments, and 3 Ladies Encampments located in every province in the Netherlands, except in Limburg. There are also lodges affiliated with the GUOOF in the country.

Norway

On April 26, 1898, *Noreg Lodge No.1* was established in *Stavanger* by the Grand Lodge of Denmark,[136] but this lodge ceased in 1903. Yet, the goal of establishing IOOF in Norway was not abandoned; past members living in Oslo eventually formed an Odd Fellows Club in 1907. As membership grew, the former charter of Noreg Lodge No.1 was re-dated and became the charter for *Norvegia Lodge No.1* on February 18, 1908. On May 28, 1909, a Rebekah Club was formed in Oslo and was subsequently instituted as the *Sct. Sunniva Rebekah Lodge No.1*. On November 2, 1919, *Norge Encampment No.1* was instituted.

When the membership became substantial, the *Grand Lodge of Norway* was instituted on August 7, 1920. During the 1960s, *Junior Odd Fellows Clubs* were instituted, which focused on humanitarian work to help disabled youth.[137] As of this date, the IOOF is one of the strongest fraternal organizations in the country with approximately 22,065 active members in 157 Odd Fellows Lodges, 132 Rebekah Lodges, 28 Patriarchs Encampments, and 26 Ladies Encampments.

Poland

The IOOF was first established in Poznan in 1876 and in Wroclaw in 1879 before Poland gained its independence. A *Regional Grand Lodge of Silesia and Poznan* was established in 1885, which opened lodges in Bydgoszcz in 1895, Gniezno in 1896, Torun in 1898, Gdansk in 1899, Pila 1899 and Grudziadz in 1901. After World War I, there were six Odd Fellows lodges working in the Polish lands, 18 lodges in the Lower Silesia, including as many as five in Wroclaw. On October 19, 1925, the *Grand Lodge of Poland* was instituted[138] and a new building for their headquarters was constructed several months thereafter. But because of the Anti-Masonic sentiments during the WWII, all fraternal organizations were made illegal in most parts of Europe that were occupied by the Nazis. The Odd Fellows, as well as other fraternities, were persecuted even though they are not a part of the Masonic Order.

On September 18, 1994, the IOOF was revived in Poland when *Sygmunt Lodge No.1* was chartered in the City of Wroclaw[139] with 60 members who received their degrees from Sweden. *Anna Rebekah Lodge No.1* was instituted on September 17, 1999.[140] This was followed by *Silesia Encampment No.1* on May 8, 2010.[141] More lodges soon followed with the help of Swedish Odd Fellows. The lodges were under the Grand Lodge of Sweden until the *Grand Lodge of Poland* was re-instituted on September 27, 2014. The event was attended by approximately 400 members and dignitaries of the Sovereign Grand Lodge, the Grand Lodge of Europe, and officers of neighboring Grand Lodges on the continent. At present, there are over 500 members belonging to 7 Odd Fellows Lodges, 2 Rebekah Lodges, and 1 Patriarchs Encampment in the country.

Spain

In 1887, petitions were submitted to the Sovereign Grand Lodge for the establishment of the IOOF in Spain by officers of a lodge in Cuba. Rafael Montoro y Valdes, a third degree member of that lodge and a Spanish Cortes in Spain, was commissioned to introduce the organization in the country.[142] However, little is known about the progress of this introduction during that time.

In 1936, IOOF members from Latin America formed Odd Fellows' Clubs in Spain and reported interest in forming a lodge in the country but WWII stalled their success.[143] In 1975, another group proposed to charter a lodge in Spain but progress was slow.[144] This changed when a *Rebekah Group of Spain* was formed in 1996 and was chartered as *Andalucia Rebekah Lodge No.1* on February 14, 1998.[145] The success of the women's branch was followed by the institution of *Costa del Sol Lodge No.1* on November 16, 2002,[146] mostly by residents of Spain who previously joined an Odd Fellows Lodge in Denmark, Norway, or Finland. There are also three Odd Fellows Clubs - in Torrevieja, Costa Blanca, and Puerto Rico in Gran Canaria.[147] These clubs are composed of members from Nordic countries but have no intention of becoming chartered lodges.

Sweden

When the Odd Fellows became prosperous and influential in Denmark, the enthusiasm reached Sweden. Odd Fellows started in the country when *Scania Odd Fellows Club* was formed in the City of Malmö on June 8, 1884. This club grew to about 45 members who were all initiated in *Denmark Lodge No.1* in Copenhagen. This group comprised *Scania Lodge No.1* in Malmo, Sweden, instituted on October 29, 1884.[148] In 1887, *Veritas Lodge No.2* was instituted and was followed by *Amicitia Lodge No.3* in 1888. Members of *Amicitia Lodge No.2* then took the initiative to establish lodges in other cities. In addition, *Suecia Encampment No.1* was instituted on October 12, 1891 under the jurisdiction of the Sovereign Grand Lodge. For a time, some lodges worked under the jurisdiction of the Grand Lodge of Denmark while others worked directly under the Sovereign Grand Lodge. This condition lasted until July 8, 1895, when the *Grand Lodge of Sweden* was eventually instituted. The first Rebekah Lodge was opened in 1967.[149] Since then, the Swedish Odd

Members gather outside an Odd Fellows Lodge in Tønsberg, Norway. Photo courtesy of the IOOF Grand Lodge of Norway.

Re-institution of the Grand Lodge of Poland of the IOOF. Photo courtesy of the Grand Lodge of Poland, IOOF, 2014.

2013 Annual Movable Conference of the Manchester Unity Oddfellows. Photo courtesy of Manchester Unity Oddfellows, 2013.

Fellows and Rebekahs have become the stronghold of the IOOF in the world with nearly 40,000 members belonging to more than 174 Odd Fellows Lodges, 115 Rebekah Lodges, 24 Patriarchs Encampments, and 20 Ladies Encampments.[150]

Switzerland

The IOOF was established in Switzerland on June 19, 1871, when *Helvetia Lodge No.1*[151] was instituted in Zurich. Shortly, more lodges followed suit, so that the *Grand Lodge of Switzerland* was quickly established on April 22, 1874.[152] The first Encampment, *Eidgenossen Encampment No.1*, was instituted in Zurich in 1888.[153] Women joined the ranks when *Anna Seiler Rebekah Lodge No.1* was instituted on April 24, 1971 in Berne. *Schweiz Ladies Encampment No.1* followed on September 30, 1989. The Odd Fellows of Switzerland has developed a corporate identity for all printed matters and advertisements. Lodge rooms are encouraged to make a good and modern impression on everybody. Also, the lodges make sure that those who apply for membership are of good reputation.[154] As of this writing, there are approximately 1,400 members in 26 Odd Fellows Lodges, 4 Rebekah Lodges, 3 Patriarchs Encampments, and 1 Ladies Encampment.

United Kingdom

There were many *Orders* of Odd Fellows in the United Kingdom during the 18th and 19th centuries. At one time, there were more than 30 Affiliated Orders across the country that bore the name Odd Fellows. The *Grand United Order of Odd Fellows Friendly Society* traces its roots with the amalgamation of the *Ancient Order* and the *Patriotic Order* on January 6, 1798. The *Manchester*

International Expansion | 151

Unity Independent Order of Odd Fellows (MUIOOF) was formed after several lodges declared their independence from the United Order beginning 1810. Both the GUOOF and the MUIOOF established Odd Fellows Lodges in many countries across the world.

When the IOOF and Manchester Unity IOOF separated in 1843, the IOOF attempted to establish lodges in the United Kingdom. On June 27, 1844, the IOOF chartered the *Friendly Ivorian Lodge No.1* in Tredegar, Wales. Other lodges were instituted in Monmouth, Stockport, and Liverpool. In 1853, the *London Order of Odd Fellows* proposed to affiliate with the Independent Order of Odd Fellows but was denied by the Grand Lodge of the United States unless the former would conform to all the usages, forms and practices of the IOOF in North America.[155] The following year, the Manchester Unity IOOF made offers to re-establish reciprocal relations with the IOOF. The Grand Lodge of the United States expressed its willingness but gave a condition that MUIOOF should adopt all the usages practiced by the IOOF. The counter-offer was not heeded by the MUIOOF although negotiations continued for many years.

Successively, the IOOF instituted *Thomas Wildey Lodge No.1* and *Anglo-American Encampment No.1* in London on November 17, 1875.[156] But both ceased operations after 1878.[157] Ultimately, the Manchester Unity IOOF and IOOF established *inter-fraternal relations* with each other and made agreements that the IOOF will not establish lodges in the United Kingdom, and vice versa. At present, the Manchester Unity Independent Order of Odd Fellows has more than 314,000 members in the country. The Grand United Order of Odd Fellows Friendly Society also has its base in the country with about 20,000 members spread across the United Kingdom, including Ireland and Scotland. Both function as fraternal organizations and friendly societies, which offer financial plans and benefits for their members.

AUSTRALIA AND ASIA PACIFIC

Australia

The Odd Fellows were founded in the country before most Australian banks, building societies or insurance companies were even conceived. It provided a great deal of security and help to thousands of Australian families for years. The IOOF and other friendly societies came into being because of a common need, and ordinary Australians, laborers, miners, carpenters and other workers banded together to provide for their own work-related needs, scant resources, and some of the medical and other essential services they lacked.[158] They sought help from no one but each other, neither from the Government nor from the wealthy.

Presumably, there were earlier Odd Fellows clubs in the country. The first recorded Independent Odd Fellows Lodge was founded by English immigrants in Sydney on February 24, 1836, under the name *Loyal Order of Independent Odd Fellows*.[159] As was the custom in those early years, the group operated both as a Grand Lodge and Lodge.[160] Like other similar groups at that time, the lodge met in a tavern "with a sliding panel between the meeting room and the adjacent dispensary which served the dual purpose of maintaining a degree of privacy as well as facilitating the passage of liquid refreshments at appropriate times."[161] The *Australian Grand Lodge* first received a charter from the *Grand Lodge of England* whose headquarters were based in Ticehurst, England, on January 22, 1846.[162] Many other independent groups, such as the *Ancient Britons*, ultimately converted to become an Odd Fellows Lodge.[163] As years passed, Grand Lodges were instituted all over Australia and New Zealand under the banner *Ancient Independent Order of Odd Fellows*.

In 1858, the *Grand Lodge of Victoria* of this *Ancient Order* made negotiations for affiliation with the Independent Order of Odd Fellows in North America. But because of distance, it was not until February 22, 1868 that the *Grand Lodge of Victoria* finally obtained a charter from the Grand Lodge of the United States. On March 4, 1878, the Grand Lodges in New South Wales, Queensland, South Australia, Tasmania, Western Australia, Victoria and New Zealand joined together to form the *Grand Lodge of Australasia*.[164] The first Encampment was also instituted on March 4, 1878. Women joined when the first Rebekah Lodge was formed on April 26, 1895.

For many years, the IOOF were a major presence in every Australian town, its membership reaching over 60,000 under the Grand Lodge of Australasia. The lodges functioned both as a fraternal organization and a mutual-aid society, which provided essential medical aid and sick pay, and generally helped those who fell on hard times.[165] As membership grew, and the funds became available, the IOOF began providing low-cost loans to members, thus helping thousands of Australian families to realize their dream of owning their own home.[166]

In 1929, however, the Grand Lodge of Victoria left the IOOF and formed an independent friendly society with mixed lodges open to both men and women. Eventually, the IOOF in Victoria became a purely friendly society with no fraternal activities but they are still represented during the sessions of the Grand Lodge of Australasia. In 1986, the IOOF in Australasia adopted the resolution to accept *beneficial* members without the need to undergo degrees of initiation while others who are fond of ceremonies can still opt to receive the degrees and become *fraternal* members. This is the situation because the Grand Lodges in Australia are registered as a friendly society with insurance, credit unions, and other forms of benefits under the name IOOF Friendly Society. For many years, the organization in Australia contributed for state benefits including Medical, Hospital, Life Assurance, Sick, and Funeral and Pharmaceutical Funds and Dispensaries.[167]

As of this writing, the IOOF in Australasia is comprised of three Grand jurisdictions: New South Wales, South Australia and Tasmania, and a few remaining lodges in New Zealand.[168] As of December 2012, there were about 2,131 members in 28 Odd Fellows Lodges, 471 members in 23 Rebekah Lodges, and 53 members in 5 Encampments.[169] There are also lodges under the *Manchester Unity Independent Order of Odd Fellows* founded as early as 1840 and the *Grand United Order of Oddfellows Friendly Society* founded in 1848. All three Affiliated Orders recently established *mutual recognition* with each other.

Indonesia

The IOOF Grand Lodge of the Kingdom of Netherlands was issued a quasi-independent charter and their leaders interpreted it as giving them jurisdiction over both continental Netherlands and its colonies and proceeded to institute lodges in the Dutch East Indies.[170] Previously, members from the Netherlands formed an Odd Fellows Club in Batavia, Java.[171] The club was eventually chartered as *India Lodge No.1* on December 25, 1922.[172] On December 25, 1923, *Kartini Rebekah Lodge No.1* was instituted.[173] In August 1930, they instituted *Ardjoeno Lodge No.1* in Sourabaya, Java. *Preanger Lodge No.3* and *Elizabeth Rebekah Lodge No.1* followed in 1934. The 2 Rebekah Lodges were abandoned during the Japanese occupation in 1940. And all lodges were

International Expansion | 153

closed when the country declared its independence and became the Republic of Indonesia.

Japan

The IOOF established *Far East Lodge No.1* in Yokohama on May 27, 1889.[174] Among the charter members was Clarence Ridgely Greathouse, who was Consul-General of Japan at that time.[175] *Kobi Lodge No.2* followed on September 16, 1891 in Kobe. When the bank where the lodge funds were deposited failed, the members in Kobe became discouraged.[176] This led to its eventual closure. On the other hand, *Far East Lodge No.1* prospered until World War II when it finally decided to cease operations because of turmoil in the country. An attempt to re-establish the IOOF in Japan was made through the efforts of some members in the Philippines who made contact with nearly 20 people in Japan. But due to more than 2 years of inaction by the Sovereign Grand Lodge, the petitioners in Japan lost their interest and consequently abandoned the plan.

China

The first attempt to establish the IOOF in China was in 1877 when Grand Representative Porter of California and the Hon. O.N. Denny of Oregon, sought permission to set up a lodge there while serving as United States Consul at Tien Tsin, China.[177] Little is known about what transpired thereafter. What is known is the existence of the *Shanghai Society of Odd Fellows* composed of about 40 members of the IOOF from different locations in the Far East.[178] In 1941, these members appealed to the Sovereign Grand Lodge to grant them a charter but was advised that it was not yet possible "on account of the unsettled and disturbed world conditions."[179] In 1945, this society was chartered as *Franklin D. Roosevelt Lodge No.1* with a membership of approximately 100.[180] A Rebekah Sisters Club for women was also formed in China.[181] Partly because China came under the rule of a Communist government, the progress of foreign organizations like the Odd Fellows was stalled.

New Zealand

The first lodge was established in New Zealand in 1843. Like the Odd Fellows in the United Kingdom and Australia, the IOOF in this country functioned both as a fraternal organization and mutual-aid society, which provided insurance benefits to its members and their families. At one time, membership reached more than 10,000 throughout the country. In October 2014, the *Grand Lodge of New Zealand* decided to close its operations and many of its lodges underwent liquidation.[182] At present, there remains only three Odd Fellows lodges in the country directly operating under the Grand Lodge of Australasia. There are also other lodges that are affiliated with the Manchester Unity IOOF and the Grand United Order of Odd Fellows Friendly Society.

Philippines

The awakening of Filipinos to a deep sense of injustice being practiced upon them by their colonizers began with "the introduction of fraternal organizations in the country and the influence of higher education obtained by those of means in the schools of Hong Kong and Europe."[183] It is recorded that a *Society of Odd Fellows* spread in the Philippines as early as 1872.[184] Prior to 1898, an *Odd Fellows Association of Manila* and several military lodges also existed in the country.[185] And, when the Philippine Islands came under American rule, it was reported that "the Order of Odd Fellows was the first largely represented in the U.S. Army."[186] During the 74th Annual Session of the Grand Lodge of the United States, D.L. Badley, who was with the

U.S. Army in the Philippines, asked permission to officially establish the IOOF in the country and was permitted to form military lodges or associations. Beginning 1899, however, an armed military conflict between Filipinos and Americans occurred so all lodge activities were suspended.

When the war ended in 1902, some groups of Odd Fellows were congregating in Manila, Iloilo, and Cebu.[187] Correspondence during the same year reported that a large number were based in Manila and Cebu and an *IOOF Club* consisting of about 150 men existed in Manila area. This convinced the Sovereign Grand Lodge to finally authorize District Deputy Grand Sire Charles H. Burritt to institute *Manila Lodge No.1* in the City of Manila on June 29, 1902.[188] Owing to the long travel from the United States to the Philippine Islands, the lodge received its charter from the Sovereign Grand Lodge only on January 29, 1903.[189]

The lodge built its first Odd Fellows Hall in 1905 and rented a part of it to other fraternal organizations namely, the Freemasons and the Knights of Pythias.[190] On June 12, 1912, *Manila Encampment No.1* was chartered. The early IOOF members consisted of prominent businessmen, government officials, judges, and soldiers. Hon. Charles Burritt, who served as the first District Deputy Grand Sire for the Philippines, was a Judge of the Court of First Instance in Bohol and the Chief of the Mining Bureau who authored the first mining laws of the country. Newton Whiting Gilbert, who served as the Acting Governor-General and Vice Governor-General of the Philippines, was also one of its early members.[191] Membership was stable at around 150 to 300 members spread all over Manila, Cebu, Iloilo, Bohol, and Zamboanga.[192]

Unfortunately, Japan declared war against the United States in 1941. At that time, the Philippine Islands was still a colony of the United States. Hours after their attack on Pearl Harbor, Japanese aircrafts launched a military strike on military base camps located in the Philippines. For many years, Filipino guerrillas and American soldiers fought together against the Japanese until 1944 when Japan finally surrendered. Nearly a million Filipinos and Americans were killed during the war and many towns and cities, including Manila, were left in ruins. Noting the situation that most likely left their building destroyed, the IOOF suspended its activities indefinitely. The organization failed to resume operations after World War II although there remained several Odd Fellows who settled in the country.

In 1985, *Watchdog Committee* was founded in the Philippines. But the group somehow lost its direction and purpose, and a merger with a more established organization was proposed. In 2008, some Watchdog members in Dumaguete City made contacts with the Sovereign Grand Lodge. Three members from the United States then traveled to the Philippines and instituted *Watchdog Lodge No.1*, *Dumaguete City Encampment No.1* and *Canton Negros Oriental No.1* on November 21, 2009. More lodges were then instituted almost every year. Notably, Manila Lodge was re-instituted as *Manila Lodge No.8* in 2015.

Instability due to lack of a national governing body led to the institution of the *Grand Lodge of the Philippines* on October 23, 2015. The event was attended by delegates from the Sovereign Grand Lodge, Grand Lodge of Australasia, Grand Lodge of Denmark and the Manchester Unity Independent Order of Odd Fellows. On August 23, 2018, the Grand Lodge of Australasia and the Grand Lodge of Philippines were further granted authority by the Sovereign Grand Lodge to form the *Grand Lodge of Asia Pacific*. After six years of fund-raising efforts, a new two-storey Odd Fellows building in Dumaguete

With the help of social media websites and a more inclusive approach in membership recruitment, the Odd Fellows in the Philippines is currently experiencing a resurgence in their membership with many younger people in their 20s, 30s, and 40s joining existing lodges and petitioning to charter new lodges in other localities. Photos by the author, 2017, and Alvin Hipolito, 2019.

City was also completed. Since its revival, more than 1000 people have been initiated into 33 Odd Fellows Lodges. There also exists 1 Rebekah Lodge, 5 Encampments and 2 Cantons of the Patriarchs Militant.

Thailand

Every year, a good number of Odd Fellows from Europe and North America travel to and even settle in Thailand. These members would informally meet in pubs and restaurants to socialize. When a tsunami hit the country in 2004, Swedish Odd Fellows raised more than SEK 1.5 million to help the victims. An additional SEK 1.2 million was donated by the Swedish Odd Fellows to construct an orphanage in Muang Mai, Phuket, Thailand. The orphanage would take care of some of the children who lost their parents during the tsunami. On January 15, 2019, an Odd Fellows Club was finally formed by 12 expats from Europe as a preparatory step in forming a lodge in due time.

Turkey

In May 1879, Rev. G.N. Shishmanian, a member of Covenant Lodge No.22 in Kentucky, sought permission to establish the IOOF in Turkey.[193] Little is known about succeeding events or the progress of Rev. Shishmanian's efforts in the last century. As of this writing, there exists no IOOF lodges in the country.

AFRICA

South Africa

In 1903, the *Grand Lodge of Australasia* sought permission to establish the IOOF in South Africa.[194] This led to the institution of *African Lodge No.1* at Johannesburg, Transvaal, in 1904.[195] But by 1906, the Secretary of the lodge reported

Being predominantly black, the Grand United Order of Odd Fellows prospered in Nigeria, Ghana, Togo and other countries in Africa as early as year 1879. GUOOF lodges continue to exist on the African continent remarkably with an abundant membership.

Photo courtesy of the Grand United Order of Oddfellows in Ghana.

that attendance in their meetings had been few because of the deplorable state of affairs in general throughout the whole country and a big number of members were scattered all over Transvaal, which made it difficult to get the members together. By the end of 1907, the lodge only had seven members in good standing.[196] The lodge ceased to exist a few years after. There were also informal IOOF clubs consisting of Australian members in the country but these groups never bothered to apply for a charter from the Sovereign Grand Lodge or any grand body.

Nigeria

On April 1, 1924, the Sovereign Grand Secretary received an application for an IOOF charter from James A. Biney, Recording Secretary of *Star of Nigeria Lodge No.9294* of the Manchester Unity IOOF located in Slatpond, Gold Coast, British West Africa. But the application was not approved because there was no IOOF member near the area who can institute the lodge.[197] The IOOF made subsequent attempts to establish a lodge in the country but also failed. But on March 30, 2007 *Nigeria Lodge No.1* was chartered in Abuja.[198] This was followed by *Lagos Lodge No.2* in Lagos on February 21, 2008, and by *Kaduma Lodge No.3* in Kaduma, on February 25, 2008.[199] At present, all 3 Odd Fellows lodges work directly under the jurisdiction of the Sovereign Grand Lodge and membership is open to both men and women.

Chapter 20

PROGRAMS AND PROJECTS

The ancient command of the Independent Order of Odd Fellows is found on the Seal of the Sovereign Grand Lodge: "We command you to visit the sick, relieve the distressed, bury the dead and educate the orphan." This, along with the ideal of Fraternity and Relief, is the reason why for more than 200 years the Odd Fellows continue to organize and support numerous charitable programs in the local, national and international level. In 1992, the IOOF was awarded the *Community Service Award* by President George Bush. The citation of the plaque he presented reads:[1]

> "Thank you for your commitment to community service. Through your generosity and hard work, you have shown that the tradition of neighbor helping neighbor is alive and well in our country. Your efforts profoundly influence the life of your community and they are a shining example for us all."

As a whole, Odd Fellows and Rebekahs raise millions of dollars every year to support a wide variety of philanthropic causes. While the individual Grand Lodges and Lodges enjoy some autonomy on what projects to support, the Sovereign Grand Lodge of the Independent Order of Odd Fellows has identified several programs and projects that all members and lodges may join and support.

IOOF Arthritis Advisory Board

In 1985, the Independent Order of Odd Fellows began supporting the Arthritis Foundation in the United States and the Arthritis Society in Canada based on their command to "relieve the distressed." Since that year, the Odd Fellows and Rebekahs have raised more than $8 million to support and fund research on arthritis.[2] Every year, lodges across the United States and Canada raise over $500,000.00 to support arthritis research.

IOOF Educational Foundation

The Educational Foundation of the Independent Order of Odd Fellows began its operation on September 20, 1927. The purpose of the Foundation is to operate a revolving loan fund for qualified students dependent, wholly or in part, on their own efforts for an education. Since the opening of the Foundation, donations of approximately $3.5 million have made it possible for over 5,000 young people to receive student loans amounting to over $7.1 million. The Foundation has expanded its educational investment for deserving students by providing several scholarships: Christine Smith Scholarship, Ingstrom Scholarship, Wirz Scholarship, Vocation Technology Scholarship, Glenn Coursey Scholarship, Continuing Education Grants, Odd Fellows and Rebekahs Education Pilgrimage Tour Scholarship, Non-Traditional Scholarship, and Davis Odd Fellows Charities, Inc.

IOOF Living Legacy Program

This program began as the idea of Past Sovereign Grand Master Wilson D. Berkey, who in 1989 noticed many dead trees in the jurisdictions that he was visiting. This aroused his concern for global tree loss, so he commissioned this worthy project as "The Living Legacy Program" of the IOOF. Planting trees has been advocated due to the ability of trees to absorb carbon dioxide, store the carbon, and release oxygen for human use. During its first implementation on June 1, 1990, members around the United States and Canada planted 162,772 trees.[3] In 1992, exactly 420,000 trees were actually planted, hundreds of shrubs, at least two rose gardens, ten flower beds on public grounds, the perpetual care of several parks, and donations of close to $12,000 in cash and checks.[4] Since the inception of the project, approximately 8 million trees have been planted by the Odd Fellows and Rebekahs in the United States and Canada.

Odd Fellows and Rebekahs Pilgrimage for Youth

This program was established by the Sovereign Grand Lodge in 1949 to provide the youth with opportunity to exchange views on education, politics, and global relations, and to develop friendships among themselves. Annually, the IOOF brings together high school students from North America and Europe for a field trip to study and observe the United Nations and visit historical sites in the United States and Canada. Expenses including transportation, meals, lodging, and sightseeing are paid by the sponsoring Odd Fellows and Rebekah Lodges. Since it was established, over 50,000 students have participated in the Pilgrimage.

IOOF Visual Research Foundation

Established in 1957, the Visual Research Foundation and World Eye Bank of the Independent Order of Odd Fellows and Rebekahs support and provide funds to advance eye research through professorships in ophthalmology at the Wilmer Eye Institute at John Hopkins School of Medicine in Baltimore, Maryland. Moreover, the World Eye Banks located in different state jurisdictions allow members of the IOOF to donate their eyes after death for corneal transplants and research.

In 1961, the Foundation's professorship in eye research was established through an endowment of $625,000. With the subsequent challenge of more research needed and its rising costs, another $1 million was added to the fund in 1987. As of 2012, the IOOF had a total endowment of $2.5 million for this program, and continues to donate at least $500,000 annually. The IOOF support to this program has made it possible for many handicapped persons to be aided, whether through corneal transplant or research breakthrough to prevent blindness.

IOOF World Hunger and Disaster Fund

The IOOF World Hunger and Disaster Fund provides relief through any humanitarian project to assist a person, persons, or groups of people in need, or in rehabilitation of their damaged properties. It provides assistance in terms of food, clothing, shelter, medical expenses, or other needs that may arise. In 1976, this Program raised $50,000 to help feed the hungry,[5] donated $35,000 to support the "Save the Rice" Congress in India, donated $5,500 to feed hungry children in Chile, and gave other amounts to the Salvation Army and International Red Cross to purchase food for destitute people.[6] Its "Love Thy Neighbor" project served refreshments to weary travelers at highway rest stops and roadside parks during heavy-travel weekends and holidays.[7] At present, this program allocates more than $7.5 million in support of relief projects annually.

Representatives of The Sovereign Grand Lodge and the IOOF Visual Research Foundation presented thier check donations to the Wilmer Eye Institute. Photo courtesy of The Sovereign Grand Lodge, IOOF, 2002.

Odd Fellows and Rebekahs Homes

The first Odd Fellows Home was built in 1872 in Pennsylvania. Eventually, almost all states and provinces in North America had a home. The endowments for and cost of operating these early homes ran in the millions and were entirely supported by the membership. These homes have provided care to thousands and afforded a home-like atmosphere and education for hundreds of orphans. Because of the works of the IOOF in the United States, then President Ronald Reagan invited Sovereign Grand Secretary Edward T. Rogers to the White House where he recognized the work of the IOOF in caring for the elderly and indigent.[8]

As times have changed, so has the concept of care-giving. Governments became involved in care-giving and Homes for the Aged are no longer considered charitable homes. The high-rise, the cottage, and the apartment complex type of living arrangements have replaced the original concept. Orphanages have been replaced by foster homes. Many jurisdictions under the Independent Order of Odd Fellows have become involved in remodeling Homes into:

- Retirement Homes
- Skilled Nursing Facilities
- Day care centers

Many of these Homes provide private rooms for residents, dining rooms, recreation rooms, hospital facilities nearby, and security and comfort in the twilight years of life. High-Rise Apartments for Senior Citizens who have retired and reached the age of 62 are also sponsored by the Odd Fellows and Rebekahs in several states and jurisdictions.

Odd Fellows and Rebekah Camps

In some states and countries, the Odd Fellows

In 1962, the Odd Fellows and Rebekahs began building high rise apartments to take care of seniors.

Photo courtesy of Odd Fellow-Rebekah Manor in Norfolk, Nebraska.

In 1984, the Odd Fellows and Rebekahs of Ontario, through its Humanitarian Services, gave Camp Trillium a grant of $5,000 to hold a one-week camp. This has now grown to two permanent camps and numerous day camps and over 2,500 campers (Children with Cancer) per year. In 2000, the Grand Master of Ontario established the "Camp Trillium, Odd Fellows and Rebekahs Capital Fund," which received donations and helped the camp with a donation of around $100,000 per year. This fund paid off the mortgage on Trillium's Office building. Eventually, the Odd Fellows and Rebekahs awarded Camp Trillium $1 million to purchase Garratt's Island, which is now known as *"Camp Trillium Odd Fellows and Rebekah Island."* Photo courtesy of Camp Trillium.

and Rebekahs own and sponsor Youth Camps and Recreation Parks. These facilities aim to provide a healthy and entertaining outdoor experience for the youth and their families. Today, the IOOF still owns and manages several Camps in Alabama, Arizona, California, Colorado, Iowa, Kentucky, Maine, Minnesota, Michigan, New Hampshire, New Mexico, Ohio, Oregon, Washington, and Wisconsin.

Odd Fellows Cemeteries

In some states or cities, Odd Fellows own cemeteries in line with their ancient command: "To Bury the Dead." While many of these cemeteries have already closed, some are still being utilized at present. Many are also registered as historic places or landmarks.

Odd Fellows Halls

Many Odd Fellows lodges across the world own buildings. Most of these halls are not just a place for lodge meetings but also serve as venue for various community and social events where people can organize fund-raising events or simply hang out and have fun. Many of these buildings are already registered as historic landmarks.

Pilgrimage to the Tomb of the Unknown Soldier and the Canadian War Memorial

The first Sunday in May has been designated for the Annual Odd Fellows and Rebekahs Pilgrimage to the Tomb of the Unknowns in Arlington, Virginia. The yearly event developed from a privilege that was afforded to the Odd Fellows and Rebekahs by 32nd President of the United States and Odd Fellow Franklin D. Roosevelt, who was in the White House from 1933 to 1945. The first Pilgrimage was on June 17, 1934. Permission for this has been granted by the Department of Army, custodian of the Arlington National Cemetery. The purpose of this Pilgrimage was not only to honor the Unknown Soldier and the Nation's War Dead, but also the IOOF members who had made the supreme sacrifice in World War I and World War II. Moreover, Odd Fellows and Rebekahs also gather on the first Sunday of June at the *Canadian War Memorial* in Ottawa, Canada, to pay homage to those brave soldiers who gave their lives for their beloved country of Canada. In other countries, Odd Fellows and Rebekahs also participate in other solemn activities to pay tribute to those who made supreme sacrifices for their country.

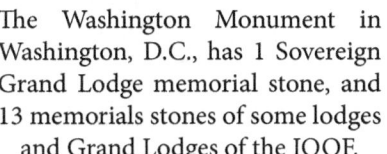

The Washington Monument in Washington, D.C., has 1 Sovereign Grand Lodge memorial stone, and 13 memorials stones of some lodges and Grand Lodges of the IOOF.

Photo by the author, 2012.

S.O.S. Children's Village

In 2003, The Sovereign Grand Lodge voted to raise more than $2 million to build an S.O.S. Children's Village in Battambang, Cambodia. This consists of homes, a kindergarten, school, social center, and medical facility for children who have lost their biological family due to personal, national, or natural disaster. In 2016, another S.O.S. Children's Village was built in Malawi, Africa, through the generous donations by the IOOF Grand Lodge of Norway.

Gate of the International Peace Garden

In the late1950s, the Independent Order of Odd Fellows raised funds to erect a Peace Tower or Entrance Gate at the International Peace Garden – a symbol of peace between the U.S. and Canada.[9] In

Every year, a number of Odd Fellows and Rebekahs from the United States and Canada travel to Pasadena, California, to volunteer in helping build and design the Odd Fellows Rebekahs Rose Float for the Annual Tournament of Roses Parade.
Photo courtesy from Odd Fellows Rebekahs Rose Float , 1977.

July of 1964, the project was dedicated by Sovereign Grand Master Murphy in the presence of some 10,000 Odd Fellows and Rebekahs from all parts of Canada and the United States.[10]

Odd Fellows Rebekahs Rose Parade Float

Since 1908 and until the present, the Odd Fellows and Rebekahs participate in the *Annual Tournament of Roses Parade* in Pasadena, California. This project is now run and managed by the Odd Fellows and Rebekahs Rose Float Organization, which provides an educational experience for the public by teaching volunteers to create and display a work of art in the annual Tournament of Roses Parade.

Chapter 21

ORGANIZATIONAL STRUCTURE

The organization of the Independent Order of Odd Fellows developed gradually. At first, lodges were self-instituted and members managed their own affairs without control and supervision from any higher organization or national governing body. But as membership increased, the lodges united themselves to form a Grand Lodge. And after Grand Lodges were established across North America and across the world, the IOOF formed the Sovereign Grand Lodge.

The historic Odd Fellows Hall in San Francisco, California, built in 1910.

Traditional collar regalia of the IOOF with corresponding jewel of office. Photo by the author, 2015.

Lodge

The local unit of the Odd Fellows is called a *Lodge*. A lodge is both the building where the members hold their meetings and the members themselves as a basic unit or branch of the Odd Fellows. A lodge may be organized upon receipt by the Grand Lodge or Sovereign Grand Lodge of a signed petition for a charter by a minimum of five (5) or more members of the Third Degree or a minimum of fifteen (15) persons qualified to become Odd Fellows in a community within a defined jurisdiction.[1] Each lodge is governed by a set of officers. In most cases, a member in good standing must attain the highest degree to be eligible to become an officer of the lodge.

The titles of the officers of a lodge slightly vary among the various Affiliated Orders of Odd Fellows. But usually, the presiding officer is called a *Noble Grand* or *Most Noble Grand*. In the Independent Order of Odd Fellows (IOOF), there are more or less sixteen officers of a lodge depending on the country or jurisdiction. Usually, five officers are elected by the members, namely: Noble Grand, Vice Grand, Recording Secretary, Financial Secretary, and Treasurer. The elected Noble Grand appoints nine additional officers: Right Supporter of the Noble Grand, Left Supporter of the Noble Grand, Warden, Conductor, Chaplain, Right Scene Supporter, Left Scene Supporter, Musician, Color Bearer, Inside Guardian, and Outside Guardian. The Vice Grand appoints two additional officers: Right Supporter of the Vice Grand and Left Supporter of the Vice Grand. Each officer usually wears a set of regalia along with jewels to denote their office and rank.

Lodge Officers, Regalia, and Their Functions

Noble Grand

His or her duty is to serve as the presiding officer of the lodge. It is also his or her duty to appoint committees and see that the lodge's program is planned in advanced. The regalia of the Noble Grand is a *scarlet collar or chain* trimmed with *white or silver* lace. The jewel of office is *crossed gavels* of white metal. Station is at the upper end of the room, in the principal chair, usually placed on an elevated platform about three steps.

Vice Grand

His or her duty is to assist in presiding meetings and assume the duties of the Noble Grand when the latter is absent. Under the direction of the Noble Grand, he or she takes charge of the inner door, helps in maintaining order, and requires members to be decorous while in the lodge. The regalia of the Vice Grand is a *blue collar or chain* trimmed with *white or silver* lace. The jewel of office is an *hour glass* of white metal. Station is at the end of the room nearest the entrance.

Secretary

This officer was formerly called *Recording Secretary*. His or her duties are to keep an accurate account of the proceedings of the lodge, write all communications, and issue all notices or summonses under the seal of the lodge. He or she also attests to all warrants or checks drawn by the lodge. A member cannot hold the two offices of Secretary and Treasurer at the same time in any Odd Fellows lodge.[2] The regalia is a *scarlet collar or chain* trimmed with *white or silver* lace. The jewel of office is *crossed quills* of white metal. Station is on the right of the Noble Grand but not on the same level.

Financial Secretary

His or her duties are to receive all monies paid to the Lodge except when otherwise provided. He or she notifies members of dues payable to the Lodge and provides them with the annual dues card or receipt. He or she also makes semi-annual and annual reports to the Grand Lodge and delivers them to the Secretary to be forwarded to the Grand Lodge or the Sovereign Grand Lodge. This position is *optional*. If there is no financial secretary, then the duties shall be assigned to the secretary. The regalia is a *scarlet collar or chain* trimmed with *white or silver* lace. The jewel of office is *crossed quills and a book* of white metal. Station is on the left of the Noble Grand but not on the same level. The Financial Secretary always sits beside or near the Treasurer.

Treasurer

His or her duties are to keep an accurate file of all monies and receipts of the lodge and write all warrants drawn by the Noble Grand and attested by the Secretary. A member cannot hold the two offices of Treasurer and Secretary at the same time in any Odd Fellows lodge.[3] The regalia is a *scarlet collar or chain* trimmed with *white or silver* lace. The jewel of office is *crossed keys* of white metal. Station is on the left of the Noble Grand but not on the same level. The Treasurer always sits beside or near the Financial Secretary

Warden

His or her duties are to take charge of the regalia and the lodge room property, place the regalia in the lodge room before opening it, remove the regalia on closing the lodge room, reporting any damage to the Noble Grand. He or she also prepares the ballot box, canvasses votes on motions when required to do so, acts as messenger, and performs such duties as may be delegated. The Warden is usually appointed by the Noble Grand but, in some lodges in Europe, the Warden is an elective officer. The regalia is a *black collar, sash, or chain* trimmed with *white or silver* lace. The jewel of office is *crossed axes* of white metal. Station is in front of the Noble Grand at the right side but not on the same level. Traditionally, the Warden holds a broad axe while on duty, which he or she uses while walking around the lodge room to collect donations from the members.

Conductor

His or her duties are to receive the candidates for initiation when they enter the lodge room and perform all duties assigned to him or her in conferring the degrees of initiation and otherwise, and assist the Warden while in the lodge. The Conductor is usually appointed by the Noble Grand but, in some lodges in Europe, the Conductor is an elective office. The regalia is a *black collar, sash, or chain* trimmed with *white or silver* lace. The jewel of office is *crossed wands* of white metal. Station is in front of the Noble Grand at the left side but not on the same level.

Chaplain

His or her duties are to lead in the opening and closing prayer in the lodge and perform all functions assigned to him or her during initiations. The Chaplain is an *optional* position. Some lodges, especially those whose members represent numerous creeds, do not have a chaplain. The regalia is a *white sash or chain* trimmed with *white or silver* lace. The jewel of office is an open *Holy Bible, Holy Book,* or *Book of Sacred Law*. Station is in the middle of one side of the room, opposite the station of the immediate Past Grand, and usually at the left side from the Noble Grand's station.

Right Supporter of the Noble Grand

His or her duties are to support the Noble Grand in keeping order in the lodge room, commands, open and close the lodge in due form, see to it that the signs are given correctly, and occupy the chair of the Noble Grand when vacated temporarily during lodge hours. The regalia is a *scarlet sash, collar or chain* trimmed *white or silver* lace. The jewel of office is a *gavel*. The station is at the right side of the Noble Grand.

Left Supporter of the Noble Grand

His or her duties are to see that all members who enter the lodge room are in proper regalia and give the signs correctly and to officiate for the Right Supporter when absent. The regalia is *scarlet sash, collar or chain* trimmed with *white or silver* lace. The jewel of office is a *gavel*. Station is at the left side of the Noble Grand.

Right Supporter of the Vice Grand

His or her duties are to observe that members give the signs correctly. He or she reports to the Noble Grand members who do not conduct themselves according to the regulations of the Order and occupy the chair of the Vice Grand when vacated temporarily during lodge hours. The regalia is a *blue sash, collar or chain* trimmed with *white or silver* lace. The jewel of office is a stylized *hour glass*. Station is at the right side of the Vice

Grand's chair.

Left Supporter of the Vice Grand

His or her duties are to assist the Right Supporter and officiate for that officer when absent. The regalia is *blue sash, collar or chain* trimmed *white or silver* lace. The jewel of office is a stylized *hour glass*. Station is at the left side of the Vice Grand's chair.

Right Scene Supporter

His or her duty is to assist during initiation, bear the wands of office during processions or funerals, and perform roles specified in the charge book. The regalia is a *white sash, collar or chain* trimmed *white or silver* lace. The jewel of office is a *burning torch*. The station is in front of the Vice Grand at the right side but not on the same level.

Left Scene Supporter

His or her duties are to assist during initiation and perform roles specified in the charge book. The regalia is a *white sash, collar or chain* trimmed *white or silver* lace. The jewel of office is a *burning torch*. The station is in front of the Vice Grand at the left side but not on the same level.

Inside Guardian

His or her duties are to guard the inner door. He or she receives the password for the degree that the lodge is open, and sees to it that all members who enter the lodge room are in proper regalia. He or she officiates for the Outside Guardian when the latter is absent. The regalia is a *scarlet sash, collar or chain* trimmed *white or silver* lace. The jewel of office is a pair of *crossed swords*. The station is beside the inner door of the lodge room. Traditionally, guardians carry a sword while on duty.

Outside Guardian

His or her duties are to see that anyone who tries to enter the lodge room is qualified, asks members to give the password before they can enter, and prevents any interference during ritualistic ceremonies. The regalia is a *scarlet sash, collar, or chain* trimmed *white or silver* lace. The jewel of office is a pair of *crossed swords*. The station is beside the outer door of the lodge room or ante-room. Guardians traditionally carry a sword while on duty.

Musician

His or her duty is to play required music or accompaniment during meetings and ceremonies. This position is *optional* and does not exist in all Odd Fellows lodges of the IOOF.

Organizational Structure | 169

The lodge room of the Reventlow Lodge No. 24 of the Independent Order of Odd Fellows in Nakskov, Denmark, founded on February 12, 1889.

The regalia is a *scarlet sash, collar, or chain* trimmed *white or silver* lace. The jewel of office is a *harp*. The station is usually on the right side of the Noble Grand's station but not on the same level. In most lodges, the musician sits by a piano or organ.

Color Bearer

His or her duty is to present and retire the flag of the country and see that it is properly cared for. This position is *optional* and does not exist in all Odd Fellows lodges of the IOOF. The regalia is a *scarlet sash, collar, or chain* trimmed *white or silver* lace. The jewel of office is the *flag of the country*. The station is in front of the Noble Grand at the right side beside the Warden.

Immediate Past Grand

After serving as Noble Grand, an individual will receive the rank and title of a Past Grand. After his or her term as Noble Grand ends, he or she will serve as Immediate Past Grand and his or her duties are

to deliver the charge to the candidate at initiation and, in many lodges, officiate as outside Conductor and assists in examining and introducing visitors. He or she may also act as Noble Grand or Vice Grand when legally called thereto. The title of Past Grand also makes him or her eligible to receive the *Grand Lodge Degree* and hold office in the Grand Lodge. The regalia is a *scarlet collar or chain* trimmed with *white or silver* lace. Collars usually have *three five-pointed stars* on each side. The jewel of office is a *five-pointed star with a heart and hand* in the center. Station is midway at one side of the room, on the right of the Noble Grand.

Trustees

Depending on the by-laws, a lodge may have at least three (3) or more Trustees who are elected at the same time as the officers of the lodge. They usually serve three (3) terms or more. They function as official agents of the lodge, and handle property and investments subject to approval of the lodge. Trustees are not officers in the same sense as

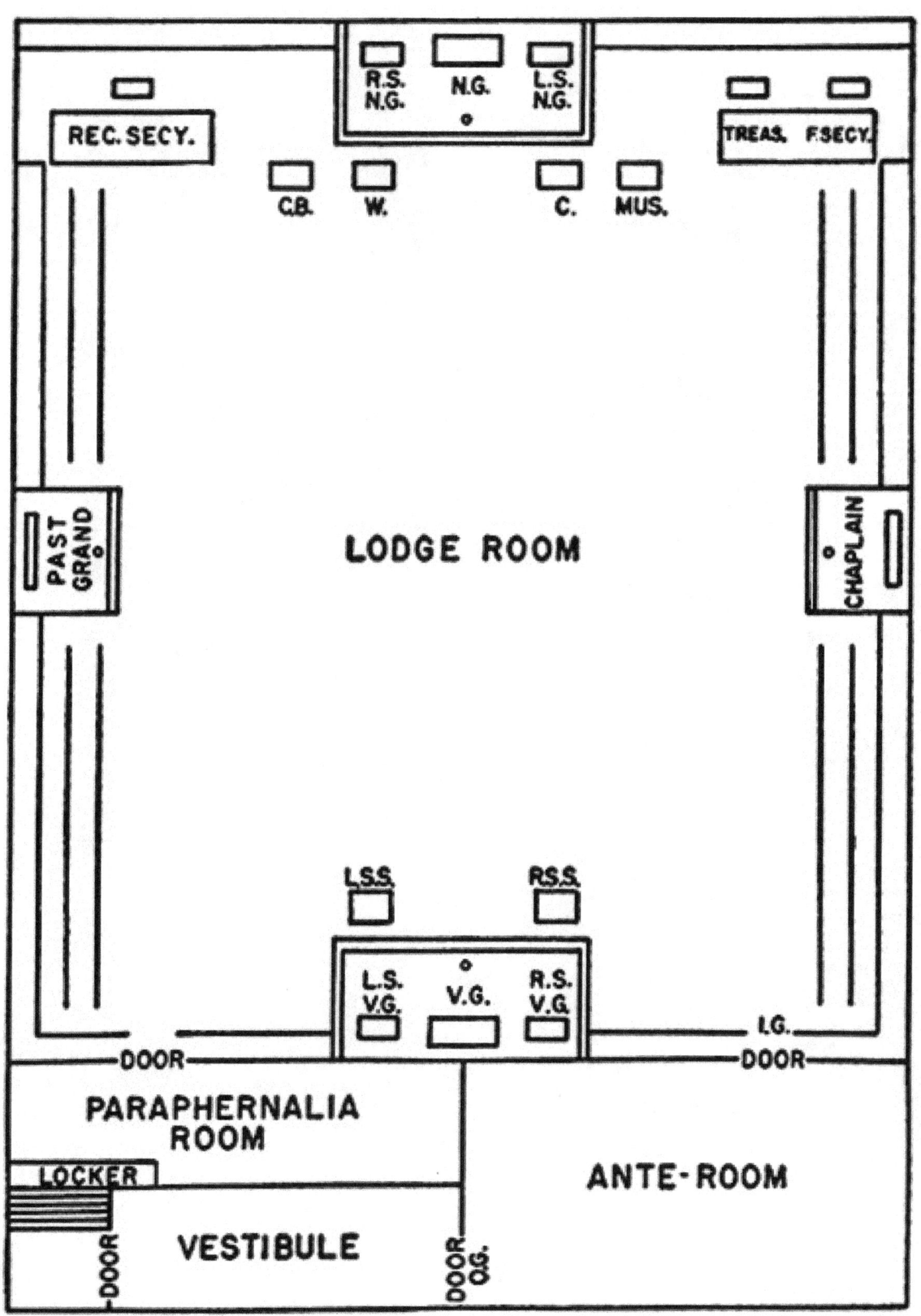

Odd Fellows' meeting rooms around the world follow similar arrangements and each officer sits at a definite location within the room. Illustration courtesy of The Sovereign Grand Lodge, IOOF.

Organizational Structure

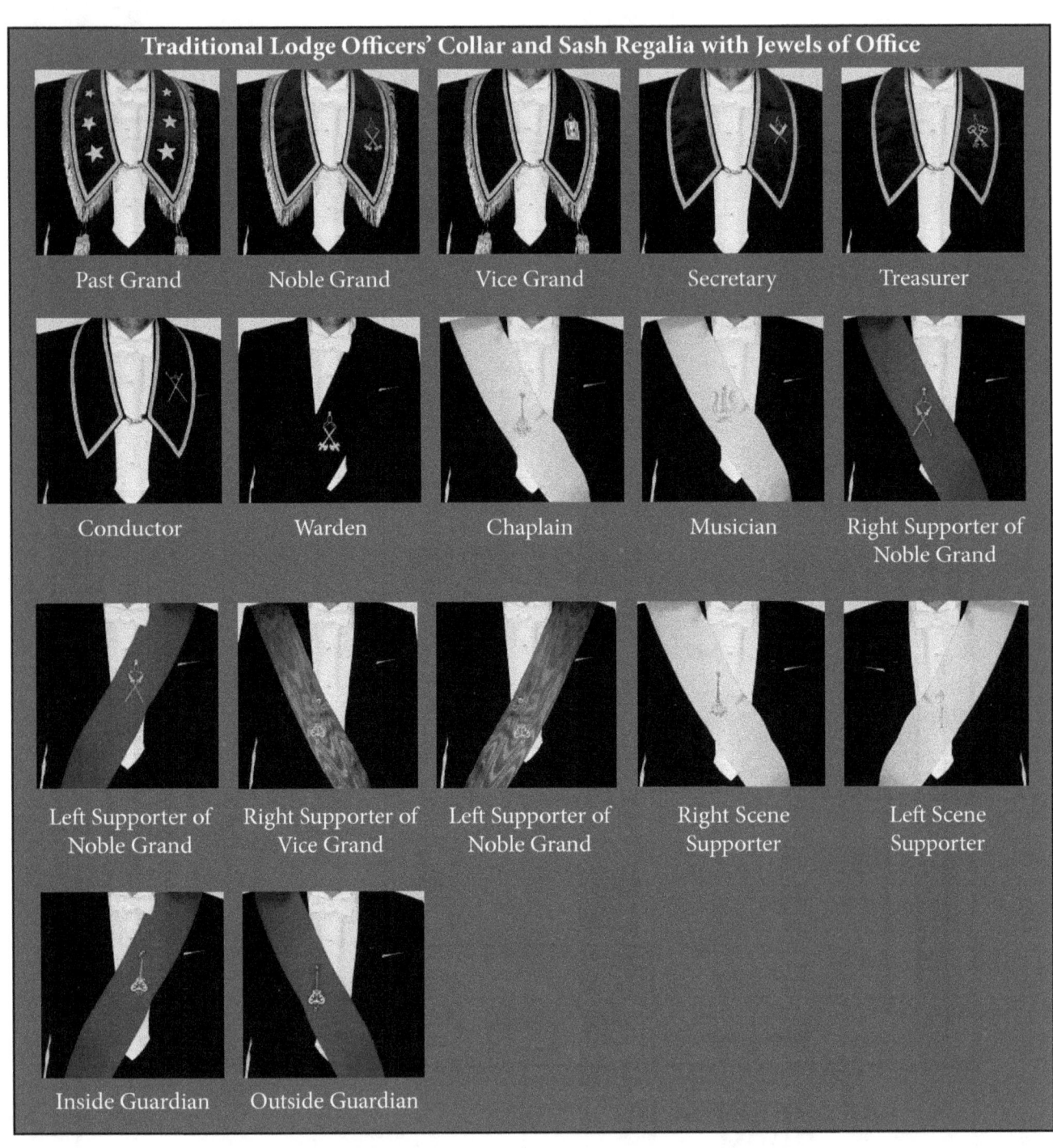

Traditional Lodge Officers' Collar and Sash Regalia with Jewels of Office

Past Grand | Noble Grand | Vice Grand | Secretary | Treasurer

Conductor | Warden | Chaplain | Musician | Right Supporter of Noble Grand

Left Supporter of Noble Grand | Right Supporter of Vice Grand | Left Supporter of Noble Grand | Right Scene Supporter | Left Scene Supporter

Inside Guardian | Outside Guardian

the elective or appointive officers so they may also hold any other office in the lodge unless prohibited by their by-laws.

Grand Lodge

Local lodges can then form a state, provincial, national or territorial organization called a *Grand Lodge*. This governing body can be organized upon the petition of five (5) or more lodges having an aggregate of at least seven (7) or more Past Grands. Each Grand Lodge has exclusive jurisdiction over all local lodges in their State, Province, nation or territory. Grand Lodges consist of Grand Representatives or Alternate Grand Representatives who are Past Grands voted by each lodge. An active lodge shall be entitled to one (1) Representative or one (1) vote for the first fifty (50) members; those lodges with more than fifty (50) members shall be entitled to an additional Representative or additional vote for each fifty (50) members.[4]

To be an officer in the Grand Lodge, a member must have attained the title of Past Grand in a lodge and must receive the *Grand Lodge Degree*. Usually, the elective officers of the Grand Lodge are as follows: Grand Master or Grand Sire, Deputy Grand Master or Deputy Grand Sire, Grand Warden, Grand Secretary, and Grand Treasurer. The appointive officers are usually the following: Grand Marshal, Grand Conductor, Grand Chaplain, Grand Musician, Grand Guardian and Grand Herald. The Grand Lodge may also provide for additional elected or appointed officers: Grand Instructor, Director of Publicity, Grand Color Bearers, etc.

Grand Lodge Officers, Regalia and Their Functions

Grand Master

Velvet collar regalia with Grand Lodge jewel of office. Photo by the author, 2015.

The Grand Master is also called the *Grand Sire* in other countries. His or her duties are to preside over the sessions and meetings of the Grand Lodge, to preserve order, and make sure that the law and mandates coincide with the general purposes and principles of the organization. He or she also presides in ceremonies in instituting new lodges, installing lodge officers, and delivery of the necessary instructions on the work of the organization. The regalia is a *scarlet collar or chain*, but color and design may vary depending on the country. The jewel of office is usually the *Sun with the Scales of Justice* made of white metal.

Deputy Grand Master

The Deputy Grand Master is also called *Deputy Grand Sire* in other countries. His or her duties are to open and close the meetings of the Grand Lodge and preside in the absence of the Grand Master. He or she also performs all duties and make visitations as may be directed by the Grand Master or the Executive Committee. The regalia is a *scarlet collar or chain*, but color and design may vary depending on the country. The jewel of office is a *Half Moon* made of white metal.

Grand Warden

His or her duty is to assist the Grand Master in maintaining law and order in the Grand Lodge. When directed by the Grand Master, he or she takes

charge of the door and presides over the sessions of the Grand Lodge in the absence of the Grand Master and Deputy Grand Master. The regalia is a *scarlet collar or chain,* but color and design may vary depending on the country. His or her jewel of office is a pair of *crossed gavels* made of white metal.

Grand Secretary

His or her duties are to keep an accurate account of the proceedings of the Grand Lodge, write all communications, and issue all notices or summonses under the seal of the Grand Lodge. Usually, the Grand Secretary manages the office and employees of the headquarters of the IOOF in the state, province, nation, or territory. The regalia is a *scarlet collar or chain,* but color and design may vary depending on the country. The jewel of office is a pair of *crossed quills* made of white metal.

Grand Treasurer

His or her duties are to receive all monies collected by the Grand Secretary, to give receipts for these, and deposit the same in depositories under the name of the Grand Lodge. He or she also signs all checks countersigned by the Grand Secretary or other designated signatory. The regalia is a *scarlet collar or chain,* but color and design may vary depending on the country. The jewel of office is a pair of *crossed keys* made of white metal.

Grand Marshal

His or her duties are to assist the Deputy Grand Master in supporting the Grand Master and to supervise the arrangements of all processions ordered or permitted by the Grand Lodge. The regalia is a *scarlet collar or chain,* but color and design may vary depending on the country. The jewel of office is a *baton* of white metal.

Grand Conductor

His or her duties are to examine the certificates for admission, and, if correct, to introduce the bearers to the Grand Lodge. He or she also assists the Grand Marshal in his or her duties. The regalia is a *scarlet collar or chain,* but color and design may vary depending on the country. The jewel of office is a *sword* of white metal.

Grand Guardian

His or her duties are to guard the inner door during Grand Lodge sessions, see to it that anyone who tries to attend the Grand Lodge

Past Grand Master

After serving his or her term, the Grand Master or Grand Sire will receive the rank and title of a Past Grand Master or Past Grand Sire and will hold such designation for a lifetime. The regalia is a *scarlet chain or collar* trimmed with *white or silver lace or fringe*, but color and design may vary depending on the country. Those who have attained the Royal Purple Degree in the Encampment (See Chapter 23) may have trimmings of yellow. The jewel of office is the *Sun with Heart and Hand* of white metal.

sessions is qualified, and ask from members the term password before they can enter. The regalia is *scarlet collar or chain,* but color and design may vary depending on the country. The jewel of office is *crossed swords* of white metal.

Grand Herald

The Grand Herald is also called the *Grand Messenger* in other countries. His or her duties are to announce the Grand Master during ceremonials, and to precede and usher the Grand Lodge officers in its processions. He or she is the messenger of the Grand Lodge and is equivalent to the outside guardian in the lodge. The regalia is *scarlet collar or chain*, but color and design may vary depending on the country. The jewel of office is a *trumpet* of white metal.

Grand Chaplain

His or her duties are to open and close the Grand Lodge with a prayer and to officiate at public ceremonials and funerals which are under special charge of the Grand Lodge. In some Grand Lodges, the Grand Chaplain is an *optional* office. The regalia is *scarlet collar or chain*, but color and design may vary depending on the country. The jewel of office is an open *Holy Bible, Holy Book* or *Book of Sacred Law* of white metal.

Grand Musician

His or her duty is to play required music or accompaniment during grand lodge sessions and ceremonies. In some Grand Lodges, the Grand Musician is *optional*. The regalia is *scarlet collar or chain*, but color and design may vary depending on the country. The jewel of office is a *harp* of white metal.

Grand Color Bearer

His or her duty is to present and retire the flag of the country, state, province, or territory during Grand Lodge sessions and see that it is properly cared for. In some Grand

Organizational Structure | 175

Lodges, the Grand Color Bearer is *optional*. The regalia is *scarlet collar or chain*, but color and design may vary depending on the country. The jewel of office is a *flag of the nation in which the* Grand Lodge *is located* made of white metal.

The Sovereign Grand Lodge

The supreme governing body of the Independent Order of Odd Fellows is the *Sovereign Grand Lodge* which consists of dues-paying Grand Lodges, Grand Encampments and Grand Bodies all over the United States and Canada.[5] Grand Lodges directly under the Sovereign Grand Lodge are represented by one (1) to three (3) votes during Sovereign Grand Lodge sessions. Each Grand Lodge with a combined membership of 1,000 or more members, based on regular and non-contributing members from Odd Fellows Lodges, Junior Lodges, Rebekah Lodges and Theta Rho Girls' Clubs; each Grand Encampment with a combined membership of 1,000 or more members, based on regular and non-contributing members from Encampments and Ladies Encampment Auxiliaries; is entitled to *two (2) Grand Representatives* or *two (2) votes*. Grand Lodges or Grand Encampments with less than 1,000 members are entitled to *one (1) Grand Representative* or *one (1) vote*.[6] The General Military Council is entitled to *one (1) Grand Representative* or *one (1) vote*.[7] The International Association of Rebekah Assemblies is entitled to *one (1) Grand Representative* or *one (1) vote*.[8] In some respects, the Sovereign Grand Lodge resembles the United States Senate in that the classification of its members secures its perpetuity. It is also similar to the United States House of Representatives in that the number of representatives is dependent on the respective constituencies. Representatives of Independent Grand Lodges, on the other hand, are *non-voting members* having the right only to make motions and debate questions.[9] In its current setting, no Grand Representative outside the jurisdiction of the United States and Canada can become an elective officer of the Sovereign Grand Lodge. So, the Sovereign Grand Lodge is really the governing body for North American jurisdictions (U.S. and Canada). But it is not an international governing body in the real sense.

The elective officers of the Sovereign Grand Lodge are as follows: Sovereign Grand Master, Deputy Sovereign Grand Master, Sovereign Grand Warden, Sovereign Grand Secretary, and Sovereign Grand Treasurer chosen among the Grand Representatives of each Grand Lodge directly under the Sovereign Grand Lodge. There are also appointed officers namely: Sovereign Grand Marshal, Sovereign Grand Conductor, Sovereign Grand Chaplain, Sovereign Grand Musician, Sovereign Grand Guardian, and Sovereign Grand Messenger. Their functions are almost synonymous with that of the Grand Lodge but their roles are on the Sovereign Grand Lodge level.

Independent Grand Lodges

Other countries outside North America where there are IOOF lodges can form *Independent Grand Lodges*. Generally, these Grand Lodges possess final and supervisory powers over the lodges within their jurisdiction and adhere only to the founding principles and ancient customs of the IOOF. These jurisdictions include the Grand Lodge of Australasia, Denmark, Finland, Germany, Iceland, Cuba, The Netherlands and Belgium, Norway, Philippines, Poland, Sweden, and Switzerland. The Sovereign Grand Master usually appoints a D*istrict Deputy Sovereign Grand Master* to serve as liaison officer between an Independent Grand Lodge and the Sovereign Grand Lodge. Typically, the District Deputy Sovereign Grand Master is the same as the

Grand Master or Grand Sire of the Grand Lodge. These Independent Grand Lodges have a seat in the International Advisory Board.

Grand Lodge of Europe

There had been discussions of establishing a governing body for the IOOF in the continent of Europe since the 1890s.[10] Grand Sires of European jurisdictions had been holding a Conference of the European Grand Sires for many years. This eventually led to the establishment of the *Federation of Independent European Jurisdictions of the Odd Fellow Order IOOF* in 1989.[11] During the same year, the leaders of the Rebekahs in Europe also established the *European Rebekah Leaders Association* (ERLA). In 2003, the Executive Committees of both the Federation and ERLA realized that the time has come to assemble both male and female leaders in one Grand body.[12]

This eventually culminated in the *Grand Lodge of Europe* in 2006.[13] This Grand Lodge is empowered to direct, supervise, and control all matters pertaining to the Independent Order of Odd Fellows within and throughout Europe except the United Kingdom of Great Britain, Northern Ireland and the Republic of Ireland, which are under the jurisdiction of the Manchester Unity Independent Order of Odd Fellows.[14] The criteria for membership and election to an office in the Grand Lodge of Europe are: 1) be a Grand Lodge Officer or Past Grand Lodge Officer in a European Jurisdiction; 2) have received the *Degree of Wisdom*.[15] The officers of the Grand Lodge of Europe are: the European Grand Sire, one male Deputy European Grand Sire, one female Deputy European Grand Sire, European Grand Secretary, Deputy European Grand Secretary, European Grand Treasurer, European Grand Marshal and European Grand Chaplain.[16]

The officers of the Independent Grand Lodges in Europe do not use the scarlet or red collar regalia like those used by Grand Lodges directly under the Sovereign Grand Lodge. To be a Grand Lodge officer in Europe, one must not only be a *Past Grand* in the Lodge but also a *Royal Purple Degree* member in the Encampment. Thus, their Grand Lodge officers wear a *purple or violet* collar regalia with *scarlet or red* upper rim decorated with *three white stars* on each side. But each IOOF Grand Lodge in Europe has a unique regalia for their Grand Sire.

Photo courtesy of The Sovereign Grand Lodge, IOOF.

Grand Lodge of Asia Pacific

In 2018, the Grand Lodge of Australasia and the Grand Lodge of the Philippines constituted themselves into the Grand Lodge of Asia Pacific to direct, supervise, and control all matters pertaining to the Independent Order of Odd Fellows within and throughout Australia, New Zealand, Asia, and the Pacific.

International Advisory Board

Before World War II, communication between the Sovereign Grand Lodge and Grand Lodges outside North America was challenging. The distance and difficulties during the war years made close relationships difficult and even severed relationships between the Sovereign Grand Lodge and several Grand Lodges in other countries. In 1946, a legislation was passed to form the International Council. The aim of the council was

The Official Certificate, otherwise known as *Annual Dues Card*, is issued annually to members in good standing after payment of their dues. This card must be presented when visiting lodges or attending Sessions of the Grand Lodge.

From the collection of Watchdog Lodge No.1, IOOF, Philippines, 1918.

to strengthen the ties between the Sovereign Grand Lodge and all Grand Lodges of the IOOF; to protect the usage, customs, and ancient teachings of the organization; exchange ideas, discuss concerns, and make endorsements to all affiliated bodies of Odd Fellows around the world. This body was renamed the *IOOF International Advisory Board* in 2012.

The Board meets a day prior to the Sovereign Grand Lodge Sessions and consist of four (4) members of the Sovereign Grand Lodge, three (3) members of the International Association of Rebekah Assemblies, one (1) from the General Military Council, three (3) from the Grand Lodge of Europe, three (3) from the Grand Lodge of Australasia, and two (2) from the *Manchester Unity Independent Order of Oddfellows Friendly Society* in the United Kingdom. The Board will be able to create recommendations to the Sovereign Grand Lodge but without legislative authority.

Funds

The IOOF raises funds through membership fees, annual dues and donations. Each individual lodge enjoy some level of financial autonomy from the Grand Lodge and the Sovereign Grand Lodge. But all funds raised by each Lodge, Grand Lodge and the Sovereign Grand Lodge are trust funds and are to be used only for the purposes collected.[17] Excess funds may be invested in safe and marketable securities.

To be a *member in good standing*, one must regularly pay his annual dues to Lodge, Grand Lodge and/or the Sovereign Grand Lodge. The amount of annual dues payable by contributing members shall be determined by the by-laws of the lodge, Grand Lodge and the Sovereign Grand Lodge. But the dues charged must be sufficient to meet the expenses and obligations of the organization.[18] Should the expenses and current liabilities for any year be in excess of the income and current assets, on hand, to an extent that it might tend to impair the financial standing of the lodge, an assessment shall be levied by the lodge on all contributing members to meet the deficiency.[19] Dues are payable in advance usually before January 31st of each year, but at the option of a member may be paid quarterly in advance.[20]

After paying the annual dues, a member in good standing is issued an *Official Certificate* or *Annual Dues Card* by the Secretary or Financial Secretary which expires after one (1) year and an *Annual Traveling Password* (ATP) which is also changed yearly. To visit other lodges and attend Sessions of any Grand Lodge, a member in good standing must present his or her Official Certificate showing dues paid up-to-date.[21] The effect of non-payment of annual dues and membership fees for one (1) year shall warrant suspension of membership in the Independent Order of Odd Fellows after being notified of arrearage and a proper record of the notice made in the minutes of the lodge.[22] However, a suspended member may have his or her membership re-instated upon payment of his or her arrears in the annual dues.

Chapter 22

INITIATION DEGREES, REGALIA, AND CUSTOMS

In order to fully understand the mission and vision of Odd Fellowship, it is a custom that candidates undergo a formal and solemn ceremony that involves a series of instructions divided into degrees. Traditionally, these degrees of initiation are presented largely by means of lectures, drama, and symbols where every stage or degree concentrates on one of the principles of the organization.

For fraternal organizations like the Odd Fellows, each degree is a time for reflection for the candidates. The goal is to give new members an experience that is unique from everyday life while imparting wise lessons and noble principles that are applicable to daily life. These rituals are also "a means by which members could define one another as brothers and sisters."[1] It is common belief that the bond between people is stronger when they share common knowledge and experiences.

An illustration of an Odd Fellows lodge meeting held inside the Gothic room of the Odd Fellows Hall in New York.
From the *Odd Fellows Family Companion*, January 3, 1852.

The local projects and social events of each lodge may vary because each city or country has its own unique culture and local needs. But the lessons in the degrees, symbols, handgrip, signs, and passwords are almost the same across the world. Understanding and learning these universal symbols of Odd Fellowship will allow members, regardless of nationality, to have a shared mission, vision, and core organizational values. By sharing private ceremonies, secret handsigns and symbols, members are also linked by a sense of exclusivity which increases group cohesion and builds a sense of belongingness.

When a member visits an Odd Fellows lodge in a different city or country, he or she will feel "at home" because the ceremonies are performed almost in the same way. Through these rituals, members are welded together and will feel a sense of belonging in their pursuit of the Odd Fellows' high ideals, ethics and teachings. But it is the lessons taught by the degrees, not the degrees themselves, which are fundamental.[2] The degrees are complementary to and not the primary purpose of the organization's existence.[3] Having shared customs and core values is very important in every organization. San Francisco Metaphysical lecturer Dadisi Sanyika observed:

> "Where there is no formal initiation process, an unconscious rite of passage will occur. This unconscious initiation will often be anti-social rather than a systematic transmission of values and knowledge. Initiation into urban street gangs is a case in point, where the aspects of initiation appear in a process that does not renew the community or its values."

There is no hazing or horseplay in the initiation rituals of Odd Fellowship. There is nothing sinister that happens inside the lodge rooms. Although a certain level of secrecy or privacy prevails around its ceremonies, the Odd Fellows is in no sense an esoteric, occult or secret society. The Independent Order of Odd Fellows has a very public agenda to promote and does not claim any secret knowledge to conceal from the public. In fact, its initiation ceremonies today are largely drawn from the Old Testament. For the most part, the initiation rituals only serve as a method of teaching the candidate the ethical lessons and core principles shared among members and, at the same time, provide a sense of mystery and fascination to both members and candidates. In the past, the degrees also provided entertainment at a time when television and other modern leisure activities did not exist as yet. If done properly, witnessing an initiation ritual is like watching a theatrical play and also gives a sense of decorum during meetings.[4]

Evolution of the Initiation

The degrees of initiation in Odd Fellowship has evolved through time. Because of the numerous *Affiliated Orders* of Odd Fellows that previously existed, there occur several variations of the initiation rituals today. Whenever new Affiliated Orders were created either through merger or secession, the older initiation rituals were often revised or completely replaced although some of the general teachings remained the same. Newer Odd Fellows' groups are usually factions of older organizations due to dissatisfaction or disagreement. Thus, for these newer groups to preserve the old records and ceremonial practices of their predecessor is unlikely.

As gleaned from past practices, a resolution is often passed by the leaders of newer Affiliated Orders to destroy older versions of the rituals to prevent any revival. Presumably, this is one reason why only a few of the printed ancient rituals survived

Rites of Passage

Because of bad publicity, the terms *initiation*, *ritual* and *rite* are widely misunderstood and often erroneously associated with witchcraft, magic, satanic cults, blood oaths, and hazing. But an *initiation* is merely defined as "a ceremony or series of actions that makes a person a member of a group or organization."[1] When prospective students are required to undergo written tests and interviews before being admitted to a college or university, this is a form of initiation. When a person is required to undergo a series of training or levels of education before being ordained as a pastor or priest in a church or before receiving a college degree, the person is actually undergoing a form of initiation. A *ritual* or *rite*, on the other hand, is defined as "a formal ceremony or series of acts that is always performed in the same way."[2] Human life involves a series of major and minor ritual practices or events. Brushing one's teeth after eating or taking a bath before sleeping are examples of simple forms of ritual. Many Christian churches use rituals, such as when the priest or pastor offers the sacraments during mass or service.

Basically, initiation rituals or *rites of passage* are "ceremonies that accompany and dramatize major events such as birth, coming-of-age of boys and girls, marriage and death, or joining a certain society".[3] Rituals tend to present themselves as "the unchanging, time-honored customs of an enduring community."[4] Examples of common rites of passage are birthday celebrations usually observed once a year, marriage ceremonies, graduation or commencement ceremonies, and funeral rites.

Circumcision is an ancient rite of passage usually performed on boys to symbolize their transition from adolescence to adulthood. Photo source: wiki-commons, public domain.

Religions, on the other hand, have more complex rituals and requirements. Baptism in religions signifies that one has joined the church and is to be considered a part of the congregation. In Catholicism, the *rite of baptism* is believed to remove the stain of original sin by Adam and Eve and brings the child or person into the community of those "reborn" in the name of Jesus. This is usually followed by a *rite of reconciliation* at about seven years of age and then by the *rite of first communion* in which the child consumes a piece of bread sanctified as the body and blood of Jesus Christ. When a child reaches age twelve, *a rite of confirmation* follows. This may be followed by a *rite of marriage* [much later], and then the *last rites* in which a dying person confesses his or her sins and is anointed with oil. In Hinduism, there are about 10 to 40 rites of passage, which also start from birth to death.[5]

These rites are therefore a part of the cultural and religious traditions of humankind. The practice of *rites of passage* or *initiation rituals* has no geographical or paternal origins. They exist in various forms in almost all cultures in the world. It is human nature that when a group of people live together as a community, they will eventually develop certain customs and practices common to their group.

Some of these ceremonies are shared by many that a population already considers them a part of public life. There are initiation rituals, however, which are not obligatory for all members of the community and is performed only for membership in a certain group. These rituals would be for joining a specific religion, fraternal organization, college fraternity or sorority, or club.[6] These practices and customs can be used for decades until newer versions take place.

A *de facto* argument suggests that the practice of initiation rituals among English fraternal organizations like the Odd Fellows was an evolution of the rites of the ancient mysteries, guilds, and journeymen associations and was influenced by people's fascination of theatrical plays. As early as the Middle Ages, "brothering" was a common ceremonial practice among trade associations and clubs in England and Scotland.[7] These customs differ across groups, but were commonly performed inside taverns and pubs, involved a lecture mixed with some horseplay and pranks, and adjourned with food and drinks for all paid for by the newcomer.[8] During the early days of Odd Fellowship, new members were admitted by way of a single degree, called a "Making" or "Initiation", and this ceremony bore very close resemblance with the "brothering" rituals practiced by journeymen and laborers.[9]

the past couple of centuries. Evidence do suggest that the succession chronologically began with the *Ancient Order of Odd Fellows*, which changed to the *Improved Order of Odd Fellows*, the *Patriotic Order of Odd Fellows*, the *Union or United Order of Odd Fellows*, and the *Manchester Unity Independent Order of Odd Fellows* from which the *Independent Order of Odd Fellows* seceded.[5]

It had been suggested that the earliest ritualistic ceremonies of the Odd Fellows consisted only of an *initiation* or *making* and a form of *opening and closing* the lodge.[6] Just like in similar English fraternal organizations, the additional degrees and dramatic work in Odd Fellowship were an evolution of later years because of the demand for additional attractions in the ceremonies.[7] The oldest surviving initiation rituals and degrees belonged to the *Order of Patriotic Odd Fellows* as revised and agreed by their Grand Lodge in London on March 12, 1797. It contained an *Opening and Closing Service*, an

During the 18th century, the candidate is blind-folded, brought into the meeting room almost naked, and assisted to walk on a set of loose wooden planks to symbolize the uncertainty of life. This rite was acceptable in the past but no longer performed since the beginning of the 19th century. However, the symbolic lessons have been preserved using other means.
Illustration by Asher Alpay as commissioned by the author, 2015.

Initiation, *White or Degree of Covenant*, *Royal Blue Degree*, and *Pink or Merit Degree*, *Royal Arch of Titus or Fidelity Degree*, and *Scarlet Degree or Priestly Degree*.[8] The degrees were conferred one after the other, one degree only every three or four months.

The oldest known *initiatory degree* was emblematic of the life of mankind. A candidate entered the lodge room stripped of his clothing, which was symbolic of birth. The imaginary road was thick with dangers. This was intended to represent the various challenges and difficulties that people encounter in real life. The eyes were blindfolded to represent ignorance and denote that in our walk through life we are in darkness and do not know what might happen tomorrow. At the end of the initiation, a scene of mortality was shown to represent the end of life, to remind the candidate that life here on earth is temporary to convince the new member to live a life of usefulness, always ready to help where help is needed. At the end of the ceremony, the Warden of the lodge explained:[9]

> "Friend, this scene represents the storm of life, when clouds and darkness are around about you, and dangers and difficulties strewn thick in your path. Learn from this scene to pity and sympathize with all unfortunates; when you hear of national calamities, remember the emblematical pains you endured."

This initiation ceremony is no longer exactly the same ceremony being practiced by the IOOF and other surviving *Affiliated Orders* today. The candidate is not stripped of his or her clothing anymore, but the general lessons are somehow identical. In 1814, the Manchester Unity Independent Order of Odd Fellows began revising the old ritualistic work. The first printed ritual of the Manchester Unity IOOF divided the degrees into the *Initiation* or *Making*;

The degrees are traditionally done with full set of costumes and props. Photo shows the Degree Team for the First Degree or Degree of Friendship during the early 1900s. Photo from the collection of the author

First Degree or *White*; *Second Degree* or *Royal Blue*, *Scarlet Degree* or *Priestly Order*.[10] There was also a lecture book that consisted of *Lectures to Prove a Secretary*, *Lectures to Prove a Vice Grand*, and *Lecture to Prove a Past Grand*.[11] This had been revised many times since 1816.[12]

For a time, the Independent Order of Odd Fellows in the United States adopted similar rituals with those of the Manchester Unity IOOF. In 1820, the Grand Lodge of the United States added the degrees of *Covenant* and *Remembrance* written by John Pawson Entwisle.[13] Both degrees appeared in the rituals of the MUIOOF and IOOF in 1826.[14] By 1835, the ritualistic work had been divided into the *Initiatory Degree, First Degree, Degree of the Covenant, Second Degree or Royal Blue, Degree of Remembrance, Scarlet Degree or Priestly Order*.[15] The same lecture book also contained merit degrees for the Secretary, Vice Grand, and Noble Grand.[16]

In 1834, the MUIOOF revised the lecture book and dropped the *degrees of the Covenant and Remembrance*. This, along with other substantial revisions, led to the separation of the MUIOOF and the IOOF. Afterwards, the IOOF further revised the ritualistic works into the *Initiatory Degree* and five degrees, namely: *White or First Degree, Pink or Second Degree (Covenant), Blue or Third Degree, Green or Fourth Degree (Remembrance)*, and *Scarlet or Fifth Degree*.[17] This system of degrees continued without material change until 1880 when the number of degrees was reduced to three. A number of amendments followed but these only involved minor alterations.

Lodge Degrees

Initiatory Degree

The Initiatory degree is an introduction to the Odd Fellows lodge. During this degree, the candidate will witness a representation of mortality, the temporary nature of life on earth, which begs the question "how will I live my life?" It is a common characteristic of many ancient rites that they begin in sorrow and gloom, but end up in life and joy. The symbolic purpose is to remind men of their weakness, their ignorance, their sinfulness of character and the shortness and uncertainty of life.[18] Being reminded of death as unstoppable, the candidate is encouraged to live a virtuous life. The regalia is a *white* collar with *white* lining.

First Degree or Degree of Friendship.

This degree reenacts an ancient story to exemplify the lesson of true friendship. True friends will help, protect, and rejoice in each other's accomplishments and will not be divided by jealous competitions and personal desires. This degree suggests that Odd Fellows stick together through good and bad times. The regalia is a *white* collar with *pink* lining.

Second Degree or Degree of Love

This degree is likewise based on an ancient story, depicting the lesson of brotherly and sisterly love which transcends race, religion or nationality. As an Odd Fellow, one is expected to make the same commitment not to look at people with prejudiced eyes. This is based on the Golden Rule: "*Do unto others as you would have them do unto you.*" The person who serves others, serves himself or herself best. The degree further teaches the candidate that fraternity, unless linked with acts of kindness, is but an empty name. The regalia is a *white* collar with *royal blue* lining.

Third Degree or Degree of Truth

In this degree, the member is introduced to the symbols of Odd Fellowship and their philosophical meanings. The candidate is reminded of the many truths they can apply in their daily lives. And that Odd Fellows must be committed to those truths. By knowing this, the member is expected to speak the truth and apply honesty in all his or her dealings with his or her church, community, lodge, and family. It reminds the member to practice truth in all actions and not just through words. The regalia is a *white* collar with *scarlet* or *red* lining.

But all these degrees are better understood when personally experienced. Traditionally, there is a minimum waiting period between receiving the Initiatory Degree, the Degree of Friendship, and all other succeeding degrees. During this period, a new member must attend lodge meetings regularly, serve on committees, and take a full and active part in the affairs of the lodge.[19] This will give the new member time to reflect on the lessons received, learn how meetings are conducted, and get to know more the other members. After attaining the Third Degree or Degree of Truth in the *Lodge*, the new member is eligible to receive higher degrees offered through branches such as the *Encampment* and the *Patriarchs Militant* (See Chapter 23).

Working Degree

In the beginning, Odd Fellows lodges open and hold their meetings in the *Initiatory Degree*. In 1881, the working degree was changed to the *Degree of Truth* or *Third Degree*.[20] The working degree reverted back to the Initiatory Degree in 1973. This is to allow a new member to participate in the

The Yreka Odd Fellows Lodge No. 19 in California annually hosts the "Cave Degree" since 1940. Customarily, the Initiatory Degree and the First Degree are conferred in the afternoon. After dinner, the participants proceed to the cave to receive the Second Degree. The next day, candidates receive the Third Degree. The 40-acre surrounding area of the cave was purchased by the IOOF in 1962. Photo courtesy of Peter Sellars, 2014.

meetings. This idea originated in Sweden and was adopted by all IOOF lodges throughout the world.

Funeral Ceremony

The funeral ceremony, sometimes referred to as the *last degree*, is performed by the members of the lodge to honor every departed member. The ceremony begins with a speech delivered by the Noble Grand and a prayer by the Chaplain. The Noble Grand then advances to the coffin and cast into it, with the right hand, the *sprig of evergreen*. The other members shall then advance to the coffin and also cast into it the sprigs of evergreen. This ceremony is in line with the duty and one of the missions of Odd Fellowship, "To bury the dead".

Handshakes, Passwords and Symbols

For each degree are confidential or private hand signs, grips, and passwords, known as *The Unwritten Work* (TUW). Historically, the Odd Fellows provided material and financial aid for their members in times of sickness, economic distress, or for finding employment when out of work. Because of this benefit, there were many instances when some people would pretend to be members to defraud or obtain funds from the lodge. So, how can the Odd Fellows verify membership and protect their funds from impostors? How can a person prove that he is a member eligible to avail himself of the fraternal benefits?

As there were no telephones at that time and the mode of communication was still very slow, secret hand signs, grips, passwords and symbols were created mainly to verify membership and protect the funds of the organization from impostors.[33] These tools are really unimportant to the outside world since they served simply the purpose of mutual recognition between members.[21] The logic behind this is almost the same why banks and people today

In the 18th and early 19th centuries, symbolism was a very important way of communicating ideas at a time when illiteracy was widespread. It allowed people from various social classes to understand each other whether or not they could read or write. Illustration courtesy of The Sovereign Grand Lodge, IOOF.

use secret PINs and passwords to protect their money from theft or fraud.

Until today, the Independent Order of Odd Fellows has preserved these hand signs, grips, passwords, and symbols mainly to honor a tradition. For many members, these still remain as a faster way of identifying each other even without the assistance of modern technology, although some think they are nonsense. Moreover, these signs and symbols stand as reminders for some of the basic ethical principles and teachings of the fraternity. Some of the moral

Initiation Degrees, Regalia, and Customs | 187

Variations of the Odd Fellows' regalia through the years

From upper left: A sash and apron of the Manchester Unity IOOF. The second photo is an early 1800s collar and apron belonging to the IOOF. The use of apron in the IOOF disappeared in 1881. The third photo is a 19th century IOOF collar regalia with officer's jewel. **From lower left:** Rope-type regalia with officer's jewel commonly used by the IOOF lodges in the Netherlands, Belgium, Cuba, and some lodges in the United States. The second photo shows the modern chain-type regalia with officer's jewel. The third photo is another version, a velvet-type regalia with officer's jewel. Photos by the author, 2019.

lessons of the IOOF are actually incorporated as symbolic meanings of the unwritten work. These signs, grips, passwords, and symbols are designed to speak one universal language to the initiated of every nationality across the world. The passwords are not translated into any other language, nor spoken other than as they are written. This is for every member to learn to give them "one universal sound as nearly as possible, so that the sound of the password will be familiar to the ear as the signs are to the eye, or the grip to the touch of the hand, to the end that an Odd Fellow of any country may be known and recognized in any part of the inhabited globe as a brother or sister." [22]

Regalia

There is a resemblance in regalia among various fraternal organizations and friendly societies with English origins. This is because almost all fraternal organizations bought their regalia from the same tailor, manufacturer, or vendor. Regalia were often mass-produced using the same materials and equipment, thus, resulting in similarities in form and design. The similarity between the Odd Fellows and Masonic regalia had led past historians to vaguely assume that Odd Fellowship copied from Freemasonry. However, the use of regalia such as the collar and the apron did not wholly originate from the Freemasons, although they might have helped popularize it.[23] Rather, this tradition originated from the English guilds. According to historian Victoria Solt Dennis:

> "It seems generally true that all the various groups, including the Odd Fellows and Freemasons, were drawing on a common folk tradition of civic and guild dress and custom."

The Manchester Unity Independent Order of Odd Fellows (MUIOOF) and Grand United Order of Odd Fellows (GUOOF) retained the use of both collars and aprons as part of their regalia. The Independent Order of Odd Fellows (IOOF), on the other hand, abandoned the use of aprons when it revised its rituals in 1881.[24] The recorded reason was to relieve the membership from the burden of the cost of too many regalia. Another plausible reason was to get rid of a public misconception.

As early as the 18th century, there had been political and religious oppositions against Freemasonry especially from the Roman Catholic Church. This worsened in the United States following the alleged murder of William Morgan by the Freemasons in 1826. Anti-Masonic sentiments by religious and political groups as well as by conspiracy theorists continued even until the present. This affected the public perception towards the IOOF and other fraternal organizations, because many people including the Church could not distinguish the Freemasons from the Odd Fellows owing to the similarities in their regalia.

In the 1870s, the Sovereign Grand Lodge even received inquiries from leaders of religious groups asking about the relationship between the Odd Fellows with the Freemasons. In fact, critics of Odd Fellowship used similarity in regalia such as the apron to support their argument that the Odd Fellows and Freemasons are one and the same (See Chapter 24). On the other hand, some Freemasons mistakenly accused the Odd Fellows as a copycat of Freemasonry, using similarities such as the use of apron as evidence for their allegations. This, among other reasons, perhaps led to why the IOOF eventually got rid of the apron and only retained the collar as official regalia.

Circa 1820, three-flapped Odd Fellows' Degree of Truth or Scarlet Degree apron showing some of the early symbols used by Odd Fellowship: heart-and-hand, all-seeing-eye, ark, sun, moon and seven stars, globe, skull and crossbones, hour glass, quiver, serpent, coffin, and bow-and-arrows. Photo by the author, 2012.

Chapter 23

BRANCHES

The Odd Fellows is analogous to a university composed of several colleges that offer different degrees under its wing. While the IOOF is a single entity, it consists of several branches that aim to serve specific interests among men, women, and youth. These branches have their own set of officers, regalia, membership fees and dues, degrees of initiation, symbolism, signs, and passwords.

Rebekahs

In the days long gone, women were expected to just stay at home. They were not allowed to go to school, own a property, practice a profession, vote, hold public office, or join civic associations. In 1846, the IOOF allowed Odd Fellows Lodges to issue official identification cards to wives and widows of members. This led to a proposal to create a Degree for women, but this idea endured years of consideration because of the legal status of women at that time.

Eventually, the IOOF deviated from the trends of those times; it became the first international fraternal organization to officially accept women when it adopted the *Rebekah Degree* on September 20, 1851. The degree was written by Schuyler Colfax, who later became the Vice President of the United States from 1869 to 1873.

The Rebekah Degree began as an honorary award only, which was conferred on wives and daughters of Odd Fellows at special lodge meetings, and recipients were known as *Daughters of Rebekah*. Later, the women were allowed to take parts in the ceremony and confer the degree on other women. The system further improved in 1868 when the Rebekahs were eventually given the right to vote and elect their own officers, charge for initiation fees, collect dues, and undertake charitable and benevolent activities. This was way before the women's rights' movement and way before women were granted suffrage by the United States government. Its success encouraged many other fraternal organizations and clubs to follow the example of the IOOF and create women's branches within their organizations.

To be a Rebekah, one must be at least sixteen (16) years old and of good character. The name Rebekah was taken from one of the prominent women in history, Rebecca, whose story started when she gave water to a stranger and his camels. Hence, a character who was charitable, generous, and kind. The Rebekahs as a sisterhood pledge themselves to follow her example. The general duties of the Rebekahs are: "*To live peaceably, do good unto all, as we have opportunity and especially to obey the Golden Rule, Whatsoever ye would that others should do unto you, do ye even so unto them.*" Traditionally, there is only one degree as still practiced in most Rebekah Lodges in North America. In European countries, however, the Rebekah Lodge ritual was revised into four (4) degrees to resemble that of the Odd Fellows Lodge, although the branch continues

"From Jerusalem to Jericho," an early illustration of the different degrees and branches within the Independent Order of Odd Fellows: Odd Fellows Lodge, Rebekah Lodge, Encampment, and Patriarchs Militant. Illustration by The Pettibone Print, 1890.

Rebekah Lodge Officers in full regalia. Photo courtesy of Georgian Rebekah Lodge No.276, 1937.

to have their own regalia, signs, passwords, and symbols.[1] The regalia is a collar or badge of *pink and green*.

The basic unit is called a *Rebekah Lodge* or *Sister Lodge*. A Rebekah Lodge is organized upon receipt by a Rebekah Assembly, Grand Lodge or Sovereign Grand Lodge of a signed petition for a charter or dispensation which must be signed by at least five (5) members who have attained the Rebekah Degree and are in good standing or upon application by at least fifteen (15) persons who are eligible for membership. The elective officers are: Noble Grand, Vice Grand, Secretary, Financial Secretary, and Treasurer. The appointive officers are: Warden, Conductor, Right Supporter of the Noble Grand, Left Supporter of the Noble Grand, Chaplain, Inside Guardian, Outside Guardian, Musician, Color Bearer, Altar Bearers, Banner Bearers, Right Supporter of the Vice Grand and Left Supporter of the Vice Grand.

The governing body for all Rebekah Lodges in a particular state, province, country, or territory is called *Rebekah Assembly*, also referred to as *Rebekah Council* in European jurisdictions. A Rebekah Assembly may be organized upon petition to the Grand Lodge of the jurisdiction for a charter by five (5) or more Rebekah Lodges, having an aggregate of seven (7) or more Past Noble Grands, in a state, province, country, or territory, but no more than one Rebekah Assembly may be chartered in the same state, province, country, or territory. When authorized by the Grand Lodge, the Rebekah Assembly has power to grant charters or dispensations for Rebekah Lodges in their jurisdiction and shall adopt legislation prescribing the methods and procedures.[2] The elective officers of a Rebekah assembly are: President, Vice President, Warden, Secretary, Treasurer, and Representative.[3] The appointive officers are: Marshal, Conductor, Chaplain, Musician, Inside Guardian and Outside Guardian. All the officers and members of the Rebekah Assembly shall be Past Presidents who have received the *Rebekah Assembly Degree*.

The *International Association of Rebekah Assemblies* (IARA) is the international governing body composed of representatives from all the Rebekah Assemblies within the jurisdiction of the Sovereign Grand Lodge. The purpose of this body is to promote Rebekahship in partnership with the Sovereign Grand Lodge. The elective officers are: President, Vice President, Warden, Secretary, and Treasurer. The appointive officers are: Marshal, Conductor, Chaplain, Musician, and two Guardians.

The peak of membership in the Rebekahs was in 1922 when they had more than 1 million active members belonging to 9,793 Rebekah Lodges.[4] Today, the Rebekahs still continue to exist as a separate branch within the IOOF, with their own set of local, national, and international officers. Like a number of Odd Fellows' Lodges in the United States that have become co-ed, membership in the Rebekahs are also open to both women and men. However, majority of the Rebekah Lodges in Europe and Latin America still limit their membership to women. In fact, only the Grand Sire of a particular Grand Lodge in Europe can join the Rebekahs.

As of this writing, there are more or less 80,000 members belonging to 1,304 Rebekah Lodges located in approximately 20 countries. A Rebekah member in good standing may also join higher branches for women such as the *Ladies Encampment Auxiliary* (LEA) and the *Ladies Auxiliary Patriarchs Militant* (LAPM), otherwise known as the *Matriarchs Militant* (MM) in Denmark and Iceland.

Encampment

The Encampment is a higher branch in the Independent Order of Odd Fellows that confers three additional degrees to Third Degree Members in good standing. The degree work in this branch is a result of evolution from additional degrees that were once conferred only to Past Grands of an Odd Fellows Lodge. These degrees originated from both England and the United States and fragmentary records would indicate that these belonged to earlier Odd Fellows groups. A ritual of the *Loyal Ancient Order of Odd Fellows*, which existed many years prior to the IOOF, opened its lodge meetings in the *Golden Rule Degree*.[5] The same ritual has the Purple Degree and its tent emblem appeared as early as 1805. These degrees were conferred and adopted by the Grand Lodge of Maryland at different times. The *Golden Rule Degree* was first conferred to five Past Grands in the United States by one Past Grand Larkham on February 22, 1821.[6] This was followed by the introduction of the *Royal Purple Degree* and the *Patriarchal Degree* in the United States in 1825. On July 6, 1827, these three additional degrees were eventually conferred in a separate branch called *Jerusalem Encampment No.1* that had 524 members at this time.[7] The Encampment degrees are based on the teachings of *Hospitality*, *Toleration*, and *Fortitude*. The motto is: *Faith*, *Hope*, and *Charity*.

To be eligible for the Encampment, one must be a Third Degree member in good standing in his or her lodge. In European countries, conferral of the Encampment Degrees is reserved for dedicated members.[8] Third degree members have to actively participate in lodge meetings and activities for at least 3 to 10 years to be invited in the Encampment. At least two years is required for a member to receive all his Encampment degrees. Upon receiving his Royal Purple Degree, the Patriarch or Matriarch is presented an Encampment ring, nearly identical for all European Jurisdictions, indicating that he or she is an active and devoted member of the Independent Order of Odd Fellows.[9] The Rebekahs also have their own higher branch called the *Ladies Encampment Auxiliary* (LEA). But since 2003, Rebekah members in North America were made eligible to join and receive the degrees in the Encampment. Male members are called *Patriarchs* while female members are called *Matriarchs*.

Encampment Degrees

Patriarchal Degree

This degree is based on the principle of *Hospitality*, and teaches transparent honesty, domestic purity, and unfeigned righteousness. The regalia is a b*lack collar* with a *black lining*.

Golden Rule Degree

This degree is based on the principle of *Toleration*, and teaches good will, and true brotherhood. It teaches that members should unite with the virtuous and good irrespective of race, religion, politics or country in the discharge of duties which all agree are paramount to universal peace and cooperation. The regalia is a b*lack collar* with a *golden yellow lining*.

Royal Purple Degree

This degree is based on the principle of *Fortitude*, and teaches, among others, alertness and determination as basis for a possible success in the journey called life. This degree is a derivation of the 1797 initiatory ceremony of the Patriotic Order. The regalia is a *purple collar* with a *golden yellow* lining.

The local branch is called an *Encampment*. A charter or dispensation for an Encampment may be issued upon a petition signed by at least five (5) Royal Purple Degree members of good standing or by at least five (5) Third Degree members. The elective officers are: Chief Patriarch or Chief Matriarch, High Priest or High Priestess, Senior Warden, Scribe, Financial Scribe, Treasurer, and Junior Warden. The appointive officers are: Guide, Inside Sentinel, Outside Sentinel, First and Second Watch, Third and Fourth Watch, and the First and Second Guard of the Tent.

The state or provincial governing body for the Encampments is called a *Grand Encampment*. A Grand Encampment may be organized upon receipt by the Sovereign Grand Lodge of a signed petition for a charter by seven (7) or more Past Chief Patriarchs of the Grand Encampment Degree from not less than three (3) Encampments within a jurisdiction of the Sovereign Grand Lodge. The petition must be accompanied by the sealed letters from the encampments certifying the rank of the Past Chief Patriarchs. Each Grand Encampment has exclusive jurisdiction over all Encampments within its jurisdiction, and may exercise all power and authority not reserved by the Sovereign Grand Lodge. The elective officers are Grand Patriarch or Grand Matriarch, Grand High Priest or Grand High Priestess, Grand Senior Warden, Grand Scribe, Grand Treasurer, Grand Junior Warden, and Grand Representatives. The appointive officers are the Grand Marshal, Grand Inside Sentinel, Grand Outside Sentinel, and such other officers as may be provided, who are appointed by the Grand Patriarch or Grand Matriarch.[10] In Europe, however, all Encampments fall directly under the authority of their Grand Lodge. As of writing, there are more or less 35,000 Patriarchs and Matriarchs belonging to 513 Encampments located in about 26 countries.

Patriarchs Militant

The Patriarchs Militant (PM) is the uniformed branch of the Independent Order of Odd Fellows, first founded by veterans as the "Patriarchal Circle" right after the American Civil War in 1865. It was a part of the Encampment for several years until it became a separate branch of the IOOF when the Sovereign Grand Lodge granted its approval in 1885. General John Cox Underwood, revered as founder, was instrumental in revising its rituals and formulating its rules and regulations.

Traditionally, membership in the Patriarchs Militant is open to Royal Purple Degree members of good standing. Beginning 2018, the qualification was lowered to Third Degree members and Rebekah Degree members of good standing. Male members are called *Chevaliers* while the female members are called *Ladies*. There are two mottoes: The first one, *Justitia Universalis*, means "*Universal Justice;*" this is the central idea of the Patriarchs Militant. The second, *Pax Aut Bellum*, means "*Peace or War*" and represents the commitment of the Patriarchs Militant to seek "Universal Justice" by peaceful means as well as the more forceful ones commemorated in our symbolism. Therefore, the interpretation of the name Patriarchs Militant is a "*peaceful ruler, serving as a soldier.*"

The basic unit is called a *Canton* with one degree. A Canton is organized upon receipt by the Department Council or the General Military Council of a signed petition for a warrant by five (5) or more members of the Patriarchs Militant Degree or ten (10) persons qualified to become members. The elective officers are: Captain, Lieutenant, Ensign, Clerk, and Accountant. The appointive officers are: Color or Banner Bearer, Guard, Chaplain, Picket, and Sentinel.

Four (4) or more Cantons, having an aggregate of seven (7) or more Past Commandants may form a *Department Council*. The Department is organized into battalions, regiments, brigades or divisions, as the strength of the forces will permit. A battalion shall consist of two (2) to six (6) cantons, a regiment of two (2) to six (6) battalions, a brigade of two (2) or more regiments and a division of two (2) or more brigades. The officers of a Battalion are: Battalion Commander shall have the rank of Major, Chief of Staff and Aide, Adjutant, Quartermaster, Inspector, Judge Advocate, Chaplain and Color Sergeant. The officers of a Regiment are: Regimental Commander with the rank of Colonel, Lieutenant Colonel, Adjutant, and optionally, Inspector, Quartermaster, Equipment Officer, Surgeon or First Aid Officer, Chaplain, Color Sergeant and Bugler. The officers of a Brigade are: Brigade Commander with the rank of Brigadier General, Chief of Staff, Military Advisor, Adjutant and optionally Inspector, Quartermaster, Judge Advocate, Equipment Officer,

Canton Washington No.1 of the Patriarchs Militant with members of the Ladies Militant. Photo from the collection of the author.

The Patriarchs Militant often held public parades in full military costumes, banners, and swords. Photo from the collection of the author.

Branches of the IOOF

The first Patriarchs Militant pilgrimage to Baltimore and Washington, held on September 21-25, 1885 at 459 Pennsylvania Avenue, Washington, D.C. Photo courtesy of The Sovereign Grand Lodge, IOOF.

Surgeon or First Aid Officer, Chaplain, Bannerette and two (2) Aides. The officers of a Division are: Division Commander with the rank of Major General, Chief of Staff, Military Advisor, Adjutant, and optionally Inspector, Quartermaster, Judge Advocate, Equipment Officer, Chaplain, Surgeon or First Aid Officer, Bannerette, and four (4) Aides.

Internationally, the *General Military Council* has general supervision over the Patriarchs Militant Army. The elective officers are: General Commanding, Deputy General Commanding, Executive Officer, Adjutant General and Quartermaster General. The Sovereign Grand Master shall be the Commander-in-Chief and the Sovereign Grand Secretary shall be the Executive Adjutant General.

Ladies Auxiliary Patriarchs Militant

On November 4, 1901, Chevalier Joseph Fairhall, together with his wife and some Rebekahs, launched the *Ladies Militant Auxiliary Association*. This group established several units across the United States called Fortresses. After much consideration, the group was eventually approved by the Sovereign Grand Lodge in 1915 as the Ladies Auxiliary Patriarchs Militant (LAPM).[11] In Denmark and Iceland, the women's branch is called the *Matriarchs Militant* (MM). The emblem of the LAPM is a *purple cross and a white rose*. The white rose symbolizes purity of thoughts and actions. The Purple cross, on the other hand, represents the cross of St. John, which signifies help and shelter and tells members to be ready to offer assistance whenever there is suffering. In 2000, the Sovereign Grand Lodge passed a legislation allowing women to directly join the Patriarchs Militant. But surprisingly, many of the women still want to retain a separate LAPM branch.

Both the PM and LAPM are purely semi-military in its character, organized for purposes of chivalric display, and are admirably fulfilling their mission through the annual "*Pilgrimage to the Tomb of the Unknown Soldier*" ceremonies held in Washington D.C., and the "*Canadian War Memorial*" in Ottawa, Ontario, Canada. Today, there is an estimated 6,000 Chevaliers and Ladies belonging to 211 Cantons located in the United States, Canada, Cuba, Denmark, Iceland, and the Philippines.

Branches for the Youth

The first proposal to form an Odd Fellows branch for the youth began in 1830 but, owing to the standing of minors in society at the time, the Grand Lodge of the United States found themselves "not yet ready for a separate Order for the youth." But due to succeeding wars in the past, a number of boys and girls in Europe and North America were growing up without fathers. This encouraged several members of the IOOF to establish unofficial clubs for the youth. The first attempt to establish a branch for sons and daughters of Odd Fellows began in Copenhagen, Denmark, when a club called *Esperanca* was established in 1887. In the Netherlands, *Jonge* (Young) *Odd Fellows Club* was formed in 1918. Other countries such as Norway and Sweden also formed groups for the youth. Sadly, very little is known about these European youth clubs. It seems that these groups did not flourish, perhaps no longer exist today, or exist in very small numbers. At present, there are four (4) youth branches officially recognized by the Sovereign Grand Lodge.

Junior Odd Fellows Lodge

The IOOF in Australia was the first to introduce the idea of Junior Lodges in 1898. The

 group was first organized with a crude organizational structure until a more formal structure paralleling the lodge system was established in 1901. In 1920, the Sovereign Grand Lodge in the United States and Canada finally passed a legislation to officially establish a youth branch. On November 21, 1921, a boys club for the youth called *Supreme Fireside, Loyal Sons of Odd Fellows* was founded by one J.H. Stotler in Kansas City, Missouri.[12]

J. H. Stotler's boys club has four degrees and each degree is devoted to a distinct lesson for the youth. The first degree teaches *fraternity*. The second degree places an emphasis on home and *devotion to parents*. The third degree teaches *patriotism* and devotion to flag and country. The fourth degree teaches the lesson of *devotion to a Deity or God*. In addition to these, there is another degree called the "Knight Degree" which is an honorary degree conferred based on actual service. The four degrees are secret while the knight degree can be conferred publicly in the presence of parents, Rebekahs, and Odd Fellows.[13]

On April 18, 1922, another group called *The Sons of Wildey for Boys* was formed in Bonham, Texas, organized by Odd Fellows for the youth but they claim that they are not totally connected with the Independent Order of Odd Fellows.[14] These two early groups eventually became the nucleus for what became the Junior Odd Fellows Lodge.

To be a member of the Junior Odd Fellows Lodge, one must be between eight (8) to eighteen (18) years old. Members who have attained the age of eighteen (18) years may receive the graduate degree and retain all rights and privileges of a member until age twenty-one (21). A member of a Junior Lodge who acquires membership in an Odd Fellows Lodge shall be a life member of the Junior Lodge so long as he remains an Odd Fellow in good standing. Adult Odd Fellows may also be elected by ballot to Senior Membership on petition accompanied by the required fees and dues. The Junior Odd Fellows participate in their own degree and meetings similar to the Odd Fellows Lodges. Their watchwords are *Fidelity, Honor and Loyalty*. Their symbolic colors are *silver and dark blue*.

The basic unit is called a *Junior Lodge*, which shall be organized upon receipt by the Grand Junior Lodge, Grand Lodge or Sovereign Grand Lodge of a signed petition for a charter by five (5) or more members of the Junior Lodge Degree or ten (10) persons qualified to become members. The elective officers of the Junior Lodge are: Chief Ruler, Deputy Ruler; Recorder, Accountant, and Treasurer. The appointive officers are: Chaplain, Warden, Conductor, Marshal, Color Bearer, Right Supporter of the Chief Ruler, Left Supporter of the Chief Ruler, Inner Sentinel, Outer Sentinel, Right Supporter of the Deputy Ruler and Left Supporter of the Deputy Ruler, Right Supporter of the Chaplain, Left Supporter of the Chaplain, Right Supporter of the Past Chief Ruler, Left Supporter of the Past Chief Ruler. At least two (2) adult Advisory Officers shall be present at all times for safety and welfare.

The state or provincial governing body is called the *Grand Junior Lodge*. A Grand Junior Lodge shall be organized upon receipt by the Grand Lodge or Sovereign Grand Lodge of a signed petition for a charter by at least three (3) Junior Lodges in good standing with the approval of the Jurisdictional Youth Committee (JYC). The elective officers of the Grand Junior Lodge are: Grand Ruler, Deputy Grand Ruler, Grand Warden, Grand Recorder, and Grand Treasurer. The appointive officers are the Grand Marshal, Grand Conductor, Grand Chaplain,

Grand Musician, Grand Inner Sentinel, Grand Outer Sentinel, Right and Left Supporters for the Grand Ruler, Past Grand Ruler and Grand Chaplain.

Theta Rho Girls' Club

In 1929, the Sovereign Grand Lodge approved the formation of *Junior Rebekah Lodges* for girls.[15] This group was ultimately renamed as the Theta Rho Girls in 1931. To be a member, one must be between eight (8) to eighteen (18) years old. Members who have attained the age of eighteen (18) years may receive the graduate degree and retain all rights privileges of a member until age twenty-one (21). The Theta Rho has one degree which encourages the girls to exert effort to improve oneself physically and mentally, build a character necessary for happiness in the home, and create an influence for good in the community.[16] The degree seeks to teach unselfishness, morality, and patriotism; to encourage mental and physical development; to develop character; to promote the sentiment that happiness is obtained only through service to God and man, and that obedience to law is necessary for preservation of government and protection of home and country. Their motto is *"Happiness through Service"* and the symbolic colors of the degree are *peach and Yale blue*.

The local branch is called a *Club* which shall be organized upon receipt of a signed petition for a charter by five (5) or more members of the Theta Rho Degree or ten (10) persons qualified to become members. But no Theta Rho Girls' Club can exist therein without the sanction of the Rebekah Assembly within that jurisdiction. The elective officers of the Theta Rho Girls' Club are: President, Vice President, Secretary, Financial Secretary, and Treasurer. The appointive officers are: Chaplain, Warden, Conductor, Marshal, Right Supporter of the President, Left Supporter of the President, First Herald, Second Herald, Third Herald, Fourth Herald, Right Supporter of the Vice President and Left Supporter of the Vice President, Inside Guardian, and Outside Guardian. At least two (2) Advisory Officers shall be present at all times for safety and welfare.

The state or provincial governing body is called the *Theta Rho Assembly* which shall be organized upon receipt of a signed petition for a charter by at least three (3) Theta Rho Girls' Clubs in good standing with the approval of the Jurisdictional Youth Committee (JYC). The elective officers of the Theta Rho Assembly are: President, Vice President, Warden, Secretary, and Treasurer. The appointive officers are: Marshal, Conductor, Chaplain, Musician, Inside Guardian, Outside Guardian, Right and Left Supporters to the President, Right and Left Supporters to the Vice President, First, Second, Third and Fourth Herald, and Color Bearer. All the officers and members of the Theta Rho Assembly shall be Past Presidents who have received the *Theta Rho Assembly Degree*.

United Youth Group

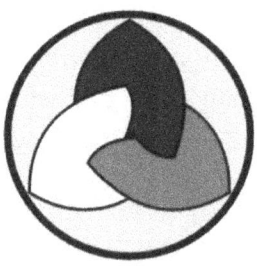

The first attempt to form a co-ed fraternal organization for the youth began in 1941 when the IOOF formed the *Alpha Rho*. The purpose was to allow the youth of both sexes an opportunity to cultivate understanding between the two sexes. But because it was not yet generally acceptable to see both boys and girls in one club, the group did not flourish. Nevertheless, when the Sovereign Grand Lodge permitted the Odd Fellows Lodge to become

Degree Staff of the St. Edwards Junior Odd Fellows Lodge No. 11 of Columbia, Missouri. Photo from *The International Odd Fellow*, September, 1972.

Degree Staff of the Starlite Theta Rho Girls' Club No. 32 of Indianola, Iowa. Photo from *The International Odd Fellow*, September, 1972.

co-ed, a second desire for a co-ed youth organization led to the formation of the *United Youth Group* (UYG).

Membership in the United Youth Group is open to all persons who believe in a Supreme Being, of good character, and are between the ages of eight

Branches of the IOOF | 203

(8) and eighteen (18) years. Members who have attained the age of eighteen (18) years may receive the graduate degree and retain all rights privileges of a member until age twenty-one (21). All members in good standing in an Odd Fellows Lodge or Rebekah Lodge may attend any UYG meeting. They may be elected by ballot to *Senior Membership* in the group on a petition accompanied by the required fee, dues, and being obligated in keeping with the ritual. However, adult members have no right to vote, and may speak only upon request or by invitation of the presiding officer. The United Youth Group seeks to teach leadership, community service, and responsibility.

The basic unit is called a *United Youth Group* formed upon a petition signed by not less than five (5) applicants, sponsored by any chartered adult branch of the IOOF. This follows a co-ed lodge setting. The elective officers of a group are: President, Vice-President, Secretary, and Treasurer. The appointive officers of a group are: Warden, Chaplain, Conductor, Guardian, Right and Left Supporters to the President who shall be appointed by the President, and Right and Left Supporters to the Vice-President who shall be appointed by the Vice-President. Meetings must be attended by an adult Advisor and Assistant Advisor to constitute a quorum for the transaction of business. The number of United Youth Groups have recently increased because several lodges in the United States, particularly in Texas and Illinois, were able to establish them.

Patriarchs Militant Cadet Corps

On September 17, 2016, the *Department Council of Virginia of the Patriarchs Militant* approved the formation of the Patriarchs Militant Cadet Corps for the Youth. This branch is connected to the Patriarchs Militant branch. The program aims to promote dignity and pride, teach the value of service to others, and prepare the youth to be useful citizens and help them grow into responsible adults and be a credit to their community. Its creed is: "*We the Cadet Corps are youth working together to reach out and do community service.*" Its motto is: "*Service is honor.*"

In establishing these youth branches, the IOOF wanted to project an atmosphere that it is a family-oriented fraternity encouraging all family members to join. The communal goal of establishing these youth branches was to teach children and youth how lodges operate, the democratic process, leadership abilities, poise, social graces, and community service. For many years, the youth branches provided boys and girls with a social support system with other boys and girls of their age bracket and a moral guide as taught in the initiations. It has also been thought that these young people are an important part of the organization's "Present" because they will eventually find involvement with Odd Fellowship meaningful and enriching so that they will become an important part of its "Future" by joining the adult lodges. Indeed, many of the dedicated leaders of the Odd Fellows and Rebekahs today began as members of these youth branches.

Unofficial Fun Groups

In 1868, some Odd Fellows were reportedly initiating people into a fun degree based on the legend of King Xerxes from Ancient Persia known as the *Oriental Order of Humility* (OOH) - a group which predated the Masonic Shriners. This additional degree was created for the purpose of fun, recreation, and amusement as an enjoyable diversion from the serious initiation ceremonies of the lodge and encampment. Many more fun groups for Odd Fellows followed thereafter, and in 1901 the

OOH added a second degree and changed its name to the Oriental Order of Humility and Perfection (OOH&P). Owing to the traditional mindsets of the national leaders at that time, these organizations faced opposition from the Sovereign Grand Lodge. Resolutions were passed declaring these fun groups illegal and demanding them to disband. The suppression continued periodically for about 50 years until the Sovereign Grand Lodge finally yielded and recognized the Ancient Mystic Order of Samaritans (AMOS) as a private club for Odd Fellows in 1951. But because this group opted not to come under the authority of the Sovereign Grand Lodge, they do not have representation in the international governing body.

Ancient Mystic Order of Samaritans

AMOS is an unofficial branch for male Odd Fellows formed as a merger of six fun groups. In 1924, the *Oriental Order of Humility and Perfection* merged with the *Imperial Order of Muscovites*, the *Pilgrim Knights of Oriental Splendor*, and the *Ancient Mystic Order of Cabiri* to form the *United Order of Splendor and Perfection*. They were joined by the *Veiled Prophets of Baghdad* in 1925 at which point the name was changed to AMOS and was subsequently joined by the *Improved Order of Muscovites* in 1927. AMOS experienced substantial growth for several years, reaching more than 100,000 members. But membership eventually declined when all fraternal organizations began losing its popularity and partly because of the traditional mindsets of its senior leaders who unwisely stood against its international expansion.

Membership is open to all Odd Fellows, whether affiliated with the IOOF, MUIOOF, or the GUOOF. The first degree, known as *Humility Degree*, is conferred by the basic unit of AMOS called a *Sanctorum*. Those who have received this degree are referred to as "*Samaritans*." The elective officers of a local Sanctorum are: Grand Monarch, Vice-Grand Monarch, Grand Counsellor, Registrar, Collector, and Banker. The appointive officers are: Grand High Executioner, Grand Chief Guide, Venerable Friar, Grand Monitor, Grand Stentoros, and Grand Herald. The second or *Perfection Degree* is usually conferred only at a Divisional or Supreme Convention held once a year confers the title of "*Sheik*." The officers of a *Supreme Sanctorum* are: Supreme Monarchos, Supreme Khalifah, Supreme Counsellor, Supreme Prince, Supreme Secretary, Supreme Treasurer, Supreme Vizier, Supreme Muezzin, and Supreme Stentoros.[17] The regalia is a *dark red fez* with *yellow tassel* for Samaritans and a *red tassel* for Sheiks. Recently, a number of new Sanctorums have been established across the United States but the total membership is still alarmingly low, which is below a thousand all over the United states and Canada.

Ladies of the Orient

The Ladies of the Orient (LOTO) is a women's fraternal organization in the United States and Canada, which had its origins as an appendant body of the Rebekahs. It was founded in Syracuse, New York, in 1915 by Emily Voorheis for the purpose of having a group dedicated to recreation and amusement as a pleasant diversion from the serious charitable work done by other groups to which the ladies already belonged. The group still exists today with a handful of members and is now open to non-Rebekahs.

The basic unit is called a *Zuanna*. The elected officers are: Great Ashayhi, Queen Ashayhi, Keeper of Traditions, Collector of Shekels, Prelate and Oriental Guide. The appointive officers are: Syndic, Guard of Zuanna, Musician, Color Bearers, Detector, Executioner, Assistant Detector, Assistant Executioner, and Captain of Degree.[18] The regalia is a *white fez* with a variety of different tassel colors to denote different officer positions.

Noble Order of Muscovites

In 1893, a group of Odd Fellows in Ohio formed the *Imperial Order of Muscovites* (IOM). Unlike most fun branches of other fraternal groups, the Muscovites opted for a Russian theme instead of the standard Middle-Eastern. The IOM additionally spawned an affiliated appendant body for women who were Rebekahs known as the *Lady Muscovites* in June of 1925. The group was active in different states throughout the Midwest and Western United States, but was disbanded in 1909 due to pressure from the Sovereign Grand Lodge. While further East, the Imperial Order re-formed and operated separately under the name *Improved Order of Muscovites*. This group continued until it merged into AMOS in 1927, but by the 1930s a portion of the membership in Oregon was unhappy with the results of the merger and left to found a new group, *The Royal Order of Muscovites*. One of the last surviving members of the Royal Order, together with younger candidates, reorganized the group as the *Noble Order of Muscovites* in 2016. This branch is now open to both men and women and no longer restrict its membership to Odd Fellows and Rebekahs. It is not an organization per se but a mere social group that will gather to put on the degree and raise some money from time to time. There are no annual dues as well. Their mission is: "*To have fun while saving the world*". The regalia of the Imperial Order was a *charcoal grey hat with a black band of fur* around the brim called by the members as a "*Busby.*" The Improved, Royal, and Noble Order instead have a *dark red busby* with a *black band of fur* around the brim.

The basic unit of the Noble Order are called *Duchies*, which are chartered by a *Kremlin*. The officers of a Kremlin are: Czar, Commandant, Royal Inspector, Grand Counselor, Grand Duke, Chronicler, Minister of Finance, Royal Inner Guard, and Royal Outer Guard. There are no national or international governing body. Once a Kremlin is chartered, each state can then operate in the best way for them, provided they follow the rules about who can be a member and the ban on hazing.

Some members of the Oriental Order of Humility and Perfection (OOH&P) wearing their fezzes during a parade in Rochester, New York. The OOH&P later merged with other fun groups to form the Ancient Mystic Order of Samaritans (AMOS). Photos courtesy of Tyler Anderson.

Branches of the IOOF | 207

Early members of the Kremlin Baku of the Imperial Order of Muscovites (IOM) in Portland, Oregon. The group survived suppression as the Improved Order, and finally, reformed as the Noble Order of Muscovites in 2016. The Muscovites also opened its membership to both men and women who are members of any fraternal organization or service club.

Photo courtesy of Kremlin Baku and the author, 2019.

Chapter 24

RELIGION, FREEMASONRY, AND WOMEN

Many of us now live in a secular country where the state is neutral in matters of religion and people are free to choose their religion without fear of government persecution. But a lot of the freedoms and principles we now enjoy - freedom of religion, religious tolerance, equality, right to vote, and democratic processes - were once secretly practiced inside the lodge rooms of so-called secret societies or fraternal organizations at a time when the monarchy and the Church held absolute control over religious and political opinions.

Fraternal organizations like Odd Fellowship and Freemasonry have long promoted religious and political tolerance within their lodge rooms. Their membership consisted of people representing different religious denominations and political backgrounds. Their lodge rooms were and still are considered neutral grounds where religious and

The Bishop of Lincoln, Rev. Dr. King, together with the Mayor, W.W. Richardson, and a political candidate, W. Crosfield, were admitted as members of the Machester Unity Independent Order of Odd Fellows in 1892.
Photo from the *Illustrated London News*, March 12, 1892.

political debates are discouraged during meetings and official events. This is mainly for the purpose of preventing disharmony and conflict between members. However, secular organizations and clubs were not widely acceptable when these fraternal organizations first started, and their religious neutrality was seen as going against the one absolutist religion that the Church espoused. Primarily because Odd Fellowship was open to anyone regardless of religious affiliation and because of its similarities with Freemasonry, it met opposition from the clergy especially of the Roman Catholic Church.

Odd Fellowship and Religion

A fundamental principle of Odd Fellowship is toleration of all religions. It professes to be predominantly a system of toleration in religion and politics. But Odd Fellowship is not a religion and a lodge is not a church. A lodge does not aim to usurp the place of the church. Members meet in the lodge room not to worship but only for purposes of "mutual counsel, the relief of distress, and the elevation of human character."[1] In fact, a number of priests and ministers actually joined while the Odd Fellows was still developing in England. In 1842, a Leeds priest lent the Odd Fellows the church and joined a lodge the next day.[2] In 1850, a priest in Preston told the members of an Odd Fellows Lodge that the "principles and practices of your Order are such that a Minister of the Gospel may entirely approve."[3] A Bishop of Winchester said that he valued being initiated as a member of the Odd Fellows and described the initiation ceremony as "a symbol of something greater."[4] But some opposition to the Order also was expressed, as when a priest refused that an Odd Fellows Lodge perform the funeral rites for a departed member, and some Roman Catholic churches refused to perform the last rites over the grave of a deceased Odd Fellow.[5] Nevertheless, there was no strict hostility from the Roman Catholic Church toward the Odd Fellows.

During the mid-19th century, however, the *Catholic Bishops of North America* became alarmed with the growth of fraternal organizations and other secular clubs. In 1893, authorities from the Roman Catholic Church sent a letter to the Sovereign Grand Lodge requesting access to the initiation rituals of the Independent Order of Odd Fellows. The purpose was for the church to decide whether Catholics might be allowed for admission to membership.[6] This was brushed aside by the Odd Fellows leadership; Grand Sire C.T. Campbell said in his report in 1893 that, "the position Odd Fellowship occupies renders it unnecessary for us to seek the recognition of any particular sect or party, though we will be pleased, at all times, to have the support of all good men, of whatever race or creed, who reverence God and seek advancement of humanity."[7] Subsequently in 1894, the Catholic Bishops of North America secured a letter from the Holy See which said that Bishops of America should endeavor to keep their believers away from the Odd Fellows.[8] About that time, Cardinal Mariano Rampolla del Tindaro advised that the instructions be applied in a flexible manner to the Odd Fellows. But the ban, if it was really a ban, applied only to North America.[9]

In August of 1958, a Swiss Odd Fellow named Clewitz had discussions for over a period of four days with a Jesuit priest in a monastery in Switzerland. These discussions were broadcasted via radio. Clewitz asked the Jesuit Father where the prohibition regarding joining the Odd Fellows could be found. The priest answered that no such prohibition existed in Europe.[10] A Carmelite priest was also asked and he answered that he was unaware of any prohibition against Odd Fellowship and that it was only Freemasonry that was expressly prohibited.[11] In 1964, a Committee was organized

On top of the Roman Catholic Church in Cebu, Philippines, is the All-seeing-eye surrounded by twelve stars, symbolizing the eye of God watching through the twelve tribes of Israel.

Photo by the Author, 2015.

The All-seeing-eye

Many people fear this symbol because of conspiracy theories on the so-called influence of Freemasonry and the Illuminati in global politics. But the All-seeing-eye, or the Eye of Providence, actually symbolizes the omniscient eye of God who continually watches over our thoughts and actions. This is not a symbol exclusively used by the Freemasons or the Illuminati but was widely and generally used by churches and many ancient societies stretching back thousands of years ago. In fact, the ancient Egyptians, Assyrians, Jews, and Christians have used the eye as a symbol of their God. Among Christians, the Holy Scriptures provide, "The eye of the Lord is in every place, beholding the evil and good" (Prov. XV.3) and "The Eye of the Lord runs to and fro throughout the whole earth, to show himself strong in behalf of them whose heart is perfect toward him" (2 Chron. XVI 9).

in Europe, which met with the *Ecumenical Council* in Rome to iron out the misunderstanding between Odd Fellowship and the Catholic Church.[12] The Committee consisted of Odd Fellows' Latin specialists Prof. Dr. Paul Pachlatka and Dr. Gustav Meyer, along with two prominent Catholics who are members of the IOOF. They initiated discussions with the Roman Catholic Church. The Committee held a meeting with Dr. Ebneter, Director of the Apologetic Institute of the Roman Catholic Young Men's Association at Zurich. The Committee showed Dr. Ebneter the Odd Fellows Hall of *Kyburg Lodge No.14* in the City of Winterthur and explained to him the stations of the officers, the opening and closing of the lodge, the symbols, and what the Odd Fellows understood as the worldwide laws to practice friendship, love, and truth.[13] After the conference, the two parties agreed that there was nothing in the Odd Fellows that was in conflict with those of the Roman Catholics. Dr. Ebneter shared that he was surprised that the Odd Fellows were involved in many worldwide humanitarian works.[14]

As soon as the controversy declined and religious leaders began to accept secular organizations, more priests, bishops, and rabbis of different religious sects became members and some even held leadership positions in the Odd Fellows. By 1965, the Odd Fellows in Germany, the Netherlands, and Switzerland had several Roman Catholic members already.[15] In 1973, Reverend Monsignor Titian Miani became the first Roman Catholic priest to become a member of the IOOF in the United States when he joined *Scio Lodge No.102* of the IOOF in Linden, California.[16] Reverend Leo Dennis Burns became the first Roman Catholic priest to serve as Grand Master of the IOOF Grand Lodge of Ontario in 1992 and became Sovereign Grand Chaplain of the Sovereign Grand Lodge.

Eventually, in 1974, it was clarified that Catholics were not forbidden to join Odd Fellows Lodges and that the Odd Fellows did not fall under the ban regarding Freemasonry. That affiliation with the Odd Fellows was not punishable by excommunication. In the changing spiritual context of the times, the Catholic Church has left its prejudicial attitude in the past, was seeking cooperation with men of goodwill, and has taken the stand that there is no justification for any ban.

It was deemed unjustified to impose a clerical ban on a Catholic regarding membership, or to cast doubt on his loyalty to his faith because of his membership in the Independent Order of Odd Fellows. Several bishops opined that if a Catholic is interested in joining the Odd Fellows, he will not be excommunicated nor have to fear any other disadvantages as far as the church is concerned, so long as he continues to perform his religious duties as a Catholic.[17] *Canon 1374 of the Code of Canon Law of 1983* forbids Catholics from joining societies which plot against the Church. By definition, Odd Fellowship does not fall under such prohibition. As an institution, it respects all recognized religions, and encourages its members to faithfully support the religion of their choice. It conforms to "law, religion, and sound morality, and does not permit anything contrary to the allegiance we owe to our country, or the duty we owe to ourselves."[18] Membership requires "no sacrifice of your opinions, no change in your relations to the state and no loosening of the obligations, which you owe to the laws and institutions under which you live."[19] To become an Odd Fellow, one must "be grateful to his or her creator, faithful to his or her country, and fraternal to his or her fellowmen".[20]

In 1991, statements were gathered from ordained ministers, rabbis, and religious leaders with reference to their membership in the Independent Order of Odd Fellows. Those denominations represented included Baptist, Christian, Episcopalian, Jewish, Latter Day Saints, Roman Catholic, United Church of Canada, and United Methodist. Within the ranks of Odd Fellowship are no doubt other denominations.

Roman Catholic priest Reverend Leo D. Burns, C.S.B., of the *Cathedral Boys High School* in Hamilton, Ontario, shared that "The beautiful thing about Odd Fellowship is that a brother and sister respects the personal beliefs of each other and yet the three links of Odd Fellowship bind us together into a close-knit family despite our varying backgrounds, as the practice of Friendship, Love, and Truth is the aim and goal of every religion." *Jewish Rabbi* David Schnitzler of New York opined that "While not a religious Order, our fraternity encompasses the noble ideals set forth in the Old Testament and is harmonious with the Jewish religion." *Latter Day Saints Elder* Jim Kotyk mentioned that he "experienced great growth from participation in the Order and have learned to appreciate the many noble men and women in the Fraternity who have set great examples in their quest to make this world a better place to live." Reverend Cela Fugate of the *First Christian Church* of Iowa attested that "As an ordained minister of the Christian Church, I have always worked and enjoyed my Rebekah Lodge and its beautiful degree work." Episcopalian minister Reverend Charles Worrell of the *Southern Episcopal Church* of Nashville, Tennessee, and Past Sovereign Grand Master of the IOOF, believes that "Odd Fellowship encompasses those high and noble teachings which make us better men...while not a religious organization, a respect for everyone's religion proves it to be composed of individuals of a faith."

These statements were printed in a brochure that has been issued especially to areas where certain religious denominations have demonstrated some objection to church members being members of the Odd Fellows, mainly because of lack of knowledge or misunderstanding of the nature of the organization.[21] At present, membership is represented by various religious denominations from Catholics, Protestants, Muslims, and others.

Odd Fellowship and Freemasonry

Freemasonry is not the original fraternity from which all other groups copied. The Odd Fellows is not and has never been a Masonic organization. Since its inception, it has been a completely separate organization. Rather, both organizations appear to have common roots and were influenced by early forms of fraternal associations such as "guilds, journeymen's associations, religious confraternities, and village youth brotherhoods."[22]

Since the Middle Ages, there have been guilds and brotherhoods for the purpose of mutual aid and protection with hierarchal rituals of initiation, oaths, and regalia. Entry into almost all of these early fraternal groups "was accompanied by some similar form of initiation."[23] For example, historian Daniel Weinbren mentioned that "the Leeds Wool-combers, London Tailors, and the Operative Masons have initiation rites that involved a blindfolded initiate calling for admittance to the lodge room, the chanting of Psalms, passages from the Old Testament, and oaths of secrecy administered by an officer in a robe."[24] Many of these guilds usually have three degrees: *Apprentices, Fellowscrafts* and *Masters*, and the leader of the guild is usually called a *Grand Master*.[25]

There were also associations of journeymen in England, also known as *Compagnonnages* in France and *Gesellenverbande* in Germany, which "attempted to defend their collective interests

Many people held membership in both the Odd Fellows and Freemasons that it is quite common to see the emblems of both fraternal organizations engraved on their gravestones. In some towns, the Odd Fellows and Freemasons share the same building to save costs with taxes, maintenance, and utility bills. Photo by the author, 2014.

Unrecorded Benefactions

In 1826, the disappearance of William Morgan damaged the public image of Freemasonry and other fraternal organizations. This resulted in the birth of the *Anti-Masonic Party*, which existed from 1828 to 1838. This was a big blow against Freemasonry and similar associations. Many lodges closed and thousands of Freemasons denounced their affiliation and dropped their membership in Freemasonry. The *Fraternal Review* (1880) published the following excerpt:

> When Freemasonry was severely under fire in 1826, and in gravest danger of extinction in the United States, Odd Fellowship came to the rescue although indirectly. The splendid work of the Odd Fellows in giving aid to their members in times of sickness and misfortunes spread among the public and had the effect of changing public opinion which was strongly averse to the secret societies because of the murder of William Morgan allegedly by the Freemasons. People began to see that these fraternal organizations were not so bad after all, and that if the Odd Fellows were doing a grand humanitarian work then the other fraternal organization is also entitled to a fair consideration and fair treatment. Hence, Freemasonry again began to rise in public esteem, thanks to the fraternal acts of Odd Fellowship, the deeds of the "reciprocal relief and kindly offices."

against the masters and to provide food, lodging, and guidance for one another as they traveled the country searching for work."[26] These journeymen associations also had an elaborate initiation ritual. They met inside taverns "where they were given food, shelter, and assistance in finding work."[27] Parallel to that of the early Odd Fellows and friendly societies in England, membership "contributed money weekly or monthly to a common fund used to pay sickness and funeral benefits for members and support the widows and orphans of those who died."[28] Some historians observed that the early Odd Fellows were "a product of a working-class tavern culture"[29] and were "much closer to the traditional journeyman's associations than to the Masonic model."[30]

When Odd Fellowship became popular, it rivaled Freemasonry in membership. Some Masonic authors then claimed that Odd Fellowship was founded as an imitation of Freemasonry, but there really is no evidence for this assertion. Even the well-known writer, journalist, and Freemason Dr. Bob James stated that "Masonic rituals themselves were far from stable or uniform across England until well into the 19th century, making even the idea of borrowing very problematic."

In fact, there were so many factions within Freemasonry. In France, the Freemasons formed the *Grand Orient de France*. This resulted in the birth of *Continental or Liberal Freemasonry*, which majority of Anglo-American Freemasons consider as clandestine or irregular. In 1751, disagreement within English Freemasonry resulted in the two rival Grand Lodges – the *Antients* and *Moderns*. These two groups were only unified in 1813. Just like Freemasonry, Odd Fellowship also experienced divisions until two of these groups ultimately formed a partial amalgamation known as the United Order of Odd Fellows in 1798. From this, the Manchester Unity of the Independent Order of Odd Fellows separated and eventually its members formed their

> **Albert Pike**
>
> Albert Pike (1809-1891) was a popular and controversial Freemason who was also a high-ranking Odd Fellow. He first joined the Independent Order of Odd Fellows and became Past Grand Master of the IOOF Grand Lodge of Arkansas. He subsequently joined the Free and Accepted Masons and became a Past Grand Master of their Grand Lodge. He is known for singlehandedly revising the degrees of the *Ancient and Accepted Scottish Rite Southern Jurisdiction* in the mid-1800s, and for writing the book, *Morals and Dogma*.

own Grand Lodge in 1814. This suggests that both Freemasonry and Odd Fellows were struggling during the 18th century and it was only in the early 19th century when both groups started to attain some organizational stability. Dr. James further noted:

> "Spry thought it was obvious because of common symbolism and the use of an oath and a degree structure... Freemasonry was, and is, in exactly the same position as those other societies - after nearly 300 years it cannot yet explain from where it 'borrowed' its rites, symbols, etc., or when it did so."

Notably, the Masonic ritual was only standardized after the union of 1813 and was further revised between 1815 and 1816.[31] Manchester Unity IOOF also revised the Odd Fellows ritual at the beginning of 1814. But its leaders were very careful in the revision process, so that in 1824 Grand Master M. Wardle of the IOOF Manchester Unity made sure that Odd Fellows Lodges prevented "expelled Masons and Orangemen from introducing Lectures, Degrees, and Obligations foreign to Odd Fellowship".[32] In North America, the IOOF formed a *Committee of Revision* in 1844. This Committee, composed of Odd Fellows who were also prominent Freemasons, met in New York to finally settle the controversy of copying.[33] They consulted every Masonic ritual that they could find to compare with that of the Odd Fellows rituals.

After a diligent investigation, they found no trace or foundation for the imputation. First, the oldest surviving rituals of Odd Fellowship and succeeding revisions did not resemble that of the rituals of Freemasonry. The degrees of Freemasonry are *Entered Apprentice, Fellowcraft,* and *Master Mason*. In Odd Fellowship, the early degrees were the *Initiatory, White or Degree of Covenant, Royal Blue Degree, Pink or Merit Degree, Royal Arch of Titus or Fidelity Degree,* and *Scarlet or Priestly Degree*. These degrees were renumbered and renamed by the IOOF as the *Initiatory, Degree of Friendship, Degree of Love* and *the Degree of Truth*.

Even the use of the apron as regalia by numerous fraternal organizations of English origin is not a proof that Odd Fellows copied or imitated Freemasonry. According to several historians and sociologists, the use of regalia or livery such as a collar or apron was a practice consequently borrowed from the customs of the craft guilds from which many other English and Scottish fraternal organizations also originated. What Freemasonry probably contributed was to help popularize it.

Yet it should be noted that Odd Fellowship is not an opposition of Freemasonry, or vice versa. Historically, there have been close ties between the two fraternal organizations stretching back at least two centuries. In March 1815, the Manchester Unity Independent Order of Odd Fellows decided not to admit an applicant for membership "in consequence of information received from the Masonic Grand Lodge."[34] Another person was rejected for membership the following year based "on the advice of the Freemasons."[35] In fact, it was not uncommon to find men who were members of both.

Many people held leadership positions in both fraternities in the past and the present. The first hospital in California was built in 1849 through a joint effort by the Odd Fellows and Freemasons. One can see pins, rings, and tombs bearing the three-link chain emblem of the Odd Fellows and the square and compass emblem of the Freemasons. It was also very common for the two groups to split the rent or share one building for their meetings. There also were several Masonic lodges that held their meetings in Odd Fellows Halls, and vice versa. Thus, cross-fertilization of lodge practices and ideas was highly possible, resulting in some similarities between the two groups. After the American civil war, both Freemasonry and Odd Fellowship became the organizational model for hundreds of fraternal organizations that would be established starting the 1860s.[36] For example, the founders of the Patrons of Husbandry "included Odd Fellows and Freemasons and the rituals and symbolism of the resulting Order drew substantial elements from each."[37]

Odd Fellowship and Women

Many years ago, women had no right to money, property, or benefits in their own. Because of their legal status, they were excluded from membership in almost all organizations. But ultimately, women were allowed to join through auxiliary groups within Odd Fellowship and in 1819, the MUIOOF in the United Kingdom organized the first female lodges.

In North America, the IOOF first recognized the importance of women when it allowed its lodges to issue official identification cards for the wives and widows of members for purposes of mutual assistance. This led to the adoption of the *Rebekah Degree* for women in 1851 which eventually culminated in becoming the female version of the Odd Fellows Lodge known as the *Rebekah Lodge*. In 1858, the GUOOF also adopted the *Ruth Degree*, which similarly became their female branch known as the *Household of Ruth*. These were the first attempts by the Odd Fellows to allow women to join at a time when it was not yet widely acceptable by the world at large to allow women to be active participants in society. In reality, however, these groups were separate branches within the organization, with their own initiation degree, symbols, regalia, and governing bodies and, in most cases, with no vote in the Grand Lodge and the Sovereign Grand Lodge level.

Sooner or later, a radical change in the roles between men and women occurred and took more women out of their homes to participate in the financial success of the family.[38] Gender equality became "a reason to alter the traditional hierarchical organizational structure of many groups."[39] The MUIOOF in the United Kingdom was quite advanced when their *Annual Movable Committee* approved the admission of female members on equal terms as men in 1898. In 1976, the *Grand Lodge of Denmark* voted to allow Rebekah Lodges to be integrated in one Grand Lodge on equal footing with the Odd Fellows, and granted them the right to speak and to vote at the Grand Lodge through their own representatives.[40] The Grand Lodge of Denmark also adopted a revised Rebekah ritual consisting of four degrees to resemble that of the four degrees in the Odd Fellows Lodge.⁴¹

In 1979, the MUIOOF in the United Kingdom elected Dorothy Merrell as their first female Grand Master and nine other women filled the same office thereafter.⁴² In Australia, the Rebekahs were given power to attend Sessions of the Grand Lodge of Australasia as full voting representatives. Grand Lodge meetings were conducted in the *Australasian Degree* expressly written for such purpose. Past Grands of Odd Fellows and Past Noble Grands of Rebekahs were made equally eligible to have this degree conferred.⁴³ To further promote equality, women members in Denmark proposed to use the name "Sister Odd Fellows" instead of Rebekahs.⁴⁴ This was approved by the Grand Lodge of Denmark in 1996.⁴⁵ In other countries, however, the Rebekahs did not want to eliminate the gender differences and did not want to become more like men.

There are women members who believe that there are actual differences between males and females which still call for sex-segregated lodges. Past President of the *International Association of Rebekah Assemblies* Sherralyn L. Robbins shared that the Rebekahs in North America do not want to become "Sister Odd Fellows." Rather, the women wanted to retain their own identity as Rebekahs and opined that some ways of women are different from those of men. For them, equality for the Rebekahs is not to eliminate the Rebekah branch but to "make sure that they have a voice and vote on matters affecting the Rebekahs."⁴⁶

There were leaders of the Sovereign Grand Lodge, however, who believed otherwise and this led to a legislation to bring women as full and equal members with men by making the Odd Fellows Lodge open to both men and women. The Sovereign Grand Lodge emphasized that this is "fair and reasonable and in compliance with federal laws in the United States."⁴⁷ At that time, it was also observed

Winifred Baulk served as the Provincial Grand Master of the MUIOOF in Hertfordshire in the 1950s. By the 1980s, Odd Fellows lodges under the Manchester Unity Independent Order of Odd Fellows (MUIOOF) became completely open to both men and women. Photo courtesy of the Manchester Unity Oddfellows.

that families were looking for opportunity to once again participate in family functions. The need for activities that include husband and wife were needed to keep families together. An increase in interest of young men and women to join the Odd Fellows Lodge was coming from couples who have never belonged to a fraternal organization or who may have some slight exposure through another group.⁴⁸ The other reason cited was economic feasibility, because the IOOF had been operating a costly separate and unequal parallel branch at a time when "separate but equal" had been found to be already unacceptable by society.⁴⁹ In August 2000, the Sovereign Grand Lodge ultimately voted to remove the word "male" from the requirement of membership in the Odd

Religion, Freemasonry, and Women | 217

Fellows Lodge.[50] At first, many of the women who joined the Odd Fellows Lodges were those who have not been members in the Rebekahs.[51] Subsequently, many Rebekahs also joined the Odd Fellows.

However, making the Odd Fellows Lodge and Rebekah Lodge co-ed is still in limbo within the IOOF. In most European countries, women themselves still prefer sex-segregated lodges. This means that the Odd Fellows Lodges are still exclusively for male members while the Rebekah Lodges or Sister Lodges remain exclusively for female members. In fact, the Grand Sire in countries in Europe is the only male by whom the Rebekah degrees can be conferred.[52] The big difference is that the Rebekah Lodges in these countries have equal voice and vote with the Odd Fellows Lodges in their Grand Lodge and in the European Grand Lodge.

In North America and the Philippines, a number of women already joined the Odd Fellows Lodge and held leadership positions in various levels of the IOOF. In 2007, Patty Olson-Fries of Oregon became the first female Grand Master of the IOOF Grand Lodge of Oregon in the United States. Emilie J. Cupp followed when she became the first female Grand Master of the IOOF Grand Lodge of Pennsylvania in 2015.[53] The following year, Darlene Parker became the first African-American woman to hold the office of Grand Master of the IOOF in Maryland.[54] The Grand Lodge of Washington has had a female Grand Master twice. And two women from Oregon had run for the position of Sovereign Grand Warden for the last two years. In 2019, Michell Heckart of Iowa was the first woman to be elected as the Sovereign Grand Warden in the Sovereign Grand Lodge.

On the other hand, the Grand United Order of Odd Fellows (GUOOF) in America and jurisdiction, still has sex-segregated lodges: Odd Fellows Lodge for men, and the Household of Ruth for women. The GUOOF in the United Kingdom, however, is already co-ed and elected their first female Grand Master in 2018.

But because a number of women still prefer to maintain their own separate branch within the IOOF, the Rebekah Lodges still exist as a branch within the IOOF. In North America, the Rebekah Lodges also opened their membership to both men and women. This means that a man and a woman can be both an Odd Fellow and Rebekah. Yet, this set-up remains contentious and may result to issues when it comes to visiting lodges in most countries in Europe. Women Odd Fellows who are not also Rebekahs may not be able to attend an Odd Fellows Lodge in Europe because they remain all-male. They may not also attend a Rebekah Lodge because they have not received the Rebekah degree. Men who are Rebekahs only may not be able to attend a Rebekah Lodge in Europe because most Rebekah Lodges there remain exclusively for females. As of 2019, it is only the IOOF Grand Lodge of Germany and the IOOF Grand Lodge of the Netherlands and Belgium that have allowed the establishment of a co-ed or mixed-gender Odd Fellows Lodge as an on-going trial. For some people, sex-segregated lodges are still needed today because some wives or girlfriends actually prevent or discourage their boyfriends or husbands from joining an Odd Fellows Lodge that has women members either because of suspicion or mistrust. This is the same with some boyfriends or husbands of women who feel uncomfortable seeing their girlfriends or wives go to a lodge meeting at night inside a building where there are other men. On the other hand, some women are against the Odd Fellows Lodge being co-ed because they are afraid that the Rebekahs will eventually go defunct. What remains undisputed is the fact that women have been valuable members of Odd Fellowship.

Chapter 25

NOTABLE MEMBERS

Odd Fellowship makes no special efforts to attract popular or famous people, whether today or in the past. Irrefutably, the first lodges were formed to serve the needs of the working class at a time when government social services were almost inexistent. Thus, majority of Odd Fellowships' early members were artisans and laborers because they were the ones who needed assistance from each other through the lodges during hard times. But these lodges soon became an early form of social networking for people from all social classes, and an initial training ground for leadership. Eventually, Odd Fellows membership included presidents, prime ministers, senators, congressmen, governors, mayors, business tycoons, and pioneers in their respective fields. Many of the early Odd Fellows were not only leaders within the fraternal organization; they also played important roles in the development of several towns, cities, states, provinces and nations. They were there to speak up on issues of local,

By late 19th and 20th centuries, many prominent people joined the Odd Fellows. Names like Presidents Ulysses Grant, Rutherford Hayes, Schuyler Colfax, and many others held leadership roles within the IOOF. *Illustration courtesy of Ainslie Heilich as commissioned by the author, 2018.*

national and international interests. People from different political parties, even ardent rivals, have had the opportunity to call themselves "brothers" within Odd Fellowship. In recognition of their contributions or leadership, some alleys, roads, streets, colleges, universities, towns, and cities have been named after some of these notable men and women.

Unfortunately, a great number of the lodges closed at the beginning of the 20th century. Thus, many records are now gone; either these were lost or misplaced. It would take years of research at various libraries, museums, cemeteries and Grand Lodge offices to come up with a complete and accurate compilation of all notable men and women who were once members of the Independent Order of Odd Fellows, Manchester Unity Independent Order of Odd Fellows, Grand United Order of Odd Fellows, International Association of Rebekah Assemblies, or the Household of Ruth. The *Political Graveyard* website enumerates a list of politicians who held membership in the Odd Fellows but no specific information is provided regarding their involvement in the organization. The author suggests that a separate book specifically dedicated to this topic be published in the near future. What follows is only an incomplete list of people whose membership were verified because newspaper accounts, journals, biographies, tombs, and other surviving records mentioned their affiliations.

PRESIDENTS, PRIME MINISTERS, AND KINGS

- **Baldwin, Sir Stanley** (1867 – 1947): Prime Minister of the United Kingdom, 1923-1929, 1935-1937.
- **Churchill, Sir Winston** (1874 – 1965): Prime Minister of United Kingdom, 1951-1955.
- **Cook, Sir Joseph** (1860 – 1947): Prime Minister of Australia, 1913-1914.
- **Davis, Jefferson Finis** (1808 – 1889): President of the Confederate States of America, 1861-1865; United States Secretary of War, 1853-57.
- **George IV** (1762 – 1830): King of the United Kingdom of Great Britain and Ireland and King of Hanover, 1820-1830.
- **Fisher, Sir Andrew** (1862 – 1928): Prime Minister of Australia, 1908-1909, 1910-1913, and 1914-1915.
- **Grant, Ulysses S.** (1822 – 1885): 18th President of the United States, 1869–1877.
- **Gustaf, Adolf VI** (1882 – 1973): King of Sweden, 1950-1973.
- **Hayes, Rutherford Birchard** (1822 – 1893): 19th President of the United States, 1877–1881; Governor of Ohio, 1868-1872, 1876-1877.
- **Harding, Warren Gamaliel** (1865 – 1923): 29th President of the United States, 1921–1923.
- **Jones, Anson** (1798-1858): 4th and last President of the Republic of Texas, 1844-1845; Grand Master of the IOOF Grand Lodge of Pennsylvania, 1831-1832 and the IOOF Grand Lodge of Texas, 1853-1854.
- **Macdonald, Sir John Alexander** (1815 – 1891): 1st Prime Minister of Canada, 1867-1873.
- **Massey, William** (1856 – 1925): 19th Prime Minister of New Zealand, 1912–25.
- **McKinley, William** (1843 – 1901): 25th President of the United States, 1897–1901; Governor of Ohio, 1892-1896).
- **Reid, Sir George Houstoun** (1845 – 1918): 4th Prime Minister of Australia, 1904–1905.
- **Roosevelt, Franklin Delano** (1882 – 1945): 32nd President of the United States, 1933–1945.

THE WHITE HOUSE
WASHINGTON

January 9, 1939

Dear Brother Gaskill:

    The one hundred twenty years that have elapsed since the founding of the Odd Fellowship in America afford a broad perspective on which to view the accomplishments of our Order in this country.

    Its record is a noble one told in terms of true brotherhood among men; the relief of sickness and distress; the care of the widow; the education of the orphan and the promotion of good will and good citizenship wherever our far-flung subordinate lodges have been established.

    In the hope that our fraternity will in the years that lie ahead ever uphold its splendid humanitarian ideals, I send fraternal greetings and good wishes.

Very sincerely yours,

Franklin D. Roosevelt

Mr. Burton A. Gaskill,
Grand Sire,
Sovereign Grand Lodge of the I.O.O.F.,
506 Guarantee Trust Building,
Atlantic City, New Jersey.

President Franklin Roosevelt's letter to Grand Sire Burton Gaskill in 1939. President Roosevelt was a member of Hyde Park Lodge No. 203 of the Independent Order of Odd Fellows in New York. The introduction of Social Security System and National Health Insurance are some of the ideas Roosevelt introduced by way of the "New Deal", which he allegedly patterned from the system of benefits previously offered by Odd Fellowship. Photo courtesy of The Sovereign Grand Lodge, IOOF

Vice-President Schuyler Colfax in full Odd Fellows' regalia. He joined South Bend Lodge No. 29 of the Independent Order of Odd Fellows in Indiana. He is regarded as author and founder of the Rebekah Degree in 1851.

Photo courtesy of The Sovereign Grand Lodge, IOOF.

VICE-PRESIDENTS

- **Barkley, Alben William** (1877 – 1956): 35th Vice-President of the United States, 1949-1953.
- **Colfax, Schuyler** (1823 – 1885): 17th Vice-President of the United States, 1869-1873; 25th Speaker of the U.S. House of Representatives, 1863-1869; founder of the Rebekah Degree established in 1851.
- **Fairbanks, Charles Warren** (1852 – 1918): 26th Vice-President of the United States, 1905-1909; Senator from Indiana from 1897-1905; namesake of several towns in Alaska, Minnesota, Oregon and Michigan.
- **Garner, John Nance III** (1868 – 1967): 32nd Vice-President of the United States, 1933-1941; 39th Speaker of the U.S. House of Representatives, 1931-1933.
- **Hendricks, Thomas Andrews** (1819 – 1885): 21st Vice-President of the United States, 1885; 16th Governor of Indiana, 1873-1877; U.S. Senator from Indiana, 1863-69; U.S. Representative from Indiana, 1851-55.

UNITED STATES SENATORS

- **Aiken, George David** (1892 – 1984): U.S. Senator from Vermont, 1941-1975; Governor of Vermont, 1937-1941; Lieutenant Governor of Vermont, 1935-1937; Member of Vermont State House of Representatives, 1931-35; Speaker of the Vermont State House of Representatives, 1933-1935.
- **Austin, Warren Robinson** (1877 – 1962): U.S. Senator from Vermont, 1931-1946; U.S. Representative to United Nations, 1947-1953; Mayor of St. Albans, Vermont, 1909.
- **Bilbo, Theodore Gilmore** (1877 – 1947): U.S. Senator from Mississippi, 1935-1947; Governor of Mississippi, 1916-1920, 1928-1932; Lieutenant Governor of Mississippi, 1912-1916; Member of Mississippi State Senate, 1908-1912.
- **Berry, George Leonard** (1882 – 1948): U.S. Senator from Tennessee, 1937-1938.
- **Black, Hugo Lafayette** (1886 – 1971): U.S. Senator from Alabama, 1927-1903; Justice of U.S. Supreme Court, 1937-1971.
- **Blease, Coleman Livingston** (1868 – 1942): U.S. Senator from South Carolina, 1925-1931; Governor of South Carolina, 1911-1915; member of South Carolina State Senate, 1905-1908; Mayor of Newberry, South Carolina, 1910; Member of South Carolina State House of Representatives, 1890-1994, 1899-1900.
- **Borah, William Edgar** (1865 – 1940): U.S. Senator from Idaho, 1907-40.
- **Brewster, Ralph Owen** (1888 – 1961): U.S. Senator from Maine, 1941-1952; U.S. Representative from Maine, 1935-1941; Governor of Maine, 1925-1929; member of Maine State Senate, 1923-1925; and member of Maine State House of Representatives, 1917-1918, 1921-1922.
- **Butler, Hugh Alfred** (1878 – 1954): U.S. Senator from Nebraska, 1941-1954.
- **Butler, Robert Reyburn** (1881 – 1933): U.S. Representative from Oregon, 1928-1933; Circuit Judge in Oregon, 1909-1911; Member of Oregon State Senate, 1913-1917, 1925-1928.
- **Byrd, Robert Carlyle** (1917 – 2010): U.S. Senator from West Virginia, 1959-2010; U.S. Representative from West Virginia, 1953-1959; Member of West Virginia State Senate, 1951-

1952; Member of West Virginia State House of Delegates, 1947-1950.
- **Capper, Arthur** (1865 – 1951): U.S. Senator from Kansas, 1919-1949.
- **Chapman, Virgil Munday** (1895 – 1951): U.S. Senator from Kentucky, 1949-1951; and U.S. Representative from Kentucky, 1925-1929, 1931-1949.
- **Clark, Bennett Champ** (1890 – 1954): U.S. Senator from Missouri, 1931-1945; Judge of U.S. Court of Appeals for the D.C. Circuit, 1945.
- **Clay, Alexander Stephens** (1853 – 1910): U.S. Senator from Georgia, 1897-1910; Member of Georgia State Senate, 1892-1894; Member of Georgia State House of Representatives, 1884-1887, 1889-1990.
- **Clements, Earle Chester** (1896 – 1985): U.S. Senator from Kentucky, 1950-1957; Governor of Kentucky, 1948-1950; U.S. Representative from Kentucky, 1945-1948; Member of Kentucky State Senate, 1942-1945.
- **Connally, Thomas Terry** (1877 – 1963): U.S. Senator from Texas, 1929-1953; U.S. Representative from Texas, 1917-1929; Member of Texas State House of Representatives, 1901-1904.
- **Cotton, Norris H.** (1900 – 1989): U.S. Senator from New Hampshire, 1954-1974, 1975; U.S. Representative from New Hampshire, 1947-1954; member of New Hampshire State House of Representatives, 1923, 1943-1945; Speaker of the New Hampshire State House of Representatives, DNA.
- **Curtis, Carl Thomas** (1905 – 2000): U.S. Senator from Nebraska, 1955-1979; and U.S. Representative from Nebraska, 1939-1955.
- **Davis, James John** (1873 – 1947): U.S. Senator from Pennsylvania, 1930-1945 and the U.S. Secretary of Labor, 1921-1930.
- **Dick, Charles William Frederick** (1858 – 1945): U.S. Senator from Ohio, 1904-1911; U.S. Representative from Ohio, 1898-1904.
- **Dill, Clarence Cleveland** (1884 – 1978): U.S. Senator from Washington, 1923-1935; Known as the "Father of the Grand Coulee Dam" and the "Father of the Radio Act".
- **Dirksen, Everett McKinley** (1896 – 1969): U.S. Senator from Illinois, 1951-1969; U.S. Representative from Illinois 1933-1949.
- **Dworshak, Henry Clarence** (1894 – 1962): U.S. Senator from Idaho, 1946-1949, 1949-1962; U.S. Representative from Idaho, 1939-1946.
- **Fessenden, William Pitt** (1806 – 1869): U.S. Senator from Maine, 1854-1864, 1865-1869; U.S. Secretary of the Treasury, 1864-1865; U.S. Representative from Maine, 1841-1843; Member of Maine State House of Representatives, 1832-1833, 1840-1841, 1845-1846, 1853-1854.
- **Flanagan, James Winright** (1805 – 1887): U.S. Senator from Texas, 1869-1875; Lieutenant Governor of Texas, 1869-1870; Member of Texas State Senate, 1856-1858; Member of Texas State House of Representatives, 1851-1852.
- **Gardner, Obadiah** (1852 – 1938): U.S. Senator from Maine, 1911-1913.
- **Gibson, Ernest William** (1901 – 1969): U.S. Senator from Vermont, 1940-1941.
- **Gibson, Ernest Willard** (1872 – 1940): U.S. Senator from Vermont, 1933-1940; U.S. Representative from Vermont, 1923-1933; Vermont Secretary of Civil and Military affairs, 1922-1923; Member of Vermont State House of Representatives, 1906; Member of Vermont State Senate, 1908.
- **Harrison, Byron Patton** (1881 – 1941): U.S. Senator from Mississippi, 1919-1941; and U.S. Representative from Mississippi, 1911-1919.
- **Hatfield, Henry Drury** (1875 – 1962): U.S.

Senator from West Virginia, 1929-1935; President of the West Virginia State Senate; Member of West Virginia State Senate, 1909-1912.

- **Hickenlooper, Bourke Blakemore** (1896 – 1971): U.S. Senator from Iowa, 1945-1969.
- **Hoey, Clyde Roark** (1877 – 1954): U.S. Senator from North Carolina, 1945-1954; Member of North Carolina State House of Representatives, 1899-1902; Member of North Carolina State Senate, 1903-1906; U.S. Representative from North Carolina, 1919-21.
- **Johnson, Edwin Carl** (1884 – 1970): U.S. Senator from Colorado, 1937-1955; Governor of Colorado, 1933-1937, 1955-1957; Lieutenant Governor of Colorado, 1931-1932; Member of Colorado State House of Representatives, 1923-1931.
- **Lennon, Alton Asa** (1906 – 1986): U.S. Senator from North Carolina, 1953-1954; U.S. Representative from North Carolina, 1957-1973; Member of North Carolina State Senate, 1947-1951.
- **Logan, Marvel Mills** (1874 – 1939): U.S. Senator from Kentucky, 1931-1939; Judge, Kentucky Court of Appeals, 1926; Kentucky State Attorney General, 1916-1917.
- **Long, Edward Vaughn** (1908 – 1972): U.S. Senator from Missouri, 1960-1968; Lieutenant Governor of Missouri, 1957-1960; Member of Missouri State Senate, 1945-1956.
- **McGill, George** (1879 – 1963): U.S. Senator from Kansas, 1930-1939; Member, U.S. Tariff Commission, 1945.
- **McKellar, Kenneth Douglas** (1869 – 1957): U.S. Senator from Tennessee, 1917-1953; and U.S. Representative from Tennessee, 1911-1917.
- **McMaster, William Henry** (1877 – 1968): U.S. Senator from South Dakota, 1925-1931; Governor of South Dakota, 1921-1925; Lieutenant Governor of South Dakota, 1917-1921; Member of South Dakota State House of Representatives, 1911-1912; Member of South Dakota State Senate, 1913-1916.
- **McNary, Charles Linza** (1874 – 1944): U.S. Senator from Oregon, 1917-1918, 1918-1944; Justice of Oregon State Supreme Court, 1913-1914.
- **Morrow, William W.** (1843 – 1929): U.S. Senator from California, 1885-1891; One of the incorporators of the American Red Cross.
- **Neely, Matthew Mansfield** (1874 – 1958): U.S. Senator from West Virginia, 1923-1929, 1931-1941, 1949-1958; Governor of West Virginia, 1941-1945; U.S. Representative from West Virginia, 1913-1921, 1945-1947; and Mayor of Fairmont, West Virginia, 1908-1910.
- **Pasco, Samuel** (1834 – 1917): U.S. Senator from Florida, 1887-1899; Member of Florida State House of Representatives, 1886-1887; Speaker of the Florida State House of Representatives, 1887.
- **Perkins, George Clement** (1839 – 1923): U.S. Senator from California, 1893-1915.
- **Robsion, John Marshall** (1873 – 1948): U.S. Senator from Kentucky, 1930; U.S. Representative from Kentucky, 1919-1930, 1935-1948.
- **Russell, Richard Brevard Jr.** (1897 – 1971): U.S. Senator from Georgia, 1933-1971; Governor of Georgia, 1931-1933; Speaker of the Georgia State House of Representatives, 1927-1931; Member of Georgia state house of representatives, 1921-1931.
- **Stanford, Amasa Leland** (1824 – 1893): U.S. Senator from California, 1885-1893; Founder of Stanford University, 1885.
- **Sheppard, Morris** (1875 – 1941): U.S. Senator from Texas, 1913-1941; U.S. Representative

from Texas, 1902-1913.
- **Shipstead, Henrik** (1881 – 1960): U.S. Senator from Minnesota, 1923-1947; a member of Minnesota State House of Representatives, 1917-1918; Mayor of Glenwood, Minnesota, 1911-1913.
- **Sterling, Thomas** (1851 – 1930): U.S. Senator from South Dakota, 1913-1925; Delegate to South Dakota State Constitutional Convention, 1889; Member of South Dakota State Senate, 1889-1890; Dean of the College of Law, University of South Dakota, 1901-1911.
- **Sumner, Charles** (1811 – 1874): U.S. Senator from Massachusetts, 1851-1874; Leading proponent of abolishing slavery to weaken the Confederacy.
- **Sutherland, Howard** (1865 – 1950): U.S. Senator from West Virginia, 1917-1923; U.S. Representative from West Virginia, 1913-1917; Member of West Virginia State Senate, 1909-1912.
- **Townsend, John Gillis Jr.** (1871 – 1964): U.S. Senator from Delaware, 1929-1941; Member of Delaware State House of Representatives, 1901-1903.
- **Vance, Zebulon Baird** (1830 – 1894): U.S. Senator from North Carolina, 1879-1894.

UNITED STATES HOUSE OF REPRESENTATIVES

- **Abernethy, Charles Laban** (1872 – 1955): U.S. Representative from North Carolina, 1922-1935.
- **Ainey, William David Blakeslee** (1864 – 1932): U.S. Representative from Pennsylvania, 1911-1915.
- **Allen, Clifford Robertson** (1912 – 1978): U.S. Representative from Tennessee, 1975-1978.
- **Allen, John Joseph, Jr.** (1899 – 1995): U.S. Representative from California, 1947-1959; Mayor of McCall, Idaho, 1989-1993.
- **Allen, Leo Elwood** (1898 – 1973): U.S. Representative from Illinois, 1933-1961.
- **Allgood, Miles Clayton** (1878 – 1977): U.S. Representative from Alabama, 1923-1935.
- **Angell, Homer Daniel** (1875 – 1968): U.S. Representative from Oregon, 1939-1955; Member Oregon State Senate, 1937-1938; Member of Oregon State House of Representatives, 1929-1931, 1935.
- **Arnold, William Wright** (1877 – 1957): U.S. Representative from Illinois, 1923-1935.
- **Ashbrook, William Albert** (1867 – 1940): U.S. Representative from Ohio, 1907-1921, 1935-1940; Member of Ohio State House of Representatives, 1905-1906.
- **Ashmore, Robert Thomas** (1904 – 1989): U.S. Representative from South Carolina, 1953-1969.
- **Aspinall, Wayne Norviel,** (1896 – 1983): U.S. Representative from Colorado, 1949-1973; Member of Colorado State Senate, 1939-1948; Member of Colorado State House of Representatives, 1931-1938; Speaker of the Colorado State House of Representatives, 1937-1938.
- **Atkeson, William Oscar,** (1854 – 1931): U.S. Representative from Missouri, 1921-1923.
- **Atwood, Harrison Henry,** (1863-1954): U.S. Representative from Massachusetts, 1895-1897; Member of Massachusetts State House of Representatives, 1887-1989, 1915, 1917-18, 1923-1924, 1927-1928.
- **Ayres, William Augustus,** (1867 – 1952): U.S. Representative from Kansas, 1915-1921, 1923-1934.
- **Baldwin, Harry Streett,** (1894 – 1952): U.S. Representative from Maryland, 1943-1947.

- **Betts, Jackson Edward** (1904 – 1993): U.S. Representative from Ohio, 1951-1973; Member of Ohio State House of Representatives, 1937-1947; Speaker of the Ohio State House of Representatives, 1945-1946.
- **Blackney, William Wallace,** (1876 – 1963): U.S. Representative from Michigan, 1935-1937, 1939-1953.
- **Bohn, Frank Probasco,** (1866-1944): U.S. Representative from Michigan, 1927-1933; Member of Michigan State Senate, 1923-1926.
- **Brantley, William Gordon** (1860 – 1934): U.S. Representative from Georgia, 1897-1913; and a member of Georgia State Senate, 1886-1887; and Georgia State House of Representatives, 1884-1885; Namesake to Brantley County, Georgia.
- **Brehm, Walter Ellsworth** (1892 – 1971): U.S. Representative from Ohio, 1943-1953; Member of Ohio State House of Representatives, 1938-1942.
- **Bankhead, William Brockman** (1874 – 1940): U.S. Representative from Alabama, 1917-1940; the Speaker of the U.S. House, 1936-1940; and Member of Alabama State House of Representatives, 1900-1902.
- **Bennett, Philip Allen** (1881 – 1942): U.S. Representative from Missouri, 1941-42; Member of Missouri State Senate, 1921-1924; Lieutenant Governor of Missouri, 1925-1929.
- **Bishop, Cecil William** (1890 – 1971): U.S. Representative from Illinois, 1941-1955; Professional football and baseball player and manager.
- **Bohn, Frank Probasco** (1866 – 1944): U.S. Representative from Michigan, 1927-1933.
- **Brand, Charles Hillyer** (1861 – 1933): U.S. Representative from Georgia, 1917-1933; Superior Court Judge in Georgia, 1906-1917; Member of Georgia State Senate, 1894-1895.
- **Brenton, Samuel** (1810 – 1857): U.S. Representative from Indiana, 1851-1853, 1855-1857; Member of Indiana State House of Representatives, 1838-1839, 1840-1841;
- **Broomfield, William** (1922 – present): U.S. Representative from Michigan, 1957-1993; Member of Michigan State Senate, 1955-56; Member of Michigan State House of Representatives, 1949-1954.
- **Browne, Thomas McLelland,** (1829 – 1891): U.S. Representative from Indiana, 1877-1891; Member of Indiana State Senate, 1863; U.S. Attorney for Indiana, 1869-1875; General in the Union Army during the American Civil War.
- **Byrns, Joseph Wellington** (1869 – 1936): U.S. Representative from Tennessee, 1909-1936; Speaker of the U.S. House, 1935-1936; Member of Tennessee State House of Representatives, 1895-1901; Speaker of the Tennessee State House of Representatives, 1899-1901; and a member of Tennessee State Senate, 1901.
- **Ball, Thomas Raymond** (1896 – 1943): U.S. Representative from Connecticut, 1939-1941; Member of Connecticut state House of Representatives, 1927-38.
- **Bankhead, William Brockman** (1874 – 1940), U.S. Representative from Alabama, 1917-1940; Speaker of the U.S. House, 1936-1940; Member of Alabama State House of Representatives, 1900-1902.
- **Barton, William Edward** (1868 – 1955): U.S. Representative from Missouri, 1931-1933; Circuit Judge in Missouri, 1923-1928, 1935-1946.
- **Beckworth, Lindley Garrison Sr.** (1913 – 984): U.S. Representative from Texas, 1939-1953, 1957-1967; Member of Texas State Senate,

1971-1972; Member of Texas State House of Representatives, 1937-1938; Judge of U.S. Customs Court, 1967-1968.
- **Belcher, Page Henry** (1899 – 1980): U.S. Representative from Oklahoma, 1951-1973.
- **Bevill, Tom** (1921 – 2005): U.S. Representative from Alabama, 1967-1997; Member of Alabama State House of Representatives, 1959-1966.
- **Blanton, Thomas Lindsay** (1872 – 1957): U.S. Representative from Texas, 1917-1929, 1930-1937; District Judge in Texas, 1908-16.
- **Boren, Lyle** (1909 – 1992): U.S. Representative from Oklahoma, 1937-1947.
- **Butler, Robert Reyburn** (1881 – 1933): U.S. Representative from Oregon, 1928-1933; Member of Oregon State Senate, 1913-1917, 1925-1928; Circuit Judge in Oregon, 1909-1911.
- **Callan, Clair Armstrong** (1920 – 2005): U.S. Representative from Nebraska, 1965-1967.
- **Campbell, Jacob Miller** (1821 – 1888): U.S. Representative from Pennsylvania, 1877-1879, 1881-1887; General in the Union Army during the American Civil War; Pennsylvania Surveyor-General, 1866-1871.
- **Candler, Ezekiel Samuel, Jr.** (1862 – 1944): U.S. Representative from Mississippi, 1901-1921.
- **Canfield, Harry Clifford** (1875 – 1945): U.S. Representative from Indiana 4th District, 1923-1933.
- **Carpenter, William Randolph,** (1894 – 1956): U.S. Representative from Kansas, 1933-1937; U.S. Attorney for Kansas, 1945-1948; and a member of Kansas State House of Representatives, 1929-1932.
- **Cartwright, Wilburn** (1891 – 1979): U.S. Representative from Oklahoma, 1927-1943; Oklahoma State Auditor, 1951-1955; Secretary of State of Oklahoma, 1947-1951; Member of Oklahoma State Senate, 1919-1922; Member of Oklahoma State House of Representatives, 1915-1918.
- **Cederberg, Elford Albin** (1918 – 2006): U.S. Representative from Michigan, 1953-1978.
- **Citron, William Michael** (1896 – 1976): U.S. Representative from Connecticut, 1935-1939; Member of Connecticut State House of Representatives, 1927-1931.
- **Christopher, George Henry** (1888 – 1959): U.S. Representative from Missouri, 1949-1951, 1955-1959.
- **Christopherson, Charles Andrew** (1871 – 1951): U.S. Representative from South Dakota, 1919-1933; Member of South Dakota State House of Representatives, 1913-1916; Speaker of the South Dakota State House of Representatives, 1915-1916.
- **Clague, Frank** (1865 – 1952): U.S. Representative from Minnesota, 1921-1933; District Judge in Minnesota, 1918-1920; Member of Minnesota State Senate, 1907-1914; Member of Minnesota State House of Representatives, 1903-1906; Speaker of the Minnesota State House of Representatives, 1905.
- **Cole, Clay** (1897 – 1965): U.S. Representative from Missouri, 1943-1949, 1953-1955.
- **Cole, William Purrington Jr.,** (1889 – 1957): U.S. Representative from Maryland, 1927-1929, 1931-1943; Judge of U.S. Customs Court, 1942-1952; Judge of U.S. Court of Customs and Patent Appeals, 1952-1957.
- **Collins, Ross Alexander** (1880 – 1968): U.S. Representative from Mississippi, 1921-1935, 1937-1943; Mississippi State Attorney General, 1911-1919.
- **Cooper, John Gordon** (1872 – 1955): U.S. Representative from Ohio, 1915-1937; Member of Ohio state House of Representatives, 1911-1915.

- **Cramton, Louis Convers** (1875 – 1966): U.S. Representative from Michigan, 1913-1931; Circuit Judge in Michigan, 1934-1941; Member of Michigan State House of Representatives, 1909-1910, 1949-1960.
- **Cumback, William** (1829 – 1905): U.S. Representative from Indiana, 1855-1857; Lieutenant Governor of Indiana, 1867-1872; U.S. Collector of Internal Revenue, 1879; Member of Indiana State Senate, 1867.
- **Cummings, Fred Nelson** (1864 – 1952): U.S. Representative from Colorado, 1933-1941.
- **Cunningham, Paul Harvey** (1890 – 1961): U.S. Representative from Iowa, 1941-1959; Member of Iowa State House of Representatives, 1933-1936.
- **Davenport, James Sanford** (1864 – 1940): U.S. Representative from Oklahoma, 1907-1909, 1911-1917; Judge, Oklahoma Criminal Court of Appeals, 1927-1931.
- **Davey, Martin Luther** (1884 – 1946): U.S. Representative from Ohio, 1918-1921, 1923-1929.
- **Davis, James Curran** (1895 – 1981): U.S. Representative from Georgia, 1947-1963; Member of Georgia State House of Representatives, 1925-1928; Superior Court Judge in Georgia, 1934-1947.
- **De Priest, Oscar Stanton** (1871 – 1951): U.S. Representative from Illinois, 1929-1935.
- **Disney, Wesley Ernest** (1883 – 1961): U.S. Representative from Oklahoma, 1931-1945; Member of Oklahoma State House of Representatives, 1919-1924.
- **Dodds, Francis Henry** (1858 – 1940): U.S. Representative from Michigan, 1909-1913.
- **Dominick, Frederick Haskell** (1877 – 1960): U.S. Representative from South Carolina, 1917-1933; Member of South Carolina state House of Representatives, 1901-1902.
- **Dorsey, Washington Emery** (1842 – 1911): U.S. Representative from Nebraska, 1885-1891.
- **Elliott, Carl Atwood** (1913 – 1999): U.S. Representative from Alabama, 1949-1965.
- **Ford, George** (1846 – 1917): U.S. Representative from Indiana, 1885-1887; Superior Court Judge in Indiana, 1914.
- **Free, Arthur Monroe** (1879 – 1953): U.S. Representative from California, 1921-1933.
- **Freer, Romeo Hoyt** (1846 – 1913): U.S. Representative from West Virginia, 1899-1901; West Virginia State Attorney General, 1901-1905; Circuit Judge in West Virginia, 1897-1899; U.S. Commercial Agent (Consul) in San Juan del Norte, 1873-1877; Member of West Virginia State House of Delegates, 1891-1892.
- **Fitzgerald, Roy Gerald** (1875 – 1962): U.S. Representative from Ohio, 1921-1931.
- **Foss, Frank Herbert** (1865 – 1947): U.S. Representative from Massachusetts, 1925-1935.
- **Fuller, Alvan Tufts** (1878 – 1958): U.S. Representative from Massachusetts, 1917-1921; Member of Massachusetts State House of Representatives, 1915.
- **Gandy, Harry Luther** (1881 – 1957): U.S. Representative from South Dakota, 1915-1921; and Member of South Dakota State Senate, 1911-1912.
- **Gasque, Allard Henry** (1873 – 1938): U.S. Representative from South Carolina, 1923-1938.
- **Gifford, Charles Laceille** (1871 – 1947): U.S. Representative from Massachusetts, 1922-1947; Member of Massachusetts State Senate, 1914-1919; Member of Massachusetts State House of Representatives, 1912-1913.
- **Gilbert, Newton Whiting** (1862 – 1939): U.S. Representative from Indiana, 1905-1906; Governor-General of the Philippine Islands,

1913; Lieutenant Governor of Indiana, 1901-05; Member of Indiana State Senate, 1897-99.
- **Gillette, Wilson Darwin** (1880 – 1951): U.S. Representative from Pennsylvania, 1941-1951; Member of Pennsylvania State House of Representatives, 1931-41.
- **Goodwin, Angier Louis** (1881 – 1975): U.S. Representative from Massachusetts, 1943-1955; Member of Massachusetts State Senate, 1929-1941; Member of Massachusetts State House of Representatives, 1925-1928.
- **Goodwin, Philip Arnold** (1905 – 1983): U.S. Representative from New York, 1933-1937.
- **Goodwin, Robert Kingman** (1882 – 1937): U.S. Representative from Iowa, 1940-1941.
- **Graham, Louis Edward** (1880 – 1965): U.S. Representative from Pennsylvania, 1939-55.
- **Gregory, William Voris** (1877 – 1936): U.S. Representative from Kentucky, 1927-1936; U.S. Attorney for the Western District of Kentucky, 1919-1922.
- **Griffith, Francis Marion** (1849 – 1927): U.S. Representative from Indiana, 1897-1905; Circuit Judge in Indiana, 1916-22; Member of Indiana State Senate, 1887-94; Lieutenant Governor of Indiana, 1891-94.
- **Guyer, Ulysses Samuel** (1868 – 1943): U.S. Representative from Kansas, 1924-1925, 1927-1943.
- **Hale, Fletcher** (1883 – 1931): U.S. Representative from New Hampshire, 1925-1931.
- **Haines, Harry Luther** (1880 – 1947): U.S. Representative from Pennsylvania, 1931-1939, 1941-1943.
- **Hall, Homer William** (1870 – 1954): U.S. Representative from Illinois, 1927-1933.
- **Hall, Philo** (1865 – 1938): U.S. Representative from South Dakota, 1907-1909; South Dakota State Attorney General, 1903-1907; Member of South Dakota State Senate, 1901-1902.
- **Hammer, William Cicero** (1865 – 1930): U.S. Representative from North Carolina, 1921-1930; U.S. Attorney for the Western District of North Carolina, 1914-1920.
- **Harsha, William Howard Jr.** (1921 – 2010): U.S. Representative from Ohio, 1961-1981.
- **Hart, Archibald Chapman** (1873 – 1935): U.S. Representative from New Jersey, 1912-1913, 1913-1917.
- **Haskell, Reuben Locke** (1878 – 1971): U.S. Representative from New York, 1915-1919.
- **Henry, Robert Kirkland** (1890 – 1946): U.S. Representative from Wisconsin, 1945-1946; Wisconsin state treasurer, 1933-1936.
- **Herlong, Albert Sydney Jr.** (1909 – 1995): U.S. Representative from Florida, 1949-1969; Member U.S. Securities and Exchange Commission, 1969-1973.
- **Hersey, Ira Greenlief** (1858 – 1943): U.S. Representative from Maine, 1917-1929; Member of Maine State Senate, 1913-1916; Member of Maine State House of Representatives, 1909-1912.
- **Hill, John Boynton Philip Clayton** (1879 – 1941): U.S. Representative from Maryland, 1921-1927; U.S. Attorney for Maryland, 1910-1915.
- **Hill, William Silas** (1886 – 1972): U.S. Representative from Colorado, 1941-1959.
- **Hinebaugh, William Henry** (1867 – 1943): U.S. Representative from Illinois, 1913-1915.
- **Holmes, Pehr Gustaf** (1881 – 1952): U.S. Representative from Massachusetts, 1931-1947.
- **Howard, Edgar** (1858 – 1951): U.S. Representative from Nebraska, 1923-1935; Lieutenant Governor of Nebraska, 1917-1919.
- **Huddleston, George** (1869 – 1960): U.S. Representative from Alabama, 1915-1937.

- **Hull, Harry Edward** (1864 – 1938): U.S. Representative from Iowa, 1915-1925.
- **Ichord, Richard Howard II** (1926 – 1992): U.S. Representative from Missouri, 1961-1981; Member of Missouri State House of Representatives, 1953-1960; Speaker of the Missouri State House of Representatives, 1959-1960.
- **Jacobsen, Bernhard Martin** (1862 – 1936): U.S. Representative from Iowa, 1931-1936.
- **James, William Francis** (1873 – 1945): U.S. Representative from Michigan, 1915-1935; Member of Michigan State Senate, 1911-1914.
- **Johnson, Luther Alexander** (1875 – 1965): U.S. Representative from Texas, 1923-1946.
- **Jonas, Charles Andrew** (1876 – 1955): U.S. Representative from North Carolina, 1929-1931; U.S. Attorney for the Western District of North Carolina, 1931-1932; Member of North Carolina State House of Representatives, 1927-1930, 1935-1938; Member of North Carolina State Senate, 1915-1918.
- **Kearns, Charles Cyrus** (1869 – 1931): U.S. Representative from Ohio, 1915-1931.
- **Kearns, Carroll Dudley** (1900 – 1976): U.S. Representative from Pennsylvania, 1947-1963.
- **Kee, John** (1874 – 1951): U.S. Representative from West Virginia, 1933-1951; Member of West Virginia State Senate, 1923-1926.
- **Keeney, Russell Watson** (1897 – 1958): U.S. Representative from Illinois, 1957-1958.
- **Keller, Kent Ellsworth** (1867 – 1954): U.S. Representative from Illinois, 1931-1941; Member of Illinois State Senate, 1913-1917.
- **Kettner, William** (1864 – 1930): U.S. Representative from California, 1913-1921.
- **Knutson, Harold** (1880 – 1953): U.S. Representative from Minnesota, 1917-1949.
- **Kunkel, John Crain** (1898 – 1970): U.S. Representative from Pennsylvania, 1939-1951, 1961-1967.
- **Lambertson, William Purnell** (1880 – 1957): U.S. Representative from Kansas, 1929-1945; Member of Kansas State House of Representatives, 1909; Speaker of the Kansas State House of Representatives, 1919-1920; Member of Kansas State Senate, 1913-1915.
- **Larrabee, Henry** (1870 – 1960): U.S. Representative from Indiana, 1931-1943; Member of Indiana State House of Representatives, 1923.
- **Lanham, Henderson Lovelace** (1888 – 1957): U.S. Representative from Georgia, 1947-1957; Member of Georgia State House of Representatives, 1929-1934, 1937-1940.
- **Larsen, William Washington** (1871 – 1938): U.S. Representative from Georgia, 1917-1933; Superior Court Judge in Georgia, 1914-1915.
- **Lord, Bert** (1869 – 1939): U.S. Representative from New York, 1935-1939; Member of New York State Senate, 1930-1934; Member of New York State Assembly, 1915-1921, 1924-1930.
- **Magee, James McDevitt** (1877 – 1949): U.S. Representative from Pennsylvania, 1923-1927.
- **Magee, Clare** (1899 – 1969): U.S. Representative from Missouri, 1949-1953.
- **Magrady, Frederick William** (1863-1954): U.S. Representative from Pennsylvania, 1925-1933.
- **Major, James Earl** (1887 – 1972): U.S. Representative from Illinois, 1923-1925, 1927-1929, 1931-1933; Judge of U.S. Court of Appeals, 1937-1956; Judge of U.S. District Court, 1933-1937.
- **Mapes, Carl Edgar** (1874 – 1939): U.S. Representative from Michigan, 1913-1939; Member of Michigan State Senate, 1909-1912; Member of Michigan State House of Representatives, 1905-1906.

Notable Members | 231

- **Martin, John Cunningham** (1880 – 1952): U.S. Representative from Illinois, 1939-1941; Illinois State Treasurer, 1933-1935, 1937-1939.
- **McGugin, Harold Clement** (1893 – 1946): U.S. Representative from Kansas, 1931-1935; Member of Kansas State House of Representatives, 1927.
- **McMaster, William Henry** (1877 – 1968): U.S. Senator from South Dakota, 1925-1931; Member of South Dakota State Senate, 1913-1916; Member of South Dakota State House of Representatives, 1911-1912.
- **Marsalis, John Henry** (1904 – 1971): U.S. Representative from Colorado, 1949-1951; District Judge in Colorado, 1955-1962.
- **Martin, John Cunningham** (1880 – 1952): U.S. Representative from Illinois, 1939-1941; Illinois State Treasurer, 1933-1935, 1937-1939.
- **McFall, John Joseph** (1918 – 2006): U.S. Representative from California, 1957-1979; Member of California State Assembly, 1951-1956; Mayor of Manteca, California, 1948-1950.
- **McGugin, Harold Clement** (1893 – 1946): U.S. Representative from Kansas, 1931-1935; Member of Kansas State House of Representatives, 1927.
- **Morey, Henry Lee** (1841 – 1902): U.S. Representative from Ohio, 1881-1884, 1889-1891.
- **Morrow, Edwin Porch** (1877 – 1935): U.S. Representative from Kentucky, 1934; Governor of Kentucky, 1919-1923; U.S. Attorney for the Eastern District of Kentucky, 1911-1914.
- **Natcher, William Huston** (1909 – 1994): U.S. Representative from Kentucky, 1953-1994.
- **Neal, William Elmer** (1875 – 1959): U.S. Representative from West Virginia, 1953-1955, 1957-1959; Member of West Virginia State House of Delegates, 1951-1952.
- **Nicholson, Donald William** (1888 – 1968): U.S. Representative from Massachusetts, 1947-1959; Member of Massachusetts State House of Representatives, 1925-1926; Member of Massachusetts State Senate, 1927-1947.
- **Odell, Benjamin Barker Jr.** (1854 – 1926): U.S. Representative from New York, 1895-1899.
- **Owen, Emmett Marshall** (1877 – 1939): U.S. Representative from Georgia, 1933-1939; Member of Georgia State House of Representatives, 1902-1906.
- **Parks, Tilman Bacon** (1872 – 1950): U.S. Representative from Arkansas, 1921-1937; Member of Arkansas State House of Representatives, 1901-1904, 1909-1910.
- **Parsons, Claude VanCleve** (1895 – 1941): U.S. Representative from Illinois, 1930-1941.
- **Peterson, James Hardin** (1894 – 1978): U.S. Representative from Florida, 1933-1951.
- **Pettit, John Upfold** (1820 – 1881): U.S. Representative from Indiana, 1855-1861; Circuit Judge in Indiana, 1853-1854, 1873-1879; Member of Indiana State House of Representatives, 1844-1845, 1865; Speaker of the Indiana State House of Representatives, 1865.
- **Pfeiffer, William Louis** (1907 – 1985): U.S. Representative from New York, 1949-1951.
- **Rainey, Henry Thomas** (1860 – 1934): U.S. Representative from Illinois, 1903-1921, 1923-1934; Speaker of the U.S. House, 1933-1934.
- **Raker, John Edward** (1863 – 1926): U.S. Representative from California, 1911-1926; Superior Court Judge in California, 1905-1910.
- **Ramey, Frank Marion** (1881 – 1942): U.S. Representative from Illinois, 1929-1931.
- **Ramsey, John Rathbone** (1862 – 1933): U.S. Representative from New Jersey, 1917-1921.
- **Ramsay, Robert Lincoln** (1877 – 1956): U.S. Representative from West Virginia, 1933-1939, 1941-1943, 1949-1953.

- **Ramspeck, Robert C. Word** (1890 – 1972): U.S. Representative from Georgia, 1929-1945; Member of Georgia State House of Representatives, 1929-1931.
- **Randell, Choice Boswell** (1857 – 1945): U.S. Representative from Texas, 1901-1913.
- **Rathbone, Henry Riggs** (1870 – 1928): U.S. Representative from Illinois, 1923-1928.
- **Reed, Chauncey William** (1890 – 1956): U.S. Representative from Illinois, 1935-1956.
- **Rogers, Byron Giles** (1900 – 1983): U.S. Representative from Colorado, 1951-1971; Colorado State Attorney General, 1936-40; Member of Colorado State House of Representatives, 1931-1935; Speaker of the Colorado State House of Representatives, 1933.
- **Salmon, William Charles** (1868 – 1925): U.S. Representative from Tennessee, 1923-1925.
- **Sasscer, Lansdale Ghiselin** (1893 – 1964): U.S. Representative from Maryland, 1939-1953; Member of Maryland State Senate, 1922-1938.
- **Scott, Frank Douglass** (1878 – 1951): U.S. Representative from Michigan, 1915-1927; Member of Michigan State Senate, 1911-1914.
- **Sears, Willis Gratz** (1860 – 1949): U.S. Representative from Nebraska, 1923-1931; Member of Nebraska State House of Representatives, 1901-1904, 1905-1922, and 1933-1948.
- **Sebelius, Keith George** (1916 – 1982): U.S. Representative from Kansas, 1969-1981; Member of Kansas State Senate, 1962-1968.
- **Sirovich, William Irving** (1882 – 1939): U.S. Representative from New York, 1927-1939; President, Industrial National Bank, DNA.
- **Schiffler, Andrew Charles** (1889 – 1970): U.S. Representative from West Virginia, 1939-1941, 1943-1945.
- **Stubbs, Henry Elbert** (1881 – 1937): U.S. Representative from California, 1933-1937.
- **Sloss, Joseph Humphrey** (1826 – 1911): U.S. Representative from Alabama, 1871-1875; Member of Illinois State House of Representatives, 1858-1859.
- **Smith, John M. C.** (1853 – 1923), U.S. Representative from Michigan, 1911-21, 1921-23; and President, First National Bank of Charlotte, 1889-1923.
- **Sproul, Elliott Wilford** (1856 – 1935): U.S. Representative from Illinois, 1921-1931.
- **Swank, Fletcher B.** (1875 – 1950): U.S. Representative from Oklahoma, 1921-1929, 1931-1935; District Judge in Oklahoma 14th District, 1915-1920; Cleveland County Judge, 1911-14.
- **Tarver, Malcolm Connor** (1885 – 1960): U.S. Representative from Georgia, 1927-1947; Superior Court Judge in Georgia, 1917-1926; Member of Georgia State Senate, 1913-1914; Member of Georgia State House of Representatives, 1909-1912.
- **Taylor, Edward Thomas** (1858 – 1941): U.S. Representative from Colorado, 1909-1941; Member of Colorado State Senate, 1896-1908.
- **Taylor, James Alfred** (1878 – 1956): U.S. Representative from West Virginia, 1923-1927; Member of West Virginia State House of Delegates, 1917-1918, 1921-1922, 1931-1932, 1937-1938; Speaker of the West Virginia State House of Delegates, 1931-1932.
- **Thom, William Richard** (1885 – 1960): U.S. Representative from Ohio, 1933-1939, 1941-1943, 1945-1947.
- **Taylor, James Willis** (1880 – 1939): U.S. Representative from Tennessee, 1919-1939; Tennessee Insurance Commissioner, 1913-1914.
- **Tirrell, Charles Quincy** (1844 – 1910): U.S. Representative from Massachusetts, 1901-1910;

Member of Massachusetts State Senate, 1881-1882; Member of Massachusetts State House of Representatives, 1872.
- **Traeger, William Isham** (1880 – 1935): U.S. Representative from California, 1933-1935.
- **Turpin, Charles Murray** (1878 – 1946): U.S. Representative from Pennsylvania, 1929-1937.
- **Tweed, William Magear** (1823 – 1878): U.S. Representative from New York, 1853-1855; Member of New York State Senate, 1868-1873.
- **Walter, Francis Eugene** (1894 – 1963): U.S. Representative from Pennsylvania, 1933-1963.
- **Weideman, Carl May** (1898 – 1972): U.S. Representative from Michigan, 1933-1935; Circuit Judge in Michigan, 1950-1967.
- **Weiss, Samuel Arthur** (1902 – 1977): U.S. Representative from Pennsylvania, 1941-1946; Member of Pennsylvania State House of Representatives, 1935-1939.
- **Willett, William Forte Jr.** (1869 – 1938): U.S. Representative from New York, 1907-1911.
- **Williamson, William Jr.** (1875 – 1972): U.S. Representative from South Dakota, 1921-1933; Circuit Judge in South Dakota, 1911-1921.
- **Wilson, Thomas Webber** (1893 – 1948): U.S. Representative from Mississippi, 1923-1929; U.S. District Judge for Virgin Islands, 1933-1935.
- **Whitley, James Lucius** (1872 – 1959): U.S. Representative from New York, 1929-1935; Member of New York State Senate, 1919-1928; Member of New York State Assembly, 1906-1910.
- **Wolcott, Jesse Paine** (1893 – 1969): U.S. Representative from Michigan, 1931-1957.
- **Woodruff, Roy Orchard** (1876 – 1953): U.S. Representative from Michigan, 1913-1915, 1921-1953.

STATE SENATORS

- **Aaron, Nathan** (1905 – 1974): Member of Connecticut State Senate, 1945-1946.
- **Abbott, Sewall** (1859 – DNA): Wester Member of New Hampshire State Senate, 1923-1925.
- **Ackroyd, Joseph** (1847 – 1915): Member of New York State Senate, 1907-1908.
- **Adams, Alfred Armstrong** (1865 – DNA): Member of Tennessee State Senate, 1903-1905, 1911-1913; Member of Tennessee State House of Representatives, 1901-1902, 1929-1930.
- **Allen, Charles E.** (1865 – DNA): Member of Nebraska State Senate, 1923, 1931, 1935.
- **Allen, George Whiting** (1854 – DNA): Member of Florida State Senate, 1879-1883; U.S. Collector of Customs, 1897-1913.
- **Allen, Harmon Gustavus** (1866 – DNA): Member of Maine State Senate, 1921-1922; Member of Maine State House of Representatives, 1919-1920, 1931-1932; Organizer and Vice-President of Sanford National Bank, DNA.
- **Allen, Mark W.** (1877 – DNA): Member of New York State Senate, 1923-1924.
- **Anthony, George Fort Donelson** (1862 – DNA): Member of Illinois State Senate, 1895-1899.
- **Arbuckle, Richard Dean** (1926 – DNA): Member of Iowa State Senate, 1971.
- **Arbuckle, Arlene** (1917 – 1989): Member of Pennsylvania State Senate, 1967-1980; Member of Pennsylvania State House of Representatives, 1959-1966.
- **Arnold, A. Otis** (1878 – 1941): Member of Illinois State Senate, 1941; Member of Illinois State House of Representatives, 1919-1929.
- **Ashworth, Ben H.** (1888 – DNA): Member of West Virginia State Senate, 1925-1928; Circuit Judge in West Virginia, 1945.

- **Avis, John Boyd** (1875 – 1944): Member of New Jersey State Senate, 1906-1908; U.S. District Judge for New Jersey, 1929-1944; Speaker of the New Jersey State House of Assembly, 1904-1905; Member of New Jersey State House of Assembly, 1902-1905.
- **Bacon, Gaspar** (1886 – 1947): Griswold Member of Massachusetts State Senate, 1925-1932; Lieutenant Governor of Massachusetts, 1934; Director, Southern Railway Co., Eliot Savings Bank, DNA.
- **Bailey, Martin Brachall** (1858 – DNA): Member of Illinois State Senate, 1901-1903, 1903-1905, 1909-1933; Member of Illinois State House of Representatives, 1894.
- **Bailey, Norman** (1859 – 1918): Member of Michigan State Senate, 1861-1862.
- **Bailey, Theodore Mead** (1862 – DNA): Member of South Dakota State Senate, 1925-1926; Member of South Dakota State House of Representatives, 1921-1922.
- **Baldwin, Frank Elmer** (1870 – 1947): Member of Pennsylvania State Senate, 1909-1912, 1917-1932; Pennsylvania State Auditor General, 1933-1937.
- **Bangham, Arthur D.** (1859 – 1918): Member of Michigan State Senate, 1901-1904.
- **Bates, Stoddard Benham** (1862 – DNA): Member of Vermont State Senate, 1923; Member of Vermont State House of Representatives, 1910.
- **Barber, Herbert Goodell** (1870 – 1947): Member of Vermont State Senate, 1912-1914; Member of Vermont State House of Representatives, 1908-1910, 1935-1937; Vermont State Attorney General, 1915-1919.
- **Barber, William Perry** (1907 – 1984): Member of Connecticut State Senate, 1943-1946; Superior Court Judge in Connecticut, 1964; and Mayor of Putnam, Connecticut, 1940.
- **Barton, Jesse Morton** (1870 – DNA): Member of New Hampshire State Senate, 1916; Member of New Hampshire State House of Representatives, 1901-1902.
- **Baumes, Caleb** (1865 – 1937): Howard Member of New York State Senate, 1919-1930; Member of New York State Assembly, 1909-1913.
- **Baxter, Witter Johnston** (1816 – 1888): Member of Michigan State Senate, 1877-1878; Member of Michigan State Board of Education, 1857-1876, 1877-1881.
- **Beebe, M. Plin** (1881 – 1941): Member of South Dakota State Senate, 1915-1916.
- **Bennett, Thomas Warren** (1831 – 1893): Member of Indiana State Senate, 1859-1861, 1865-1867; General in the Union Army during the American Civil War.
- **Bentley, James Lynwood** (1904 – 1975): Member of Georgia State Senate, 1945-1946; Member of Georgia State House of Representatives, 1941-1944.
- **Barkley, James Robert** (1869 – 1948): Member of Iowa State Senate, 1945-1947.
- **Beardsley, William S.** (1901 – 1954): Member of Iowa State Senate, 1933-1941; Member of Iowa State House of Representatives, 1947-1948.
- **Bishop, Otto William** (1875 – 1966): Member of Michigan State Senate, 1935-1948.
- **Blake, Raymond** (1896 – 1984): Member of Vermont State Senate, 1965; Member of Vermont State House of Representatives, 1937-1939, 1959.
- **Blood, Robert Oscar** (1887 – 1975): Member of New Hampshire State Senate, 1937-1940; Member of New Hampshire State House of Representatives, 1935.
- **Boner, Floyd D.** (1878 – 1969): Member of West

Virginia State Senate, 1945-1952.
- **Brereton, Henry E. H.** (1865 – 1957): Member of New York State Senate, 1927-1932; Member of New York State Assembly, 1911-1917.
- **Bright, William H.** (1863 – DNA): Member of New Jersey State Senate, 1919-1927.
- **Brown, Thomas C.** (1870 – 1952): Member of New York State Senate, 1925-1930.
- **Buckley, Monroe Leer** (1905 – 1979): Member of Kentucky State Senate, 1936-1939; Member of Kentucky State House of Representatives, 1932-1933.
- **Burhans, Earl L.** (1883 – 1945): Member of Michigan State Senate, 1937-1942; Member of Michigan State House of Representatives, 1931-1934; Member of University of Michigan Board of Regents, 1942.
- **Burritt, Fred W.** (1875 – 1948): Member of Michigan State Senate, 1943-1948.
- **Burrows, Warren Booth** (1877 – 1952): Member of Connecticut State Senate, 1927-1928; Connecticut State Attorney General, 1931-1935; U.S. District Judge for Connecticut, 1928-1930; Member of Connecticut State House of Representatives, 1925-1926.
- **Burrus, John T.** (1877 – DNA) Member of North Carolina State Senate, 1931-1935.
- **Busbee, Charles Manly** (1845 – 1909): Member of North Carolina State Senate, 1875-1876; Member of North Carolina State House of Representatives, 1885-1886; Postmaster at Raleigh, North Carolina, 1894-1898.
- **Bussey, Thomas H.** (1857 – 1937): Member of New York State Senate, 1911- 1914.
- **Butt, Festus Orestes** (1875 – 1972): Member of Arkansas State Senate, DNA; member of Arkansas State House of Representatives, DNA.
- **Buttrick, Allan Gordon** (1876 – DNA): Member of Massachusetts State Senate, 1906; Member of Massachusetts State House of Representatives, 1904.
- **Buxton, Willis George** (1856 – DNA): Member of New Hampshire State Senate, 1897-1898; Member of New Hampshire State House of Representatives, 1895.
- **Buzzell, Hodgdon C.** (1878 – DNA): Member of Maine State Senate, 1925; Member of Maine State House of Representatives, 1919-1920.
- **Cammack, James William** (1869 – DNA): Member of Kentucky State Senate, 1904-1907; Kentucky State Attorney General, 1927-1931; Circuit Judge in Kentucky, 1907-1916.
- **Carrigan, Charles E.** (1871 – DNA): Member of West Virginia State Senate, 1903-1906.
- **Casto, Boyd Cleo** (1892 – 1951): Member of West Virginia State Senate, 1939-1942.
- **Chapman, Maro Spaulding** (1839 – 1907): Member of Connecticut State Senate, 1885-1886; Member of Connecticut State House of Representatives, 1882.
- **Chernenko, John G.** (1924 – DNA): Member of West Virginia State Senate, 1983- 1994.
- **Cherry, Robert Gregg** (1891 – 1957): Member of North Carolina State Senate, 1941-1943; Governor of North Carolina, 1945-1949; Member of North Carolina State House of Representatives, 1931-1940; Speaker of the North Carolina State House of Representatives, 1937; Mayor of Gastonia, North Carolina, 1919-1923.
- **Christensen, John** (1890 – 1970): Member of Connecticut State Senate, 1943; Member of Connecticut State House of Representatives, 1933-1942.
- **Clark, William Judson** (1825 – DNA): Member of Connecticut State Senate, 1883-1884.
- **Cole, Ernest E.** (1871 – 1949): Member of New

York State Senate, 1923-1926; New York Commissioner of Education, 1940; Member of New York State Assembly, 1920-1922.

- **Condon, Richard William** (1867 – DNA): Member of Washington State Senate, 1905-1909, 1925-1930.
- **Cornen, Peter P.** (1815 – 1893): Member of Connecticut State Senate, 1867; Member of Connecticut State House of Representatives, 1871.
- **Coughanour, William Albert** (1851 – 1936): Member of Idaho State Senate, 1896.
- **Cox, Louis Sherburne** (1874 –DNA): Member of Massachusetts State Senate, 1906; Superior Court Judge in Massachusetts, 1918-1937.
- **Clark, Herbert Augustus** (1873 – DNA): Member of Maine State Senate, 1921-1924.
- **Cram, Harry** (1871 – DNA): Lorenzo Member of Maine State Senate, 1923-1926; Member of Maine State House of Representatives, 1921-1922.
- **Cranor, Ozro N.** (1855 – 1933): Member of Indiana State Senate, 1893-1895; Member of Indiana State House of Representatives, 1889.
- **Crisona, James J.** (1907 – 2003): Member of New York State Senate, 1955-1957; Justice of New York Supreme Court, 1959-1960; Borough President of Queens, New York, 1958-1959; and Member of New York State Assembly, 1946.
- **Crossley, James Judson** (1869 – 1957): Member of Iowa State Senate, 1900-1907; U.S. Attorney for the 4th District of Alaska Territory, 1909-1914; U.S. Attorney for the 3rd District of Alaska Territory, 1908-1909.
- **Culbert, Albert E.** (1862 – 1939): Member of Ohio State Senate, 1921-1922.
- **Culkin, William Edgar** (1861 – 1949): Member of Minnesota State Senate, 1895-1897.
- **Davenport, William Aiken** (1869 – DNA): Member of Massachusetts State Senate, 1935-1936; Member of Massachusetts State House of Representatives, 1899-1900.
- **Davis, George Allen** (1858 – DNA): Member of New York State Senate, 1896-1910.
- **Davis, Gilbert Asa** (1835 – DNA): Member of Vermont State Senate, 1876-1878; Member of Vermont State House of Representatives, 1872-1876.
- **Davis, Marion Leslie** (1879 – DNA): Member of North Carolina State Senate, 1911-1914; Member of North Carolina State House of Representatives, 1907-1908, 1915-1916.
- **Davison, Harold King** (1893 – DNA): Member of New Hampshire State Senate, 1929-1930; Member of New Hampshire Governor's Council, 1939-1940; Municipal Judge in New Hampshire, 1940; Member of New Hampshire State House of Representatives, 1921-1928; Speaker of the New Hampshire State House of Representatives, 1927-1928.
- **Deal, Edson Hart** (1903 – 1967): Member of Idaho State Senate, 1941-1950; Secretary of State of Idaho, 1967; Lieutenant Governor of Idaho, 1951-1955.
- **Decker, Alpheus P.** (1887 – 1965): Member of Michigan State Senate, 1951-1954; Member of Michigan State House of Representatives, 1935-1950.
- **Dixon, George C.** (1810 – 1871): Member of Illinois State Senate, 1935-1943; Mayor of Dixon, Illinois, 1931-1934; Member of Illinois State House of Representatives, 1929-1931.
- **Donnelly, Philip Matthew** (1891 – 1961): Member of Missouri State Senate, 1925-1944; Member of Missouri State House of Representatives, 1923-1924.
- **Duncan, Cullen Steger** (1889 – 1964): Member of Missouri State Senate, 1939-1942; Member

of Missouri State House of Representatives, 1937-1938.

- **Eddy, Don J.** (1911 – DNA): Member of West Virginia State Senate, 1943-1952; Circuit Judge in West Virginia, 1960-1969; Member of West Virginia State House of Delegates, 1941-1942.
- **Edwards, Albert Edwin** (1879 – DNA): Member of Washington State Senate, 1937-1952; Member of Washington State House of Representatives, 1933-1936, 1955-1963.
- **Erickson, Edgar C.** (1895 – DNA): Member of Massachusetts State Senate, 1933-1936.
- **Ewert, Adolph W.** (1865 – DNA): Member of South Dakota State Senate, 1909-1910; South Dakota State Treasurer, 1913-1917.
- **Evans, William Franklin** (1883 – DNA): Member of North Carolina State Senate, 1913-1914.
- **Fairbanks, Alfred Gerry** (1822 – 1896): Member of New Hampshire State Senate, 1893-1894; Member of New Hampshire State House of Representatives, 1881-1882; Hillsborough County Commissioner, 1883-1889.
- **Fancher, Isaac Alger** (1833 – DNA): Member of Michigan State Senate, 1875-1876; Member of Michigan State House of Representatives, 1873-1874.
- **Farrington, Frank George** (1872 – 1933): Member of Maine State Senate, 1921-1924; Member of Maine State House of Representatives, 1917-1920; Speaker of the Maine State House of Representatives, 1919-1920.
- **Fehling, Edward William** (1880 – 1957): Member of Michigan State Senate, 1935-1938.
- **Fields, Harvey Goodwyn** (1884 – unknown): Member of Louisiana State Senate, 1916-1920; Member of Louisiana Public Service Commission, 1927-1936; U.S. Attorney for the Western District of Louisiana, 1937-1945.
- **Floyd, Charles Miller** (1861 – 1923): Member of New Hampshire State Senate, 1899-1900; Member of New Hampshire Governor's Council, 1904.
- **Folsom, LeRoy Rowell** (1870 – 1951): Member of Maine State Senate, 1919-1922; Member of Maine Governor's Council, 1923-1927; Member of Maine State House of Representatives, 1907.
- **Forsyth, Joseph H.** (1879 – DNA): Member of New Jersey State Senate, 1927-1928.
- **Freehafer, Albertus LeRoy** (1868 – 1940): Member of Idaho State Senate, 1908; Member of Idaho State House of Representatives, 1906.
- **Freed, Tilghman A.** (1895 – DNA): Member of Pennsylvania State Senate, 1951-1954; Member of Pennsylvania State House of Representatives, 1939-1940, 1943-1946.
- **Furbish, Harry Albert** (1867 – DNA): Member of Maine State Senate, 1905-1906; Member of Maine State House of Representatives, 1903-1904, 1919-1920.
- **Garcelon, Donald Dean Frye** (1880 – 1960): Member of Maine State Senate, 1921-1922; Member of Maine State House of Representatives, 1917-1920.
- **Gansser, Augustus Herbert** (1872 – 1951): Member of Michigan State Senate, 1915-1918, 1923-1932; Member of Michigan State House of Representatives, 1911-1912.
- **Gardner, Oliver Max** (1882 – 1947): Member of North Carolina State Senate, 1911-1912, 1915-1916; Lieutenant Governor of North Carolina, 1917-1921.
- **Gaskill, Job Hillman** (1804 – 1886): Member of New Jersey State Senate, 1868-1870; Member of New Jersey State House of Assembly, 1854.
- **Gibbs, Joshua Preston** (1868 – 1947):

Member of North Carolina State Senate, 1935; Member of North Carolina State House of Representatives, 1921-1922.

- **Gibson, Benjamin Joseph** (1881 – 1949): Member of Iowa State Senate, 1916-1918; Iowa State Attorney General, 1921-1927.
- **Grant, Wilbur Gill** (1906 – 1964): Member of South Carolina State Senate, 1943-1964; Member of South Carolina State House of Representatives, 1935-1938, 1941-1942.
- **Green, William** (1872 – 1952): Member of Ohio State Senate, 1911-1915.
- **Grimes, William C.** (1876 – DNA): Member of West Virginia State Senate, 1909-1912.
- **Gunning, Thomas P.** (1882 – 1943): Member of Illinois State Senate, 1931-1943.
- **Gladstone, Louis I.** (1927 – DNA): Member of Connecticut State Senate, 1959-1961.
- **Grosvenor, Ebenezer Oliver** (1820 – 1910): Member of Michigan State Senate, 1859-1860, 1863-1864; Member of University of Michigan Board of Regents, 1880-1887; Michigan State Treasurer, 1867-1870; Lieutenant Governor of Michigan, 1865-1866.
- **Hagaman, Harry T.** (1869 – 1952): Member of New Jersey State Senate, 1920-1922; Member of New Jersey State House of Assembly, 1917-1919.
- **Hager, Philip Jr.** (1872 – 1966): Member of West Virginia State Senate, 1921-1924.
- **Haigis, John William** (1881 – 1960): Member of Massachusetts State Senate, 1915-1916, 1923-1926; Trustee of the University of Massachusetts, 1940-1956; Massachusetts State Treasurer, 1929-1930; Member of Massachusetts State House of Representatives, 1909-1912.
- **Haines, William Thomas** (1854 – 1919): Member of Maine State Senate, 1889-1893; Maine State Attorney General, 1897-1900; Member of Maine State House of Representatives, 1895.
- **Haley, Cornelius F.** (1875 – DNA): Member of Massachusetts State Senate, 1927-1936; Member of Massachusetts State House of Representatives, 1919-1920.
- **Hall, Othniel D.** (1902 – 1983): Member of West Virginia State Senate, 1943-1946; Member of West Virginia State House of Delegates, 1941-1942, 1959-1960.
- **Hamlin, Howard Hutchins** (1902 – DNA): Member of New Hampshire State Senate, 1937-1939.
- **Halliburton, Wesley** (1822 – 1890): Member of Missouri State Senate, 1883-1886.
- **Hannah, William Johnson** (1867 – DNA): Member of North Carolina State Senate, 1913-1914.
- **Hansen, Harry W.** (1884 – DNA): Member of Colorado State Senate, 1929-1932.
- **Hanmer, William E.** (1879 – 1966): Member of Connecticut State Senate, 1945-1946; Member of Connecticut State House of Representatives, 1941-1944.
- **Harmer, Hardin Roads** (1899 – 1963): Member of West Virginia State Senate, 1943-1948.
- **Harmer, Harvey Walker** (1865 – 1961): Member of West Virginia State Senate, 1901-1904, 1919-1922; Member of West Virginia State House of Delegates, 1895-1896, 1929-1930, 1943-1948.
- **Hatcher, Glenn D.** (1905 – DNA): Member of West Virginia State Senate, 1961-1968; Member of West Virginia State House of Delegates, 1957-1958.
- **Helgerson, Gustav Holden** (1875 – 1965): Member of South Dakota State Senate, 1913-1914; South Dakota State Treasurer, 1917-1921; Member of South Dakota State House of Representatives, 1909-1912.
- **Higgins, George Neil** (1900 – 1982): Member

of Michigan State Senate, 1945-1946, 1949-1954; Member of Michigan State House of Representatives, 1939-1944.

- **Hill, John Sprunt** (1869 – DNA): Member of North Carolina State Senate, 1933-1935.
- **Hoke, Joseph Thatcher** (1835 – DNA): Member of West Virginia State Senate, 1867-1869; Member of West Virginia State House of Delegates, 1887-1888; U.S. Consul in Windsor, 1897-1907.
- **Hughes, Harold B.** (1911 – 1997): Member of Michigan State Senate, 1961-1964.
- **Ingersoll, John Nathaniel** (1817 – 1881): Member of Michigan State Senate, 1861-1862; Member of Michigan State House of Representatives, 1849, 1869-1870.
- **Isler, Samuel W.** (1882 – DNA): Member of Indiana State Senate, 1943-1944.
- **Jamiel, Morphis A.** (1921 – 2013): Member of Rhode Island State Senate, DNA; Member of Rhode Island State House of Representatives, DNA.
- **Johnson, Davis B.** (1880 – DNA): Member of Ohio State Senate, 1929.
- **Jones, Edward E.** (1867 – DNA): Member of Pennsylvania State Senate, 1917-1924; Member of Pennsylvania State House of Representatives, 1907-1909.
- **Kahle, I. Dana** (1875 – DNA): Member of Pennsylvania State Senate, 1935-1938; Member of Pennsylvania State House of Representatives, 1927-1931.
- **Kahlo, Charles** (1840 – DNA), Member of Indiana State Senate, 1879-1881.
- **Kaley, Frank E.** (1856 – DNA), Member of New Hampshire State Senate, 1901-1902; Member of New Hampshire Governor's Council, 1903.
- **Karickhoff, Orton R.** (1905 – DNA): Member of West Virginia State Senate, 1947-1950; Member of West Virginia State House of Delegates, 1972.
- **Karcher, Horatio S.** (1868 – 1939): Member of Michigan State Senate, 1923-1928.
- **Keeler, Edwin Olmstead** (1846 – 1923): Member of Connecticut State Senate, 1897-1900; Lieutenant Governor of Connecticut, 1901-1903; Member of Connecticut State House of Representatives, 1893-1896.
- **Kelso, Daniel** (1803 – 1857): Member of Indiana State Senate, 1842-1843; Member of Indiana State House of Representatives, 1833-1835, 1848-1849.
- **Kendall, Robert C.** (1819 – 1869): Member of Indiana State Senate, 1851-1852.
- **Kenrick, John** (1857 – DNA): Member of Massachusetts State Senate, 1893-1894; Member of Massachusetts State House of Representatives, 1891.
- **Kent, James V.** (1847 – 1918): Member of Indiana State Senate, 1877-1879; Circuit Judge in Indiana, 1896-1902.
- **Keyes, Otis McCullough** (1854 – 1937): Member of Indiana State Senate, 1899-1901; Member of Indiana State House of Representatives, 1905.
- **Knerr, Edwin J.** (DNA): Member of Rhode Island State Senate, 1911.
- **Knight, John** (1871 – DNA): Member of New York State Senate, 1917-1931; Federal Judge, 1931.
- **Laughlin, Edward E.** (1887 – DNA): Member of Illinois State Senate, 1937-1941, 1943-1953; Member of Illinois State House of Representatives, 1935-1937.
- **Lewis, John Nelson** (1847 – DNA): Member of Connecticut State Senate, 1897; Member of Connecticut State House of Representatives, 1889, 1891.
- **Lewis, Griffith Walker** (1863 – DNA):

Member of New Jersey State Senate, 1910-1912; President, G.W. Lewis & Son, DNA; President, Burlington Electric Light & Power Co., DNA; Member of New Jersey State House of Assembly, 1907-1909.
- **Lewis, John Nelson** (1847 – DNA): Member of Connecticut State Senate, 1897; Member of Connecticut State House of Representatives, 1889, 1891.
- **Liebowitz, Simon J.** (1906 – 1998): Member of New York State Senate, 1960-1968.
- **Lindsley, Myron Plato** (1825 – 1883): Member of Wisconsin State Senate, 1873-74.
- **Loder, LeRoy W.** (1883 – DNA): Member of New Jersey State Senate, 1932-1934; Judge of the Common Pleas Court in New Jersey, 1914-1919.
- **Lowry, John Augusta Way Jr.** (1848 – 1899): Member of Louisiana State Senate, 1893.
- **Love, Thomas Bell** (1870 – 1948): Member of Texas State Senate, 1927-1930; Texas Commissioner of Insurance and Banking, 1907-1910; Member of Texas State House of Representatives, 1902-1907; Speaker of the Texas State House of Representatives, 1906-1907.
- **Lusk, Clayton Riley** (1872 – DNA): Member of New York State Senate, 1919-1924.
- **MacKay, John D.** (1913 – DNA): Member of Massachusetts State Senate, 1930-1936.
- **Magness, James M.** (1872 – DNA): Member of South Dakota State Senate, 1933-1934.
- **Maine, Ernest Orrin** (1890 – 1977): Member of Rhode Island State Senate, 1949-1957; and a member of Rhode Island State House of Representatives, 1947-1949;
- **Mallery, Charles R.** (1888 – DNA): Member of Pennsylvania State Senate, 1935-1962.
- **Marsden, Arthur** (1880 – DNA): Willard Member of Connecticut State Senate, 1911-1912, 1919-1920; Member of Connecticut State House of Representatives, 1909-1910, 1913-1918, 1921-1922.
- **Martin, Alpheus** (1873 – 1941): Member of West Virginia State Senate, 1939-1941; Member of West Virginia State House of Delegates, 1935-1938.
- **Martin, Vincent A. (**1870 – DNA): Member of Michigan State Senate, 1917-1918, 1925-1928.
- **Miles, Charles Gardner** (1879 – DNA): Member of Massachusetts State Senate, 1933-1936.
- **McAllister, Frank Winton** (1873 – 1948): Member of Missouri State Senate, 1905-1912; Missouri State Attorney General, 1917-1921.
- **McBride, Claude B.** (1883 – DNA): Member of Indiana State Senate, 1935-1942.
- **McCulty, Roy L.** (1889 – DNA): Member of West Virginia State Senate, 1957-1960; Member of West Virginia State House of Delegates, 1943-1954.
- **McDougall, John E.** (1860 – DNA): Member of South Dakota State Senate, 1903-1904; Lieutenant Governor of South Dakota, 1905-1907; Member of South Dakota State House of Representatives, 1901-1902.
- **McRae, Duncan** (1869 – DNA): Member of Michigan State Senate, 1917-1922.
- **Moore, Andrew L.** (1870 – 1935): Member of Michigan State Senate, 1933-1935.
- **Moyse, George G. (**1878 – DNA): Member of Massachusetts State Senate, 1925-1936; Member of Massachusetts State House of Representatives, 1920-1924.
- **Mumford, Earl Milham** (1889 – DNA): Member of South Dakota State Senate, 1933-1936; Member of South Dakota State House of Representatives, 1923-1924.
- **Nason, Arthur Leroy** (1872 – DNA): Member

of Massachusetts State Senate, 1910-12, 1919-20; and a member of Massachusetts State House of Representatives, 1906-09, 1917-18.

- **Newton, Charles** (1861 – DNA): Damon Member of New York State Senate, 1915-1918; New York State Attorney General, 1919-1922.
- **Newton, Frank T.** (1867 – 1931): Member of Michigan State Senate, 1909-1912.
- **Nuckols, Jack A.** (1912 – DNA): Member of West Virginia State Senate, 1952-1961.
- **Nutting, Edward H.** (1869 – DNA): Member of Massachusetts State Senate, 1931-1936; Member of Massachusetts State House of Representatives, 1913, 1915-1916, 1918, 1923-1930.
- **Owlett, G. Mason** (1892 – 1956): Member of Pennsylvania State Senate, 1933-1940.
- **Oyler, Samuel Petitt** (1819 – 1898): Member of Indiana State Senate, 1865-1867; Circuit Judge in Indiana, 1869-1870.
- **Parker, Otey Roy** (1902 – 1991): Member of West Virginia State Senate, 1955-1966.
- **Payne, Abner Clinton** (1871 – DNA): Member of North Carolina State Senate, 1913-1914.
- **Pinkerton, Alfred** S. (1856 – 1922): Member of the Massachusetts State Senate and 58th President of the Massachusetts Senate, 1892 – 1893; Grand Master of the Grand Lodge of Massachusetts of the IOOF, 1888-1889; Grand Sire of The Sovereign Grand Lodge of the IOOF, 1898-1899.
- **Phelps, Charles** (1852 – 1940): Member of Connecticut State Senate, 1893-1894; Tolland County State's Attorney, 1904-1915; Connecticut State Attorney General, 1899-1903; Secretary of State of Connecticut, 1897-1899; Member of Connecticut State House of Representatives, 1885.
- **Purkitt, Claude Fouts** (1875 – 1930): Member of California State Senate, 1914-1922; Superior Court Judge in California, 1921-1928.
- **Penney, Harvey A.** (1866 – DNA): Member of Michigan State Senate, 1917-1926; Member of Michigan State House of Representatives, 1915-1916.
- **Peterson, William R.** (1894 – 1992): Member of Connecticut State Senate, 1947-1949; Member of Connecticut State House of Representatives, 1939-1943.
- **Pierce, Albert** (1876 – DNA): Member of Massachusetts State Senate, 1935-1936.
- **Pilgrim, Charles Clarke** (1874 – DNA): Member of New Jersey State Senate, 1918-20; a member of New Jersey State House of Assembly, 1915-16; Speaker of the New Jersey State House of Assembly, 1916.
- **Potter, William W.** (1869 – 1940): Member of Michigan State Senate, 1899-1900.
- **Prall, Horace Griggs** (1881 – 1951): Member of New Jersey State Senate, 1928-1936; Member of New Jersey State House of Assembly, 1926-1927.
- **Pulver, Seth Quarles** (1879 – 1943): Member of Michigan State Senate, 1927-1928; Member of Missouri State House of Representatives, 1933-1934.
- **Quinn, William Merrill** (1886 – 1958): Member of Missouri State Senate, 1935-1958.
- **Rankin, George Jr.** (1869 – 1949): Member of Pennsylvania State Senate, 1935-1938.
- **Reed, Carl B.** (1873 – DNA): Member of Iowa State Senate, 1919-1926; District Judge in Iowa, 1926-1933.
- **Reed, Perry A. C.** (1871 – DNA): Member of Nebraska State Senate, 1919-1933; Member of Nebraska State House of Representatives, 1917.
- **Riggen, John Clarence** (1882 – 1946): Member

of Missouri State Senate, 1943-1946.
- **Ritch, William Gillett** (1830 – 1904): Member of Wisconsin State Senate, 1867; Secretary of New Mexico Territory, 1880.
- **Rogers, John I.** (1910 – 1994): Member of West Virginia State Senate, 1969-1972; Member of West Virginia State House of Delegates, 1939-1948, 1951-1954.
- **Sarraf, George J.** (1901 – 1966): Member of Pennsylvania State Senate, 1956-1966; Member of Pennsylvania State House of Representatives, 1935-1956.
- **Saylor, Henry D.** (1857 – DNA): Member of Pennsylvania State Senate, 1895-1898; U.S. Consul in Matanzas, 1898-1899.
- **Sayre, Bradford** (1912 – DNA): Member of West Virginia State Senate, 1955-1957, 1969-1972; Member of West Virginia State House of Delegates, 1945-1950.
- **Searcy, Lemuel Newland** (1882 – 1944): Member of Missouri State Senate, 1927-1930, 1935-1942.
- **Sexton, Jesse Dewitt** (1885 – unknown): Member of Missouri State Senate, 1937-1948.
- **Sharpe, William R. Jr.** (1928 – 2009): Member of the West Virginia State Senate, 1960–1980, 1984–2009.
- **Sherill, Miles Osborne** (1841 – DNA): Member of North Carolina State Senate, 1885-1886, 1893-1894; Member of North Carolina State House of Representatives, 1882-1883.
- **Smith, Frank A.** (1876 – 1947): Member of Michigan State Senate, 1931-1932; Member of Michigan State House of Representatives, 1915-1924.
- **Smith, Jacob David** (1870 – 1945): Member of West Virginia State Senate, 1929-1932.
- **Snow, George W.** (1842 – 1927): Member of South Dakota State Senate, 1889-1890, 1899-1900; Lieutenant Governor of South Dakota, 1901-1905.
- **Snyder, L. B.** (1893 – 1964): Member of West Virginia State Senate, 1937-1940.
- **Sones, Charles Wesley** (1859 – 1944): Member of Pennsylvania State Senate, 1911-1930, 1933-1938.
- **Spears, Jacob Franklin Sr.** (1899 – 1946): Member of Texas State Senate, 1937-1946; Member of Texas State House of Representatives, 1934-1936.
- **Stacy, Ted T.** (1923 – DNA): Member of West Virginia State Senate, 1983-1986; Member of West Virginia State House of Delegates, 1959-1960, 1969-1970, 1973-1979.
- **Straight, Henry E.** (1864 – 1945): Member of Michigan State Senate, 1913-1916; Member of Michigan State House of Representatives, 1909-1912.
- **Talbott, Richard Edward** (1867 – 1949): Member of West Virginia State Senate, 1915-1918; West Virginia State Treasurer, 1933.
- **Taft, Arthur M.** (1854 – DNA): Member of Massachusetts State Senate, 1906-1907; Member of Massachusetts State House of Representatives, 1901-1906.
- **Taft, Herbert James** (1860 – DNA): Member of New Hampshire State Senate, 1905-1906; Member of New Hampshire State House of Representatives, 1890-1891.
- **Taylor, Walter Ross** (1858 – DNA): Member of Michigan State Senate, 1909-1912, 1915-1916.
- **Thompson, Edward Jackson** (1901 – unknown): Member of Pennsylvania State Senate, 1935-1938.
- **Thompson, George L.** (1864 – 1941): Member of New York State Senate, 1915-1941; Member of New York State Assembly, 1909-1910, 1912.
- **Town, Calvin Jay** (1875 – 1942): Member

of Michigan State Senate, 1933-1942; Member of Michigan State House of Representatives, 1919-1924, 1927-1928.
- **Tuttle, Arthur J.** (1868 – 1944): Member of Michigan State Senate, 1907-1910; U.S. District Judge for the Eastern District of Michigan, 1912-1944; U.S. Attorney for the Eastern District of Michigan, 1911-1912; President, Peoples Bank of Leslie, DNA.
- **Wallace, William Luxon** (1889 – 1974): Member of Kentucky State Senate, 1921-1924.
- **Walsh, James F.** (1864 – DNA): Member of Connecticut State Senate, 1903-1904, 1907-1908; Speaker of the Connecticut State House of Representatives, 1919-20; a member of Connecticut State House of Representatives, 1901-1902, 1919-1920; Connecticut State Treasurer, 1905-1907.
- **Ward, David Elmer** (1909 – DNA): Member of Florida State Senate, 1939-1942.
- **Watson, De Vere** (1893 – 1982): Member of Iowa State Senate; 1940, 1944.
- **Webb, Nathan** (1808 – unknown): Member of Michigan State Senate, 1861-1862.
- **Webber, William L.** (1825 – 1901): Member of Michigan State Senate, 1875.
- **Wemple, William W.** (1862 – DNA): Member of New York State Senate, 1907-1908; Member of New York State Assembly, 1903-1906.
- **Wesselius, Sybrant** (1859 – 1926): Member of Michigan State Senate, 1889.
- **Wheeler, Edward Warren** (1876 – DNA): Member of Maine State Senate, 1909-1910; Member of Maine Governor's Council, 1913-14.
- **White, Blanchard H.** (1864 – DNA): Member of New Jersey State Senate, 1913-1915, 1920-1921; Member of New Jersey State House of Assembly, 1910-1912.
- **White, Mont Z.** (1872 – DNA): Member of West Virginia State Senate, 1911-1914, 1923-1934; President of the West Virginia State Senate, 1925-1932.
- **Wilkins, Aaron Milton** (1854 – 1910): Member of New Hampshire State Senate, 1903-1904.
- **Wilson, Allen Crane Tibbetts** (1866 – DNA): Member of Maine State Senate; Member of Maine State House of Representatives, 1919-1922.
- **Williams, Ralph D.** (1928 – DNA): Member of West Virginia State Senate, 1971-1986.
- **Wiseman, Perry N.** (1869 – DNA): Member of West Virginia State Senate, 1929-1936.
- **Wolff, Joseph C.** (1849 – unknown): Member of New York State Senate, 1894-1895; Member of New York State Assembly, 1893.
- **Woodruff, Ari Harrison** (1888 – DNA): Member of Michigan State Senate, 1925-1932; Member of Michigan State House of Representatives, 1915-1924.
- **Wragg, Samuel H.** (1882 – DNA): Member of Massachusetts State Senate, 1925-1936; Member of Massachusetts State House of Representatives, 1919-1924.
- **Wright, George W.** (18720 – DNA): Member of South Dakota State Senate, 1911-1914.

STATE HOUSE OF REPRESENTATIVES

- **Agens, Martyn Livingston** (1855 – 1909): Member of Michigan State House of Representatives, 1905-1909.
- **Alexander, Cassius L.** (1875 – DNA): Member of Pennsylvania State House of Representatives, 1915-1916.
- **Amerson, Harvey Sandburg** (1875 – 1943): Member of Michigan State House of

Representatives, 1911-1912.
- **Ames, Albert Alonzo** (1842 – 1911): Member of Minnesota State House of Representatives, 1867.
- **Allan, George Herman** (1861 – DNA): Member of Maine State House of Representatives, 1901-1903, 1914, 1919-1920.
- **Allmon, Ray N.** (1918 – 2004): Member of Missouri State House of Representatives, 1965.
- **Allred, Linville H.** (1876 – 1965): Member of North Carolina State House of Representatives, 1911-1914.
- **Anderson, Andrew F.** (1857 – DNA): Member of Michigan State House of Representatives, DNA.
- **Anderson, Louis Edwin** (1884 – 1955): Member of Michigan State House of Representatives, 1929-1932, 1941-1954.
- **Atwater, Clifford J.** (1858 – DNA): Member of Connecticut State House of Representatives, 1898-1900.
- **Austin, Charles W.** (1869 – DNA): Member of Michigan State House of Representatives, 1909-1912.
- **Bacon, John Lement** (1862 – DNA): Member of Vermont State House of Representatives, 1892, 1908; and Vermont State Treasurer, 1898-1906.
- **Bailey, Alanson Cooper** (1850 – DNA): Member of New Hampshire State House of Representatives, 1895-1897.
- **Bates, John Lewis** (1859 – 1946): Member of Massachusetts State House of Representatives, 1894-1899; Speaker of the Massachusetts State House of Representatives, 1897-1899.
- **Becker, Christian** (1851 – 1917): Member of Pennsylvania State House of Representatives, 1913-16.
- **Bennett, John William** (1865 – DNA): Member of Georgia State House of Representatives, 1892-1896.
- **Bennett, Silas J.** (1874 – unknown): Member of North Carolina State House of Representatives, 1913-1914.
- **Boe, Nils Andreas** (1913 – 1992): Member of South Dakota State House of Representatives, 1951-1958; Speaker of the South Dakota State House of Representatives, 1955-1958.
- **Boutwell, Harvey Lincoln** (1860 – DNA): Member of Massachusetts State House of Representatives, 1895-1898.
- **Bowie, Thomas C.** (1876 – DNA): Member of North Carolina State House of Representatives, 1909-1910, 1913-1916, 1921-1922.
- **Boyd, Berl** (1896 – DNA): Member of Kentucky State House of Representatives, 1922.
- **Boyd, James P.** (1869 – 1964): Member of Missouri State House of Representatives, 1911-1916, 1945-1950; Speaker of the Missouri State House of Representatives, 1915-1916.
- **Bragdon, William H.** (1868 – DNA): Member of Maine State House of Representatives, 1919-22.
- **Briggs, Alexander B.** (1850 – DNA): Member of Rhode Island State House of Representatives, 1887-1888.
- **Brooks, John B.** (1871 – DNA): Member of Pennsylvania State House of Representatives, 1898-1899.
- **Burkett, Franz Upham** (1887 – DNA): Member of Maine State House of Representatives, 1931-1932; Maine State Attorney General, 1937-1940.
- **Burrows, Robert O. Sr.** (1899 – DNA): Member of Iowa State House of Representatives, 1951.
- **Butler, Luna Ermal** (1904 – 1970): Member of Missouri State House of Representatives, 1945-1952, 1955-1960, 1963-1966.

- **Cahill, Horace Tracy** (1894 – 1976): Member of Massachusetts State House of Representatives, 1928; Lieutenant Governor of Massachusetts, 1939-1945.
- **Cameron, Colin J.** (1879 – 1958): Member of Massachusetts State House of Representatives, 1936.
- **Carlton, Pritchard Sylvester** (1878 – DNA): Member of North Carolina State House of Representatives, 1913-1914.
- **Carroll, Howard Robert** (1907 – 2000): Member of Michigan State House of Representatives, 1943-1944, 1947-54; Circuit Judge in Michigan, 1956-1977.
- **Carroll, John H.** (1849 – DNA): Member of South Dakota State House of Representatives, 1903-1908.
- **Carter, William A.** (1874 – DNA): Member of Oregon State House of Representatives, 1901;
- **Casey, Mike** (1899 – DNA): Member of West Virginia State House of Representatives, 1939-1952, 1959-1968.
- **Catlin, Ashmon H.** (1869 – 1955): Member of Michigan State House of Representatives, 1911-1914.
- **Cherry, Edgar** (1865 – DNA): Manning Member of Maine State House of Representatives, DNA.
- **Chew, Jacob E.** (1863 – DNA): Member of Michigan State House of Representatives, 1917-20.
- **Clark, G. T.** (1905 – DNA): Member of Iowa State House of Representatives, 1950.
- **Clark, B.** (1927 – DNA): Member of Michigan State House of Representatives, 1965-1972.
- **Chastain, Robert E.** (1890 – DNA): Member of Georgia State House of Representatives, 1941-1942, 1945-1946, 1949-1950, 1953-1956.
- **Conary, Wiley C.** (1880 – DNA): Member of Maine State House of Representatives, 1917-1920.
- **Corn, Russell** (1903-1973): Member of Missouri State House of Representatives, 1947-1962. Mayor of Willow Springs, Missouri, DNA.
- **Cornwell, John Lee** (1872 – DNA): Member of North Carolina State House of Representatives, 1911-1914.
- **Cornick, Raymond** (1889 – DNA): Member of Iowa State House of Representatives, 1950.
- **Cooper, Clyde Eugene** (1885 – 1963): Member of Michigan State House of Representatives, 1947-1960.
- **Crabbe, Charles C.** (1878 – DNA): Member of Ohio State House of Representatives, 1918-1922; Ohio State Attorney General, 1923-27.
- **Christensen, Parley Parker** (1869 – DNA): Member of Utah State House of Representatives, 1910-1912.
- **Cruce, W. D. "Bill"** (1904 – 1972): Member of Missouri State House of Representatives, 1947-1952.
- **Daniels, William Taylor** (1874 – 1951): Member of Iowa State House of Representatives, 1911-1914.
- **Deadman, Richard Hector** (1872 – 1962): Member of Michigan State House of Representatives, 1939-1950.
- **Denman, Harris Edward** (1859 – 1944): Member of Ohio State House of Representatives, 1913-1914.
- **Darin, Frank Peter** (1899 – 1958), Member of Michigan State House of Representatives, 1925-1932.
- **Davis, William Raymond** (1877 – DNA): Member of Ohio State House of Representatives, 1913-1914.
- **Dempster, Charles W.** (1879 – 1941): Member of Montana State House of Representatives, 1901-1902; and a member of California State

Assembly, 1931-1934.
- **Devin, William Augustus** (1871 – DNA): Member of North Carolina State House of Representatives, 1911-1914.
- **Dodge, Frank L.** (1853 – 1929): Member of Michigan State House of Representatives, 1883-1886;
- **Dows, William Greene** (1864 – 1926): Member of Iowa State House of Representatives, 1897-1899.
- **DeMunbrun, L. A.** (DNA): Member of Kentucky State House of Representatives, 1946.
- **Dunsmore, Andrew B.** (1866 – 1938): Member of Pennsylvania State House of Representatives, 1905-1909.
- **Dusenbury, Frank H**. (1878 – DNA): Member of Michigan State House of Representatives, 1923-1932, 1935-1949;
- **Duvall, Milton Francis** (1896 – 1990): Member of Missouri State House of Representatives, 1945-1952.
- **Early, John Levering** (1896 – 1999): Member of Florida State House of Representatives, 1933-1939; Municipal Judge in Florida, 1944-1946.
- **Early, Samuel St. Clair** (1824 – 1882): Member of Indiana State House of Representatives, 1857-1859.
- **Eastman, Charles Sumner** (1864 – 1939): Member of South Dakota State House of Representatives, 1907-1908.
- **Edwards, William Kirkpatrick** (1820 – 1878): Member of Indiana State House of Representatives, 1846-1851, 1859, 1873; Speaker of the Indiana State House of Representatives, 1873.
- **Ehringhaus, John Christoph Blucher** (1882 – 1949): Member of North Carolina State House of Representatives, 1905-1908.
- **Fairbanks, George Chandler** (1852 – 1931): Member of Massachusetts State House of Representatives, 1909.
- **Farquhar, J. S. N.** (1881 – DNA): Member of Missouri State House of Representatives, 1921-1922, 1945-1950.
- **Feighner, Len W.** (1862 – 1948): Member of Michigan State House of Representatives, 1929-1932.
- **Fernald, Roy Lynde** (1901 – DNA): Member of Maine State House of Representatives, 1931-1932.
- **Foote, David** (1897 – 1973): Member of Wyoming State House of Representatives, 1939, 1943-1951.
- **Forney, Alva Clark** (1871 – 1956): Member of South Dakota State House of Representatives, 1921-1924; Lieutenant Governor of South Dakota, 1925-1927.
- **Gardiner, William Tudor** (1892 – 1953): Member of Maine State House of Representatives, 1921-1926; Speaker of the Maine State House of Representatives, 1925-1926.
- **Gerber, Fredrick Jr.** (1870 – 1941): Member of South Dakota State House of Representatives, 1919-1922
- **Gillespie, L. G.** (1875 – DNA): Member of Nebraska State House of Representatives, 1935-1936.
- **Gmelich, Jacob Friedrich** (1839 – 1914): Member of Missouri State House of Representatives, 1895-1896; Lieutenant Governor of Missouri, 1909-1913; Missouri State Treasurer, 1905-1909.
- **Greeley, Horace Wesley** (1857 – DNA): Member of Maine State House of Representatives, 1919-1920.
- **Greene, Luther D.** (1867 – 1959): Member of Missouri State House of Representatives, 1945-1950.

- **Griffin, Mallie Asa** (1869 – DNA): Member of North Carolina State House of Representatives, 1913-1914.
- **Haight, Charles F.** (1865 – 1954): Member of Michigan State House of Representatives, 1923-1932, 1935-1936; Municipal Judge in Michigan, 1911-18.
- **Haley, Addison E.** (1844 – DNA): Member of Maine State House of Representatives, 1873.
- **Hallock, Edwin** (1840 – DNA): Member of Connecticut State House of Representatives, 1897-1898, 1903-1906.
- **Hamilton, Robert K.** (1905 – 1986): Member of the Pennsylvania State House of Representatives, 1941-1946, 1949-1972; Speaker of the Pennsylvania House of Representatives, 1965-1966.
- **Harrington, Ralph Earl** (1881 – DNA): Member of Nebraska State House of Representatives, 1923-1926.
- **Hankins, Dewey Love** (1898 – 1976): Member of Missouri State House of Representatives, 1956.
- **Hays, J. O.** (1882 DNA): Member of Missouri State House of Representatives, 1947-1948.
- **Hazlewood, Lee** (1819 – 1887): Member of Indiana State House of Representatives, 1881.
- **Heal, William Arthur** (1867 DNA): Member of Maine State House of Representatives, 1921-1922.
- **Hill, Austin** (1917 – DNA): Member of Missouri State House of Representatives, 1947-1954.
- **Hinton, James Sidney** (1834 – 1892): Member of Indiana State House of Representatives, 1881.
- **Hutchinson, William O.** (1880 – DNA): Member of Vermont State House of Representatives, 1910.
- **Jakway, James Jencks** (1862-1949): Member of Michigan State House of Representatives, 1913-1914.
- **Jewett, Victor Francis** (1881-DNA): Member of Massachusetts State House of Representatives, 1913-1932.
- **Kelley, John Inzer** (1891 – DNA): Member of Georgia State House of Representatives, 1925-1926.
- **Kennedy, Peter** (1829 – 1903): Member of Indiana State House of Representatives, 1875.
- **Kercheval, Samuel Edward** (1847 – 1910): Member of Indiana State House of Representatives, 1887.
- **Kruse, John D.** (1893 – 1971): Member of Michigan State House of Representatives, 1943-1954.
- **Kelly, John Tillmon** (1860 – DNA): Member of Indiana State House of Representatives, 1895.
- **Kennedy, Peter** (1829 – 1903): Member of Indiana State House of Representatives, 1875.
- **Kenner, James B.** (1846 – 1910): Member of Indiana State House of Representatives, 1881.
- **Kircher, Fred L.** (1891 – 1960): Member of Michigan State House of Representatives, 1939-1946.
- **Kistler, Clarence E.** (1869 – 1947): Member of Michigan State House of Representatives, 1917-1918, 1929-1932.
- **Knaggs, Daniel A.** (1887 – 1957): Member of Michigan State House of Representatives, 1943-1944.
- **Jackman, Ernest Eugene** (1884 – DNA): Member of Nebraska State House of Representatives, 1927-1931.
- **Foster, Henry Clay** (1843 – 1890): Member of Georgia State House of Representatives, 1870-1872.
- **Frazer, William Defrees** (1849 – DNA): Member of Indiana State House of Representatives, 1881-1883.

- **Flansburg, Leonard A.** (DNA): Member of Nebraska State House of Representatives, 1917.
- **Gillespie, L. G.** (1875 – DNA): Member of Nebraska State House of Representatives, 1935-1936.
- **Griffin, Elihu** (1830 – 1887), Member of Indiana State House of Representatives, 1859.
- **Ginsburg, Bernard** (1898 – DNA): Member of Massachusetts State House of Representatives, 1925-1926, 1929-1930.
- **Grossman, Joseph B.** (1892 – 1990): Member of Massachusetts State House of Representatives, 1927-28; and member of Massachusetts Governor's Council, 1933-36.
- **Halsted, Charles L.** (1894 – 1968), Member of Minnesota State House of Representatives, 1937-1947.
- **Harrington, Ralph Earl** (1881 – DNA): Member of Nebraska State House of Representatives, 1923-1926.
- **Hayes, William H. I.** (1848 – 1907): Member of Massachusetts State House of Representatives, 1893-1899, 1902, 1904-07.
- **Hazlewood, Lee** (1819 – 1887): Member of Indiana State House of Representatives, 1881.
- **Heebner, William D.** (1848 – DNA): Member of Pennsylvania State House of Representatives, 1885-88.
- **Hedrick, John T.** (1836 – 1896): Member of Indiana State House of Representatives, 1873.
- **Hench, Samuel Mortier** (1846 – 1932): Member of Indiana State House of Representatives, 1891-1893.
- **Henderson, Alexander H.** (1841 – 1902): Member of Indiana State House of Representatives, 1883.
- **Hermann, Harry** (1872 – 1964): Member of Michigan State House of Representatives, 1939-1944, 1947-1954.
- **Hinton, James Sidney** (1834 – 1892): Member of Indiana State House of Representatives, 1881.
- **Hitch, Calvin Milton** (1869 – DNA): Member of Georgia State House of Representatives, 1896-1897; U.S. Consul in Nottingham, 1915-1920; Basel, 1924-1929; and U.S. Consul General in Wellington, 1932.
- **Jackman, Ernest Eugene** (1884 – DNA): Member of Nebraska State House of Representatives, 1927-1931.
- **Johnson, Albert Williams** (1872 – DNA): Member of Pennsylvania State House of Representatives, 1901-1902; U.S. District Judge for the Middle District of Pennsylvania, 1925; District Judge in Pennsylvania, 1912-1922.
- **Joslin, Chauncey** (DNA): Member of Michigan State House of Representatives, 1844; Circuit Judge in Michigan, 1882-1887.
- **LaChapelle, Joseph Blanchard** (1860 – 1927): Member of Nebraska State House of Representatives, 1927.
- **Lambert, Francis Eddy** (1860 – 1924): Member of Indiana State House of Representatives, 1894-1998.
- **Leonard, Edwin F.** (1862 – 1931): Member of Massachusetts State House of Representatives, 1906-1907.
- **Lawrence, Walter Edward** (1905 – 1967): Member of Massachusetts State House of Representatives, 1939-1944.
- **Leslie, Harry Guyer** (1878 – 1937): Member of Indiana state house of representatives, 1923-1927; Speaker of the Indiana State House of Representatives, 1925-1927.
- **Lewis, Isaac Chauncey** (1812 – 1893): Member of Connecticut State House of Representatives, 1848, 1859, 1862, 1866.
- **Lewis, Lynn J.** (1876 – 1938): Member

of Michigan State House of Representatives, 1915-1920.

- **Libby, Jesse Felt** (1857 – 1936): Member of New Hampshire state House of Representatives, 1903, 1905.
- **Light, John Henry** (1855 – DNA): Member of Connecticut State House of Representatives, 1899-1901; Speaker of the Connecticut State House of Representatives, 1901-1902; Connecticut State Attorney General, 1910-1915.
- **Linton, John Park** (1833 – 1892): Member of Pennsylvania State House of Representatives, 1866-1867;
- **Little, Carl O.** (1899 – 1988): Member of Michigan State House of Representatives, 1961-68.
- **MacKay, Alexander M.** (1881 – 1952): Member of Michigan State House of Representatives, 1937-1952.
- **Macomber, Charles Leonard** (1841 – DNA): Member of Maine State House of Representatives, 1919-1920.
- **Mahnkey, Charles Douglas** (1902 – 2004): Member of Missouri State House of Representatives, 1935-1936, 1945-1950.
- **Meins, Walter Robertson** (1883 –DNA): Member of Massachusetts State House of Representatives, 1912.
- **Martin, George Washington** (1841 – 1914): Member of Kansas State House of Representatives, 1883.
- **Metzgar, Carl W.** (1981 – present): Member of the Pennsylvania State House of Representatives, 2009 – present.
- **McCall, William S.** (DNA): Member of Missouri State House of Representatives, 1943-1944.
- **McCauley, Hugh Maxwell** (1879 – 1949): Member of Missouri State House of Representatives, 1945-1948.
- **McCreary, William Miller** (1837 – 1916): Member of Iowa State House of Representatives, 1904-1906.
- **McCurdy, John A**. (1841 – 1925): Member of Ohio State House of Representatives, 1897.
- **McLean, William Edward** (1832 – 1906): Member of Indiana State House of Representatives, 1861, 1867-1868.
- **Miller, Leo** (1892 – 1955): Member of Michigan State House of Representatives, 1950-1955.
- **Mittendorf, Forrest** (1906 – DNA): Member of Missouri State House of Representatives, 1939-1946, 1953-1954.
- **Moore, John W.** (1871 – DNA): Member of Michigan State House of Representatives, 1918.
- **Morley, Francis Dean** (1897 – 1976): Member of Michigan State House of Representatives, 1933-1938.
- **Nash, James L.** (1829 – 1896): Member of Indiana State House of Representatives, 1875.
- **Nelson, Hugo A.** (1894 – 1971): Member of Michigan State House of Representatives, 1945-1954.
- **Newhall, George H**. (1850 – 1923): Member of Massachusetts State House of Representatives, 1894-1895, 1906-08, 1923.
- **Newkirk, Henry Wirt** (1854 – DNA): Member of Michigan State House of Representatives, 1893-1894, 1907-1910, 1917-1918.
- **Nicholas, William H.** (1892 – DNA): Member of Iowa State House of Representatives, 1947; Lieutenant Governor of Iowa, 1951-1953, 1957-1959.
- **Norvell, Ernest Campbell** (1870 – 1941): Member of Tennessee State House of Representatives, 1917-1925.
- **Parrish, Albert T.** (1883 – DNA): Member of Missouri State House of Representatives,

1939-1942, 1955-1956.
- **Partridge, Benjamin Franklin** (1822 – 1892): Member of Michigan State House of Representatives, 1881-1882; Michigan Land Commissioner, 1877-1878; General in the Union Army during the American Civil War.
- **Pears, Don R.** (1899 – 1992): Member of Michigan State House of Representatives, 1951-1962, 1965-1970; Speaker of the Michigan State House of Representatives, 1959-1962.
- **Peeples, Thomas H.** (1882 DNA): Member of South Carolina State House of Representatives, 1911-1912, 1925-1926; South Carolina State Attorney General, 1913-1918.
- **Pendleton, Harris** (1845 – DNA): Member of Connecticut State House of Representatives, 1886.
- **Perry, Doctrine Clark** (1868 – DNA): Member of North Carolina State House of Representatives, 1913-1914.
- **Pettit, Henry Corbin** (1863 – 1913): Member of Indiana State House of Representatives, 1895-97; Speaker of the Indiana State House of Representatives, 1897.
- **Pomeroy, Albert Nevin** (1859 – 1927): Member of Pennsylvania State House of Representatives, 1895-1896, 1901-1902.
- **Randall, Charles A.** (1846 – DNA): Member of Pennsylvania State House of Representatives, 1887-1890;
- **Ratliff, Joseph Clayton** (1827 – 1909): Member of Indiana State House of Representatives, 1875.
- **Rawleigh, William Thomas** (1870 – DNA): Member of Illinois State House of Representatives, 1911-1912.
- **Reed, James Edward** (1888 – DNA): Member of Nebraska State House of Representatives, 1931.
- **Roberts, Gallatin** (1878 – DNA): Member of North Carolina State House of Representatives, 1911-1916.
- **Roe, Charles Silas** (1897 – 1959): Member of Missouri State House of Representatives, 1935-1938.
- **Rohlfs, Harry E.** (1902 – 1974): Member of Michigan State House of Representatives, 1965-1970.
- **Russell, Richard Brevard** (1861 – 1938): Member of Georgia State House of Representatives, 1882-1888.
- **Ryan, Emmett C.** (1887 – DNA): Member of South Dakota State House of Representatives, 1937-1938.
- **Sackett, Carl Leroy** (1876 – DNA): Member of Wyoming State House of Representatives, 1919-1920; First Vice-President, Sheridan Trust & Savings Bank, 1928-34.
- **Smith, Ballard** (1821 – 1866): Member of Indiana State House of Representatives, 1855-1857; Speaker of the Indiana State House of Representatives, 1857; Circuit Judge in Indiana, 1858-59.
- **Smith, Oliver Saxton** (1881 – DNA): Member of Michigan State House of Representatives, 1945-1946;
- **Smithpeter, Charles W.** (1873 – 1955): Member of Missouri State House of Representatives, 1945-1952.
- **Spencer, George A.** (1906 – DNA): Member of Missouri State House of Representatives, 1947-1952.
- **Stedronsky, John** (1872 – DNA): Member of South Dakota State House of Representatives, 1915-1918.
- **Stephenson, Joseph Burton** (1861 – DNA): Member of North Carolina State House of Representatives, 1913-1914, 1919-1920, 1929.
- **Stevens, William Everett** (1886 – DNA):

Member of Missouri State House of Representatives, 1935-1936, 1947-1948.
- **Stites, Robert C.** (1915 – 1981): Member of Michigan State House of Representatives, 1967-1970.
- **Tillett, Durant Howard** (1883 – DNA): Member of North Carolina State House of Representatives, 1907, 1913-1914.
- **Thomson, James Francis** (1891 – 1973): Member of Michigan State House of Representatives, 1929-1930.
- **Thorington, Justus** (1848 – 1927): Member of Michigan State House of Representatives, 1903-1904.
- **Trask, Eliphalet** (1806 – 1890): Member of Massachusetts State House of Representatives, 1856-1857, 1862; Lieutenant Governor of Massachusetts, 1858-61.
- **Underwood, Alexander L.** (1814 – 1870): Member of Indiana State House of Representatives, 1853.
- **Valder, Clarence A.** (1872 – 1954): Member of Nebraska State House of Representatives, 1929-1931.
- **Vawter, David G.** (1824 – 1884): Member of Indiana State House of Representatives, 1867.
- **Vickrey, Absalom M.** (1822 – 1886): Member of Indiana State House of Representatives, 1885.
- **Wallace, Charles Slover** (1864 – DNA): Member of North Carolina State House of Representatives, 1909-1914.
- **Wallace, Robert Moore** (1847 – 1914): Member of New Hampshire State House of Representatives, 1877-1878.
- **Wallace, Sumner** (1856 – 1920): Member of New Hampshire State House of Representatives, 1885; Member of New Hampshire Governor's Council, 1899-1900.
- **Warner, Joseph Everett** (1884 – DNA): Member of Massachusetts State House of Representatives; Speaker of the Massachusetts State House of Representatives, 1919-1920.
- **Webster, Harvey L.** (1867 – DNA): Member of Nebraska State House of Representatives, 1920-1923.
- **Wheeler, Alton Chapman** (1877 – DNA): Member of Maine State House of Representatives, 1911-1914; One of the Founders of the Paris Trust Company, DNA.
- **Whinrey, Walter William** (1905 – DNA): Member of Missouri State House of Representatives, 1939-1948.
- **Williams, Philip John** (1901 – DNA): Member of Michigan State House of Representatives, 1947-1948.
- **Wilson, John Stockbridge Patten Ham** (1860 – DNA): Member of Maine State House of Representatives, 1910.
- **Witty, Lee T.** (1859 – 1931): Member of Missouri State House of Representatives, 1903-1906, 1923-1924, 1927-1931.
- **Wolcott, L. J.** (1849 – DNA): Member of Michigan State House of Representatives, 1910-1917.
- **Woolfolk, Edgar Bailey** (1865 – 1956): Member of Missouri State House of Representatives, 1899-1902. He was circuit judge in Missouri, 1912-43.
- **Worthington, Marvin Lee** (1940 – 2000): Member of Kentucky State House of Representatives, 1978-2000.
- **Wright, Hamilton Mercer** (1852 – DNA): Member of Michigan State House of Representatives, 1883-86; and Mayor of Bay City, Michigan, 1887-89, 1895-97.

GOVERNORS

- **Anderson, Victor Emanuel** (1902 – 1962): Governor of Nebraska, 1955-1959; Member of Nebraska Unicameral Legislature, 1949-1950.
- **Arthur, Harold John** (1904 – 1971): Governor of Vermont, 1950-1951; Lieutenant Governor of Vermont, 1949-1950.
- **Barron, William Wallace** (1911 – 2002): Governor of West Virginia, 1961-1965.
- **Bates, John Lewis** (1859 – 1946): Governor of Massachusetts, 1903-1905; Lieutenant Governor of Massachusetts, 1900-1903.
- **Bennett, Thomas Warren** (1831 – 1893): Governor of Idaho Territory, 1871-1875.
- **Beardsley, William S.** (1901 – 1954): Governor of Iowa, 1949-1954.
- **Bigler, John** (1805 – 1871): Governor of California, 1852-1856; U.S. Minister to Chile, 1857- 1861.
- **Blood, Robert Oscar** (1887 – 1975): Governor of New Hampshire, 1941-1945.
- **Boe, Nils Andreas** (1913 – 1992): Governor of South Dakota, 1965-1969; Lieutenant Governor of South Dakota, 1963-1965.
- **Brandon, William Woodward** (1868 – 1934): Governor of Alabama, 1923-1927.
- **Brewster, Ralph Owen** (1888 – 1961): Governor of Maine, 1925-1929.
- **Brucker, Wilber Marion** (1894 – 1968): Governor of Michigan, 1931-1932; U.S. Secretary of the Army; Michigan State Attorney General, 1928-1930.
- **Bryan, Charles Wayland** (1867 – 1945): Governor of Nebraska, 1923-1925, 1931-1935.
- **Capper, Arthur** (1865 – 1951): Governor of Kansas, 1915-1919.
- **Cherry, Robert Gregg** (1891 – 1957): Governor of North Carolina, 1945-1949.
- **Clark Alonzo Monroe** (1868 – 1952): Governor of Wyoming, 1931-1933; Secretary of State of Wyoming, 1927-1935.
- **Clauson, Clinton Amos** (1895 – 1959): Governor of Maine, 1959; U.S. Collector of Internal Revenue for Maine, 1934-1953.
- **Clements, Earle Chester** (1896 – 1985): Governor of Kentucky, 1948-1950.
- **Conley, William Gustavus** (1866 – 1940): Governor of West Virginia, 1929-1933; West Virginia State Attorney General, 1908-1913.
- **Cornwell, John Jacob** (1867 – 1953): Governor of West Virginia, 1917-1921.
- **Dale, Charles Milby** (1893 – 1978): Governor of New Hampshire, 1945-1949.
- **Daly, Dominick** (1798 – 1868): Governor of Prince Edward Island, 1854-1859; Governor of South Australia, 1862-1868.
- **Davey, Martin Luther** (1884 – 1946): Governor of Ohio, 1935-1939.
- **Davis, Jonathan McMillan** (1871 – 1943): Governor of Kansas, 1923-1925.
- **Donnelly, Philip Matthew** (1891 – 1961): Governor of Missouri, 1945-49, 1953-1957.
- **Dorsey, Hugh Manson** (1871 – 1948): Governor of Georgia, 1917-1921.
- **Drake, Francis Marion** (1830 – 1903): Governor of Iowa, 1896-1898; General in the Union Army during the American Civil War; Namesake of Drake University.
- **Emmerson, Louis Lincoln** (1863 – 1941): Governor of Illinois, 1929-1933; Secretary of State of Illinois, 1917-1929.
- **Ehringhaus, John Christoph Blucher** (1882 – 1949): Governor of North Carolina, 1933-1937.
- **Fitzgerald, Frank Dwight** (1885 – 1939): Governor of Michigan, 1935-1936; Secretary of

State of Michigan, 1931-1934.
- **Floyd, Charles Miller** (1861 – 1923): Governor of New Hampshire, 1907-1909.
- **Fuller, Alvan Tufts** (1878 – 1958): Governor of Massachusetts, 1925-1929.
- **Furnas, Robert Wilkinson** (1824 – 1905): Governor of Nebraska, 1873-1875; Member of Nebraska Territorial Legislature, 1856; Member of University of Nebraska Board of Regents, 1869-1875.
- **Gardiner, William Tudor** (1892 – 1953): Governor of Maine, 1929-1933.
- **Gibson, Ernest William** (1901 – 1969): Governor of Vermont, 1947-1950.
- **Gore, Howard Mason** (1887 – 1947): Governor of West Virginia, 1925-29; U.S. Secretary of Agriculture, 1924-1925; West Virginia Commissioner of Agriculture, 1931-1933.
- **Gray, Isaac Pusey** (1828 – 1895): Governor of Indiana, 1880-1881, 1885-1889; U.S. Minister to Mexico, 1893-1895; Lieutenant Governor of Indiana, 1877-1880.
- **Gunderson, Carl** (1864 – 1933): Governor of South Dakota, 1925-1927; Lieutenant Governor of South Dakota, 1921-1925.
- **Haines, William Thomas** (1854 – 1919): Governor of Maine, 1913-1915.
- **Haight, Henry Huntly** (1825 – 1878): Governor of California, 1867-1871.
- **Hart, Louis Folwell** (1862 – 1929): Governor of Washington, 1919-1925; Lieutenant Governor of Washington, 1913-1919.
- **Hatfield, Henry Drury** (1875 – 1962): Governor of West Virginia, 1913-1917.
- **Hawley, James Henry** (1847 – 1929): Governor of Idaho, 1911-1913.
- **Hickenlooper, Bourke Blakemore** (1896 – 1971): Governor of Iowa, 1943-1945; Lieutenant Governor of Iowa, 1939-1943.
- **Hoey, Clyde Roark** (1877 – 1954): Governor of North Carolina, 1937-1941
- **Hunt, George Wylie Paul** (1859 – 1934): Governor of Arizona, 1912-1917, 1917-1919, 1923-1929, 1931-1933; U.S. Minister to Siam, 1920-1921.
- **Hyde, Arthur Mastick** (1877 – 1947): Governor of Missouri, 1921-1925; U.S. Secretary of Agriculture, 1929-1933.
- **Johnson, Edwin Carl** (1884 – 1970): Governor of Colorado, 1955-1957.
- **Kerner, Otto Jr.** (1908 – 1976): Governor of Illinois, 1961-68; Judge of U.S. Court of Appeals, 1968-74.
- **Knight, Goodwin Jess** (1896 – 1970): Governor of California, 1953-1959; Lieutenant Governor of California, 1947-1953.
- **Kump, Herman Guy** (1877 – 1962): Governor of West Virginia, 1933-1937; Circuit Judge in West Virginia, 1929-1932.
- **Landon, Alfred Mossman** (1887 – 1987): Governor of Kansas, 1933-1937.
- **Leader, George Michael** (1918 – 2013): Governor of Pennsylvania, 1955-1959.
- **Leslie, Harry Guyer** (1878 – 1937): Governor of Indiana, 1929-1933.
- **Martin, John Wellborn** (1884 – 1958): Governor of Florida, 1925-1929.
- **Meyner, Robert Baumle** (1908 – 1990): Governor of New Jersey, 1954-1962.
- **McFarland, Ernest William** (1894 – 1984): Governor of Arizona, 1955-1959.
- **McKelvie, Samuel Roy** (1881 – 1956): Governor of Nebraska, 1919-1923; and Lieutenant Governor of Nebraska, 1913-1915.
- **McMaster, William Henry** (1877 – 1968): Governor of South Dakota, 1925-1931.
- **Moody, Daniel James Jr.** (1893 – 1966): Governor of Texas, 1927-1931; Texas State

Attorney General, 1925-27.
- **Morrow, Edwin Porch** (1877 – 1935): Governor of Kentucky, 1919-1923.
- **Morton, Oliver Perry** (1823 – 1877): Governor of Indiana, 1861-67; Grand Master of the IOOF Grand Lodge of Indiana, 1854-1855.
- **Nash, George Kilborn** (1842 – 1904): Governor of Ohio, 1900-1904.
- **Neely, Matthew Mansfield** (1874 – 1958): Governor of West Virginia, 1941-1945.
- **Neville, M. Keith** (1884 – 1959): Governor of Nebraska, 1917-1919.
- **Nice, Harry Whinna** (1877 – 1941): Governor of Maryland, 1935-1939.
- **Odell, Benjamin Barker Jr.** (1854 – 1926): Governor of New York, 1901-1905.
- **O'Neill, C. William** (1916 – 1978): Governor of Ohio, 1957-1959.
- **Osborn, Chase Salmon** (1860 – 1949): Governor of Michigan, 1911-1912.
- **Perkins, George Clement** (1839-1923): Governor of California, 1880-1883.
- **Richardson, Friend William** (1865 – 1943): Governor of California, 1923-1927; California State Treasurer, 1915-23.
- **Roberts, Albert Houston** (1868 – 1946): Governor of Tennessee, 1919-1921.
- **Robertson, James Brooks Ayers** (1871 – 1938): Governor of Oklahoma, 1919-1923.
- **Rolph, James Jr.** (1869 – 1934): Governor of California, 1931-1934.
- **Russell, Richard Brevard Jr.** (1897 – 1971): Governor of Georgia, 1931-1933.
- **Sampson, Flemon Davis** (1875 – 1967): Governor of Kentucky, 1927-1931; Judge, Kentucky Court of Appeals, 1917-1924.
- **Steunenberg, Frank** (1861 – 1905): Governor of Idaho, 1897-1901.
- **Stanford, Amasa Leland** (1824 – 1893): Governor of California, 1862-1863.
- **Stelle, John H.** (1891 – 1962): Governor of Illinois, 1940-1941; Lieutenant Governor of Illinois, 1937-1940; and Treasurer of Illinois State, 1935-1937.
- **Trumbull, John Harper** (1873 – 1961): Governor of Connecticut, 1925-1931; Lieutenant Governor of Connecticut, 1925.
- **Vance, Zebulon Baird** (1830 – 1894): Governor of North Carolina, 1862-1865, 1877-1879.
- **Warren, Earl** (1891 – 1974): Governor of California, 1943–1953.

MAYORS

- **Abbott, Carroll Waite** (1855 – 1921): Mayor of Waterville, Maine, 1898.
- **Abbott, Walter W.** (1894 – unknown): Mayor of Rome, New York, 1942-1943.
- **Alexander, Cassius L.** (1875 – DNA): Mayor of Corry, Pennsylvania, 1909-1914, 1917-1922, 1929.
- **Aldridge, George** (1856 – 1922): Washington Mayor of Rochester, New York, 1894.
- **Ames, Albert Alonzo** (1842 – 1911): Mayor of Minneapolis, Minnesota, 1876-1877, 1882-1884, 1886-1889, 1901-1902.
- **Anderson, Victor Emanuel** (1902 – 1962): Mayor of Lincoln, Nebraska, 1950-1953.
- **Annin, Bert Alexander** (1872 – 1938): Mayor of Fullerton, California, 1928-1930.
- **Baker, George Luis** (1868 – 1941): Mayor of Portland, Oregon, 1917-1933.
- **Baird, Paul Revere** (1889 – DNA): Mayor of Waterville, Maine, 1925.
- **Baldwin, Frank L.** (1863 – 1938): Mayor of Youngstown, Ohio, 1906-1907.

- **Barber, Albert M.** (1846 – 1927): Mayor of Charlotte, Michigan, DNA.
- **Barney, Carl F.** (1878 – DNA): Mayor of Marion, Indiana, 1935-1942.
- **Bartlett, Charles Henry** (1872 – 1941): Mayor of Evanston, Illinois, 1925-1937.
- **Becker, Lawrence** (1869 – 1947): Mayor of Hammond, Indiana, 1904-1911; Superior Court Judge in Indiana, 1911-1914, 1934-1946.
- **Bennett, Charles** (1838 – 1903): Mayor of Charlotte, Michigan, 1897-1898.
- **Bennett, Thomas Warren** (1831 – 1893): Mayor of Richmond, Indiana, 1869-1871, 1877-1883, 1885-1887.
- **Berg, James** (1876 – 1944): Mayor of Mt. Vernon, New York, 1928-1931.
- **Bingham, John David** (1884 – 1942): Mayor of Alpena, Michigan, 1930-1940.
- **Blethen, George Herbert** (1865 – DNA): Mayor of Rockland, Maine, 1911-1913.
- **Broening, William Frederick** (1870 – 1953): Mayor of Baltimore, Maryland, 1919-1923, 1927-1931.
- **Brunnerm, Henry G.** (1885 – 1963): Mayor of Mansfield, Ohio, 1918-1924.
- **Bryan, Charles Wayland** (1867 – 1945): Mayor of Lincoln, Nebraska, 1915-1917, 1935-1937.
- **Bundlie, Gerhard J.** (1889 – 1966): Mayor of St. Paul, Minnesota, 1930-1932.
- **Bunker, Luther G.** (1868 – DNA): Mayor of Waterville, Maine, 1907-1908.
- **Burrit, Charles H.** (1854 – 1927): Mayor of Buffalo, Wyoming, 1881-1897; Chief of Mining Bureau and Judge of the Court of First Instance of Leyte, Philippines, 1898-1907; Author of the Coal Measures of the Philippines and the Spanish Mining Law.
- **Bruce, Alexander Bern** (1853 – DNA): Mayor of Lawrence, Massachusetts, 1886-1887.
- **Bruton, John Fletcher** (1861 – DNA): Mayor of Wilson, North Carolina, 1894-1896.
- **Call, Conley** (1931 – 2017): Mayor of North Wilkesboro, North Carolina, 1993-2001; Grand Master of the Grand Lodge of North Carolina of the IOOF, DNA; and Sovereign Grand Master of The Sovereign Grand Lodge of the IOOF, 1999-2000.
- **Candler, Ezekiel Samuel, Jr.** (1862 – 1944): Mayor of Corinth, Missouri, 1933-1937.
- **Carroll, Regis** (1932 – 2019): Mayor of Dunlevy, Pennsylvania, DNA.
- **Carson, Joseph Kirtley Jr.** (1891 – DNA): Mayor of Portland, Oregon, 1933-1940.
- **Campkin, Algernon S.** (DNA): Mayor of Cambridge, England, 1911-1912.
- **Cederberg, Elford Albin** (1918 – 2006): Mayor of Bay City, Michigan, 1949-1952.
- **Chabo, C. C.** (DNA): Mayor of Gillette, Wyoming, 1898-1899.
- **Cherry, Edgar** (1865 – DNA): Mayor of Eastport, Maine, 1914-1915.
- **Cherry, Robert Gregg** (1891 – 1957): Mayor of Gastonia, North Carolina, 1919-1923.
- **Childs, Edwin O.** (1876 – DNA): Mayor of Newton, Massachusetts, 1914-1929, 1936-1939.
- **Clauson, Clinton Amos** (1895 – 1959): Mayor of Waterville, Maine, 1956-1957.
- **Coburn, Jesse Milton** (1853 – 1923): Mayor of South Norwalk, Connecticut, 1898-1899.
- **Cobb, Theodore Gettys** (1867 – DNA): Mayor of Morganton, North Carolina, 1903-1904.
- **Cole, Alvah H.** (1884 – 1970), Mayor of Highland Park, New Jersey, 1948-1951.
- **Coleman, William Thomas** (1867 – DNA): Mayor of Elmira, New York, 1905.
- **Conley, William Gustavus** (1866 – 1940): Mayor, Kingwood, West Virginia, 1906-1908.
- **Coombs, Charles Robert** (1862 – DNA): Mayor

of Belfast, Maine, 1915.
- **Corn, Russell** (1903-1973): Mayor of Willow Springs, Missouri, DNA.
- **Coughanour, William Albert** (1851 – 1936): Mayor of Payette, Idaho, 1897-1899, 1900-1901, 1907-1911.
- **Craig, Louis G.** (1908 – DNA): Mayor of Weston, West Virginia, 1961-1967.
- **Cummings, Homer Stillé** (1870 – 1956): Mayor of Stamford, Connecticut, 1900-1902, 1904-1906.
- **Cummings, Charles S.** (1856 – DNA): Mayor of Auburn, Maine, 1922-1925.
- **Davey, Martin Luther** (1884 – 1946): Mayor of Kent, Ohio, 1914-1918.
- **Davis, Frank E.** (1851 – DNA): Mayor of Gloucester, Massachusetts, 1898.
- **Dixon, George C.** (1810 – 1871): Mayor of Dixon, Illinois, 1931-1934.
- **Duncan, Cullen Steger** (1889 – 1964): Mayor of New Franklin, Missouri, DNA.
- **Dunlap, Samuel Benjamin** (1888 – DNA): Mayor of Caldwell, Idaho, 1938-1939.
- **Dunton, Arthur James** (1871 – DNA): Mayor of Bath, Maine, 1914-1915.
- **Early, John Levering** (1896 – 1999): Mayor of Sarasota, Florida, 1951-1952.
- **Edwards, William Kirkpatrick** (1820 – 1878): Mayor of Terre Haute, Indiana, 1853-1855.
- **Emmons, Willis Talmon** (1858 – DNA): Mayor of Saco, Maine, 1887-1890, 1928-1929.
- **Eisenhower, Nathan M.** (1811 – 1879), Mayor of Reading, Pennsylvania, 1865-1867.
- **English, Charles Reid** (1886 – DNA): Mayor of Red Bank, New Jersey, 1931-1939.
- **Finkbeiner, Orval Carl** (1910 – 1967), Mayor of Sandusky, Michigan, 1945-1967.
- **Flood, Frank H.** (1851 – DNA): Mayor of Elmira, New York, 1900-1902.
- **Fones, Civilion** (1836 – 1907), Mayor of Bridgeport, Connecticut, 1886-1888.
- **Foss, Frank Herbert** (1865 – 1947): Mayor of Fitchburg, Massachusetts, 1917-1920.
- **Frank, Charles** (1842 – 1911): Mayor of Mishawaka, Indiana, 1905-1906.
- **Gerow, Daniel Joseph** (1864 – 1950): Mayor of Sturgis, Michigan, 1930-1931.
- **Goodwin, Angier Louis** (1881 – 1975): Mayor of Melrose, Massachusetts, 1921-1923.
- **Gordon, William Warring** (1874 – 1963), Mayor of Kansas City, Kansas, 1923-1926.
- **Guyer, Ulysses Samuel** (1868 – 1943): Mayor of Kansas City, Kansas, 1909-1910.
- **Hall, Clark** (DNA): Mayor of Conway, Pennsylvania, DNA.
- **Hall, Philo** (1865 – 1938): Mayor of Brookings, South Dakota, 1894-1895.
- **Halvorson, Halvor Langdon** (1881 – DNA): Mayor of Minot, North Dakota, 1911-1915.
- **Hamilton, Wilson H.** (1877 – DNA): Mayor of Sigourney, Iowa, 1906-1908.
- **Hammer, William Cicero** (1865 – 1930): Mayor of Asheboro, North Carolina, 1895-1899.
- **Hansen, Harry W.** (1884 – DNA): Mayor of Craig, Colorado, 1920-1921.
- **Harmer, Harvey Walker** (1865 – 1961): Mayor of Clarksburg, West Virginia, 1906-1907.
- **Hart, Ray** (1872 – DNA): Mayor of Midland, Michigan, 1899-1900.
- **Hawley, James Henry** (1847 – 1929): Mayor of Boise, Idaho, 1903-1905.
- **Hayward, Nelson** (1810 – 1857): Mayor of Cleveland, Ohio, 1843-1844.
- **Hershey, Harry B.** (1885 – 1967): Mayor of Taylorville, Illinois, 1922-1926.
- **Hogg, James Robert** (1863-1934): Mayor of Poplar Bluff, Missouri, 1897-1899.
- **Holmes, Pehr Gustaf** (1881 – 1952): Mayor of

Worcester, Massachusetts, 1917-1919.
- **Horne, William Edgar** (DNA): Mayor of Westminster, England, 1923-1924.
- **Hyer, Lewis Spencer** (1839 – 1909): Mayor of Rahway, New Jersey, 1874-1875, 1888, 1889-1891.
- **Ingersoll, John Nathaniel** (1817 – 1881): Mayor of Corunna, Michigan, DNA.
- **James, William Francis** (1873 – 1945): Mayor of Hancock, Michigan, 1908-1910.
- **Jeffries, Edward John Jr.** (1900 – 1950): Mayor of Detroit, Michigan, 1940-1948.
- **Johnson, John Augustus** (1842 – 1907): Mayor of Fargo, North Dakota, 1885-1886, 1896-1902, 1906-1907.
- **Joslin, Chauncey** (DNA): Mayor of Ypsilanti, Michigan, 1858-1859.
- **Keeler, Edwin Olmstead** (1846 – 1923): Mayor of Norwalk, Connecticut, 1893-1894.
- **Kercheval, Samuel Edward** (1847 – 1910): Mayor of Rockport, Indiana, DNA.
- **Knaggs, Daniel A.** (1887 – 1957): Mayor of Monroe, Michigan, 1934-1939.
- **Knight, Charles A.** (1870 – DNA): Mayor of Gardiner, Maine, 1905-1906
- **Kopriver, Frank Jr.** (1906 – 1985), Mayor of Duquesne, Pennsylvania, 1947-1960.
- **Kump, Herman Guy** (1877 – 1962): Mayor of Elkins, West Virginia, 1922-1923.
- **Latimer, Thomas Erwin** (1879 – 1937): Mayor of Minneapolis, Minnesota, 1935-1937.
- **Law, Levi J.** (1854 – 1909), Mayor of Cadillac, Michigan, 1889-1890.
- **Lawrence, Walter Edward** (1905 – 1967): Mayor of Medford, Massachusetts, 1944-1950.
- **Lemp, John** (1838 – 1912): Mayor of Boise, Idaho, 1875-1876.
- **Leonard, Edwin F.** (1862 – 1931): Mayor of Springfield, Massachusetts, 1921-1924.
- **Lewis, Isaac Chauncey** (1812 – 1893): Mayor of Meriden, Connecticut, 1870-1872.
- **Lind, Peter** (1851 – unknown): Mayor of West Bay City, Michigan, 1896-1901.
- **Lindsley, Myron Plato** (1825 – 1883): Mayor of Green Bay, Wisconsin, 1865.
- **Lovingood, S. W.** (1865 – DNA): Mayor of Murphy, North Carolina, 1896.
- **Lull, Francis Wayland** (1872 – DNA): Mayor of Wetumpka, Alabama, 1910-1914.
- **Mackie, Gerald E.** (1910 – 2000): Mayor of Hastings, Nebraska, 1952-1953, 1956.
- **Madden, Walter** (1873 – DNA): Mayor of Trenton, New Jersey, 1908-1911.
- **Mallory, Hugh Shepperd Darby** (1848 – 1920): Mayor of Selma, Alabama, 1885-1887.
- **Martin, George Washington** (1841 – 1914): Mayor of Junction City, Kansas, 1883-1884.
- **Martin, John S.** (1886 – DNA): Mayor of LaPorte, Indiana, 1943-1944.
- **Martin, John Wellborn** (1884 – 1958): Mayor of Jacksonville, Florida, 1917-1923.
- **Marshall, George Sidney** (1869 – 1956): Mayor of Columbus, Ohio, 1910-1911.
- **Maxson, Grove T.** (DNA): Mayor of Cortland, New York, 1907-1908.
- **McFall, John Joseph** (1918 – 2006): Mayor of Manteca, California, 1948-1950.
- **Miller, John L.** (1821 – 1907): Mayor of Corsicana, Texas, 1877-1880.
- **Mowbray, George W.** (1847 – 1910): Mayor of Tulsa, Oklahoma, 1903-1904; Grand Master of the IOOF Grand Lodge of Indian Territory of the IOOF, DNA; Instrumental in building the Odd Fellows Home in Checotah, Oklahoma.
- **Munson, Clara Cynthia** (1861 – 1938): Mayor of Warrenton, Oregon, 1913-1914; First woman to be elected as Mayor in the State of Oregon.
- **Neal, William Elmer** (1875 – 1959): Mayor of

- Huntington, West Virginia, 1925-1928.
- **Newhall, George H.** (1850 – 1923): Mayor of Lynn, Massachusetts, 1913-1917.
- **Newkirk, Henry Wirt** (1854 – DNA): Mayor of Ann Arbor, Michigan, 1931-1933.
- **Paddock, Hilem F.** (1871 – 1922): Mayor of Saginaw, Michigan, 1915-1919.
- **Page, Herman L.** (1818 – 1873): Mayor of Milwaukee, Wisconsin, 1859-1960.
- **Patterson, P. John**, (1849 – 1921): Mayor of Irvona, Pennsylvania, 1994 – 2018.
- **Patterson, William Worth** (1849 – 1921): Mayor of Ashland, Kentucky, 1886-1889.
- **Payne, John Grove** (1872-1967): Mayor of Oil City, Pennsylvania, 1931-1939.
- **Pettit, Henry Corbin** (1863 – 1913): Mayor of Wabash, Indiana, 1888-1890.
- **Pettyjohn, Russell L.** (1921 – present), Mayor of Lititz, Pennsylvania, 1994 – 2009.
- **Phillips, Kim Y.** (1962 – present), Mayor of Shenandoah, Pennsylvania, 2010 – present.
- **Pierce, George H.** (1851 – 1902): Mayor of Olean, New York, 1923-29.
- **Prinz, Gottfried Adolph** (1851 – 1902): Mayor of Cullman, Alabama, 1876-1877.
- **Raymond, John Marshall** (1852 – DNA): Mayor of Salem, Massachusetts, 1886-1889.
- **Rawleigh, William Thomas** (1870 – DNA): Mayor of Freeport, Illinois, 1909-1911.
- **Reedy, Raymond S.** (1939 – 2016): Mayor of Lititz, Pennsylvania, 1974-1985.
- **Rettig, Valentine** (1846 – DNA): Mayor of Corning, New York, 1905-1907.
- **Rice, Frank James** (1869 – 1917): Mayor of New Haven, Connecticut, 1910-1917.
- **Rice, John Campbell** (1864 – 1937): Mayor of Caldwell, Idaho, 1901.
- **Robinson, Clarence** (DNA): Mayor, Tecumseh, Oklahoma, 1917-1918.
- **Rodenbeck, Julius** (DNA): Mayor of Rochester, New York, 1902-1903.
- **Rolph, James Jr.** (1869 – 1934): Mayor of San Francisco, California, 1912-1931.
- **Rosenberg, David** (1946 – present): Mayor of Davis, California, 1986-1988, 1994-1996; Grand Master of IOOF Grand Lodge of California, 2015-2016.
- **Saunders, Mark Ashton** (1883 – 1974): Mayor of Kewanee, Illinois, 1935-1943.
- **Shakley, Dean R.** (1937 – 2017): Mayor of Parker, Pennsylvania, DNA.
- **Schlesinger, Val** (1857 – 1924), Mayor of Fredericktown, Missouri, 1900.
- **Schwoob, Jacob Macomb** (1874-1932), Mayor of Cody, Wyoming, 1903-1905.
- **Shearer, George H.** (1825 – 1894), Mayor of Bay City, Michigan, 1885-1887.
- **Sloss, Joseph Humphrey** (1826 – 1911): Mayor of Tuscumbia, Alabama, DNA.
- **Smith, Clarence W.** (1853 – 1937): Mayor of Johnstown, New York, 1914-1915, 1918-1919.
- **Spears, Jacob Franklin Sr.** (1899 – 1946): Mayor of Tarpon Springs, Florida, 1921.
- **Stedronsky, John** (1872 – DNA): Mayor of Wagner, South Dakota, 1911-1914.
- **Szczyglak, Andrew J.** (1976 – present): Mayor of Shenandoah, Pennsylvania, 2012 – present.
- **Taylor, James Willis** (1880 – 1939): Mayor of La Follette, Tennessee, 1910-1912.
- **Taylor, Walter Ross** (1858 – DNA): Mayor of Kalamazoo, Michigan, 1905.
- **Thayer, Charles Frederick** (1852 – present): Mayor of Norwich, Connecticut, 1900-1908, 1911.
- **Tomko, Richard E.** (1947 – present): Mayor of Saint Clair, Pennsylvania, 1986-1906, 2014 – present.
- **Trask, Eliphalet** (1806 – 1890): Mayor of

- Springfield, Massachusetts, 1855.
- **Tunis, Elmer** (1872 – present): Mayor of Elwood, Indiana, 1917-1918, 1943-1944, 1950-1951.
- **Uhlman, Wesley Carl** (1935 – DNA): Mayor of Seattle, Washington, 1969-1978.
- **Van Eps, John E.** (1822 – 1908): Mayor of Mt. Clemens, Michigan, 1885-1887.
- **Wallace, Charles Slover** (1864 – DNA): Mayor of Morehead City, North Carolina, 1906-1908.
- **Warren, Nathan A.** (1856 – 1944): Mayor of Yonkers, New York, 1908-1909.
- **Watson, Alfred E.** (1875 – 1960): Mayor of Yonkers, New York, 1923.
- **Webber, William L.** (1825 – 1901): Mayor of East Saginaw, Michigan, 1873-1874.
- **Wheatley, Leon F.** (1872 – 1944): Mayor of Hornell, New York, 1934-37.
- **Wilson, Clifford Brittin** (1879 – 1943): Mayor of Bridgeport, Connecticut, 1911-21; Lieutenant Governor of Connecticut, 1915-1921.
- **Wilson, John Stockbridge Patten Ham** (1860 – DNA): Mayor of Auburn, Maine, 1900-1901.
- **Woodruff, Roy Orchard** (1876 – 1953): Mayor of Bay City, Michigan, 1911-1913.
- **Wolcott, L. J.** (1849 – DNA): Mayor of Albion, Michigan, 1887.

JUSTICES, JUDGES, AND STATE ATTORNEYS

- **Adams, John Taylor** (1873 – 1942): Chief Justice of Colorado Supreme Court, 1931-1935; Justice of Colorado State Supreme Court, 1925-1935.
- **Anderson, Harry Bennett** (1879 – 1935): U.S. District Judge for the Western District of Tennessee, 1926-1935.
- **Andrews, Thomas Galphin** (1892 – 1942): Justice of Oklahoma State Supreme Court, 1929-1935; Author of the book, Jericho Road or the Philosophy of Odd Fellowship.
- **Annabel, Floyd W.** (1886 – 1944): Justice of New York State Supreme Court, 1935.
- **Anderson, John William** (1871 – 1954): Justice of Iowa State Supreme Court, 1933-1938.
- **Ailshie, James Franklin** (1868 – 1947): Chief Justice of Idaho State Supreme Court, 1907-1909, 1913-1915, 1939-1941, 1945-1946; Justice of Idaho State Supreme Court, 1903-1914, 1935-1947.
- **Atwell, William Hawley** (1869 – 1961): U.S. District Judge for the Northern District of Texas, 1923-1954.
- **Babcock, Fred Jason** (1891 – 1973): Idaho State Attorney General, 1931-1933.
- **Baker, Andrew Jackson** (1832 – 1911): Iowa State Attorney General, 1885-1889; Missouri State Attorney general, 1871-1873.
- **Ballard, Wade Hampton III** (1924 – 2006): U.S. Attorney for the Southern District of West Virginia, 1969-1970.
- **Bell, Reason Chesnutt** (1880 – 1862): Chief Justice of Georgia Supreme Court, 1943-1946; Justice of Georgia State Supreme Court, 1932-1943, 1946-1949; and Judge, Georgia Court of Appeals, 1922-1932.
- **Black, Hugo Lafayette** (1886 – 1971): Justice of U.S. Supreme Court, 1937-1971.
- **Bridgeman, Richard B.** (1875 – 1948): Circuit Judge in Missouri Circuit Court, 1933-1946.
- **Brown, George M. J** (1864 – 1934): Justice of Oregon State Supreme Court, 1920-1933.
- **Burch, Newton Dexter** (1871 – 1931): Judge of South Dakota State Supreme Court, 1926-1931.
- **Burden, Oliver D.** (1873 – unknown): U.S. Attorney for the Northern District of New York, 1923-1936.
- **Burket, Jacob F.** (1837 – 1906), Chief justice of Ohio State Supreme Court, 1897; and Justice of

Ohio State Supreme Court, 1893-1901.

- **Burnett, George Henry** (1853 – 1927): Chief Justice of Oregon State Supreme Court, 1921-1922, 1927; and Justice of Oregon State Supreme Court, 1911-1927.
- **Bushnell, Robert Tyng** (1896 – 1949): Massachusetts State Attorney General, 1941-1945.
- **Cahill, Horace Tracy** (1894 – 1976): Superior Court Judge in Massachusetts, 1947-1973.
- **Candler, John Slaughter** (1861 – 1941): Justice of Georgia State Supreme Court, 1902-1906.
- **Candler, Thomas Slaughter** (1890 – 1971): Justice of Georgia State Supreme Court, 1945-1966.
- **Carlstrom, Oscar E.** (1878 – 1948), Illinois state attorney general, 1925-1933.
- **Chase, Harrie Brigham** (1889 – 1969): Justice of Vermont State Supreme Court, 1927-1929; Judge of U.S. Court of Appeals, 1929-1954.
- **Cluff, Harvey H.** (1872 – 1941): Utah state attorney general, 1921-1929.
- **Coshow, Oliver Perry** (1863 – 1937): Chief Justice of Oregon State Supreme Court, 1929-1931; Justice of Oregon State Supreme Court, 1924-1931.
- **Cox, Louis Sherburne** (1874 – 1961): Justice of Massachusetts State Supreme Court, 1937-1940.
- **Dalton, Sidna Poage** (1892 – 1965): Chief Justice of Missouri State Supreme Court, 1956-1958; Justice of Missouri State Supreme Court, 1950-1965.
- **Davies, John C.** (1857 – 1925): New York State Attorney General, 1899-1902.
- **Davis, Fred Henry** (1894 – 1937): Chief Justice of Florida State Supreme Court, 1933-1935; Justice of Florida State Supreme Court, 1931-1937.
- **Dean, James Renwick** (1862 – 1936): Justice of Nebraska State Supreme Court, 1908-10, 1917-1935.
- **Deaver, Bascom S.** (1882 – DNA): U.S. District Judge for the Middle District of Georgia, 1928-1936; U.S. Attorney for the Middle District of Georgia, 1926-1928.
- **Dehnke, Herman** (1887 – 1979): Circuit judge in Michigan, 1928-1959.
- **Devin, William Augustus** (1871 – 1959): Justice of North Carolina State Supreme Court, 1935-1940.
- **Farrington, Frank George** (1872 – 1933): Justice of Maine State Supreme Court, 1928-1933.
- **Flansburg, Leonard A.** (DNA): Justice of Nebraska State Supreme Court, 1920-1923; and District Judge in Nebraska, 1918-1920.
- **Fletcher, Robert Virgil** (1869 – 1960): Justice of Mississippi State Supreme Court, 1908-1909.
- **Frazer, James Somerville** (1824 – 1893): Justice of Indiana State Supreme Court, 1865-1871.
- **Frick, Joseph E.** (1848 – 1927): Chief Justice of Utah State Supreme Court, 1910-1912, 1917-1919; and Justice of Utah State Supreme Court, 1906-1927.
- **Gardner, Bunk** (1875 – 1960): U.S. District Judge for Canal Zone, 1938-1948; U.S. Attorney for the Western District of Kentucky, 1935-1938; and District Judge in Kentucky 1st District, 1916-1922.
- **Garrigues, James Edward** (1852 – 1946): Chief Justice of Colorado Supreme Court, 1919-1921; Justice of Colorado State Supreme Court, 1910-21.
- **Hall, Charles P.** (1876 – DNA): District Judge in Minnesota 1st District Court, 1929-1947.
- **Hallam, Oscar** (1865-1945): Justice of Minnesota State Supreme Court, 1923.
- **Hamilton, Wilson H.** (1877 – DNA): Justice of Iowa State Supreme Court, 1935-1940; Chief

Justice of Iowa State Supreme Court, 1937.
- **Hanft, Hugo O.** (1871 – 1949): District Judge in Minnesota 2nd District, 1915-1932; Municipal Judge in Minnesota, 1906-1914.
- **Heard, Oscar Edwin** (1856 – 1940): Justice of Illinois State Supreme Court, 1924-1933; and Judge, Illinois Appellate Court, 1919-1924.
- **Hershey, Harry B.** (1885 – 1967): Justice of Illinois State Supreme Court, 1951-1966.
- **Holbrook, Donald E.** (1909 – 1986): Judge of the Michigan Court of Appeals, 1965-1978.
- **Holcomb, Oscar Raymond** (1869 – 1948): Chief Justice of Washington State Supreme Court, 1919-1921; Justice of Washington State Supreme Court, 1915-1927, 1927-1931.
- **House, Byron O.** (1902 – 1969): Chief justice of Illinois State Supreme Court-60; justice of Illinois State Supreme Court, 1957-1969.
- **Hunter, Robert T.** (1907 – 2000): Chief Justice of Washington State Supreme Court, 1971; Justice of Washington State Supreme Court, 1957-1977.
- **Ittner, Anthony F.** (1872 – DNA): Circuit Judge in Missouri, 1923-1927.
- **Johnson, John T.** (1856 – DNA): Chief justice of Oklahoma State Supreme Court, 1925.
- **Jones, Buell Fay** (1892 – 1947): South Dakota state attorney general, 1923-1929.
- **Lansden, Dick Latta** (1869 – 1924): Justice of Tennessee State Supreme Court, 1916.
- **Levy, Aaron Jefferson** (1881 – 1955): Justice of New York Supreme Court, 1924-1951.
- **Lester, Eugene F.** (1871 – 1940): Chief justice of Oklahoma State Supreme Court-1932; Justice of Oklahoma State Supreme Court, 1924-1931.
- **Liebowitz, Simon J.** (1906 – 1998): Justice of New York Supreme Court, 1969-1975.
- **Matthews, John Aaron** (1876 – DNA): Justice of Montana state Supreme Court, 1919-1931.
- **Maughmer, Frederic Hine** (1899 – 1972): Circuit judge in Missouri, 1947-1955.
- **McFarland, Ernest William** (1894 – 1984): Justice of Arizona State Supreme Court, 1965-1971.
- **Messmore, Fred W.** (DNA): Justice of Nebraska State Supreme Court, 1937-1965.
- **Nash, George Kilborn** (1842 – 1904): Justice of Ohio State Supreme Court, 1883-1985.
- **Nichols, David A.** (1917 – 1997): Justice of Maine State Supreme Court, 1988.
- **O'Neill, C. William** (1916 – 1978): Justice of Ohio State Supreme Court, 1960.
- **Parker, Jay S.** (1895 – 1969), Justice of Kansas State Supreme Court, 1943; Kansas State Attorney General, 1939-1943.
- **Peterson, K. Berry** (1891 – 1851): Arizona State Attorney General, 1929-1933.
- **Phelps, James Ivey** (1875 – 1947): Justice of Oklahoma State Supreme Court, 1925-1929, 1935.
- **Poffenbarger, George** (1861 – 1951): Judge of West Virginia State Court of Appeals, 1901-1922.
- **Potter, William W.** (1869 – 1940): Justice of Michigan State Supreme Court, 1928-1940; Chief Justice of Michigan State Supreme Court, 1935; Michigan State Attorney General, 1927-1928.
- **Raker, John Edward** (1863 – 1926): Superior Court Judge in California, 1905-1910.
- **Raney, William Edgar KC,** (1859 – 1933): 10th Attorney General of Ontario, 1919-1923.
- **Reid, Neil E.** (1871 – 1956): Chief justice of Michigan State Supreme Court, 1951; Justice of Michigan State Supreme Court, 1944-1956.
- **Reid, Leonard C.** (1887 – DNA): Circuit Judge in Illinois, 1945.
- **Reed, David W.** (DNA - present): Superior Court Judge in California, 2009-present; Grand Master of the Grand Lodge of California of the IOOF, 2016-2017.

- **Rees, Warren J.** (1908 – 1988): Justice of Iowa State Supreme Court, 1969-1980.
- **Rice, John Campbell** (1864 – 1937): Justice of Idaho State Supreme Court, 1916-22.
- **Rodenbeck, Adolph Julius** (1862 – 1960): Justice of New York State Supreme Court, 1916-1932.
- **Rosenberg, David** (1946 – present): Superior Court Judge in California, 2003 – present; Grand Master of IOOF Grand Lodge of California, 2015-2016.
- **Russell, Richard Brevard** (1861 – 1938): Chief Justice of Georgia Supreme Court, 1923-1938; Judge, Georgia Court of Appeals, 1907-1916; Circuit Judge in Georgia, 1898-1906.
- **Ryan, Howard C.** (1916 – 2008): Justice of Illinois State Supreme Court, 1970-1990.
- **Sharpe, Edward MacGlen** (1887 – 1975): Chief Justice of Michigan State Supreme Court, 1941, 1949, 1956; Justice of Michigan State Supreme Court, 1934-1957.
- **Sherwood, Carl G.** (1855 – 1938): Justice of South Dakota State Supreme Court, 1922-1931.
- **Spencer, Harry A.** (1903 – 2007): Justice of Nebraska State Supreme Court, 1961-1979.
- **Thompson, Floyd Eugene** (1887 – 1960): Justice of Illinois State Supreme Court, 1928.
- **Thompson, George King** (1887 – 1979): Justice of Iowa State Supreme Court, 1951-1965.
- **Vanover, Paris Roscoe Sr.** (1863 – 1927): Circuit Judge in Kentucky, 1920-1921.
- **Wallace, Robert Moore** (1847 – 1914): Justice of New Hampshire State Supreme Court, 1893-1901; Superior Court Judge in New Hampshire, 1901-1913.
- **Warner, Joseph Everett** (1884 – DNA): Superior Court Judge in Massachusetts, 1940-1949; Massachusetts State Attorney General, 1928-1935.
- **Warren, Earl** (1891 – 1974): Chief Justice of the U.S. Supreme Court, 1953–1969.
- **Woods, Homer Boughner** (1869 – 1941): Judge of West Virginia Supreme Court of Appeals, 1925-36.
- **Yeager, John Walter** (1891 – 1967): Justice of Nebraska State Supreme Court, 1940-65.

OTHERS

- **Adams, Hunter Doherty** (1945 – present): Physician, social activist, and founder of the *Gesundheit! Institute* in 1971; His life was portrayed by actor Robin Williams' in the 1998 movie, "Patch Adams".
- **Ames, Hermes Luther** (1865 – 1920): Member of New York State Assembly, 1918-1920.
- **Ambler, Charles H.** (1876 – 1957): Member of West Virginia State House of Delegates, 1951-1954.
- **Austin, Wallace Ray** (1888 – unknown): Member of New York State Assembly, 1923-1933.
- **Armstrong, William George** (1810 – 1900): Founder of the Armstrong Whitworth manufacturing empire; instrumental in the construction of Cragside in Northumberland, the first house in the world to be lit by hydroelectricity.
- **Bachmann, Charles F.** (1915 – 1983): Member of West Virginia State House of Delegates, 1957-1960.
- **Baensch, Emil** (1857 – 1939): Lieutenant Governor of Wisconsin, 1895-1899.
- **Bagley, Willis Gaylord Clark** (1873 – 1943): Iowa State Treasurer, 1939-1943.
- **Bailey, Robert Melville** (1875 – 1960): Pioneer music educator in the Bahamas.
- **Banfield, Thomas Jacob** (1895 – 1976): Member

of New York state assembly, 1934.

- **Barnes, William** (1801 – 1886): English writer, poet, minister, and philologist.
- **Barnhart, Hugh A.** (1892 – 1986): President, Rochester Telephone Co., 1934; heeceived the Indiana Telephone Man of the Year Award in 1959 and USITA's Distinguished Service Award in 1971.
- **Barr, George Andrew** (1873 – DNA): Trustee, University of Illinois, 1924-1936.
- **Barr, Robert** (1802 – 1839), Texas Republic Postmaster General, 1836-1839.
- **Beard, Charles R.** (1879 – 1965): Member of West Virginia State House of Delegates, 1915-1916, 1925-1930, 1935-1936, 1939-1940, 1943-1948.
- **Becker, Conrad F.** (1905 – 1965):, Illinois State Treasurer, 1945-1947.
- **Bell, Frank Thomas** (1883 – 1970): Promoter of Grand Coulee Dam and other federal dam projects.
- **Bedford, Homer Franklin** (1880 – 1968): Colorado State Treasurer, 1933-1934, 1937-1938, 1941-1942, 1945-1946, 1949-1950, 1953-1954, 1957-1958, 1963-1966; Colorado State Auditor, 1935-1937, 1939-1941, 1947-1949, 1951-1953, 1955-1957, 1959-1963.
- **Belknap, Rodney B.** (1924 – 2009): Member of West Virginia State House of Delegates, 1957-1960, 1969-1974.
- **Bennett, James Fay** (1888 – 1957): Member of West Virginia State House of Delegates, 1929-1930.
- **Bertil, Gustaf Oskar Carl Eugén** (1912 – 1997): Duke of Halland, Sweden, 1912–1997.
- **Billheimer, John C.** (1857 – 1918): Indiana State Auditor, 1906-1910; U.S. Consul in Zanzibar, 1898.
- **Blanchard, Nathan Weston** (1831 – 1917): Founder of the City of Santa Paula, California; First Noble Grand of Santa Paula Odd Fellows Lodge of the IOOF.
- **Bloch, Maurice** (1891 – 1929): Member of New York State Assembly, 1915-1929.
- **Bloom, Earl D.** (1871 – 1930): Lieutenant Governor of Ohio, 1917-1919, 1923-1925, 1927-1928.
- **Blue, Arthur Grant** (1864 – 1952): Member of New York State Assembly, 1907-1908.
- **Bodenwein, Theodore** (1864 – 1939): Secretary of State of Connecticut, 1905-1909.
- **Bolander, Henry Nicholas** (1831 – 1897): California superintendent of Public Instruction, 1871-1875.
- **Bower, Emma Eliza** (1852 – 1937): American physician, club-woman, and newspaper owner, publisher, and editor. She served as the Great Record Keeper of the Ladies of the Maccabees (LOTM).
- **Bowers, John C.** (1811 – 1873): Abolitionist and one of the founders of the Grand United Order of Odd Fellows in Pennsylvania and several other civic groups such as the Pennsylvania Anti-Slavery Society.
- **Bowman, Thomas DeWitt** (DNA): U.S. Consul General in Budapest, 1925-1926; Belfast, 1926-1931; Santiago, 1932; Naples, 1938; Johannesburg, 1943; and Canton, 1947.
- **Bowyer, George** (1811 – 1883): 7th Baronet and early British politician.
- **Booth, Don** (1932 – unknown): Member of West Virginia State House of Delegates, 1959-1960.
- **Bryan, William Jennings** (1860 – 1925): U.S. Secretary of State, 1913-1915.
- **Buhrmaster, John H.** (1876 – DNA): Member of New York State Assembly, 1932-1933; Director and Vice-president, Glenville Bank, DNA.

- **Burgdorf, Andrew D.** (1892 – DNA): Member of New York State Assembly, 1934-1938
- **Burhyte, Orlando Walter** (1855 – unknown): Member of New York State Assembly, 1907-1909.
- **Brady, William C.** (1852 – unknown): Member of New York State Assembly, 1905-1909.
- **Brady, William E.** (1889 – 1970): Member of New York State Assembly, 1940-1962.
- **Brand, Franklin Marion** (1880 – 1963): Member of West Virginia State House of Delegates, 1919-1920, 1943-1944.
- **Breedlove, Sarah "Madam C.J. Walker"** (1867 – 1919): African American entrepreneur, philanthropist, and a political and social activist; Leading member of the Household of Ruth of the Grand United Order of Odd Fellows.
- **Brown, Martin L.** (1867 – 1947): Member of West Virginia State House of Delegates, 1929-1930.
- **Brougham, Henry Peter** (1778 – 1868): British statesman who became Lord Chancellor of Great Britain, 1830-1834; Early members of the Manchester Unity Independent Order of Odd Fellows in 1814.
- **Bruce, Homer Mayne** (1909 – 1975): Secretary of State of Colorado, 1953-55.
- **Buzzerd, Simeon Strother** (1869 – 1959): Member of West Virginia State House of Delegates, 1929-1930.
- **Cameron, Isaac B.** (1851 – 1930): Ohio Treasurer of State, 1900-04.
- **Canada, William Wesley** (1850 – 1921): U.S. Consul in Veracruz, 1897-1918.
- **Chapel, Charles Edward** (1904 – 1967): Member of California State Assembly, 1950-1966.
- **Chapin, Edwin Hubbell** (1814 – 1880): Universalist minister, author, lecturer, and social reformer, and was one of the most popular speakers in America from the 1840s until his death.
- **Chaplin, Sir Charles Spencer "Charlie"** (1889 – 1977): Iconic comedian and actor.
- **Chisum, John Simpson** (1824 – 1884): Prominent and wealthy cattle baron in the American West in the mid-to-late 19th century; The "Chisum Trail' of Denton, Texas, is named after him; Founding member of Denton Odd Fellows Lodge No. 82 of the IOOF.
- **Cheney, Guy Warren** (1886 – 1939): Member of New York State Assembly, 1937-1939.
- **Cobbett, William** (1763 – 1835): Member of Parliament for Oldham, England, 1832–1835.
- **Cole, Ernest** (1871 – 1949): Commissioner of Education of the State of New York, 1940-1942.
- **Cole, George B.** (1851 – DNA): Member of New Jersey State Assembly, 1910-1911.
- **Congdon, Cassius** (1870 – DNA): Member of New York State Assembly, 1924-1929.
- **Cook, Alonzo B.** (1866 – DNA): Massachusetts state auditor, 1915-1923.
- **Corwin, Edward K.** (1873 – DNA): Member of New York State Assembly, 1933-1935, 1943-1944.
- **Coyne, Clarence Edward** (1881 – 1929): Secretary of state of South Dakota, 1922-1927; Lieutenant Governor of South Dakota, 1929.
- **Cote, Edmond** (1863 – DNA): Member of Massachusetts Governor's Council, 1931-1936.
- **Craig, Louis G.** (1908 – DNA): Member of West Virginia State House of Delegates, 1957-1960, 1963-1966.
- **Cravey, Zachariah Daniel** (1894 – 1966): Georgia state game and fish commissioner, 1934-1937; Georgia natural resources commissioner,

1941-1943.

- **Cuney, Norris Wright** (1846 – 1898): Member of Republican National Committee from Texas, 1886; U.S. Collector of Customs, 1889.
- **Cusack, Lee** (1885 – 1951): Member of West Virginia State House of Delegates, 1927-1932.
- **Darling, Carl E.** (1903 – DNA): Member of New York State Assembly, 1936-1942.
- **Davis, Paul B.** (1870 – DNA): Member of West Virginia State House of Delegates, 1961-1962.
- **Delker, Edward A. "Eddie"** (1906 – 1997): former Major League Baseball infielder who played for the Philadelphia Phillies and St. Louis Cardinals professional baseball, 1929-33.
- **De Cordova, Jacob Raphael** (1808 – 1868): Founder of Waco City, Texas; Founder Lone Star Odd Fellows Lodge No. 1 of the IOOF in 1838; Grand Master of the Grand Lodge of Texas of the IOOF, 1860-1861.
- **DeRousse, Louis Theodore** (1844 – 1921): Member of New Jersey State Assembly, 1895-1897; Speaker of the New Jersey State House of Assembly, 1896.
- **De Young, Charles** (1846 – 1880): Pioneer journalist, co-founder and first Editor-in-Chief of the San Francisco Chronicle.
- **Dickson, Moses** (1824 – 1901): American abolitionist; Founder of the The Knights of Liberty, International Order of Twelve Knights and Daughters of Tabor; Co-founder of Lincoln University.
- **Downs, N. T.** (1874 – DNA): Member of West Virginia State House of Delegates, 1941-1946.
- **Dwelle, Georgia** R. (1884 – 1977): First female African-American Physician; Leading member of the Household of Ruth.
- **Evans, George** (1882 – DNA): Member of West Virginia State House of Delegates, 1937-1938, 1941-1946.
- **Ericsson, John** (1803 – 1889): Swedish-American inventor; Designer of the U.S. Navy's first screw-propelled steam-frigate USS *Princeton*, in partnership with Captain Robert Stockton, and the first armored ship with a rotating turret, USS *Monitor*, in partnership with Cornelius H. DeLamater.
- **Faber, Hiram Oliver** (1878 – 1961): Member of West Virginia State House of Delegates, 1931.
- **Farley, Rush Floyd** (1887 – DNA): Member of West Virginia State House of Delegates, 1941-1942.
- **Fitzwygram, Sir Frederick Wellington John** (1823 – 1904): 4th Baronet, and member of Parliament for Hampshire South, 1884-1885
- **Fowler, Matthew J.** (1879 – DNA): President, Haverhill Cooperative Bank.
- **Gibson, Robert Lawrence** (1895-1966): Member of West Virginia State House of Delegates, 1931-1932, 1941-1942.
- **Gilbert, William "Billy"** (1894 – 1971): American comedian and actor known for his comic sneeze routines.
- **Gaunt, Alfred Calvin** (1882 – 1959): Member of Massachusetts Governor's Council, 1947-1948.
- **Gilpatric, George Harold** (1881 – 1927): Connecticut State Treasurer, 1919-1924.
- **Guilbert, Walter D.** (1844 – 1911): Ohio State Auditor, 1896-1909.
- **Grant, Julia** (1826 – 1902): First Lady of the United States, 1869-1877.
- **Hackleman, Pleasant Adams** (1814 – 1862): lawyer, politician and Union General during the American Civil War; Namesake of Hackleman, Indiana; Grand Master of the Grand Lodge of Indiana of the IOOF, 1857-1858.
- **Ehrlich, Harold B.** (1902 – DNA): Member of New York State Assembly, 1934-1944.

- **Evans, Sir George de Lacy** (1787 – 1870): British Army General and Member of Parliament, 1830, 1831-32, 1833-41, 1846-65.
- **Hallock, Joseph Nelson** (1861 – 1942): Member of New York State Assembly, 1899-1901.
- **Harshaw, Henry Baldwin** (1842 – 1900): Wisconsin State Treasurer, 1887-91; Namesake of Harshaw, Wisconsin.
- **Hayes, Lucy Webb** (1831 – 1889): First Lady of the United States, 1877-1881; Past Grand of Lincoln Rebekah Lodge of the IOOF.
- **Hersman, Mark K.** (1904 – DNA): Member of West Virginia State House of Delegates, 1955-1960.
- **Hood, Solomon Porter** (1853 – 1943): U.S. Minister to Liberia, 1922-1926; U.S. Consul General in Monrovia, 1922-1924.
- **Hopkins, A. A.** (1873 – DNA): Member of West Virginia State House of Delegates, 1939-1942.
- **Howell, Harry U.** (1923 – DNA): Member of West Virginia State House of Delegates, 1965-1970.
- **Irvin, Edward G.** (1893 – 1982): Founder of Kappa Alpha Psi Fraternity, Inc.
- **Ives, Burl Icle Ivanhoe** (1909 – 1995): American Singer, actor and writer.
- **Ivy, Vernettie Oscar Greene** (1876 – 1967): a member of the Arizona House of Representatives, DNA; President of the Rebekah Assembly of Arizona, DNA.
- **Johnson, Henry Lincoln** (1870 – 1925): Recorder of Deeds for the District of Columbia, 1912-1916.
- **Jones, Fleming Adolphus Jr.** (1895 – DNA): Member of West Virginia State House of Delegates, 1935-1942, 1945-1948.
- **Jones, John Luther Casey** (1863 – 1900): Local hero who sacrificed himself to save the passengers of his train in 1900.
- **Kaminsky, George** (1906 – DNA): Member of New York State Assembly, 1935-1936.
- **Kelley, Nathan B.** (1808 – 1871): American architect who designed the Ohio statehouse.
- **Kidd, Paul H.** (1907 – 1965): Member of West Virginia State House of Delegates, 1936, 1939-1940, 1947-1952, 1955-1960, 1963-1965.
- **Kincaid, Hugh A.** (1911 – DNA): Member of West Virginia State House of Delegates, 1955-1956, 1959-1962, 1965-1978.
- **Lacy, Benjamin Rice** (1854 – 1929): North Carolina State Treasurer, 1901-1929.
- **Lawson, Edgar C.** (1898 – DNA): West Virginia State Auditor, 1929-1933;
- **Leonard, Walter Anderson** (1880 – DNA): U.S. Vice Consul in Kehl, 1908; U.S. Consul in Stavanger, 1912-1914; Colombo, 1914-1919; Stockholm, 1924; Warsaw, 1926-1929; Bremen, 1932-1935; and U.S. Consul General in Stockholm, 1935-1936; Tallinn, 1938.
- **Lindbergh, Charles Augustus** (1902 – 1974): American aviator, author, inventor, explorer and environmental activist.
- **Loch, Sir Charles** (1849 – 1923): English Social worker whose life was spent working to improve the welfare of the poor and disadvantaged.
- **Lowe, Alfred D.** (1850 – DNA): Member of New York State Assembly, 1907-1909; Director, Depauville Telephone Exchange.
- **Mace, H. Clay** (1888 – DNA): Member of West Virginia State House of Delegates, 1939-1942.
- **MacCollum, Isaac James** (1889 – DNA): Lieutenant Governor of Delaware, 1941-1945.
- **Marble, Harry Ray** (1876 – DNA): Member of New York State Assembly, 1934-1950.
- **Mariner, Paul** (1953 – present): International football player, coach and manager of Plymouth Argyle and Toronto FC.

- **Marks, Haskell Harold** (1880 – DNA): Member of New York State Assembly, 1929-1933.
- **Marks, Samuel** (1861 – DNA): Member of New York State Assembly, 1909.
- **Mason, Edwyn E.** (1916 – DNA): Member of New York State Assembly, 1953-1972.
- **Matney, Thomas Graham** (1889 – 1976): Member of West Virginia State House of Delegates, 1951-1952, 1955-1956, 1959-1964.
- **Mecherle, George Jacob** (1877 – 1951): Founder of State Farm Insurance, 1922-1937.
- **Miller, Frank G.** (DNA): Member of New York State Assembly, 1930-1937.
- **Montgomery, James** (1771 – 1854): British hymn writer, poet, and abolitionist.
- **Mullins, Sylvester** (1906 – DNA): Member of West Virginia State House of Delegates, 1947-1954.
- **McCormick, Judson D.** (1928 – unknown): Member of West Virginia State House of Delegates, 1953-1954, 1957-58.
- **McIntosh, William Alexander** (1833 – 1912): Member of Kansas State Legislature, 1866-1867.
- **MacNab, Sir Allan Napier** (1798 – 1862): 1st Baronet and Premier of the Province of Canada before Canadian Confederation, 1854–1856.
- **McWhorter, Matthew Lauren** (1889 – 1985): Member of Georgia Public Service Commission, 1936-1961.
- **Neal, Jacob Alexander** (1881 – DNA): Member of West Virginia State House of Delegates, 1919-20, 1933-40, 1953-54, 1965-66.
- **Northcott, William Allen** (1854 – 1917), Lieutenant Governor of Illinois, 1897-1905.
- **Norton, Eugene R.** (1856 – DNA): Member of New York State Assembly, 1906-07, 1913, 1919-20.
- **Nye, Olin Tracy** (1874 – DNA): Member of New York State Assembly, 1901-1904.
- **Ogden, Peter** (DNA – 1852), Founder of Grand United Order of Odd Fellows in North America.
- **Otto, Charles A. Jr.** (1888 – DNA): Member of New Jersey State Assembly, 1927-1933.
- **Outterson, James Andrew** (1858 – DNA): Member of New York State Assembly, 1902-1903.
- **Patton, John K.** (1856 – DNA): Member of New York State Assembly, 1898-1907.
- **Pauley, Harry R.** (1907 – DNA): Speaker of the West Virginia State House of Delegates, 1958-1959; Member of West Virginia State House of Delegates, 1937-1940, 1949-1954, 1957-1960, 1963-1966, 1969-1974.
- **Peck, John G.** (1865 – DNA): Member of New York State Assembly, 1922-1924.
- **Peck, Oliver** (1971 – present): Tattoo artist and celebrity judge of the TV show "Ink Master".
- **Pembleton, John G.** (1880 – DNA): Member of New York State Assembly, 1912-1913.
- **Perry, Joseph Flintlock** (1898 – DNA): Member of West Virginia state house of delegates, 1941-42.
- **Pike, Albert** (1809 – 1891): Brigadier General, philosopher and writer; Author of the revised degrees of the Ancient and Accepted Scottish Rite Southern Jurisdiction, 1855; and Morals and Dogma of Freemasonry, 1871; Grand Master of the IOOF Grand Lodge of Arkansas, 1852-1853.
- **Prather, Earl** (1903 – 1967): Member of West Virginia State House of Delegates, 1949-1952.
- **Ralston, William Chapman** (1826 – 1875): Founder of the Bank of California.
- **Rankin, Barrick Samuel** (1872 – 1939): Member of West Virginia State House of Delegates, 1929-1932.
- **Reitsma, Doreen Patterson** (1927 – 2000): First woman wren of the Royal Canadian Navy.

- **Rice, William Marsh** (1816 – 1900): Founder of Rice University.
- **Richards, Evan Mathew** (1821 – 1880): Member of U.K. Parliament for Cardiganshire, 1868-1874.
- **Roberts, George Madison** (1830 – 1915): Member of California State Assembly, 1875-1877.
- **Robbins, Corilla** (1842 – 1927): Early pioneer of Boise, Idaho; first woman suffragette and feminist in Boise; first woman to ride Boise's automobile; first woman to go on an airplane ride; 3rd President of the Rebekah Assembly of Idaho.
- **Robinson, William Benjamin** (1797 – 1873): Member of the Legislative Assembly of Upper Canada, 1830-1840; One of the early members of the Independent Order of Odd Fellows in Canada.
- **Robinson, James R.** (1885 – DNA): Member of New York State Assembly, 1923-1936.
- **Roche, Frances Ruth** (1908 – 1993): Baroness Fermoy; confidante of Queen Elizabeth, and the maternal grandmother of Princess Diana.
- **Russel, Andrew** (1856 – 1934): Illinois State Auditor of Public Accounts, 1917-1925; Illinois State Treasurer, 1909-1911, 1915-1917.
- **Sapp, Glenn** (1920 – DNA): Member of West Virginia State House of Delegates, 1955-1956, 1959-1960;
- **Savile, Sir George** (1726 – 1784): 8th Baronet and early English politician.
- **Sitton, Relief W. "Lefie"** (1851 – 1939): Pioneer of Oregon and well known as a children's welfare worker, philanthropist and civic leader; Namesake of Sitton Elementary School in Portland, Oregon.
- **Scanes, Frederick H. Jr.** (1906 – 1974): Member of West Virginia State House of Delegates, 1949-1956.
- **Sheppard, William Taylor** (1877 – DNA): Member of West Virginia State House of Delegates, 1927-1930.
- **Shearer, James Buchanan** (1823 – 1896): Member of University of Michigan Board of Regents, 1880-1887.
- **Shillaber, Benjamin P.** (1814 – 1890): American editor and humorist.
- **Skelton, Richard "Red"** (1913 – 1997): American Comedian and actor.
- **Simpson, E. L.** (1895 – DNA): Member of West Virginia State House of Delegates, 1939-1942.
- **Springer, Charles Henry** (1857 – 1916): Member of New York State Assembly, 1914.
- **Stein, Joseph I.** (1880 – DNA): Member of New York State Assembly, 1877.
- **Sterling, Frederick E.** (1869 – DNA): Lieutenant Governor of Illinois, 1921-33; and Illinois State Treasurer, 1919-1921.
- **Stidham, Jerry E.** (1909 – DNA): Member of West Virginia State House of Delegates, 1947-1952.
- **Struble, John T.** (1828 – 1916): One of the early pioneer of the State of Iowa; charter member of Eureka Odd Fellows Lodge of the IOOF.
- **Summers, Isabelle McCullough** (1887 – DNA): Member of New Jersey state house of assembly, 1926-1927.
- **Swanson, Wayne R.** (1914 – DNA): Nebraska State Treasurer, 1967-1975; Member of Nebraska Railway Commission, 1957-1967.
- **Sweetland, Monroe Marsh** (1860 – 1944): One of the founding fathers of Delta Chi Fraternity in the United States.
- **Taylor, Lucy Hobbs** (1833 – 1910): First American woman to finish Dentistry.
- **Thomas, Joseph Henry** (1823 – 1908): Founding member of the Berkeley Institute; Founding

Lucy Hobbs Taylor (1833-1920) became the first American woman to earn a *Doctor of Dental Surgery* degree in 1866. After her husband died, she spent most of her time on activities of her Rebekah Lodge and became a staunch supporter of the women's rights movement.

father of Odd Fellowship in the Bahamas Islands.
- **Thompson, L. E.** (1906 – DNA): Member of West Virginia State House of Delegates, 1952, 1954.
- **Thompson, Lorenzo Dow** (1873 – 1951): Missouri State Auditor, 1925-1929; and Missouri State Treasurer, 1921-1925.
- **Trego, Reno W.** (1877 – 1961): Member of Wisconsin State Assembly, 1937-1940.
- **Trexler, Harry Clay** (1854 – 1933): one of the founding directors of The Pennsylvania Power and Light Company, 1920; The Harry C. Trexler Trust continue to benefit the people and community of Lehigh County, Pennsylvania.
- **Underwood, John Cox** (1840 – 1913): Lieutenant Governor of Kentucky, 1875-1979; and revered as the Founder of the Patriarchs Militant branch of the IOOF.
- **Vaughan, William L.** (1866 – DNA): Member of New York State Assembly, 1922-1933.
- **Wadlin, John F.** (1953 – DNA): Member of New York State Assembly, 1941-1953.
- **Wallace, Thomas Ross** (1848 – 1929): U.S. Consul in Crefeld, 1901-1907; Jerusalem, 1907-1910; Martinique, 1910-1924.
- **Weiford, Arnold O.** (1927 – DNA): Member of West Virginia State House of Delegates, 1957-1958.
- **Weinfeld, Morris** (1898 – DNA): Member of New York State Assembly, 1924-1927.
- **Welch, Thomas E.** (1930 – DNA): Member of West Virginia State House of Delegates, 1955-1958.
- **Wildey, Thomas** (1782 – 1861): Founder of the Independent Order of Odd Fellows in North America.
- **Wilkes, John** (1725 – 1797): early English radical, journalist and politician.
- **Wilson, Cecil W.** (1913 – DNA): Member of West Virginia State House of Delegates, 1939.
- **Winegar, Isaac Milton** (1816 – 1901): early pioneer of the State of Michigan; and Justice of the Peace of Byron Center, Michigan, 1848-1849.
- **White, Everett Edison** (1881 – DNA): Member of West Virginia State House of Delegates, 1929-1934, 1936-1940, 1947-1958.
- **Whitcomb, Forman E.** (1866 – DNA): Member of New York State Assembly, 1918-1932.
- **Whiting, George Addison** (1827 – 1903): Member of California State Assembly, 1871-1873.
- **Whittlesey, William Seward** (1840 – 1917): Postmaster at Rochester, New York, 1907-1911.
- **Wilcox, Orin S.** (1898 – unknown): Member of New York State Assembly, 1945-1965.
- **Woodward, Howard E.** (1892 – unknown): Member of West Virginia State House of Delegates, 1935-1936
- **Yale, John Reed** (1855 – 1925): Member of New York State Assembly, 1902-1913, 1921-1925.

Past Grand Sires and Past Sovereign Grand Masters

Past Grand Sires		
Name	Term	Jurisdiction
Thomas Wildey	1825-1833	Baltimore, MD
James Gettys	1833-1835	Georgetown, DC
Samuel H. Perkins	1837-1840	Philadelphia, PA
Zenas B. Glazier	1840-1841	Wilmington, DE
John A. Kennedy	1841-1843	New York City, NY
Howell Hopkins	1843-1845	Philadelphia, PA
Thomas Sherlock	1845-1847	Cincinnati, OH
Horn R. Kneass	1847-1849	Philadelphia, PA
Robert H. Griffin	1849-1851	Savannah, GA
Wm. W. Moore	1851-1853	Washington, DC
Wilmot G. DeSaussure	1853-1855	Charleston, SC
William Ellison	1855-1857	Boston, MA
George W. Race	1857-1858	New Orleans, LA
Samuel Craighead	1858-1860	Dayton, OH
Robert D. Boylston	1860-1862	Winnsborough, S
James B. Nicholson	1862-1864	Philadelphia, PA
Isaac M. Vietch	1864-1866	St. Louis, MO
James P. Sanders	1866-1868	Yonkers, NY
E. D. Farnsworth	1868-1870	Nashville, TN
Frederick D. Stuart	1870-1872	Washington, DC
Cornelius A. Logan	1872-1874	Leavenworth, KS
Milton J. Durham	1874-1876	Lexington, KY
John W. Stokes	1876-1878	Philadelphia, PA
John B. Harmon	1878-1880	San Francisco, CA
Luther J. Glenn	1880-1882	Atlanta, GA
Erie J. Leech	1882-1884	Keokuk, IA
Henry F. Garey	1884-1886	Baltimore, MD
John H. White	1886-1888	Albion, NY
John C. Underwood	1888-1890	Covington, KY
Charles M. Busbee,	1890-1892	Raleigh, NC
C. T. Campbell	1892-1894	London, ON
John W. Stebbins	1894-1896	Rochester, NY
Fred Carleton	1896-1898	Austin, TX
Alfred S. Pinkerton	1898-1900	Worcester, MA

A. C. Cable	1900-1902	Cincinnati, OH
John B. Goodwin	1902-1904	Baltimore, MD
R. E. Wright	1904-1906	Allentown, PA
E. S. Conway	1906-1908	Chicago, IL
John L. Nolen	1908	Nashville, TN
Wm. L. Kuykendall	1908-1910	Saratoga, WY
John B. Cockrum	1910-1912	Indianapolis, IN
C. A. Keller	1912-1914	San Antonio, TX
Robert T. Daniel	1914	Griffin, GA
J. B. A. Robertson	1915-1916	Oklahoma City, OK
Frank C. Goudy	1916-1918	Denver, CO
Henry V. Borst	1918-1920	Amsterdam, NY
Joseph Oliver	1921-1922	Toronto, ON
Lucian J. Easton	1922-1924	St. Joseph, MO
Herbert A. Thompson	1924-1926	Detroit, MI
Ernest W. Bradford	1926-1927	Washington, DC
Leon S. Merrill,	1927-1928	Orono, ME
Frank Martin	1928-1929	Boise, ID
M. M. Logan	1929-1930	Bowling Green, KY
Clement D. Rinehart	1930-1931	Jacksonville, FL
Joseph Powley	1931-1932	Toronto, ON
William F. Jackson	1932-1933	Fort Scott, KS
James H. Davis	1933-1934	Tacoma, WA
William A. Pittinger	1934-1935	Duluth, MN
Parke P. Deans	1935-1936	Richmond, VA
George E. Hershman	1936-1937	Crown Point, IN
Thomas G. Andrews	1937-1938	Oklahoma City, OK
Burton A. Gaskill	1938-1939	Mays Landing, NJ
George S. Starrett	1939-1940	Columbia, MO
James A. Hagerman	1940-1941	Saskatoon, SK
Lynn J. Irwin	1941-1943	Des Moines, IA
J. Paul Kuhn	1943-1944	Aurora, IL
D. D. Monroe	1944-1946	Clayton, NM
Past Sovereign Grand Masters		
C. A. Wheeler	1946-1947	Austin, TX
Arthur Charles Tiemeyer	1947-1948	Baltimore, MD
Frederick L. Phelps	1948-1949	Middletown, CT
Edward M. Sharpe	1949-1950	Bay City, MI

Miles E. Peck	1950-1951	Sioux Falls, SD
Joe Looney	1951-1952	Wewoka, OK
P. V. Ibbetson	1952-1953	Port Arthur, ON
James R. French	1953-1954	Greybull, WY
Tellie F. Aston	1954-1955	Sherman, TX
H. Sanders Anglea	1955-1956	Nashville, TN
L. S. Bridges	1956-1957	Baton Rouge, LA
James M. Elliott	1957-1958	Alliance, OH
Fred L. Pardee	1958-1958	Little Rock, AR
E. O. Richards	1959-1960	Chappell, NE
Gene J. Bianchi	1960-1961	Oakdale, CA
Verdie A. Dodds	1961-1962	Lexington, MA
Oakford A. Schalick	1962-1963	Elmer, NJ
C. Everett Murphy	1963-1964	Kingfisher, OK
Kermit R. Cofer	1964-1965	Water Valley, MS
James Main	1965-1966	Vancouver, BC
A. M. Black	1966-1967	Knoxville, IA
Harold L. Scott	1967-1968	Linn, WV
Chester J. Hunnicutt	1968-1969	Powell, WY
Donald R. Smith	1969-1970	Linden, CA
Samuel J. Patterson	1970-1971	Philadelphia, PA
J. Ray King	1971-1972	Sutherland, NE
J. Edward Stallings	1972-1973	Griffin, GA
Shelby McCauley	1973-1974	Prescott, AZ
Frank L. Shrives	1974-1975	Portland, OR
J. Douglas Moore	1975-1976	Perth-Andover, NB – AP
Jack O. Morrow	1976-1977	Boise, ID
Corwin E. Havill	1977-1978	Casper, WY
Hugh J. Bradley	1978-1979	Hendersonville, TN
Eugene C. Mount	1979-1980	Oklahoma City, OK
William H. England	1980-1981	Syracuse, NY
Meriel D. Harris	1981-1982	Somerset, KY
Lloyd G. Cranston	1982-1983	Calgary, AB
Ronald W. Hughes	1983-1984	Dallas, TX
Lorin D. Swift	1984-1985	Sacramento, CA
George E. Shaw	1985-1986	Worcester, MA
James P. Sadler	1986-1987	Nashville, TN
Percy J. Henry	1987-1988	New Iberia, LA

Horace H. Childress	1988-1989	Sapulpa, OK
Wilson D. Berkey	1989-1990	Lakeside, AZ
Robert D. Irving	1990-1991	Sacramento, CA
Carl C. Williams	1991-1992	Clarksburg, WV
Lloyd D. Shelvey	1992-1993	Grandview, MB
Charles E. Worrell Sr.	1993-1994	Nashville, TN
J. W. Frederick Laycock	1994-1995	Paris, KY
Wayne N. Reynolds	1995-1996	Reno, NV – NC
Louis E. Fancher Jr.	1996-1997	Greenwood, MS
Martin Elson	1997-1998	New York, NY
Connie Mac Riley	1998-1999	Omaha, NE
Conley Call	1999-2000	North Wilkesboro, NC
Arthur A. Craig	2000-2001	Buckley, WA
Harry V. Lohman	2001-2002	Largo, MD – DC
Jon R. Petersen	2002-2003	Lead Hill, AR – AZ
Henry L. Dupray	2003-2004	Wilmington, NC
C. LaVaughn Lawson	2004-2005	Perry, OK
Michael W. Dutton	2005-2006	Nashville, TN
Robert J. Robbins	2006-2007	Golden, CO
Richard S. Kim	2007-2008	Kaneohe, HI
Richard G. Proulx	2008-2009	Green Bay, WI
Paul J. Cuminale	2009-2010	Claymont, DE – CT
George L. Glover III	2010-2011	Coventry, RI
Delmar L. Burns	2011-2012	Germantown, OH
Charles L. Renninger	2012-2013	Largo, MD – DC
Robert W. Smith	2013-2014	Bourbonnais, IL
Jimmy C. Humphrey	2014-2015	Savannah, GA
Danny W. Wood	2015-2016	Springtown, TX
W. Larry Ferguson	2016-2017	Elkins, WV
John A. Miller, Sr.	2017-2018	Warren, CT
Douglas E. Pittman	2018-2019	Canon City, CO
E. Wesley Nelson	2019-2020	Calgary, AB

Sovereign Grand Lodge Sessions

Session	Place of Meeting
1850	Cincinnati, Ohio
1851	Baltimore, Maryland
1852	Baltimore, Maryland
1853	Philadelphia, PA
1854	Baltimore, Maryland
1855	Baltimore, Maryland
1856	Baltimore, Maryland
1857	Baltimore, Maryland
1858	Baltimore, Maryland
1859	Baltimore, Maryland
1860	Nashville, TN
1861	Baltimore, Maryland
1862	Baltimore, Maryland
1863	Baltimore, Maryland
1864	Boston, MA
1865	Baltimore, Maryland
1866	Baltimore, Maryland
1867	New York City, NY
1868	Baltimore, Maryland
1869	San Francisco, CA
1870	Baltimore, Maryland
1871	Chicago, IL
1872	Baltimore, Maryland
1873	Baltimore, Maryland
1874	Atlanta, GA
1875	Indianapolis, IN
1876	Philadelphia, PA
1877	Baltimore, Maryland
1878	Baltimore, Maryland
1879	Baltimore, Maryland
1880	Toronto, ON
1881	Cincinnati, OH
1882	Baltimore, MD
1883	Providence, RI
1884	Minneapolis, MN

1885	Baltimore, MD
1886	Boston, MA
1887	Denver, CO
1888	Los Angeles, CA
1889	Columbus, OH
1890	Topeka, KS
1891	St. Louis, MO
1892	Portland, OR
1893	Milwaukee, WI
1894	Chattanooga, TN
1895	Atlantic City, NJ
1896	Dallas, TX
1897	Springfield, IL
1898	Boston, MA
1899	Detroit, MI
1900	Richmond, VA
1901	Indianapolis, IN
1902	Des Moines, IA
1903	Baltimore, MD
1904	San Francisco, CA
1905	Philadelphia, PA
1906	Toronto, ON
1907	St. Paul, MN
1908	Denver, CO
1909	Seattle, WA
1910	Atlanta, GA
1911	Indianapolis, IN
1912	Winnipeg, MB
1913	Minneapolis, MN
1914	Atlantic City, NJ
1915	San Francisco, CA
1916	Chattanooga, TN
1917	Louisville, KY
1918	St. Louis, MO
1919	Baltimore, MD
1920	Boston, MA
1921	Toronto, ON
1922	Detroit, MI

1923	Cincinnati, OH
1924	Jacksonville, FL
1925	Portland, OR
1926	Philadelphia, PA
1927	Hot Springs, AR
1928	Montreal, PQ
1929	Houston, TX
1930	Indianapolis, IN
1931	Winnipeg, MB
1932	Denver, CO
1933	Springfield, IL
1934	Toronto, ON
1935	Atlantic City, NJ
1936	New York City, NY
1937	Milwaukee, WI
1938	Oklahoma City, OK
1939	Minneapolis, MN
1940	Huntington, WV
1941	Des Moines, IA
1943	Chicago, IL
1944	Toronto, ON
1945	- Postponed due to World War II -
1946	Columbus, OH
1947	Winnipeg, MB
1948	St. Paul, MN
1949	Sacramento, CA
1950	Philadelphia, PA
1951	Indianapolis, IN
1952	Dallas, TX
1953	Atlanta, GA
1954	Colorado Springs, CO
1955	Chicago, IL
1956	Omaha, NE
1957	Miami, Florida
1958	Memphis, TN
1959	Pittsburgh, PA
1960	Long Beach, CA
1961	Phoenix, AZ

1962		Montreal, PQ
1963		Louisville, KY
1964		Minneapolis, MN
1965		Chicago, IL
1966		Philadelphia, PA
1967		Calgary, AB
1968		Miami Beach, FL
1969		Baltimore, MD
1970		Gatlinburg, TN
1971		Vancouver, BC
1972		Cincinnati, OH
1973		New York City, NY
1974		Philadelphia, PA
1975		Portland, OR
1976		Denver, CO
1977		Oklahoma City, OK
1978		San Antonio, TX
1979		Jackson, MS
1980		Toronto, ON
1981		St. Louis, MO
1982		Pittsburgh, PA
1983		Winnipeg, MB
1984		Albuquerque, NM
1985		Indianapolis, IN
1986		New Orleans, LA
1987		Portland, OR
1988		Winston-Salem, NC
1989		Reno, NV
1990		Nashville, TN
1991		Edmonton, AB
1992		Atlanta, GA
1993		Rosemont, IL
1994		Sacramento, CA
1995		Denver, CO
1996		Nashville, TN
1997		Kansas City, MO
1998		Kiamesha Lake, NY
1999		Sea Tac, WA

2000	Rosemont, IL
2001	Winston-Salem, NC
2002	Wichita, KS
2003	Halifax, NS
2004	St. Louis, MO
2005	London, ON
2006	Winston-Salem, NC
2007	Denver, CO
2008	Winnipeg, MB
2009	Santa Clara, CA
2010	Kansas City, MO
2011	Winston-Salem, NC
2012	Cincinnati, OH
2013	Schaumburg, IL
2014	Victoria, BC
2015	Fort Worth, TX
2016	Rapid City, SD
2017	St. Louis, MO
2018	Baltimore, Maryland
2019	Winston-Salem, North Carolina
2020	- Postponed due to Covid-19 pandemic -

Always grateful to Officers of The Sovereign Grand Lodge and International Association of Rebekah Assemblies and the Staff

From Right: Sovereign Grand Secretary Bro. Terry Barrett, Suzie Robertson+, former International Association of Rebekah Assemblies Secretary Vivian Pursell, Kelly Westbrook, Bill Pursell, Brenda Nelson and Louie Blake Saile Sarmiento at the International Headquarters of The Sovereign Grand Lodge of the Independent Order of Odd Fellows in Winston-Salem, North Carolina, USA. Photo by author, 2014.

Notes

Chapter 1 - Introduction

1. James Spry, *The History of Odd Fellowship: Its Origin, Tradition and Objectives* (London: J.R.H. Spry, 1866), 2-5; Michael Streeter, B*ehind Closed Doors* (United Kingdom: New Holland Publishers, 2008), 153-155.

2. John Kennedy Melling, *Discovering London's Guilds and Liveries* (United Kingdom: Shire Publications, 2002), 11; Elvin James Curry, *The Red Blood of Odd Fellowship* (Maryland: Elvin Curry, 1903), 62-68; Simon Cordery, *British Friendly Societies, 1750-1914* (New York: Palgrave Macmillan, 2003), 17; Michael Streeter, *Behind Closed Doors* (United Kingdom: New Holland Publishers, 2008), 153-155.

3. Elvin James Curry, *The Red Blood of Odd Fellowship* (Maryland: Elvin Curry, 1903), 209-253

4. Elvin James Curry, *The Red Blood of Odd Fellowship* (Maryland: Elvin Curry, 1903), 75-84.

5. Paschal Donaldson, *The Odd Fellows' Pocket Companion* (Ohio: R.W. Carroll & Co, 1881), 13.

6. Grand Lodge of Ontario and J.B. King, *Odd Fellowship* (Toronto: Independent Odd Fellow Print, 1907), 4-5.

7. Thomas G. Andrews, *The Jericho Road* (Oklahoma: William Thomas Co, 1937); Benson M. Powell, *The Triple Links* (Kansas: Ed G. Moore and Son, 1900); Sovereign Grand Lodge, *Ritual of a Lodge of Odd Fellows of The Sovereign Grand Lodge of the Independent Order of Odd Fellows* (United States: Sovereign Grand Lodge, I.O.O.F., 2004).

8. Ibid.

9. Charles H. Brooks, *The Official History ad Manual of the Grand United Order of Odd Fellows* (Pennsylvania: Odd Fellows Journal Print, 1903), 228.

10. Sovereign Grand Lodge, *Journal of Proceedings of the International Council, Independent Order of Odd Fellows, 1999-2001* (U.S.A: Sovereign Grand Lodge, 2001), 17.

11. Thomas G. Beharrell, *The Brotherhood: Being a Presentation of Odd Fellowship* (Indiana: Brotherhood Publishing Co., 1875), 9-16; Thomas G. Andrews, *The Jericho Road* (Oklahoma: William Thomas Co, 1937), 12-13; Sovereign Grand Lodge, *Ritual of a Lodge of Odd Fellows of The Sovereign Grand Lodge of the Independent Order of Odd Fellows* (United States: Sovereign Grand Lodge, I.O.O.F., 2004).

12. Thomas G. Beharrell, *The Brotherhood: Being a Presentation of Odd Fellowship* (Indiana: Brotherhood Publishing Co., 1875), 29; Sovereign Grand Lodge, *Ritual of a Lodge of Odd Fellows of The Sovereign Grand Lodge of the Independent Order of Odd Fellows* (United States: Sovereign Grand Lodge, I.O.O.F., 2004).

13. Sovereign Grand Lodge, *Ritual of a Lodge of Odd Fellows of The Sovereign Grand Lodge of the Independent Order of Odd Fellows* (United States: Sovereign Grand Lodge, I.O.O.F., 2004); Thomas G. Andrews, *The Jericho Road* (Oklahoma: William Thomas Co, 1937), 75-110.

14. Ibid.

15. Ibid.

16. Ritual of the Manchester Unity Independent Order of Odd Fellows (1824)

17. Thomas G. Beharrel, T*he Brotherhood: Being a Presentation of the Principles of Odd Fellowship* (Indiana: Brotherhood Publishing Company, 1875), 74-76; Sovereign Grand Lodge, *Ritual of a Lodge of Odd Fellows of The Sovereign Grand Lodge of the Independent Order of Odd Fellows* (United States: Sovereign Grand Lodge, I.O.O.F., 2004).

18. Sovereign Grand Lodge, *Journal of Proceedings of the Sovereign Grand Lodge, I.O.O.F* (North Carolina, Sovereign Grand Lodge, 1995), 302.

19. Ibid.

20. Sovereign Grand Lodge, *Ritual of a Lodge of Odd Fellows of The Sovereign Grand Lodge of the Independent Order of Odd Fellows* (United States: Sovereign Grand Lodge, I.O.O.F., 2004).

21. Ibid.

22. Sovereign Grand Lodge, *Ritual of a Lodge of Odd Fellows of The Sovereign Grand Lodge of the Independent Order of Odd Fellows* (United States: Sovereign Grand Lodge, I.O.O.F., 2004); Thomas G. Andrews, *The Jericho Road* (Oklahoma: William Thomas Co, 1937), 75-110.

23. Thomas G. Beharrell, *The Brotherhood: Being a Presentation of the Principles of Odd Fellowship* (Indiana: Brotherhood Publishing Company, 1875), 12.

24. Ibid.

25. Ibid.

26. Grand Lodge of Denmark, Ritual of the Odd Fellows Lodge (Denmark: Grand Lodge of Denmark, 1978).

27. Ibid.

28. George Emery and J. C. Herbert Emery, *A Young Man's Benefit* (London: McGill-Queen's University Press, 1999).

29. Tom Reedy and Nita Thurman, *Denton Lodge No.82, I.O.O.F.: A History 1859-2009* (Maine: Acme Bookbinding, 2009), 131-134.

30. Sovereign Grand Lodge, *Code of General Laws* (2012).

31. Sovereign Grand Lodge, *Ritual of a Lodge of Odd Fellows of The Sovereign Grand Lodge of the Independent Order of Odd Fellows* (United States: Sovereign Grand Lodge, I.O.O.F., 2004).

General Purposes

1. Sovereign Grand Lodge, Members Handbook:

Independent Order of Odd Fellows (North Carolina: Sovereign Grand Lodge, 2013), 11.

Chapter 2 - The Name
1. Don R. Smith and Wayne Roberts, *The Three Link Fraternity* (California: Linden Publications, 1993), 5; Peter Sellars, T*he History of the Independent Order of Odd Fellows in the City of San Francisco,* (California: Privately printed, 2007), 4-5.
2. Michael Streeter, *Behind Closed Doors* (London: New Holland Publishers, 2008), 153-155
3. R.H. Moffrey, *A Century of Odd Fellowship* (United Kingdom: Manchester Unity Independent Order of Oddfellows, 1910),16; Michael Streeter, *Behind Closed Doors* (London: New Holland Publishers, 2008), 153-155; John Kennedy Melling, *Discovering London's Guilds and Liveries* (United Kingdom: Shire Publications, 2002), 11; Simon Cordery, *British Friendly Societies, 1750-1914* (New York: Palgrave Macmillan, 2003), 17.
4. *European History Quarterly* (London: SAGE), vol. 16 (1986), 25-45; Mary Ann Clawson, *Constructing Brotherhood: Class, Gender, and Fraternalism* (New Jersey: Princeton University Press, 1989), 3.
5. *European History Quarterly* (London: SAGE), vol. 16 (1986), 25-45.
6. L. Hamel Cooke, *Democracy and Odd Fellowship* (Canada: L. Hamel Cooke, 1943), 7-9.
7. Peter Swift Seibert, *Fraternally Yours: Identify Fraternal Groups and Their Emblems* (Pennsylvania: Schiffer Publishing, 2012), 88.
8. Harriet Wain McBride, *Fraternal Regalia in America, 1865 to 1918* (Ohio: Ohio State University, 2000), 81.
9. Ibid.
10. Elvin James Curry, *The Red Blood of Odd Fellowship* (Maryland: Elvin Curry, 1903), 66.
11. Daniel Weinbren, *The Oddfellows 1810-2010: 200 Years of Making Friends and Helping People* (Lancaster: Carnegie Publishing, 2012), 33-34.

An Edifying Explanation
1. Ward-Stillson Co., *Ancient Ritual of the Order of Patriotic Odd Fellows: Revised and agreed to in the Grand Lodge held at London, England, March 12, 1797* (Michigan: Kalamazoo Publishing,n.d.), 23.

Chapter 3 - Legends and Origins
1. Mary Ann Clawson, *Constructing Brotherhood: Class, Gender, and Fraternalism* (New Jersey: Princeton University, 1989), 15.
2. Noel P. Gist, *Culture Patterning in Secret Society Ceremonials* (North Carolina: University of North Carolina Press, 1936), 497-505.
3. Mary Ann Clawson, *Constructing Brotherhood: Class, Gender, and Fraternalism* (New Jersey: Princeton University, 1989), 15. "The lodges of the nineteenth and twentieth century America were the descendants of an earlier European fraternalism. Guilds, journeyman societies, religious confraternities, and village youth brotherhoods were all forms of fraternal association, making it one of the most widespread and culturally central modes of organization in the late medieval and early modern Europe."
4. Charles H. Brooks, *The Official History ad Manual of the Grand United Order of Odd Fellows* (Pennsylvania: Odd Fellows Journal Print, 1903), 5-7; Paschal Donaldson, *The Odd Fellows Text Book* (Philadelphia: Moss & Brother, 1852), 1
5. Paschal Donaldson, *The Odd Fellows Text Book* (Philadelphia: Moss & Brother, 1852), 19.
6. Henry Leonard Stillson, *The Official History of Odd Fellowship* (Massachusetts: Fraternity Publishing Company, 1900), 23; Paschal Donaldson, The Odd Fellows Text Book (Philadelphia: Moss & Brother, 1852), 18.
7. Victoria Solt Dennis, *Discovering Friendly and Fraternal Societies* (United Kingdom: Shire Publications, 2008), 4; Robert Moffrey, *The Rise and Progress of the Manchester Unity of the Independent Order of Oddfellows* (United Kingdom: Grand Master & Board of Directors of the Order, 1904), 2.
8. Steven A. Epstein, *Wage labor and guilds in Medieval Europe* (North Carolina: University of North Carolina Press, 1991), 11-33.
9. Emmanuel Rebold and J. Fletcher Brennan, A *General History of FreeMasonry in Europe: Based upon the Ancient Documents Relating to and the Monuments Erected by this Fraternity from its foundation in the year 715 BC to present time* (Ohio: Cincinnati American Masonic publishing association, 1868), 34-154; Daniel Weinbren, T*he Oddfellows 1810-2010: 200 Years of Making Friends and Helping People* (Lancaster: Carnegie Publishing, 2012), 7.
10. William Sewell, *Work and Revolution in France: The Language of Labor from the Old Regime to 1848* (New York: Cambridge University Press, 1980).
11. 'By 1423 there were over 100 guilds. New ones formed, and amalgamations occurred'. Roy Porter, *London: A Social History* (United Kingdom: Penguin, 2000), 29. See also John Kennedy Melling, *Discovering London's Guilds and Liveries* (United Kingdom: Shire Publications, 2002), 34-106.
12. John Kennedy Melling, *Discovering London's Guilds and Liveries* (United Kingdom: Shire Publications, 2002), 46.
13. Ibid, 68-69.

14. Ibid, 68-69.
15. Ibid, 47-48.
16. Ibid, 52.
17. Joshua Toulmin Smith, *English Gilds* (London: N. Trubner & Co., London, 1870). See also Victoria Solt Dennis, Discovering Friendly and Fraternal Societies (United Kingdom: Shire Publishing, 2008), 4.
18. Elvin James Curry, *The Red Blood of Odd Fellowship* (Maryland: Elvin Curry, 1903), 62-65. See also Roy Porter, London: A social history (United Kingdom: Penguin, 2000), 29.
19. Henry Leonard Stillson, *The Official History of Odd Fellowship* (Massachusetts: Fraternity Publishing Company, 1900), 33-37. See also Joshua Toulmin Smith, *English Gilds* (London: N. Trubner & Co., London, 1870).
20. Ibid, 34-35.
21. Porter, *London: A Social History* (United Kingdom: Penguin, 2000), 29.
22. John Weber, *An Illustrated Guide of the Lost Symbol* (New York: Sensei Publications, 2009), 12.
23. Ibid, 12-13.
24. John Kennedy Melling, *Discovering London's Guilds and Liveries* (United Kingdom: Shire Publications, 2002), 84.
25. John Weber, *An Illustrated Guide of the Lost Symbol* (New York: Sensei Publications, 2009), 13.
26. Tom Reedy and Nita Thurman, *Denton Lodge No.82, I.O.O.F.: A History 1859-2009* (Maine: Acme Bookbinding, 2009), 7.
27. Ibid.
28. John Kennedy Melling, *Discovering London's Guilds and Liveries* (United Kingdom: Shire Publications, 2002), 11;
29. Mary Ann Clawson, *Constructing Brotherhood: Class, Gender, and Fraternalism* (New Jersey: Princeton University, 1989), 3; *European History Quarterly* (London: SAGE), vol. 16 (1986), 25-45;
30. *European History Quarterly* (London: SAGE), vol. 16 (1986), 25-45;
31. Mary Ann Clawson, *Constructing Brotherhood: Class, Gender, and Fraternalism* (New Jersey: Princeton University, 1989), 3.
32. Ibid, 118.
33. Paschal Donaldson, *The Odd Fellows Text Book* (Philadelphia: Moss & Brother, 1852), 22.
34. Ibid.
35. Ibid.

Ancient Noble Order of Bucks
1. W.J. Parre, *Quatuor Coronatum: Being the Transactions of the Quatuor Coronati Lodge No. 2076, London, Volume 3* (London: W. J. Parre, 1840), 140; Clark, *British Clubs and Societies: 1580-1800* (New York: Oxford University Press, 2002), 76; P.D., A candid enquiry into the principles and practices of the most ancient and honourable society of Bucks (London: C. Kiernan, 1770).
2. Elvin James Curry, *The Red Blood of Odd Fellowship* (Maryland: Elvin Curry, 1903), 6-9.
3. Ibid, 68-69.
4. W.J. Parre, 150
5. Henry Leonard Stillson, *The Official History of Odd Fellowship* (Massachusetts: Fraternity Publishing Company, 1900), 41
6. W.J. Parre, 153.
7. Stillson, 40.
8. W.J. Parre, 149.
9. Curry, 71.
10. Stillson, 40.
11. Ibid, 41.

Chapter 4 - Early English Clubs and Their Practices
1. Henry Leonard Stillson, *The Official History of Odd Fellowship* (Massachusetts: Fraternity Publishing Company, 1908), 21.
2. 'The first members were toiling laborers. Their daily labor barely sufficed to procure them daily bread. When sickness came, gaunt and terrible want was not far off. When one loses a job, he lacked the means to seek employment elsewhere and support their families meanwhile. When on the bed of disease or death, none could spare time to smooth the creased pillow, or moisten the fevered lips, or speak calmness to the delirious mind'. See Rev. A.B. Grosh, *The Odd-Fellows Improved Pocket Manual* (New York: Clark & Maynard, 1873), 29-30. See also Geoffrey Blainey, *Odd Fellows: A history of IOOF Australia* (Sydney: Allen & Unwin, 1991), 3. He mentioned that the typical Odd Fellow in England in the eighteenth century was an artisan with an income higher than that of a laborer and lower than that of a clerk or self-employed tradesman.
3. 'The early English Lodges were supported, and their members relieved, by each member and visitor paying a penny to the secretary on entering the lodge. If a member needed aid, a sufficient sum will be given to him. If out of work, he was furnished with a card and funds to reach the next lodge'. W.W. Wallace, *The Odd-Fellows' Keepsake: A Concise History of Odd-Fellowship in the United States* (New York: Office of the Mirror of the Times, 1850), 18-25.
4. Daniel Defoe, *An Essay upon Projects* (London: R.R. for Tho. Cockerill, 1697), 118-119.
5. Simon Cordery, *British Friendly Societies, 1750-1914* (New York: Palgrave Macmillan, 2003), 22.
6. Ibid.

7. Ibid, 34-35.
8. Henry Leonard Stillson, *The Official History of Odd Fellowship* (Massachusetts: Fraternity Publishing Company, 1900), 50.
9. Ibid.
10. Tal P. Shaffner, *Odd Fellowship Illustrated: In an Address delivered before the Grand Lodge of Kentucky* (New York: Russel Brothers Publishers, 1875), 43-44.
1. Rev. A.B. Grosh, *Odd Fellows Improved Pocket Manual* (New York: Clark & Maynard, 1873), 27.

Chapter 5 - Industrial Revolution

1. Jonathan Downs, *The Industrial Revolution: Britain, 1770-1810* (United Kingdom: Shire Publications, 2010).
2. Goeffrey Blainey, *Odd Fellows: A History of IOOF Australia* (Australia: Allen & Unwin, 1991), 3.
3. Simon Cordery, *British Friendly Societies, 1750-1914* (New York: Palgrave Macmillan, 2003).

Chapter 6 - Government Suppression

1. Compiled by various authors, *A History of the Holy Catholic Inquisition* (Philadelphia: Perkins, Marvin and Co, 1835).
2. David B. Barrett, *Secret Societies: An unbiased history of our desire for secret knowledge* (Philadelphia: Running Press, 2007), 82. See also Colin Robert Bowling, *A New Order of the Ages* (Indiana: iUniverse, 2011), 232.
3. Armstrong Starkey, *War in the Age of Enlightenment, 1700-1789* (Connecticut: Praeger Publishers, 2003). See also Robert Wokler, Rousseau, *the Age of Enlightenment, and Their Legacies* (New Jersey: Princeton University Press, 2012).
4. Michael Streeter, *Behind Closed Doors* (London: New Holland Publishers, 2008), 105. For example, "Nicolas de Bonneville, a known radical who played a part in the French Revolution, was member of the Freemasons and allegedly had close links with a prominent member of the Illuminati". See also Michael L. Kennedy, *The Jacobin Clubs in the French Revolution 1793-1795* (New York: Berghahn Books, 2000). He mentioned that the term Jacobin Club popularly applies to all supporters of left-wing revolutionary political movement that had been the most famous political club of the French Revolution.
5. Ibid, 101-105.
6. Michael Howard, *Secret Societies: Their Influence and Power from Antiquity to Present Day* (Vermont: Destiny Books, 2008), 74-78.
7. Michael Streeter, *Behind Closed Doors* (London: New Holland Publishers, 2008), 91-93. See also Una Birch, *Secret Societies: Illuminati, Freemasons and the French Revolution* (Florida: Ibis Press, 2007).
8. Victoria Solt Dennis, *Discovering Friendly and Fraternal Societies* (United Kingdom: Shire Publications, 2008), 13.
9. Ibid, 9-11.
10. Manchester Unity Independent Order of Oddfellows, "*The Oddfellows Over the Years*", accessed July 20, 2017, https://www.oddfellows.co.uk/About-us/Over-the-Years.
11. Ibid.
12. Victoria Solt Dennis, *Discovering Friendly and Fraternal Societies* (United Kingdom: Shire Publications, 2008), 73. He mentioned that friendly societies provided common ground for middle and working class individuals to cooperate, and for members of different strata within working class to meet. See also Jasper Ridley, *The Freemasons: A history of the world's most powerful secret society* (New York: Arcade Publishing, 2011).

Chapter 7 - Revival

1. *Early Reminiscences of Odd Fellowship, The Covenant, and Official Magazine of the Grand Lodge of the United States I.O.O.F.*, Volume 1 (1842), 80.
2. Charles H. Brooks, *The Official History ad Manual of the Grand United Order of Odd Fellows* (Pennsylvania: Odd Fellows Journal Print, 1903), 9-10. It is accepted that the Manchester Unity Independent Order of Odd Fellows seceded from the United Order of Odd Fellows in London which is usually mentioned as Union Order or United Order.
3. The Union Order or Grand United Order embraced all Lodges in England until 1813, when the first split or secession occurred. The seceding Lodges formed a union and styled themselves "Independent Order of Odd Fellows, Manchester Unity".
4. Brooks, *The Official History and Manual of the Grand United Order of Odd Fellows in America*, 12.
5. "Oddfellows Welcome", *Grand United Order of Oddfellows*, accessed October 25, 2017, https://www.guoofs.com/.
6. The Oddfellows' Magazine of 1888 refers to the 'Free and Independent Order of Odd Fellows' in Dover.
7. Dennis, *Discovering Friendly and Fraternal Societies*, 92-94. See also entry for the Odd Fellows in Gilman, Peck and Colby, T*he New International Encyclopedia*, 783.

Chapter 8 - Rise of the Manchester Unity Oddfellows

1. Simon Cordery, *British Friendly Societies, 1750-1914* (New York: Palgrave Macmillan, 2003), 40.
2. Daniel Weinbren, *The Oddfellows 1810-2010: 200 years of making friends and helping people* (Lancaster: Carnegie Publishing, 2012).
3. Henry Leonard Stillson, *The Official History of Odd Fellowship* (Massachusetts: Fraternity Publishing Company, 1900), 50.

4. Don R. Smith and Wayne Roberts, *The Three Link Fraternity* (California: Linden Publications, 1993), 6. See also Henry Leonard Stillson, *The Official History of Odd Fellowship* (Massachusetts: Fraternity Publishing Company, 1900), 50-51.

5. R.H. Moffrey, *A Century of Odd Fellowship* (United Kingdom: Manchester Unity Independent Order of Oddfellows, 1910), 65-67.

6. Simon Cordery, *British Friendly Societies, 1750-1914* (New York: Palgrave Macmillan, 2003), 115.

7. *The Times*, January 4, 1944.

8. Manchester Unity Independent Order of Odd Fellows Friendly Society, *Ritual of the Independent Order of Odd Fellows Manchester Unity Friendly Society: For the Use of District Officers* (Manchester: Manchester Unity Independent Order of Odd Fellows Manchester Unity Friendly Society, 1989), 26.

9. Ibid, 62-79.

10. Ibid, 100-118.

11. Ibid, 121.

12. Sovereign Grand Lodge of the IOOF, *Journal of Proceedings of the International Council of the Independent Order of Odd Fellows, 1999-2001* (United States of America: Sovereign Grand Lodge, 2001), 49.

13. Manchester Unity Independent Order of Odd Fellows Manchester Unity Friendly Society, *Ritual of the Independent Order of Odd Fellows Manchester Unity Friendly Society: For the Use of District Officers* (Manchester: Manchester Unity Independent Order of Odd Fellows Manchester Unity Friendly Society, 1989), 87-89.

14. Sovereign Grand Lodge of the IOOF, *Journal of Proceedings of the One Hundred and Sixty-First Annual Communication of the Sovereign Grand Lodge of the Independent Order of Odd Fellows, 1987 (Volume LXXV)* (Winston-Salem: The Sovereign Grand Lodge of the I.O.O.F., 1988), 37.

15. Sovereign Grand Lodge of the IOOF, *Journal of Proceedings of the International Council of the Independent Order of Odd Fellows, 1999-2001* (United States of America: Sovereign Grand Lodge, 2001), 51.

16. Ibid.

17. Manchester Unity Independent Order of Oddfellows Friendly Society, "About the Oddfellows Friendly Society", accessed 25 October 2017, https://www.oddfellows.co.uk/about/

Chapter 9 - Odd Fellowship in North America

1. Robert Macoy, *General History, Cyclopedia, and Dictionary of Freemasonry* (New York, Masonic Publishing Company, 1870), 271. Macoy (1870) mentioned the the Odd Fellows was introduced in the United States as early as 1799 when a lodge was constituted in Connecticut, in 1802 in Baltimore in and in 1806 in New York.

2. Aaron Burt Grosh, *A Manual of Odd Fellowship* (New York, Clark & Maynard, 1882), 31-36.

3. Elvin J. Curry, *Red Blood of Odd Fellowship* (Baltimore: Elvin J. Curry, 1903), 75.

4. Sovereign Grand Lodge of the IOOF, *Journal of Proceedings of the One Hundred and Forty-Third Annual Communication of the Sovereign Grand Lodge of the Independent Order of Odd Fellows, 1969 (Volume LVII)* (Baltimore: The Sovereign Grand Lodge of the I.O.O.F., 1970), 478.

5. Ibid.

6. Ibid.

7. Curry, *The Red Blood of Odd Fellowship*, 80.

8. Grosh, *A Manual of Odd Fellowship*, 32-33.

9. Curry, *The Red Blood of Odd Fellowship*, 128-132. Curry (1903) mentioned that there was a tendency in most men of all social gathering to be convivial in their habits. Members meet to eat and drink and sing festive songs. See also Donaldson, The Odd Fellows' Text Book and Manual, 36. See also Ridgely, History of American Odd Fellowship, 26-27. The original charter issued by Duke of York Lodge in 1820 states that the lodge was chartered for the encouragement and support of brothers of the said Order, when on travel or otherwise. It was the tradition of the Lodge to assist members when traveling, sick or in distress.

10. Clawson, *Constructing Brotherhood: Class, Gender, and Fraternalism* (New Jersey: Princeton University, 1989), 120.

11. Stillson, *The Official History of Odd Fellows*, 67.

12. Aaron Burt Grosh, *A Manual of Odd Fellowship* (New York, Clark & Maynard, 1882), 30.

13. Aaron Burt Grosh, *A Manual of Odd Fellowship* (New York, Clark & Maynard, 1882), 40. Grosh (1882) mentioned that one of the first acts of the Grand Lodge of the United States was to step out in advance of nearly all social organizations of that period by decreeing that in no case should any refreshment except water be used in any of the lodge rooms.

14. Powley, *Concise History of Odd Fellowship* (Revised edition), 14-15.

15. Stillson, *The Official History of Odd Fellowship*, 234.

16. Streeter, *Behind Closed Doors* (United Kingdom: New Holland Publishers, 2008), 153-155.

17. Moffrey, *A Century of Odd Fellowship*, 46.

18. Powley, *Concise History of Odd Fellowship* (Revised edition), 17.

19. Stillson, *Official History of Odd Fellowship: The Three Link Fraternity*, 99-100. Stillson (1900) mentioned that a resolution to dissolve ties with Manchester Unity was

adopted on September 23, 1842, and was reaffirmed on September 22, 1843.
20. Sovereign Grand Lodge of the IOOF, *Journal of Proceedings of the One Hundred and Sixty-First Annual Communication of the Sovereign Grand Lodge of the Independent Order of Odd Fellows, 1987 (Volume LXXV)*, 35.
21. Ibid.
22. Ibid.
23. Brooks, T*he Official History ad Manual of the Grand United Order of Odd Fellows,* 11;
24. Sovereign Grand Lodge of the IOOF, *Journal of Proceedings of the Right Worthy Grand Lodge of the United States, and the Sovereign Grand Lodge of the Independent Order of Odd Fellows, 1941-1944 (Volume XL)* (Baltimore: The Sovereign Grand Lodge of the I.O.O.F., 1945), 1130.
25. Ibid, 1131.

Three Odd Links
1. Edward Stallings, Searching for Treasures (North Carolina: Sovereign Grand Lodge), 12.
2. Ibid.
3. Ibid.

African-American Odd Fellows
1. Charles Brooks, *The Official History ad Manual of the Grand United Order of Odd Fellows* (Pennsylvania: Odd Fellows Journal Print, 1903), 12.
2. Ibid, 12-14.
3. Archives of Maryland, *"Freedom's Friend Lodge No. 1024: Black Mutual Aid Society; Saint Michaels, Maryland"*, Archives of Maryland, n.d., accessed October 4, 2017, http://msa.maryland.gov/megafile/msa/speccol/sc5400/sc5496/051800/051882/html/51882bio.html
4. David Hackett, *The Prince Hall Freemasons and the African American Church: The Labors of Grand Master and Bishop James Walker Hood, 1831-1918,* Church History, 69:4 (December 2000), 770-802.

Chapter 10 - The Gold Rush
1. H.W. Brands, *The Age of Gold: The California Gold Rush and the New American Dream*, (New York: Doubleday, 2003), 30.
2. G.H. Tinkham, *The Half Century of California Odd Fellowship* (Stockton, CA: Record Publishing Co, 1906), 14.
3. Unknown author, *An Illustrated History of San Joaquin County, California* (Chicago: The Lewis Publishing Company, 1890), 52.
4. Ibid.
5. Unknown author, *An Illustrated History of San Joaquin County, California* (Chicago: The Lewis Publishing Company, 1890), 52.
6. R. Cherny, M.A. Irwin, and A.M. Wilson, *California Women and Politics: From the Gold Rush to the Great Depression* (Nebraska: University of Nebraska Press, 2011), 29; See also G.H. Tinkham, *The Half Century of California Odd Fellowship* (Stockton, CA: Record Publishing Co., 1906), 15.
7. Ibid.
8. Ibid.
9. Peter Sellars, *The History of the Independent Order of Odd Fellows in the City of San Francisco* (CA: Sellars, 2007), 14.
10. G. Blainey, *Odd Fellows: A History of IOOF Australia* (Australia: Allen & Unwin, 1991), 4.
11. Ibid, 11-12.
12. H.L. Stillson, *The Official History of Odd Fellowship: The Three Link Fraternity* (MA: The Fraternity Publishing Company, 1900), 389; See also G..H. Tinkham, *The Half Century of California Odd Fellowship*, 10-12.
13. G.H. Tinkham, *The Half Century of California Odd Fellowship*, 21-24.
14. H.L. Stillson, *The Official History of Odd Fellowship: The Three Link Fraternity*, 471.
15. G. Blainey, *Odd Fellows: A History of IOOF Australia*, 20-21.
16. G.H. Tinkham, *The Half Century of California Odd Fellowship*, 146.
17. Sellars, *The History of the Independent Order of Odd Fellows in the City of San Francisco*; See also F. Christy and D. Smith, *Six Links of Fellowship: Sovereign Grand Lodge Sessions in California* (California: Linden Publications, 1995).

The California Seal
1. G.H. Tinkham, *The Half Century of California Odd Fellowship*, 13.
2. R. Sullivan, *Royal Arch of Enoch: The Impact of Masonic Rituals, Philosophy and Symbolism* (Rocket Science Productions, 2011), 431-432.
3. Ibid.

Chapter 11 - American Civil War
1. Bruce Catton, *The Civil War* (Boston: Houghton Mifflin Company, 2004), 10.
2. Ibid.
3. Ibid.
4. Ibid.
5. Drew Gilpin Faust, *This Republic of Suffering: Death and the American Civil War* (New York: Alfred A. Knope, 2008), 3.
6. Sovereign Grand Lodge of the IOOF, *Journal of Proceedings of the Right Worthy Grand Lodge of the United*

States, and the Sovereign Grand Lodge of the Independent Order of Odd Fellows, from its Formation in February, 1858-1862 (Volume IV)* (Baltimore: The Sovereign Grand Lodge of the I.O.O.F., 1884), 331..

7. McBride, *The Golden Age of Fraternalism: 1870-1910*, Heredom, Volume 12, 2005, 4.

8. Sovereign Grand Lodge of the IOOF, *Journal of Proceedings of the Right Worthy Grand Lodge of the United States, and the Sovereign Grand Lodge of the Independent Order of Odd Fellows, from its Formation in February, 1863-1867 (Volume V)* (Baltimore: The Sovereign Grand Lodge of the I.O.O.F., 1876), 3637-3638. "I have received a communication from brother John C. Smith, P.G. Patriarch of the Order, and Colonel of the 96th Illinois Volunteers, dated in line of battle Atlanta Mountains, Georgia, May 25, 1864, informing me of the destruction of many of the Lodge rooms in that jurisdiction by the occupation of the belligerent armies, and consequent scattering of the furniture and books. He was fortunate enough to secure some of the charge books, which he conveyed to me to the notice of the Grand Lodge.

9. Ross, *Odd Fellowship: Its History and Manual*, 158.

10. Stillson, *The Official History of Odd Fellowship: The Three Link Fraternity*, 128-129.

11. Ibid.

12. Ibid.

13. Sovereign Grand Lodge of the IOOF, *Journal of Proceedings of the Right Worthy Grand Lodge of the United States, and the Sovereign Grand Lodge of the Independent Order of Odd Fellows, from its Formation in February, 1858-1862 (Volume IV)*, 3410-3412.

14. Ibid, 3411.

15. Stillson, *The Official History of Odd Fellowship: The Three Link Fraternity*, 131.

16. Sovereign Grand Lodge of the IOOF, *Journal of Proceedings of the Right Worthy Grand Lodge of the United States, and the Sovereign Grand Lodge of the Independent Order of Odd Fellows, from its Formation in February, 1858-1862 (Volume IV)*, 3411.

17. Ibid.

18. Sovereign Grand Lodge of the IOOF, *Journal of Proceedings of the Right Worthy Grand Lodge of the United States, and the Sovereign Grand Lodge of the Independent Order of Odd Fellows, from its Formation in February, 1863-1867 (Volume V)*, 3736.

19. Ibid.

20. Ibid.

21. Sovereign Grand Lodge of the IOOF, *Journal of Proceedings of the Right Worthy Grand Lodge of the United States, and the Sovereign Grand Lodge of the Independent Order of Odd Fellows, from its Formation in February, 1863-1867 (Volume V)*, 3880.

22. Stillson, *The Official History of Odd Fellowship: The Three Link Fraternity*, 134-135.

23. *The Odd Fellow's Companion*, Oct.1865, 115.

24. Ibid.

25. Ibid.

26. Stillson, *The Official History of Odd Fellowship: The Three Link Fraternity*, 200.

27. William Barnes in J. Edward Stallings, *Searching for Treasures* (North Carolina: Sovereign Grand Lodge, IOOF, n.d.), 33.

28. Ibid.

29. Ibid.

30. Sovereign Grand Lodge of the IOOF, *Journal of Proceedings of the Right Worthy Grand Lodge of the United States, and the Sovereign Grand Lodge of the Independent Order of Odd Fellows, from its Formation in February, 1863-1867 (Volume V)*, 3734-3740.

31. Sovereign Grand Lodge of the IOOF, *Journal of Proceedings of the Right Worthy Grand Lodge of the United States, and the Sovereign Grand Lodge of the Independent Order of Odd Fellows, from its Formation in February, 1858-1862 (Volume IV)*, 3763.

32. William Barnes in J. Edward Stallings, *Searching for Treasures* (North Carolina: Sovereign Grand Lodge, IOOF., n.d.), 33.

33. Ibid.

34. Ibid.

35. Ibid.

36. Ibid.

37. Ibid.

38. Ibid.

39. *The American Odd Fellow*, October 1865, Vol.4, No.10, 337-345

40. Ibid.

41. Ibid.

42. Ibid.

43. Ibid.

44. Ibid.

45. Ibid.

46. Ibid.

47. Ibid.

48. Ibid.

Andersonville Prison Camp

1. Mike Wright, *What they didn't teach you about the civil war* (New York: The Random House Publishing Group, 1996), 154.

2. Members of the Odd Fellows and masonic fraternities receive special aid from their respective brothers from inside and outside of prison" in Robert Scott Davis, *Andersonville Civil War Prison. South Carolina* (South Carolina: The History Press, 2010), 34.

3. Ralph Bates, *Billy and Dick from Andersonville Prison to the White House* (California: Sentinel Publishing, 1910), 33.
4. Mike Wright, *What they didn't teach you about the civil war* (New York: The Random House Publishing Group, 1996), 154-155.
5. Lessel Long, *Twelve Months in Andersonville* (Indiana: Thad and Mark Butler Publications, 1886), 50-53

The Essence of Fraternity
1. William Barnes in J. Edward Stallings, *Searching for Treasures* (North Carolina: Sovereign Grand Lodge, IOOF, n.d.), 34.

Chapter 12 - Golden Age of Fraternalism
1. Arthur Schlesinger, *Biography of a Nation of Joiners, American Historica Review,* 50 (October 1994), 1-25.
2. Stinchcombe in James, *Social Structure and Organizations, Handbook of Organizations* (March Ed.), 142-143.
3. David Beito, *From Mutual Aid to the Welfare State: Fraternal Societies and Social Services, 1890-1967* (Chapel Hill: University of North Carolina Press, 2000), 17.
4. Ibid.
5. Mark Carnes, *Secret Ritual and Manhood in Victorian America* (New Haven: Yale University, 1989), 85.
6. W.S. Harwood, *Secret Societies in America, North American Review,* 164, (May 1897), 617-624.
7. Ibid.
8. Ibid.
9. Ibid.
10. Noel Gist, *Structure and Process in Secret Societies, Social Forces* 16(3), March 1938, 349-357.
11. Ibid.
12. W.S. Harwood,, *Secret Societies in America, North American Review,* 164, (May 1897), 617-624.
13. Ibid.
14. Stillson, *Official History of Odd Fellowship: The Three Link Fraternity,* 525
15. Stillson, *Official History of Odd Fellowship: The Three Link Fraternity,* 482.
16. Annual Reports of the Grand Lodges to the Sovereign Grand Lodge ending December 31 from 1900 to 1910.
17. Sovereign Grand Lodge of the IOOF, *Journal of Proceedings of the Right Worthy Grand Lodge of the United States, and the Sovereign Grand Lodge of the Independent Order of Odd Fellows, 1911-1912(Volume XXV)* (Baltimore: The Sovereign Grand Lodge of the I.O.O.F., 1913), 184-185.
18. In 1921, Manchester Unity Independent Order of Odd Fellows report around 928,003 members and the Grand United Order of Odd Fellows estimated more than 300,000 members.
19. Sovereign Grand Lodge of the IOOF, *Journal of Proceedings of the Right Worthy Grand Lodge of the United States, and the Sovereign Grand Lodge of the Independent Order of Odd Fellows, 1921-1922 (Volume XXX)* (Baltimore: The Sovereign Grand Lodge of the I.O.O.F., 1923), 418-424.
20. Sovereign Grand Lodge of the IOOF, *Journal of Proceedings of the Right Worthy Grand Lodge of the United States, and the Sovereign Grand Lodge of the Independent Order of Odd Fellows, 1929-1930 (Volume XXXIV)* (Baltimore: The Sovereign Grand Lodge of the I.O.O.F., 1931), 55.
21. Ibid, 60.
22. Sovereign Grand Lodge of the IOOF, *Journal of Proceedings of the Right Worthy Grand Lodge of the United States, and the Sovereign Grand Lodge of the Independent Order of Odd Fellows, 1893-1894 (Volume XVI),* 13857
23. David Beito, *From Mutual Aid to the Welfare State: Fraternal Societies and Social Services, 1890-1967* (Chapel Hill: University of North Carolina Press, 2000), 9-12.
24. Ibid.
25. Ibid.
26. Ibid.
27. Ibid.
28. Annual Reports of the Grand Lodges to the Sovereign Grand Lodge ending December 31 from 1900 to 1910.
29. Annual Reports of the Grand Lodges to the Sovereign Grand Lodge ending December 31 from 1900 to 1910.
30. Sovereign Grand Lodge of the IOOF, *Journal of Proceedings of the Right Worthy Grand Lodge of the United States, and the Sovereign Grand Lodge of the Independent Order of Odd Fellows, 1911-1912(Volume XXV)* (Baltimore: The Sovereign Grand Lodge of the I.O.O.F., 1913), 206.
31. David Beito, *From Mutual Aid to the Welfare State: Fraternal Societies and Social Services, 1890-1967* (Chapel Hill: University of North Carolina Press, 2000).
32. Wolfe, *Album of Odd Fellows Home* (12th Rev. Ed.), 12
33. Sovereign Grand Lodge of the IOOF, *Journal of Proceedings of the Right Worthy Grand Lodge of the United States, and the Sovereign Grand Lodge of the Independent Order of Odd Fellows, 1931-1932 (Volume XXXV)* (Baltimore: The Sovereign Grand Lodge of the I.O.O.F., 1933), 723.

Chapter 13 - World War I
1. Sovereign Grand Lodge of the IOOF, *Journal of Proceedings of the Right Worthy Grand Lodge of the United States, and the Sovereign Grand Lodge of the Independent Order of Odd Fellows, 1915-1916 (Volume XXVII)* (Baltimore: The Sovereign Grand Lodge of the I.O.O.F.,

1917), 366.
2. Sovereign Grand Lodge of the IOOF, *Journal of Proceedings of the Right Worthy Grand Lodge of the United States, and the Sovereign Grand Lodge of the Independent Order of Odd Fellows, 1915-1916 (Volume XXVII)*, 95.
3. Ibid.
4. Ibid.
5. Ibid.
6. Sovereign Grand Lodge of the IOOF, *Journal of Proceedings of the Right Worthy Grand Lodge of the United States, and the Sovereign Grand Lodge of the Independent Order of Odd Fellows, 1915-1916 (Volume XXVII)*. 49-350.
7. Sovereign Grand Lodge of the IOOF, *Journal of Proceedings of the Right Worthy Grand Lodge of the United States, and the Sovereign Grand Lodge of the Independent Order of Odd Fellows, 1917-1918 (Volume XXVIII)*, 67.
8. Ibid, 359.
9. Ibid, 303.
10. Sovereign Grand Lodge of the IOOF, *Journal of Proceedings of the Right Worthy Grand Lodge of the United States, and the Sovereign Grand Lodge of the Independent Order of Odd Fellows, 1915-1916 (Volume XXVII)*, 113.
11. Ibid, 376.
12. Sovereign Grand Lodge of the IOOF, *Journal of Proceedings of the Right Worthy Grand Lodge of the United States, and the Sovereign Grand Lodge of the Independent Order of Odd Fellows, 1913-1914 (Volume XXVI)*, 515-516.
13. Sovereign Grand Lodge of the IOOF, *Journal of Proceedings of the Right Worthy Grand Lodge of the United States, and the Sovereign Grand Lodge of the Independent Order of Odd Fellows, 1915-1916 (Volume XXVII)*, 89.
14. Ibid, 91.
15. Ibid, 104.
16. Ibid, 104.
17. Ibid, 109.
18. Sovereign Grand Lodge of the IOOF, *Journal of Proceedings of the Right Worthy Grand Lodge of the United States, and the Sovereign Grand Lodge of the Independent Order of Odd Fellows, 1919-1920 (Volume XXVIX)*, 56-71.
19. Ibid.
20. Ibid, 69.
21. Ibid.
22. Ibid, 17.
23. Sovereign Grand Lodge of the IOOF, *Journal of Proceedings of the Right Worthy Grand Lodge of the United States, and the Sovereign Grand Lodge of the Independent Order of Odd Fellows, 1915-1916 (Volume XXVII)*, 65.
24. Ibid.
25. Sovereign Grand Lodge of the IOOF, *Journal of Proceedings of the Right Worthy Grand Lodge of the United States, and the Sovereign Grand Lodge of the Independent Order of Odd Fellows, 1923-1924 (Volume XXXI)*, 30.
26. Sovereign Grand Lodge of the IOOF, *Journal of Proceedings of the Right Worthy Grand Lodge of the United States, and the Sovereign Grand Lodge of the Independent Order of Odd Fellows, 1917-1918 (Volume XXVIII)*, 168.
27. Ibid, 252.
28. Ibid, 252.
29. Sovereign Grand Lodge of the IOOF, *Journal of Proceedings of the Right Worthy Grand Lodge of the United States, and the Sovereign Grand Lodge of the Independent Order of Odd Fellows, 1917-1918 (Volume XXVIII)*, 517.
30. Ibid, 252.
31. Ibid.
32. Ibid, 308.
33. Sovereign Grand Lodge of the IOOF, *Journal of Proceedings of the Right Worthy Grand Lodge of the United States, and the Sovereign Grand Lodge of the Independent Order of Odd Fellows, 1919-1920 (Volume XXVIX)*, 21.
34. Sovereign Grand Lodge of the IOOF, *Journal of Proceedings of the Right Worthy Grand Lodge of the United States, and the Sovereign Grand Lodge of the Independent Order of Odd Fellows, 1917-1918 (Volume XXVIII)*, 284.
35. Ibid, 168.
36. Sovereign Grand Lodge of the IOOF, *Journal of Proceedings of the Right Worthy Grand Lodge of the United States, and the Sovereign Grand Lodge of the Independent Order of Odd Fellows, 1919-1920 (Volume XXVIX)*, 73.
37. Sovereign Grand Lodge of the IOOF, *Journal of Proceedings of the Right Worthy Grand Lodge of the United States, and the Sovereign Grand Lodge of the Independent Order of Odd Fellows, 1917-1918 (Volume XXVIII)*, 302.
38. Ibid, 322-323.
39. Sovereign Grand Lodge of the IOOF, *Journal of Proceedings of the Right Worthy Grand Lodge of the United States, and the Sovereign Grand Lodge of the Independent Order of Odd Fellows, 1919-1920 (Volume XXVIX)*, 334-336.
40. Ibid.
41. Sovereign Grand Lodge of the IOOF, *Journal of Proceedings of the Right Worthy Grand Lodge of the United States, and the Sovereign Grand Lodge of the Independent Order of Odd Fellows, 1919-1920 (Volume XXVIX)*, 334-336.
42. Annual Reports to the Sovereign Grand Lodge, I.O.O.F., from 1914-1919.
43. Sovereign Grand Lodge of the IOOF, *Journal of Proceedings of the Right Worthy Grand Lodge of the United States, and the Sovereign Grand Lodge of the Independent Order of Odd Fellows,1917-1918 (Volume XXVIII)*, 383.
44. Ibid, 366.
45. Ibid, 64.
46. Ibid, 66.

47. Ibid, 369.
48. Ibid, 376.
49. Ibid, 377.
50. Ibid, 365.
51. Ibid, 64.
52. Annual Report of Rebekah Lodges to the Sovereign Grand Lodge, I.O.O.F. year ending December 31, 1919.
53. Annual Reports to the Sovereign Grand Lodge, I.O.O.F., from 1914-1919.
54. Sovereign Grand Lodge of the IOOF, *Journal of Proceedings of the Right Worthy Grand Lodge of the United States, and the Sovereign Grand Lodge of the Independent Order of Odd Fellows, 1919-1920 (Volume XXVIX)*, 424.
55. Ibid, 425
56. Ibid, 438.
57. Ibid, 438.
58. Ibid, 450-451.
59. Ibid, 450-451.
60. Ibid, 450-451.
61. Ibid, 428.
62. Sovereign Grand Lodge of the IOOF, *Journal of Proceedings of the Right Worthy Grand Lodge of the United States, and the Sovereign Grand Lodge of the Independent Order of Odd Fellows, 1921-1922 (Volume XXX)*, 13.
63. Daniel Weinbren, *The Oddfellows 1810-2010: 200 Years of making friends and helping people* (United Kingdom: Carnegie Publishing, 2010), 314.
64. Nina Mjagkij, *Organizing Black America: An Encyclopedia of African American Associations* (New York: Garland Publishing, 2001), 219.
65. Sovereign Grand Lodge of the IOOF, *Journal of Proceedings of the Right Worthy Grand Lodge of the United States, and the Sovereign Grand Lodge of the Independent Order of Odd Fellows, 1921-1922 (Volume XXX)*, 18.
66. Ibid.
67. Ibid, 77.
68. Ibid.
69. Ibid, 352.
70. Ibid.
71. Ibid, 77.
72. Ibid.
73. Sovereign Grand Lodge of the IOOF, *Journal of Proceedings of the Right Worthy Grand Lodge of the United States, and the Sovereign Grand Lodge of the Independent Order of Odd Fellows, 1921-1922 (Volume XXX)*,150-151.
74. Sovereign Grand Lodge of the IOOF, *Journal of Proceedings of the Right Worthy Grand Lodge of the United States, and the Sovereign Grand Lodge of the Independent Order of Odd Fellows, 1929-1930 (Volume XXXIV)*, 467.

The Great Parade
1. Sovereign Grand Lodge of the IOOF, *Journal of Proceedings of the Right Worthy Grand Lodge of the United States, and the Sovereign Grand Lodge of the Independent Order of Odd Fellows, 1919-1920 (Volume XXVIX)*, 660.

Illinois Degree Day
1. Sovereign Grand Lodge of the IOOF, *Journal of Proceedings of the Right Worthy Grand Lodge of the United States, and the Sovereign Grand Lodge of the Independent Order of Odd Fellows, 1919-1920 (Volume XXVIX)*, 428.
2. Ibid.
3. Ibid.

Chapter 14 - The Great Depression
1. Sovereign Grand Lodge of the IOOF, *Journal of Proceedings of the Right Worthy Grand Lodge of the United States, and the Sovereign Grand Lodge of the Independent Order of Odd Fellows, 1933-1934 (Volume XXXVI)*, 724.
2. Ibid.
3. Ibid, 727.
4. Robert Stewart, *The Illustrated Encyclopedia of Historical Facts from the Dawn of Christian Era to the Present Day* (United States: Barnes and Noble, 2002), 228.
5. Sovereign Grand Lodge of the IOOF, *Journal of Proceedings of the Right Worthy Grand Lodge of the United States, and the Sovereign Grand Lodge of the Independent Order of Odd Fellows, 1933-1934 (Volume XXXVI)*, 47.
6. Ibid.
7. Sovereign Grand Lodge of the IOOF, *Journal of Proceedings of the Right Worthy Grand Lodge of the United States, and the Sovereign Grand Lodge of the Independent Order of Odd Fellows, 1931-1932 (Volume XXXV)*, 397.
8. Ibid, 112.
9. Sovereign Grand Lodge of the IOOF, *Journal of Proceedings of the Right Worthy Grand Lodge of the United States, and the Sovereign Grand Lodge of the Independent Order of Odd Fellows,1929-1930 (Volume XXXIV)*, 90.
10. Ibid, 76.
11. Ibid, 79.
12. Ibid, 42.
13. Ibid.
14. Sovereign Grand Lodge of the IOOF, *Journal of Proceedings of the Right Worthy Grand Lodge of the United States, and the Sovereign Grand Lodge of the Independent Order of Odd Fellows, 1931-1932 (Volume XXXV)*, 397.
15. Ibid.
16. Ibid, 399-400.
17. Ibid, 440.
18. Ibid, 440.
19. Ibid.
20. Sovereign Grand Lodge of the IOOF, *Journal of Proceedings of the Right Worthy Grand Lodge of the United*

States, and the Sovereign Grand Lodge of the Independent Order of Odd Fellows, 1937-1938 (Volume XXXVIII), 45.
21. Sovereign Grand Lodge of the IOOF, *Journal of Proceedings of the Right Worthy Grand Lodge of the United States, and the Sovereign Grand Lodge of the Independent Order of Odd Fellows,* 1929-1930 (Volume XXXIV), 103-107.
22. Sovereign Grand Lodge of the IOOF, *Journal of Proceedings of the Right Worthy Grand Lodge of the United States, and the Sovereign Grand Lodge of the Independent Order of Odd Fellows,* 1931-1932 (Volume XXXV), 460.
23. Sovereign Grand Lodge of the IOOF, *Journal of Proceedings of the Right Worthy Grand Lodge of the United States, and the Sovereign Grand Lodge of the Independent Order of Odd Fellows,* 1933-1934 (Volume XXXVI), 17.
24. Sovereign Grand Lodge of the IOOF, *Journal of Proceedings of the Right Worthy Grand Lodge of the United States, and the Sovereign Grand Lodge of the Independent Order of Odd Fellows,* 1931-1932 (Volume XXXV), 746.
25. Sovereign Grand Lodge of the IOOF, *Journal of Proceedings of the Right Worthy Grand Lodge of the United States, and the Sovereign Grand Lodge of the Independent Order of Odd Fellows,* 1933-1934 (Volume XXXVI), 16-17.
26. Sovereign Grand Lodge of the IOOF, *Journal of Proceedings of the Right Worthy Grand Lodge of the United States, and the Sovereign Grand Lodge of the Independent Order of Odd Fellows,* 1923-1924 (Volume XXXI), 727.
27. Sovereign Grand Lodge of the IOOF, *Journal of Proceedings of the Right Worthy Grand Lodge of the United States, and the Sovereign Grand Lodge of the Independent Order of Odd Fellows,* 1933-1934 (Volume XXXVI), 746.
28. Ibid.
29. Ibid.
30. Ibid.
31. Ibid, 747.
32. Sovereign Grand Lodge of the IOOF, *Journal of Proceedings of the Right Worthy Grand Lodge of the United States, and the Sovereign Grand Lodge of the Independent Order of Odd Fellows,* 1929-1930 (Volume XXXIV). 85.
33. Jeffrey Charles, *Service Clubs in American Society* (Chicago: University of Illinois Press, 1993).
34. Sovereign Grand Lodge of the IOOF, *Journal of Proceedings of the Right Worthy Grand Lodge of the United States, and the Sovereign Grand Lodge of the Independent Order of Odd Fellows,* 1949-1950 (Volume XLII), 479.
35. Sovereign Grand Lodge of the IOOF, *Journal of Proceedings of the Right Worthy Grand Lodge of the United States, and the Sovereign Grand Lodge of the Independent Order of Odd Fellows,* 1951-1952 (Volume XLIII), 455.
36. Sovereign Grand Lodge of the IOOF, *Journal of Proceedings of the Right Worthy Grand Lodge of the United States, and the Sovereign Grand Lodge of the Independent Order of Odd Fellows,* 1933-1934 (Volume XXXVI), 747.
37. Sovereign Grand Lodge of the IOOF, *Journal of Proceedings of the Right Worthy Grand Lodge of the United States, and the Sovereign Grand Lodge of the Independent Order of Odd Fellows,* 1917-1918 (Volume XXVIII), 252.
38. Jason Kaufman, *For the Common Good? American Civic Life and the Golden Age of Fraternity* (New York: Oxford University Press, 2002), 29.
39. Robert Stewart, *The Illustrated Encyclopedia of Historical Facts from the Dawn of Christian Era to the Present Day* (United States: Barnes and Noble, 2002), 231.
40. Amy Gutmann, *Democracy and the Welfare State* (New Jersey: Princeton University Press, 1988), 3.
41. Sovereign Grand Lodge of the IOOF, *Journal of Proceedings of the Right Worthy Grand Lodge of the United States, and the Sovereign Grand Lodge of the Independent Order of Odd Fellows,* 1917-1918 (Volume XXVIII, 70.
42. Lynn Dumenil, *The Oxford Encyclopedia of American Social History* (United States: Oxford University Press, 2012), 415.
43. Sovereign Grand Lodge of the IOOF, *Journal of Proceedings of the Right Worthy Grand Lodge of the United States, and the Sovereign Grand Lodge of the Independent Order of Odd Fellows,* 1931-1932 (Volume XXXV), 727.
44. Sovereign Grand Lodge of the IOOF, *Journal of Proceedings of the Right Worthy Grand Lodge of the United States, and the Sovereign Grand Lodge of the Independent Order of Odd Fellows,* 1933-1934 (Volume XXXVI), 48.
45. Sovereign Grand Lodge of the IOOF, *Journal of Proceedings of the Right Worthy Grand Lodge of the United States, and the Sovereign Grand Lodge of the Independent Order of Odd Fellows,* 1931-1932 (Volume XXXV), 727. 479.
46. Sovereign Grand Lodge of the IOOF, *Journal of Proceedings of the Right Worthy Grand Lodge of the United States, and the Sovereign Grand Lodge of the Independent Order of Odd Fellows,* 1951-1952 (Volume XLIII), 57.
47. Ibid.
48. Sovereign Grand Lodge of the IOOF, *Journal of Proceedings of the Right Worthy Grand Lodge of the United States, and the Sovereign Grand Lodge of the Independent Order of Odd Fellows,* 1931-1932 (Volume XXXV), 474.
49. Ibid, 475.
50. Ibid, 527.
51. Ibid, 527.

Chapter 15 - World War II
1. Robert Stewart, *The Illustrated Encyclopedia of Historical Facts from the Dawn of Christian Era to the Present Day* (United States: Barnes and Noble, 2002), 239.
2. Ibid, 242.

3. Sovereign Grand Lodge of the IOOF, *Journal of Proceedings of the Right Worthy Grand Lodge of the United States, and the Sovereign Grand Lodge of the Independent Order of Odd Fellows, 1941-1944 (Volume XL)*, 967.
4. Ibid.
5. Ibid, 16.
6. Ibid.
7. Sovereign Grand Lodge of the IOOF, *Journal of Proceedings of the Right Worthy Grand Lodge of the United States, and the Sovereign Grand Lodge of the Independent Order of Odd Fellows, 1949-1950 (Volume XLII)*, 28.
8. Sovereign Grand Lodge of the IOOF, *Journal of Proceedings of the Right Worthy Grand Lodge of the United States, and the Sovereign Grand Lodge of the Independent Order of Odd Fellows, 1941-1944 (Volume XL)*, 17.
9. Ibid.
10. Ibid, 439.
11. Sovereign Grand Lodge of the IOOF, *Journal of Proceedings of the Right Worthy Grand Lodge of the United States, and the Sovereign Grand Lodge of the Independent Order of Odd Fellows, 1945-1948 (Volume XLI)*, 151.
12. Ibid, 48.
13. Ibid, 434-435.
14. Sovereign Grand Lodge of the IOOF, *Journal of Proceedings of the Right Worthy Grand Lodge of the United States, and the Sovereign Grand Lodge of the Independent Order of Odd Fellows, 1941-1944 (Volume XL)*, 410-411.
15. Ibid, 810.
16. Ibid, 54.
17. Ibid, 480.
18. Ibid, 482-483.
19. Ibid, 480.
20. Ibid, 1205.
21. Ibid, 440.
22. Ibid, 973.
23. Ibid, 973.
24. Ibid, 974.
25. Ibid, 973-975.
26. Sovereign Grand Lodge of the IOOF, *Journal of Proceedings of the Right Worthy Grand Lodge of the United States, and the Sovereign Grand Lodge of the Independent Order of Odd Fellows, 1941-1944 (Volume XL)*, 1291. See also Address of the Honorable Dana Porter, Minister of Planning and Development for the Province of Ontario, to the I.O.O.F. (1944).
27. Sovereign Grand Lodge of the IOOF, *Journal of Proceedings of the Right Worthy Grand Lodge of the United States, and the Sovereign Grand Lodge of the Independent Order of Odd Fellows, 1941-1944 (Volume XL)*, 684.
28. Ibid, 1215.
29. Ibid.
30. Ibid, 766.
31. Sovereign Grand Lodge of the IOOF, *Journal of Proceedings of the Right Worthy Grand Lodge of the United States, and the Sovereign Grand Lodge of the Independent Order of Odd Fellows, 1945-1948 (Volume XLI)*, 44-45.
32. Sovereign Grand Lodge of the IOOF, *Journal of Proceedings of the Right Worthy Grand Lodge of the United States, and the Sovereign Grand Lodge of the Independent Order of Odd Fellows, 1949-1950 (Volume XLII)*, 632-633.
33. Ibid.
34. Sovereign Grand Lodge of the IOOF, *Journal of Proceedings of the Right Worthy Grand Lodge of the United States, and the Sovereign Grand Lodge of the Independent Order of Odd Fellows, 1941-1944 (Volume XL)*, 743.
35. Ibid.
36. Ibid, 764.
37. Sovereign Grand Lodge of the IOOF, *Journal of Proceedings of the Right Worthy Grand Lodge of the United States, and the Sovereign Grand Lodge of the Independent Order of Odd Fellows, 1960 (Volume XLVIII)*, 356.
38. Sovereign Grand Lodge of the IOOF, *Journal of Proceedings of the Right Worthy Grand Lodge of the United States, and the Sovereign Grand Lodge of the Independent Order of Odd Fellows, 1945-1948 (Volume XLI)*, 917-918.
39. Ibid, 918.
40. Ibid, 1108.
41. Ibid, 1258.
42. Ibid, 927.
43. Sovereign Grand Lodge of the IOOF, *Journal of Proceedings of the Right Worthy Grand Lodge of the United States, and the Sovereign Grand Lodge of the Independent Order of Odd Fellows, 1945-1948 (Volume XLI)*, 927.
44. Ibid, 932.
45. Ibid.
46. Sovereign Grand Lodge of the IOOF, *Journal of Proceedings of the Right Worthy Grand Lodge of the United States, and the Sovereign Grand Lodge of the Independent Order of Odd Fellows, 1941-1944 (Volume XL)*, 466.
47. Ibid, 466.
48. Sovereign Grand Lodge of the IOOF, *Journal of Proceedings of the Right Worthy Grand Lodge of the United States, and the Sovereign Grand Lodge of the Independent Order of Odd Fellows, 1945-1948 (Volume XLI)*, 91.
49. Ibid.
50. Ibid.
51. Ibid, 391-399.
52. Ibid.
53. Sovereign Grand Lodge of the IOOF, *Journal of Proceedings of the Right Worthy Grand Lodge of the United States, and the Sovereign Grand Lodge of the Independent Order of Odd Fellows, 1949-1950 (Volume XLII)*, 364.
54. Sovereign Grand Lodge of the IOOF, *Journal of Proceedings of the Right Worthy Grand Lodge of the United*

States, and the Sovereign Grand Lodge of the Independent Order of Odd Fellows, 1941-1944 (Volume XL), 449.
55. Sovereign Grand Lodge of the IOOF, *Journal of Proceedings of the Right Worthy Grand Lodge of the United States, and the Sovereign Grand Lodge of the Independent Order of Odd Fellows, 1949-1950 (Volume XLII),* 824.
56. Ibid.
57. Sovereign Grand Lodge of the IOOF, *Journal of Proceedings of the Right Worthy Grand Lodge of the United States, and the Sovereign Grand Lodge of the Independent Order of Odd Fellows, 1964 (Volume LII),* 165).
58. *Ritual of a Junior Lodge under the Jurisdiction of the Sovereign Grand Lodge of the Independent Order of Odd Fellows* (United States: Sovereign Grand Lodge, I.O.O.F., 1930).
59. *Ritual of Theta Rho Girls Club under the Jurisdiction of the Sovereign Grand Lodge of the Independent Order of Odd Fellows* (United States: Sovereign Grand Lodge, I.O.O.F., 1975).
60. Sovereign Grand Lodge of the IOOF, *Journal of Proceedings of the Right Worthy Grand Lodge of the United States, and the Sovereign Grand Lodge of the Independent Order of Odd Fellows, 1949-1950 (Volume XLII),* 523.
61. Peter Sellars, *The History of the Independent Order of Odd Fellows in the City of San Francisco* (California: Privately printed, 2007), 131.
62. Sovereign Grand Lodge of the IOOF, *Journal of Proceedings of the Right Worthy Grand Lodge of the United States, and the Sovereign Grand Lodge of the Independent Order of Odd Fellows, 1945-1948 (Volume XLI),* 120.
63. Ibid.
64. Ibid, 120-121.
65. Ibid, 937.
66. Ibid, 194-219.
67. Sovereign Grand Lodge of the IOOF, *Journal of Proceedings of the Right Worthy Grand Lodge of the United States, and the Sovereign Grand Lodge of the Independent Order of Odd Fellows, 1949-1950 (Volume XLII),* 450.
68. Sovereign Grand Lodge of the IOOF, *Journal of Proceedings of the Right Worthy Grand Lodge of the United States, and the Sovereign Grand Lodge of the Independent Order of Odd Fellows, 1945-1948 (Volume XLI),* 593-625.
69. Sovereign Grand Lodge of the IOOF, *Journal of Proceedings of the Right Worthy Grand Lodge of the United States, and the Sovereign Grand Lodge of the Independent Order of Odd Fellows, 1951-1952 (Volume XLIII),* 71.
70. Sovereign Grand Lodge of the IOOF, *Journal of Proceedings of the Right Worthy Grand Lodge of the United States, and the Sovereign Grand Lodge of the Independent Order of Odd Fellows, 1949-1950 (Volume XLII),* 450.
71. Ibid, 200-205.
72. Ibid.
73. Sovereign Grand Lodge of the IOOF, *Journal of Proceedings of the Right Worthy Grand Lodge of the United States, and the Sovereign Grand Lodge of the Independent Order of Odd Fellows, 1951-1952 (Volume XLIII),* 793.
74. Speech by Grand Sire J. Paul Kuhn during the 1944 Sovereign Grand Lodge Sessions.
75. Ibid.
76. Sovereign Grand Lodge of the IOOF, *Journal of Proceedings of the Right Worthy Grand Lodge of the United States, and the Sovereign Grand Lodge of the Independent Order of Odd Fellows, 1949-1950 (Volume XLII),* 598.
77. Sovereign Grand Lodge of the IOOF, *Journal of Proceedings of the Right Worthy Grand Lodge of the United States, and the Sovereign Grand Lodge of the Independent Order of Odd Fellows, 1949-1950 (Volume XLII),* 711.
78. Ibid.
79. Ibid, 599.
80. Sovereign Grand Lodge of the IOOF, *Journal of Proceedings of the Right Worthy Grand Lodge of the United States, and the Sovereign Grand Lodge of the Independent Order of Odd Fellows, 1951-1952 (Volume XLIII),* 234.
81. Ibid.
82. Ibid, 235.
83. Sovereign Grand Lodge of the IOOF, *Journal of Proceedings of the Right Worthy Grand Lodge of the United States, and the Sovereign Grand Lodge of the Independent Order of Odd Fellows, 1949-1950 (Volume XLII),*478; Sovereign Grand Lodge of the IOOF, *Journal of Proceedings of the Right Worthy Grand Lodge of the United States, and the Sovereign Grand Lodge of the Independent Order of Odd Fellows, 1951-1952 (Volume XLIII),* 225-227;
84. Sovereign Grand Lodge of the IOOF, *Journal of Proceedings of the Right Worthy Grand Lodge of the United States, and the Sovereign Grand Lodge of the Independent Order of Odd Fellows, 1949-1950 (Volume XLII),* 940.
85. Sovereign Grand Lodge of the IOOF, *Journal of Proceedings of the Right Worthy Grand Lodge of the United States, and the Sovereign Grand Lodge of the Independent Order of Odd Fellows, 1949-1950 (Volume XLII),* 478. It was mentioned that Prince Bertil, Duke of Halland, was initiated as a member of the Odd Fellows Order in Sweden on May 22, 1950.
86. Sovereign Grand Lodge of the IOOF, *Journal of Proceedings of the Right Worthy Grand Lodge of the United States, and the Sovereign Grand Lodge of the Independent Order of Odd Fellows, 1949-1950 (Volume XLII),* 1259.
87. Sovereign Grand Lodge of the IOOF, *Journal of Proceedings of the Right Worthy Grand Lodge of the United States, and the Sovereign Grand Lodge of the Independent Order of Odd Fellows, 1931-1932 (Volume XXXV),* 38.
88. Ibid.
89. Ibid.

90. Ibid.

Duke of Halland

1. Sovereign Grand Lodge of the Independent Order of Odd Fellows, *Journal of Proceedings of the Right Worthy Grand Lodge of the United States, and the Sovereign Grand Lodge of the Independent Order of Odd Fellows, 1949-1950 (Volume XLII)* (Baltimore: The Sovereign Grand Lodge of the I.O.O.F., 1951), 478.

Chapter 16 - Civil Rights and Racial Integration

1. Sovereign Grand Lodge of the Independent Order of Odd Fellows. *Journal of Proceedings of the Right Worthy Grand Lodge of the United States, and the Sovereign Grand Lodge of the Independent Order of Odd Fellows, from its Formation in February, 1876-1878 (Volume IX)*, 7179.
2. Russell Brooker, *The American Civil Rights Movement 1865-1950* (Maryland: Lexington Books, 2017), 98.
3. Ira Katznelson and Martin Shefter, *Shaped by War and Trade: International Influences on American Political Development* (New Jersey: Princeton University Press, 2002), 149.
4. Charles H. Brooks, *The Official History and Manual of the Grand United Order of Odd Fellows in America: A Chronological Treatise* (Pennsylvania: C.H. Brooks, 1902), 72.
5. Henry Louis Gates, Jr. & Evelyn Brooks Higginbotham, *African American Lives* (NY: Oxford University Press, 2004), 702-703.
6. Adrienne Shadd, *The Journey from Tollgate toe Parkway: African Canadians in Hamilton* (Toronto: National Heritage Books, 2010), 173.
7. Nancy Stearns Theiss, "One of the oldest African American organizations in Kentucky celebrates 145 years," *Courier Journal*, August 29, 2017, accessed October 4, 2017, https://www.courier-journal.com/story/news/local/oldham/2017/08/29/one-oldest-african-american-organizations-kentucky-celebrates-145-years/610308001/
8. John Stauffer, *The Works of James McCune Smith: Black Intellectual and Abolitionist* (New York: Oxford University Press, 2006), 159.
9. Ibid.
10. Morrill, Monica. "Frederick Douglass Today: 200 Years Later," *Selous Foundation for Public Policy Research*, February 27, 2018, accessed August 30, 2018, http://sfppr.org/2018/02/frederick-douglass-today-200-years-later/
11. Nicholas Buccula, *The Political Thought of Frederick Douglass: In Pursuit of American Liberty* (NY: New York University Press, 2012), 95.
12. Linda Duyer, "In 1880: Frederick Douglas speaks at Salisbury Courthouse," *Dorchester Banner*, February 25, 2015, Accessed August 30, 2018, https://www.dorchesterbanner.com/dorchester/1880-frederick-douglas-speaks-salisbury-courthouse/
13. Ibid.
14. Lester Salamon, *The State of Nonprofit America* (District of Columbia: Bookings Institution Press, 2002), 526.
15. Theda Skopol, Ariane Liazos and Marshal Ganz, *What a Mighty Power We Can be: African American Fraternal Groups and the struggle for Racial Equality* (New Jersey: Princeton University Press, 2006), 36 -37.
16. Leslie Alexander and Walter Rucker, *Encyclopedia of African American History* (California: ABC-CLIO, 2010), 155.
17. Nicholas Guyatt, *Bind Us Apart: How Enlightened Americans Invented Racial Segregation* (UK: Oxford University Press, 2016), 10.
18. Nicholas Guyatt, *Bind Us Apart: How Enlightened Americans Invented Racial Segregation* (UK: Oxford University Press, 2016), 4.
19. James W. Loewen, *Sundown Towns: A hidden Dimension of American Racism* (New York: The New Press, 2005).
20. William Richter, *Historical Dictionary of the Civil War and Reconstruction* (Toronto: The Scarecrow Press, 2012), 137.
21. Darren Ferry, *Uniting in Measures of Common Good: The Construction of Liberal Identities in Central Canada* (Quebec: McGill Queen's University Press, 2008), 160.
22. Sovereign Grand Lodge of the IOOF, *Journal of Proceedings of the Right Worthy Grand Lodge of the United States, and the Sovereign Grand Lodge of the Independent Order of Odd Fellows, from its Formation in February, 1874-1875 (Volume VIII)*, 6347.
23. Sovereign Grand Lodge of the IOOF, *Journal of Proceedings of the Right Worthy Grand Lodge of the United States, and the Sovereign Grand Lodge of the Independent Order of Odd Fellows, 1879-1881 (Volume X)*, 7918.
24. Sovereign Grand Lodge of the Independent Order of Odd Fellows, *Journal of Proceedings of the Right Worthy Grand Lodge of the United States, and the Sovereign Grand Lodge of the Independent Order of Odd Fellows, 1887-1888 (Volume XIII)* (Columbus, Ohio: The Sovereign Grand Lodge of the I.O.O.F., 1889), 11122.
25. Ann Curthoys and Marilyn Lake, *Connected Worlds: History in Transnational Perspective* (Canberra: Australian National University, 2005),
26. Sovereign Grand Lodge of the IOOF, *Journal of Proceedings of the Right Worthy Grand Lodge of the United States, and the Sovereign Grand Lodge of the Independent Order of Odd Fellows, 1919-1920 (Volume XXVIX)*, 398-399.
27. Ibid, 398-399

28. Ibid, 400.
29. Ibid, 398-399.
30. Sovereign Grand Lodge of the IOOF, *Journal of Proceedings of the One Hundred and Fortieth Annual Communication of the Sovereign Grand Lodge of the Independent Order of Odd Fellows, 1966 (Volume LIV)*, 476.
31. Ibid, 477.
32. Ibid, 478.
33. Ibid, 476.
34. Ibid, 250.
35. Sovereign Grand Lodge of the IOOF, *Journal of Proceedings of the One Hundred and Fortieth Annual Communication of the Sovereign Grand Lodge of the Independent Order of Odd Fellows, 1966 (Volume LIV)*, 450.
36. Ibid, 476.
37. Sovereign Grand Lodge of the IOOF, *Journal of Proceedings of the One Hundred and Thirty-Second Annual Communication of the Sovereign Grand Lodge of the Independent Order of Odd Fellows, 1968 (Volume LVI)*, 475.
38. Sovereign Grand Lodge of the IOOF, *Journal of Proceedings of the One Hundred and Thirty-Sixth Annual Communication of the Sovereign Grand Lodge of the Independent Order of Odd Fellows, 1962 (Volume XLVX)*, 202.
39. Sovereign Grand Lodge of the IOOF, *Journal of Proceedings of the One Hundred and Fortieth Annual Communication of the Sovereign Grand Lodge of the Independent Order of Odd Fellows, 1966 (Volume LIV)*, 246.
40. Sovereign Grand Lodge of the IOOF, *Journal of Proceedings of the One Hundred and Forty-First Annual Communication of the Sovereign Grand Lodge of the Independent Order of Odd Fellows, 1967 (Volume LV)*, 363.
41. Sovereign Grand Lodge of the IOOF, *Journal of Proceedings of the One Hundred and Thirty-Sixth Annual Communication of the Sovereign Grand Lodge of the Independent Order of Odd Fellows, 1962 (Volume XLVX)*, 59; Sovereign Grand Lodge of the IOOF, *Journal of Proceedings of the One Hundred and Thirty-Sixth Annual Communication of the Sovereign Grand Lodge of the Independent Order of Odd Fellows, 1962 (Volume XLVX)*, 345.
42. Sovereign Grand Lodge of the IOOF, *Journal of Proceedings of the One Hundred and Thirty-Seventh Annual Communication of the Sovereign Grand Lodge of the Independent Order of Odd Fellows, 1963 (Volume LI)*, 305.
43. Sovereign Grand Lodge of the IOOF, *Journal of Proceedings of the One Hundred and Thirty-Eight Annual Communication of the Sovereign Grand Lodge of the Independent Order of Odd Fellows, 1964 (Volume LII)*, 213.
44. Sovereign Grand Lodge of the IOOF, *Journal of Proceedings of the One Hundred and Fortieth Annual Communication of the Sovereign Grand Lodge of the Independent Order of Odd Fellows, 1966 (Volume LIV)*, 474.
45. Rachael Pacella, "*Towson business owner is Odd Fellows' first female African-American leader,*" The Baltimore Sun, June 1, 2016, accessed August 30, 2017, http://www.baltimoresun.com/news/maryland/baltimore-county/towson/ph-tt-darlene-parker-0525-20160526-story.html
46. Sovereign Grand Lodge of the IOOF, *Journal of Proceedings of the One Hundred and Sixty-Seventh Annual Communication of the Sovereign Grand Lodge of the Independent Order of Odd Fellows, 1993 (Volume LXXXI)*, 75.
47. Ibid.

Arnett and McKinley
1. Charles Carey, African-American Political Leaders, (New York: Facts On File, 2004), 6-7.
1. Odd Fellows Journal, Vol.3, January 11, 1900.
2. Ibid.
3. Ibid.

Chapter 17 - Decline of Fraternalism
1. Sovereign Grand Lodge of the IOOF, *Journal of Proceedings of the One Hundred and Sixty-Eight Annual Communication of the Sovereign Grand Lodge of the Independent Order of Odd Fellows, 1994 (Volume LXXXII)*, 593.
2. Dave Rosenberg, *The Future of Odd Fellowship: Evolution and Change* (2015), 107.
3. Sovereign Grand Lodge of the IOOF, *Journal of Proceedings of the One Hundred and Sixty-Eight Annual Communication of the Sovereign Grand Lodge of the Independent Order of Odd Fellows, 1994 (Volume LXXXII)*, 631.
4. Sovereign Grand Lodge of the IOOF, *Journal of Proceedings of the One Hundred and Sixty-Third Annual Communication of the Sovereign Grand Lodge of the Independent Order of Odd Fellows, 1989 (Volume LXXVII)*, 139.
5. Sovereign Grand Lodge of the IOOF, *Journal of Proceedings of the One Hundred and Sixty-Eight Annual Communication of the Sovereign Grand Lodge of the Independent Order of Odd Fellows, 1994 (Volume LXXXII)*, 599.
6. Sovereign Grand Lodge of the IOOF, *Journal of Proceedings of the One Hundred and Fifty-Seventh Annual Communication of the Sovereign Grand Lodge of the*

Independent Order of Odd Fellows, 1983 (Volume LXXI), 390.

7. Dave Rosenberg, *The Future of Odd Fellowship: Evolution and Change* (2015), 230.

8. Dave Rosenberg, *The Future of Odd Fellowship: Evolution and Change* (2015), 10.

9. Sovereign Grand Lodge of the IOOF, *Journal of Proceedings of the One Hundred and Sixty-Eight Annual Communication of the Sovereign Grand Lodge of the Independent Order of Odd Fellows, 1994 (Volume LXXXII)*, 593.

10. Sovereign Grand Lodge of the IOOF, *Journal of Proceedings of the One Hundred and Thirty-Sixth Annual Communication of the Sovereign Grand Lodge of the Independent Order of Odd Fellows, 1962 (Volume XLVX)*. 423.

11. Sovereign Grand Lodge of the IOOF, *Journal of Proceedings of the One Hundred and Thirty-Seventh Annual Communication of the Sovereign Grand Lodge of the Independent Order of Odd Fellows, 1963 (Volume LI)*, 487

12. Sovereign Grand Lodge of the IOOF, Journal of Proceedings of the One Hundred and Forty-First Annual Communication of the Sovereign Grand Lodge of the Independent Order of Odd Fellows, 1967 (Volume LV)., 431.

13. Sovereign Grand Lodge of the IOOF, *Journal of Proceedings of the One Hundred and Thirty-Seventh Annual Communication of the Sovereign Grand Lodge of the Independent Order of Odd Fellows, 1963 (Volume LI)*, 487.

14. Sovereign Grand Lodge of the IOOF, *Journal of Proceedings of the One Hundred and Thirty-Sixth Annual Communication of the Sovereign Grand Lodge of the Independent Order of Odd Fellows, 1962 (Volume XLVX)*. 52-53.

15. Sovereign Grand Lodge of the IOOF, *Journal of Proceedings of the One Hundred and Fortieth Annual Communication of the Sovereign Grand Lodge of the Independent Order of Odd Fellows, 1966 (Volume LIV)*, 51.

16. Sovereign Grand Lodge of the IOOF, *Journal of Proceedings of the One Hundred and Thirty-Sixth Annual Communication of the Sovereign Grand Lodge of the Independent Order of Odd Fellows, 1962 (Volume XLVX)*, 52-53.

17. Sovereign Grand Lodge of the IOOF, *Journal of Proceedings of the One Hundred and Thirty-Sixth Annual Communication of the Sovereign Grand Lodge of the Independent Order of Odd Fellows, 1962 (Volume XLVX)*, 52-53.

18. Sovereign Grand Lodge of the IOOF, *Journal of Proceedings of the One Hundred and Fifty-Seventh Annual Communication of the Sovereign Grand Lodge of the Independent Order of Odd Fellows, 1983 (Volume LXXI)*, 387.

19. Sovereign Grand Lodge of the IOOF, *Journal of Proceedings of the One Hundred and Sixty-Eight Annual Communication of the Sovereign Grand Lodge of the Independent Order of Odd Fellows, 1994 (Volume LXXXII)*, 49.

20. Sovereign Grand Lodge of the IOOF, *Journal of Proceedings of the One Hundred and Fortieth Annual Communication of the Sovereign Grand Lodge of the Independent Order of Odd Fellows, 1966 (Volume LIV)*, 52.

21. Sovereign Grand Lodge of the IOOF, *Journal of Proceedings of the One Hundred and Thirty-Sixth Annual Communication of the Sovereign Grand Lodge of the Independent Order of Odd Fellows, 1962 (Volume XLVX)*, 56-57.

22. Ibid, 52-53.

23. Sovereign Grand Lodge of the IOOF, *Journal of Proceedings of the One Hundred and Sixty-Eight Annual Communication of the Sovereign Grand Lodge of the Independent Order of Odd Fellows, 1994 (Volume LXXXII)*, 593.

24. Sovereign Grand Lodge of the IOOF, *Journal of Proceedings of the One Hundred and Fortieth Annual Communication of the Sovereign Grand Lodge of the Independent Order of Odd Fellows, 1966 (Volume LIV)*, 465.

25. Sovereign Grand Lodge of the IOOF, *Journal of Proceedings of the One Hundred and Sixty-Eight Annual Communication of the Sovereign Grand Lodge of the Independent Order of Odd Fellows, 1994 (Volume LXXXII)*, 593.

26. Ibid.

27. Ibid.

28. Sovereign Grand Lodge of the IOOF, *Journal of Proceedings of the One Hundred and Thirty-Second Annual Communication of the Sovereign Grand Lodge of the Independent Order of Odd Fellows, 1968 (Volume LVI)*, 85.

29. Sovereign Grand Lodge of the IOOF, *Journal of Proceedings of the One Hundred and Fifty-Sixth Annual Communication of the Sovereign Grand Lodge of the Independent Order of Odd Fellows, 1982 (Volume LXX)*, 389.

30. Sovereign Grand Lodge of the IOOF, *Journal of Proceedings of the One Hundred and Forty-Third Annual Communication of the Sovereign Grand Lodge of the Independent Order of Odd Fellows, 1969 (Volume LVII)*, 523.

31. Ibid.

32. Sovereign Grand Lodge of the IOOF, *Journal of Proceedings of the One Hundred and Sixty-Eight Annual Communication of the Sovereign Grand Lodge of the Independent Order of Odd Fellows, 1994 (Volume LXXXII)*, 593.

33. Sovereign Grand Lodge of the IOOF, *Journal of Proceedings of the One Hundred and Thirty-Second Annual Communication of the Sovereign Grand Lodge of the Independent Order of Odd Fellows, 1968 (Volume LVI)*, 57.

34. Sovereign Grand Lodge of the IOOF, Journal of Proceedings of the One Hundred and Forty-Third Annual Communication of the Sovereign Grand Lodge of the Independent Order of Odd Fellows, 1969 (Volume LVII), 523.

35. Ibid, 480.

36. Ibid

37. Sovereign Grand Lodge of the IOOF, *Journal of Proceedings of the One Hundred and Thirty-Second Annual Communication of the Sovereign Grand Lodge of the Independent Order of Odd Fellows, 1968 (Volume LVI)*, 83.

38. Dave Rosenberg, *The Future of Odd Fellowship: Evolution and Change* (2015), 107.

39. Patrick Healy, "*A Ritual Gone Fatally Wrong Puts Light on Masonic Secrecy*," New York Times, March 10, 2004, accessed August 30, 2017, https://www.nytimes.com/2004/03/10/nyregion/a-ritual-gone-fatally-wrong-puts-light-on-masonic-secrecy.html

40. Sovereign Grand Lodge of the IOOF, *Journal of Proceedings of the One Hundred and Sixty-Sixth Annual Communication of the Sovereign Grand Lodge of the Independent Order of Odd Fellows, 1992 (Volume LXXX)*, 259.

41. Sovereign Grand Lodge of the IOOF, *Journal of Proceedings of the One Hundred and Fifty-Fifth Annual Communication of the Sovereign Grand Lodge of the Independent Order of Odd Fellows, 1981 (Volume LXVIX)*, 164.

42. Sovereign Grand Lodge of the IOOF, *Journal of Proceedings of the One Hundred and Fifty-first Annual Communication of the Sovereign Grand Lodge of the Independent Order of Odd Fellows, 1977 (Volume LXV)*, 245.

43. Sovereign Grand Lodge of the IOOF, *Journal of Proceedings of the One Hundred and Sixty-Sixth Annual Communication of the Sovereign Grand Lodge of the Independent Order of Odd Fellows, 1992 (Volume LXXX)*, 259.

44. Sovereign Grand Lodge of the IOOF, *Journal of Proceedings of the One Hundred and Sixty-Fourth Annual Communication of the Sovereign Grand Lodge of the Independent Order of Odd Fellows, 1990 (Volume LXXVIII)*, 44.

45. Dave Rosenberg, *The Future of Odd Fellowship: Evolution and Change* (2015), 93.

46. Sovereign Grand Lodge of the IOOF, *Journal of Proceedings of the One Hundred and Forty-Eight Annual Communication of the Sovereign Grand Lodge of the Independent Order of Odd Fellows, 1974 (Volume LXII)*, 279-280.

47. Sovereign Grand Lodge of the IOOF, *Journal of Proceedings of the One Hundred and Sixty-Seventh Annual Communication of the Sovereign Grand Lodge of the Independent Order of Odd Fellows, 1993 (Volume LXXXI)*, 45.

48. Sovereign Grand Lodge of the IOOF, *Journal of Proceedings of the One Hundred and Forty-Eight Annual Communication of the Sovereign Grand Lodge of the Independent Order of Odd Fellows, 1974 (Volume LXII)*, 279-280.

49. Sovereign Grand Lodge of the IOOF, *Journal of Proceedings of the One Hundred and Sixty-Eight Annual Communication of the Sovereign Grand Lodge of the Independent Order of Odd Fellows, 1994 (Volume LXXXII)*, 604.

50. Ibid.

51. Sovereign Grand Lodge of the IOOF, *Journal of Proceedings of the One Hundred and Sixty-Seventh Annual Communication of the Sovereign Grand Lodge of the Independent Order of Odd Fellows, 1993 (Volume LXXXI)*, 43.

52. Sovereign Grand Lodge of the IOOF, *Journal of Proceedings of the One Hundred and Fifty-Sixth Annual Communication of the Sovereign Grand Lodge of the Independent Order of Odd Fellows, 1982 (Volume LXX)*, 61.

53. Sovereign Grand Lodge of the IOOF, *Journal of Proceedings of the One Hundred and Seventy-Third Annual Communication of the Sovereign Grand Lodge of the Independent Order of Odd Fellows, 1999 (Volume LXXXVII)*, 479.

54. Sovereign Grand Lodge of the IOOF, *Journal of Proceedings of the One Hundred and Forty-Third Annual Communication of the Sovereign Grand Lodge of the Independent Order of Odd Fellows, 1969 (Volume LVII)*, 13.

55. Sovereign Grand Lodge of the IOOF, *Journal of Proceedings of the One Hundred and Seventy-Third Annual Communication of the Sovereign Grand Lodge of the Independent Order of Odd Fellows, 1999 (Volume LXXXVII)*, 320.

56. Sovereign Grand Lodge of the IOOF, *Journal of Proceedings of the One Hundred and Sixtieth Annual*

Communication of the Sovereign Grand Lodge of the Independent Order of Odd Fellows, 1986 (Volume LXXIV), 43.
57. Sovereign Grand Lodge of the IOOF, *Journal of Proceedings of the One Hundred and Sixty-First Annual Communication of the Sovereign Grand Lodge of the Independent Order of Odd Fellows, 1987 (Volume LXXV)*, 50.
58. Ibid.
59. Ibid.
60. Dave Rosenberg, *The Future of Odd Fellowship: Evolution and Change* (2015), 84.
61. Ibid.
62. Dave Rosenberg, *The Future of Odd Fellowship: Evolution and Change* (2015), 112.
63. Sovereign Grand Lodge of the IOOF, *Journal of Proceedings of the One Hundred and Seventy-Fifth Annual Communication of the Sovereign Grand Lodge of the Independent Order of Odd Fellows, 2001 (Volume LXXXVIX)*, 32.
64. Dave Rosenberg, *The Future of Odd Fellowship: Evolution and Change* (2015), 296-297.
65. Sovereign Grand Lodge of the IOOF, *Journal of Proceedings of the One Hundred and Sixty-Eight Annual Communication of the Sovereign Grand Lodge of the Independent Order of Odd Fellows, 1994 (Volume LXXXII)*, 630.
66. Sovereign Grand Lodge of the IOOF, *Journal of Proceedings of the One Hundred and Fifty-Eight Annual Communication of the Sovereign Grand Lodge of the Independent Order of Odd Fellows, 1984 (Volume LXXII)*. 16.
67. Sovereign Grand Lodge of the IOOF, *Journal of Proceedings of the One Hundred and Seventieth Annual Communication of the Sovereign Grand Lodge of the Independent Order of Odd Fellows, 1996 (Volume LXXXIV)*, 352.
68. Sovereign Grand Lodge of the IOOF, *Journal of Proceedings of the One Hundred and Forty-Third Annual Communication of the Sovereign Grand Lodge of the Independent Order of Odd Fellows, 1969 (Volume LVII)*, 68.
69. Sovereign Grand Lodge of the IOOF, *Journal of Proceedings of the One Hundred and Seventieth Annual Communication of the Sovereign Grand Lodge of the Independent Order of Odd Fellows, 1996 (Volume LXXXIV)*, 352.
70. Sovereign Grand Lodge of the IOOF, *Journal of Proceedings of the One Hundred and Thirty-Second Annual Communication of the Sovereign Grand Lodge of the Independent Order of Odd Fellows, 1968 (Volume LVI)*, 29.
71. Sovereign Grand Lodge of the IOOF, *Journal of Proceedings of the One Hundred and Fifty-Sixth Annual Communication of the Sovereign Grand Lodge of the Independent Order of Odd Fellows, 1982 (Volume LXX)*, 392.
72. Sovereign Grand Lodge of the IOOF, *Journal of Proceedings of the One Hundred and Thirty-Second Annual Communication of the Sovereign Grand Lodge of the Independent Order of Odd Fellows, 1968 (Volume LVI)*, 29.
73. Ibid.
74. Sovereign Grand Lodge of the IOOF, *Journal of Proceedings of the One Hundred and Sixty-Seventh Annual Communication of the Sovereign Grand Lodge of the Independent Order of Odd Fellows, 1993 (Volume LXXXI)*, 35.
75. Ibid.
76. Sovereign Grand Lodge of the IOOF, *Journal of Proceedings of the One Hundred and Sixty-Eight Annual Communication of the Sovereign Grand Lodge of the Independent Order of Odd Fellows, 1994 (Volume LXXXII)*, 606.
77. Ibid.
78. Ibid, 43.
79. Sovereign Grand Lodge of the IOOF, *Journal of Proceedings of the One Hundred and Sixtieth Annual Communication of the Sovereign Grand Lodge of the Independent Order of Odd Fellows, 1986 (Volume LXXIV)*, 261.
80. Sovereign Grand Lodge of the IOOF, *Journal of Proceedings of the One Hundred and Sixty-Eight Annual Communication of the Sovereign Grand Lodge of the Independent Order of Odd Fellows, 1994 (Volume LXXXII)*, 43.
81. Sovereign Grand Lodge of the IOOF, *Journal of Proceedings of the One Hundred and Sixty-Seventh Annual Communication of the Sovereign Grand Lodge of the Independent Order of Odd Fellows, 1993 (Volume LXXXI)*, 371.
82. Ibid.
83. Sovereign Grand Lodge of the IOOF, *Journal of Proceedings of the One Hundred and Sixty-Eight Annual Communication of the Sovereign Grand Lodge of the Independent Order of Odd Fellows, 1994 (Volume LXXXII)*, 606.
84. Sovereign Grand Lodge of the IOOF, *Journal of Proceedings of the One Hundred and Fifty-Seventh Annual Communication of the Sovereign Grand Lodge of the Independent Order of Odd Fellows, 1983 (Volume LXXI)*, 387.
85. Ibid.
86. Ibid.

87. Ibid.

88. Ibid.

89. Sovereign Grand Lodge of the IOOF, *Journal of Proceedings of the One Hundred and Sixty-Eight Annual Communication of the Sovereign Grand Lodge of the Independent Order of Odd Fellows, 1994 (Volume LXXXII),* 631.

90. Sovereign Grand Lodge of the IOOF, *Journal of Proceedings of the One Hundred and Forty-Sixth Annual Communication of the Sovereign Grand Lodge of the Independent Order of Odd Fellows, 1972 (Volume LX),* 469.

91. Sovereign Grand Lodge of the IOOF, *Journal of Proceedings of the One Hundred and Sixty-Third Annual Communication of the Sovereign Grand Lodge of the Independent Order of Odd Fellows, 1989 (Volume LXXVII),* 289.

92. Ibid.

93. Sovereign Grand Lodge of the IOOF, *Journal of Proceedings of the One Hundred and Thirty-Second Annual Communication of the Sovereign Grand Lodge of the Independent Order of Odd Fellows, 1968 (Volume LVI),* 87.

94. Sovereign Grand Lodge of the IOOF, *Journal of Proceedings of the One Hundred and Sixty-Eight Annual Communication of the Sovereign Grand Lodge of the Independent Order of Odd Fellows, 1994 (Volume LXXXII),* 631.

95. Sovereign Grand Lodge of the IOOF, *Journal of Proceedings of the One Hundred and Sixty-First Annual Communication of the Sovereign Grand Lodge of the Independent Order of Odd Fellows, 1987 (Volume LXXV),* 206.

96. Sovereign Grand Lodge of the IOOF, *Journal of Proceedings of the One Hundred and Sixty-Seventh Annual Communication of the Sovereign Grand Lodge of the Independent Order of Odd Fellows, 1993 (Volume LXXXI).* 44.

97. Ibid, 44.

98. Sovereign Grand Lodge of the IOOF, *Journal of Proceedings of the One Hundred and Thirty-Seventh Annual Communication of the Sovereign Grand Lodge of the Independent Order of Odd Fellows, 1963 (Volume LI),* 12.

99. Sovereign Grand Lodge of the IOOF, *Journal of Proceedings of the One Hundred and Sixty-Third Annual Communication of the Sovereign Grand Lodge of the Independent Order of Odd Fellows, 1989 (Volume LXXVII),* 301.

100. Sovereign Grand Lodge of the IOOF, *Journal of Proceedings of the One Hundred and Thirty-Second Annual Communication of the Sovereign Grand Lodge of the Independent Order of Odd Fellows, 1968 (Volume LVI).* 288.

101. Ibid.

102. Ibid, 289.

103. Sovereign Grand Lodge of the IOOF, *Journal of Proceedings of the One Hundred and Sixty-Seventh Annual Communication of the Sovereign Grand Lodge of the Independent Order of Odd Fellows, 1993 (Volume LXXXI),* 351.

104. Ibid.

105. Ibid.

106. Sovereign Grand Lodge of the IOOF, *Journal of Proceedings of the One Hundred and Sixty-Eight Annual Communication of the Sovereign Grand Lodge of the Independent Order of Odd Fellows, 1994 (Volume LXXXII),* 596.

107. Ibid, 604.

108. Ibid.

109. Ibid, 625.

110. Sovereign Grand Lodge of the IOOF, *Journal of Proceedings of the One Hundred and Sixty-Eight Annual Communication of the Sovereign Grand Lodge of the Independent Order of Odd Fellows, 1994 (Volume LXXXII),* 604-605.

111. Ibid, 625.

112. Ibid.

113. Sovereign Grand Lodge of the IOOF, *Journal of Proceedings of the One Hundred and Sixty-Ninth Annual Communication of the Sovereign Grand Lodge of the Independent Order of Odd Fellows, 1995 (Volume LXXXIII),* 298.

114. Ibid.

115. Sovereign Grand Lodge of the IOOF, *Journal of Proceedings of the One Hundred and Sixty-Sixth Annual Communication of the Sovereign Grand Lodge of the Independent Order of Odd Fellows, 1992 (Volume LXXX),* 36.

116. Sovereign Grand Lodge of the IOOF, *Journal of Proceedings of the One Hundred and Sixty-Sixth Annual Communication of the Sovereign Grand Lodge of the Independent Order of Odd Fellows, 1992 (Volume LXXX),* 295.

117. Sovereign Grand Lodge of the IOOF, *Journal of Proceedings of the One Hundred and Sixty-Sixth Annual Communication of the Sovereign Grand Lodge of the Independent Order of Odd Fellows, 1992 (Volume LXXX),* 295.

118. Ibid.

119. Sovereign Grand Lodge of the IOOF, *Journal of Proceedings of the One Hundred and Thirty-Eight Annual Communication of the Sovereign Grand Lodge of the Independent Order of Odd Fellows, 1964 (Volume LII),* 12.

120. Sovereign Grand Lodge of the IOOF, *Journal of*

Proceedings of the One Hundred and Thirty-Second Annual Communication of the Sovereign Grand Lodge of the Independent Order of Odd Fellows, 1968 (Volume LVI), 93.

121. Sovereign Grand Lodge of the IOOF, *Journal of Proceedings of the One Hundred and Sixty-Eight Annual Communication of the Sovereign Grand Lodge of the Independent Order of Odd Fellows, 1994 (Volume LXXXII)*, 43-44.

122. Ibid.

123. Sovereign Grand Lodge of the IOOF, *Journal of Proceedings of the One Hundred and Sixty-Third Annual Communication of the Sovereign Grand Lodge of the Independent Order of Odd Fellows, 1989 (Volume LXXVII)*, 289.

124. Sovereign Grand Lodge of the IOOF, *Journal of Proceedings of the One Hundred and Forty-Third Annual Communication of the Sovereign Grand Lodge of the Independent Order of Odd Fellows, 1969 (Volume LVII)*, 58.

125. Sovereign Grand Lodge of the IOOF, *Journal of Proceedings of the One Hundred and Thirty-Eight Annual Communication of the Sovereign Grand Lodge of the Independent Order of Odd Fellows, 1964 (Volume LII)*, 61.

126. Sovereign Grand Lodge of the IOOF, *Journal of Proceedings of the One Hundred and Sixty-Third Annual Communication of the Sovereign Grand Lodge of the Independent Order of Odd Fellows, 1989 (Volume LXXVII)*, 140.

127. Sovereign Grand Lodge of the IOOF, *Journal of Proceedings of the One Hundred and Fifty-Fifth Annual Communication of the Sovereign Grand Lodge of the Independent Order of Odd Fellows, 1981 (Volume LXVIX)*, 18.

128. Sovereign Grand Lodge of the IOOF, *Journal of Proceedings of the One Hundred and Fifty-Ninth Annual Communication of the Sovereign Grand Lodge of the Independent Order of Odd Fellows, 1985 (Volume LXXIII)*, 45.

129. Sovereign Grand Lodge of the IOOF, *Journal of Proceedings of the One Hundred and Forty-Third Annual Communication of the Sovereign Grand Lodge of the Independent Order of Odd Fellows, 1969 (Volume LVII)*, 57.

130. Sovereign Grand Lodge of the IOOF, *Journal of Proceedings of the One Hundred and Sixty-Seventh Annual Communication of the Sovereign Grand Lodge of the Independent Order of Odd Fellows, 1993 (Volume LXXXI)*, 324.

131. Ibid, 351.

132. Sovereign Grand Lodge of the IOOF, *Journal of Proceedings of the One Hundred and Forty-Third Annual Communication of the Sovereign Grand Lodge of the Independent Order of Odd Fellows, 1969 (Volume LVII)*, 73.

133. Sovereign Grand Lodge of the IOOF, *Journal of Proceedings of the One Hundred and Thirty-Sixth Annual Communication of the Sovereign Grand Lodge of the Independent Order of Odd Fellows, 1962 (Volume XLVX)*, 50.

134. Ibid.

135. Sovereign Grand Lodge of the IOOF, *Journal of Proceedings of the One Hundred and Sixty-First Annual Communication of the Sovereign Grand Lodge of the Independent Order of Odd Fellows, 1987 (Volume LXXV)*, 205.

136. Sovereign Grand Lodge of the IOOF, *Journal of Proceedings of the One Hundred and Forty-Third Annual Communication of the Sovereign Grand Lodge of the Independent Order of Odd Fellows, 1969 (Volume LVII)*, 510.

137. Ibid.

138. Sovereign Grand Lodge of the IOOF, *Journal of Proceedings of the One Hundred and Seventy-Third Annual Communication of the Sovereign Grand Lodge of the Independent Order of Odd Fellows, 1999 (Volume LXXXVII)*, 480.

139. Ibid.

140. Sovereign Grand Lodge of the IOOF, *Journal of Proceedings of the One Hundred and Sixty-Fifth Annual Communication of the Sovereign Grand Lodge of the Independent Order of Odd Fellows, 1991 (Volume LXXVIV)*, 286.

141. Ibid.

142. Sovereign Grand Lodge of the IOOF, *Journal of Proceedings of the One Hundred and Seventy-Third Annual Communication of the Sovereign Grand Lodge of the Independent Order of Odd Fellows, 1999 (Volume LXXXVII)*, 480.

143. Sovereign Grand Lodge of the IOOF, *Journal of Proceedings of the One Hundred and Seventieth Annual Communication of the Sovereign Grand Lodge of the Independent Order of Odd Fellows, 1996 (Volume LXXXIV)*, 351.

144. Ibid.

145. Sovereign Grand Lodge of the IOOF, *Journal of Proceedings of the One Hundred and Forty-Third Annual Communication of the Sovereign Grand Lodge of the Independent Order of Odd Fellows, 1969 (Volume LVII)*, 153.

146. Sovereign Grand Lodge of the IOOF, *Journal of Proceedings of the One Hundred and Forty-First Annual Communication of the Sovereign Grand Lodge of the Independent Order of Odd Fellows, 1967 (Volume LV)*, 126.

147. Sovereign Grand Lodge of the IOOF, *Journal of Proceedings of the One Hundred and Forty Annual Communication of the Sovereign Grand Lodge of the Independent Order of Odd Fellows, 1966 (Volume LIV)*, 300.

148. Ibid, 447.

149. Sovereign Grand Lodge of the IOOF, *Journal of Proceedings of the One Hundred and Sixty-Seventh Annual Communication of the Sovereign Grand Lodge of the Independent Order of Odd Fellows, 1993 (Volume LXXXI)*, 351.

150. Sovereign Grand Lodge of the IOOF, *Journal of Proceedings of the One Hundred and Fifty-Sixth Annual Communication of the Sovereign Grand Lodge of the Independent Order of Odd Fellows, 1982 (Volume LXX)*, 33.

151. Sovereign Grand Lodge of the IOOF, *Journal of Proceedings of the One Hundred and Thirty-Seventh Annual Communication of the Sovereign Grand Lodge of the Independent Order of Odd Fellows, 1963 (Volume LI)*, 442.

152. Sovereign Grand Lodge of the IOOF, *Journal of Proceedings of the One Hundred and Thirty-Sixth Annual Communication of the Sovereign Grand Lodge of the Independent Order of Odd Fellows, 1962 (Volume XLVX)*, 353.

153. Sovereign Grand Lodge of the IOOF, *Journal of Proceedings of the One Hundred and Thirty-Second Annual Communication of the Sovereign Grand Lodge of the Independent Order of Odd Fellows, 1968 (Volume LVI)*, 86.

154. Sovereign Grand Lodge of the IOOF, *Journal of Proceedings of the One Hundred and Fifty-first Annual Communication of the Sovereign Grand Lodge of the Independent Order of Odd Fellows, 1977 (Volume LXV)*, 48.

155. Ibid, 51.

156. Ibid, 48.

157. Sovereign Grand Lodge of the IOOF, *Journal of Proceedings of the One Hundred and Fifty-Sixth Annual Communication of the Sovereign Grand Lodge of the Independent Order of Odd Fellows, 1982 (Volume LXX)*, 34.

158. Sovereign Grand Lodge of the IOOF, *Journal of Proceedings of the One Hundred and Forty-Sixth Annual Communication of the Sovereign Grand Lodge of the Independent Order of Odd Fellows, 1972 (Volume LX)*, 461.

159. Sovereign Grand Lodge of the IOOF, *Journal of Proceedings of the One Hundred and Fifty-Seventh Annual Communication of the Sovereign Grand Lodge of the Independent Order of Odd Fellows, 1983 (Volume LXXI)*, 18.

160. Sovereign Grand Lodge of the IOOF, *Journal of Proceedings of the One Hundred and Sixty-Seventh Annual Communication of the Sovereign Grand Lodge of the Independent Order of Odd Fellows, 1993 (Volume LXXXI)*, 351.

161. Sovereign Grand Lodge of the IOOF, *Journal of Proceedings of the One Hundred and Fifty-Seventh Annual Communication of the Sovereign Grand Lodge of the Independent Order of Odd Fellows, 1983 (Volume LXXI)*, 18-19.

162. Ibid.

163. Sovereign Grand Lodge of the IOOF, *Journal of Proceedings of the One Hundred and Forty-Sixth Annual Communication of the Sovereign Grand Lodge of the Independent Order of Odd Fellows, 1972 (Volume LX)*, 459.

164. Sovereign Grand Lodge of the IOOF, *Journal of Proceedings of the One Hundred and Fifty-Fifth Annual Communication of the Sovereign Grand Lodge of the Independent Order of Odd Fellows, 1981 (Volume LXVIX)*, 18.

165. Sovereign Grand Lodge of the IOOF, *Journal of Proceedings of the One Hundred and Fifty-Seventh Annual Communication of the Sovereign Grand Lodge of the Independent Order of Odd Fellows, 1983 (Volume LXXI)*, 19.

166. Sovereign Grand Lodge of the IOOF, *Journal of Proceedings of the One Hundred and Fifty-Ninth Annual Communication of the Sovereign Grand Lodge of the Independent Order of Odd Fellows, 1985 (Volume LXXIII)*, 45.

167. Sovereign Grand Lodge of the IOOF, *Journal of Proceedings of the One Hundred and Seventieth Annual Communication of the Sovereign Grand Lodge of the Independent Order of Odd Fellows, 1996 (Volume LXXXIV)*, 603.

168. Sovereign Grand Lodge of the IOOF, *Journal of Proceedings of the One Hundred and Seventy-Second Annual Communication of the Sovereign Grand Lodge of the Independent Order of Odd Fellows, 1998 (Volume LXXXVI)*, 277.

169. Sovereign Grand Lodge of the IOOF, *Journal of Proceedings of the One Hundred and Sixty-Seventh Annual Communication of the Sovereign Grand Lodge of the Independent Order of Odd Fellows, 1993 (Volume LXXXI)*, 351.

170. Sovereign Grand Lodge of the IOOF, *Journal of Proceedings of the One Hundred and Fifty-first Annual Communication of the Sovereign Grand Lodge of the Independent Order of Odd Fellows, 1977 (Volume LXV)*, 213.

171. Sovereign Grand Lodge of the IOOF, *Journal of Proceedings of the One Hundred and Fifty-Ninth Annual*

Communication of the Sovereign Grand Lodge of the Independent Order of Odd Fellows, 1985 (Volume LXXIII), 45.
172. Sovereign Grand Lodge of the IOOF, *Journal of Proceedings of the One Hundred and Seventy-Fifth Annual Communication of the Sovereign Grand Lodge of the Independent Order of Odd Fellows, 2001 (Volume LXXXVIX)*, 51.
173. Ibid.
174. Ibid.

Meeting Presidents
1. Sovereign Grand Lodge of the IOOF, *Journal of Proceedings of the One Hundred and Thirty-Sixth Annual Communication of the Sovereign Grand Lodge of the Independent Order of Odd Fellows, 1962 (Volume XLVX)*, 215-216.
2. Sovereign Grand Lodge of the IOOF, *Journal of Proceedings of the One Hundred and Thirty-Seventh Annual Communication of the Sovereign Grand Lodge of the Independent Order of Odd Fellows, 1963 (Volume LI)*, 180.
3. Sovereign Grand Lodge of the IOOF, *Journal of Proceedings of the One Hundred and Forty-Fourth Annual Communication of the Sovereign Grand Lodge of the Independent Order of Odd Fellows, 1970 (Volume LVIII)*, 52.
4. Ibid.
5. Sovereign Grand Lodge of the IOOF, *Journal of Proceedings of the One Hundred and Fifty-Sixth Annual Communication of the Sovereign Grand Lodge of the Independent Order of Odd Fellows, 1982 (Volume LXX)*, 34-35.
6. Ibid.

Chapter 18 - Signs of Rediscovery
1. Sovereign Grand Lodge of the IOOF, *Journal of Proceedings of the One Hundred and Fifty-first Annual Communication of the Sovereign Grand Lodge of the Independent Order of Odd Fellows, 1977 (Volume LXV)*, 48.
2. Dave Rosenberg, *The Future of Odd Fellowship: Evolution and Change* (California: Dave Rosenberg, 2015), 226.
3. Taya Flores, "*Fraternal, Service groups battle declining membership: Elks, Rotarians and Other Fraternal Groups Struggle to Attract Younger Members*", Journal & Courier, October 11, 2014, accessed August 30, 2017, https://www.jconline.com/story/news/2014/10/11/fraternal-service-groups-battle-declining-membership/16874977/
4. Sovereign Grand Lodge of the IOOF, *Journal of Proceedings of the One Hundred and Seventy-Fifth Annual Communication of the Sovereign Grand Lodge of the Independent Order of Odd Fellows, 2001 (Volume LXXXVIX)*, 310.
5. Sovereign Grand Lodge of the IOOF, *Journal of Proceedings of the Right Worthy Grand Lodge of the United States, and the Sovereign Grand Lodge of the Independent Order of Odd Fellows, 1931-1932 (Volume XXXV)*, 14.
6. Sovereign Grand Lodge of the IOOF, *Journal of Proceedings of the One Hundred and Forty-Fourth Annual Communication of the Sovereign Grand Lodge of the Independent Order of Odd Fellows, 1970 (Volume LVIII)*, 224.
7. Lisa Hix, "*Decoding Secret Societies: What are those Old Boys' Clubs Hiding?,*" Collectors Weekly, October 3, 2012, accessed August 30, 2017, https://www.collectorsweekly.com/articles/decoding-secret-societies/
8. Sovereign Grand Lodge of the IOOF, *Journal of Proceedings of the One Hundred and Seventy-Seventh Annual Communication of the Sovereign Grand Lodge of the Independent Order of Odd Fellows, 2003 (Volume XCI)*, 121.
9. Sovereign Grand Lodge of the IOOF, Journal of Proceedings of the I.O.O.F (North Carolina: Sovereign Grand Lodge, 1989), 452.
10. Sovereign Grand Lodge of the IOOF, *Journal of Proceedings of the One Hundred and Seventy-Ninth Annual Communication of the Sovereign Grand Lodge of the Independent Order of Odd Fellows, 2005 (Volume XCIII)*, 43.
11. Sovereign Grand Lodge of the IOOF, *Journal of Proceedings of the One Hundred and Eighty-Second Annual Communication of the Sovereign Grand Lodge of the Independent Order of Odd Fellows, 2008 (Volume XCVI)*, 140
12. Sovereign Grand Lodge of the IOOF, *Journal of Proceedings of the One Hundred and Eighty-Fourth Annual Communication of the Sovereign Grand Lodge of the Independent Order of Odd Fellows, 2010 (Volume XCVIII)*, 16-17; 126
13. Ibid.
14. Sovereign Grand Lodge of the IOOF, *Journal of Proceedings of the One Hundred and Seventy-Fifth Annual Communication of the Sovereign Grand Lodge of the Independent Order of Odd Fellows, 2001 (Volume LXXXVIX)*, 319.
15. Sovereign Grand Lodge of the IOOF, *Journal of Proceedings of the One Hundred and Fifty-Fifth Annual Communication of the Sovereign Grand Lodge of the Independent Order of Odd Fellows, 1981 (Volume LXVIX)*, 2.
16. Rick Braggy, interview with the author, June 15, 2012.
17. Ibid.

18. Vic Anton Somoza, interview with the author, November 10, 2014.
19. Thomas Roam, interview with the author through facebook, June 5, 2018.
20. Dave Rosenberg, *The Future of Odd Fellowship: Evolution and Change* (California: Dave Rosenberg, 2015), 58.
21. Dave Rosenberg, *The Future of Odd Fellowship: Evolution and Change* (2015), 172.
22. Dave Rosenberg, "*9 Steps to Help Resuscitate a Failing Lodge*", Davis Odd Fellows Lodge No.169, February 26, 2018, accessed May 30, 2018, http://davislodge.org/9-steps-help-resuscitate-failing-lodge/
23. Dave Rosenberg, *The Future of Odd Fellowship: Evolution and Change* (California, Dave Rosenberg, 2015), 32.
24. Dave Rosenberg, *The Future of Odd Fellowship: Evolution and Change* (California, Dave Rosenberg, 2015), 225.
25. Dave Rosenberg, *The Future of Odd Fellowship: Evolution and Change* (California, Dave Rosenberg, 2015), 169.
26. Ibid.
27. Sovereign Grand Lodge of the IOOF, *Journal of Proceedings of the One Hundred and Forty-Third Annual Communication of the Sovereign Grand Lodge of the Independent Order of Odd Fellows, 1969 (Volume LVII)*, 532.
28. Dave Rosenberg, *The Future of Odd Fellowship: Evolution and Change* (California: Dave Rosenberg, 2015), 142.
29. Scott Shaw, interview with the author, August 20, 2014.
30. Sovereign Grand Lodge, *Journal of Proceedings of the One Hundred and Seventy-Fifth Annual Communication of the Sovereign Grand Lodge of the Independent Order of Odd Fellows, 2001 (Volume LXXXVIX)*, 310.
31. Sovereign Grand Lodge, *Journal of Proceedings of the One Hundred and Sixty-Fifth Annual Communication of the Sovereign Grand Lodge of the Independent Order of Odd Fellows, 1991 (Volume LXXVIV)*, 285.
32. Dave Rosenberg, *The Future of Odd Fellowship: Evolution and Change* (California: Dave Rosenberg, 2015), 264.
33. Sovereign Grand Lodge of the IOOF, *Journal of Proceedings of the One Hundred and Fifty-first Annual Communication of the Sovereign Grand Lodge of the Independent Order of Odd Fellows, 1977 (Volume LXV)*, 47.
34. Ibid.
35. Dave Rosenberg, The Future of Odd Fellowship: Evolution and Change, 29.
36. Chris Saur, "*Centennial: Odd Fellows Lodge is a Community Powerhouse*," *Davis Enterprise*, June 2, 2017, accessed October 2, 2017, https://www.davisenterprise.com/local-news/centennial-odd-fellows-lodge-is-a-community-service-powerhouse/
37. Dave Rosenberg, The Future of Odd Fellowship: Evolution and Change, 132.
38. Dave Rosenberg, *The Future of Odd Fellowship: Evolution and Change*, 58.
39. Rachel Watts, "*The Experienced Three Links Owners Get Their Priorities from the Odd Fellows*," *Dallas Observer*, July 25, 2013, accessed October 4, 2017, http://www.dallasobserver.com/music/the-experienced-three-links-owners-get-their-priorities-from-the-odd-fellows-6430224 http://www.dallasobserver.com/music/the-experienced-three-links-owners-get-their-priorities-from-the-odd-fellows-6430224
40. Ross, Robyn. "*Antiques and 'Ink Master' Play Roles in Renaissance of Fading Fraternal Order,*" New York Times, May 10, 2014, accessed October 2, 2017, https://www.nytimes.com/2014/05/11/us/antiques-and-ink-master-play-roles-in-renaissance-of-fading-fraternal-order.html
41. Dave Rosenberg, *The Future of Odd Fellowship: Evolution and Change* (California: Dave Rosenberg, 2015), 92.
42. Dave Rosenberg, *The Future of Odd Fellowship: Evolution and Change* (California: Dave Rosenberg, 2015), 28.
43. Linda Sailer, "*Restoring the Odd Fellows Lodge: Members helping do the work, one room at a time*", *The Dickinson Press*, February 13, 2016, accessed October 2, 2017, http://www.thedickinsonpress.com/lifestyle/3947511-restoring-odd-fellows-lodge-members-helping-do-work-one-room-time
44. Sovereign Grand Lodge of the IOOF, *Journal of Proceedings of the One Hundred and Seventy-Fourth Annual Communication of the Sovereign Grand Lodge of the Independent Order of Odd Fellows, 2000 (Volume LXXXVIII)*, 43.
45. Ibid, 43.
46. Ibid, 44.
47. Dave Rosenberg, *The Future of Odd Fellowship: Evolution and Change*, 63.
48. Sovereign Grand Lodge of the IOOF, *Journal of Proceedings of the One Hundred and Sixty-Seventh Annual Communication of the Sovereign Grand Lodge of the Independent Order of Odd Fellows, 1993 (Volume LXXXI)*, 35.
49. Robyn Ross, "*Antiques and 'Ink Master' Play Roles in Renaissance of Fading Fraternal Order*", New York Times, May 10, 2014, accessed October 4, 2017, https://www.nytimes.com/2014/05/11/us/antiques-and-ink-master-

play-roles-in-renaissance-of-fading-fraternal-order.html
50. Dave Rosenberg, *The Future of Odd Fellowship: Evolution and Change*, 155.
51. Ibid.
52. Sovereign Grand Lodge of the IOOF, *Journal of Proceedings of the One Hundred and Forty-Third Annual Communication of the Sovereign Grand Lodge of the Independent Order of Odd Fellows, 1969 (Volume LVII)*, 72.
53. Ibid.
54. Dave Rosenberg, *The Future of Odd Fellowship: Evolution and Change*, 264.
55. Dave Rosenberg, *The Future of Odd Fellowship: Evolution and Change*, 132.
56. Ibid, 264.
57. Ibid, 237-238.
58. Ibid, 41.
59. Sovereign Grand Lodge of the IOOF, *Journal of Proceedings of the One Hundred and Sixty-Fourth Annual Communication of the Sovereign Grand Lodge of the Independent Order of Odd Fellows, 1990 (Volume LXXVIII)*, 297.
60. Sovereign Grand Lodge of the IOOF, *Journal of Proceedings of the One Hundred and Sixty-First Annual Communication of the Sovereign Grand Lodge of the Independent Order of Odd Fellows, 1987 (Volume LXXV)*, 49.
61. Ashley Ford, "*Horace Bratcher Honored with Odd Fellows Meritorious Award*", Daily Light, March 30, 2018, accessed October 3, 2017, http://waxahachietx_com.gm5-txstage.newscyclecloud.com/news/20180330/horace-bratcher-honored-with-odd-fellows-meritorious-award
62. Dave Rosenberg, *The Future of Odd Fellowship: Evolution and Change*, 61.
63. Jynnette Neal, "*Join the Club: Old-School Networking Made Cool Again*", Advocate Oak Cliff, September 26, 2017, accessed on October 3, 2017 https://oakcliff.advocatemag.com/2017/09/join-club-old-school-networking-made-cool/
64. Dave Moore, "*Dallas Odd Fellows Reviving Old-school Social Network*", Dallas Innovates, February 23, 2017, accessed October 3, 2017, https://www.dallasinnovates.com/dallas-odd-fellows-reviving-old-school-social-network/
65. Amy Smart, "*For First Time in 151 Years, Woman Leads Victoria Odd Fellows*", Times Colonist, January 17, 2015, accessed October 4, 2017, http://www.timescolonist.com/news/local/for-first-time-in-151-years-woman-leads-victoria-odd-fellows-1.1734684
66. Sara Hayden, "*Odd Fellows Ensure No One is Odd Man Out*", Half Moon Bay Review, December 26, 2017, accessed January 5, 2018, https://www.hmbreview.com/news/odd-fellows-ensures-no-one-is-odd-man-out/article_b6e4da60-eaa0-11e7-9421-3b5f60770def.html
67. Elizabeth Kalfsbeek, "*Reborn Arbuckle Odd Fellows Revitalizing Community*", Daily Democrat, December 9, 2009, accessed January 5, 2018, http://www.dailydemocrat.com/article/zz/20090209/NEWS/902099769
68. Dave Rosenberg, *The Future of Odd Fellowship: Evolution and Change*, 188.
69. Sovereign Grand Lodge of the IOOF, *Journal of Proceedings of the One Hundred and Sixty-Eight Annual Communication of the Sovereign Grand Lodge of the Independent Order of Odd Fellows, 1994 (Volume LXXXII)*, 297.
70. Sovereign Grand Lodge of the IOOF, *Journal of Proceedings of the One Hundred and Sixty-Seventh Annual Communication of the Sovereign Grand Lodge of the Independent Order of Odd Fellows, 1993 (Volume LXXXI)*, 298.
71. Ibid.
72. Sovereign Grand Lodge of the IOOF, *Journal of Proceedings of the One Hundred and Sixty-Fourth Annual Communication of the Sovereign Grand Lodge of the Independent Order of Odd Fellows, 1990 (Volume LXXVIII)*, 45.
73. Sovereign Grand Lodge of the IOOF, *Journal of Proceedings of the One Hundred and Seventy-Sixth Annual Communication of the Sovereign Grand Lodge of the Independent Order of Odd Fellows, 2002 (Volume XC)*, 34.
74. Ibid.

Chapter 19 - International Expansion
1. Sovereign Grand Lodge of the IOOF, *Journal of Proceedings of the Right Worthy Grand Lodge of the United States, and the Sovereign Grand Lodge of the Independent Order of Odd Fellows, from its Formation in February, 1879-1881 (Volume X)*, 8215,
2. Sovereign Grand Lodge of the IOOF, *Journal of Proceedings of the Right Worthy Grand Lodge of the United States, and the Sovereign Grand Lodge of the Independent Order of Odd Fellows, from its Formation in February, 1879-1881 (Volume X)*, 7918.
3. Sovereign Grand Lodge of the IOOF, *Journal of Proceedings of the Right Worthy Grand Lodge of the United States, and the Sovereign Grand Lodge of the Independent Order of Odd Fellows, 1882-1884 (Volume XI)*, 8842.
4. Stillson, *The Three Link Fraternity*, 420-421.
5. Ibid, 424.
6. Ibid, 425.
7. Ibid, 448.
8. Ibid, 425-426.
9. Ibid, 438.

10. Ibid, 440.
11. Ibid, 444-460.
12. Ibid, 474.
13. Ibid, 463
14. Ibid, 467.
15. Ibid, 474.
16. Sovereign Grand Lodge of the Independent Order of Odd Fellows. *Journal of Proceedings of the Right Worthy Grand Lodge of the United States, and the Sovereign Grand Lodge of the Independent Order of Odd Fellows, 1882-1884 (Volume XI)*, 9164.
17. Sovereign Grand Lodge of the Independent Order of Odd Fellows. *Journal of Proceedings of the Right Worthy Grand Lodge of the United States, and the Sovereign Grand Lodge of the Independent Order of Odd Fellows, 1923-1924 (Volume XXXI)*, 425.
18. Ibid, 418.
19. Sovereign Grand Lodge of the Independent Order of Odd Fellows. *Journal of Proceedings of the Right Worthy Grand Lodge of the United States, and the Sovereign Grand Lodge of the Independent Order of Odd Fellows, 1925-1926 (Volume XXXII)*, 90-91
20. Sovereign Grand Lodge of the Independent Order of Odd Fellows. *Journal of Proceedings of the One Hundred and Fifty-Seventh Annual Communication of the Sovereign Grand Lodge of the Independent Order of Odd Fellows, 1983 (Volume LXXI)*. 21.
21. Website of the Grand Lodge of Cuba www.oddfellowsencuba.cubava.cu
22. Sovereign Grand Lodge of the Independent Order of Odd Fellows. *Journal of Proceedings of the One Hundred and Eighty-First Annual Communication of the Sovereign Grand Lodge of the Independent Order of Odd Fellows, 2007 (Volume XCV)*, 152. See also Sovereign Grand Lodge of the Independent Order of Odd Fellows. *Journal of Proceedings of the One Hundred and Eighty-Second Annual Communication of the Sovereign Grand Lodge of the Independent Order of Odd Fellows, 2008 (Volume XCVI)*, 156.
23. Sovereign Grand Lodge of the Independent Order of Odd Fellows. *Journal of Proceedings of the Right Worthy Grand Lodge of the United States, and the Sovereign Grand Lodge of the Independent Order of Odd Fellows, 1882-1884 (Volume XI)*, 8843.
24. Sovereign Grand Lodge of the Independent Order of Odd Fellows. *Journal of Proceedings of the Right Worthy Grand Lodge of the United States, and the Sovereign Grand Lodge of the Independent Order of Odd Fellows, 1885-1886 (Volume XII)*, 9860.
25. Sovereign Grand Lodge of the Independent Order of Odd Fellows. *Journal of Proceedings of the One Hundred and Seventieth Annual Communication of the Sovereign Grand Lodge of the Independent Order of Odd Fellows, 1996 (Volume LXXXIV)*, 39.
26. Sovereign Grand Lodge of the Independent Order of Odd Fellows. *Journal of Proceedings of the One Hundred and Seventy-First Annual Communication of the Sovereign Grand Lodge of the Independent Order of Odd Fellows, 1997 (Volume LXXXV)*, 23.
27. Sovereign Grand Lodge of the Independent Order of Odd Fellows. *Journal of Proceedings of the Right Worthy Grand Lodge of the United States, and the Sovereign Grand Lodge of the Independent Order of Odd Fellows, 1905-1906 (Volume XXII)*, 539.
28. Sovereign Grand Lodge of the IOOF, *Journal of Proceedings of the One Hundred and Forty-Seventh Annual Communication of the Sovereign Grand Lodge of the Independent Order of Odd Fellows, 1973 (Volume LXI)*, 65.
29. Sovereign Grand Lodge of the IOOF, *Journal of Proceedings of the One Hundred and Forty-Ninth Annual Communication of the Sovereign Grand Lodge of the Independent Order of Odd Fellows, 1975 (Volume LXIII)*, 39-51.
30. Sovereign Grand Lodge of the IOOF, *Journal of Proceedings of the One Hundred and Seventy-Fourth Annual Communication of the Sovereign Grand Lodge of the Independent Order of Odd Fellows, 2000 (Volume LXXXVIII)*. 29.
31. Sovereign Grand Lodge of the IOOF, *Journal of Proceedings of the One Hundred and Seventy-Eight Annual Communication of the Sovereign Grand Lodge of the Independent Order of Odd Fellows, 2004 (Volume XCII)*, 113.
32. Robert Macoy, *General History, Cyclopedia, and Dictionary of Freemasonry*, 271.
33. Sovereign Grand Lodge of the IOOF, *Journal of Proceedings of the Right Worthy Grand Lodge of the United States, and the Sovereign Grand Lodge of the Independent Order of Odd Fellows, 1901-1902 (Volume XX)*, 55.
34. Sovereign Grand Lodge of the IOOF, *Journal of Proceedings of the Right Worthy Grand Lodge of the United States, and the Sovereign Grand Lodge of the Independent Order of Odd Fellows, 1911-1912(Volume XXV)*, 78-79.
35. Sovereign Grand Lodge of the IOOF, *Journal of Proceedings of the Right Worthy Grand Lodge of the United States, and the Sovereign Grand Lodge of the Independent Order of Odd Fellows, 1911-1912(Volume XXV)*, 80-81.
36. Sovereign Grand Lodge of the IOOF, *Journal of Proceedings of the One Hundred and Seventy-Eight Annual Communication of the Sovereign Grand Lodge of the Independent Order of Odd Fellows, 2004 (Volume XCII)*, 113.
37. Sovereign Grand Lodge of the IOOF, *Journal of*

Proceedings of the Right Worthy Grand Lodge of the United States, and the Sovereign Grand Lodge of the Independent Order of Odd Fellows, 1876-1878 (Volume IX), 6871.

38. Ibid, 6749.

39. Sovereign Grand Lodge of the IOOF, *Journal of Proceedings of the Right Worthy Grand Lodge of the United States, and the Sovereign Grand Lodge of the Independent Order of Odd Fellows, 1874-1875 (Volume VIII)*, 5996.

40. Sovereign Grand Lodge of the IOOF, *Journal of Proceedings of the Right Worthy Grand Lodge of the United States, and the Sovereign Grand Lodge of the Independent Order of Odd Fellows, 1876-1878 (Volume IX)*, 6749.

41. Sovereign Grand Lodge of the IOOF, *Journal of Proceedings of the One Hundred and Thirty-Ninth Annual Communication of the Sovereign Grand Lodge of the Independent Order of Odd Fellows, 1965 (Volume LIII)*, 45.

42. Sovereign Grand Lodge of the IOOF, *Journal of Proceedings of the One Hundred and Forty-First Annual Communication of the Sovereign Grand Lodge of the Independent Order of Odd Fellows, 1967 (Volume LV)*, 285.

43. Sovereign Grand Lodge of the IOOF, *Journal of Proceedings of the One Hundred and Seventieth Annual Communication of the Sovereign Grand Lodge of the Independent Order of Odd Fellows, 1996 (Volume LXXXIV)*. 40.

44. Ibid.

45. Sovereign Grand Lodge of the IOOF, *Journal of Proceedings of the One Hundred and Seventieth Annual Communication of the Sovereign Grand Lodge of the Independent Order of Odd Fellows, 1996 (Volume LXXXIV)*, 98.

46. Sovereign Grand Lodge of the IOOF, *Journal of Proceedings of the One Hundred and Seventy-Third Annual Communication of the Sovereign Grand Lodge of the Independent Order of Odd Fellows, 1999 (Volume LXXXVII)*, 124.

47. Sovereign Grand Lodge of the IOOF, *Journal of Proceedings of the Right Worthy Grand Lodge of the United States, and the Sovereign Grand Lodge of the Independent Order of Odd Fellows, 1876-1878 (Volume IX)*, 6749.

48. Sovereign Grand Lodge of the IOOF, *Journal of Proceedings of the Right Worthy Grand Lodge of the United States, and the Sovereign Grand Lodge of the Independent Order of Odd Fellows, 1901-1902 (Volume XX)*, 195.

49. Sovereign Grand Lodge of the IOOF, *Journal of Proceedings of the One Hundred and Forty-First Annual Communication of the Sovereign Grand Lodge of the Independent Order of Odd Fellows, 1967 (Volume LV)*, 46.

50. Sovereign Grand Lodge of the IOOF, *Journal of Proceedings of the Right Worthy Grand Lodge of the United States, and the Sovereign Grand Lodge of the Independent Order of Odd Fellows, 1907-1908 (Volume XXIII)*, 74; 437.

51. Sovereign Grand Lodge of the IOOF, *Journal of Proceedings of the Right Worthy Grand Lodge of the United States, and the Sovereign Grand Lodge of the Independent Order of Odd Fellows, 1907-1908 (Volume XXIII)*, 437.

52. Ibid.

53. Sovereign Grand Lodge of the IOOF, *Journal of Proceedings of the Right Worthy Grand Lodge of the United States, and the Sovereign Grand Lodge of the Independent Order of Odd Fellows, 1951-1952 (Volume XLIII)*, 47

54. Sovereign Grand Lodge of the IOOF, *Journal of Proceedings of the One Hundred and Forty-Fourth Annual Communication of the Sovereign Grand Lodge of the Independent Order of Odd Fellows, 1970 (Volume LVIII)*, 56-57.

55. Sovereign Grand Lodge of the IOOF, *Journal of Proceedings of the One Hundred and Forty Annual Communication of the Sovereign Grand Lodge of the Independent Order of Odd Fellows, 1966 (Volume LIV)*, 68.

56. Sovereign Grand Lodge of the IOOF, *Journal of Proceedings of the One Hundred and Forty-First Annual Communication of the Sovereign Grand Lodge of the Independent Order of Odd Fellows, 1967 (Volume LV)*, 47.

57. Sovereign Grand Lodge of the IOOF, *Journal of Proceedings of the One Hundred and Seventieth Annual Communication of the Sovereign Grand Lodge of the Independent Order of Odd Fellows, 1996 (Volume LXXXIV)*, 40.

58. Sovereign Grand Lodge of the IOOF, *Journal of Proceedings of the Right Worthy Grand Lodge of the United States, and the Sovereign Grand Lodge of the Independent Order of Odd Fellows, from its Formation in February, 1847-1852 (Volume II)*, 1213.

59. Ibid.

60. Sovereign Grand Lodge of the IOOF, *Journal of Proceedings of the One Hundred and Sixtieth Annual Communication of the Sovereign Grand Lodge of the Independent Order of Odd Fellows, 1986 (Volume LXXIV)*, 42.

61. Sovereign Grand Lodge of the IOOF, *Journal of Proceedings of the One Hundred and Sixty-First Annual Communication of the Sovereign Grand Lodge of the Independent Order of Odd Fellows, 1987 (Volume LXXV)*, 39.

62. Sovereign Grand Lodge of the IOOF, *Journal of Proceedings of the One Hundred and Sixty-Eight Annual Communication of the Sovereign Grand Lodge of the Independent Order of Odd Fellows, 1994 (Volume LXXXII)*, 55.

63. Ibid.

64. Sovereign Grand Lodge of the IOOF, *Journal of Proceedings of the Right Worthy Grand Lodge of the United States, and the Sovereign Grand Lodge of the Independent

Order of Odd Fellows, 1929-1930 (Volume XXXIV), 719.
65. Ibid.
66. Sovereign Grand Lodge of the IOOF, *Journal of Proceedings of the One Hundred and Seventy-Ninth Annual Communication of the Sovereign Grand Lodge of the Independent Order of Odd Fellows, 2005 (Volume XCIII)*, 21.
67. Sovereign Grand Lodge of the IOOF, *Journal of Proceedings of the Right Worthy Grand Lodge of the United States, and the Sovereign Grand Lodge of the Independent Order of Odd Fellows, 1923-1924 (Volume XXXI)*, 64.
68. Sovereign Grand Lodge of the IOOF, *Journal of Proceedings of the Right Worthy Grand Lodge of the United States, and the Sovereign Grand Lodge of the Independent Order of Odd Fellows, 1923-1924 (Volume XXXI)*, 64.
69. Sovereign Grand Lodge of the IOOF, *Journal of Proceedings of the One Hundred and Thirty-Second Annual Communication of the Sovereign Grand Lodge of the Independent Order of Odd Fellows, 1968 (Volume LVI).)*, 121.
70. Sovereign Grand Lodge of the IOOF, *Journal of Proceedings of the One Hundred and Fifty-first Annual Communication of the Sovereign Grand Lodge of the Independent Order of Odd Fellows, 1977 (Volume LXV)*, 215.
71. Sovereign Grand Lodge of the IOOF, *Journal of Proceedings of the One Hundred and Seventy-Fourth Annual Communication of the Sovereign Grand Lodge of the Independent Order of Odd Fellows, 2000 (Volume LXXXVIII)*. 24.
72. Sovereign Grand Lodge of the IOOF, *Journal of Proceedings of the Right Worthy Grand Lodge of the United States, and the Sovereign Grand Lodge of the Independent Order of Odd Fellows, 1911-1912(Volume XXV)*, 52.
73. Sovereign Grand Lodge of the IOOF, *Journal of Proceedings of the Right Worthy Grand Lodge of the United States, and the Sovereign Grand Lodge of the Independent Order of Odd Fellows, 1931-1932 (Volume XXXV)*, 36.
74. Ibid.
75. Ibid.
76. Website of the Odd Fellows in Belgium http://oddfellowsbelgium.com/
77. Sovereign Grand Lodge of the IOOF, *Journal of Proceedings of the Right Worthy Grand Lodge of the United States, and the Sovereign Grand Lodge of the Independent Order of Odd Fellows, 1931-1932 (Volume XXXV)*, 43.
78. Ibid.
79. Sovereign Grand Lodge of the IOOF, *Journal of Proceedings of the Right Worthy Grand Lodge of the United States, and the Sovereign Grand Lodge of the Independent Order of Odd Fellows, 1923-1924 (Volume XXXI)*, 432.
80. Sovereign Grand Lodge of the IOOF, *Journal of Proceedings of the One Hundred and Seventieth Annual Communication of the Sovereign Grand Lodge of the Independent Order of Odd Fellows, 1996 (Volume LXXXIV)*, 584.
81. Sovereign Grand Lodge of the IOOF, *Journal of Proceedings of the One Hundred and Seventy-Second Annual Communication of the Sovereign Grand Lodge of the Independent Order of Odd Fellows, 1998 (Volume LXXXVI)*, 278.
82. Sovereign Grand Lodge of the IOOF, *Journal of Proceedings of the One Hundred and Seventy-Third Annual Communication of the Sovereign Grand Lodge of the Independent Order of Odd Fellows, 1999 (Volume LXXXVII)*, 491.
83. Ibid.
84. Sovereign Grand Lodge of the IOOF, *Journal of Proceedings of the Right Worthy Grand Lodge of the United States, and the Sovereign Grand Lodge of the Independent Order of Odd Fellows, from its Formation in February, 1876-1878 (Volume IX)*, 7532.
85. Sovereign Grand Lodge of the IOOF, *Journal of Proceedings of the Right Worthy Grand Lodge of the United States, and the Sovereign Grand Lodge of the Independent Order of Odd Fellows, 1882-1884 (Volume XI)*, 9164.
86. Sovereign Grand Lodge of the IOOF, *Journal of Proceedings of the One Hundred and Seventy-Third Annual Communication of the Sovereign Grand Lodge of the Independent Order of Odd Fellows, 1999 (Volume LXXXVII)*, 490.
87. The Grand Lodge of Europe IOOF, *10 years* (Latvia: United Press Poligrafija Corporation, 2017), 24.
88. See official website of the Grand Lodge of Denmark https://www.oddfellow.dk/loger-lejre-cantons
89. Sovereign Grand Lodge of the IOOF, *Journal of Proceedings of the One Hundred and Eighty-Eight Annual Communication of the Sovereign Grand Lodge of the Independent Order of Odd Fellows, 2014 (Volume XCXI)*.128
90. See official website of the Odd Fellows in Estonia http://oddfellow.ee/
91. Sovereign Grand Lodge of the IOOF, *Journal of Proceedings of the One Hundred and Sixty-Seventh Annual Communication of the Sovereign Grand Lodge of the Independent Order of Odd Fellows, 1993 (Volume LXXXI)*, 509.
92. Sovereign Grand Lodge of the IOOF, *Journal of Proceedings of the One Hundred and Sixty-Ninth Annual Communication of the Sovereign Grand Lodge of the Independent Order of Odd Fellows, 1995 (Volume LXXXIII)*, 37. Sovereign Grand Lodge of the IOOF, *Journal of Proceedings of the One Hundred and Sixty-Seventh Annual Communication of the Sovereign Grand*

Lodge of the Independent Order of Odd Fellows, 1993 (Volume LXXXI), 324.

93. Sovereign Grand Lodge of the IOOF, *Journal of Proceedings of the One Hundred and Sixty-First Annual Communication of the Sovereign Grand Lodge of the Independent Order of Odd Fellows, 1987 (Volume LXXV)*, 37.

94. Sovereign Grand Lodge of the IOOF, *Journal of Proceedings of the Right Worthy Grand Lodge of the United States, and the Sovereign Grand Lodge of the Independent Order of Odd Fellows, 1925-1926 (Volume XXXII)*, 47

95. Sovereign Grand Lodge of the IOOF, *Journal of Proceedings of the Right Worthy Grand Lodge of the United States, and the Sovereign Grand Lodge of the Independent Order of Odd Fellows, 1927-1928 (Volume XXXIII)*, 131.

96. The Grand Lodge of Europe IOOF, *10 years* (Latvia: United Press Poligrafija Corporation, 2017), 27.

97. Sovereign Grand Lodge of the IOOF, *Journal of Proceedings of the Right Worthy Grand Lodge of the United States, and the Sovereign Grand Lodge of the Independent Order of Odd Fellows, 1903-1904 (Volume XXI)*, 17.

98. The Grand Lodge of Europe IOOF, *10 years*, 27.

99. Sovereign Grand Lodge of the IOOF, *Journal of Proceedings of the Right Worthy Grand Lodge of the United States, and the Sovereign Grand Lodge of the Independent Order of Odd Fellows, 1887-1888 (Volume XIII)*, 10710.

100. Sovereign Grand Lodge of the IOOF, *Journal of Proceedings of the Right Worthy Grand Lodge of the United States, and the Sovereign Grand Lodge of the Independent Order of Odd Fellows, 1887-1888 (Volume XIII)*, 11159.

101. Sovereign Grand Lodge of the IOOF, *Journal of Proceedings of the Right Worthy Grand Lodge of the United States, and the Sovereign Grand Lodge of the Independent Order of Odd Fellows, 1887-1888 (Volume XIII)*, 111175.

102. Sovereign Grand Lodge of the IOOF, *Journal of Proceedings of the Right Worthy Grand Lodge of the United States, and the Sovereign Grand Lodge of the Independent Order of Odd Fellows, 1893-1894 (Volume XVI)*, 13857

103. Sovereign Grand Lodge of the IOOF, *Journal of Proceedings of the Right Worthy Grand Lodge of the United States, and the Sovereign Grand Lodge of the Independent Order of Odd Fellows, 1895-1896 (Volume XVII)*, 14345.

104. Sovereign Grand Lodge of the IOOF, *Journal of Proceedings of the Right Worthy Grand Lodge of the United States, and the Sovereign Grand Lodge of the Independent Order of Odd Fellows,1897-1898 (Volume XVIII)*, 15296.

105. Sovereign Grand Lodge of the IOOF, *Journal of Proceedings of the Right Worthy Grand Lodge of the United States, and the Sovereign Grand Lodge of the Independent Order of Odd Fellows, 1901-1902 (Volume XX)*, 635.

106. Ibid.

107. Sovereign Grand Lodge of the IOOF, *Journal of Proceedings of the Right Worthy Grand Lodge of the United States, and the Sovereign Grand Lodge of the Independent Order of Odd Fellows, 1905-1906 (Volume XXII)*, 130

108. Sovereign Grand Lodge of the IOOF, *Journal of Proceedings of the Right Worthy Grand Lodge of the United States, and the Sovereign Grand Lodge of the Independent Order of Odd Fellows, 1901-1902 (Volume XX)*, 636-637.

109. Sovereign Grand Lodge of the IOOF, *Journal of Proceedings of the Right Worthy Grand Lodge of the United States, and the Sovereign Grand Lodge of the Independent Order of Odd Fellows, 1931-1932 (Volume XXXV)*, 45

110. Ibid.

111. Ibid.

112. Sovereign Grand Lodge of the IOOF, *Journal of Proceedings of the fifteenth Communication of the International Council of the Independent Order of Odd Fellows held in Lucerne, Switzerland, May 18 to May 21, 1990*, 31.

113. Sovereign Grand Lodge of the IOOF, *Journal of Proceedings of the International Council, Independent Order of Odd Fellows, 1999-2001*, 496.

114. Stillson, 478-479.

115. Stillson, 481.

116. Stillson, 482.

117. Ibid.

118. Ibid.

119. Sovereign Grand Lodge of the IOOF, *Journal of Proceedings of the Right Worthy Grand Lodge of the United States, and the Sovereign Grand Lodge of the Independent Order of Odd Fellows, from its Formation in February, 1871-1873*, 5270.

120. Ibid, 5653.

121. Sovereign Grand Lodge of the IOOF, *Journal of Proceedings of the Right Worthy Grand Lodge of the United States, and the Sovereign Grand Lodge of the Independent Order of Odd Fellows, 1933-1934 (Volume XXXVI)*, 43.

122. Ibid.

123. Sovereign Grand Lodge of the IOOF, *Journal of Proceedings of the Right Worthy Grand Lodge of the United States, and the Sovereign Grand Lodge of the Independent Order of Odd Fellows, 1951-1952 (Volume XLIII)*, 594.

124. Sovereign Grand Lodge of the IOOF, *Journal of Proceedings of the One Hundred and Forty-Third Annual Communication of the Sovereign Grand Lodge of the Independent Order of Odd Fellows, 1969 (Volume LVII)*, 485.

125. Sovereign Grand Lodge of the Independent Order of Odd Fellows. *Journal of Proceedings of the Right Worthy Grand Lodge of the United States, and the Sovereign Grand Lodge of the Independent Order of Odd Fellows,1897-1898 (Volume XVIII)*, 15791-15792.

126. Sovereign Grand Lodge of the IOOF, *Journal of*

Proceedings of the One Hundred and Thirty-Seventh Annual Communication of the Sovereign Grand Lodge of the Independent Order of Odd Fellows, 1963 (Volume LI), 479

127. Ibid.

128. Sovereign Grand Lodge of the IOOF, *Journal of Proceedings of the One Hundred and Fifty-Ninth Annual Communication of the Sovereign Grand Lodge of the Independent Order of Odd Fellows, 1985 (Volume LXXIII)*, 44.

129. Sovereign Grand Lodge of the IOOF, *Journal of Proceedings of the One Hundred and Seventy-Third Annual Communication of the Sovereign Grand Lodge of the Independent Order of Odd Fellows, 1999 (Volume LXXXVII)*, 480.

130. Sovereign Grand Lodge of the IOOF, *Journal of Proceedings of the Right Worthy Grand Lodge of the United States, and the Sovereign Grand Lodge of the Independent Order of Odd Fellows, 1893-1894 (Volume XVI)*, 13248.

131. Sovereign Grand Lodge of the IOOF, *Journal of Proceedings of the Right Worthy Grand Lodge of the United States, and the Sovereign Grand Lodge of the Independent Order of Odd Fellows, 1895-1896 (Volume XVII)*, 14272.

132. Sovereign Grand Lodge of the IOOF *Journal of Proceedings of the Right Worthy Grand Lodge of the United States, and the Sovereign Grand Lodge of the Independent Order of Odd Fellows, 1897-1898 (Volume XVIII)*, 15787.

133. Sovereign Grand Lodge of the IOOF, *Journal of Proceedings of the Right Worthy Grand Lodge of the United States, and the Sovereign Grand Lodge of the Independent Order of Odd Fellows, from its Formation in February, 1876-1878 (Volume IX)*, 7178.

134. Note: *The journal I brought with me was destroyed by termites. I will find the source again when I visit the Sovereign Grand Lodge headquarters.*

135. Sovereign Grand Lodge of the IOOF, *Journal of Proceedings of the Right Worthy Grand Lodge of the United States, and the Sovereign Grand Lodge of the Independent Order of Odd Fellows, 1921-1922 (Volume XXX)*, 77.

136. Sovereign Grand Lodge of the IOOF, *Journal of Proceedings of the Right Worthy Grand Lodge of the United States, and the Sovereign Grand Lodge of the Independent Order of Odd Fellows,1897-1898 (Volume XVIII)*, 15792.

137. Sovereign Grand Lodge of the IOOF, *Journal of Proceedings of the One Hundred and Forty-Third Annual Communication of the Sovereign Grand Lodge of the Independent Order of Odd Fellows, 1969 (Volume LVII)*, 516.

138. Sovereign Grand Lodge of the IOOF, *Journal of Proceedings of the Right Worthy Grand Lodge of the United States, and the Sovereign Grand Lodge of the Independent Order of Odd Fellows, 1925-1926 (Volume XXXII)*, 526

139. Sovereign Grand Lodge of the IOOF, *Journal of Proceedings of the One Hundred and Sixty-Eight Annual Communication of the Sovereign Grand Lodge of the Independent Order of Odd Fellows, 1994 (Volume LXXXII)*, 347.

140. The Grand Lodge of Europe IOOF, *10 years* (Latvia: United Press Poligrafija Corporation, 2017), 38.

141. Ibid.

142. Sovereign Grand Lodge of the IOOF, *Journal of Proceedings of the Right Worthy Grand Lodge of the United States, and the Sovereign Grand Lodge of the Independent Order of Odd Fellows, 1887-1888 (Volume XIII)*, 10710-10711.

143. Sovereign Grand Lodge of the IOOF, *Journal of Proceedings of the Right Worthy Grand Lodge of the United States, and the Sovereign Grand Lodge of the Independent Order of Odd Fellows, 1935-1936 (Volume XXXVII)*, 411.

144. Sovereign Grand Lodge of the IOOF, *Journal of Proceedings of the One Hundred and Forty-Ninth Annual Communication of the Sovereign Grand Lodge of the Independent Order of Odd Fellows, 1975 (Volume LXIII)*, 588.

145. The Story, SosterLoge Andalucia Nr.1, http://www.loge69.dk:80/andalus/omvorLoge.htm

146. History, Broder Loge Costa del Sol Nr.1, http://www.loge69.dk:80/costa/omvorLoge.htm

147. The Grand Lodge of Europe IOOF, *10 years* (Latvia: United Press Poligrafija Corporation, 2017), 25.

148. Sovereign Grand Lodge of the IOOF, *Journal of Proceedings of the Right Worthy Grand Lodge of the United States, and the Sovereign Grand Lodge of the Independent Order of Odd Fellows, 1882-1884 (Volume XI)*, 9506.

149. Sovereign Grand Lodge of the IOOF, *Journal of Proceedings of the One Hundred and Forty-Third Annual Communication of the Sovereign Grand Lodge of the Independent Order of Odd Fellows, 1969 (Volume LVII)*, 265.

150. The Grand Lodge of Europe IOOF, *10 years* (Latvia: United Press Poligrafija Corporation, 2017), 39.

151. Sovereign Grand Lodge of the IOOF, *Journal of Proceedings of the Right Worthy Grand Lodge of the United States, and the Sovereign Grand Lodge of the Independent Order of Odd Fellows, from its Formation in February, 1871-1873 (Volume VII)*, 4984.

152. Stillson, 500.

153. Sovereign Grand Lodge of the IOOF, *Journal of Proceedings of the Right Worthy Grand Lodge of the United States, and the Sovereign Grand Lodge of the Independent Order of Odd Fellows, 1887-1888 (Volume XIII)*, 11111.

154. Sovereign Grand Lodge of the IOOF, *Journal of Proceedings of the One Hundred and Sixty-Fifth Annual Communication of the Sovereign Grand Lodge

of the Independent Order of Odd Fellows, 1991 (Volume LXXVIV), 286.

155. Powley, *Concise History of Odd Fellowship*, 20.

156. Sovereign Grand Lodge of the IOOF, *Journal of Proceedings of the Right Worthy Grand Lodge of the United States, and the Sovereign Grand Lodge of the Independent Order of Odd Fellows, 1876-1878 (Volume IX)*, 1876.

157. Ibid, 7535.

158. Sovereign Grand Lodge of the IOOF, *Journal of Proceedings of the One Hundred and Sixty-Sixth Annual Communication of the Sovereign Grand Lodge of the Independent Order of Odd Fellows, 1992 (Volume LXXX)*, 323.

159. Sovereign Grand Lodge of the IOOF, *Journal of Proceedings of the One Hundred and Forty-First Annual Communication of the Sovereign Grand Lodge of the Independent Order of Odd Fellows, 1967 (Volume LV)*, 46.

160. Sovereign Grand Lodge of the IOOF, *Journal of Proceedings of the One Hundred and Sixty-Sixth Annual Communication of the Sovereign Grand Lodge of the Independent Order of Odd Fellows, 1992 (Volume LXXX)*, 321.

161. Ibid.

162. Goeffrey Blainey, *Odd Fellows: A History of IOOF Australia*, 15.

163. Ibid, 35.

164. Sovereign Grand Lodge of the IOOF, *Journal of Proceedings of the Right Worthy Grand Lodge of the United States, and the Sovereign Grand Lodge of the Independent Order of Odd Fellows, from its Formation in February, 1876-1878 (Volume IX)*, 7531.

165. Sovereign Grand Lodge of the IOOF, *Journal of Proceedings of the One Hundred and Sixty-Sixth Annual Communication of the Sovereign Grand Lodge of the Independent Order of Odd Fellows, 1992 (Volume LXXX)*, 323.

166. Ibid, 321.

167. Sovereign Grand Lodge of the IOOF, *Journal of Proceedings of the One Hundred and Forty-Third Annual Communication of the Sovereign Grand Lodge of the Independent Order of Odd Fellows, 1969 (Volume LVII)*, 509.

168. Sovereign Grand Lodge of the IOOF, *Journal of Proceedings of the One Hundred and Eighty-Sixth Annual Communication of the Sovereign Grand Lodge of the Independent Order of Odd Fellows, 2012*, 18-19.

169. Sovereign Grand Lodge of the IOOF, *Journal of Proceedings of the One Hundred and Eighty-Sixth Annual Communication of the Sovereign Grand Lodge of the Independent Order of Odd Fellows, 2012*, 18-19.

170. Sovereign Grand Lodge of the IOOF, *Journal of Proceedings of the Right Worthy Grand Lodge of the United States, and the Sovereign Grand Lodge of the Independent Order of Odd Fellows, 1931-1932 (Volume XXXV)*, 36.

171. Sovereign Grand Lodge of the IOOF, *Journal of Proceedings of the Right Worthy Grand Lodge of the United States, and the Sovereign Grand Lodge of the Independent Order of Odd Fellows, 1923-1924 (Volume XXXI)*, 112.

172. Ibid.

173. Ibid.

174. Sovereign Grand Lodge of the IOOF, *Journal of Proceedings of the Right Worthy Grand Lodge of the United States, and the Sovereign Grand Lodge of the Independent Order of Odd Fellows, 1889-1890 (Volume XIV)*, 11498

175. Ibid, 11576.

176. Sovereign Grand Lodge of the IOOF, *Journal of Proceedings of the Right Worthy Grand Lodge of the United States, and the Sovereign Grand Lodge of the Independent Order of Odd Fellows, 1893-1894 (Volume XVI)*, 13860.

177. Sovereign Grand Lodge of the IOOF, *Journal of Proceedings of the Right Worthy Grand Lodge of the United States, and the Sovereign Grand Lodge of the Independent Order of Odd Fellows, from its Formation in February, 1876-1878 (Volume IX)*.

178. Sovereign Grand Lodge of the IOOF, *Journal of Proceedings of the Right Worthy Grand Lodge of the United States, and the Sovereign Grand Lodge of the Independent Order of Odd Fellows, 1939-1940 (Volume XXXIX)*. 668; Sovereign Grand Lodge of the IOOF, *Grand Lodge of the United States, and the Sovereign Grand Lodge of the Independent Order of Odd Fellows, 1941-1944 (Volume XL)*, 16-17.

179. Ibid.

180. Sovereign Grand Lodge of the IOOF, *Journal of Proceedings of the Right Worthy Grand Lodge of the United States, and the Sovereign Grand Lodge of the Independent Order of Odd Fellows, 1945-1948 (Volume XLI)*, 120.

181. Ibid.

182. Sovereign Grand Lodge of the IOOF, *Journal of Proceedings of the One Hundred and Eighty-Sixth Annual Communication of the Sovereign Grand Lodge of the Independent Order of Odd Fellows, 2012*, 18-19.

183. Oscar William Coursey, *History and Geography of the Philippine Islands*, 24

184. Ibid.

185. Sovereign Grand Lodge of the IOOF, *Journal of Proceedings of the Right Worthy Grand Lodge of the United States, and the Sovereign Grand Lodge of the Independent Order of Odd Fellows,1897-1898 (Volume XVIII)*, 15768

186. Sovereign Grand Lodge of the IOOF, *Journal of Proceedings of the Right Worthy Grand Lodge of the United States, and the Sovereign Grand Lodge of the Independent Order of Odd Fellows, 1901-1902 (Volume XX)*, 99.

187. Sovereign Grand Lodge of the IOOF, *Journal of*

Proceedings of the Right Worthy Grand Lodge of the United States, and the Sovereign Grand Lodge of the Independent Order of Odd Fellows, 1901-1902 (Volume XX), 643.

188. Sovereign Grand Lodge of the IOOF, *Journal of Proceedings of the Right Worthy Grand Lodge of the United States, and the Sovereign Grand Lodge of the Independent Order of Odd Fellows, 1905-1906 (Volume XXII)*, 131.

189. Sovereign Grand Lodge of the IOOF, *Journal of Proceedings of the Right Worthy Grand Lodge of the United States, and the Sovereign Grand Lodge of the Independent Order of Odd Fellows, 1903-1904 (Volume XXI)*, 62.

190. Sovereign Grand Lodge of the IOOF, *Journal of Proceedings of the Right Worthy Grand Lodge of the United States, and the Sovereign Grand Lodge of the Independent Order of Odd Fellows, 1905-1906 (Volume XXII)*,.131.

191. Sovereign Grand Lodge of the IOOF, *Journal of Proceedings of the Right Worthy Grand Lodge of the United States, and the Sovereign Grand Lodge of the Independent Order of Odd Fellows, 1911-1912(Volume XXV)*, 520.

192. Sovereign Grand Lodge of the IOOF, *Journal of Proceedings of the Right Worthy Grand Lodge of the United States, and the Sovereign Grand Lodge of the Independent Order of Odd Fellows, 1905-1906 (Volume XXII)*, 132.

193. Sovereign Grand Lodge of the IOOF, *Journal of Proceedings of the Right Worthy Grand Lodge of the United States, and the Sovereign Grand Lodge of the Independent Order of Odd Fellows, from its Formation in February, 1879-1881 (Volume X)*, 7918.

194. Sovereign Grand Lodge of the IOOF, *Journal of Proceedings of the Right Worthy Grand Lodge of the United States, and the Sovereign Grand Lodge of the Independent Order of Odd Fellows, 1903-1904 (Volume XXI)*, 63.

195. Sovereign Grand Lodge of the IOOF, *Journal of Proceedings of the Right Worthy Grand Lodge of the United States, and the Sovereign Grand Lodge of the Independent Order of Odd Fellows, 1903-1904 (Volume XXI)*, 553.

196. Sovereign Grand Lodge of the IOOF, *Journal of Proceedings of the Right Worthy Grand Lodge of the United States, and the Sovereign Grand Lodge of the Independent Order of Odd Fellows, 1907-1908 (Volume XXIII)*, 125.

197. Sovereign Grand Lodge of the IOOF, *Journal of Proceedings of the Right Worthy Grand Lodge of the United States, and the Sovereign Grand Lodge of the Independent Order of Odd Fellows, 1923-1924 (Volume XXXI)*, 430-431.

198. Sovereign Grand Lodge of the IOOF, *Journal of Proceedings of the One Hundred and Eighty-First Annual Communication of the Sovereign Grand Lodge of the Independent Order of Odd Fellows, 2007 (Volume XCV)*, 152.

199. Sovereign Grand Lodge of the IOOF, *Journal of Proceedings of the One Hundred and Eighty-Second Annual Communication of the Sovereign Grand Lodge of the Independent Order of Odd Fellows, 2008 (Volume XCVI)*, 156.

Chapter 20 - Programs and Projects

1. Sovereign Grand Lodge of the Independent Order of Odd Fellows. *Journal of Proceedings of the One Hundred and Sixty-Sixth Annual Communication of the Sovereign Grand Lodge of the Independent Order of Odd Fellows, 1992* (Winston-Salem: The Sovereign Grand Lodge of the I.O.O.F., 1993), 345.

2. Sovereign Grand Lodge of the Independent Order of Odd Fellows, *Journal of Proceedings of the One Hundred and Eighty-Fifth Annual Communication of the Sovereign Grand Lodge of the Independent Order of Odd Fellows, 2011* (Winston-Salem: The Sovereign Grand Lodge of the I.O.O.F., 2012), 65.

3. Sovereign Grand Lodge of the Independent Order of Odd Fellows, *Journal of Proceedings of the One Hundred and Sixty-Fourth Annual Communication of the Sovereign Grand Lodge of the Independent Order of Odd Fellows, 1990* (Winston-Salem: The Sovereign Grand Lodge of the I.O.O.F., 1991), 241.

4. Sovereign Grand Lodge of the Independent Order of Odd Fellows, *Journal of Proceedings of the One Hundred and Sixty-Sixth Annual Communication of the Sovereign Grand Lodge of the Independent Order of Odd Fellows, 1992* (Winston-Salem: The Sovereign Grand Lodge of the I.O.O.F., 1993), 285.

5. Sovereign Grand Lodge of the Independent Order of Odd Fellows, *Journal of Proceedings of the One Hundred and Fifty-first Annual Communication of the Sovereign Grand Lodge of the Independent Order of Odd Fellows, 1977* (Baltimore: The Sovereign Grand Lodge of the I.O.O.F., 1978), 49.

6. Ibid, 30.

7. Ibid, 50.

8. Sovereign Grand Lodge of the Independent Order of Odd Fellows, *Journal of Proceedings of the One Hundred and Fifty-Sixth Annual Communication of the Sovereign Grand Lodge of the Independent Order of Odd Fellows, 1982* (Winston-Salem: The Sovereign Grand Lodge of the I.O.O.F., 1983), 35.

9. Sovereign Grand Lodge of the Independent Order of Odd Fellows, *Journal of Proceedings of the One Hundred and Thirty-Sixth Annual Communication of the Sovereign Grand Lodge of the Independent Order of Odd Fellows, 1962* (Baltimore: The Sovereign Grand Lodge of the I.O.O.F., 1963), 43.

10. Sovereign Grand Lodge of the Independent Order of Odd Fellows. *Journal of Proceedings of the One Hundred and Forty Annual Communication of the Sovereign Grand*

Lodge of the Independent Order of Odd Fellows, 1966 (Baltimore: The Sovereign Grand Lodge of the I.O.O.F., 1967), 467.

Chapter 21 - Organizational Structure
1. Code of General Laws of the Sovereign Grand Lodge, IOOF (2017).
2. Ibid.
3. Ibid.
4. Ibid.
5. Ibid.
6. Ibid.
7. Ibid.
8. Ibid.
9. Ibid.
10. The Grand Lodge of Europe IOOF, *10 years* (Latvia: United Press Poligrafija Corporation, 2017), 9.
11. Ibid.
12. Ibid.
13. Sovereign Grand Lodge of the Independent Order of Odd Fellows, *Journal of Proceedings of the One Hundred and Eighty-Third Annual Communication of the Sovereign Grand Lodge of the Independent Order of Odd Fellows, 2009* (Volume XCVII), 350.
14. Ibid, 21.
15. Sovereign Grand Lodge of the IOOF, *Journal of Proceedings of the One Hundred and Eighty-Fourth Annual Communication of the Sovereign Grand Lodge of the Independent Order of Odd Fellows, 2010* (Volume XCVIII), 21.
16. Sovereign Grand Lodge of the IOOF, *Journal of Proceedings of the One Hundred and Eighty-Third Annual Communication of the Sovereign Grand Lodge of the Independent Order of Odd Fellows, 2009* (Volume XCVII), 21.
17. Sovereign Grand Lodge of the IOOF, *Journal of Proceedings of the One Hundred and Sixty-Third Annual Communication of the Sovereign Grand Lodge of the Independent Order of Odd Fellows, 1989* (Volume LXXVII), 18.
18. Ibid.
19. Ibid.
20. Ibid.
21. Ibid.
22. Ibid.

Chapter 22 - Degrees, Regalia and Customs
1. Mary Ann Clawson, *Constructing Brotherhood: Class, Gender, and Fraternalism*, 24-25.
2. Sovereign Grand Lodge of the IOOF, *Journal of Proceedings of the One Hundred and Sixty-Eight Annual Communication of the Sovereign Grand Lodge of the Independent Order of Odd Fellows, 1994* (Volume LXXXII), 607.
3. Sovereign Grand Lodge of the IOOF, *Journal of Proceedings of the One Hundred and Forty-Third Annual Communication of the Sovereign Grand Lodge of the Independent Order of Odd Fellows, 1969* (Volume LVII), 533.
4. Clawson, *Constructing Brotherhood: Class, Gender, and Fraternalism*, 24-25.
5. Henry Leonard Stillson, *The Official History of Odd Fellowship* (Massachusetts: Fraternity Publishing Company, 1900), 739.
6. Stillson, *The Official History of Odd Fellowship*, 740.
7. Ibid.
8. *Ancient Ritual of the Order of Patriotic Odd Fellows: Revised and agreed to in the Grand Lodge held at London, England, March 12, 1797.*
9. Ibid, 12.
10. Henry Leonard Stillson, *The Official History of Odd Fellowship*, 745.
11. Ibid, 745.
12. Ibid.
13. Ibid, 746.
14. Ibid.
15. Ibid.
16. Ibid.
17. Stillson, 746-747.
18. Aaron Burt Grosh, *A Manual of Odd Fellowship* (New York: Clark & Maynard, 1882), 1380.
19. Sovereign Grand Lodge of the IOOF, *Journal of Proceedings of the One Hundred and Forty-Third Annual Communication of the Sovereign Grand Lodge of the Independent Order of Odd Fellows, 1969* (Volume LVII), 532.
20. Joseph Powley, *Concise History of Odd Fellowship* (Toronto: The Grand Lodge of Ontario IOOF, 1943), 22.
21. Sovereign Grand Lodge of the IOOF, *Journal of Proceedings of the One Hundred and Sixty-Eight Annual Communication of the Sovereign Grand Lodge of the Independent Order of Odd Fellows, 1994* (Volume LXXXII), 608.
22. Sovereign Grand Lodge of the IOOF, *Journal of Proceedings of the One Hundred and Fifty-Fifth Annual Communication of the Sovereign Grand Lodge of the Independent Order of Odd Fellows, 1981* (Volume LXVIX), 23.
23. Victoria Solt Dennis, *Discovering Friendly and Fraternal Societies* (United Kingdom: Shire Publications, 2008).
24. Joseph Powley, *Concise History of Odd Fellowship*, 22.

Rites of Passage

1. Webster's Dictionary
2. Webster's Dictionary
3. Catherine Bell, *Ritual: Perspectives and Dimensions*, 94.
4. Ibid, 210.
5. Ibid, 98-99.
6. Eliade, 2.
7. John Michael Greer, *The Element Encyclopedia of Secret Societies* (New York: Barnes and Nobles, 2008)
8. Ibid.
9. Ibid.

Chapter 23 - Branches
1. Sovereign Grand Lodge of the IOOF, *Journal of Proceedings of the One Hundred and Seventy-Third Annual Communication of the Sovereign Grand Lodge of the Independent Order of Odd Fellows, 1999 (Volume LXXXVII)*, 490.
2. Ibid.
3. Ibid.
4. Sovereign Grand Lodge of the IOOF, *Journal of Proceedings of the Right Worthy Grand Lodge of the United States, and the Sovereign Grand Lodge of the Independent Order of Odd Fellows, 1921-1922 (Volume XXX)* (Baltimore: The Sovereign Grand Lodge of the I.O.O.F., 1923), 418-424.
5. Powley, *Concise History of Odd Fellowship*, 35.
6. Ibid.
7. Nathan Billstein, *A Brief History of The Encampment Branch of the IOOF* (Baltimore: Nathan Billstein, 1927), 7-8.
8. Sovereign Grand Lodge of the IOOF, *Journal of Proceedings of the One Hundred and Sixty-Ninth Annual Communication of the Sovereign Grand Lodge of the Independent Order of Odd Fellows, 1995 (Volume LXXXIII)*, 305.
9. Ibid.
10. Ibid.
11. Sovereign Grand Lodge of the IOOF, *Concise History of the International Association of Ladies' Auxiliary Patriarchs Militant, IOOF*, 29.
12. Sovereign Grand Lodge of the IOOF, *Journal of Proceedings of the Right Worthy Grand Lodge of the United States, and the Sovereign Grand Lodge of the Independent Order of Odd Fellows, 1921-1922 (Volume XXX)*, 335.
13. Ibid, 543.
14. Sovereign Grand Lodge of the IOOF, *Journal of Proceedings of the Right Worthy Grand Lodge of the United States, and the Sovereign Grand Lodge of the Independent Order of Odd Fellows, 1921-1922 (Volume XXX)*, 337.
15. Sovereign Grand Lodge of the IOOF, *Journal of Proceedings of the Right Worthy Grand Lodge of the United States, and the Sovereign Grand Lodge of the Independent Order of Odd Fellows, 1929-1930 (Volume XXXIV)*, 269.
16. *Ritual of Theta Rho Girls' Club under the Jurisdiction of the Sovereign Grand Lodge of the Independent Order of Odd Fellows* (United States: Sovereign Grand Lodge, I.O.O.F., 1975).
17. *Ritual of The Ancient, Mystic Order of Samaritans of the United States and Canada* (Cleveland: Supreme Sanctorum, 1935).
18. *Ritual of The Ladies of the Orient of the United States and Canada* (Supreme Royal Zuanna, n.d.).

Chapter 24 - Religion, Freemasonry, and Women
1. Sovereign Grand Lodge Independent Order of Odd Fellows, *Ritual of a Lodge of Odd Fellows of The Sovereign Grand Lodge of the Independent Order of Odd Fellows* (North Carolina: Sovereign Grand Lodge, I.O.O.F., 2004), 65.
2. Danial Weinbren, *The Oddfellows 1810-2010: 200 Years of Making Friends and Helping People* (Lancaster: Carnegie Publishing, 2012), 61.
3. Ibid, 62.
4. Ibid, 62.
5. Ibid, 61.
6. Sovereign Grand Lodge of the Independent Order of Odd Fellows, *Journal of Proceedings of the Right Worthy Grand Lodge of the United States, and the Sovereign Grand Lodge of the Independent Order of Odd Fellows, 1893-1894 (Volume XVI)* (Baltimore: The Sovereign Grand Lodge of the I.O.O.F., 1895), 13250.
7. Ibid.
8. Sovereign Grand Lodge of the Independent Order of Odd Fellows, *Journal of Proceedings of the One Hundred and Forty-Eight Annual Communication of the Sovereign Grand Lodge of the Independent Order of Odd Fellows, 1974 (Volume LXII)* (Baltimore: The Sovereign Grand Lodge of the I.O.O.F., 1975), 246.
9. *Ibid.*
10. Sovereign Grand Lodge of the Independent Order of Odd Fellows, *Journal of Proceedings of the One Hundred and Thirty-Ninth Annual Communication of the Sovereign Grand Lodge of the Independent Order of Odd Fellows, 1965 (Volume LIII)*. Baltimore: The Sovereign Grand Lodge of the I.O.O.F., 1966), 240.
11. *Ibid*, 241.
12. Sovereign Grand Lodge of the Independent Order of Odd Fellows, *Journal of Proceedings of the One Hundred and Thirty-Eight Annual Communication of the Sovereign Grand Lodge of the Independent Order of Odd Fellows, 1964 (Volume LII)* (Baltimore: The Sovereign Grand

Lodge of the I.O.O.F., 1965), 64.

13. Sovereign Grand Lodge of the Independent Order of Odd Fellows, *Journal of Proceedings of the One Hundred and Thirty-Ninth Annual Communication of the Sovereign Grand Lodge of the Independent Order of Odd Fellows, 1965 (Volume LIII)* (Baltimore: The Sovereign Grand Lodge of the I.O.O.F., 1966), 239.

14. *Ibid.*

15. *Ibid.*

16. Sovereign Grand Lodge of the Independent Order of Odd Fellows, *Journal of Proceedings of the One Hundred and Sixty-Seventh Annual Communication of the Sovereign Grand Lodge of the Independent Order of Odd Fellows, 1993 (Volume LXXXI).* (Winston-Salem: The Sovereign Grand Lodge of the I.O.O.F., 1994), 51.

17. Sovereign Grand Lodge of the Independent Order of Odd Fellows, *Journal of Proceedings of the One Hundred and Forty-Eight Annual Communication of the Sovereign Grand Lodge of the Independent Order of Odd Fellows, 1974 (Volume LXII)* (Baltimore: The Sovereign Grand Lodge of the I.O.O.F., 1975), 246.

18. Sovereign Grand Lodge Independent Order of Odd Fellows, *Ritual of a Lodge of Odd Fellows of The Sovereign Grand Lodge of the Independent Order of Odd Fellows* (North Carolina: Sovereign Grand Lodge, I.O.O.F., 2004), 56.

19. Ibid, 65.

20. Ibid, 65.

21. Sovereign Grand Lodge of the Independent Order of Odd Fellows, *Journal of Proceedings of the One Hundred and Sixty-Fifth Annual Communication of the Sovereign Grand Lodge of the Independent Order of Odd Fellows, 1991 (Volume LXXIV)* (Winston-Salem: The Sovereign Grand Lodge of the I.O.O.F., 1992), 434.

22. Mary Ann Clawson, Constructing Brotherhood: Class, Gender, and Fraternlism (New Jersey: Princeton University Press, 1989), 15.

23. John Michael Greer, The Element Encyclopedia of Secret Societies (New York: Barnes and Nobles, 2008), 101.

24. Weinbren, *The Oddfellows 1810-2010: 200 Years of Making Friends and Helping People*, 48.

25. Ibid.

26. Clawson, Constructing Brotherhood: Class, Gender, and Fraternlism, 3.

27. Ibid, 40.

28. John Michael Greer, *The Element Encyclopedia of Secret Societies* (New York: Barnes and Nobles, 2008), 135.

29. Clawson, Constructing Brotherhood: Class, Gender, and Fraternlism, 118.

30. Ibid, 118.

31. Weinbren, *The Oddfellows 1810-2010: 200 Years of Making Friends and Helping People*, 50.

32. Manchester Unity Independent Order of Odd Fellows, Lectures used by the Manchester District (Manchester: Mark Wardle, P.G. and C.S., 1824), 3.

33. J. Edward Stallings, Searching for Treasures (North Carolina: The Sovereign Grand Lodge IOOF, n.d.), 8.

34. Weinbren, *The Oddfellows 1810-2010: 200 Years of Making Friends and Helping People*, 51.

35. Ibid, 50.

36. Clawson, Constructing Brotherhood: Class, Gender, and Fraternlism, 112.

37. Greer, *The Element Encyclopedia of Secret Societies*, 193.

38. Sovereign Grand Lodge of the Independent Order of Odd Fellows, *Journal of Proceedings of the One Hundred and Sixty-Ninth Annual Communication of the Sovereign Grand Lodge of the Independent Order of Odd Fellows, 1995 (Volume LXXXIII)* (Winston-Salem: The Sovereign Grand Lodge of the I.O.O.F., 1996), 48.

39. Sovereign Grand Lodge of the Independent Order of Odd Fellows. *Journal of Proceedings of the One Hundred and Seventy-Third Annual Communication of the Sovereign Grand Lodge of the Independent Order of Odd Fellows, 1999 (Volume LXXXVII)* (Winston-Salem: The Sovereign Grand Lodge of the I.O.O.F., 2000), 488.

40. Sovereign Grand Lodge of the Independent Order of Odd Fellows. *Journal of Proceedings of the One Hundred and Seventieth Annual Communication of the Sovereign Grand Lodge of the Independent Order of Odd Fellows, 1996 (Volume LXXXIV)* (Winston-Salem: The Sovereign Grand Lodge of the I.O.O.F., 1997), 373.

41. Sovereign Grand Lodge of the IOOF, *Journal of Proceedings of the One Hundred and Seventy-Third Annual Communication of the Sovereign Grand Lodge of the Independent Order of Odd Fellows, 1999 (Volume LXXXVII)*, 490.

42. Weinbren, *The Oddfellows 1810-2010: 200 Years of Making Friends and Helping People*, 331-332.

43. Sovereign Grand Lodge of the Independent Order of Odd Fellows, *Journal of Proceedings of the One Hundred and Seventy-Sixth Annual Communication of the Sovereign Grand Lodge of the Independent Order of Odd Fellows, 2002 (Volume XC)* (Winston-Salem: The Sovereign Grand Lodge of the I.O.O.F., 2003), *33.*

44. Sovereign Grand Lodge of the Independent Order of Odd Fellows, *Journal of Proceedings of the One Hundred and Seventy-Third Annual Communication of the Sovereign Grand Lodge of the Independent Order of Odd Fellows, 1999 (Volume LXXXVII)* (Winston-Salem: The Sovereign Grand Lodge of the I.O.O.F., 2000), 278.

45. Sovereign Grand Lodge of the Independent Order of Odd Fellows, *Journal of Proceedings of the One Hundred*

and Seventy-Second Annual Communication of the Sovereign Grand Lodge of the Independent Order of Odd Fellows, 1998 (Volume LXXXVI) (Winston-Salem: The Sovereign Grand Lodge of the I.O.O.F., 1999), 277.

46. Sovereign Grand Lodge of the Independent Order of Odd Fellows, *Journal of Proceedings of the One Hundred and Seventy-Third Annual Communication of the Sovereign Grand Lodge of the Independent Order of Odd Fellows, 1999*, 504.

47. Sovereign Grand Lodge of the Independent Order of Odd Fellows, *Journal of Proceedings of the One Hundred and Seventy-Second Annual Communication of the Sovereign Grand Lodge of the Independent Order of Odd Fellows, 1998*, 2.

48. Sovereign Grand Lodge of the Independent Order of Odd Fellows, *Journal of Proceedings of the One Hundred and Seventy-Fifth Annual Communication of the Sovereign Grand Lodge of the Independent Order of Odd Fellows, 2001 (Volume LXXXVIX)* (Winston-Salem: The Sovereign Grand Lodge of the I.O.O.F., 2002), 20.

49. Sovereign Grand Lodge of the Independent Order of Odd Fellows, *Journal of Proceedings of the One Hundred and Seventy-Second Annual Communication of the Sovereign Grand Lodge of the Independent Order of Odd Fellows, 1998*, 2.

50. Sovereign Grand Lodge of the Independent Order of Odd Fellows, *Journal of Proceedings of the One Hundred and Seventy-Fifth Annual Communication of the Sovereign Grand Lodge of the Independent Order of Odd Fellows, 2001 (Volume LXXXVIX)* (Winston-Salem: The Sovereign Grand Lodge of the I.O.O.F., 2002), 20.

51. Sovereign Grand Lodge of the Independent Order of Odd Fellows. *Journal of Proceedings of the One Hundred and Seventy-Fourth Annual Communication of the Sovereign Grand Lodge of the Independent Order of Odd Fellows, 2000 (Volume LXXXVIII)* (Winston-Salem: The Sovereign Grand Lodge of the I.O.O.F., 2001), 20.

52. Sovereign Grand Lodge of the Independent Order of Odd Fellows, *Journal of Proceedings of the One Hundred and Sixty-Ninth Annual Communication of the Sovereign Grand Lodge of the Independent Order of Odd Fellows, 1995 (Volume LXXXIII)* (Winston-Salem: The Sovereign Grand Lodge of the I.O.O.F., 1996), 300-301.

53. Franklin Lacava, "Hopwood woman breaks mold as leader of Odd Fellows", Triblive, July 18, 2015, accessed January 22, 2019, http://triblive.com/news/fayette/8717029-74/fellows-odd-cupp

54. Rachael Pacella, "*Towson business owner is Odd Fellows' first female African-American leader*", Towson Times, June 1, 2016, January 22, 2019, http://www.baltimoresun.com/news/maryland/baltimore-county/towson/ph-tt-darlene-parker-0525-20160526-story.html

Bibliography

I. Published Books

Alexander, Leslie and Rucker, Walter. *Encyclopedia of African American History.* California: ABC-CLIO, 2010.

Andrews, Thomas. *The Jericho Road.* Oklahoma: William Thomas Co, 1937.

Barrett, David. *Secret Societies: An unbiased history of our desire for secret knowledge.* Philadelphia: Running Press, 2007.

Bates, Ralph. *Billy and Dick from Andersonville Prison to the White House.* California: Sentinel Publishing, 1910.

Beharrell, Thomas. *Odd Fellows Monitor and Guide.* Indianapolis: Robert Douglass, 1883.

Beharrell, Thomas. *The Brotherhood: Being a Presentation of Odd Fellowship.* Indiana: Brotherhood Publishing Co., 1875.

Beito, David. *From Mutual Aid to the Welfare State: Fraternal Societies and Social Services, 1890-1967.* Chapel Hill: University of North Carolina Press, 2000.

Bell, Catherine. *Ritual: Perspectives and Dimensions.* New York: Oxford University Press, 1997.

Birch, Una. *Secret Societies: Illuminati, Freemasons and the French Revolution.* Florida: Ibis Press, 2007.

Blainey, Goeffrey. *Odd Fellows: A History of IOOF Australia.* Australia: Allen & Unwin, 1991.

Bowling, Colin Robert. *A New Order of the Ages.* Indiana: iUniverse, 2011.

Brands, H.W. *The Age of Gold: The California Gold Rush and the New American Dream.* New York: Doubleday, 2003.

Brooker, Russell. *The American Civil Rights Movement 1865-1950.* Maryland: Lexington Books, 2017.

Brooks, Charles. *The Official History ad Manual of the Grand United Order of Odd Fellows.* Pennsylvania: Odd Fellows Journal Print, 1903.

Buccula, Nicholas. *The Political Thought of Frederick Douglass: In Pursuit of American Liberty.* New York: New York University Press, 2012.

Carey, Charles. *African-American Political Leaders.* New York: Facts On File, 2004.

Carnes, Mark. *Secret Ritual and Manhood in Victorian America.* New Haven: Yale University, 1989.

Catton, Bruce. *The Civil War.* Boston: Houghton Mifflin Company, 2004.

Charles, Jeffrey. *Service Clubs in American Society.* Chicago: University of Illinois Press, 1993.

Cherny, Robert, Irwin, Mary Ann, and Wilson, Ann Marie. *California Women and Politics: From the Gold Rush to the Great Depression.* Nebraska: University of Nebraska Press, 2011.

Clark, Peter. *British Clubs and Societies 1580-1800: The Origins of an Associational World.* New York: Oxford University Press, 2000.

Clark, Peter. *British Clubs and Societies: 1580-1800.* New York: Oxford University Press, 2002.

Clawson, Mary Ann. *Constructing Brotherhood: Class, Gender, and Fraternalism*. New Jersey: Princeton University Press, 1989.

Compiled by various authors, *A History of the Holy Catholic Inquisition*. Philadelphia: Perkins, Marvin and Co., 1835.

Cooke, L. Hamel. *Democracy and Odd Fellowship*. Canada: L. Hamel Cooke, 1943.

Cordery, Simon. *British Friendly Societies, 1750-1914*. New York: Palgrave Macmillan, 2003.

Coursey, Oscar William. *History and Geography of the Philippine Islands*. South Dakota: Educator School Supply Co., 1903.

Curry, Elvin James. *The Red Blood of Odd Fellowship*. Maryland: Elvin Curry, 1903.

Curthoys, Ann and Lake, Marilyn. *Connected Worlds: History in Transnational Perspective*. Canberra: Australian National University, 2005.

Davis, Robert Scott. *Andersonville Civil War Prison. South Carolina*. South Carolina: The History Press, 2010.

Defoe, Daniel. An *Essay upon Projects*. London: R.R. for Tho. Cockerill, 1697.

Dennis, Victoria Solt. *Discovering Friendly and Fraternal Societies*. United Kingdom: Shire Publications, 2008.

Donaldson, Paschal. *The Odd Fellows Text Book*. Philadelphia: Moss & Brother, 1852.

Donaldson, Paschal. *The Odd Fellows' Pocket Companion*. Ohio: R.W. Carroll & Co, 1881.

Douglas, David Charles. *English Historical Documents*. United Kingdom: Oxford University Press, 1959.

Downs, Jonathan. *The Industrial Revolution: Britain, 1770-1810*. United Kingdom: Shire Publications, 2010.

Dumenil, Lynn. *The Oxford Encyclopedia of American Social History*. United States: Oxford University Press, 2012.

Emery, George and Emery, J. C. Herbert. *A Young Man's Benefit*. London: McGill-Queen's University Press, 1999.

Epstein, Steven. *Wage labor and guilds in Medieval Europe*. North Carolina: University of North Carolina Press, 1991.

Faust, Drew Gilpin. *This Republic of Suffering: Death and the American Civil War*. New York: Alfred A. Knope, 2008.

Ferry, Darren. *Uniting in Measures of Common Good: The Construction of Liberal Identities in Central Canada*. Quebec: McGill Queen's University Press, 2008.

Ford, Henry. *Symbolism of Odd Fellowship*. New Orleans: Cornerstone Book Publishers, 2013.

Gates, Jr., Henry Louis and Higginbotham, Evelyn Brooks. *African American Lives*. New York: Oxford University Press, 2004.

Gilman, Daniel Coit, Peck, Harry Thurston and Colby, Frank Moore. *The New International Encyclopedia*. New York: Dodd, Mead & Company, 1906.

Gist, Noel. *Patterning in Secret Society Ceremonials*. North Carolina: University of North Carolina Press, 1936.

Gosden, Peter Henry John Heather. *The Friendly Societies in England, 1815-1875*. United Kingdom: University of Manchester Press, 1961.

Greer, John Michael. *The Element Encyclopedia of Secret Societies*. New York: Barnes and Nobles, 2006.

Grosh, Aaron Burt. *The Odd Fellow's Manual*. Philadelphia: H.C. Peck & Theo Bliss, 1860.

Grosh, Aaron Burt. *The Odd-Fellows Improved Pocket Manual*. New York: Clark & Maynard, 1873.

Grosh, Aaron Burt. *A Manual of Odd Fellowship. New York:* New York: Clark & Maynard, 1882.

Gutmann, Amy. *Democracy and the Welfare State*. New Jersey: Princeton University Press, 1988.

Guyatt, Nicholas. *Bind Us Apart: How Enlightened Americans Invented Racial Segregation*. United Kingdom: Oxford University Press, 2016.

Howard, Michael. *Secret Societies: Their Influence and Power from Antiquity to Present Day*. Vermont: Destiny Books, 2008.

Katznelson, Ira and Shefter, Martin. *Shaped by War and Trade: International Influences on American Political Development*. New Jersey: Princeton University Press, 2002.

Kaufman, Jason. *For the Common Good? American Civic Life and the Golden Age of Fraternity*. New York: Oxford University Press, 2002.

Kelly, Cindy. *Outdoor Culture in Baltimore: A Historical Guide to Public Art in the Monumental City*. Maryland: The John Hopkins University Press, 2011.

King, J.B. and the Grand Lodge of Ontario, IOOF. *Odd Fellowship*. Toronto: Independent Odd Fellow Print, 1907.

Loewen, James. *Sundown Towns: A hidden Dimension of American Racism*. New York: The New Press, 2005.

Long, Lessel. *Twelve Months in Andersonville*. Indiana: Thad and Mark Butler Publications, 1886.

Macoy, Robert. *General History, Cyclopedia, and Dictionary of Freemasonry*. New York, Masonic Publishing Company, 1870.

McBride, Harriet Wain. *Fraternal Regalia in America, 1865 to 1918*. Ohio: Ohio State University, 2000.

Melling, John Kennedy. *Discovering London's Guilds and Liveries*. United Kingdom: Shire Publications, 2002.

Mjagkij, Nina. *Organizing Black America: An Encyclopedia of African American Associations*. New York: Garland Publishing, 2001.

Moffrey, Robert. *The Rise and Progress of the Manchester Unity of the Independent Order of Oddfellows*. United Kingdom: Grand Master & Board of Directors of the Order, 1904.

Moffrey, Robert. *A Century of Odd Fellowship*. United Kingdom: Manchester Unity Independent Order of Oddfellows, 1910.

Parre, W.J. *Quatuor Coronatum: Being the Transactions of the Quatuor Coronati Lodge No. 2076, London, Volume 3* (London: W. J. Parre, 1840).

P.D. A *candid enquiry into the principles and practices of the most ancient and honourable society of Bucks*. London: C. Kiernan, 1770.

Porter, Roy. *London: A Social History*. United Kingdom: Penguin, 2000.

Powell, Benson. *The Triple Links*. Kansas: Ed G. Moore & Son, 1900.

Powley, Joseph. *Concise History of Odd Fellowship*. Toronto: The Grand Lodge of Ontario IOOF, 1943.

Powley, Joseph. *Concise History of Odd Fellowship (Revised edition)*. Toronto: Macoomb Publishing, 1952.

Reedy, Tom and Thurman, Nita. *Denton Lodge No.82, I.O.O.F.: A History 1859-2009*. Maine: Acme Bookbinding, 2009.

Rebold, Emmanuel, and Brennan, J. Fletcher. *A general History of Free-Masonry in Europe: Based upon the Ancient Documents Relating to and the Monuments Erected by this Fraternity from its foundation in the year 715 BC to present time*. Ohio: Cincinnati American Masonic publishing association, 1868.

Richter, William. *Historical Dictionary of the Civil War and Reconstruction*. Toronto: The Scarecrow Press, 2012

Ridgely, James Lot. *History of American Odd Fellowship: The First Decade*. Baltimore: James Lot Ridgely, 1878.

Ridley, Jasper. *The Freemasons: A history of the world's most powerful secret society*. New York: Arcade Publishing, 2011.

Rosenberg, Dave. *The Future of Odd Fellowship: Evolution and Change*. California: Dave Rosenberg, 2015.

Ross, Theodore. *Odd Fellowship: Its History and Manual*. New York: M.W. Hazen Co., 1888.

Salamon, Lester. *The State of Nonprofit America*. District of Columbia: Bookings Institution Press, 2002.

Seibert, Peter Swift. *Fraternally Yours: Identify Fraternal Groups and Their Emblems*. Pennsylvania: Schiffer Publishing, 2012.

Sellars, Peter. *The History of the Independent Order of Odd Fellows in the City of San Francisco*. California: Peter Sellars, 2007.

Sewell, William. *Work and Revolution in France: The Language of Labor from the Old Regime to 1848*. New York: Cambridge University Press, 1980.

Shadd, Adrienne. *The Journey from Tollgate toe Parkway: African Canadians in Hamilton*. Toronto: National Heritage Books, 2010.

Smith, Donald and Roberts, Wayne. The *Three Link fraternity*. California: Linden Publications, 1993.

Skopol, Theda, Liazos, Ariane and Ganz, Marshal. *What a Mighty Power We Can be: African American Fraternal Groups and the struggle for Racial Equality*. New Jersey: Princeton University Press, 2006.

Smith, Joshua Toulmin. *English Gilds*. London: N. Trubner & Co., London, 1870.

Spry, James. *The History of Odd Fellowship: Its Origin, Tradition and Objectives*. London: J.R.H. Spry, 1866.

Stallings, J. Edward. *Searching for Treasures*. North Carolina: Sovereign Grand Lodge, IOOF, n.d.

Starkey, Armstrong. *War in the Age of Enlightenment, 1700-1789*. Connecticut: Praeger Publishers, 2003.

Stauffer, John. *The Works of James McCune Smith: Black Intellectual and Abolitionist*. New York: Oxford University Press, 2006.

Stewart, Robert. *The Illustrated Encyclopedia of Historical Facts from the Dawn of Christian Era to the Present Day*. United States: Barnes and Noble, 2002.

Streeter, Michael. *Behind Closed Doors*. United Kingdom: New Holland Publishers, 2008.

Stillson, Henry Leonard. *The Official History of Odd Fellowship*. Massachusetts: Fraternity Publishing Company, 1900.

Stillson, Henry Leonard. *The Official History of Odd Fellowship*. Massachusetts: Fraternity Publishing Company, 1908.

Sovereign Grand Lodge of the Independent Order of Odd Fellows. *Members Handbook: Independent Order of Odd Fellows*. Winston-Salem: Sovereign Grand Lodge, 2013.

Sullivan, Robert. *Royal Arch of Enoch: The Impact of Masonic Rituals, Philosophy and Symbolism*. Rocket Science Productions, 2011.

Tinkham, George. *The Half Century of California Odd Fellowship*. Stockton, CA: Record Publishing Co., 1906.

Unknown Author, *An Illustrated History of San Joaquin County, California*. Chicago: The Lewis Publishing Company, 1890.

Wallace, W.W. *The Odd-Fellows' Keepsake: A Concise History of Odd-Fellowship in the United States*. New York: Office of the Mirror of the Times, 1850.

Weber, John. *An Illustrated Guide of the Lost Symbol*. New York: Sensei Publications, 2009.

Weinbren, Daniel. *The Oddfellows 1810-2010: 200 Years of Making Friends and Helping People*. Lancaster: Carnegie Publishing, 2012.

Wokler, Robert. *Rousseau, the Age of Enlightenment, and Their Legacies*. New Jersey: Princeton University Press, 2012.

Wolfe, Joseph. *Album of Odd Fellows Home*. Minnesota: J.F. Wolf Company, 1927.

Wright, Mike. *What they didn't teach you about the civil war*. New York: The Random House Publishing Group, 1996.

II. Journal of Proceedings

Sovereign Grand Lodge of the Independent Order of Odd Fellows. *Journal of Proceedings of the Right Worthy Grand Lodge of the United States, and the Sovereign Grand Lodge of the Independent Order of Odd Fellows, from its Formation in February, 1821-1846 (Volume I)*. Baltimore: The Sovereign Grand Lodge of the I.O.O.F., 1893.

Sovereign Grand Lodge of the Independent Order of Odd Fellows. *Journal of Proceedings of the Right Worthy Grand Lodge of the United States, and the Sovereign Grand Lodge of the Independent Order of Odd Fellows, from its Formation in February, 1847-1852 (Volume II)*. Baltimore: The Sovereign Grand Lodge of the I.O.O.F., 1888.

Sovereign Grand Lodge of the Independent Order of Odd Fellows. *Journal of Proceedings of the Right Worthy Grand Lodge of the United States, and the Sovereign Grand Lodge of the Independent Order of Odd Fellows, from its Formation in February, 1853-1857 (Volume III)*. Baltimore: The Sovereign Grand Lodge of the I.O.O.F., 1884.

Sovereign Grand Lodge of the Independent Order of Odd Fellows. *Journal of Proceedings of the Right Worthy Grand Lodge of the United States, and the Sovereign Grand Lodge of the Independent Order of Odd Fellows, from its Formation in February, 1858-1862 (Volume IV)*. Baltimore: The Sovereign Grand Lodge of the I.O.O.F., 1884.

Sovereign Grand Lodge of the Independent Order of Odd Fellows. *Journal of Proceedings of the Right Worthy Grand Lodge of the United States, and the Sovereign Grand Lodge of the Independent Order of Odd Fellows, from its Formation in February, 1863-1867 (Volume V)*. Baltimore: The Sovereign Grand Lodge of the I.O.O.F., 1876.

Sovereign Grand Lodge of the Independent Order of Odd Fellows. *Journal of Proceedings of the Right Worthy Grand Lodge of the United States, and the Sovereign Grand Lodge of the Independent Order of Odd Fellows, from its Formation in February, 1868-1870 (Volume VI)*. Baltimore: The Sovereign Grand Lodge of the I.O.O.F., 1880.

Sovereign Grand Lodge of the Independent Order of Odd Fellows. *Journal of Proceedings of the Right Worthy Grand Lodge of the United States, and the Sovereign Grand Lodge of the Independent Order of Odd Fellows, from its Formation in February, 1871-1873 (Volume VII)*. Baltimore: The Sovereign Grand Lodge of the I.O.O.F., 1893.

Sovereign Grand Lodge of the Independent Order of Odd Fellows. *Journal of Proceedings of the Right Worthy Grand Lodge of the United States, and the Sovereign Grand Lodge of the Independent Order of Odd Fellows, from its Formation in February, 1874-1875 (Volume VIII)*. Baltimore: The Sovereign Grand Lodge of the I.O.O.F., 1876.

Sovereign Grand Lodge of the Independent Order of Odd Fellows. *Journal of Proceedings of the Right Worthy Grand Lodge of the United States, and the Sovereign Grand Lodge of the Independent Order of Odd Fellows, from its Formation in February, 1876-1878 (Volume IX)*. Baltimore: The Sovereign Grand Lodge of the I.O.O.F., 1884.

Sovereign Grand Lodge of the Independent Order of Odd Fellows. *Journal of Proceedings of the Right Worthy Grand Lodge of the United States, and the Sovereign Grand Lodge of the Independent Order of Odd Fellows, from its Formation in February, 1879-1881 (Volume X)*. Baltimore: The Sovereign Grand Lodge of the I.O.O.F., 1887.

Sovereign Grand Lodge of the Independent Order of Odd Fellows. *Journal of Proceedings of the Right Worthy Grand Lodge of the United States, and the Sovereign Grand Lodge of the Independent Order of Odd Fellows, 1882-1884 (Volume XI)*. Baltimore: The Sovereign Grand Lodge of the I.O.O.F., 1884.

Sovereign Grand Lodge of the Independent Order of Odd Fellows. *Journal of Proceedings of the Right Worthy Grand Lodge of the United States, and the Sovereign Grand Lodge of the Independent Order of Odd Fellows, 1885-1886 (Volume XII)*. Columbus, Ohio: The Sovereign Grand Lodge of the I.O.O.F., 1888.

Sovereign Grand Lodge of the Independent Order of Odd Fellows. *Journal of Proceedings of the Right Worthy Grand Lodge of the United States, and the Sovereign Grand Lodge of the Independent Order of Odd Fellows, 1887-1888 (Volume XIII)*. Columbus, Ohio: The Sovereign Grand Lodge of the I.O.O.F., 1889.

Sovereign Grand Lodge of the Independent Order of Odd Fellows. *Journal of Proceedings of the Right Worthy Grand Lodge of the United States, and the Sovereign Grand Lodge of the Independent Order of Odd Fellows, 1889-1890 (Volume XIV)*. Columbus, Ohio: The Sovereign Grand Lodge of the I.O.O.F., 1891.

Sovereign Grand Lodge of the Independent Order of Odd Fellows. *Journal of Proceedings of the Right Worthy Grand Lodge of the United States, and the Sovereign Grand Lodge of the Independent Order of Odd Fellows, 1891-1892 (Volume XV)*. Columbus, Ohio: The Sovereign Grand Lodge of the I.O.O.F., 1893.

Sovereign Grand Lodge of the Independent Order of Odd Fellows. *Journal of Proceedings of the Right Worthy Grand Lodge of the United States, and the Sovereign Grand Lodge of the Independent Order of Odd Fellows, 1893-1894 (Volume XVI)*. Baltimore: The Sovereign Grand Lodge of the I.O.O.F., 1895.

Sovereign Grand Lodge of the Independent Order of Odd Fellows. *Journal of Proceedings of the Right Worthy Grand Lodge of the United States, and the Sovereign Grand Lodge of the Independent Order of Odd Fellows, 1895-1896 (Volume XVII)*. Baltimore: The Sovereign Grand Lodge of the I.O.O.F., 1898.

Sovereign Grand Lodge of the Independent Order of Odd Fellows. *Journal of Proceedings of the Right Worthy Grand Lodge of the United States, and the Sovereign Grand Lodge of the Independent Order of Odd Fellows, 1897-1898 (Volume XVIII)*. Baltimore: The Sovereign Grand Lodge of the I.O.O.F., 1899.

Sovereign Grand Lodge of the Independent Order of Odd Fellows. *Journal of Proceedings of the Right Worthy Grand Lodge of the United States, and the Sovereign Grand Lodge of the Independent Order of Odd Fellows, 1899-1900 (Volume XVIX)*. Baltimore: The Sovereign Grand Lodge of the I.O.O.F., 1901.

Sovereign Grand Lodge of the Independent Order of Odd Fellows. *Journal of Proceedings of the Right Worthy Grand Lodge of the United States, and the Sovereign Grand Lodge of the Independent Order of Odd Fellows, 1901-1902 (Volume XX)*. Baltimore: The Sovereign Grand Lodge of the I.O.O.F., 1903.

Sovereign Grand Lodge of the Independent Order of Odd Fellows. *Journal of Proceedings of the Right Worthy Grand Lodge of the United States, and the Sovereign Grand Lodge of the Independent Order of Odd Fellows, 1903-1904 (Volume XXI)*. Baltimore: The Sovereign Grand Lodge of the I.O.O.F., 1905.

Sovereign Grand Lodge of the Independent Order of Odd Fellows. *Journal of Proceedings of the Right Worthy Grand Lodge of the United States, and the Sovereign Grand Lodge of the Independent Order of Odd Fellows, 1905-1906 (Volume XXII)*. Baltimore: The Sovereign Grand Lodge of the I.O.O.F., 1907.

Sovereign Grand Lodge of the Independent Order of Odd Fellows. *Journal of Proceedings of the Right Worthy Grand Lodge of the United States, and the Sovereign Grand Lodge of the Independent Order of Odd Fellows, 1907-1908 (Volume XXIII)*. Baltimore: The Sovereign Grand Lodge of the I.O.O.F., 1909.

Sovereign Grand Lodge of the Independent Order of Odd Fellows. *Journal of Proceedings of the Right Worthy Grand Lodge of the United States, and the Sovereign Grand Lodge of the Independent Order of Odd Fellows, 1909-1910 (Volume XXIV)*. Baltimore: The Sovereign Grand Lodge of the I.O.O.F., 1911.

Sovereign Grand Lodge of the Independent Order of Odd Fellows. *Journal of Proceedings of the Right Worthy Grand Lodge of the United States, and the Sovereign Grand Lodge of the Independent Order of Odd Fellows, 1911-1912(Volume XXV)*. Baltimore: The Sovereign Grand Lodge of the I.O.O.F., 1913.

Sovereign Grand Lodge of the Independent Order of Odd Fellows. *Journal of Proceedings of the Right Worthy Grand Lodge of the United States, and the Sovereign Grand Lodge of the Independent Order of Odd Fellows, 1913-1914 (Volume XXVI)*. Baltimore: The Sovereign Grand Lodge of the I.O.O.F., 1915.

Sovereign Grand Lodge of the Independent Order of Odd Fellows. *Journal of Proceedings of the Right Worthy Grand Lodge of the United States, and the Sovereign Grand Lodge of the Independent Order of Odd Fellows, 1915-1916 (Volume XXVII)*. Baltimore: The Sovereign Grand Lodge of the I.O.O.F., 1917.

Sovereign Grand Lodge of the Independent Order of Odd Fellows. *Journal of Proceedings of the Right Worthy Grand Lodge of the United States, and the Sovereign Grand Lodge of the Independent Order of Odd Fellows, 1917-1918 (Volume XXVIII)*. Baltimore: The Sovereign Grand Lodge of the I.O.O.F., 1919.

Sovereign Grand Lodge of the Independent Order of Odd Fellows. *Journal of Proceedings of the Right Worthy Grand Lodge of the United States, and the Sovereign Grand Lodge of the Independent Order of Odd Fellows, 1919-1920 (Volume XXVIX)*. Baltimore: The Sovereign Grand Lodge of the I.O.O.F., 1921.

Sovereign Grand Lodge of the Independent Order of Odd Fellows. *Journal of Proceedings of the Right Worthy Grand Lodge of the United States, and the Sovereign Grand Lodge of the Independent Order of Odd Fellows, 1921-1922 (Volume XXX)*. Baltimore: The Sovereign Grand Lodge of the I.O.O.F., 1923.

Sovereign Grand Lodge of the Independent Order of Odd Fellows. *Journal of Proceedings of the Right Worthy Grand Lodge of the United States, and the Sovereign Grand Lodge of the Independent Order of Odd Fellows, 1923-1924 (Volume XXXI)*. Baltimore: The Sovereign Grand Lodge of the I.O.O.F., 1925.

Sovereign Grand Lodge of the Independent Order of Odd Fellows. *Journal of Proceedings of the Right Worthy Grand Lodge of the United States, and the Sovereign Grand Lodge of the Independent Order of Odd Fellows, 1925-1926 (Volume XXXII)*. Baltimore: The Sovereign Grand Lodge of the I.O.O.F., 1927.

Sovereign Grand Lodge of the Independent Order of Odd Fellows. *Journal of Proceedings of the Right Worthy Grand Lodge of the United States, and the Sovereign Grand Lodge of the Independent Order of Odd Fellows, 1927-1928 (Volume XXXIII)*. Baltimore: The Sovereign Grand Lodge of the I.O.O.F., 1929.

Sovereign Grand Lodge of the Independent Order of Odd Fellows. *Journal of Proceedings of the Right Worthy Grand Lodge of the United States, and the Sovereign Grand Lodge of the Independent Order of Odd Fellows, 1929-1930 (Volume XXXIV)*. Baltimore: The Sovereign Grand Lodge of the I.O.O.F., 1931.

Sovereign Grand Lodge of the Independent Order of Odd Fellows. *Journal of Proceedings of the Right Worthy Grand Lodge of the United States, and the Sovereign Grand Lodge of the Independent Order of Odd Fellows, 1931-1932 (Volume XXXV)*. Baltimore: The Sovereign Grand Lodge of the I.O.O.F., 1933.

Sovereign Grand Lodge of the Independent Order of Odd Fellows. *Journal of Proceedings of the Right Worthy Grand Lodge of the United States, and the Sovereign Grand Lodge of the Independent Order of Odd Fellows, 1933-1934 (Volume XXXVI)*. Baltimore: The Sovereign Grand Lodge of the I.O.O.F., 1935.

Sovereign Grand Lodge of the Independent Order of Odd Fellows. *Journal of Proceedings of the Right Worthy Grand Lodge of the United States, and the Sovereign Grand Lodge of the Independent Order of Odd Fellows, 1935-1936 (Volume XXXVII)*. Baltimore: The Sovereign Grand Lodge of the I.O.O.F., 1937.

Sovereign Grand Lodge of the Independent Order of Odd Fellows. *Journal of Proceedings of the Right Worthy Grand Lodge of the United States, and the Sovereign Grand Lodge of the Independent Order of Odd Fellows, 1937-1938 (Volume XXXVIII)*. Baltimore: The Sovereign Grand Lodge of the I.O.O.F., 1939.

Sovereign Grand Lodge of the Independent Order of Odd Fellows. *Journal of Proceedings of the Right Worthy Grand Lodge of the United States, and the Sovereign Grand Lodge of the Independent Order of Odd Fellows, 1939-1940 (Volume XXXIX)*. Baltimore: The Sovereign Grand Lodge of the I.O.O.F., 1941.

Sovereign Grand Lodge of the Independent Order of Odd Fellows. *Journal of Proceedings of the Right Worthy Grand Lodge of the United States, and the Sovereign Grand Lodge of the Independent Order of Odd Fellows, 1941-1944 (Volume XL)*. Baltimore: The Sovereign Grand Lodge of the I.O.O.F., 1945.

Sovereign Grand Lodge of the Independent Order of Odd Fellows. *Journal of Proceedings of the Right Worthy Grand Lodge of the United States, and the Sovereign Grand Lodge of the Independent Order of Odd Fellows, 1945-1948 (Volume XLI)*. Baltimore: The Sovereign Grand Lodge of the I.O.O.F., 1946.

Sovereign Grand Lodge of the Independent Order of Odd Fellows. *Journal of Proceedings of the Right Worthy Grand Lodge of the United States, and the Sovereign Grand Lodge of the Independent Order of Odd Fellows, 1949-1950 (Volume XLII)*. Baltimore: The Sovereign Grand Lodge of the I.O.O.F., 1951.

Sovereign Grand Lodge of the Independent Order of Odd Fellows. *Journal of Proceedings of the Right Worthy Grand Lodge of the United States, and the Sovereign Grand Lodge of the Independent Order of Odd Fellows, 1951-1952 (Volume XLIII)*. Baltimore: The Sovereign Grand Lodge of the I.O.O.F., 1953.

Sovereign Grand Lodge of the Independent Order of Odd Fellows. *Journal of Proceedings of the Right Worthy Grand Lodge of the United States, and the Sovereign Grand Lodge of the Independent Order of Odd Fellows, 1953-1954 (Volume XLIV)*. Baltimore: The Sovereign Grand Lodge of the I.O.O.F., 1955.

Sovereign Grand Lodge of the Independent Order of Odd Fellows. *Journal of Proceedings of the Right Worthy Grand Lodge of the United States, and the Sovereign Grand Lodge of the Independent Order of Odd Fellows, 1955-1956 (Volume XLV)*. Baltimore: The Sovereign Grand Lodge of the I.O.O.F., 1957.

Sovereign Grand Lodge of the Independent Order of Odd Fellows. *Journal of Proceedings of the Right Worthy Grand Lodge of the United States, and the Sovereign Grand Lodge of the Independent Order of Odd Fellows, 1957-1958 (Volume XLVI)*. Baltimore: The Sovereign Grand Lodge of the I.O.O.F., 1959.

Sovereign Grand Lodge of the Independent Order of Odd Fellows. *Journal of Proceedings of the One Hundred and Thirty-Third Annual Communication of the Sovereign Grand Lodge of the Independent Order of Odd Fellows, 1959 (Volume XLVII)*. Baltimore: The Sovereign Grand Lodge of the I.O.O.F., 1960.

Sovereign Grand Lodge of the Independent Order of Odd Fellows. *Journal of Proceedings of the One Hundred and Thirty-Fourth Annual Communication of the Sovereign Grand Lodge of the Independent Order of Odd Fellows, 1960 (Volume XLVIII)*. Baltimore: The Sovereign Grand Lodge of the I.O.O.F., 1961.

Sovereign Grand Lodge of the Independent Order of Odd Fellows. *Journal of Proceedings of the One Hundred and Thirty-Fifth Annual Communication of the Sovereign Grand Lodge of the Independent Order of Odd Fellows, 1961 (Volume XLVIX)*. Baltimore: The Sovereign Grand Lodge of the I.O.O.F., 1962.

Sovereign Grand Lodge of the Independent Order of Odd Fellows. *Journal of Proceedings of the One Hundred and Thirty-Sixth Annual Communication of the Sovereign Grand Lodge of the Independent Order of Odd Fellows, 1962 (Volume XLVX)*. Baltimore: The Sovereign Grand Lodge of the I.O.O.F., 1963.

Sovereign Grand Lodge of the Independent Order of Odd Fellows. *Journal of Proceedings of the One Hundred and Thirty-Seventh Annual Communication of the Sovereign Grand Lodge of the Independent Order of Odd Fellows, 1963 (Volume LI)*. Baltimore: The Sovereign Grand Lodge of the I.O.O.F., 1964.

Sovereign Grand Lodge of the Independent Order of Odd Fellows. *Journal of Proceedings of the One Hundred and Thirty-Eight Annual Communication of the Sovereign Grand Lodge of the Independent Order of Odd Fellows, 1964 (Volume LII)*. Baltimore: The Sovereign Grand Lodge of the I.O.O.F., 1965.

Sovereign Grand Lodge of the Independent Order of Odd Fellows. *Journal of Proceedings of the One Hundred and Thirty-Ninth Annual Communication of the Sovereign Grand Lodge of the Independent Order of Odd Fellows, 1965 (Volume LIII)*. Baltimore: The Sovereign Grand Lodge of the I.O.O.F., 1966.

Sovereign Grand Lodge of the Independent Order of Odd Fellows. *Journal of Proceedings of the One Hundred and Forty Annual Communication of the Sovereign Grand Lodge of the Independent Order of Odd Fellows, 1966 (Volume LIV)*. Baltimore: The Sovereign Grand Lodge of the I.O.O.F., 1967.

Sovereign Grand Lodge of the Independent Order of Odd Fellows. *Journal of Proceedings of the One Hundred and Forty-First Annual Communication of the Sovereign Grand Lodge of the Independent Order of Odd Fellows, 1967 (Volume LV)*. Baltimore: The Sovereign Grand Lodge of the I.O.O.F., 1968.

Sovereign Grand Lodge of the Independent Order of Odd Fellows. *Journal of Proceedings of the One Hundred and Thirty-Second Annual Communication of the Sovereign Grand Lodge of the Independent Order of Odd Fellows, 1968 (Volume LVI)*. Baltimore: The Sovereign Grand Lodge of the I.O.O.F., 1969.

Sovereign Grand Lodge of the Independent Order of Odd Fellows. *Journal of Proceedings of the One Hundred and Forty-Third Annual Communication of the Sovereign Grand Lodge of the Independent Order of Odd Fellows, 1969 (Volume LVII)*. Baltimore: The Sovereign Grand Lodge of the I.O.O.F., 1970.

Sovereign Grand Lodge of the Independent Order of Odd Fellows. *Journal of Proceedings of the One Hundred and Forty-Fourth Annual Communication of the Sovereign Grand Lodge of the Independent Order of Odd Fellows, 1970 (Volume LVIII)*. Baltimore: The Sovereign Grand Lodge of the I.O.O.F., 1971.

Sovereign Grand Lodge of the Independent Order of Odd Fellows. *Journal of Proceedings of the One Hundred and Forty-Fifth Annual Communication of the Sovereign Grand Lodge of the Independent Order of Odd Fellows, 1971 (Volume LVIX)*. Baltimore: The Sovereign Grand Lodge of the I.O.O.F., 1972.

Sovereign Grand Lodge of the Independent Order of Odd Fellows. *Journal of Proceedings of the One Hundred and Forty-Sixth Annual Communication of the Sovereign Grand Lodge of the Independent Order of Odd Fellows, 1972 (Volume LX)*. Baltimore: The Sovereign Grand Lodge of the I.O.O.F., 1973.

Sovereign Grand Lodge of the Independent Order of Odd Fellows. *Journal of Proceedings of the One Hundred and Forty-Seventh Annual Communication of the Sovereign Grand Lodge of the Independent Order of Odd Fellows, 1973 (Volume LXI)*. Baltimore: The Sovereign Grand Lodge of the I.O.O.F., 1974.

Sovereign Grand Lodge of the Independent Order of Odd Fellows. *Journal of Proceedings of the One Hundred and Forty-Eight Annual Communication of the Sovereign Grand Lodge of the Independent Order of Odd Fellows, 1974 (Volume LXII)*. Baltimore: The Sovereign Grand Lodge of the I.O.O.F., 1975.

Sovereign Grand Lodge of the Independent Order of Odd Fellows. *Journal of Proceedings of the One Hundred and Forty-Ninth Annual Communication of the Sovereign Grand Lodge of the Independent Order of Odd Fellows, 1975 (Volume LXIII)*. Baltimore: The Sovereign Grand Lodge of the I.O.O.F., 1976.

Sovereign Grand Lodge of the Independent Order of Odd Fellows. *Journal of Proceedings of the One Hundred and Fiftieth Annual Communication of the Sovereign Grand Lodge of the Independent Order of Odd Fellows, 1976 (Volume LXIV)*. Baltimore: The Sovereign Grand Lodge of the I.O.O.F., 1977.

Sovereign Grand Lodge of the Independent Order of Odd Fellows. *Journal of Proceedings of the One Hundred and Fifty-first Annual Communication of the Sovereign Grand Lodge of the Independent Order of Odd Fellows, 1977 (Volume LXV)*. Baltimore: The Sovereign Grand Lodge of the I.O.O.F., 1978.

Sovereign Grand Lodge of the Independent Order of Odd Fellows. *Journal of Proceedings of the One Hundred and Fifty-second Annual Communication of the Sovereign Grand Lodge of the Independent Order of Odd Fellows, 1978 (Volume LXVI)*. Baltimore: The Sovereign Grand Lodge of the I.O.O.F., 1979.

Sovereign Grand Lodge of the Independent Order of Odd Fellows. *Journal of Proceedings of the One Hundred and Fifty-Third Annual Communication of the Sovereign Grand Lodge of the Independent Order of Odd Fellows, 1979 (Volume LXVII)*. Baltimore: The Sovereign Grand Lodge of the I.O.O.F., 1980.

Sovereign Grand Lodge of the Independent Order of Odd Fellows. *Journal of Proceedings of the One Hundred and Fifty-Fourth Annual Communication of the Sovereign Grand Lodge of the Independent Order of Odd Fellows, 1980 (Volume LXVIII)*. Baltimore: The Sovereign Grand Lodge of the I.O.O.F., 1981.

Sovereign Grand Lodge of the Independent Order of Odd Fellows. *Journal of Proceedings of the One Hundred and Fifty-Fifth Annual Communication of the Sovereign Grand Lodge of the Independent Order of Odd Fellows, 1981 (Volume LXVIX)*. Winston-Salem: The Sovereign Grand Lodge of the I.O.O.F., 1982.

Sovereign Grand Lodge of the Independent Order of Odd Fellows. *Journal of Proceedings of the One Hundred and Fifty-Sixth Annual Communication of the Sovereign Grand Lodge of the Independent Order of Odd Fellows, 1982 (Volume LXX)*. Winston-Salem: The Sovereign Grand Lodge of the I.O.O.F., 1983.

Sovereign Grand Lodge of the Independent Order of Odd Fellows. *Journal of Proceedings of the One Hundred and Fifty-Seventh Annual Communication of the Sovereign Grand Lodge of the Independent Order of Odd Fellows, 1983 (Volume LXXI)*. Winston-Salem: The Sovereign Grand Lodge of the I.O.O.F., 1984.

Sovereign Grand Lodge of the Independent Order of Odd Fellows. *Journal of Proceedings of the One Hundred and Fifty-Eighth Annual Communication of the Sovereign Grand Lodge of the Independent Order of Odd Fellows, 1984 (Volume LXXII)*. Winston-Salem: The Sovereign Grand Lodge of the I.O.O.F., 1985.

Sovereign Grand Lodge of the Independent Order of Odd Fellows. *Journal of Proceedings of the One Hundred and Fifty-Ninth Annual Communication of the Sovereign Grand Lodge of the Independent Order of Odd Fellows, 1985 (Volume LXXIII)*. Winston-Salem: The Sovereign Grand Lodge of the I.O.O.F., 1986.

Sovereign Grand Lodge of the Independent Order of Odd Fellows. *Journal of Proceedings of the One Hundred and Sixtieth Annual Communication of the Sovereign Grand Lodge of the Independent Order of Odd Fellows, 1986 (Volume LXXIV)*. Winston-Salem: The Sovereign Grand Lodge of the I.O.O.F., 1987.

Sovereign Grand Lodge of the Independent Order of Odd Fellows. *Journal of Proceedings of the One Hundred and Sixty-First Annual Communication of the Sovereign Grand Lodge of the Independent Order of Odd Fellows, 1987 (Volume LXXV)*. Winston-Salem: The Sovereign Grand Lodge of the I.O.O.F., 1988.

Sovereign Grand Lodge of the Independent Order of Odd Fellows. *Journal of Proceedings of the One Hundred and Sixty-Second Annual Communication of the Sovereign Grand Lodge of the Independent Order of Odd Fellows, 1988 (Volume LXXVI)*. Winston-Salem: The Sovereign Grand Lodge of the I.O.O.F., 1989.

Sovereign Grand Lodge of the Independent Order of Odd Fellows. *Journal of Proceedings of the One Hundred and Sixty-Third Annual Communication of the Sovereign Grand Lodge of the Independent Order of Odd Fellows, 1989 (Volume LXXVII)*. Winston-Salem: The Sovereign Grand Lodge of the I.O.O.F., 1990.

Sovereign Grand Lodge of the Independent Order of Odd Fellows. *Journal of Proceedings of the One Hundred and Sixty-Fourth Annual Communication of the Sovereign Grand Lodge of the Independent Order of Odd Fellows, 1990 (Volume LXXVIII)*. Winston-Salem: The Sovereign Grand Lodge of the I.O.O.F., 1991.

Sovereign Grand Lodge of the Independent Order of Odd Fellows. *Journal of Proceedings of the One Hundred and Sixty-Fifth Annual Communication of the Sovereign Grand Lodge of the Independent Order of Odd Fellows, 1991 (Volume LXXVIV)*. Winston-Salem: The Sovereign Grand Lodge of the I.O.O.F., 1992.

Sovereign Grand Lodge of the Independent Order of Odd Fellows. *Journal of Proceedings of the One Hundred and Sixty-Sixth Annual Communication of the Sovereign Grand Lodge of the Independent Order of Odd Fellows, 1992 (Volume LXXX)*. Winston-Salem: The Sovereign Grand Lodge of the I.O.O.F., 1993.

Sovereign Grand Lodge of the Independent Order of Odd Fellows. *Journal of Proceedings of the One Hundred and Sixty-Seventh Annual Communication of the Sovereign Grand Lodge of the Independent Order of Odd Fellows, 1993 (Volume LXXXI)*. Winston-Salem: The Sovereign Grand Lodge of the I.O.O.F., 1994.

Sovereign Grand Lodge of the Independent Order of Odd Fellows. *Journal of Proceedings of the One Hundred and Sixty-Eighth Annual Communication of the Sovereign Grand Lodge of the Independent Order of Odd Fellows, 1994 (Volume LXXXII)*. Winston-Salem: The Sovereign Grand Lodge of the I.O.O.F., 1995.

Sovereign Grand Lodge of the Independent Order of Odd Fellows. *Journal of Proceedings of the One Hundred and Sixty-Ninth Annual Communication of the Sovereign Grand Lodge of the Independent Order of Odd Fellows, 1995 (Volume LXXXIII)*. Winston-Salem: The Sovereign Grand Lodge of the I.O.O.F., 1996.

Sovereign Grand Lodge of the Independent Order of Odd Fellows. *Journal of Proceedings of the One Hundred and Seventieth Annual Communication of the Sovereign Grand Lodge of the Independent Order of Odd Fellows, 1996 (Volume LXXXIV)*. Winston-Salem: The Sovereign Grand Lodge of the I.O.O.F., 1997.

Sovereign Grand Lodge of the Independent Order of Odd Fellows. *Journal of Proceedings of the One Hundred and Seventy-First Annual Communication of the Sovereign Grand Lodge of the Independent Order of Odd Fellows, 1997 (Volume LXXXV)*. Winston-Salem: The Sovereign Grand Lodge of the I.O.O.F., 1998.

Sovereign Grand Lodge of the Independent Order of Odd Fellows. *Journal of Proceedings of the One Hundred and Seventy-Second Annual Communication of the Sovereign Grand Lodge of the Independent Order of Odd Fellows, 1998 (Volume LXXXVI)*. Winston-Salem: The Sovereign Grand Lodge of the I.O.O.F., 1999.

Sovereign Grand Lodge of the Independent Order of Odd Fellows. *Journal of Proceedings of the One Hundred and Seventy-Third Annual Communication of the Sovereign Grand Lodge of the Independent Order of Odd Fellows, 1999 (Volume LXXXVII)*. Winston-Salem: The Sovereign Grand Lodge of the I.O.O.F., 2000.

Sovereign Grand Lodge of the Independent Order of Odd Fellows. *Journal of Proceedings of the One Hundred and Seventy-Fourth Annual Communication of the Sovereign Grand Lodge of the Independent Order of Odd Fellows, 2000 (Volume LXXXVIII)*. Winston-Salem: The Sovereign Grand Lodge of the I.O.O.F., 2001.

Sovereign Grand Lodge of the Independent Order of Odd Fellows. *Journal of Proceedings of the One Hundred and Seventy-Fifth Annual Communication of the Sovereign Grand Lodge of the Independent Order of Odd Fellows, 2001 (Volume LXXXVIX)*. Winston-Salem: The Sovereign Grand Lodge of the I.O.O.F., 2002.

Sovereign Grand Lodge of the Independent Order of Odd Fellows. *Journal of Proceedings of the One Hundred and Seventy-Sixth Annual Communication of the Sovereign Grand Lodge of the Independent Order of Odd Fellows, 2002 (Volume XC)*. Winston-Salem: The Sovereign Grand Lodge of the I.O.O.F., 2003.

Sovereign Grand Lodge of the Independent Order of Odd Fellows. *Journal of Proceedings of the One Hundred and Seventy-Seventh Annual Communication of the Sovereign Grand Lodge of the Independent Order of Odd Fellows, 2003 (Volume XCI)*. Winston-Salem: The Sovereign Grand Lodge of the I.O.O.F., 2004.

Sovereign Grand Lodge of the Independent Order of Odd Fellows. *Journal of Proceedings of the One Hundred and Seventy-Eight Annual Communication of the Sovereign Grand Lodge of the Independent Order of Odd Fellows, 2004 (Volume XCII)*. Winston-Salem: The Sovereign Grand Lodge of the I.O.O.F., 2005.

Sovereign Grand Lodge of the Independent Order of Odd Fellows. *Journal of Proceedings of the One Hundred and Seventy-Ninth Annual Communication of the Sovereign Grand Lodge of the Independent Order of Odd Fellows, 2005 (Volume XCIII)*. Winston-Salem: The Sovereign Grand Lodge of the I.O.O.F., 2006.

Sovereign Grand Lodge of the Independent Order of Odd Fellows. *Journal of Proceedings of the One Hundred and Eightieth Annual Communication of the Sovereign Grand Lodge of the Independent Order of Odd Fellows, 2006 (Volume XCIV)*. Winston-Salem: The Sovereign Grand Lodge of the I.O.O.F., 2007.

Sovereign Grand Lodge of the Independent Order of Odd Fellows. *Journal of Proceedings of the One Hundred and Eighty-First Annual Communication of the Sovereign Grand Lodge of the Independent Order of Odd Fellows, 2007 (Volume XCV)*. Winston-Salem: The Sovereign Grand Lodge of the I.O.O.F., 2008.

Sovereign Grand Lodge of the Independent Order of Odd Fellows. *Journal of Proceedings of the One Hundred and Eighty-Second Annual Communication of the Sovereign Grand Lodge of the Independent Order of Odd Fellows, 2008 (Volume XCVI)*. Winston-Salem: The Sovereign Grand Lodge of the I.O.O.F., 2009.

Sovereign Grand Lodge of the Independent Order of Odd Fellows. *Journal of Proceedings of the One Hundred and Eighty-Third Annual Communication of the Sovereign Grand Lodge of the Independent Order of Odd Fellows, 2009 (Volume XCVII)*. Winston-Salem: The Sovereign Grand Lodge of the I.O.O.F., 2010.

Sovereign Grand Lodge of the Independent Order of Odd Fellows. *Journal of Proceedings of the One Hundred and Eighty-Fourth Annual Communication of the Sovereign Grand Lodge of the Independent Order of Odd Fellows, 2010 (Volume XCVIII)*. Winston-Salem: The Sovereign Grand Lodge of the I.O.O.F., 2011.

Sovereign Grand Lodge of the Independent Order of Odd Fellows. *Journal of Proceedings of the One Hundred and Eighty-Fifth Annual Communication of the Sovereign Grand Lodge of the Independent Order of Odd Fellows, 2011 (Volume XCIX)*. Winston-Salem: The Sovereign Grand Lodge of the I.O.O.F., 2012.

Sovereign Grand Lodge of the Independent Order of Odd Fellows. *Journal of Proceedings of the One Hundred and Eighty-Sixth Annual Communication of the Sovereign Grand Lodge of the Independent Order of Odd Fellows, 2012 (Volume XCX)*. Winston-Salem: The Sovereign Grand Lodge of the I.O.O.F., 2013.

Sovereign Grand Lodge of the Independent Order of Odd Fellows. *Journal of Proceedings of the One Hundred and Eighty-Seventh Annual Communication of the Sovereign Grand Lodge of the Independent Order of Odd Fellows, 2013 (Volume XCXI)*. Winston-Salem: The Sovereign Grand Lodge of the I.O.O.F., 2014.

Sovereign Grand Lodge of the Independent Order of Odd Fellows. *Journal of Proceedings of the One Hundred and Eighty-Eight Annual Communication of the Sovereign Grand Lodge of the Independent Order of Odd Fellows, 2014 (Volume XCXI)*. Winston-Salem: The Sovereign Grand Lodge of the I.O.O.F., 2015.

Sovereign Grand Lodge of the Independent Order of Odd Fellows. *Journal of Proceedings of the fifteenth Communication of the International Council of the Independent Order of Odd Fellows held in Lucerne, Switzerland, May 18 to May 21, 1990*. Winston-Salem: The Sovereign Grand Lodge of the I.O.O.F., 1990.

Sovereign Grand Lodge of the Independent Order of Odd Fellows. *Journal of Proceedings of the International Council, Independent Order of Odd Fellows, 1999-2001*. Winston-Salem: The Sovereign Grand Lodge of the I.O.O.F., 2001.

III. Initiation Rituals

Grand Lodge of Maryland and the United States. *Lectures and Charges of the Degrees of the Independent Order of Odd Fellowship*. Maryland: Grand Lodge of Maryland and the United States, I.O.O.F., 1820.

Manchester Unity Independent Order of Odd Fellows Manchester Unity Friendly Society. *Ritual of the Independent Order of Odd Fellows Manchester Unity Friendly Society: For the Use of District Officers*. Manchester: Manchester Unity Independent Order of Odd Fellows Manchester Unity Friendly Society, 1989.

Manchester Unity Independent Order of Odd Fellows. *Lectures used by the Manchester District*. Manchester: Mark Wardle, P.G. and C.S., 1824.

Ritual of The Ancient, Mystic Order of Samaritans of the United States and Canada (Cleveland: Supreme Sanctorum, 1935).

Ritual of The Ladies of the Orient of the United States and Canada (Supreme Royal Zuanna, n.d.)

Sovereign Grand Lodge Independent Order of Odd Fellows. *Ritual of a Lodge of Odd Fellows of The Sovereign Grand Lodge of the Independent Order of Odd Fellows*. North Carolina: Sovereign Grand Lodge, I.O.O.F., 2004.

Sovereign Grand Lodge Independent Order of Odd Fellows. *Ritual of a Junior Lodge under the Jurisdiction of the Sovereign Grand Lodge of the Independent Order of Odd Fellows*. Maryland: Sovereign Grand Lodge, IOOF, 1930.

Sovereign Grand Lodge Independent Order of Odd Fellows. *Ritual of Theta Rho Girls Club under the Jurisdiction of the Sovereign Grand Lodge of the Independent Order of Odd Maryland*: Sovereign Grand Lodge, IOOF, 1975.

Ward-Stillson Co. *Ancient Ritual of the Order of Patriotic Odd Fellows: Revised and agreed to in the Grand Lodge held at London, England, March 12, 1797*. Michigan: Kalamazoo Publishing, n.d.

IV. Internet Sources

Archives of Maryland. "*Freedom's Friend Lodge No. 1024: Black Mutual Aid Society; Saint Michaels, Maryland*". *Archives of Maryland*, n.d. Accessed October 4, 2017, http://msa.maryland.gov/megafile/msa/speccol/sc5400/sc5496/051800/051882/html/51882bio.html

Duyer, Linda. "*In 1880: Frederick Douglas speaks at Salisbury Courthouse.*" *Dorchester Banner*, February 25, 2015. Accessed August 30, 2018, https://www.dorchesterbanner.com/dorchester/1880-frederick-douglas-speaks-salisbury-courthouse/

Flores, Taya. "*Fraternal, Service groups battle declining membership: Elks, Rotarians and Other Fraternal Groups Struggle to Attract Younger Members.*" *Journal & Courier*, October 11, 2014. Accessed August 30, 2017, https://www.jconline.com/story/news/2014/10/11/fraternal-service-groups-battle-declining-membership/16874977/

Ford, Ashley. "*Horace Bratcher Honored with Odd Fellows Meritorious Award.*" *Daily Light*, March 30, 2018. Accessed October 3, 2017, http://waxahachietx_com.gm5-txstage.newscyclecloud.com/news/20180330/horace-bratcher-honored-with-odd-fellows-meritorious-award

Hayden, Sara. "*Odd Fellows Ensure No One is Odd Man Out.*" *Half Moon Bay Review*, December 26, 2017. Accessed January 5, 2018, https://www.hmbreview.com/news/odd-fellows-ensures-no-one-is-odd-man-out/article_b6e4da60-eaa0-11e7-9421-3b5f60770def.html

Healy, Patrick. "*A Ritual Gone Fatally Wrong Puts Light on Masonic Secrecy*," New York Times, March 10, 2004. Accessed August 30, 2017, https://www.nytimes.com/2004/03/10/nyregion/a-ritual-gone-fatally-wrong-puts-light-on-masonic-secrecy.html.

Hix, Lisa. "*Decoding Secret Societies: What are those Old Boys' Clubs Hiding?*" *Collectors Weekly*, October 3, 2012. Accessed August 30, 2017, https://www.collectorsweekly.com/articles/decoding-secret-societies/

Kalfsbeek, Elizabeth. "*Reborn Arbuckle Odd Fellows Revitalizing Community*". *Daily Democrat*, December 9, 2009. Accessed January 5, 2018, http://www.dailydemocrat.com/article/zz/20090209/NEWS/902099769

Lacava, Franklin, "Hopwood woman breaks mold as leader of Odd Fellows". Triblive, July 18, 2015. Accessed January 22, 2019, http://triblive.com/news/fayette/8717029-74/fellows-odd-cupp

Manchester Unity Independent Order of Odd Fellows, "*The Oddfellows Over the Years*", Accessed July 20, 2016, https://www.oddfellows.co.uk/About-us/Over-the-Years.

Manchester Unity Independent Order of Odd Fellows, "*About the Oddfellows Friendly Society*", Accessed July 20, 2018, https://www.oddfellows.co.uk/about/

Moore, Dave. "*Dallas Odd Fellows Reviving Old-school Social Network.*" *Dallas Innovates*, February 23, 2017. Accessed October 3, 2017, https://www.dallasinnovates.com/dallas-odd-fellows-reviving-old-school-social-network/

Morrill, Monica. "*Frederick Douglass Today: 200 Years Later.*" *Selous Foundation for Public Policy Research*, February 27, 2018. Accessed August 30, 2018, http://sfppr.org/2018/02/frederick-douglass-today-200-years-later/

Neal, Jynnette. "*Join the Club: Old-School Networking Made Cool Again.*"*Advocate Oak Cliff*, September 26, 2017. Accessed October 3, 2017, https://oakcliff.advocatemag.com/2017/09/join-club-old-school-networking-made-cool/

Pacella, Rachael. "*Towson business owner is Odd Fellows' first female African-American leader.*" *The Baltimore Sun*, June 1, 2016. Accessed August 30, 2017, http://www.baltimoresun.com/news/maryland/baltimore-county/towson/ph-tt-darlene-parker-0525-20160526-story.html

Rosenberg, Dave. "*9 Steps to Help Resuscitate a Failing Lodge*". Davis Odd Fellows Lodge No.169, February 26, 2018. Accessed May 30, 2018, http://davislodge.org/9-steps-help-resuscitate-failing-lodge/

Ross, Robyn. "*Antiques and 'Ink Master' Play Roles in Renaissance of Fading Fraternal Order.*" *New York Times*, May 10, 2014. Accessed October 2, 2017, https://www.nytimes.com/2014/05/11/us/antiques-and-ink-master-play-roles-in-renaissance-of-fading-fraternal-order.html

Sailer, Linda. "*Restoring the Odd Fellows Lodge: Members helping do the work, one room at a time.*" *The Dickinson Press*, February 13, 2016. Accessed October 2, 2017, http://www.thedickinsonpress.com/lifestyle/3947511-restoring-odd-fellows-lodge-members-helping-do-work-one-room-time

Saur, Chris. "*Centennial: Odd Fellows Lodge is a Community Powerhouse.*" Davis Enterprise, June 2, 2017. Accessed October 2, 2017, https://www.davisenterprise.com/local-news/centennial-odd-fellows-lodge-is-a-community-service-powerhouse/

Smart, Amy. "*For First Time in 151 Years, Woman Leads Victoria Odd Fellows.*" *Times Colonist*, January 17, 2015. Accessed October 4, 2017, http://www.timescolonist.com/news/local/for-first-time-in-151-years-woman-leads-victoria-odd-fellows-1.1734684

Theiss, Nancy Stearns. "*One of the oldest African American organizations in Kentucky celebrates 145 years.*" *Courier Journal*, August 29, 2017. Accessed October 4, 2017, https://www.courier-journal.com/story/news/local/oldham/2017/08/29/one-oldest-african-american-organizations-kentucky-celebrates-145-years/610308001/

Watts, Rachel. "The Experienced Three Links Owners Get Their Priorities from the Odd Fellows." *Dallas Observer*, July 25, 2013. Accessed October 4, 2017, http://www.dallasobserver.com/music/the-experienced-three-links-owners-get-their-priorities-from-the-odd-fellows-6430224

V. Periodical, Newspapers and Other Sources

Address of the Honorable Dana Porter, Minister of Planning and Development for the Province of Ontario, to the I.O.O.F. (1944).

Annual Reports of the Grand Lodges to the Sovereign Grand Lodge ending December 31 from 1900 to 1910.

Annual Reports of the Grand Lodges to the Sovereign Grand Lodge ending December 31 *from 1914-1919.*

Annual Report of the Rebekah Lodges to the Sovereign Grand Lodge, I.O.O.F. year ending December 31, 1919.

Code of General Laws of the Sovereign Grand Lodge of the Independent Order of Odd Fellows (2012).

European History Quarterly (London: SAGE), vol. 16 (1986).

Early Reminiscences of Odd Fellowship. *The Covenant, and Official Magazine of the Grand Lodge of the United States I.O.O.F.*, vol. 1 (1842).

English Westerners' Society. *English Westerners' Tally Sheet*. Vol.33-38 (1986).

Gilman, Peck and Colby. *The New International Encyclopedia*.

Hackett, David. *The Prince Hall Freemasons and the African American Church: The Labors of Grand Master and Bishop James Walker Hood, 1831-1918*, Church History, 69:4 (December 2000).

Harwood, W.S. *Secret Societies in America*, North American Review, 164, (May 1897).

Noel Gist, *Structure and Process in Secret Societies*, Social Forces 16(3), March 1938.

McBride, *The Golden Age of Fraternalism: 1870-1910, Heredom*, Volume 12, 2005.

Odd Fellows Journal, Vol.3, January 11, 1900.

Pacific Appeal, Number 11, November 8, 1873.

Speech by Grand Sire J. Paul Kuhn *during the 1944 S.G.L Sessions.*

Stinchcombe in James, *Social Structure and Organizations, Handbook of Organizations* (March Ed.).

Schlesinger, Arthur. *Biography of a Nation of Joiners*, American Historical Review, 50 (October 1994).

The American Odd Fellow, October 1865, Vol.4, No.10.

The Odd Fellow's Companion, October 1865.

The Oddfellows' Magazine of 1888.

The Times, January 4, 1944.

VI. Interviews

Harald Thoen (Past Grand Sire of the Grand Lodge of Norway, I.O.O.F.), interview with the author, August 19, 2012.

Rick Braggy (Member, Sycamore Lodge No. 129, Hayward, California), interview with the author, June 15, 2012.

Scott Shaw (Past Grand, Columbia Lodge No.2, Victoria, British Columbia, Canada), interview with the author, August 20, 2014.

Thomas Roam (Member), interview with the author through facebook, June 5, 2018.

Vic Anton Somoza (Past Grand, Watchdog Odd Fellows Lodge No.1, Dumaguete, Philippines), interview with the author, November 10, 2014.

VII. Official Websites

www.glpaioof.org

www.guoofs.com

www.ioofsa.org.au

www.oddfellows.ch

www.oddfellows.co.uk

www.oddfellows.de

www.oddfellow.dk

www.oddfellow.ee

www.oddfellow.fi

www.oddfellow.is

www.oddfellows.nl

www.oddfellow.no

www.odd-fellows.org

www.oddfellows.ph

www.oddfellows.pl

www.oddfellow.se

Index

A

Adams, Hunter Doherty
   Patch Adams 263
Adams, John Taylor 260
African-American Civil Rights 96
Ailshie, James Franklin 260
Anderson, Victor Emanuel 253
Andersonville Prison Camp 56
Anti-miscegenation laws 97
Arnett, Benjamin William 97
Asiatic Brethren 29
atheism
   atheist 63

B

Baldwin, Stanley 220
Barkley, Alben William 223
Barnes, William 59, 264
Bell, Reason Chesnutt 260
Bertil, Duke of Halland
   Prince Bertil 93
Bertil, Gustaf Oskar Carl Eugén
   Prince Bertil 264
Bigler, John 253
Black, Hugo Lafayette 260
Bowers, John C. 96
Breedlove, Sarah 265
Brenton, Samuel 227
Brewster, Ralph Owen 253
Brucker, Wilber Marion 253
Buck, Ancient Noble Order of 14
Burnett, George Henry 261
Byrd, Robert Carlyle
   Senator Byrd 223

C

Call, Conley 256
Camp Trillium
   Odd Fellows and Rebekahs Island 162
Canterbury Tales 8
Chaplin, Charles Spencer
   Charlie Chaplin 265
Chaucer, Geoffrey 8
Chisum, John Simpson
   Chisum Trail 265
Christianity 12
Churchill, Winston 220
Colfax, Schuyler 49

collegia
   collegium 11
Communism 108
compagnons 15
Coshow, Oliver Perry 261

D

Dalton, Sidna Poage 261
Davis, Fred Henry 261
Davis, Jefferson F. 56
Defoe, Daniel 18
Devin, William Augustus 261
Douglass, Frederick 96

E

Emmerson, Louis 253
Encampment 194
Enlightenment, Age of
   Enlightenment era 28
Ericsson, John 266
Eye, All-Seeing
   All-seeing-eye 211

F

Fairbanks, Charles Warren 223
Farrington, Frank George 261
Fisher, Andrew 220
Fitzgerald, Frank Dwight 253
Frazer, James Somerville 261
Free Gardeners, Ancient Order of 13
Freemasonry
   Freemasons 61
friendly society 11

G

Gardiner, William Tudor 254
Garner, John Nance III 223
Garrigues, James Edward 261
George IV 220
Gold Rush 51
Grand United Order of Odd Fellows
   GUOOF 2
Grant, Julia 266
Grant, Ulysses
   Ulysses Grant 57
guilds
   craft guilds
      trade guilds 1

Gustaf VI Adolf 220

H

Hamilton, Wilson 261
Handshakes 187
Harding, Warren 220
Hatfield, Henry Drury 254
Hayes, Rutherford
   Rutherford Hayes 97
Hayes, Rutherford Birchard 220
Hendricks, Thomas Andrews 223
Holcomb, Oscar Raymond 262
Hook, Thomas 51
Hunter, Robert 262
Hunt, George 254

I

Illuminati
   Bavarian Illuminati 28
Independent Order of Odd Fellows
   IOOF 2
Initiation Ceremony
   Initiatory Degree 41
Insurance
   Life insurance
      Health insurance 66

J

Jacobin Clubs 28
Jim Crow laws 97
Johnson, John 262
Jones, Anson 220
journeymen associations 1
Junior Odd Fellows Lodge
   Junior Odd Fellows 200

K

Kerner, Otto Jr. 254
Key, Leroy 56
Knight, Goodwin 254
Knights of the Light 29

L

Lindbergh, Charles Augustus 267

M

Macdonald, John Alexander 220
Manchester Unity Independent Order of Odd Fellows
   Manchester Unity Oddfellows
      MUIOOF 2

Mariner, Paul 267
masons
   operative masons 13
Massey, William 220
McFarland, Ernest William 254
McKinley, William 97, 220
McMaster, William 254
Montgomery, James 22
Morrow, William 225
Morse, Dr. John 51
Morton, Oliver 255
Muscovites
   Muscovites, Imperial Order of
      Muscovites, Improved Order of
         Muscovites, Noble Order of 208

N

Nazis
   Nazi Party 85

O

Oddur Golf Club 147
Ogden, Peter 49, 268
Orient, Ladies of the
   LOTO 205

P

Passwords 187
Patriarchs Militant
   PM
      LAPM 196
Patriotic Odd Fellows, Order of 10
Peck, Oliver 268
Perkins, George Clement 255
Pike, Albert 215
Potter, William 262
Prince Hall Freemasons 97
Prohibition era 127

Q

Quong Tart 99

R

Ralston, William Chapman 268
Rebekah Lodge
   Rebekah Assembly
      International Association of Rebekah Assemblie 50
Reid, George Houstoun 220
Reid, Neil 262
Reitsma, Doreen Patterson 268

Index | 335

Rice, William Marsh
   Rice University 269
Richardson, Friend 255
Rites of Passage
   Rite
      Ritual 181
Roman Catholic
   Church 211
Roosevelt, Franklin
   Franklin Delano Roosevelt 82
Roosevelt, Franklin Delano 220
Rose Parade
   Tournament of Roses Parade 164
Russell, Richard Brevard 263
Ruth Degree
   Household of Ruth 101–340
Ruth, Household of
   Household of Ruth
      Ruth Degree 101

S

Samaritans, Ancient Mystic Order of
   AMOS 205
secret societies
   secret society 209
Self-institution 18
Sharpe, Edward MacGlen 263
Skelton, Richard
   Red Skelton 269
Slavery
   slaves 55
Stanford, Amasa Leland
   Stanford University 225
Supreme Being 2

Symbolism
   symbols 187

T

Taylor, Lucy Hobbs 269
Temperance Movement
   Temperance 123
Theta Rho Girls' Club 201
Thiu, Nguyen Van
   Nguyen Van Thiu 116
Travelling password
   Annual Travelling Password
      ATP 19
Tyndale, William 28

U

Underwood, John Cox 270
United Youth Group
   UYG 203

V

Volunteerism
   volunteer 127

W

Warren, Earl 263
Wildey, Thomas 44
Wilkes, John 270
Winn, A.M. 51
Witchcraft
   witches 28
women's suffrage 50

THE FIRST PUBLICATION OF THIS BOOK WAS MADE POSSIBLE BECAUSE OF THE GENEROUS SUPPORT OF THE FOLLOWING:

Major Sponsors

Grand Lodge of Pennsylvania
Independent Order of Odd Fellows

Grand Lodge of Denmark
Independent Order of Odd Fellows

Hopkins Lodge No.87
of Bristol, Pennsylvania

Walker Lodge No.306
of Philadelphia, Pennsylvania

Rockville Centre Lodge No.279
of Rockville Centre, New York

Minor Sponsors

Grand Lodge of Sweden, IOOF | Grand Lodge of Texas, IOOF | Grand Lodge of Maryland, IOOF | Upper Falls Lodge No.175 | North Point Lodge No.4 | Towson Lodge No.79 | Baltimore City Lodge No.57 | State College Lodge No.1032 | William F. Packer Encampment No.127 | Bob Simoni | Debra LaVergne | Johanna Norton | Michael Zurell | Jan-Hugo Nihlen | Hans Thronström | Eilif Henriksen | Isleifur Gislason | James Harrington | Daniel Weinbren | Dan Woolever | Loretta Kaskey | Jason Walt | Bjørn-Arne Connolly | Eddie LeBoeuf III | Lars Kirkeby | Alice Legg | Roy King | Danilo Lopez | Frances Peterson | Michael Milan | Christopher Milan | Len Taylor | Ronald Aughenbaugh | Benjamin Kadow | Antoinette Vasta | Robert Chaney | Jamie List | Tattie Sarmiento | Christopher Faulkner | Bernadette Maradane Sarmiento-Faulkner | Stacey Layne | John Cain |

THANK YOU VERY MUCH FOR BELIEVING IN THIS PROJECT!

Sponsors and Supporters

About the Author

Louie Blake Saile Sarmiento finished his Associate in Health Science Education in 2007; Bachelor of Science in Psychology with Certificate in Human Resource Management and Certificate in Women's Studies in 2010; Master of Arts in Industrial/Organizational Psychology in 2013; and Juris Doctor (Law) degree in 2020. With a wide range of academic backgrounds, he uses various quantitative and qualitative research methodologies in his writings. He does not rely solely on old history books and manuals written many years ago but also conducts interviews, surveys, SWOT analysis, case studies and consults the most recent dissertations, thesis and expert opinions of historians, sociologists, organizational psychologists, lawyers and other academic scholars.

He is instrumental in re-establishing Odd Fellowship in the Philippines. He is a Past Grand and Past District Deputy Sovereign Grand Master of the Independent Order of Odd Fellows. He is credited for connecting thousands of members from various countries when he created and managed the first social media groups and pages of the Independent Order of Odd Fellows from 2009-2019. He is also credited for writing and creating most of the modern literature and infographics about Odd Fellowship on the internet at a time when the organization had almost zero presence online, including the first YouTube videos and the Wikipedia entries about the Odd Fellows. Because of his contributions, he was appointed as Public Relations Coordinator and member of both the Communications Committee and the Revitalization Committee of the Sovereign Grand Lodge from 2012-2015. He was based at the Odd Fellows International Headquarters in North Carolina for an aggregate period of three years where he had full access and was able to read from cover-to-cover all the journals, history books, manuals, rituals, secret works and artifacts related to the Odd Fellows. He traveled widely for more than six years to conduct research and case studies about the Odd Fellows and similar fraternal organizations; visited over a hundred Lodges and several Grand Lodges across the United States and Canada; read and reviewed volumes of records, minutes and books; observed meetings and initiations; and interviewed local, national and international leaders.

He is an advocate for the preservation of historical fraternal organizations, service clubs and civic associations. He is a member of all branches of the Independent Order of Odd Fellows (IOOF), including the Rebekah Lodge, Encampment and Patriarchs Militant. He is also affiliated with the Grand United Order of Odd Fellows (GUOOF); Ancient Mystic Order of Samaritans (AMOS); Noble Order of Muscovites (Muscovites); International Order of DeMolay (IOD); International Order of Free Gardeners (IOFG); Universal Druid Order (UDO); Ordo Supremus Militaris Templi Hierosolymitani - Regency (OSMTH); Knights of Rizal (KOR); The Fraternal Order of Eagles - Philippine Eagles (TFOE-PE); and Tau Gamma Phi or Triskelion Grand Fraternity (TGP). He now enjoys living a secluded and peaceful life while focusing on his career. As a hobby, he writes and collects books, antiques and artifacts related to fraternal organizations, service clubs and other civic associations.

Other Books by the Author

This illustrated book, **Ancient Rites of Odd Fellowship: Revisiting the Revised Ritual of the Order of Patriotic Odd Fellows, 1797**, is published for preservation and educational purposes. This is for the benefit of members, scholars, researchers and historians alike who want to gain more knowledge about the origins, history and evolution of the ancient rites of Odd Fellowship. It is not the objective of this book to divulge the secret workings of Odd Fellowship to the uninitiated. This ritual has been published to the public in the past and copies are available in public libraries. This is also considered ancient and no longer practiced by existing Odd Fellows' organizations today.

This illustrated book, **Odd Fellows: Brief History and Introduction to the Degrees, Symbols, Teachings, and Organization of Patriarchal Odd Fellowship**, aims to provide the reader a brief history of the Encampment, along with an introduction to its degrees, symbols, teachings and regalia; also covering the organizational structure and functions of the officers of the Encampment and the Grand Encampment. The Encampment, also known as Patriarchal Odd Fellowship, is a higher branch of the Independent Order of Odd Fellows that confers three additional degrees to Third Degree or Degree of Truth members in good standing: Patriarchal Degree, Golden Rule Degree and Royal Purple Degree. The degrees are based on the lessons of Hospitality, Toleration and Fortitude. The motto is Faith, Hope, and Charity.

The aim of this illustrated book, **Odd Fellows Manual: Modern Guide to the Origin, History, Rituals, Symbols and Organization of the Independent Order of Odd Fellows,** is to create a 21st century reference book highlighting the essentials of the Independent Order of Odd Fellows. This book hopes to acquaint potential candidates, members and leaders with a straight-forward approach of its origin and history, philosophy and purposes, degrees, teachings, symbols, regalia, jewels of office and organizational structure. But this does not aim to teach the rituals itself or any of its grips, signs and passwords. This does not also aim to supplant the Code of General Laws but only to emphasize some of the generally accepted rules within the IOOF.

About the Author

For suggestions and inquiries:

louieblakesailesarmiento@gmail.com

facebook.com/louieblakesailesarmientoauthor

instagram.com/louieblakesailesarmiento

twitter.com/LouieBlake

youtube.com/IOOF1819

www.ingramcontent.com/pod-product-compliance
Lightning Source LLC
Chambersburg PA
CBHW080602170426

43196CB00017B/2877